Africa: From Mystery to Maze

Africa: From Mystery to Maze

Critical Choices for Americans

Volume XI

Edited by

Helen Kitchen

Lexington Books
D.C. Heath and Company
Lexington, Massachusetts
Toronto

Library of Congress Cataloging in Publication Data

Main entry under title:
Africa, from mystery to maze.

(Critical choices for Americans ; 11)
Includes index.
1. Africa—politics and government—1960- Addresses, essays, lectures.
2. Africa—Economic conditions—1945- Addresses, essays, lectures.
I. Kitchen, Helen A. II. Series.
DT30.A346   320.9'6'03   75-44729
ISBN 0-669-00425-1   Sept 677

Published simultaneously in Canada.

Printed in the United States of America.

International Standard Book Number: 0-669-00425-1

Library of Congress Catalog Card Number: 75-44729

Foreword

The Commission on Critical Choices for Americans, a nationally representative, bipartisan group of forty-two prominent Americans, was brought together on a voluntary basis by Nelson A. Rockefeller. After assuming the Vice Presidency of the United States, Mr. Rockefeller, the chairman of the Commission, became an ex officio member. The Commission's assignment was to develop information and insights which would bring about a better understanding of the problems confronting America. The Commission sought to identify the critical choices that must be made if these problems are to be met.

The Commission on Critical Choices grew out of a New York State study of the Role of a Modern State in a Changing World. This was initiated by Mr. Rockefeller, who was then Governor of New York, to review the major changes taking place in federal-state relationships. It became evident, however, that the problems confronting New York State went beyond state boundaries and had national and international implications.

In bringing the Commission on Critical Choices together, Mr. Rockefeller said:

As we approach the 200th Anniversary of the founding of our Nation, it has become clear that institutions and values which have accounted for our astounding progress during the past two centuries are straining to cope with the massive problems of the current era. The increase in the tempo of change and the vastness and complexity of the wholly new situations which are evolving with accelerated change, create a widespread sense that our political and social system has serious inadequacies.

We can no longer continue to operate on the basis of reacting to crises, counting on crash programs and the expenditure of huge sums of money to solve our problems. We have got to understand and project present trends, to take command of the forces that are emerging, to extend our freedom and wellbeing as citizens and the future of other nations and peoples in the world.

Because of the complexity and interdependence of issues facing America and the world today, the Commission has organized its work into six panels, which emphasize the interrelationships of critical choices rather than treating each one in isolation.

The six panels are:

Panel I: Energy and its Relationship to Ecology, Economics and World Stability;

Panel II: Food, Health, World Population and Quality of Life;

Panel III: Raw Materials, Industrial Development, Capital Formation, Employment and World Trade;

Panel IV: International Trade and Monetary Systems, Inflation and the Relationships Among Differing Economic Systems;

Panel V: Change, National Security and Peace;

Panel VI: Quality of Life of Individuals and Communities in the U.S.A.

The Commission assigned, in these areas, more than 100 authorities to prepare expert studies in their fields of special competence. The Commission's work has been financed by The Third Century Corporation, a New York not-for-profit organization. The corporation has received contributions from individuals and foundations to advance the Commission's activities.

The Commission is determined to make available to the public these background studies and the reports of those panels which have completed their deliberations. The background studies are the work of the authors and do not necessarily represent the views of the Commission or its members.

This volume is one of the series of volumes the Commission will publish in the belief that it will contribute to the basic thought and foresight America will need in the future.

> WILLIAM J. RONAN
> *Acting Chairman*
> Commission on Critical Choices
> for Americans

Members of the Commission

LEO CHERNE
   Executive Director, Research Institute
   of America, Inc.

JOHN S. FOSTER, JR.
   Vice President for Energy Research
   and Development, TRW, Inc.

LUTHER H. FOSTER
   President, Tuskegee Institute

NANCY HANKS
   Chairman, National Endowment for the Arts

BELTON KLEBERG JOHNSON
   Texas Rancher and Businessman

CLARENCE B. JONES
   Former Editor and Publisher,
   The New York Amsterdam News

JOSEPH LANE KIRKLAND
   Secretary–Treasurer, AFL-CIO

JOHN H. KNOWLES, M.D.
   President, Rockefeller Foundation

DAVID S. LANDES
   Leroy B. Williams Professor of History
   and Political Science, Harvard University

MARY WELLS LAWRENCE
   Chairman and Chief Executive Officer,
   Wells, Rich, Greene, Inc.

SOL M. LINOWITZ
   Senior Partner of Coudert Brothers

EDWARD J. LOGUE
   Former President and Chief Executive Officer,
   New York State Urban Development Corporation

EDWARD TELLER
   Senior Research Fellow, Hoover Institution
   on War, Revolution and Peace,
   Stanford University

ARTHUR K. WATSON*
   Former Ambassador to France

MARINA VON NEUMANN WHITMAN
   Distinguished Public Service Professor
   of Economics, University of Pittsburgh

CARROLL L. WILSON
   Professor, Alfred P. Sloan
   School of Management,
   Massachusetts Institute of Technology

GEORGE D. WOODS
   Former President, World Bank

Members of the Commission served on the panels. In addition, others assisted the panels.

BERNARD BERELSON
Senior Fellow
President Emeritus
The Population Council

C. FRED BERGSTEN
Senior Fellow
The Brookings Institution

ORVILLE G. BRIM, JR.
President
Foundation for Child Development

LESTER BROWN
President
Worldwatch Institute

LLOYD A. FREE
President
Institute for International Social Research

*Deceased

J. GEORGE HARRAR
Former President
Rockefeller Foundation

WALTER LEVY
Economic Consultant

PETER G. PETERSON
Chairman of the Board
Lehman Brothers

ELSPETH ROSTOW
Dean, Division of General and Comparative Studies
University of Texas

WALT W. ROSTOW
Professor of Economics and History
University of Texas

SYLVESTER L. WEAVER
Communications Consultant

JOHN G. WINGER
Vice President
Energy Economics Division
Chase Manhattan Bank

Preface

It is less than two decades since the British and French agreed to decolonize the bulk of Africa, thus opening the way for emergence of four dozen independent African states. Their politics, their drive for recognition and for influence coupled with their limited experience and transitional problems make the new Africa a volatile continent. The literature on Africa to date has given remarkably little attention to the specific concerns that may confront the United States and its relationship with Africa.

Africa: From Mystery to Maze is one of seven geographic studies prepared for the Commission on Critical Choices for Americans, under the coordination of Nancy Maginnes Kissinger. Companion volumes cover Western Europe, the Soviet Empire, the Middle East, China and Japan, Southern Asia, and Latin America. In myriad ways, America's goals, interests, and prosperity over the next decade will depend significantly on its relations with, and the shape of, the world around it. The world has grown closer together and more interdependent as our own country and other nations find it impossible today to solve domestic problems in isolation of other countries' needs and priorities.

Helen Kitchen's study fills a gap in the current literature on Africa. She looks at Africa in terms of the human, functional, and regional problems and challenges the continent will present to American policymakers in the next decade, rather than relations with specific leaders or states, any of which may vanish or veer in any of several different directions in the search for identity and nationhood. The contributors have been chosen to present various points of view. Among them are a number of respected American, European, and African scholars, as well as an American banker and a defense planner with long African experience. Together, they provide information and insights that are essential to the understanding of a continent that is large in our concerns.

—W.J.R.

Acknowledgments

From the outset, every effort has been made to conduct the Africa Area Study in as open a manner as possible. Toward this end, I sent a letter to some 1,600 members of the multinational African Studies Association in the fall of 1974 welcoming an expression of their views on the central concerns of this book; a similar invitation was extended to the Afro-American membership of the African Heritage Studies Association. The response to these and other initiatives was gratifying, sometimes overwhelming. The diversity of views and perceptions on the critical choices confronting the United States in Africa, as well as those confronting Africans, contributed significantly to the central premise of the book as set forth in my opening essay.

It follows that no specialist whose contribution appears within these covers wrote his essay in an ivory tower. The authors of papers touching on economic matters met for an all-day session in Washington in May 1975 to discuss each other's first drafts; invited commentators for this roundtable were Professor Henry S. Bienen, Chairman of the Department of Politics at Princeton University, and former U.S. Ambassador to Zambia Oliver L. Troxel. A Communications Round Table of 25 African and American journalists held in Washington under the joint sponsorship of the Overseas Liaison Committee of the American Council on Education and the Washington Task Force on African Affairs provided an unusual opportunity to expose W.A.J. Payne's views on the media to critical evaluation and to update our material on francophone Africa. Subgroup meetings on southern Africa were organized for or by John Marcum throughout the United States. All chapters have gone through at least two drafts, often several. Each chapter has evolved out of extensive discussion and has been critically reviewed by those who share, and those who do not share, the writer's perceptions. The editorial process has been rigorous.

Because so many here and in Africa and Europe have given so generously of their time in working with me and with the contributing writers in broadening the scope of our vision, it is impossible here to thank all persons and institutions individually. In any case, my list would be incomplete since each contributing writer carried on correspondence and held meetings on his own in the course of preparing and refining his chapter.

Mention must be made, however, of some major working papers prepared at my specific request. An examination of the changing character of Africa's constituency in the United States by Daniel G. Matthews and Francis A. Kornegay, Jr. of the African Bibliographic Center will be expanded to book length and published independently in late 1976 or early 1977. Both of these contributors participated in a meeting at my home on the constituency and the media, and were supportive of the Africa Area Study of the Commission on Critical Choices in many other ways. Fred C. Hadsel, Executive Director of the George C. Marshall Research Foundation, contributed a working paper on Soviet and Chinese activity in Africa. Dr. Hadsel's paper, reflecting insights gained in the course of a long career in African affairs that included service as United States Ambassador to Ghana and to the Somali Republic, was omitted only because the events of 1975 and early 1976 created major overlaps of content with other chapters. Another provocative contribution was journalist Russell Warren Howe's paper on the spread of Islam in Africa, a subject now covered in a different context in Manfred Halpern's chapter, "Changing Connections to Multiple Worlds: The African as Individual, Tribesman, Nationalist, Muslim, Christian, Traditionalist, Transformer, and as a World Neighbor, Especially with Israel and the Arabs." Robert I. Fleming and a group of Nigerian businessmen contributed a working paper on American business in West Africa, and journalist Bruce Oudes' contributions included invaluable field research, insightful critiques of manuscripts, and a never-ending flow of innovative ideas that could easily have extended this study to several volumes. James D. Farrell, Information Editor at the Brookings Institution, edited major economic chapters and provided supportive counsel in many other areas as well. Reather Kelly, who worked with me at *Africa Report* in the 1960s, consented to join me in yet another enterprise, combining the roles of editorial secretary, accountant, and general envoy of good will.

To all those in the United States, Africa, Europe, and the Middle East—academicians, government officials, journalists, and concerned citizens—who shared their views and their time so generously with us in the preparation of this book, I express the hope that your trust has not been misplaced.

Helen Kitchen

Contents

List of Tables

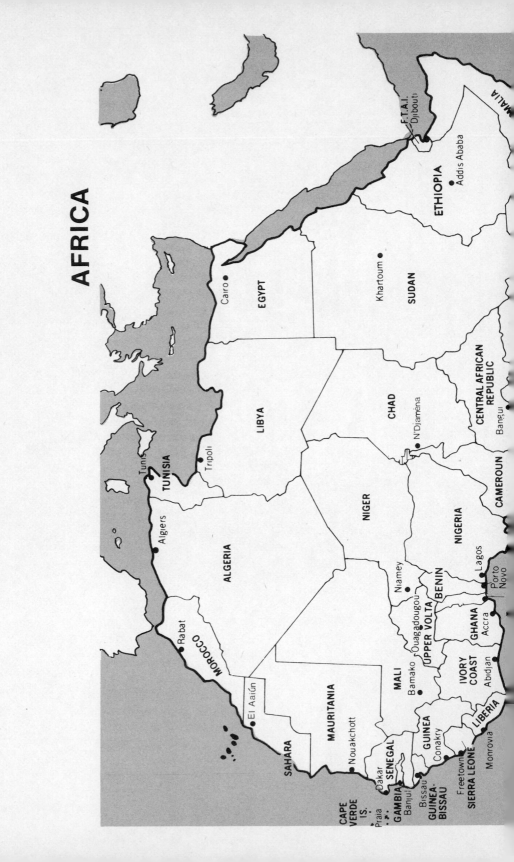

AFRICA

TUNISIA
Tunis
Algiers
Tripoli

MOROCCO
Rabat

El Aaiún

SAHARA

MAURITANIA
Nouakchott

ALGERIA

LIBYA

NIGER
Niamey

MALI
Bamako

Ouagadougou
UPPER VOLTA

EGYPT
Cairo

CHAD
N'Djaména

SUDAN
Khartoum

ETHIOPIA
Addis Ababa

F.T.A.I.
Djibouti

SOMALIA

CENTRAL AFRICAN
REPUBLIC
Bangui

CAMEROUN

NIGERIA
Lagos
Porto
Novo
BENIN
GHANA
Accra

IVORY
COAST
Abidjan

LIBERIA
Monrovia

GUINEA
Conakry

SIERRA LEONE
Freetown

GUINEA-
BISSAU
Bissau

GAMBIA
Banjul

SENEGAL
Dakar

CAPE
VERDE
IS.
Praia

Reprinted by courtesy of Africa Report (New York)

The Critical Choices:
An Overview

Helen Kitchen

It is the basic premise of this book that the single most "critical" choice for Americans in relation to Africa is one of perception.

Was the conflict in Angola a Cold War turning point foreshadowing a new era of Soviet-led marxist imperialism in a previously westernized area—or a factional power struggle only ephemerally and opportunistically "ideological"? Has time already run out for those who believe it is possible to achieve an orderly evolution toward racial justice in southern Africa? Should the more than four million whites who hold the reins of political and economic power in the Republic of South Africa be perceived as "white Africans" or as implanted Europeans? Do the labels "radical," "moderate," "pro-communist," "anti-American" have any lasting meaning in black Africa? Or are all African regimes of the late twentieth century—whatever their rhetoric and whether military or civilian—still largely preoccupied with the distribution of privilege and power within the middle-class elite that inherited authority at the end of the colonial interlude?

Should American involvement in Africa be primarily reactive to the degree of involvement of other world powers? To the support given by African governments to the position of the United States on non-African issues in international forums? To the acute human needs of a continent in which are located 18 of the 29 nations classified by the United Nations as the world's least developed? To the opportunities for mutual economic benefits that present themselves as the extent of Africa's subsoil resources becomes better known? Or should we perceive Africa as a vast body of land around which the United States Navy and merchant fleet must find their way to reach areas of greater priority? To what extent should American policy toward Africa be influenced by the consideration that some ten percent of our citizens are of African descent, and that

Afro-Americans increasingly identify with the pressures of their ethnic kin for an end to privileged white minority rule in southern Africa?

The contributors to this volume look at Africa through prisms shaped by differing disciplinary interests, differing ideological preferences, and differing life experiences. It is an article of faith with me that choices, especially "critical" ones, should be made in full comprehension—not just positive or negative judgments, but factual and empathetic comprehension—of the various ways in which a given problem or situation or constellation of problems is understood by those most informed and concerned. Thus it is by design that the radical Afro-American anthropologist/journalist W.A.J. Payne and New York banker David L. Buckman find themselves together in these pages. Philippe Lemaitre's assumptions concerning world economic trends over the next quarter century derive from a marxist conceptual framework that is rejected by economists Andrew M. Kamarck and William I. Jones. Kamarck and Jones, in turn, often interpret the same economic data quite differently—thus justifying a degree of substantive overlap in Chapters V and XI. Defense analyst William H. Lewis and theorist Manfred Halpern only occasionally see the same Africa.

What knits these dozen perceptions into a coherent whole is the obligation each participant undertook to dispense with platitudes and generalities. Oversimplifiers of African issues will not be comfortable with the commentaries to be found in these pages. It is an understatement to say that the record of United States policy toward Africa is described and evaluated in a forthright manner. At the same time, we do not patronize by glossing over the shortcomings of contemporary African political behavior; we seek to understand the shortcomings by examining them in an analytical framework that is not uniquely African but related to universal human experience.

John Marcum's characterization of the leaders of the splintered Angolan nationalist movement of 1974 is a case in point: "Because their range of action (and often their lifespan) was so limited, most were unable fully to transcend the parochial bounds of primary ethnic (or regional) loyalties or of class ties. Clandestinity left its mark too. Decimated by infiltrators and corroded by the insecurities and tensions of underground politics, Angola's nationalists became obsessively distrustful of everyone, including each other."

Similarly, Ali Mazrui draws on an American parallel to convey a sense of certain kinds of intertribal violence in contemporary black Africa: "The fact that the various indigenous cultures that make up all but a handful of African states speak different languages and are, or may be, products of different cultural histories, sharpens the sense of distinctiveness from other groups, even when a people are politicized and nation-minded. . . . It is not an exaggeration to say that African culture groups can at times see themselves as no less different from each other than Americans saw the Vietnamese. The ease with which some American military personnel could commit atrocities such as My Lai arose out of a sense of cultural distance between themselves and their victims great enough to result in a certain degree of dehumanization. Many African communities, though forced by the colonial experience to share the same borders, feel virtually as distant from some of their compatriots as those involved at My Lai. A crucial problem for African governments is how to promote greater identification across these cultural chasms."

Perhaps the most important message that this book offers to present and future policymakers and their critics—both in Africa and the United States—is embodied in Manfred Halpern's introductory essay: "Africans are entering into a great breaking. Relationships established yesterday or millennia ago are being shattered. Nobody thought that the first decades of independence would be easy. But the era of great breaking was believed by most to have been accomplished when almost all Africans freed themselves from colonialism. The next phase was foreseen as a time of making, not breaking. . . . To trust and care in the midst of a great breaking is the most difficult and most necessary task confronting us all in the modern age. It means moving beyond the drifting and bargaining and the moments of seeming stability to acknowledge this crisis openly . . . with all its great dangers and opportunities."

This theme of the changing connections of Africans to their multiple worlds—of the uncertainty that arises from the "great breaking" of previously accepted loyalties—is touched upon in every contribution. Projecting the future role of the media in black Africa, Payne concludes: "Even as African journalists become technically more proficient, the media in which they work will continue to be instruments of an authoritarian elite until or unless there is a fundamental reorganization of African society." Lemaitre agrees, believing that the ultimate impact of the more "socialist," more "self-consciously indigenous" regimes of Africa will depend on developments not yet predictable—on "the way the internal economic structure develops, the paths of class-formation, and the focus of political education"—and that the choices now being made "may only be properly and seriously weighed in the period after next, the one beginning about the year 2000." Halpern makes the same point in a different framework: ". . . the fact is that no communist anywhere in the world knows, in published theory or tested practice, how to turn the African society we have been describing into a communist society from its present starting point."

In his analysis of political prospects in South Africa, Marcum warns that "unless and until South Africa . . . achieve(s) some kind of fundamental change in its racial caste system, it will remain a magnet for trouble." Moreover, if Africans ever gain the organizational capacity and collective audacity to withhold their labor, no amount of force that Pretoria could muster would be sufficient to "put the Humpty Dumpty of a fractured race-caste social economy together again."

Economic geographer William A. Hance cautions that the significance of the so-called Sahelian drought of 1968-74 extends far beyond the Sahel itself: "The issues involved include some of the more difficult problems facing mankind: the growing strain of increasing populations; producing enough food, not just in quantity but also in nutritive quality, to feed the expanding populations; improving the standard of life of the earth's billions; and the potential conflicts arising from the inequalities between the more advanced peoples and economies and those that remain among the poor, the underdeveloped, and the nonindustrial."

In his wide-ranging examination of the search for an aid policy, Jones questions the utility of aid as a means of cultivating an African regime for strategic purposes in the present period of "great breaking": "Should the United States aid Ian Smith's Rhodesia for the sake of America's chrome supply? Leaving moral compunctions aside, few would bet on the longevity of the white Rhodesian regime or be willing to invest aid in cultivating it. What applies to Rhodesia applies, perhaps less dramatically, to other parts of Africa. . . . Instability gives rise not only to the possibility of a regime's replacement by force, but also to the possibility of arbitrary action. After Russia's careful cultivation of Guinea, that country's refusal to allow Soviet planes to land at the Russian-built airport during the Cuban missile crisis must have seemed arbitrary indeed in Moscow. The Russians may wonder whether such behavior (or an equally unpredictable coup) will destroy the returns on their investment in Guinean bauxite as well."

Lewis pursues this same doubt in writing of the dilemma that faced the United States government in determining whether to continue to aid an Ethiopia that "seemed on the brink of major if not revolutionary change" after the overthrow of Emperor Haile Selassie: "Yet the fact remained that the United States government had little familiarity with most of the members of the Military Council, and lacked the leverage and skills to influence the outcome of the policy deliberations of this unstable coalition."

The American concern for stability (meaning the status quo) in areas such as Africa has rested on the assumption that instability is artificially induced by communist troublemakers. In fact, neither the Soviet Union nor Cuba nor China created the Angolas and Rhodesias of Africa; they are, among other things, a product of the particular character of Western colonial rule experienced by these countries. The Russians did not get the "upper hand" in Somalia because the Somalis are ripe for communism (though some of the present in-group may be marxist) but because the Somalis are exceptionally poor and welcomed help from any quarter—perhaps especially from a country that shared their interest in the extent to which the United States was helping a next-door neighbor, Ethiopia, whose intentions were suspect. China did not build the Tan-Zam railway because Tanzania and Zambia were infested with maoists, but because Peking accepted (as other potential aid sources did not) that this railroad had enormous symbolic significance for a desperate, landlocked Zambia as well as economic importance for both countries. The reasons the Russians have port facilities in Guinea may have less to do with President Sékou Touré's avowed ideology than with the disabling effects of France's peremptory "lock, stock, and barrel" departure in 1958 after Guinean voters rejected membership in an envisaged Franco-African community.

To talk of retaliation against Moscow or Peking or Havana for responding to invitations to support deeply felt political, social, or economic needs in Africa may serve larger geopolitical purposes (that is not for me to say), but in Africa it elevates Russians, Chinese, or Cubans to a heroic stature they could not achieve on their own. The problems that need solving are genuine African ones, and we should not determine our role on the basis of whether communists get there first. The United States will repeatedly find itself on the losing side in Africa so long as it opts in favor of short-run stability or longer run instability under tyrannical rulers, black or white, while allowing others to orchestrate short-run instability into the kind of changes that could create more secure roads on which Africa might move toward a just society.

To "fight communism" in alliance with either black or white partners may (as in Zaire in the 1960s) or may not (as in Angola in the 1970s) forestall effective expression of the "instability" of social change. But it is not possible to render Africa stable by force of arms. In these circumstances, American interests and Africa's as well are best served by supporting those perilously few institutions and leaders committed to reweaving Africa's fragmented societies into a new fabric that would extend the benefits of self-government from the privileged few to that still largely ignored world of the urban and rural poor.

In the three decades since World War II, the one constant in American policy toward Africa has been the tendency to think of Africa as an appendage of our security interests in Western Europe, the Middle East, and Asia. As Lewis points out in Chapter IX, the long periods of benign neglect, punctuated by the interventions in the Congo in the 1960s and in Angola in 1975, can only be understood in this context. In short, we have never had, and do not yet have, an Africa policy. It is the implicit conclusion of this book that Africa deserves a policy.

If we have learned only one lesson from Angola, it should be that we must come to terms with Africa as it is, and not with Africa as a mirror image of ourselves. There were many miscalculations in our handling of the Angolan issue, as Marcum sets forth at length, but none was more crucial than the failure to recognize that Africans have had more experience with racism than with communism, and that, in African eyes, the intervention of South Africa in a black African crisis is of a different order than that of the Soviet Union or Cuba. This is understandably illogical in Washington, but it is entirely logical in Lagos.

It is my view, however, that the United States should not exchange one set of blinders for another. We should not try to outdo the rhetoric of those who call for all-out war within the Republic of South Africa, because to do so would mean that we have learned nothing from our own history. Knowing that more than a half million Americans died in the course of a civil war triggered in part by issues having to do with the rights of blacks to be full and equal citizens of the United States, we should have a deeply compassionate interest in all efforts to achieve racial justice in southern Africa with the loss of as few lives as possible. Among other considerations, Americans should recognize that the effects of a major race war in Africa would extend far beyond that continent, with the ominous prospect of encouraging further racial polarization in the United States.

The prospect of avoiding a major race war becomes more remote if we make pariahs of the Vorsters of southern Africa who have opted (albeit belatedly and now out of calculated self-interest) to try to build bridges between blacks and whites within and outside the Republic. There is considerable reason to doubt that the "solution" South Africa has devised—separate development—will work in the long run. But a significant number of black South Africans whose commitment to their own people cannot be questioned have come to believe that the "homeland" concept can serve as a wedge—a beginning, not an end. In the case of South Africa's decision to grant independence to the Transkei "homeland" in October 1976, as in so many other issues involving Africa, we are not qualified to take an adamant position prematurely. When, and if, the member-states of the Organization of African Unity decide that the Republic's black-governed spinoff is a politically viable African state, then we might well follow the OAU's lead. In any case, what useful purpose do we serve by demeaning those Xhosa of the Transkei who have made the painful decision to gamble on Pretoria's offer of half a loaf? If the United States is to make a constructive contribution to the future of southern Africa, this can best be accomplished in a spirit of humility appropriate to our own unfinished experience. Marcum's footnote (or caveat) to this generalization warrants underscoring, however: "The United States [must not allow] the Soviet Union to push it into an alliance with an embattled white minority attempting to maintain a privileged status quo from which we continue to enjoy economic profit. Instead, it would do well to encourage South Africa to interpret the loneliness of its intervention in Angola as evidence that . . . acceptance by black Africans is a prerequisite to healthy relations between the two countries."

In sharing these and other concerns with Africa, we should relate to "radicals" and "moderates" alike on a basis of mutuality of interest, and in ways that will help to build Africa's collective strength and self-reliance. To build this self-reliance is Africa's (and our) best hope of avoiding a superpower collision in Africa. Thus, while Washington may not always like their rhetoric or their votes in world forums, it is the Nyereres, the Kaundas, the Machels, and the Seretse Khamas of Africa who should be encouraged in their willingness to commit their personal political futures to the effort to move Africa toward a coherence of its own.

We should also take the Organization of African Unity seriously. It is perhaps true, as Claude E. Welch writes in these pages, that "the most important single accomplishment of the Organization of African Unity is that it has survived for nearly a decade and a half"; but the fact that no state has resigned since the association was founded in 1963, and that none of the 18 countries achieving independence since that time has declined to join, renders the OAU something more than a token pancontinental ritual. Indeed, the very fact of survival "has established an accepted pattern of cooperation among heads of state, some norms of conflict resolution, and acceptance by non-Africans of the OAU's focal role." The commitment of Africa's heads of state—now numbering 48—to air differences on a regular basis at the highest level of decisionmaking "is a significant accomplishment unparalleled by any pancontinental body outside Africa." The OAU's failures, but also its success in maintaining a nucleus around which some level of pan-African unity persists against all odds, "can be contributed in part to the absence of any single overriding bloc or dominant leader." It is in Africa's interest, and in our interest, to build on these strengths and worry less about the annual predictions of the association's imminent collapse.

Although this book was conceived as an examination of the critical choices that will or could confront the United States in relation to Africa over the next decade or so, much of its substance is concerned with the critical choices that face Africans. If the central choice for Americans in relation to Africa is one of perception and vision, so also is "re-visioning" the critical choice facing Africa itself. Such re-visioning entails dire risks as well as transforming opportunities. For choosing to open one's eyes at this new turning point in Africa's history requires the capacity to look beyond the present incoherence to still more dissolution, and beyond that to the rejoining of African relationships in new ways.

The subtle shift of emphasis that has occurred as this book was being written is, in itself, a policy recommendation.

I

Changing Connections to Multiple Worlds: The African as Individual, Tribesman, Nationalist, Muslim, Christian, Traditionalist, Transformer, and as a World Neighbor, Especially with Israel and the Arabs

Manfred Halpern

Africans are entering into a great breaking. Relationships established yesterday or millennia ago are being shattered. Nobody thought that the first decades of independence would be easy. But the era of great breaking was believed by most to have been accomplished when almost all Africans freed themselves from colonialism. The next phase was foreseen as a time of making, not breaking. Nation-building became the watchword; and if the parties and bureaucracies are not functioning according to their announced ideologies, they nonetheless coordinate a far larger network of political bargaining than ever existed before in Africa. A growing body of skilled labor and an ever larger number of educated men and women are clearly in process of building a more comprehensive economic and governmental infrastructure. Why, then, call this new era a time of breaking, crippling, and drifting in Africa?

There is no way of seeing the true dimensions of this new incoherence and suffering through old lenses, Western or African. We need a new theory—a new way of seeing human relationships.[1] This essay starts from such a re-vision. Since everything written hereafter—including our radical criticism of changes in African society—makes sense only if the reader is willing (at least for the span of this essay) to share our new lenses, we must begin by clarifying the three concepts that will guide our entire discussion. These terms are emanation, incoherence, and transformation. They become decisive criteria for explaining and predicting how Africans—and everyone else in the world—are dealing with the concrete problems of modernization.

Emanation is a concept that will allow us to come to terms with all relationships that any people regard as sacred—sacred in the larger sense that each individual in such a relationship sees himself as the embodiment of a

mysterious and overwhelmingly powerful source.[a] In Africa, we shall discuss
tribe, ethnic group, nation, Islam, and Christianity from this perspective. What
we shall find is that Africans, like all of the rest of us, now live in a world in
which devoted loyalty to the unquestioned or unquestionable can cripple and
destroy even as it continues to inspire.

Emanation is any relationship in which individuals yield entirely to collabo-
rating with a source of mysterious and overwhelming power, repressing all
conflict with it. They accept or reject change as that source wills. Justice is
experienced in this relationship as unquestioning devotion to that source of
one's being, and therefore also as receiving total security for one's self.

All of us began life in emanation—as children without power adequate to fend
for ourselves. We necessarily yield much of our identity to the mysterious and
overwhelming power of our mothers until we free ourselves enough to risk losing
total security. Some fathers and mothers in all societies seek to retain all
members of their household as emanations of themselves. Others in every society
treat their property, their employees, or ideas in this way. Emanation is not,
however, simply a child's way of life. All over the world, many individuals spend
all of their lives submerged as emanations of another—of a political movement, a
dogma, or a leader.

The traditional African, precisely in this way, sees himself as an extension,
not only of his own kinship group, but of the land and spirits and gods that
constitute the cosmos of his tribe and his ethnic community. This is also the
relationship that links the loyal Algerian or Mozambican to his nation for whose
birth and preservation so many have already died; without any need for
cost-benefit analysis, they could not imagine a higher cause. In this same
archetypal form, African Christians have accepted a God whose emanation of
power is great enough to protect them against all the African emanations that
once enveloped them and against the insecurities that lie beyond traditional
society. So also do African Muslims see themselves as embodiments of a
charismatic Community of Believers which, by its nature, cannot fall into error.

Wherever one lives in the world, one cannot escape the searing difficulties of
living within inherited relationships of emanation. As Ali Mazrui demonstrates in
his analysis of tribal conflict in Burundi elsewhere in this volume, no one lodged
within a sacred, emanational container, however large or small its size, is capable
of seeing humanity as a single species. Within each separate vessel, people see,
hear, feel, think, eat, marry, raise children, dress, manage, hope quite differently.

---

[a]In this new theory of human relations, emanation is one of eight qualitatively different
relations which, together, constitute the human capacity for dealing simultaneously with
these five central issues—continuity and change, collaboration and conflict, and the
achieving of justice. Part of the power of this theory derives from the fact that it can be
demonstrated that there are only eight types of relationship for dealing with these five
central issues—whether in intrapersonal, interpersonal, intragroup, or intergroup relations or
in man's relationship to concepts or to the sacred. Emanation, therefore, is not a term of
convenience offered for the sake of the present argument, but a term for a real choice
among specifiable alternatives.

To overcome this segmentation, the nationalist seeks to create a larger but similar container to substitute for the many within his own country. The political broker tries to create a new state, if not yet a nation, by offering to make connections among the many containers. The racist believes only his own pseudo-species to be legitimately human. These different roads into the future constitute vital distinctions within the world of emanations. But none free individuals from being the unquestioning embodiment of a group, so that they might freely discover and cooperate with others.

Modernization: Transforming Human Relationships

If one sees modernization, as many people do, as a combination of saving capital, investing in industrialization, and improving agricultural production, transportation, and communications, working intelligently, hard, and steadily, and providing strong, institutionalized, planned, and stable political leadership, then one must conclude that emanation has sometimes proved a great help. Some gods inspire sustained hard work and capital accumulation in their service; gods and other sources of emanation have inspired strong leaders and enthusiastic followers in economic as well as political endeavors. Indeed, if one follows most current cookbooks on modernization, one is told that the best recipe is to combine just such portions of emanation with enough technocrats who have already left their containers but care only about efficiency. This is undeniably one of the most powerful ways of gaining and, while it lasts, preserving, power and profits in the modern world. "Capitalism" and "socialism" are usually added labels which sometimes stand for different ways of sharing such power and profit and, sometimes, for different ways of hiding how they are shared. This kind of concoction, though it is modern, is not modernization. Modernization is something else.

There would be no point talking about the "modern" world unless something fundamentally new had come about to distinguish it from a world now being lost. Modernization cannot mean saving, investing, working hard and efficiently under strong, stable leadership to produce any new product, say widgets, or more widgets by far than ever before. The Chinese knew how to increase silk production in this way millennia ago. Surely the essence of modernization is the process by which (1) people free themselves for the first time to create any new relationship to themselves, others, or nature that they have never known before but that they now recognize as valuable; and (2) feel free and make themselves capable of evaluating any old or new relationship, and, therefore, of choosing whether to nourish or else end it. Modernization is the persistent capability to create the fundamentally new in all human relationships—persistently, so that relationships may move toward compassion, justice, beauty, and truth.

As long as a human being is the embodiment of somebody or something else, he cannot analyze, experiment, criticize, create, or produce on his own. This is the price of total security: the enchantment or enchainment of emanation. Neither tribesman, Christian, Muslim, patriot—patriot of Zaire, Iran, or the United States—can modernize as long as he or she is caught in the embrace of emanation.

It follows that to modernize does not mean to Europeanize, not even for Europeans, whether Eastern, Western, or trans-Atlantic. To modernize means to begin by shattering the container which has kept any person the embodiment of another. The revolution of modernization is the first revolution in the history of mankind which is worldwide, and certainly more fundamental and far-reaching than any which preceded it, because it touches every human relationship.

This revolution of modernization does not demonstrate its seriousness of purpose by breaking heads. If the heads which rise thereafter do not recognize what process of transformation is at stake in modernization, they will grow new halos of emanation, even if now styled "revolutionary." A much greater pain than the physical dying of a few is at stake in this revolution. What is at stake is the spiritual, intellectual, psychological, social, political, economic, and personal loss for all of deeply rooted relationships. The first harvest of the revolution of modernization necessarily is incoherence.

Substitutes for Modernization

Incoherence creates the risk and opportunity of human choice. Most leaders in Africa, as in the rest of the world, have so far chosen to pay ever increasing costs for repressing, masking, and profiting from incoherence. Incoherence means an inability or unwillingness to agree on a relationship which would allow self or other to deal simultaneously with continuity and change, collaboration and conflict, and the achieving of justice in their relationships with each other or in their relation to a concrete problem.

Most leaders in Africa refuse to acknowledge the pervasive and growing depth of incoherence. They prefer to speak instead of mere strains, imbalances, or difficulties, or to see the problem as one calling for the repression of particular individuals and groups as malcontents, just as colonial governments once saw and repressed African nationalists as "a vocal minority of agitators."

Not only most political leaders but also most theories of "development" tend to be silent about incoherence, thus helping to mask it. Leaders and theorists tend to focus attention on the dynamics of seizing or stabilizing power, but seldom ask what difference, if any, particular persons, movements, armed forces, or ideologies make to the transformation of human relationships. Public institutions, private corporations, and economic productivity have grown in selected sectors of many African countries. What has also grown is the number of people unconnected to and, worse, disconnected from the future by such new development. To speak of growth does not describe the price paid by people in cutting themselves off from traditional relationships in order to make this new world function effectively; or else, the price paid in the inefficient and uneconomical functioning of these new forms of growth thanks to the fact that these forms are being exploited by people for the benefit of established emanational connections or else individually and opportunistically milked, since there seem no longer to be any over-awing limits.

The leaders and students of "development" also tell us of prolonged periods of successful bargaining linking modern and traditional segments of African society; but we are often not told the price of bargaining among chiefs, businessmen, bureaucrats, party leaders, and army officers, or who pays that price. If we knew only (as conventional wisdom has it) of a choice between systems of bargaining and systems of tyranny, we could cut our discussion short by congratulating Africans on having so far turned to bargaining much more often than to tyranny, and in having so far hamstrung all intended tyranny through networks of bargaining. If we were interested only in making moral judgments, we could restrict ourselves to observing that participation and justice are unequally distributed within and among African countries. We are concerned with something more fundamental. For the first time in African history, there is not only more pain and frustration than ever before over participation and justice, but more incapacity relative to that anguish. Relationships, and not only things, fall short, and both are going up in price, if not always in value. This shortfall in relationships is what we need to look into.

Why Transformation Is Especially Difficult in Africa

The great majority of the new African elite does not yet know how to connect to the rest of its people. Like the great majority of elites in the rest of the world, most of the new African elite knows nothing about the process of transformation. Also, like most other elites, it cares more about something else—preserving and enlarging its own power.

It is especially difficult to connect people again in Africa. Its majority lives, and still intends to live, a life endowed in all its relationships by an overarching emanation that allows no questioning of fundamental relations or of most details associated with them. In other parts of the world, large numbers of people also exist in such relationships but they have for a longer time been recognized as traditionalists or conservatives. In contrast to traditional man, the traditionalist or conservative knows himself to be championing just one of several competing alternatives. Knowing that, he has already suffered a fundamental change. He is no longer a person who can take himself and his world for granted, as given, beyond question and remedy. The traditionalist has to fight for his position and therefore must come to know his position. As we shall see, men of tradition are beginning to turn into men of traditionalism in Africa also. For some time to come, however, modern leaders in Africa who have succeeded in defeating or gaining the support of traditionalists cannot count on having dealt at all with the men of tradition. People who already see themselves as pulling strings may, at most, be pushing strings. This inability of leaders to connect to other people is likely to remain great in Africa for some time yet.

Africa is a continent of many distinct horizons bounded by family, lineage group, ethnicity, language, culture, and religion. African elites who care about the integrity, dignity, and destiny of human beings need to know a great deal more about their various peoples than most other elites do. Transformation cannot begin except where people are now. In the face of these difficulties and vulnerabilities, the process of beginning conscious, deliberate, creative change is rendered more difficult by the growing reluctance of African elites to allow either foreign or domestic scholars to investigate the different values and cultures of their peoples. Then the past remains unredeemed, and therefore an unconscious and all the heavier a burden; the present remains manacled, and the dialogue between past and present covert or repressed.

Direct bargaining and brokerage are above all the types of relationships taking the place, or else attempting to mask the loss, of emanation in Africa. By these means, the new governments are able to connect themselves directly and (through political brokers) indirectly everywhere in the country. Nation-building thus appears to make progress. Certainly such relationships also create openings for new kinds of moral, intellectual, political, social, and economic movement by any individual African beyond the established emanational containers.

There is nothing wrong with bargaining and brokerage as such. But bargaining and brokerage, by their very nature, only serve to exchange what already exists; they cannot bring the new into being. They can trade only in convertible values; they can trade new values for old only by pretending that the former are also old. Thus the bureaucrat in charge of education may bargain successfully with the new military junta for an increase in appropriations in exchange for closer military supervision of the curriculum. This renewed coherence in this particular bargaining relationship does not alter an education which prepares the majority for unavailable careers, cuts off premature school-leavers from old and new roots alike, and introduces the discontented to no other alternatives. The excluded can then know only how to rebel against the very nature and rules of this kind of education and of the life for which it is supposed to prepare.

The tribesman may seem to be content to see the local party leader who is bent on social mobilization—or, in a more conservative vein, the ruler's henchman who is organizing demonstrations of affection—route his requests through the tribesman's own headman. Both modern and traditional forms of coherence would seem to be maintained. Something else is in fact taking place in such transactions between the people of tradition, the traditionalists (the people for whom tradition has become an ideology), and the non-traditional center. The people of tradition in most cases yield a half-trusting, half-fearful, but in any case not a knowledgeable support to those who know how to realize claims upon a non-traditionalist center. As they stand by, still dreaming of what was once the only reality, the people of tradition are being subverted by their would-be protectors. For a traditionalist is a person who has come to have an interest in the dream, and so also in the continued sleep of the dreamer in the midst of vast changes in the lives of the man of tradition and of the traditionalist. Subverted also because the traditionalist can protect only selected items of tradition, and tradition is by its nature a web and not sets of particular strands. Subverted because traditional man, by nature, does not know how to select strands and is at the mercy of the traditionalist in supporting the latter's choices. The traditionalists, in turn, are subverted by the non-traditional center, which strengthens their legitimacy by using them as brokers even while undermining them through the tasks which they are being asked to carry out, and by preventing them from guarding inherited emanational limits.

Precisely because most new African elites fashion connections in this way, they turn these new connections into veils which mask incoherence. The break with inherited forms of emanation—which is necessary for anyone who means to enter the road to transformation—is not allowed to come to people's attention. This decisive break is masked in three ways. The center offers a leader who presents himself as a new source of emanation, mysterious and overwhelming in his power. In truth, of course, no human being, all by himself, is any such thing. The local patron (chief, headman, or local party man) offers himself in the same manner, whether as a traditionalist or modernist, as the local link in such a chain of emanations. The miracles performed by these new men of emanation (apart from novel skills, sheer arbitrary willfulness, well-arranged ceremonies, or good luck) are those of direct bargains which trade in part on bits of emanation which are not supposed to have lost their mystery.

In this way the day is saved for the time being for the now powerful, both at the center and locally. But only the day, each day, because the Wizard of Oz, busy working smoke-machines and amplifying his voice, is not likely for long to be able to keep people from peering behind the curtain, because it is, after all, only a curtain. Also, Africans are more likely to insist on peering behind the curtain than many other people whose well-established institutions and social structures are more effective in inhibiting such peering or whose secret police is already too efficient.

All bargains of this kind are, by their nature, only particular bargains, and open to renegotiation as soon as the balance of power changes. One might be tempted to call this flexibility one of the small blessings of instability. The trouble is that all the faking and bargaining precludes the building of capacity— at the center or locally—to overcome the underlying incoherence. Time is being bought, but, fundamentally, for no creative purpose.

Meanwhile, vital resources are being wasted or distorted. Traditional security is being undermined but replaced only by an opportunistic linking of old and new power-brokers; at the same time, the artful preservation of emanational containers prevents the emergence of a critical, creative imagination and the building of the fundamentally new. The political and social system comes, in fact, to be based upon the consent of the already powerful (or those ready and able to join the already powerful) to the masking of incoherence. There is also an economic price: direct bargaining and brokerage require the immediate and invidious distribution and consumption of already existing resources. One can try to offer long-term incentives for production, but they may not be convincing to those who see others getting their rewards now.

There are, no doubt, Africans both at the center and locally who not only seem content but are content with how this system operates. Such contentment is a case of false consciousness, i.e., a consciousness that is unaware of demonstrably subverted or broken connections. It is far more difficult in emanation than in any other form of relationship to become aware that the relationship is, in fact, disintegrating—so powerful is the sense of total security which it radiates. However, when emanation finally breaks, no other relationship induces so powerful a reaction either of a violence fueled by a sense of betrayal or the obverse of such violence, namely intense apathy or intense despair. What bargaining and brokerage mask is the potential for civil war or passive resistance. No doubt some of the bargaining is half-consciously or even conscientiously designed to ward off such dangers. However, no new solidarity can be founded through such means.

All this discussing and negotiating can seem to be modern, national, democratic, and traditionally African—modern in its pay-off, national in the scope of its network, democratic in its pluralism, and African in its resemblance to the management of intratribal affairs. It is none of these, though many leaders find it in their interest to pretend that it is. It is neither democratic nor traditional, since leadership has come to depend crucially upon the counterfeit of emanation, namely covert manipulation, so that power will appear to be mysterious and overwhelming. Moreover, what is being traded suffers from several vital deficiencies: the center trades in socialism or capitalism and in the extension of its power, but finds the concrete expressions of its values—e.g., schools, credits, roads, participation in national institutions—accepted by most only as particular gains and not as living symbols of an entirely new way of life. In the small number of African countries actually tending toward socialism, the national party and government seek to re-educate and reorganize people for the sake of a change in patterns of life rather than a change only in certain segmented particulars. Beyond a few small and still scattered networks of relationships, this transformation usually comes to a halt because the center is not yet able to guide people into a whole network of new relationships. That will require the creation of a critical mass of conscious, critical, creative people experienced (or with enough courage to experiment) with new and just connections to people and problems. To settle meanwhile for an extension of central power can be justified in the name of transformation only if a nucleus of transforming individuals and relationships (and not merely a more loyal, efficient cadre) is actually being created in the time being purchased by other means.

The corruptive effect of these other means on the center and the local community is much greater if the government is committed to transformation. For what such governments especially need is participation. Participation is most likely to *seem* to be forthcoming when the bargain involves a trade of underlying loyalties between the center and the local community. But the fact is there is no similarity whatever between the loyalties which the transforming center requires and those to which the local community adheres. The essential requirement of bargaining and brokerage is missing, namely convertible values. This abyss comes to be masked by offering particulars for particulars, and pretending to a shared wholeness of which these are alleged to be tokens.

The substitutions we have been analyzing are a way of seeming to stay in business, bargain after bargain, but the hidden price is too high. It is a way which encourages clever manipulation, but not wisdom; it encourages a shrewd concern for how well the mask fits and therefore creates a large cover for official irrationality and, in those not shrewd, a powerful and irrational resentment. The resentment is irrational because the powerless are powerless in part because they have not been allowed to understand how things work. There is no shared vision of social purpose or justice. It remains for some a way of becoming wealthy, since it identifies and therefore permits exploitation of anxiety and encourages opportunism, but it is not a way of sustaining creative productivity.

Varieties of Connections Among Africans

We have been examining the toll taken by most present efforts to try new bargaining among and beyond people caught in emanation—the most common mode by which African elites have tried to avoid confronting the revolution of modernization. Now we ask at what cost present patterns of emanation are still being preserved in Africa—since few consciously, critically, and creatively attend to their transformation—and at what cost these patterns are breaking.

The African as an Individual

We have described the traditional African as experiencing himself or herself above all as the emanation of a mysterious and overwhelming source. The richness and complexity of such a relationship deserves elaboration. Nothing would be more erroneous than to conclude that a tribesman does not think for himself, but acts only as an embodiment of the tribe. Behind the term "tribe," as a visiting journalist or distant observer might use it, there lies in fact a whole chain of emanations. This chain reaches from the individual to his living and immediate family, his ancestors, his kinship group, his age-group, and often various other secret and public associations within his tribe, his ethnic group, and the sacred spirits of his entire cosmos.

An African novelist, Noni Jabavu, may therefore write in her *Ochre People* that "a person is a person (is what he is) because of and through other people,"[2] or Boubou Hamma speak of a "collective and religious whole in which man is never alone."[3] Even so, it is a life of many vital individual choices. Only the individual can give concrete life at every moment to the particular intersection of all these emanations. Each individual is free to connect himself more intensely to some relationships in this chain of emanations than to others. Individuals also risk being overcome by particular emanational forces and, depending upon the connection made, experience visions, prophetic utterances, psychosomatic illness, or witchcraft. In cases of seeming conflict or confusion, the tribesman participates in discussions or divinations about the conflicts or seeks judgment, mediation, or arbitration from rulers likely to take him and all his relationships personally into account. In such a world, each African individual can discover his own uniqueness.

The limits imposed by the chains of emanation upon individual creativity in Africa are in some respects less severe, in others more severe, than those normally accepted by modern scientists working within a prevailing paradigm, i.e., a framework of envisioning and working with relationships. The African tribesman's paradigm opens up a whole way of life; the scientist's paradigm is usually restricted to problems like plasma physics or structural-functional sociology and, beyond those limits, the scientist may know less that is sure, meaningful, purposeful, good, or beautiful about life than any African tribesman. In many areas of life, a scientist may not even know how to find out, at least on terms he would consider valid in his own work. Within the African's paradigm, intuitions and deep feelings are greatly cherished. In the world of the scientist, they count for nothing unless validated by other means. In the technological world the scientists have helped to build, the rest of the people are also expected to conform to this same diminution of part of man's consciousness.[4] In the emanational world of the African tribesman, all particular beings and events are experienced as expressions of the sacred. In the world of the scientist, only that which can be manipulated counts.

The scientist usually struggles hard against revolutions that would overthrow his prevailing paradigm.[5] Nonetheless, the scientific community is able to survive such changes, since the outcome of any such revolution so far has normally been a paradigm once again contained within the same limits which we have been describing. African tribesmen have in the past also created new empires, new tribes by secession, and new ways of life. Such transformations in vision and work have never before in Africa destroyed life as lived within the limits created by chains of emanation, but only substituted one closed system of emanations for another. In the modern age, no closed containers—precisely because they are closed—are safe from destruction. To maintain closed, fixed systems of any sort now demands covert manipulation and repression. In the light of our comparison between the paradigm of the tribesman and the paradigm of the scientist, modernization cannot mean simply trading new scientific paradigms for old African paradigms. What is required in the modern age is not one particular method or set of answers, but the capacity to persist in transforming paradigms as new problems, vision, work, and values arise.

Scientific-technocratic-bureaucratic systems are undoubtedly more powerful than any other contemporary network that binds people—demonstrably more powerful for purposes of production, administration, and destruction. Power is only beginning to be mobilized in Africa in this form, and in most instances foreigners still play a major role in such organizations. Most African individuals who are becoming available for new forms of linking with others have not entered technocratic society. Instead, most of them follow a particular person.

How is it that strong, personalist leadership can emerge in much of Africa from the matrix of its seeming opposite, that chain of emanations commonly called the tribe? Our explanation is consonant with our analysis of what it is to be a traditional man. In this period of African history, one can still grow up feeling one's self to be the blessed and powerful manifestation of such an entire chain of emanation. But one can also separate or distance one's self from the tribe, and still feel and express this power within one's self—but without any longer feeling bound solely to one's own tribe. At this point, a crucial choice is made. Some then no longer feel accountable to any other individual or group, and become confidence men. Others feel free and powerful enough to devote themselves to any new group of people which is drawn to them. For, as either kind of leader, one comes to have as one's followers all those who, upon their separation or distancing, search for a new total security. In a world dominated by relationships of emanation, one becomes either the source (which requires grace and wisdom, or else great gall and shrewdness at covert manipulation) or one becomes much more often in desperate need and hope the embodiment of the source.

Such an explanation for the emergence of one particularly prevalent type of African leader and follower has the advantage of explaining individual behavior without resorting to explanations regarding the cult of particular personalities, pseudopsychological analyses of individual disorders, or a general condemnation of the quality of African leadership. Nonetheless, this kind of analysis does allow us to distinguish between leaders who attend to the overcoming of incoherence in their society, and leaders who seek to profit from incoherence and from its mere repression while they enjoy willfulness, prestige, and luxury as long as they can.

No African leader can avoid bargaining and brokerage, nor the likely conspiracy of rivals. However, the transforming leader may be able to use bargaining and brokerage for the sake of persuading people to take the first step toward transformation, e.g., by giving special seeds and priority in fertilizers to those who join cooperatives. (Obviously, cooperatives are not forms of community which can therefore be held together as a community merely by constantly renewed bargaining.) Transforming leaders are able to act differently because of a critical distinction between them and the exploiters of incoherence. They have not only cut themselves off from the original chain of emanations, thus creating space for their own ego, but they have also become conscious of their own consciousness and of the meaning and value of alternative patterns of action open to their societies. This difference in consciousness is the necessary beginning, without which no turn to a new creativity, a new linking with others, and new just means is possible.

The present structure of African society creates exceptionally high obstacles for the progress of such conscious new leadership. In their traditional form, tribes today confront *each* nation in which they are wholly (or sometimes only in part) contained with somewhere between 20 and 200 worldviews more different from each other than Christianity, Judaism, and Islam. For the latter developed for the most part in centuries of articulate and prolonged conflict with, and adaptation from, each other. In Africa, such encounters among African worldviews were much more limited in premodern times. Intrinsic to the traditional tribe is that it shuts out nonmembers as total strangers. Not that most tribes therefore shunned all contact with each other; most knew well how to honor as well as to insulate passing strangers of any kind, and how to create carefully defined places for merchants or for conquered people. Ideas were also exchanged. But the central thrust was against openness unless the new could be totally assimilated by the overwhelming power of one's own tribal emanation.

The tribe raises problems for modernization not only in its contemporary traditional form but, at least as powerfully, in its modern form as tribalism. Tribalism (a term that is to tribe as traditionalism is to tradition) turns an organic unit into a defense mechanism. Tribalism organizes conflict among individuals and units who, as tribesmen, usually had no contact with each other. Tribalism is a problem of *modern* Africa. It covers quite different modes of defense. It may involve use of the power of the particular tribe to put pressure on the government to satisfy the same modern expectation (e.g., for schools, roads) which other tribes are raising in the same competition. It may involve defense by a tribe, or by several tribes never united before, against government actions which would upset tribal authority. Tribalism may involve favoring by the government of some tribes over others or carefully rewarding them in accordance with their strength.

What neither government nor tribesman can any longer depend upon in the age of tribalism is that the tribe in fact benefits from such arrangements.

Tribalism, like traditionalism, is selective in its loyalties. The support from the center may, in fact, end up reinforcing the power of an individual African political or economic entrepreneur, or of his family. Tribalism may also have quite a different meaning in the city than in the countryside. In the city, tribalism may connect individuals from several tribes by their new loyalty to the same larger ethnic roots. Tribalism may even fictitiously but potently connect diverse people into "tribes," since tribes were initially the only form of organization these migrants knew. In the countryside, the tribe has, on the whole, become more decentralized than before: local headmen rather than tribal chiefs now often hold decisive power, and may therefore speak for "tribalism" rather than tribe.[b]

The persistence of tribes and the new growth of tribalism means that no government can hope to adopt a single policy toward all "survivals of the past." African governments must come to know what actual relationships are being practiced, and how to change them. And no government and no group of individuals will be able to change existing relationships until there is a critical mass of transformers in each locality, or at least in each locality which supplies crucial modern services to its immediate neighboring communities. New human relations can only be initiated and practiced by human beings and not by decree or exhortation. That critical mass of transformers is far from being developed in any African country.

Africans as Citizens

The patterns of relationships among individuals and groups described in the preceding sections came to be delimited in the modern age within particular containers arbitrarily created by colonial regimes and currently ratified by all independent African regimes. These containers, initially altogether unrelated to tribal or ethnic limits, now constitute the nations of Africa.[c]

It would be easy—and wrong—to exaggerate the difference between African nations and Western and Eastern European nations. Southern and northern Italians are just beginning to meet each other; the Spanish, French, Czechoslovak, and Yugoslav governments still fear that stronger regional self-determination instead of centralized rule might give encouragement to centrifugal forces; the USSR opposes the free migration of Jews principally because non-Russians will soon constitute a majority of the USSR and their free movement, in any sense of

---

[b]It does not matter that "tribe" and "ethnicity" have become terms increasingly uncertain in their boundaries and controversial in their applicability in African life. Quite the contrary. Our discussion is formulated in terms of emanational containers precisely in order to indicate that individuals were shaped by vessels within vessels, and that all these vessels are now turning into crucibles.

[c]Swaziland, Lesotho, and the Somali Republic are among the few African nations that are ethnic units.

these terms, worries their rulers; the blacks of the United States are divided on whether to integrate with white society on terms already developed by white society. East and West Germans, having lived apart for centuries, and united for less than a century, are now building quite different societies apart from each other again.

What is truly different about African nations is that the inherited sacred containers within most nations are greater in number than in any European state except the Soviet Union, and the peoples within the containers are still more compellingly self-contained, and less acquainted with other contained peoples in their nation than is true of the nations of any other continent. On the other hand, this means that political and cultural development is still wide open in Africa. If the Baganda no longer dominate Ugandan politics from their power center in the kingdom of Buganda, but a northern Muslim named Amin rules the entire nation instead, the question of linkage between ethnicity, religion, and politics remains far from settled. In Great Britain, some of the Scots, Welsh, and Irish are beginning to feel that two centuries of rule primarily by the English has not done them that much good. In Belgium, the Flemings are beginning to fight hard against Walloon dominance. In the latter two cases, it will be much harder to make rapid changes in the structure of power than in Africa. But it is likely to become easier to resolve this kind of issue sooner in Europe than in Africa on the basis of the merit of individuals rather than the power of ethnicity.

Whether national boundaries were initially arbitrary or not, boundaries as such on any continent help to create nations whatever happens within the enclosure. African nations, by now, differ from each other by virtue of the fact that lines have been drawn and enforced. They therefore differ in terms of the containers which define the starting points of the connecting and disconnecting—the binding and the loosening—for each of the peoples of each nation. African nations differ in the *premodern* evolution of their patterns of relationship, the patterns imposed upon them by colonial regimes, and the circumstances under which they regained freedom to reshape these patterns themselves. They also differ in their contentment or discontent with existing patterns of relationships and in the resources they already possess for transforming them. Finally, they differ in their power as collective bargaining units with the rest of the world and secessionist groups within.

There is one thing that is true of all African nations as of 1976. All are being held together primarily by small groups at the center seeking to preserve and enhance their power and to move others through direct bargaining and resort to brokers. Much more rarely than during the period of initial state formation or nation-building in Europe, so far at least, is direct force being used. Even when the military rules, it has so far become only the final arbiter of all bargainings. There are, as yet, only small minorities in Africa who mean to alter these patterns for the sake of transforming African society. What is scarce in Africa are citizens—people ready to collaborate with strangers (i.e., someone not living within your emanational container; i.e., most people) in shared public purpose when such a purpose necessarily involves the transformation of individual and society.[6]

Africans and Two World Religions

The most misleading way to begin a discussion of Christians and Muslims in Africa would be to recite statistics. Christianity first arrived in North Africa in the first century, Islam during the seventh century—each in the century of its birth. Both, however, have scored their most rapid advance since the beginning of the nineteenth century. Christian churches claim a membership of just over 100 million (which may, or may not, include African separatist churches), while some 98 million are reported by some sources to be Muslims. Although it is said that Muslims have been gaining, in recent years, about 10 converts for every one new Christian, about half of all Africans remain—in the vocabulary of Muslims and Christians—pagans.

I rather doubt that God keeps score this way. I think it can be shown that no politician or scholar who cares about man's relationship to God or society would find it helpful to start from here. Much more that is certain about connecting and disconnecting in Africa follows from knowing who a person is and what tribe and nation he belongs to than from knowing that he is a Christian or Muslim. There are, as we shall see, many quite different ways of being a Christian or a Muslim in Africa. That is why wholesale labels mislead, and so do numbers, unless they add up, which they do not, to the same experience. As for the experience, theologians, who know very well what ought to be practiced, may not always be the most reliable witnesses.

Africans as Muslims. Islam—meaning literally "surrender," a surrender which brings the peace of God—was revealed as a sacred way of life to Muhammad, a prophet in the Arabian cities of Mecca and Medina during the early part of the seventh century after Christ. Muslims—that is, "those who surrender themselves" in this way—regard Islam as God's final revelation to mankind. Over half a billion people from West Africa to the Persian Gulf to the Soviet Union to China to the Philippines to the United States now call themselves Muslims.

Islam is, in contrast to Christianity, not only a religion but a way of life. For traditional Muslims, the separation of the sacred and the secular is evidence of a breach in life. Muslims strive for a practice in which all realms of life hang together and are experienced as manifestations of the sacred.

Islam offers a larger variety of religious experiences than Christianity, especially since it has neither an institutionalized church hierarchy nor keen interest in elaborating theological uniformities or distinctions, and willingly integrates many existing local traditions. In order to make some sense of the large number of different Islamic expressions in black Africa, let us speak of three major trends which are also to be found in the rest of the Muslim world.

One such tendency is to emphasize an explicit code of righteousness which serves to sustain a community of believers—a community overarching the other communities to which the adherent continues to belong. A second tendency focuses on the theory and practice of individual, social, and cosmological transformation. It champions not order but fundamental and permanent revolution. This movement has given rise to most of Islam's greatest philosophers and saints, and many of its political leaders, over the past 1300 years.

The Islamic philosophy of transformation is reflected in the practice of part of the third Islamic tendency well known in Africa—the Islamic brotherhoods. Under that conventionally accepted name hide two different, if overlapping, experiences. All Islamic brotherhoods in black Africa are founded upon a chain of emanational sources—a contemporary charismatic sheikh who inspires his followers to practice the rituals and devotions of the original founder of the order. The latter was himself usually a contributor to the theory of transformation. Among other orders, the emanation of the sacred shone powerfully enough in the deeds of the founder, if not especially in his ideas, to inspire generations of solidarity and devotion.

The power of an Islamic code of righteousness which sustains a community larger than the tribe must be analyzed primarily in terms of the issues raised for Africans by the modern age. Most sub-Saharan Africans who converted to Islam became Muslims (as others became Christians) sometime during the nineteenth and twentieth centuries. The unique attraction of Islam is that, alone among all the religions, ideologies, or ways of life competing in Africa, it offers a higher and sacred integration of existing forms of relationship. That was also one of Islam's principal attractions before the modern age, accounting for individual conversions, for the ease in integrating entire tribes conquered from the north, and for the success of African Muslim empires which lasted for centuries, as in northern Nigeria. In the modern age, this attraction becomes much more poignant and pervasive. For the first time, large numbers of individuals are in need of new and larger forms of integration, but also fear to give up what remains of their inherited ties. Here Islam offers its umbrella with such confidence because it perceives itself as a faith based upon God's final revelations.

How does Islam bring about a higher integration of individual, society, and cosmos? By offering an already familiar archetype—chains of emanation—in new, enlarged, and more explicit concrete forms. The basic model is this: A single, all-powerful God becomes the final source of power for all still accepted or already attenuated gods, spirits, values, and rituals of the tribe; God's community of believers becomes the final source of emanation for the individual and his tribe; God's explicit code of righteousness becomes the final container of all Muslim, pre-Muslim, and post-Muslim rituals and relationships which do not directly contradict what really counts in Islam—submission to God and to his charismatic community. And since this last rule places submission to God and community at the center of Islam rather than submission to any particular dogma of faith or action, the actual codes of righteousness which bind Muslims to each other in Africa differ greatly from actual community to actual community. It is the archetypal chain of Islamic emanations which remains the same, however rich or narrow, unique or universal, obeyed or neglected may be its concrete manifestations. Islam is a container that knows how to contain, and thus enlarge upon, containers of emanation. This is not a flexibility known to most Christian missionaries in Africa.

Islamic communities can therefore provide a new and larger solidarity for people from various tribes arriving in cities where they would otherwise remain forlorn strangers, without asking them to cut themselves off from their own history. In the countryside, the spread of Islam creates peaceful connections and opportunities for people who did not previously share any overarching values. In each instance, the community develops the scope and texture of its own emanational network.

Thus, Islamic criminal law has been applied almost nowhere in Muslim areas of black Africa; Islamic family law almost everywhere, but with important variations regarding such issues as inheritance and women's rights. Changes in Islamic law are coming about now in even more variegated ways—by substitution of modern codes from other Muslim or non-Muslim countries, by casuistic reinterpretation, and by neglect.

It is therefore not helpful to focus a discussion of Islam, as so many scholars do, on its "Five Pillars." The first of these is bearing witness to the fact that "there is no God but God and Muhammad is his Prophet." It is crucial that repeating this statement three times before witnesses makes one a Muslim, and Muslims repeat and meditate upon this statement every day to the end of their lives. The second pillar is praying five times a day, the first one just before dawn breaks. Few Muslims pray five times a day. The third pillar is fasting, especially during the entire month of Ramadan when no food nor drink nor sexual intercourse may be had by the believer from dawn to dusk. Some abstain; others get up very late, and wait eagerly for the evening's feast; some do not abstain at all. The fourth pillar is giving alms. Some do; some give little. The fifth pillar is going on a pilgrimage to Mecca. In 1974, over 300,000 Muslims—or less than 0.01 percent of the world's Muslim population—came from around the globe.[7] In some parts of Africa, for example among the Fulani, large numbers go every year; elsewhere, the number is much smaller. "The Five Pillars of Islam" are not the most solid positions upon which to erect generalizations about Islam anywhere, including Africa.

Nonetheless, it is possible to generalize about Islam in Africa as communities based upon codes of righteousness. It is a way of life in which *explicit* rules of behavior emanating from a more universal good assume a much larger significance and cover a much larger area of life than the codes of the tribe. Correspondingly, the father becomes more important than the mother, the husband more important than the wife. As part of this movement to legal authority and rationality, the teacher, trader, and judge become more important than the chief and earlier traditional workers of the spirit. Ritual cleanliness also becomes more important. Temperance, with regard to alcohol, increases in value. Personal dignity and integrity are thus reinforced by a larger sense of what is specifically and purposefully required in life, and by the larger social solidarity which not only unites but can be reunited, in case of conflicts, through mediation, judgment, teaching, and the force of consensus.

The religious brotherhoods, more prominent in West Africa than in East Africa (with the notable exception of the Sudan), place greater emphasis than the communities which we have just described on the blessings that flow through the person of the sheikh who leads them and through the practice of particular rituals. The protection of emanation thus looms larger among the brotherhoods than explicit legal rationality.

Differences among the brotherhoods therefore depend upon two factors: (1) the charismatic power of the sheikh or marabout, which certainly differs from generation to generation and can change within a lifetime, since misfortunes will be held against him; (2) the rituals being practiced, which may vary from meditation to recitations of litanies (*dhikr*) to ecstatic exercises. Among the Murids of Senegal[8] and the Ansars of the Sudan, the faithful are encouraged to earn their blessings by working at lower than prevailing wages on the peanut plantations (among the former) or the cotton plantations (among the latter) owned by the sheikh. Obedience to the sheikh is at the heart of such work, not a Protestant-type work ethnic.

The seat (*zawiya*) of the brotherhood often becomes a place of asylum, charity, marketing, education, mediation, divination, and healing. A new web of connections is thus established, based upon trust in a personally and ritually mediated god and community, transcending, without denying, the tribe.[d]

What difference does Islam make in creating new bonds among Africans— bonds that help to unite people for the tasks of modernization? We have already seen that it is misleading to speak of Islam in Africa. Muslim communities of various persuasions, yes; also an increasing number of individual Muslims redefining their own way, but not Islam. Islam does not serve to unite all Muslims within any single country. To be the member of a brotherhood is by no

---

[d]I have neglected to speak about Muslims in Africa who are not themselves Africans. Asians from the Indian subcontinent or Iran, whether orthodox (*Sunni*) or heterdox (*Shi'a*) Muslims, have tended (in contrast to many Muslim Arabs) not to intermarry with Africans. The Asian Muslims have therefore tended to function primarily as a commercial caste but, despite centuries of residence, have had little cultural or religious impact on their African neighbors. The only exception has been the still small heretical Ahmadiya sect, founded on the Indian subcontinent about 1880, and now proselytizing in about 33 countries around the world. It emphasizes charity, peacefulness, and draws on the values of other religions as well. Arabs in black Africa have as often been Christians as Muslims.

means to be in favor of "brotherhoods." To be oriented toward a legalistic code of righteousness is often to be opposed to brotherhoods generally, since they place so much more trust in the emanation of persons and prayerful chants. Islam, which has only for a few decades during 1300 years united all Muslim Arabs (namely during most of the first 50 years of Islam's expansion and sometimes, but much more rarely, against a common enemy thereafter) is unlikely ever to unite all Muslim Africans. If it did, such Islamic unity would shatter in turn the national unity of all African states containing non-Muslims.

The Sudan, sometimes viewed as the cultural crossroads of Arab and black Africa, is a good example of the issues at stake in Islam as well as of their likely movement. The struggle for the independence of the Sudan was led by secular university graduates and trade unionists as much as by members of two religious brotherhoods. In this country, where two-thirds of the people are Muslim, the first major decision of the Sudanese at the time of independence in 1956 was to reject union with Egypt, its neighbor, which also contains an overwhelmingly Muslim majority. The next 15 years after independence saw, above all, a battle for control between (and among) the secular leadership and the leadership of the brotherhoods in which, by 1969, the most powerful of the latter were defeated. Meanwhile, the decade-long civil war between the Muslim north and the non-Muslim south was, in fact, being waged not, appearances to the contrary, over problems touching Islam, but over problems of participation in a modern government. No one in the north imagined that these problems could be solved by southerners (Christians and animists of various denominations) converting to Islam. The resolution of the conflict involved taking the varieties of contemporary African experience seriously and allowing them to be represented and to work toward further change.

Islam in Africa differs in many important ways from the experience of Arabs with Islam. Islam originally arrived in black Africa by several routes—by conquest from the north, by the influence of caravan traders from the north and sea traders from the east, by conversion by charismatic Muslim brotherhood leaders coming primarily from the north. Some Africans recall Arab Muslims as slave raiders and slave traders; others converted to Islam in order to avoid becoming subject to slavery; most Africans never met Muslims in this way. All these original encounters have lost their importance by now on two grounds: they occurred, at minimum, more than a century ago and it was during the past century that most Muslims in black Africa became Muslims. In turn, this means that the roots of Islam in black Africa are not comparable in depth to those of North Africa, the Middle East, or South or Southeast Asia. There is no shared memory which would resonate through the entire northern third of Africa, or any but small segments of it, to a call to resurrect Islamic institutions, laws, ideas, or leadership, or to bring about a renaissance of Islam, or to reestablish Islamic unity.

Such a flowering of Islam is unlikely to happen in black Africa, even if Islam continues to increase in membership. The obstacles are many. The flexibility of African Islam—which allows it to constitute itself as an umbrella of umbrellas—not only leads to quite autonomous varieties of expression, but also, by its very tolerance, leads to an avoidance of facing clearly the fundamentally new issues raised by modernization. The two main tendencies of Islam in Africa—communities based upon a code of righteousness and brotherhoods centering around a charismatic personality—have been elsewhere in the Muslim world among the tendencies least open to, and least creative in dealing with, fundamental change. Nowhere in black Africa have organized Muslim communities (in contrast to individual Muslims such as Sékou Touré) taken an important role (much less a leading role) in the struggle for modernization. In a number of areas (for example, in northern Nigeria), organized Islam was reluctant even to move toward national independence.

During the period of colonial rule, Islam played initially an innovative role in some regions even while already playing a conservative role in other regions. In areas of new conversion, Islam opened up to Africans participation in a larger, universalist way of life without placing them under Christian, which was then also to say European, supervision. Where Islam was already established prior to European conquest, Muslim authorities gladly lent themselves to an arrangement of indirect rule whereby the colonial rulers reinforced the authority of Muslim rulers (as in northern Nigeria) while both joined in claiming reluctance to innovate except as it might be useful to the authority of both, on the ground that orthodox Muslim law was based upon God's final revelation. In areas where brotherhoods were important, some sheikhs allowed themselves to be purchased by colonial rulers into advocating political quiescence, a matter of particular concern to rulers since brotherhoods throughout Islamic history have tended to be especially prone to revolutionary activity.[e] Even in the postcolonial period, those Islamic institutions which were established in the precolonial period, or which were reinforced by the kind of symbiotic relationship we have described during the colonial period, have tended to be among the most conservative African institutions.

Although Muslims have larger and more flexible connections than those which link solely to a tribe—connections which initially gave them greater strengths—Muslims are not exempt from the fate of tribal Africans. In truth, Muslims cannot modernize unless, for example, their schools emphasize critical analysis and creativity rather than memorization, and until women are free to express their own potential freely in a culture whose public life then ceases to be

---

[e]Brotherhood sheikhs were vulnerable to such purchase (though not all allowed themselves to be bought) for two particular reasons. When the membership of the brotherhood is deeply devoted to the sheikh, his arrest or exile (for that was often the threatened alternative to accepting favors from the colonial rulers) is likely to cause deep disarray in the community. When the sheikh comes into his position through family inheritance, as is often the case, his need for grace may exceed his grasp, and political and economic aid may be acceptable to him as a helpful substitute.

the monopoly of men. But the central fact is that Muslims will not feel free to make these changes until they have freed themselves of emanational ties in which such changes remain unthinkable.

Just such changes are taking place. They are accomplished in the first instance by taking advantage of the multiplicity of African containers (which Islam never failed to recognize) and speaking in behalf of changes in the name of the nation, or of Africa, or of community as if it were a modern version of the tribe or of an Islam which can be shown to be wearing modern garments in other parts of the Muslim world. The task of changing Islam as a set of interrelated ideas and practices is not being placed on the agenda. The emphasis is on changing human beings who are also Muslims.[9]

Africans as Christians. It is characteristic of the modern age that the concrete advantages possessed by people during one phase of change often become the concrete disadvantages of the next phase. To become a Christian during the colonial period meant for many Africans the only available opportunity to receive modern medicines and medical treatment and to learn reading and writing and modern economic skills. Until after World War II, most colonial governments provided financial and logistical support to mission schools instead of making a serious effort to create a public educational system. This policy, which served to limit the growth of literacy and gave a particular character to the new African political elite thus shaped, also complicated the role of mission schools (and of Christianity in general) in the postcolonial period.

In sum, to become a Christian was to prepare one's self to enter a world of dramatically greater political, material, and, God willing, spiritual power than had ever been contained within the tribe. There were limits to entering, since Christianity remained until independence an enterprise primarily under European control. Although some Christian churches (by no means all of them) had once shared in the leadership of the struggle against the slave trade, and some individual European theologians took a stand against the colonial political or social structure or against the pervasive economic exploitation, the position of Christianity as such was ambiguous. The structure of the missionary enterprise mirrored the structure of colonial society generally: whites held all leading positions. No African Catholic bishops or cardinals were appointed until after independence. One important difference must be noted. Christian missionaries lived among Africans, sharing practical and spiritual experiences, as few other Europeans did.

In view of these obstacles to full acceptance, Africans turned in two directions during the colonial period. They became Muslims, for reasons we have already indicated, but to which we can now add the following, by way of comparison. Islam was far less color-conscious than Christianity. It was being spread primarily by Africans and under African leadership. Islam also offered participation in a worldwide way of life, without European control or paternalism. Though Christianity offered only a religion and not, in its modern form, a way of life, it sharply condemned as both barbaric and immoral many customs, values, and ideas of tribal life. Thereby, Christianity created a gap which it did not and could not fill. Islam, by contrast, accepted most aspects of tribal life, including polygamy, initiation ceremonies, graven images, and propitiation of spirits, and augmented this inheritance through its own way of life. Islam, unlike Christianity in Africa, had no reservations about dancing as part of religious worship, nor did it have Christianity's austere notions about singing or participation in devotions by the congregation. Islam emphasized righteous behavior in community, solidarity, justice, equality among believers, hierarchy among Africans (but not with regard to Europeans), and personal intercession with, or direct emanation from, God. Christianity focused its work on charity and salvation, and the inculcation of doctrines, and in this sense offered a more individualistic religion.

Many Africans who were touched by the power of Christianity but chafed under its European supervision and outlook created their own separate Christian churches. There are thousands of these in Africa by now. In these churches, prophecy, healing, and spiritual guidance became an expression of African inspiration; Jesus and Moses were seen as black; African sounds and rhythms returned to the rituals of worship, and Christianity became community-centered. Since justice, equality, and the Holy Spirit often became major inspirations for such religious solidarity groups, these churches were often treated as breeding grounds of subversion by colonial regimes and with utmost reserve by European-sponsored Christian churches.

Great pain and the desire for salvation continues to attract followers to these syncretist churches. Since they alternate between securing balm for the soul or pursuing a millenarian politics (or else concentrate on one of these purposes), they cannot hope to sustain unity among large groups of Africans in the pursuit of problem-solving in the realm of modernization.

Although the World Council of Churches and other ecumenical groups have become increasingly active in organizing strong Christian pressures for domestic social justice in Africa—targeting especially on the tolerance by multinational business interests of apartheid in South Africa—European-inspired Christian churches of Africa still largely pursue a policy of caution in political affairs. Paradoxically, some of the more notable exceptions can be found among white churches in South Africa, where the issues of racial injustice and minority rule are now often openly engaged. This apolitical stance of African Christianity arises in part from the inheritance of these churches. They taught catechism and individual offering of service, not a social gospel. The rural congregations cannot hope to offer national leadership; some of the urban congregations have become ingrown and frozen status groups in remembrance of an earlier European rank-ordering.

There are more powerful causes for this lack of Christian leadership. The new political authorities will not allow it. They intend to monopolize, or at least direct, all political action. But it would be misleading to stop here. The great majority of Africans now taking leading roles in politics, administration, and business were trained in Christian mission schools. President Julius Nyerere of Tanzania is only one of many prominent Africans thus educated who knew that the struggle for national independence and social justice in Africa would require fundamentally new forms of organization outside the church.

For this reason also, one must speak differently about the break required of Christians (in contrast to Muslims) before they can participate effectively in modernization. Christianity at its best in Africa created perhaps above all a sense that one must take one's own soul seriously and that caring matters. It also taught vital skills. (By contrast, Muslim schools in Africa taught primarily an Arabic which is to contemporary Arabic as Latin is to Italian, and memorization of the Koran and of commentaries on it in that form of Arabic.)

Christianity, as we have seen, also left by virtue of its concentration on doctrinal religion great gaps in its vision of life. That opens at least two possibilities. One is that religion becomes a private matter reinforced on Sundays, leaving the rest of the week to such inner light as may illuminate the profitable or such rules as one cares to remember. The other possibility is that one comes to know that, with God's help, one needs to find one's own way. In the former case, Christianity becomes a fig-leaf for any modern appearance. In the latter case, the believers can postpone the testing of received Christianity, though not the testing of the theories through whose practice, with God's help, they are finding their own way.

Christianity in this latter form leaves openings which do not demand breaking with Christianity, though the guidance it provides for entering into these openings remains to be clarified. If Africans themselves take this task of clarification seriously—considering that Protestants are divided and the present Pope is unlikely to be heard by all Catholics in the same way—their earlier connection with the West will not matter for much longer. These connections are indeed likely to be ever more quickly put into question. Though the Pope refused for a second time in 1974 to permit the cultural Africanization of Catholic services, this trend is likely to prove irresistible. Also in 1974, the All Africa Conference of Churches, which claims to speak for over a hundred African churches and about a third of Africa's professing Christians, called upon all American and European churches to keep their missionaries at home.[10] Missionary schools almost everywhere by now have become state schools in Africa. The next generation of Africans will not be trained primarily as Christians or Muslims but as citizens. There is no modern center for all of Christianity, and, after a while, in terms of contemporary influences, the origins of African Christianity in Europe will matter as little as the origins of European Christianity in the Middle East.

The Christians likely to be in the greatest difficulty resemble the Muslims likely to be in the greatest trouble—namely those who found their religious answer before the modern age. Ethiopia turned to Christianity in the fourth century. It has been defending its own Coptic faith ever since—a faith which also sustained royal power and vast churchly and lordly landholdings—against pagans and Muslims. Since the 1960s, Ethiopia's royal government welcomed technological, industrial, and military changes which it hoped would further strengthen its power. Established power, including Coptic institutions and norms, neglected the hungry in times of drought and remained opposed to modernization, and were unable to make any contribution to the search for new forms of society which began after the overthrow of Emperor Haile Selassie in 1974.

Africa's Connections in Foreign Affairs

The post-traditionalists who rule most African countries today (in contrast, for example, to the predominance of white traditionalists in Rhodesia) are freer from the constraints of inherited domestic loyalties than most governments in the world when they make choices in foreign policy. Africans are freer because the underlying loyalties upon which we concentrate in this essay do not carry any necessary consequences for foreign affairs in the minds of traditional people or post-traditional leaders.

African countries are likely for some decades to come to suffer from time to time the rule of traditionalists, such as that exercised by the late President Tombalbaye of Chad until his overthrow in 1975. Chad's "cultural revolution," as he called it (traditionalists are selectively informed), demanded that every prominent individual undergo the initiation rites of the president's ethnic group, the Saras, in what then became a ritual of sadistic purification. To create the illusion of stability of enforcing, even through official terror, selected aspects of tradition, is necessarily also to turn xenophobic at the same time. To turn xenophobic is, however, more obviously destructive in Africa than in societies based on a single ethnicity. A traditionalist in Africa can only be moved by the tradition—or the novel, selective resurrection of the traditions—of his tribe.[f] Xenophobia therefore threatens the neighboring tribe, and not only the stranger from abroad.

Not inherited loyalties but the breaking of them define the limits and issues of what is to be done in foreign affairs. Foreign connections can be used either as a weight in the internal power game of bargaining and brokerage or they can be used as an aid to modernization. For years there have been cold warriors in the West who believed that loans, investments, and arms could help a strongman, backed by the military, police, bureaucrats, and technocrats, to establish

---

[f]This fact seriously limited the circle of membership in the Mau Mau during its guerrilla warfare in Kenya prior to independence. The Mau Mau drew its ranks primarily from the Kikuyu.

"bulwarks" of domestic stability and international (i.e., Western-controlled) security. This kind of internal power game is by its very nature unstable and inhibits modernization. Undoubtedly, foreign support can help to render some cycles of "stability" in this power game more rather than less profitable for some in Africa and abroad. It is much more doubtful whether foreign nations can do much directly either to lengthen or shorten any cycle of stability. Either the promise of greater prosperity or the threat of greater repression, whether or not either is reinforced by resources from abroad, can spur rivals to try for power. Outsiders who become politically or professionally committed to maintaining or undermining such "stability" in an African country are wasting resources on results that cannot help but remain marginal in either direction.

Cold warriors in the West imagine that things could be worse: if such bargaining and brokerage were no longer to work, civil wars would be likely to break out, and secessions based on tribal, tribalist, and conflicting modern ideologies could succeed, as they threatened to in the Congo (Zaire) in 1960, in Nigeria in 1966, and in Ethiopia in 1975. This danger is real enough in all of Africa. In traditional Arab society, rebellion and secession were established as legitimate phases of bargaining, as the strike and lockout are in labor-capital relations in the United States. In most of Africa today, rebellion and secession are usually intended as ends, and only in defeat become means to a new integration. What the reality of this danger exposes is the intrinsic fragility of African systems based upon bargaining and brokerage without the overarching solidity of a shared source of emanation or a shared commitment to transformation. It follows from our analysis of the patterning and breaking of emanation in Africa that no bargaining and brokerage, however often resurrected or prolonged, can lead to a shared network of emanations or to transformation. On the contrary, the attempt to preserve this system from within or without leads to its repeated disintegration.

The other, worse, alternative to the present system imagined by Western cold warriors is the conversion of Africa to communism. But the fact is that no communist anywhere in the world knows, in published theory or tested practice, how to turn the African society we have been describing into a communist society from its present starting point.

The real choice for Africans, then, is to use foreign alignments and aid for helping to fuel the cycles of seeming stability and actual instability, or for supporting the process of modernization. How such choices may be made, and what they might mean, is best examined in the concrete context of Africa's relations with Israel and the Muslim nations of the Arab world.

Relations with Israel: An Illustration
of Limits and Potentials

We enter into this discussion by way of Israel because it is, together with the Arab states, among Africa's closest neighbors, and because the Israelis have been more in touch with African nations since the latters' independence than any except the great powers. Above all, the changing ties of Israel and the Arab states with Africa illuminate some of the most fundamental trends of the past and future decade in the new connections which Africans are fashioning among themselves and with others.

Israel, born only about a decade before the majority of African states began to come into independent being, entered more rapidly and more extensively into relations with this continent than any other state in the world, barring only the three leading Western powers. By early 1972, Israel had 32 diplomatic missions in Africa, accompanied in most instances by technical aid programs. About 300 Israeli experts then worked in Africa, while about 700 African trainees went to Israel each year. Israelis and Africans engaged in joint projects, for example in merchant shipping lines, mechanized agriculture, and hotel construction, as well as trade (Israel imported some $20.4 million worth from black Africa in 1972, while exporting to the extent of $37.4 million).

Israel, faced by a hostile Arab world, needed to win sympathy elsewhere in the Third World. From Israel, Africans could gain knowledge in nation-building, in cooperative farming, and in building medium-sized enterprises without the more demanding political pressures that often accompany aid from the great powers. Nonetheless, it would be more accurate even for the decade prior to 1973 to speak of *an* Israeli presence in Africa rather than *the* Israeli presence. Its aid program always remained small—about $10 million a year for the entire continent. It was a presence made relatively more significant for a time by the growing need of Africa for assistance in a context of declining aid from Western powers, still modest help from the Soviet Union and China, and the absence, until the 1970s, of important offers of technical or financial help from the Arab world.

Other than the Scandinavian countries, Israel was one of the few small countries in the world which took an interest in African countries generally, and hence it was noticed and appreciated. Africa's relationship with Israel, even during this heyday, was limited by certain hesitations on both sides. Though Israeli experts were generally willing to work with their own hands (rather than merely advise and direct) far more than most other foreigners except people in the American Peace Corps, the Israeli government was concerned only to win good will. Its principal aim was to persuade African governments not to vote with the Arab states; it was not Israel's primary aim to help Africans transform their society. At the same time, while a number of countries, especially Tanzania, drew upon Israeli experience in building cooperative communities, they were wary of having a significant number of foreign advisers involved in this major political task. In other projects which also demanded a concentration upon transforming human relationships, African governments were not always willing to accept the need for changing old habits, or on their own to continue, revise, and enlarge Israeli-sponsored pilot projects, nor did Israeli priorities—any more than the priorities of the USSR, China, or the great Western powers—call for pressing such issues.

The governments on both sides spoke about cooperation in "modernization," but not in the sense that we use the term in this essay. The willingness of Israel, and such countries as Zaire, Ethiopia, and Uganda, to join in "modernizing" African military and police forces referred to cooperation in making them more powerful and efficient. The point is not to diminish the value of what was accomplished by the Israelis in particular, but to discover in African-Israeli experience the likely potentials and limits of future African connections with other foreigners.

If the primary Israeli interest in Africa was to win international support, the interest of most African nations was, in fact, exactly the same. From this fact arose the destruction, by 1973, of Israel's position in Africa. If the African nations, now constituting one-third of the membership of the United Nations, were united and could unitedly bargain with others, their number would give them great strength. By 1970, as Claude Welch writes elsewhere in this book, almost all the conflicts between black Africa and Arab-African states had been dampened down under the aegis of the Organization of African Unity, and Arab North Africans were contributing more than one-third of the OAU's annual budget. The basis was thus being created for united bargaining with other groupings, most obviously and most immediately the rest of the Arab states— who are altogether 18, including the six in Africa. What is at stake for the black African states is creating more favorable international terms for acquiring the resources needed for their internal development, and help in ending white supremacy in South Africa and Rhodesia. No single small nation, such as Israel, can compete with the help which a whole group of nations can offer in this respect. Not even a great power can compete in this situation unless it is serious in using its power for these purposes. Generating pressure for the return of territories lost to Israel in the 1967 war was the principal Arab concern.

Shortly after the Yom Kippur/Ramadan war of October 1973, all African states except Malawi, Mauritius, Lesotho, Swaziland, and South Africa broke relations with Israel. The official explanations given by African governments for their actions touched upon important African interests, but the causes publicly cited were not decisive. These same reasons had been advanced earlier, but only a handful of African states had broken relations with Israel prior to 1973. African governments pointed out that Israel had since 1967 occupied Arab territory taken by force. Since most black African countries are tribal and linguistic conglomerates and every border in Africa was created arbitrarily at European bargaining tables in the nineteenth century, postindependence national leaders have been exceedingly sensitive to the possible domino effect of any attempt to adjust any border more "realistically." In the dozen years of its existence, the Organization of African Unity has devoted more time and energy to the reconciliation of interstate border disputes than to any other category of problem.

Since African strength in votes, chairmen, and committee membership is especially real and visible in the United Nations, African nations are especially concerned to demonstrate the reality of United Nations power by having UN resolutions carried into practice. With regard to Security Council Resolution 242 of 1967 and 338 of 1973, Africans believe that Israel has deliberately delayed returning occupied territories, and thus disregarded the UN. During the 1973 war, moreover, Egypt also won attentive concern in Africa when it called Israel's crossing of the Suez Canal—which was meant to outflank the advancing Egyptian army in the Sinai—an "invasion of Africa."

African governments also noted that Israel's total trade with South Africa was rising to equal (in 1973) its total trade with black Africa. At the same time that the Israeli government was asking for world support for free emigration from the USSR, it remained silent about severe restrictions imposed even on the internal migration of the black majority of South Africa. The Arab argument that Israel was by its very nature a "colonialist settler state" comparable with South Africa was less persuasive, as evidenced by the fact that most African governments indicated that they would renew relations with Israel once Israel had withdrawn to its pre-1967 territory.

These arguments, focusing on racial justice, opposition to forceful occupation of another nation's territory, and respect for the United Nations, are deeply felt by Africans, and were already significantly hampering Israeli relations with Africa prior to 1973. But the sudden and dramatic disintegration of Israeli connections with Africa came on other grounds.

Relations with Arab Nations: An Illustration
of Limits and Potentials

For the first time in modern history, the Arabs were effectively united in October 1973. That made them a much more promising ally for Africans than before. Far more important, the Arabs, unlike the Africans, had discovered an immediately effective weapon against the industrial nations—oil. The Arabs appeared to be at once united, wealthy, and powerful friends.

In fact, of course, these qualifications were more apparent than real. It is not true that *all* Arab states are wealthy in oil. At least half of them are not, and about two-thirds of all Arabs live in states that have no oil or not enough to export it. Unity has not been, nor is it likely to remain, characteristic of Arabs. The year 1973 is exceptional not only as a moment of Arab unity, but as a moment when Arab governments could agree even on what to do about Israel. Usually, they cannot even agree on that. The unity in the Arab world in 1976, which is already no longer that of 1973, is being bought by the money of some of the oil-rich nations. This kind of dependency, based upon constantly renewed bargaining in the fact of eroding emanational containers of faith and community, is no more likely than in Africa to create either a new overarching emanation or a creative transformation of human relationships. The new unity, wealth, and power of the Arabs mask an underlying incoherence, and also a gap between wealthy and poor Arab nations.

The oil-rich Arab nations, insofar as they are also conservative nations eager to preserve their social structure at home and their investments in the West, may be willing to use their power to strike in behalf of certain principles at specific nations—Israel or South Africa. They are unlikely to risk damaging their own investments and monetary holdings abroad by placing several industrial nations simultaneously under duress in order to win better conditions for the poor nations of the world. The oil-rich Arab states have begun to aid selectively, but none has yet taken the initiative to offer oil at a lower rate to poor states than to rich states.[g] And Africa (see Chapter V) is the continent containing the largest number of poor states in the world, reading upward from the bottom of the list.

Are there other central concerns that might in the future link Africans and Arabs? Let us consider the worst and the best case. The worst possibility is, obviously, neocolonialism practiced by the Arabs. But the Arabs cannot gain economic and political dominance by sending additional Arab traders to Africa. Their talent in Africa has so far gone largely into commerce, real estate, construction, and finance, not large-scale production and management. The Arabs are far from ready to create and manage their own multinational corporations at home or abroad, even though they can be expected to invest in existing giants. The rich Arab nations are not willing at all to alienate themselves from Third World support by using oil prices or supplies threateningly or seductively to bring selected African countries into their orbit. Nor are they capable of doing so. Iran is already the principal supplier of oil to East Africa, and Nigeria stands increasingly ready as an alternative supplier to the rest of Africa. Particular Arab states (never in unison) may act to provide money or weapons to particular African regimes or counterelites, with the same marginal results that every other outsider has experienced. It is simply too late in history for any foreigner successfully to establish *new* empires of *direct* rule in Africa. Empires of indirect rule depend upon technocratic-bureaucratic-cultural power and efficiency which only the United States, Britain, France, and multinational corporations are now able to supply. This conflict with African modernization is increasingly understood, and in some African countries opposition is already polarizing around this point. Israelis were not, and Arabs are not, fighting in this league.[11]

The best case is collaboration on humanitarian grounds, and for that it is too early in the Arab world. It is, obviously, too early everywhere in the world for such collaboration except, primarily, on the part of individuals and certain voluntary associations. In order for humanitarianism to become a strong motive

[g]Nigeria, one of the principal suppliers of oil to the United States, has not taken any such initiatives either.

among people, one must have experienced being wounded one's self, and that means knowing that one has lost the all-embracing security of inherited emanation, at least with regard to the problem at issue. The sense of barrier among pseudospecies is then overcome, and one comes to care for one's fellow human being in whom one recognizes the same wounds—the same breaking and the same need for transformation. This kind of collaboration is different from supporting those who share one's own traditions (e.g., Muslim or Christian) or becoming a missionary for one's own solutions or becoming paternalistic or being merely pragmatic, offering gifts and loans to people practical enough to ask sympathetically what is wanted in return. The wounds of change are too painful; the incoherence too great; the transformation too serious for such easy (i.e., temporary and marginal) connections. As William I. Jones shows in his chapter on aid in this volume, the increasing wealth and power of the Arabs, like that of their foreign predecessors on the African continent, will not soon be used for transforming acts of collaboration.

As half the Arab states grow richer and more powerful, there will be more Africans to speak a rhetoric of enticement and justification—whether Islamic or revolutionary in tenor—in the hope that it may prove rewarding with such Arabs. Africans, like other peoples, are not short of specialists in knowing who and what is up at any given moment, and how to make and cover bets accordingly. It will not do, however, to use "Islam," or "Arabs," or "revolution" as a label for what is likely to be spreading in Africa.[h] The decisive difference remains the distinction between opportunism (whatever the new opportunities) and transformation.

The Critical Choices—for Africans and Americans

This essay has asked what kind of African relationships are being created, preserved, or destroyed, and what kind of human capacity is being crippled or nourished by them. To look at politics everywhere, including Africa, from this perspective is also to make a fundamental choice—as fundamental as deciding instead, as others do in this volume, to look at Africans strategically, economically, institutionally, or in terms of specific gains or opportunities. To accept any way whatever of looking at things is at the same time to choose what has meaning, significance, value (and what does not), and what the better and worse alternatives are.

[h]Zaire's President Mobutu was raised as a Christian, yet he has moved easily from ties with the American CIA to visits with Israel to dialogue with China. President Idi Amin of Uganda is a Muslim. That did not keep him from working with Israeli military aides and accepting an Israeli military decoration while commander of his country's armed forces before he took political power, breaking relations with Israel after he came to power, and ousting Muslim Asians from Uganda after being in power. The Muslim Sékou Touré in Guinea and the Catholic Julius Nyerere in Tanzania both transformed a number of significant relationships in their countries.

To accept the perspectives of this essay is to recognize that we will not understand Africa, be helpful to Africa, or even pay enough attention to Africa unless we integrate our connection to change in Africa with our most important concern: the quality and direction of human relations among the human species. As a small part of this "we," i.e., as Americans, we shall be capable of participating in consciously and creatively shaping this change only insofar as we come to understand and act upon this issue as well in our own society. Otherwise, other people will not and should not risk trust in our caring.

To trust and care in the midst of a great breaking is the most difficult and the most necessary task confronting all of us in the modern age. It means moving beyond the drifting and bargaining and the moments of seeming stability to acknowledge this crisis openly—"crisis"—a word which literally means "separating," with all its great dangers and opportunities. Acknowledging such a crisis is no small matter. It means recognizing the terror of chaos and ignorance; living with the fact that one knows that one does not yet know what to do next, and allowing one's self to discover and test new relationships.

How does this movement from chaos to creativity come about? When one ceases to be the unquestioning embodiment of another, one experiences a new freedom and a new energy. The mysterious and overwhelming source of energy which had previously been experienced only as located in the other is now discovered within. To liberate one's own source of emanation liberates previously repressed energy. One is therefore also freed to discover and test alternative patterns of relationships within and without, and to experiment with different concrete manifestations of them.

This is what we mean by transformation—precisely this movement from the shattering of containers in which one is mysteriously contained by others to the conscious (and not masked or repressed) experience of incoherence to participation in the creating and choosing of new patterns of human relationships. We have been using the term "modernization" for this process of transformation, and only this process of transformation, whenever it takes place in the modern age.

Modernization, by its nature, is a radical revolution. For in the course of this struggle with one's self and with others, one comes to recognize that the "ultimate" source of emanation specified by any tradition leaves much of human experience untouched. No single, current, concrete expression of that source, whether of fixed words, faith, relationships, or rituals, can hope to maintain forever our connection to the infinite richness of the undifferentiated source. In turn, of course, each concrete relationship legitimized as fixed and final by the established "ultimate" source of emanation is then also recognized as a fetish. Thus all human experience becomes available for analysis, new creation and experimentation.

There was nothing wrong with any emanational container in Africa until it prevented Africans from renewing their connections to the movement of life.

Otherwise, containers are always a mercy several times over. Containers protect those who are still coming to birth within them or do not yet possess the strength to survive without them. Containers are not to be rejected simply because they are old. We may not yet have caught on to their symbolic meaning; we may find new symbolic meaning in them; we may recover their hidden meaning as a new experience for us. When we find that our containers no longer fit us, containers also remain a mercy because they then define, for any time and place, exactly what needs next to be overcome. Once we have taken courage to break and escape from old pots, we must, of course, learn next how to become potters ourselves.

The task of fashioning new and just links to one's own inner self, to others, and to concrete problems is by its very nature a task for each African. It is not a business that is solved simply by leaving—by becoming an ex-tribesman, an ex-Muslim or an ex-Christian. It cannot be left solely to leaders, administrators, managers, philosophers, ideologists, technocrats, investors, or other top personnel. A new consciousness and a new creativity and a new ability to link with others cannot be commanded into being. Leaders can do a great deal to guide such a movement: to organize enough power to remove barriers to transformation, to marshal resources, to teach, to exemplify. Such guides, however, are needed for fashioning new links at all levels, not only at the center, and the guide who already knows how to create one new connection is very likely in need of guidance in another connection—whether at the center or locally. None of these statements is drawn from any prevailing ideology. They are criteria of action and participation that follow analytically for anyone who requires a persistent capacity to overcome incoherence because he or she has ceased to be the embodiment of another.

No universal genius is required to guide such transformation, and certainly no guides toward becoming British, French, Soviet, Chinese, American, or even postideological technocratic man. Only those are capable of being guides who have already themselves made that journey—not all journeys, but a particular journey through particular links and breaks which constitute a particular problem, and who understood their way through this particular problem as an instance of the way of transformation. At minimum, guides who have not met that particular problem before, but who have the courage, energy, and insight of a previous journey to know one of the first steps. They begin by honoring, and not by masking, the fact that this journey begins from a feeling of apathy, betrayal, despair, and confusion. Such guides also know that stability and change do not—cannot—go together, and therefore, for a time, maintain or create some connections while transforming others. Such guides know that successful new bargains or obediences or other forms of manipulation are not signs of successful transformation. What is required is evidence of new consciousness and creativity and ability to link with others on the part of those who once began as followers. No new society can emerge until all—or at least, most—individuals in it know how to participate in constructing new networks of connections among each other in lieu of old containers.

The problem of modernization—or transformation—is not resolved by achieving greater technical know-how and efficiency—though they can be very helpful in their place. The heart of modernization lies in taking the terror and beauty of breaking and recreating human relationships seriously. The core of modernization is not getting richer and more powerful. Surely it does mean providing a minimum decency of food, health, education, and housing for everyone, especially since we now know, as a human species, how to accomplish this for the first time in our history. Hardly any black African nation is likely, in the next decade, to become as rich or powerful as any of the world's leading multinational corporations which have branches within it or buy its principal commodities. Some African nations may therefore nationalize some of these corporations. However, even such a shift in power is not modernization. Certainly it matters who controls technological-bureaucratic institutions, and to what purpose they work. Just developing more such public or private institutions, or taking possession of them, would merely put Africa closer to the shape of life in the United States, the Soviet Union, Japan, and most of Western Europe. Life then becomes a powerful web of calculated instrumental rationality for the minority working within that network, while most other human values—such as liberty, beauty, affection, goodness, joy—are neglected. No underlying human bonds can be fashioned on grounds of economic rationality, efficiency, and power alone.

There is one major distinction between most of Africa and most of the industrialized countries. In Africa, emanational containers are still the major obstacles to modernization; in the industrialized world, technological-bureaucratic institutions, both public and private, have become the most powerful barriers to modernization. The greatest vulnerability of Africa, therefore, is that its human relationships will be torn apart and rearranged by technological-bureaucratic forces much stronger than any which Africans are now organizing for the sake of their own transformation.[1 2]

Modernization is the touchstone of our analysis because the central problem in Africa is the breaking and remaking of ways of life.[1 3] All inherited and present webs of emanation—personal, tribal, national, Muslim, Christian—will be tested primarily by their ability to respond to the breaking of established connections within and between individuals and groups and with the values and concepts that people had once been able to take for granted. To transform relationships after such incoherence (which is no mere matter of adaptation or improvement) and to realize in practice new ultimate values and meaning is a task which directly challenges all groups whose very virtue was believed to lie in having already contained all answers.

All new infrastructures drawing upon new ways of using physical resources more efficiently must be tested by the same criteria. Many among the present

African elite may come to pride themselves upon the greater power and competence of African armies, police, and bureaucracy resulting from improved modern productivity, transportation, and communication. An "advance" in infrastructure unconnected to the transformation of society could well lead to a shift in Africa from an emphasis upon direct bargaining and brokerage to an emphasis upon more effective subjection, i.e., instrumental rationality, tyranny, and aggression—a shift from bad to worse.

The worst possibility is fascism, which returns by means of covert manipulation, terror, and violence to a new but final emanation, seeking to contain once and for all, in the midst of profound changes, the loyalties of all. Fascism is the costliest and yet the most seductive of all temptations. It seems to promise a return to what most people in the world have recently experienced as the most traumatic loss—the total security and stability of emanation. Especially in an age of incoherence, nothing seems at first glance more desirable or easier than to accept the now death-dealing offer of a return to such total security. This temptation is a major threat in Africa, as almost everywhere else.

The other choice in Africa, as everywhere else, is transforming strangers into fellow human beings who are moved to collaborate for common public purpose.

Notes

1. The basic elements of this theory are briefly sketched in Manfred Halpern, "Four Contrasting Repertories of Human Relations in Islam: Two Pre-Modern and Two Modern Ways of Dealing with Continuity and Change, Collaboration and Conflict and the Achieving of Justice," in L. Carl Brown and Norman Itzkowitz (eds.), *Psychology and Near Eastern Studies* (Princeton: Darwin Press, 1976). The theory is developed in full in Manfred Halpern, *The Dialectics of Transformation in Politics, Personality, and History*, forthcoming.

2. Noni Jabavu, *Ochre People* (New York: St. Martin's Press, 1963), p. 69, quoted by James Olney, *Tell Me Africa, An Approach to African Literature* (Princeton: Princeton University Press, 1973), pp. 285-286.

3. Boubou Hama, in *Kotia-Nima*, Vol. 2 of 3 volumes (Paris: Presence Africaine, 1968-1969), p. 15, quoted by Olney, in *ibid*, p. 55.

4. We are here following Carl Gustav Jung's conception of consciousness as having four faces—sensation, thinking, feeling, and intuition. These aspects of consciousness make us aware (to simplify and segment the contribution of each) of what is, what it is, the value of it, and its hidden context. See C. G. Jung, *Psychological Types* (Princeton: Princeton University Press, 1971).

5. See Thomas S. Kuhn, *The Structure of Scientific Revolutions* (Chicago: University of Chicago Press, second enlarged edition, 1970), from whom I have also drawn the conception of paradigm.

6. For a carefully detailed and penetrating analysis of the significance and consequences of bargaining and political brokerage, but appreciated from a different perspective, see the works of my colleague, Henry Bienen, *Tanzania, Party Transformation and Economic Development*, expanded edition (Princeton: Princeton University Press, 1970), and *Kenya, The Politics of Participation and Control* (Princeton: Princeton University Press, 1974).

7. *The Washington Post*, November 1, 1974.

8. See V. Monteil, "Une Confrerie Musulmane: les Mourides du Senegal," in *Archives de Sociologie des Religions* (Paris, 1962), No. 14, pp. 77-102.

9. The preceding analysis of Islam in Black Africa has drawn upon facts, but much less on the perspectives, offered in the following works: James Kritzeck and William H. Lewis (eds.), *Islam in Africa* (New York: Van Nostrand-Reinhold Company, 1969)—a book which also offers valuable bibliographies; and the volumes by J. Spencer Trimingham, *Islam in the Sudan* (London: Oxford University Press, 1949), *A History of Islam in West Africa* (London: Oxford University Press, 1962), *Islam in East Africa* (London: Edinburgh House Press, 1962), and *The Influence of Islam Upon Africa* (New York: Praeger, 1968). A number of crucial questions about Islam in Africa were defined more than a decade ago by Thomas Hodgkin and remain unanswered. See his "Islam, History and Politics," *Journal of Modern African Studies*, Vol. 1, No. 1 (1963), pp. 91-97.

10. "Missionaries' Moratorium Tied to African Liberation," *The Washington Post*, January 17, 1975.

11. On Israel's relationship with Africa, I have drawn especially upon Susan Arelia Gitelson, *Israel's African Setback in Perspective* (Jerusalem: Hebrew University, 1974) and Leopold Laufer, *Israel and the Developing Countries* (New York: Twentieth Century Fund, 1967). On Egypt in Africa, see Tareq Y. Ismael, *The UAR in Africa* (Evanston, Illinois: Northwestern University Press, 1971).

12. We have thus introduced five of the eight archetypal forms of relationship which allow self and other to deal simultaneously with continuity and change, collaboration and conflict, and the achieving of justice. These five relationships are emanation, incoherence, transformation, direct bargaining, and buffering. (In the formal statement of the theory, brokerage is subsumed under the term "buffering," since a concept, and not only a person, may also serve to mediate between ourselves and others.) Although we do little with the remaining three archetypal relationships in this essay, a brief indication should be made of what is missing. Isolation is a relationship in which individuals or groups agree upon one mode of collaboration—to refrain from demanding anything of each other. Both sides collaborate in avoiding all conflict intended to lead to change in, with, or by the other. This kind of relationship is, obviously, dying out in Africa. Subjection is a relationship in which I control others as a means to my own end, whether I base this control on the naked powers of the logic of

deductive reasoning, on standards of efficiency, or simply on the power of the gun.

Boundary-management is a relationship in which self and other are both entitled to claim an autonomous zone of jurisdiction based on some explicit principle of law or competence. Such autonomous zones of jurisdiction both internally and in relation to others define the special power of modern bureaucracy as well as modern corporations, private or public. Boundary-management of this kind is beginning to increase in strength in Africa, but not all so-called African "bureaucracies" are as yet marked by it in practice. One of the important characteristics of bargaining and brokerage in Africa therefore is that its societies as a whole are not yet dominated by private or public jurisdictions of autonomous power. Whenever such power already exists, as in a marketing board or a large corporation, it does, however, enter into bargaining with a more sustained and better organized strength than others who are not entitled to such claims.

13. In *The Dialectics of Transformation in Politics, Personality, and History*, we show that this process of transformation has been experienced and discussed in this same underlying form in Africa, Europe, the Middle East, the Far East, and among American Indians for at least two millennia. If there were not such an archetypal pattern which all human beings can experience under these circumstances, incoherence could only lead to anarchy, either constituted of broken connections or of new connections we would not know how to share. Our theory, by resting upon the human experience of archetypal patterns, is therefore not culture-bound. What distinguishes transformation—which has been experienced before in human history—from modernization, i.e., transformation in the modern age, is that now all concrete inherited forms of human relationships are coming apart and can never permanently be put into any fixed, final form again. Never before the modern age were all human relationships in motion in this way.

II The Anatomy of Violence in Contemporary Black Africa

Ali A. Mazrui

It was in 1959 that the Hutu of what is now the Republic of Rwanda rose against the Tutsis, who had ruled and despised the numerically superior Hutu for generations. An estimated 20,000 lives were lost in the blood bath that followed, and five times that number fled for refuge to neighboring countries. By the time Rwanda became an independent republic in 1962, the government was indisputably Hutu. In neighboring Burundi, where the same two ethnic communities also shared a nation in approximately the same proportions, the Tutsi have remained in power. A government assertion in 1972 of the discovery of a plot to overthrow the Tutsi regime initiated a wave of reprisals that resulted in the deaths of upward to 100,000 citizens, the great majority of them Hutu. Many more thousands fled the country.

Between these two massacres, violent eruptions also had taken place elsewhere in sub-Saharan Africa. The shaky passage of the Belgian Congo into independence in 1960, as a result of an abrupt turnaround in Belgian colonial policy that left little time for transitional preparations, was followed by four years of turbulence and instability at various levels of Zairian society. In Nigeria in January 1966, a particularly violent military coup, spearheaded by middle grade Ibo officers from the Eastern Region, swept away the federal parliamentary regime that had governed in Lagos since British rule ended in 1960. An Ibo, General J.T.U. Aguiyi-Ironsi, was designated head of a new Supreme Military Council. A few months later, backlash by the Hausa of Nigeria's most populous Northern Region resulted in the butchering of thousands of Ibo in a communal uprising. The stage was set for the outbreak in 1967 of a brutal civil war that did not end until 1970, with the reintegration of the Ibo-led Biafran secessionists into the mainstream of Nigerian political life the eventual result.

45

A civil war of even longer duration was that of the Sudan, where, as the British departure began in 1955, the black south, religiously oriented toward traditional African belief systems or Christianity, began its struggle for autonomy in the face of a massive military effort by the primarily Arab and Muslim north to consolidate a unitary state. Several hundred thousand lives were lost in the Sudanese civil war before it came to a negotiated end early in 1972.

Africa's numerous coups and counter-coups since independence—totalling no less than 50 between 1960 and 1975—have varied widely in the degree of violence experienced. In contrast to the execution of a significant number of the previous political elite which characterized the end of parliamentary rule in Nigeria, the overthrow of President Kwame Nkrumah in neighboring Ghana in 1966 was remarkably low key. Many of Nkrumah's senior officials were jailed, of course, but there was very little killing; it was not even necessary to impose a curfew in the capital city of Accra. The removal of President Yakubu Gowon from power in Nigeria in 1975 was even more staid.

Then there have been coups which started off as relatively nonviolent, but deteriorated over time under various pressures. In this category are the overthrow of the civilian regime of President Milton Obote by General Idi Amin in Uganda in 1971, and what was termed "the gradual coup" by the Ethiopian military in 1974. In the case of the Uganda coup, there was brutality against "loyalists" within the armed forces from the outset, but Amin's treatment of civilian members of the previous government was initially conciliatory, even magnanimous. Instead of being jailed (as were Nkrumah's closest advisors in Ghana) or killed (as were many members of the regime of Prime Minister Sir Abubakar Tafawa Balewa in the first military coup in Nigeria), Uganda's ousted civilian officials were, for a time, ignored. Many found refuge in the most luxurious hotel in Kampala. The magnanimity eroded as Amin consolidated his power, however, and former ministers of the Obote government began to disappear; in most cases, it seems clear, they were murdered. Many unarmed civilians belonging to the "wrong tribe" also suffered, sometimes with systematic torture preceding the final *coup de grace*. Within the armed forces, interethnic violence gradually culminated in massive reprisals against those whose loyalty to the Amin regime was in doubt.

In February 1975, the new military regime in Ethiopia, angered and frustrated by the secessionist movement in the strategically important coastal province of Erithrea, deliberately wiped out two villages near the Erithrean city of Asmara on the suspicion that the population of the villages included rebels in hiding. A few months previously, the regime had executed a number of former members of deposed Emperor Haile Selassie's Imperial elite, including two former prime ministers.

In 1973, Chad's President N'Garta Tombalbaye inaugurated a "cultural revolution" in his country, designed to emphasize afresh African "authenticity" and reduce the heavy weight of Western (notably French) civilization. In 1974, press reports referred to the forceful "initiation" of westernized Chadians, ranging from college professors to Christian priests, to help them dewesternize their minds and hearts. *The New York Times*, for example, reported in October that "the ordeals are known to include floggings, mock burials, drugging and acts of humiliation."[1] Other coverage, in a similar vein, reported that a number of Protestant clergymen who resisted this initiation rite lost their lives.

These acts of violence experienced by Africa in the decade and a half following the end of all but the remnants of the colonial era demand, first, to be understood. Beyond the causes, what are the short and longer term consequences of what has occurred? Most importantly and most urgently, how can Africa move toward institutionalizing the resolution of conflicts within nations, as it has sought to do (through the Organization of African Unity) in resolving disputes between nations? A start has to be made by interpreting black violence. Diagnosis does not lead directly to solutions, and Africans themselves may need to try various experiments concurrently with the exploration of causes, but understanding is the first step.

Three Kinds of Violence

Three broad types of large-scale violence have occurred in Africa since 1955. First, of course, there has been violence arising from the effort to define the proper boundaries of a political community. A civil war which results from an attempt by one ethnic or geographical unit to secede from a country whose boundaries were set in the last century by European colonial powers without much regard for ethnic or geographical realities falls into this category. The Nigerian civil war and the Sudanese civil war both arose out of a profound dissatisfaction with the inherited frontiers of nationhood, as did the American civil war a century earlier.

A second type of violence is concerned with redefining the purposes and policies of a political community whose boundaries are acceptable to the contenders. This type of violence can also result in a civil war, especially if the different groups are ideologically divided, and if each seeks to control the center at whatever cost. The Spanish civil war in the 1930s falls into this second category, since it was concerned with the issue of who should control Madrid and rule Spain, rather than with the boundaries of Spain.

A third kind of violence is not primarily concerned with the frontiers of a given political community or the domestic purposes of that community, but rather arises as a result of pressures emanating from the wider environment in which a community must function. Violence sparked by "environmental" pressures includes, in the first instance, situations in which a crisis in one African country spills over and affects another African country. The civil war in the Congo (now Zaire) in the early 1960s resulted in the bombing of Ugandan villages by planes of the central Congolese government, partly on the assumption that the Uganda government was supporting Congolese dissidents fighting to unseat the central government. Similarly, the confrontations beginning in 1971 between Tanzania and Uganda, resulting at times in border clashes, stemmed from post-coup violence within Uganda, and the degree to which Tanzania took sides in the quarrels among Ugandans.

Environmentally induced violence has a second and larger dimension, in that international events only indirectly or incidentally involving Africa can profoundly affect political and social stability in individual African countries. To what extent did the fall of the price of cocoa on the international market, combined with the relative monoculture of the Ghanaian export economy, contribute to the fall of Kwame Nkrumah? Analysis relating violence in African countries to larger international geopolitical issues, perhaps especially the global distribution of resources and the terms of trade and aid, is fundamental to the understanding of some important trends in less-developed societies.

There is yet another sense of environment to be considered in any diagnosis of African violence: the basic relationship between man and nature. A natural calamity can precipitate acts of violence. Floods which destroy food resources can arouse new levels of selfish acquisitiveness among starving peoples. A prolonged drought can impel neighbor to fight neighbor, or the ruled to rise against rulers. It is arguable that the fall of the decade-old government of President Hamani Diori in Niger in 1974 was directly connected with the Sahel drought, the hardships which had resulted from it, and widespread dissatisfaction with the government's distribution of aid received from abroad.

In reality, of course, these three categories of violence are seldom neatly differentiated. There are times when violence has multiple causes, and it can be difficult to distinguish whether the primary factor is a challenge to the boundaries of the political community, the policies being pursued in the name of that community, or pressures from the larger environment in which that community functions. But a quest for an understanding of the dynamics of violent behavior in African countries involves an effort to distinguish between these levels, and to explore which factors are amenable to ameliorative measures.

While the nature of violence itself can be separated into these broad categories or levels, African violence at any level must also be studied in terms of the local cultural, economic, and demographic contexts in which it occurs. It is to these cultural, economic, and demographic factors that we now turn, with the object of relating them to the three levels of civil strife.

The Cultural Contexts of African Violence

Most African countries have mutiple indigenous cultures, with an overlay of Western or Islamic culture as well. The relationship between the various indigenous cultures, though at times tense, is not, in the modern period at least, a relationship of domination or conquest. The Ibo do not attempt to convert the Yoruba to Ibo culture, nor does Yoruba culture exercise hegemony over the Hausa. We might characterize this multiplicity of indigenous cultures in most African countries as horizontal cultural pluralism.

The relationship between Western culture and each separate African culture, on the other hand, is one of domination and conversion. Because of its global prestige, and because of the prior thrust of colonial penetration, Western culture has been a conquering system of values in Africa, leaving many indigenous cultures on the defensive. The relationship between Kikuyu and English culture, or between the ways of the Saras in Chad and the values of the French, is a relationship of dominion and conquest. It is a relationship of vertical cultural dualism. In countries such as Kenya and Chad, this egalitarian diversity of indigenous systems of values coexists with a hierarchical relationship between the indigenous systems collectively and the technologically superior Western civilization. Horizontal cultural pluralism coexists with vertical cultural dualism.

Certain forms of violence arise out of the delicacy of this balancing act. The fact that the various indigenous cultures that make up all but a handful of African states speak different languages and are, or may be, products of different cultural histories, sharpens the sense of distinctiveness from other groups, even when a people are politicized and nation-minded. Should there be a scramble for opportunities in schools, or for jobs in the civil service, or for business opportunities in the marketplace, the tension of competition can reactivate the sense of primordial distinctiveness. It is not an exaggeration to say that African culture groups can at times see themselves as no less different from each other than Americans saw the Vietnamese. The ease with which some American military personnel could commit atrocities such as My Lai arose out of a sense of cultural distance between themselves and their victims great enough to result in a certain degree of dehumanization. Many African communities, though forced by the colonial experience to share the same borders, feel virtually as distant from some of their compatriots as those involved at My Lai. A crucial problem for African governments is how to promote greater identification across these cultural chasms.

The Hausa in northern Nigeria regarded the enterprising Ibo, to all intents and purposes, as foreigners in their midst, endangering their sense of security and their jobs and economic opportunities. When the Hausa rose against the Ibo in their midst in 1966, and killed them in thousands, the My Lai factor of cultural distance (that is, the incapacity to recognize each other as fellow citizens of the same political community) was clearly involved. To that extent, violence arising out of horizontal cultural pluralism in African societies in indicative of a deep unhappiness about the current boundaries of the political community and, implicitly or explicitly, a wish that these could be redefined. Major ethnic eruptions in Africa are indeed cases of the first level of civil strife discussed at the outset of this essay.

But when violence erupts because of the vertical cultural dualism, manifesting tensions between those who have adopted Western culture and those who have not, the quarrel may be about who should exercise ultimate authority (the intellectuals or those who are not intellectuals), or about national directions and purposes, or both of these issues. In any case, boundaries of the political community are not in question.

The distinction between disagreements over concrete policies and disagreements over who holds power is important, though the two are often intertwined. Tensions between the westernized and the nonwesternized African are often focused on the central issue of who shall rule the country, or who shall determine its directions, and not necessarily or very precisely on what those directions should be. Thus, nonwesternized military rulers in Africa sometimes pursue foreign policies which are not very different from those followed by their more westernized civilian counterparts prior to the military takeover. The coup had to do with the wielding of power, and the ethnic factor may or may not have been vital. Indeed, it is not unusual for nonwesternized military rulers to come from almost precisely the same ethnic groups as the westernized civilian rulers they overthrew.

A major form of violence emanating from vertical cultural dualism is violence perpetrated against intellectuals. This is what happened in Zaire (then the Democratic Republic of the Congo) in 1964, when thousands of moderately educated Africans were killed in Stanleyville and other outposts of opposition to the Kinshasa-based central government. A pattern of intolerance toward at least certain sections of the educated class also gradually emerged in Uganda following Idi Amin's coup of 1971. Although the atmosphere in Uganda was not neatly anti-intellectual, enough intellectuals suffered, or began to feel insecure, to result in a significant exodus of some of the best educated Ugandans, including civilian officials, army officers, and academicians. Nairobi, Dar es Salaam, Lusaka, and London have become major centers of Ugandan refugees; and the University of Nairobi, the University of Zambia, the University of Dar es Salaam, the London School of Economics, and Brigham Young University in Salt Lake City have been among the beneficiaries of the academic exodus.

In Zaire and in Uganda, anti-intellectualism interacted with ethnic regional factors. In Burundi, the interaction is even clearer. The brutality against the Hutu in 1972 concentrated overwhelmingly on those with "leadership potential," which often meant those with some degree of Western education. Many Hutu students were dragged screaming from classrooms in schools, colleges, or the university, and killed. Many were betrayed by their Tutsi fellow students, some by their Tutsi teachers and professors. Since then, educators in Burundi have found Hutus reluctant to go beyond the equivalent of junior high school. A teacher has been quoted as saying that "you can be sure the Tutsi will have no Hutu competition for a long time to come."[2] The Hutu saw what happened to so many who had some education.

In Chad the moves against the educated class before the coup of April 1975 were more clearly a case of tense vertical cultural dualism, as the Tombalbaye government carried forward its effort to restore some respect for ancestral ways in Chad. The government of Mobutu Sésé Séko in Zaire is committed to a similar program of cultural authenticity, seeking to reduce the dominating influence of Euro-Christian civilization in the life of Zairian society. Leaders such as Tombalbaye and Mobutu Sésé Séko have not hesitated to apply strong and sometimes brutal pressure in the pursuit of greater parity between the imported culture and the indigenous pluralistic heritage.

Violence emanating from vertical cultural dualism has its ancestry in Africa's particular relationship with the broader global environment. Africa has been penetrated so disproportionately by an alien civilization that many countries have chosen their rulers on the basis of who has acquired the literary and verbal skills of Western culture. There are still countries where no person can become a member of parliament, even if he speaks a dozen indigenous African languages, if he does not have an adequate command of the imperial language from Europe. On the other hand, a person could become a member of parliament without knowing a single indigenous language, not even that of his constituents. One African constitution after another has given considerable preeminence to the imported language, and has virtually ignored the wealth of horizontal linguistic pluralism. African educational institutions have been designed to transmit Western civilization, with relatively little sensitivity even now to local civilizations. Violent eruptions between the westernized and the nonwesternized in Africa are a reflection of the extent to which the Eurocentrism of world culture has become an aspect of African domestic realities.

The Economic Contexts of African Violence

At least until the energy panic began in 1973, the world appeared doomed to a rigid stratification between an affluent northern hemisphere consisting of North America, Europe, the Soviet Union, and Japan, and, on the other side of the economic divide, the less developed and more indigent countries of Africa, much of Asia, and much of Latin America. An international class system had emerged, and the gap between the poor and the rich seemed to be widening.

Two equations have been shattered as a result of the energy crisis. First, the assumption that a country must be economically developed in order to be economically powerful has been rendered obsolete. Since 1973, it has become increasingly clear that a country like Saudi Arabia can be immensely powerful economically, while remaining underdeveloped at the same time. Also shattered was the equation that "underdeveloped countries" are "poor countries." We now know that a country can be underdeveloped and not poor.

These modifications in the international stratification system resulting from the successes of the Organization of Petroleum-Exporting Countries have not changed the fact, however, that the bulk of the African continent is still both underdeveloped and poor. The great majority of the poorest nations of the world are within the African continent—the so-called "Fourth World." And yet even the poorest of Africa's poor have been shocked out of their primordial complacency by the Western demonstration impact. The expectations of the peoples of countries such as Niger, Tanzania, Rwanda, Burundi, and the Central African Republic have risen far beyond those of their forefathers, yet the capacity of any government to approximate those dreams is still incredibly low.

Ted Robert Gurr has defined the resulting phenomenon of relative deprivation as a "perceived discrepancy between men's value expectations and their value capabilities"—the discrepancy between the goods and conditions of life to which people believe they are rightfully entitled, on the one hand, and the goods and conditions they think they are capable of attaining or maintaining, given the social means available to them:

The primary causal sequence in political violence is first the development of discontent, second the politicization of that discontent, and finally its actualization in violent action against political objects and actors. Discontent arising from the perception of relative deprivation is the basic, instigating condition for participants in collective violence. The linked concepts of discontent and deprivation comprise most of the psychological states implicit or explicit in such theoretical notions about the causes of violence as frustration, alienation, drive and goal conflicts, exigency, and strain. . . .[3]

But Gurr assumes too readily that relative deprivation manifests itself directly in politically conscious discontent. Economic disadvantage and awareness of relative deprivation can also result in forms of violence which are not directly politicized, even though the ancestry is ultimately political. Violence in the black ghettos of Detroit, Chicago, or New York, may not be politically conscious violence, but its ancestry can be traced in part to the economic deprivations of ghetto areas and the response of the dwellers to the stratification system of which the ghetto is a part.

We now know that the incidence of violence is higher in disadvantaged ghetto conditions within an otherwise affluent society than it is in the rest of the society. Moreover, far more ghetto violence is committed by the underprivileged against other underprivileged people than it is against the well-to-do. In New York City, eight out of every nine murders committed by black people have other blacks as their victims. The brutality is often both intraclass and intraracial.[4] Is there a similar ghetto syndrome in relation to the international system of stratification? Are poor countries more prone to violence than affluent countries?

Such a formulation oversimplifies the issue, to be sure, but there is a residual area of legitimate analogy between domestic ghettos and international ghettos such as Burundi and Rwanda. The issue is not simply one of being poor, but one of being poor in relation to an affluent environment. It is also an issue of being poor in a situation of rapidly shifting values and accelerated social change.

In the case of Harlem or Detroit, sheer physical mobility and regional migration patterns are significant factors in accelerating social change. New people come in from poorer or more bigoted parts of the United States, seek to establish themselves in conditions of discrimination and indigence, and gradually drift toward looser mores and weaker social inhibitions. In the case of poor countries, social change may be accelerated by internal migration from rural to urban areas, increased interpenetration as ethnic groups move into each other's ancestral regions, and selective but highly visible upward social mobility for a conspicuous few following independence. Vertical cultural dualism contributes to the fluidity, as traditional values lose their grip under the impact of the conquering Western alternatives. Because the new values of the West are only partially assimilated, the result can be, at least for a time, a kind of normative void, an area of conflicting values and mutually negating social inhibitions.

Thus, the ghetto complex of Chicago and Detroit begins to manifest itself in conditions at once different and profoundly comparable. The people of Rwanda, Burundi, Uganda, and Chad are in varying degrees aware of the broad possibilities of the modern world, and at the same time keenly and definitely aware of their predicament. As the gap between what is ideally feasible and what has practically been actualized yawns in cruel mockery, the ghetto complex starts its evil game. The poor kill the poor, the exploited turn against those in a similar predicament. Just as black kills black in Harlem, black kills black in Uganda, Zaire, and the Central African Republic. Relative deprivation once again looms into relevance, when those who live in the slums begin to sense that there are happier gardens in suburbia. But, Gurr's theory to the contrary, relative deprivation need not be directly politicized in order to result in politically derived violence. The poor may kill the indigent and still not fully perceive the political roots of their mutual brutality.

Not all inequalities contributing to bloodshed in Africa arise from such environmental causes, however. Some are traditionally and primordially domestic. Once again, the striking example lies in the violent history between the Tutsi and Hutu in Rwanda and Burundi.

The Hutu, a Bantu people, arrived in this region from the southwest and began to cultivate the land. And then, a thousand years ago, the Tutsi, with a cattle-raising culture, drifted into the area. The Tutsi were physically tall and slender, with physical attributes more characteristic of Ethiopia and Somalia than of Bantu Africa proper. In due time, a feudal system based on cattle was established—a social contract by which the Hutu were provided with some cattle in exchange for service to the Tutsi in perpetuity. The Tutsi hegemony persisted after Germany colonized the Tutsi and the Hutu in 1885, and remained in force when the Belgians assumed the trusteeship of Ruanda-Urundi after World War I.

As the two peoples entered the second half of the twentieth century, a faint awareness that things need not be what they were began to dawn on the Hutu. As a Hutu intellectual explained to a Western journalist in 1973: "The Tutsis were taught from birth that they were superior and they believed it. We were taught that we were inferior and we believed it. So, in effect, we were inferior until we made ourselves believe otherwise."[5]

The rise of modern and egalitarian forms of African nationalism after World War II set the stage for the slaughters which have devastated the lives of these two communities in two different countries since 1959:

The era of independence, with its emphasis on majority rule, also meant that the leaders of the Hutus began to feel the power of their numbers. On the other hand, the Tutsis—only 15 percent of the population of Burundi, 10 percent of Rwanda—began to feel deep fears about their place in societies where power might go to the majority. These two feelings—inferiority by the Hutus, fear by the Tutsis—probably account for most of the terrible bloodshed of the last ten years.[6]

This had been a clear case of domestic stratification, going back centuries before Europeans established colonial rule, and therefore a system of stratification that is independent of the vertical cultural dualism which characterizes political elites in some other African countries.

Culturally, Hutu and Tutsi are in fact much closer than most other communities in Africa are to each other. Within Rwanda, the lingua franca of both groups is Kinyaruanda, while Kirundi is the common tongue in neighboring Burundi. In the case of the Tutsi and the Hutu, then, the problem is not one of cultural distance resulting in an incapacity to recognize each other as compatriots. Rather, it is a problem of such cultural closeness that the lower caste majority could no longer accept the Tutsi minority as legitimate overlords. In the ultimate analysis, the Hutu-Tutsi violence has to do with defining the proper boundaries of a political community. If the two groups had been of comparable size, the best answer might have been a neat ethnic exchange of populations between Rwanda and Burundi, with Rwanda becoming an entirely Hutu country, and Burundi a Tutsi country. Had this been feasible, the two countries might have become among the very few truly homogenous nation-states in the classical West European sense within Africa. Such a neat exchange of populations is bedevilled, however, by the considerable difference in numbers between the Hutus and Tutsis.

The Demographic Context of African Violence

As matters now stand, Rwanda and Burundi are among the most densely populated countries in Africa, and among the more densely populated in the world. Conservative estimates put Rwanda's population at 370 per square mile, and Burundi's at 225. This contrasts with a population density of less than 20 per square mile in neighboring Tanzania.[7]

How much significance should be attached to the fact that mainland Tanzania is at once one of the most sparsely populated countries of middle Africa and also one of the least politically violent political entities in Africa? The question which arises is whether there is indeed a correlation between density of population and certain levels of political violence in multi-ethnic countries not yet beyond the danger of violence over the proper boundaries of the political community. The question of causality becomes even more pertinent when one notes the marked difference between the island of Zanzibar and mainland Tanzania, again in density of population and in scale of violence.

This is not to suggest that demography is the root cause of the violence in Rwanda, Burundi, or Zanzibar, because more immediate causes are obvious in each instance. It is not even suggested here that demography is ever likely to be a sufficient condition, in and of itself, to set off violent political eruptions. All that is being asked is whether demography might, given other conditions, tilt the balance. In this connection, René Lemarchand has observed that the most salient combination of environmental and situational factors likely to generate more pressures in Rwanda and Burundi in the years ahead include: "an explosive population growth in both Rwanda and Burundi, far exceeding the economic capabilities of either state and hence reinforcing the conditions of chronic instability and ethnic strife inherent in their respective social systems."[8]

The demographic situation in Africa in the modern period has been aggravated by two major developments: the rapid decline of the death rate as a result of improvements in medical and sanitation facilities, and the emergence of legally defined national boundaries constituting serious political impediments to mass migrations. In Rwanda and Burundi, a lack of awareness of the implications of population growth and traditional ignorance about contraception (reinforced by the negative influence of the dominant Roman Catholic Church on these matters) have also conspired to intensify the population problem. The population growth rate in Rwanda is at least 3.5 percent per annum; in Burundi at least three percent. Both are high in absolute terms, and dangerously high given the existing high density.

Before the Europeans came with their concern about carefully defined territorial boundaries, black Africa had its own safety valves for population pressures. Migration to an unused area of land some 50 to 100 miles away was the simplest mechanism. Indeed, the British historian Roland Oliver has likened the momentous phenomenon of Bantu migration and expansion in Africa in past centuries to the European settlement of America and Australia rather than to the Teutonic invasion in Europe in the Middle Ages. That is to say, Oliver saw Bantu migration as more of a population explosion than conquest, although conquest often accompanied population growth.[9] In any case, the coming of the territorial nation-state shut off these primordial safety valves for relieving the pressure for scarce resources.

Another chapter in this book deals with the low incidence of conflict during the postcolonial era over redefinition of national boundaries. Periodic border clashes between Kenya and Somalia, or Morocco and Algeria, or Chad and Sudan, or Upper Volta and Dahomey notwithstanding, the conflict-potential of African boundaries remains relatively low, considering the arbitrariness with which these boundaries were drawn by European imperial powers in the nineteenth and early twentieth centuries. What has not been adequately examined by scholars is the conflict-potential within each territorial entity emanating from the placement of national boundaries. It is a mistake to assume that the only violence generated by boundaries is violence over or about those boundaries. Rwanda, Burundi, and Tanzania again are cases in point.

It is in part an accident of European rather than African history that Rwanda and Burundi did not become part of what is now mainland Tanzania. All three territories were ruled by Germany before World War I. Each imperial power calculated the administrative convenience of determining which of its colonies was separate from which and in what manner. Had both Rwanda and Burundi become part of sparsely populated Tanganyika (now mainland Tanzania), the scale of migration of the Hutu and Tutsi within the broader area might have been enough to ease the tensions of population pressure that built up in the landlocked enclaves to which these two communities were in fact confined by the borders drawn by German administrators.

Moreover, since neither Hutu nor Tutsi would have been in a position to gain ascendancy in the central government in Dar es Salaam, their power to inflict damage upon each other would have been reduced. Certainly neither would be in control of an army. Outbreaks of violence between the two communities would be handled by a central government with its own institutions of pacification and stabilization. It is even conceivable that the Hutu and the Tutsi, because they are culturally very much alike and share a common language, might have found a basis of solidarity against other groups in a large Tanzania, and united to compete for electoral advantage or patronage. An alternative scenario might have found the Hutu and the Tutsi mobilizing as a united Kinyaruanda force within the area covered by Rwanda and Burundi to become a separatist movement within Tanzania. Such a scenario could also lead to violence, but the scale would have been different.

After World War I terminated Germany's role as a colonial power, Tanganyika became a mandate of the League of Nations and was entrusted to Britain for administration. Rwanda and Burundi were entrusted by the League to Belgium, which administered them virtually as an integrated political system (Ruanda-Urundi). All three territories later became mandates of the United Nations. The bypassing of this opportunity to integrate the Hutu and the Tutsi into a larger territorial entity set the scene for the demographic pressures, ethnic rivalry, competition for the control of the means of destruction, and periodic eruptions of mutual brutality that have thus far marked Rwanda's and Burundi's history in the latter half of the century. In the absence of open frontiers for migration, many Hutu in Burundi simply wait until the next round of brutality, knowing that one has a better chance of escaping to refuge and political asylum in neighboring countries under the immediate pressure of brutality. Ironically, borders become tighter when violence ceases, and those who remain behind quietly await another confrontation with fate.

The placement of Uganda's borders also has contributed to that country's internal violence. It is an irony of history that Idi Amin might easily have been a non-Ugandan had the border been drawn a few miles differently to take account of ethnic realities. The ethnic groups in political power since the military coup in 1971 are from the north of the country, but they spread over into neighboring states because colonial-era boundary makers took little account of ethnicity. Segments of General Amin's own tribe, the Kakwa, are in the Sudan and Zaire, as well as in Uganda, and he has not hesitated to recruit ethnic compatriots from the Sudan and Zaire into the Ugandan military. By 1975, a sizable proportion of Uganda's armed forces consisted of non-Ugandans, exercising considerable authority and power over the population. Had the boundaries been drawn in a way which made West Nile District of Uganda part of the Sudan, as a number of administrators during the British colonial period recommended, the history of violence in Uganda could have been dramatically different. All the Kakwa would have been part of the Sudan.

Looking at Africa as a whole, the conclusion is inescapable that there would have been violence whichever way the Europeans had defined the borders of their colonies. But viewed from the perspective of individual entities as they now exist, it is clear that certain alternative territorial definitions would have had less violent potential. Uganda probably would have experienced less violence if the West Nile were part of the Sudan; and the Hutu and the Tutsi might have brutalized each other on a more limited scale if both were subject to the government of Tanzania's President Julius Nyerere in Dar es Salaam, and both were without the military instruments of mutual destruction. Nigeria would have had a less violent history since independence if north and south had been separate states.

The interplay between demographic factors and the geopolitics of boundaries is implicit in the earlier discussion of the Hutu-Tutsi confrontation. Demography in Africa has political relevance in relation not only to density of population but also to concentrations of population, and relative sizes of the different ethnic groups within a given area, and the competition for resources.

Density is to be distinguished from concentration in the sense that the latter refers to migratory patterns which result in major concentrations either in urban areas or in more prosperous subregions. The national density might be low, and yet a particular city or a particular region might have a high concentration of people.

The size of the different ethnic groups is also important. On balance, large ethnic groups converging on the center of the nation, and competing for power and influence, run greater risk of violent conflict than small ethnic groups scattered more widely. To understand the high incidence of ethnic tension in Kenya and Uganda, one must take account of the fact that each of these countries entered into independence with at least one large ethnic community which was centrally located, critical in national affairs, and had access to certain political, economic, and educational advantages. Under British rule, the Baganda were not only the largest ethnic community in Uganda but also the most centrally located in terms of proximity to the capital city, the most responsive to the new economic and cultural civilization which came with the British, and the most favored. In the first years after Uganda became independent, the "Buganda issue"—in effect, the power position of what was known as the kingdom of Buganda—was a major source of tension. The conflict potential of the Baganda role in Uganda has been overshadowed since the 1971 military coup by the quarrels within the armed forces involving northern ethnic groups in particular. But the Baganda remain Uganda's largest ethnic community and the now-quiescent "Buganda issue" may once again emerge in national affairs once the internecine military conflicts of the erratic Amin period have become history.

The tensions between the Kikuyu and the Luo in Kenya, both large communities by African standards, also illustrate the relevance of size to the style of competition. Although Kenya as of the mid-1970s has been spared some of the convulsions that have characterized Ugandan and Nigerian history in the previous decade, all three countries illustrate an ominous interplay between ethnicity, size, location, density, and concentration. In Nigeria the cost was heavy, both at the time of the eruptions against the Ibo in 1966 in the Northern Region, and in the course of the civil war from 1967 to 1970. Helping to set the stage for the Hausa-Ibo violence of 1966 and the subsequent Biafran secessionist movement and civil war were the exceptionally large size of Nigeria's Ibo, Hausa, and Yoruba communities; the location, concentration, and uneven prosperity of these communities; and the fragility of the regionally and ethnically balanced federal government.

Similarly the Mau Mau insurrection against the British presence in colonial Kenya during the 1950s can be related to the concentration of land-hungry Kikuyu in a finite area overlooking large areas of relatively underutilized farmland reserved for European settlers. The land hunger and population explosion in Kikuyuland, combined with rising expectations fed in part by the nearness of fertile land reserved for others, propelled much of the community from frustration into open rebellion. In retrospect, one can say that the Mau Mau uprising set in motion a major reconsideration of colonialism, and was a significant factor in moving Britain (and subsequently France and Belgium) more rapidly than had theretofore been envisaged in the direction of releasing its African colonies.

The Special Case of Southern Africa

Southern Africa presents a special mixture of primary and tertiary violence—of violence concerned with redefining the political community and violence related to the wider international environment. Primary violence in southern Africa has been both interracial (white against black) and intraracial (black against black). The Angolan tragedy illustrates how easily tertiary violence against colonialism can evolve into an acute primary struggle when a fragile, ethnically divided country suddenly becomes an independent nation. The unfinished story of Rhodesia (Zimbabwe) has already involved both interracial violence (black against white) and eruptions of internecine black violence.

The contemporary political morality of black Africa is supportive of anticolonial violence in general and, in rhetoric at least, of violence directed against governments ruled by white minorities. This acceptance of interracial violence in the name of national liberation is, however, a relatively recent development. Earlier phases of African nationalism were characterized by a strong distrust of violence as a strategy of liberation.

The ideological history of President Kenneth Kaunda of Zambia is particularly instructive, because it mirrors the shift which has taken place. Kaunda's early nationalist views were greatly influenced by Mohandas Gandhi. Although violence was a tempting strategy for those who were denied alternative means of correcting injustices, Kaunda stood firmly for *satyagraha*, or passive resistance: "I could not lend myself to take part in any [violent] campaigns. I reject absolutely violence in any of its forms as a solution to our problem."[10]

Kaunda has always been basically a pragmatist rather than a philosopher, and his commitment to nonviolence did not arise from a romantic assumption that man was essentially peaceful. On the contrary, Kaunda accepted that man, "just like any other animal," is violent.[11] What was distinctive about man, in Kaunda's view, was that he was capable of disciplining or modifying his own nature by cultivating certain aspects or partially repressing others: ". . . we must understand that non-violence is, as Mahatma Gandhi described it, a 'big experiment in man's development towards a higher realization of himself.' . . . Man . . . is violent. But he has so many finer qualities than other animals that we should entertain this Gandhi thought. . . ."[12]

Kaunda remained an ardent Gandhian throughout that phase of his life in which he was a nationalist agitating against British rule. But when Northern Rhodesia (now Zambia) began the transition to independence under Kaunda's prime ministership in 1964, he was propelled almost immediately into a painful test of his rejection of violence "in any of its forms as a solution to our problems." In July 1964—just three months before Zambia was to become fully independent—a "state of emergency" was declared after the separatist Lumpa Church of prophetess Alice Lenshina rose in fanatical and violent protest partly against a requirement that its members declare their political loyalty to the new government by joining the ruling United National Independence Party. Some

600 persons died in the several weeks before Alice Lenshina agreed to surrender herself in exchange for a pledge that there would not be reprisals against her followers.[13] A major landmark in the evolution of Kaunda's view of violence is reflected in his pledge to parliament at the height of the Lumpa affair: "My government will spare no efforts to bring them down as quickly as possible. Even if it means other people calling me savage then I am going to be one."[14]

The Lumpa uprising awakened Kaunda to the realization that *satyagraha* was conceived as a strategy for winning self-government, and that Gandhi himself had never been placed in the position of having to adapt its principles to the changed circumstances in which a leader is placed when he must administer a government. Kaunda's acceptance of the reality that governing a given territory is likely to involve the use of force, or at least the demonstrated potential to use force, was next called into play in 1965, when the white minority regime in neighboring (Southern) Rhodesia unilaterally declared the colony's independence from Britain. Kaunda was among the most vocal advocates of the use of military force against the illegal regime, even inviting British forces to use Zambia as a staging area for operations against the Smith regime.

In the 1970s, however, Kaunda's basic preference for peaceful solutions reemerged in his support for South African Prime Minister Vorster's venture in détente and dialogue (rather than violent confrontation) as a means of working out the future of southern Africa. It is an ironic twist of history that Kaunda should rediscover his Gandhian roots through a South African mentor; for it was in South Africa that Gandhi first experimented with *satyagraha*. Is the ghost of Gandhi still walking in southern Africa? Can "soul force" destroy apartheid in the fullness of time?

My own view is that the region is likely to need both Gandhians and guerrillas before racial equity finally prevails. In any case, the achievement of racial equity is only the first phase of the evolving drama of southern Africa; the political and ethnic cleavages between blacks in this part of the continent will require even longer term remedial treatment by Africans who care.

From Understanding to Action

Although the Mau Mau insurrection illustrates that violent eruptions can sometimes serve positive functions in Africa, the continent will not be fully liberated to focus on genuine nation-building until ways of moderating and mitigating violent confrontations between its own peoples are devised. Given the causes and consequences of violence considered in this chapter, it is quite clear that no immediate solutions are likely or even feasible. The cases of New York, Detroit, and Chicago are disturbing reminders that our understanding of the sociology of violence is not even remotely matched by a capacity to find solutions to known social problems. Despite exhaustive exploration of the dynamics of ghetto violence in the United States, these three cities remain among the most violent in the world.

Nevertheless, any society which knows that it contains the elements of violence has an obligation to work toward the creation, through experimentation, of mechanisms for the gradual moderation and containment of the inevitable eruptions. Progress toward conflict resolution in Africa will necessarily involve a combination of judicial, administrative, and diplomatic processes and institutions.

Toward Judicial Mechanisms for Conflict Resolution

For purposes of this discussion, we define judicial mechanisms for conflict resolution as those mechanisms which require (1) a body of law on which to base decisions, (2) officials with legal expertise to interpret and administer this body of law, and (3) a system of sanctions that can be applied with some degree of effectiveness against those found guilty of violating the law.

Is it within the realm of possiblity that the Organization of African Unity could establish an All-Africa Supreme Tribunal of Justice? At first glance, a proposal for a coherent continental court system with an appellate tribunal at its pinnacle sounds so ambitious as to be sheer fantasy. In fact, however, a significant number of African countries have already had experience, even after independence, with legal and judicial systems pyramiding into a final court of appeal located outside their borders. Of special interest is the role of the Privy Council in London in resolving important legal questions affecting African countries which are or were members of the [British] Commonwealth of Nations.

The issue of the "lost counties" of Bunyoro in Uganda is an instructive case in point. During the British colonial period these two counties had been transferred from the jurisdiction of the kingdom of Bunyoro to the kingdom of Buganda as a reward for certain services rendered by Buganda to the imperial authorities. Bunyoro repeatedly challenged this transfer, and by the 1950s was beginning to discuss the retrieval of the "lost counties" in legal and judicial terms. In 1958, the Queen was petitioned with a request that the case be submitted to the Privy Council for judgment; but the Secretary of State for the Colonies advised that the issues in dispute were political rather than legal, and that Privy Council review was not appropriate.

Bunyoro did not give up, however. At the 1961 Constitutional Conference in London in preparation for Uganda's independence, agreement was reached that a referendum would be held after independence to determine once and for all whether the populace of the "lost counties" considered themselves part of Buganda or Bunyoro. Then, in anticipation of the referendum, the Kabaka (king) of Buganda decided to settle several thousand Baganda ex-servicemen in the disputed counties in the hope of swelling the pro-Buganda vote. When the Uganda government ruled in 1964 that the Baganda ex-servicemen did not qualify to vote in the referendum, on the grounds that they were not on the 1962 voting register of the areas concerned (essentially, a disqualification on the basis of an inadequate period of residence), Buganda appealed to the Uganda High Court against the holding of the referendum. Buganda's argument was that some 9,000 legal residents of the counties (the ex-servicemen who had moved into the disputed areas since 1962) had been disqualified from voting.

When Buganda lost the case in the High Court, the Kabaka carried the appeal to the Privy Council in London. The referendum was held in November 1964, while the Privy Council was still considering the issue; but all concerned recognized that the phraseology of the constitutional provision on the disputed counties allowed for the possibility of declaring the results of the referendum null and void if the ·Privy Council should rule in Buganda's favor. The referendum resulted in a victory for Bunyoro, and the constitution of Uganda was amended accordingly to affirm the change in the status of the "lost counties." In April 1965, the Privy Council dismissed the Buganda appeal.

The significance of this complex sequence lies not in the final outcome, but in the fact that an issue of momentous implications within Uganda (involving (1) the rival claims of two subregions, and (2) a confrontation between the central government of the country as a whole and the king of Uganda's largest ethnic community) was voluntarily taken out of Uganda altogether in an appeal to the highest appellate court of the Commonwealth. This precedent is not unique to Uganda, of course. In all of the former British colonies in Africa, the constitutional arrangement devised at the time of independence specified that certain issues could be carried to the Privy Council as the final court of appeal if and when a litigant had exhausted the local legal system. Indeed, almost every former British colony, including Canada and Australia, originally had at the pinnacle of its legal system an appeal to the Privy Council. Although each Commonwealth member, in due course, conferred ultimate legal jurisdiction to a local court of appeal, the function of the Privy Council was understood, respected, and utilized even after independence.

While it would no longer be politically acceptable to resort to a court of appeal outside Africa altogether, particularly one linked to the former imperial power, the precedent of the Privy Council suggests that the creation of a high tribunal of justice with jurisdiction over the continent as a whole is not beyond the realm of practical possibility. If such an appellate tribunal existed, an aggrieved group would first seek redress within the court system of its own country. Depending upon the outcome, and assuming that the issue fell within the clearly defined domain of the All-Africa Supreme Tribunal of Justice, the highest court of the individual country concerned could rule to allow for higher appeal to the continental supreme court. Since much of the violence of Africa is interethnic, a priority step in developing continental judicial mechanism would have to be agreement on a regional code of social justice. The case of the Tutsi in Burundi is only the most flagrant example of the existence in Africa of communities which have been accorded, because of certain preexisting historical circumstances, an advantageous position in relation to other ethnic groups. In Uganda, the charge is made that the Baganda not only enjoyed a certain preeminence during British colonial rule and in the early years of independence, but even now have access to a disproportionate share of opportunities, including those in educational institutions and the civil service, and perhaps increasingly in the economy since the expulsion of the Asian mercantile element.

Thus the Baganda, like the Ibos in Nigeria and the Luo in Kenya, pose a different kind of issue than the Tutsis of Burundi. If a particular ethnic group is more enterprising than some of its neighbors, or more hard-working and imaginative, should its members be rewarded for its skills and drive? The predominance of Luo among academics deemed suitable for appointment to positions of influence and authority at the University of Nairobi, and the high visibility of Ibo scholars at the University of Ibadan, have, at one time or another, created acute tensions in Kenya and Nigeria. Should an African university pursue a conscious policy of ethnic diversification of the academic staff, thus discriminating against communities that are already over-represented in favor of communities that are underprivileged? Or should African universities continue to utilize the criteria of merit, making academic appointments regardless of whether adherence to these criteria increases or diminishes the preponderance of particular ethnic groups? Put more broadly, should a regional code of justice explicitly permit the utilization of a calculus to redress ethnic imbalance in African countries? Or should Africa as a region opt for a system of merit, regardless of ethnic affiliation?

Sometimes violence in Africa is precipitated by such secondary issues as the number of children from a particular ethnic group that have done well in the Higher School Certificate, and have therefore become eligible for university admission, as against the number of successful candidates from a rival ethnic group. Should an All-Africa Supreme Tribunal of Justice include within its jurisdiction questions of collective equity? The experience with affirmative action in the United States suggests that a clear dilemma can arise in determining, on one side, the rights of *individuals* and their claim to be judged on merit, and, on the other, the rights of previously underprivileged *groups* to a better chance in the grand arena of influence and opportunity. Both in Africa and the United States, issues demanding judicial adroitness arise when an ethnic calculus is invoked to help redress imbalances of the past. In some countries of Africa, the problems are compounded by the high risk of ethnic violence created by these imbalances.

Any large-scale, officially sanctioned or officially permitted violence in an African country, threatening or seeming to threaten the liquidation of a particular ethnic group, could be deemed an offense against the body politic of the African continent as a whole. This would be consistent with the determination by the Allied governments after World War II that genocide against the Jewish people fell within the definition of "crimes against humanity." In my view, it is entirely conceivable that, by the 1990s, Africa will have evolved a judicial and legal system under which certain "crimes against the African people" will be defined in terms virtually indistinguishable from those applied at Nuremberg to "crimes against humanity."

Toward Administrative Institutions for
Conflict Resolution

The evolution of the kind of judicial process I have envisaged in the preceding pages would involve the corollary development of administrative machinery, partly in support of the judicial process and partly parallel to it. The Organization of African Unity, like all international governmental organizations, is better equipped to respond to interstate violence than to cope with intrastate eruptions. Under the terms of the 1963 OAU charter, as another chapter in this book explains, a serious border clash between Rwanda and Burundi can and should activate the OAU machinery, whereas the internal massacre of either the Hutu in Burundi or the Tutsi in Rwanda is outside the charter's terms of reference.

How, then, can domestic massacres be deliberately internationalized in Africa short of actual war between, say, Rwanda and Burundi? Although political considerations would seem to rule out the creation of an OAU police force in the foreseeable future, an OAU Human Rights Committee working in combination with an OAU Ombudsman is not an unreasonable interim possibility. It would be a step in the right direction to set up machinery for internal regional censure, even though sanctions would be lacking initially.

Censurable offenses would need to be narrowly defined in a protocol to the charter of the Organization of African Unity. Large-scale violence in which a government seemingly is guilty of either direct complicity or of dereliction in protecting the innocent could be handled (1) judicially through the All-Africa Supreme Tribunal of Justice or (2) administratively and politically through a motion of censure initiated by the Ombudsman. Under this second alternative, the motion could first be submitted by the Ombudsman to the OAU's newly activated Committee on Human Rights and, with its approval, to the Assembly of the heads of state and government of the OAU. The Ombudsman and subsequently the committee would accept evidence from all sides. The Assembly, after examining all the evidence accumulated, would listen to the Ombudsman as the administrative "prosecutor" and to the member state as the defendant, and then vote on the motion of censure.

It is important to remember that the drafters of the charter of the

Organization of African Unity were by no means insensitive to issues of violence. But the OAU was founded at a moment in Africa's history when there was greater sensitivity to the threat of violence directed against those in authority than to violence that might be committed by those in authority. Sylvanus Olympio, the prestigous president of Togo, had been assassinated only a few months earlier in 1963 and President Kwame Nkrumah of neighboring Ghana was widely believed to have helped to engineer the insurrection which resulted in the violent overthrow of the Togolese government. Olympio's assassination involved two issues which came to be regarded as offenses of crucial concern to all OAU heads of state: the political murder of a head of state, and suspected subversion from a neighboring country. The OAU charter, reflecting the primary concerns of its drafters in the year 1963, established these two offences as fundamental wrongs. Article 3 of the charter affirms "unreserved condemnation, in all its forms, of political assassination as well as of subversive activities on the part of neighboring states or any other states."

Looked at another way, it can be said that Article 3 sets an important precedent by clearly defining two incontrovertible offenses against the African people on which all heads of government assembled in Addis Ababa in 1963 could agree. Because the decisionmakers at the OAU's founding were heads of government, this overriding concern with their own vulnerability in the wake of events in Togo was understandable. In the dozen years since 1963, however, most violence and conflict in Africa has been of a different sort. Accordingly, it is time for the Organization of African Unity to define more decisively additional areas of censure.

But how can the Organization of African Unity be expected to create an effective system of censure for its large and diverse membership when, for example, the smaller and older Organization of American States seems incapable of achieving the consensus required to censure the post-Allende government of Chile for its slaughter of innocent people who served the previous regime? Indeed, the Organization of American States has yet to censure its senior member, the United States, for the participation of the Central Intelligence Agency in the events which led to the murder of President Allende—an example of subversion more firmly substantiated than the participation of Kwame Nkrumah in the assassination of Togo's Sylvanus Olympio. Perhaps the answer to the question posed at the beginning of this paragraph lies in the very fact that, in the limited areas of violence to which the OAU has addressed itself, it has been more courageous and effective than its sister organization in the western hemisphere.

Precisely what role would an all-African Ombudsman, serving under the aegis of the OAU, perform in holding governments accountable for indirect aggression against other governments and for perpetration of brutality against their own citizens? Would an Ombudsman as an institution be more acceptable to some OAU member states if it had an association with the United Nations and thus constituted a part of a global system?

Let us consider some practical examples of the ways in which the Ombuds-man might respond to initiatives by an aggrieved citizen, a group of citizens, or a neighboring state directly affected by a violent eruption in a given African country. The problem of fleeing refugees and the burdens placed on host countries is particularly pertinent.

In July 1973, President Julius Nyerere of Tanzania called on the Organization of African Unity to use its good offices to end the fighting in Burundi between the governing Tutsi and the more numerous but underprivileged Hutus. While acknowledging that it was indeed the established policy of the OAU to avoid interference in the internal affairs of member states, Nyerere held that this narrow reading of the charter should not preclude the organization from initiating efforts to mediate in an instance where tens of thousands of people were dying. In a telegram to President Yakubu Gowon of Nigeria, serving in rotation as 1973 chairman of the OAU, Nyerere argued that "both humanity and the cause of peace in Africa demand that we concern ourselves actively."

Burundi's head of state, Colonel Michel Micombero, also appealed to General Gowon, but his request was for the OAU to intervene in what Micombero perceived as a crisis between his country and Tanzania. Nyerere countered that there was no real problem between Tanzania and Burundi per se, and that the crisis in relations between the two countries arose only because violence within Burundi spilled over into Tanzania. Forty thousand Burundi refugees had fled to Tanzania by 1973, and two attacks on Tanzanian villages had resulted in the killing of more than 80 people by Burundi troops. Under the circumstances, it was logical for the president of Tanzania to appeal to the Organization of African Unity—not only out of a sense of compassion for the Hutu, but also because the resources of the Tanzania government were being severely taxed by the influx of refugees resulting from a situation of such great brutality next door.[15]

Nyerere's 1973 cable to the OAU chairman can be interpreted as a forward step in Africa's groping search for a systematic way of dealing with flagrant violence. In effect, a case was emerging for an Ombudsman operating under the aegis of the Organization of African Unity—with staff and resources to accumulate evidence and with access both to the sources of the violence and refugees in neighboring countries.

It is not clear if the OAU could survive the stresses and strains of the kind of passionate controversy that could arise if the organization expanded its purview in this way, but the need is so acute that the risk is worth taking. Isolation and the threat of ostracism have proved to be effective forms of pressure in Africa before, suggesting that censure by fellow Africans in an institutionalized form could moderate excesses by individual African governments. As recounted in another chapter of this book, one reason that so many African governments fell in line and broke relations with Israel in 1973 was the simple fear of being left in splendid isolation. And there was some evidence, however modest, that even

Uganda's General Idi Amin cared enough about his stature in the Organization of African Unity to make an effort to reduce violence and arbitrariness in Uganda before taking his turn as host to the OAU summit meeting in 1975, and as chairman of the Assembly of heads of state and government for 1975-76. Some observers hazarded the guess that Amin would have executed (instead of banished) former Foreign Minister Elizabeth Bagaya, just as he had apparently arranged the killing in 1974 of Bagaya's predecessor in the Foreign Office, had he not been concerned that a boycott might deny him the glory of serving as 1975 host to the OAU.

What these examples suggest is that collective African opinion, though not effective against every regime in Africa, has *some* power over *some* regimes. It follows that an organized campaign of ostracism could have a moderating influence in some instances. Here again, parallels from other regions of the world are instructive.

The Organization of American States embarked on the isolation of Cuba in 1962, and it seems almost certain that Cuba would sooner or later have had to moderate its repressive internal police methods and hemispheric strategies substantially had the Soviet Union not come to the rescue. The Arab world has also had its deviants in international politics. Collective Arab censure has not always succeeded in preventing either independent foreign policy postures or domestic repression by individual governments, but public opinion throughout the Arab world has been a factor which each Arab government has had to take into account. In the 30 years of its existence, the Arab League has sometimes served as an instrument for exhortation and has succeeded in discouraging at least some member governments from risking censure by their fellow Arabs on a narrowly defined range of policies and issues.

Partly because Africa is so much more fragmented than either Latin America or the Arab world, more structured instruments would seem to be required. An Ombudsman, for example, could serve as the crucial linkage between the proposed legal system of social justice pyramiding toward an All-Africa Supreme Tribunal of Justice and the more traditional diplomatic mechanisms for handling conflict resolution. Since Africa's Ombudsman would have both judicial and diplomatic functions, the diplomatic area must be examined in its own right. And it is to this that we must now turn.

Toward Diplomatic Mechanisms for
Conflict Resolution

An Ombudsman under the aegis of the Organization of African Unity is likely to be more acceptable to a wider number of African states if it constitutes a part of a global system. This brings us to the role of the United Nations. Two existing UN devices come to mind: the "uniting for peace" resolution passed by the

General Assembly in 1950, and the 1974 precedent of suspending a member state from the General Assembly.

Hans J. Morgenthau has set forth the five main features of the "uniting for peace" resolution in these terms:

(1) A provision that the General Assembly could meet in 24 hours if the Security Council were prevented by the veto from exercising its primary responsibility for international peace and security.

(2) A provision that in such cases the General Assembly could make recommendations to member states for collective measures, including the use of armed forces.

(3) A recommendation that each member state should maintain within its national armed forces elements that could promptly be made available for possible service as United Nations units.

(4) The establishment of a Peace Observation Commission to observe and report in any area where international tension existed.

(5) The creation of the Collective Measures Committee to study and report on the ways and means to strengthen international peace and security in accordance with the charter of the United Nations.[16]

The "uniting for peace" resolution was invoked at the urgent behest of the United States at the time of the Korean crisis. The Security Council took the initial step of applying collective security provisions of the charter against North Korea, but this action was only possible because the Soviet Union had temporarily absented itself. When the Soviet representative resumed his seat, the Security Council was paralyzed by the Soviet veto. The United States then turned to the more representative General Assembly (over which the United States then had effective control) for collective action. The resulting collective action included the use of armed forces in Korea under the flag of the United Nations.

If the "uniting for peace" resolution is to be used to support Ombudsmanship in Africa, the concept of "peace" would require redefinition to include genocide or comparable large-scale violence preventable by collective action. Since the General Assembly must endorse such a redefinition, wherever it originates, the redefinition would have to be perceived as keyed to the interests and concerns of the Third World majority that holds voting power in the Assembly. In order to pass such a resolution, the General Assembly as now constituted would have to balance humanitarian concerns with a recognition that very raw sensibilities of many Third World countries are involved. The issue is a legitimate one for the Third World to decide, since the kind of large-scale violence covered by a redefinition of the concept of "peace" in the "uniting for peace" resolution cannot, in the 1970s, any longer be blamed simply on "Western imperialism."

A "uniting for peace" resolution encompassing certain levels of domestic violence within its purview would be a long way from world government; but acceptance of the principle that the General Assembly as a collective body has the authority to impose restraints on outright excesses by individual member states, even when these excesses are purely domestic in scope, could moderate or contain at least certain forms of brutality. Although the concern of this essay is with violence in Africa, the amended "uniting for peace" resolution would apply equally to countries ranging from Pakistan and Bangladesh to Chile, from Indonesia to Northern Ireland, from Uganda to the Philippines.

The temporary suspension of South Africa voted by the General Assembly in November 1974 was a precedent-shattering motion of censure against a member state. Just as the United States in 1950 took the Korean case to the General Assembly because of the frustrating impasse in the Security Council, so the African states in 1974 took their case against South Africa to the General Assembly for the same reason. The effort to get the Security Council to expel South Africa altogether from the world organization had foundered when the United States, Britain, and France all used their veto power to kill the motion.

The General Assembly does not have the power to expel a state from membership in the United Nations, but it concluded that it could determine who should deliberate within its own proceedings. Accordingly, on November 12, 1974, by a vote of 91 to 22, the General Assembly voted to suspend South Africa from participation in the current session. The vote, which outraged the United States and much of Western Europe, was certainly among the factors which moved United States Ambassador to the UN John Scali to denounce what he called the "tyranny of the majority" in the General Assembly in a speech later in the same session. African diplomats, on their part, find it difficult to see why the manner in which the 1974 censure of South Africa's system of apartheid was achieved was any more "tyrannical" than the tactics used by the United States in 1950 to assure UN intervention in Korea. Although suspension was unparalleled in the history of the world organization, it was no more unparalleled (and more limited in scope) than the "uniting for peace" resolution introduced by the United States a quarter century earlier.

In any case, critics of the 1974 resolution of censure against South Africa overlook some positive longer term implications of the precedent established by its passage. Because of the immediate historical background of most countries in Africa and Asia, and the vividness of their memories of colonialism's humiliations, the issue of racial discrimination is certain to achieve greater consensus in a Third World forum than is the issue of genocide. Even though genocide in absolute terms is a greater sin against humanity than racism, moral issues tend to be perceived in the context of historical conditioning. An overwhelming majority of the countries represented in the United Nations are comprised of citizens previously humiliated by white people, and it may take some time before a balanced perspective between racism and genocide is achieved in any genuine "world" organization.

Until this more balanced perspective is achieved, mechanisms for censuring man's inhumanity to man (now seen primarily as racism) should be allowed to become institutionalized, so that they can one day be used to impose limitations on other forms of aberrant behavior. The suspension of South Africa in 1974 could provide a precedent for the suspension of a Burundi or a Rwanda, if they are still unrepentent in their genocidal tendencies ten years hence. What has been invoked against one sin against humanity, racism, could one day be invoked against another, genocide.

There is no escaping the fact that it may take more than one generation to moderate Africa's tensions and the eruptions they cause. It may also take more than an interstate judicial system in Africa; administrative processes in Africa and other regions; and/or diplomatic processes involving the United Nations. To the extent that environmental violence in Africa relates to the total global scene, the global system as a whole may have to undergo reform or restructuring in the direction of greater economic equity and social justice before particular manifestations of tension can be controlled.

Out of the blood of Burundi, the agony of Uganda, the scars of Nigeria, the stains of Chile, the ashes of Bangladesh, the racism of the United States, the pained frustrations of Czechoslovakia, the silenced voices of the Soviet Union, and the sheer exhaustion and lack of imagination of the United Kingdom, a new world order could one day emerge.

A Postscript: Some Lessons from Watergate

Shortly after Uganda's President Idi Amin was elected to the 1975-76 chairmanship of the Organization of African Unity, Kenya's most influential journalist, editor-general George Githii of the *Daily Nation*, discussed the larger implications of this development in two major articles in his newspaper. Referring to "the carnage that has been going on in Uganda since Amin took over power . . . [and started] his type of tyranny which knows of no right or wrong except the single-minded pursuit of power," Githii suggested that Amin was only an exaggeration of a more widespread phenomenon:

When ruling presidents enter prison cells and spit on their opponents, when others go to prison cells personally to execute their detainees, when whole ethnic groups are mercilessly decimated on the spurious ground of national security, clearly men and women of goodwill and conscience must ask themselves whether they ought to be in league with people whose hands are immersed in the blood of innocent people, with states whose soil is replete with skeletons of people whose crime appears to be that they were born of certain tribes and not others.[17]

All members of the Organization of African Unity should be reminded, Githii wrote, that they are individually and collectively signatories of the 1948 Universal Declaration of Human Rights and therefore "bound to respect the precepts of the declaration about inalienable human rights—the right to life, property, movement, speech and worship among others."[18] Given the manner in which "former colonial subjects have become, with alarming rapidity, oppressors of their kith and kin" since independence, there was an urgent need for a renewed reaffirmation of the will to respect human rights and the rule of law and "to speak out when human life is violated."

Conceding that the OAU lacked the status of a supranational federal institution, Githii argued that public censure of a government by its peers has been underestimated as a moral weapon in Africa. Simply by exposing offending governments to both African and world opinion, the OAU could exert significant power. He called for "some kind of social contract," to be administered and adjudicated partly by an all-African court empowered "to monitor and investigate atrocities and abuse of law by member states." Such a court should be required to make public its findings on human rights issues both at the annual meetings of the OAU and at the time atrocities were being committed.

George Githii is one example of many concerned and imaginative Africans who are groping for effective mechanisms to prevent moral anarchy in Africa. A central issue in all such deliberations is how and by whom the head of state of an African country might be tried for crimes committed against the people he governs.

While judgment of a president's performance by his "peers" poses particular problems in a contemporary Africa lacking in stable institutions, recent events have demonstrated that the question of whether an incumbent head of state can be tried in a court of law remains unresolved in the United States too. We know that there is a workable constitutional device by which an incumbent American president can be divested of the protective status of "presidenthood" (impeachment), but we still do not know for certain whether he can be tried in a court of law *before* he is removed from office. Before President Nixon resigned as a result of the Watergate affair, the Special Prosecutor considered the possibility of starting legal proceedings against the president—and abandoned the idea precisely because of the constitutional ambiguity. For the same reasons, the Watergate jury decided against indicting the sitting president as a co-conspirator.

Although a sitting president is, de facto, above the law, a former president may be tried for offenses committed while he was still in office. It seems to be the prevailing constitutional opinion in the United States (pending a definitive decision by the Supreme Court at some future date) that a president can only become legally *actionable* when he is no longer in office. Although political realities in the United States were such that Richard Nixon was not indicted and tried even after he ceased to be president, it required a complete and unconditional pardon from his successor to establish this immunity.

By this comparative analysis I do not mean to equate former President Nixon's behavior with that of, say, Idi Amin. On the contrary, I realize that Nixon would have fallen from power much sooner than he did if he had manifested an insensitivity to human life in the United States remotely comparable to his callousness towards human life in Cambodia and Vietnam. An American president can get away with authorizing the killing of any number of foreigners on foreign soil, but he would risk a very great deal if he were to effect the murder (or even the silencing) of a single irritating American journalist at home. By contrast, an African president can get away with having thousands of his compatriots killed on his personal orders—but few would dare risk deliberately ordering the murder of a single expatriate journalist. American constitutional arrangements have traditionally tolerated the authorization of all manner of violence abroad by presidential fiat—but sharply limited abuse of physical power at home. By contrast, the lack of established constitutional arrangements in most African states allows a president great leeway in the range of brutality he can inflict on his own citizenry—but custom limits the capacity for maltreatment of foreigners within (or outside) the national boundaries.

While Africa should not aspire to emulate the broad and sometimes frightening interpretation of "national interests" that has developed in the United States over time, Africa would do well to study some of the constitutional devices by which Americans limit their rulers' capacity to do harm to disaffected citizens.

If the device of impeachment were feasible in Africa, it would mitigate many injustices. But impeachment rests on a doctrine of domestic political accountability, and a society which has not yet evolved a system of regular elections is unlikely to be able to develop workable impeachment procedures. Although the history of the doctrine of impeachment in England provides some contrary evidence, the morality of elections usually has to evolve before the morality of impeachment can be effective. Thus Africa is unlikely to find a way to impeach unfit presidents before it learns to elect its leaders freely. In the interim, as I have argued earlier in this chapter, public opinion is the most promising device for encouraging the development of moral accountability in Africa.

Three levels of public opinion might be brought to bear on an African president—public opinion in his own society, public opinion on the African continent, and public opinion at the broader international level. In Western societies, where the citizenry routinely pass judgment on a governing regime in periodic elections, the most important level of public opinion in influencing the performance of a head of government is domestic. In Africa, on the other hand, we are more likely to have a situation in which a president is less affected by domestic opinion than by regional and continental opinion. An African dictator's domestic advisors are likely to have been reduced to sycophants and flatterers; his Western or other foreign advisors tend to avoid "moral issues" concerning the ruler's treatment of his own people—and concentrate instead on either "technical" advice or advice reflecting extra-African interests in the country. Any moral persuasion to ameliorate his policies in the area of human rights must, in the final analysis, come from fellow Africans whom he cannot ignore but over whom he does not have authority.

Although regional African opinion has the greatest potential for exercising moral influence on African rulers, this influence is not yet strong enough to seat or unseat an African president. Some member states of the Organization of African Unity have on occasion, but not consistently, acted on the principle that it is within the purview of the OAU to try to unseat a head of government who is not operating in the African interest and to attempt to prevent the removal of a head of government who is. The most explicit effort to remove a head of government was that directed against Moise Tshombe in 1964 when he became prime minister of Zaire; techniques of ostracism and boycott were used not only by individual members of the organization but also by OAU officials. The unofficial charge against Tshombe was "treason," in the sense that he was believed by many to have sold the independence of an African state to a foreign interest in consideration of personal advantage. This was the nearest Africa has come to the collective impeachment of an African leader. On the other hand, when Presidents Kwame Nkrumah of Ghana and Milton Obote of Uganda were overthrown in military coups, some members of the OAU attempted to use the organization's machinery to reinstate them. All three cases revealed the weaknesses of the OAU in dealing with those who already have captured the reins of power in their own societies.

If Africa (like the United States) cannot try those who are in positions of ultimate power in a court of law, and if (unlike the United States) Africa cannot effectively start impeachment proceedings to remove an unfit leader from power, what then is the answer? One intermediate stage for Africa may be to try malevolent heads of state who have been removed from power. A president who has been displaced would thus become subject to prosecution for inhumane acts committed *before* he was overthrown. Since the impartiality of the political successors of the accused leader would be in doubt, and pressures on individual judges within the fallen leader's country might preclude a fair trial, any legal action against a former head of state or government would be moved to an independent pan-African court—for example, the proposed All-African Supreme Tribunal of Justice.

Let us consider how this might work in practice. If the former president were to be captured in his own country, the succeeding regime would be legally bound to hand him over to the custody of the chairman of the Organization of African Unity until judicial proceedings could get under way. A former president who managed to escape to another African state would be handed over to the custodial authorities of the All-African Supreme Tribunal, assuming that he has been indicted by the Supreme Tribunal or *in absentia* in his own country.

What if the fallen leader should seek political asylum outside of Africa? The answer is that there is a clear need for international law to be altered enough to allow for extradition treaties not only between state and state but also between a state and a regional international political entity. If a deposed leader should escape to, say, Paris, London, or Lisbon, the courts there would assess whether the offenses for which the refugee was charged were subject to extradition. Whenever appropriate, indicted former African rulers would be handed over to the custody of the legal arm of the Organization of African Unity. The time must come when brutal Third World rulers are not lightly given asylum in Western countries.

Such a system of future accountability would add one more factor to the calculations that incumbent African presidents would have to take into account in acting brutally against their own citizens. While a sitting president might still be above the law, he would now have to consider that pan-African law operates the morning after the night of power. An Idi Amin or Bokassa—no longer in office and domestically in disgrace—would ultimately have to face the drumbeat of collective African justice.

What happens if the accused is found guilty? In creating a pan-African court, the Organization of African Unity would have to decide at the outset if such a court would be empowered to impose capital punishment. As long as "ordinary" citizens in all African countries are subject to capital punishment—and this is the situation at the present time—it can be argued that former presidents should not be exempt. In the event that capital punishment was imposed by the All-Africa Supreme Tribunal, the chairman of the OAU would logically be the one to make arrangements for the execution.

But what if the pan-African court determines that the punishment should be imprisonment? In this case, the convicted leader might be given the right to choose the African country in which he would prefer to be imprisoned. While he could be expected to choose a country likely to be sympathetic to him and to treat him well, he would have to be imprisoned for a designated period or until such time as the judicial arm of the OAU found it appropriate to review his case.

And what if an indicted former president is finally found innocent of the crimes with which he is charged? This would not enhance his chances of his getting his job back as president. Once a president is overthrown, it should not be up to the OAU to reinstate him; indeed, any attempt by the OAU to interfere in the internal political arrangements of a member state in this way would endanger the modest experiment in judicial institutionalization. A fallen president who is found innocent of charges against him should simply be set free to go as a private individual. Where appropriate, however, the OAU might intercede on the former president's behalf to persuade the new government of his country to allow the former leader to return home as a free man.

But justice is not simply a case of punishing the wicked; it should include rewards for virtue. Thus, the OAU should not only create procedures and institutions for punishing offending presidents; it should also find methods of honoring examples of unusual service or compassion among its members.

Since its inception, the OAU has chosen its chairmen from the ranks of the heads of state. And except when the annual Assembly has been held at the OAU headquarters in Addis Ababa, the host president of an OAU summit meeting has been chosen by acclamation as next chairman. In the second of his two articles in the *Daily Nation*, Githii proposed that, if it is deemed necessary to choose the OAU chairman from the ranks of reigning presidents, members should do so by secret ballot from a list of candidates nominated by member states and not simply opt for whatever leader is taking his turn as host to the annual Assembly. Indeed, Githii argues that consideration should be given to the transformation of the chairmanship into a full-time, supra-African post:

Officials of the Secretariat of the organization's headquarters, according to the OAU Charter, are full-time staff; they cannot hold offices in their home countries simultaneously with offices in the organization's headquarters. This is how it should be. For although they are Africans, they serve two different entities and there are occasions when a conflict of loyalty, or indeed ambition, may arise. . . . It seems logical that the same principle should be applied with regard to the position of chairmanship, or Presidency, of the OAU.[19]

On this point, it seems to me that Githii underestimates the role of status in African politics. An OAU chairman who is not also head of state would be far less influential in dealing with national leaders than a chairman who still had a power base independent of the organization. A compromise innovation that might deserve a gamble would be to choose the OAU chairman from among respected former heads of state, with the option of reelecting the same person up to a maximum of five years. A particularly promising candidate among the present crop of former African presidents is General Yakubu Gowon of Nigeria. Of all the heads of state who have fallen from power, his exit was the most dignified. He accepted the fait accompli with grace; promptly dedicated himself to the service of his country in an alternative capacity should he be needed; and had the humility to register himself as an undergraduate at Warwick University in England only a few months after he had been honored (as a distinguished head of state) with an honorary Doctorate of Laws from Cambridge University. Gowon's capacity for humility and humaneness, combined with his unique experience in presiding over Nigeria's civil war and the reintegration of the nation that followed, qualify him to be seriously considered as a future full-time chairman of the Organization of African Unity. To do so would be one way that Africa could reward leaders who have sought to bring dignity and compassion into the governing process, even as it explores ways of punishing those who bring disgrace and misery to Africa.

Notes

1. Henry Kamm, "Chad Tribal Rite Disrupting Nation," *The New York Times*, October 13, 1974.

2. See the article by Thomas A. Johnson, *The New York Times*, June 6,

1973; and the article by Frederick Hunter, *The Christian Science Monitor*, June 4, 1973.

3. Ted Robert Gurr, *Why Men Rebel* (Princeton, N.J.: Princeton University Press, 1971), pp. 12-13.

4. *The New York Times*, August 5, 1973.

5. *The New York Times*, June 6, 1973.

6. Stanley Meisler, "Rwanda and Burundi: Decade of Independence—and Murder," *The Washington Post*, May 22, 1973. Copyright, 1973, *Los Angeles Times*. Reprinted by permission.

7. Consult U.N. Statistical Year Books for 1970 and 1971. The density for Rwanda and Burundi is also analyzed by René Lemarchand in his essay, "The Military in Former Belgian Africa," in Catherine M. Kelleher (ed.), *Political-Military Systems: Comparative Perspectives* (Beverly Hills and London: Sage Publications, 1974), p. 91.

8. Lemarchand, *ibid*., p. 101.

9. Roland Oliver, "The Problem of Bantu Expansion," *Journal of African History*, VII (1966), pp. 361-376. Consult also George Peter Murdock, *Africa: Its Peoples and Their Culture History* (New York: McGraw-Hill Book Company, 1959), Part 8, "Expansion of the Bantu," pp. 271-313.

10. See Kenneth Kaunda and Collin Morris, *Black Government* (Lusaka: United Society for Christian Literature, 1960).

11. See *New Africa*, Vol. 5, No. 1 (January 1963), p. 4.

12. *Ibid.*

13. See Andrew D. Roberts, "The Lumpa Church of Alice Lenshina," in Robert I. Rotberg and Ali A. Mazrui (eds.), *Protest and Power in Black Africa* (New York: Oxford University Press, 1970), pp. 513-568. Also, Fergus Macpherson, *Kenneth Kaunda of Zambia: The Times and The Man* (Lusaka: Oxford University Press, 1974), especially pp. 410-411, 442-443. See also James W. Fernandez, "The Lumpa Uprising: Why?", *Africa Report* (November 1964).

14. Reported in the *Uganda Argus*, August 7, 1975.

15. For a report in the United States of Nyerere's request for OAU mediation in Burundi, see *The New York Times*, July 18, 1973.

16. Hans J. Morgenthau, *Politics Among Nations: The Struggle for Power and Peace* (New York: Alfred A. Knopf, 1963 edition), p. 310.

17. George Githii, "Wanted: An African Court of Justice," *Daily Nation* (Nairobi), July 28, 1975.

18. *Ibid.*

19. George Githii, "OAU Chairmanship: Time to Change the System," *Daily Nation* (Nairobi), July 29, 1975.

III Southern Africa after the Collapse of Portuguese Rule

John A. Marcum

For many years southern Africa[a] has confronted the United States with a black versus white, a moral versus material, dilemma. As an outside party with a significant financial stake in the status quo of this industrializing, mineral-rich area, the United States responded ambivalently over several decades to the mounting criticism of the racial policies practiced by governing white minorities in the Republic of South Africa, Rhodesia, and the Portuguese "overseas provinces" of Angola, Mozambique, and Guinea-Bissau. Conflicting economic, strategic, and political concerns, and a negative assessment of the chances that indigenous forces would muster the skills, military resources, and will to overthrow white rule, all contributed to the equivocations in U.S. policy.

In the view of successive American administrations, African insurgency movements did not offer a "realistic or supportable" means of correcting political systems that were admittedly grossly unjust to the overwhelming majority of the population. Any hope for creative change in southern Africa depended, it was believed, upon attitude reform among the 4.5 million whites who dominated 36 million other persons living in the region.[1] A methodical analysis of the southern African situation made by a National Security Council (NSC) Interdepartmental Group for Africa in 1969 questioned "the depth and permanence of black resolve" and concluded that "military realities rule out a black victory at any stage." It also asserted that militarily and economically weak African revolutionaries who employed violence could only solidify white fears, prejudice, and resistance to change—and thus hurt the very people they purported to serve.[2]

---

[a]In this book, the term southern Africa refers to the one-sixth of the continent, roughly two million square miles, lying to the south of the northern borders of Angola, Zambia, and Mozambique.

In making and perpetuating these assumptions, American policymakers miscalculated, in much the same fundamental way that they had miscalculated in Vietnam and that the French had miscalculated in Algeria. Not only did Washington planners underestimate indigenous rebel capacity; they also erred in assuming an unflagging resolve on the part of at least one white ruling group, the Portuguese, to pay the costs of protracted wars of attrition against African liberation movements. Perhaps American vision was clouded by unconscious racial bias. At no point did the authors of the 1969 NSC study question the durability of Portuguese resolve. Instead, they predicted "continued stalemate" because "the rebels cannot oust the Portuguese and the Portuguese can contain but not eliminate the rebels."[3] The security analysts ignored an elementary fact of life: for rebels to "win" it is necessary only for incumbents to "lose."

Although the absence of a free press and other democratic institutions differentiated the political context of Portugal from that of the United States or France, indications of severe stress were there for those with eyes to see: mounting military casualties (11,000 dead, 30,000 wounded) and defections; increasing incidence of anti-regime terrorism and sabotage in Portugal itself; economic dislocation (an inflation rate of 22 percent by 1973); and massive emigration (1.5 million). On April 25, 1974, an association of battle-weary Portuguese officers who had organized within a dissident Armed Forces Movement (AFM) overthrew the government that had locked them into an unending, unwinnable war. Just weeks after their most celebrated and flamboyant peer, General António de Spínola, had published a myth-shattering book in which he declared that Portugal could not win its African wars,[4] the young captains and majors of the AFM seized power and began to liquidate Portugal's colonial empire. In so doing, they liquified the politics of all of white-dominated southern Africa.

Responses to Mozambique's Independence

The Mozambique Liberation Front (FRELIMO) was formed in 1962, over a year after the insurgency against Portuguese rule had begun in Angola, as a merger of small exile groups of regional (Tete), ethnic (Maconde) and emigrant labor (Bulawayo railway) origins. The moving force was Dr. Eduardo Mondlane, an American-educated sociologist.[5] Military training in Algeria and staging bases in Tanzania permitted FRELIMO to prepare and mount guerrilla operations in northern Mozambique beginning in September 1964. Following the assassination of Mondlane in 1969, the movement came under the direction of Samora Machel, a young, Algerian-trained military commander from the southern district of Gaza. Using classical guerrilla tactics, FRELIMO raided, mined, parried, then slithered and ambushed its way southward, infesting the district of Tete and spreading its political message and structure ever farther into the

303,000 square-mile territory which stretched along 1,500 miles of the East African coast. FRELIMO was associated in an interterritorial alliance with the outlawed African National Congress (ANC) of South Africa. It was assisted by Chinese instructors and Soviet arms. And it was committed to a multiracial, socialist rule. Why, then, did the achievement of independence in June 1975 not put Mozambique on a collision course with white/capitalist South Africa?

The FRELIMO-Pretoria Détente

Having been forewarned by its own military intelligence of serious slippage in Portugal's efforts to contain African insurgency in Mozambique,[6] the government of South Africa made a quick, hard, and sober choice. Possibly profiting from the lessons of Vietnam, Algeria, and Portuguese Africa, Prime Minister Balthazar Johannes Vorster resisted temptations to back efforts to create a "moderate alternative" in Mozambique. Avoiding the slippery path of intervention, he refused to support white diehards who made a clumsy effort to seize power in September 1974, refrained from assisting fractious African dissidents (the Mozambique National Coalition led by Uria Simango) or separatists (advocates of a north of the Zambezi state of "Rumbezia"), and came to terms, instead, with the movement that had led the insurgency, FRELIMO. In so doing, he assumed for South Africa a startling, forceful, and conflictual role in what was to be a recasting of political structures and relationships in a region of Africa two-thirds the size of the United States.

There were also strong reasons why FRELIMO, despite its revolutionary ethos, would wish for at least a temporary modus vivendi with South Africa. Although Portugal's Armed Forces Movement had opted to minimize chances of a chaotic power struggle by bypassing elections and granting power directly to the movement which had led the struggle against them, FRELIMO had yet to consolidate its authority in a sprawling country of nine million people. Whereas FRELIMO had leadership and organizational strength in Lourenço Marques and the peripheral areas of its insurgency, it had not succeeded in penetrating the country's major population centers either militarily or politically. In a sense, the Portuguese collapse had come too soon. FRELIMO needed more time to mobilize support among such ethno-linguistic communities as the more than two million Makua-Lomwe of the north-central coast and to secure its sway in centers of white or regional particularism such as Beira.

Thus in the period leading up to and following independence on June 25, 1975, FRELIMO was obliged to concentrate singlemindedly on establishing its political authority. It created a formal party structure extending down to local *groupas dynamizadores* to carry out political education and exercise worker control in factories and offices. It obliged all whites to carry identity cards (because their loyalty was doubted), thereby creating a mirror image of South

Africa where all Africans must bear "passes." It enacted an extremely tough security law. Under this law the director of a new National Service of Popular Security can have persons arrested, and "given over to the competent police authority, sent to court, or to camps for re-education" should they commit "subversion, sabotage, or acts directed against the People's Power and its representatives, against the national economy or against the objectives of the Popular Republic of Mozambique." There is no appeal, no habeas corpus.[7]

Moves to reorganize and eliminate "corruption" from ranks that included many who had served under the Portuguese led to an abortive revolt by several hundred soldiers and policemen just six months after independence. And in keeping with its firmly stated marxist ideology and populist ethos, the new FRELIMO government moved to curtail the religious and educational role of foreign missionaries and to nationalize the professions of law and medicine. Determined to build an egalitarian society, FRELIMO undertook to create medical and paramedical services for an African populace that had been inadequately served under the colonial system. But the shortrun effect of abolishing private practice was to speed the exodus of doctors, whose numbers were down from something over 300 to about 50 by early 1976. This exodus, in turn, encouraged more departures from among the some 50,000 Europeans then remaining in the country.

Paradoxically, then, the immediate consequence of FRELIMO's decision to embark upon the radical reconstruction of Mozambican society on the heels of Portugal's hasty exit was to heighten the country's dependency on South Africa. The flight of over 120,000 Europeans, including technicians, civil servants, and teachers, left FRELIMO with a precarious hold on the wheel. Although Western predictions of a dramatic economic collapse seemed culture bound (the bulk of the populace depended on subsistence farming and, overall, the economy was too little developed, too underindustrialized to "collapse"), FRELIMO was obliged to accept technical help from South Africa to keep its railroads and harbors functioning and reduce the danger of large-scale urban unemployment and disaffection. As of early 1976, Mozambique also depended on South Africa: (1) for half of its port and railroad foreign currency earnings of $150 million a year, which in turn constituted a third of all its foreign earnings; (2) for special deferred mine worker wage payments in gold, formerly pocketed by Portugal, worth up to $140 million a year on the free market; and (3) for purchase of 90 percent of the hydroelectric power produced at the Cabora Bassa dam.

Rejecting as "suicidal" any notion of an immediate withdrawal of Mozambican labor from South Africa,[8] FRELIMO officials sought to gain time for the "battle of national reconstruction" in which they would reorganize the country's agriculture and begin to exploit its untapped resources in coal, iron, copper, gold, manganese, chrome, nickel, and natural gas. Responding affirmatively to FRELIMO's pragmatic external relations policy, South Africa sought to ingratiate itself by offering a variety of aid, including help to modernize the port of

Lourenço Marques, renamed Maputo, so that it could handle containerized cargo.[9]

Myopia in Washington

The modus vivendi taking shape between Mozambique and South Africa presented the United States with what one might have predicted would be welcomed in Washington as a splendid opportunity to further a process of change that could ultimately ease the political-racial constraints on American economic and strategic relations with southern Africa as a whole. FRELIMO made the opportunity more explicit by an unexpected gesture.

Despite the record of close American association with Portugal during ten years of African insurgency in Mozambique, it was an American official, Assistant Secretary of State for African Affairs Donald B. Easum, who was the first foreign diplomat to be granted a formal audience by the transitional FRELIMO government set up in mid-1974. Following a meeting with FRELIMO President Samora Machel in Dar es Salaam, Easum was accorded several hours of serious exchange with Prime Minister Joaquim Chissano and members of his cabinet in Maputo. The Mozambicans invoked the past, but they also presented a frank picture of their transitional economic plight and requested American assistance.

Subsequently, FRELIMO's avowedly marxist leaders exhibited a remarkable degree of independence in dealing with their longtime Soviet benefactors. They denied the Soviet Navy use of Mozambique ports, publicly rebuked the Russians for exerting undue political pressure, and accorded preferred diplomatic status to the Chinese.[10] Influenced by and linked to the government of President Julius Nyerere of Tanzania, which had harbored and succored FRELIMO during a decade of anti-colonial struggle, Mozambique's new regime looked to the Tanzanian model in devising its egalitarian goals, concentrating on agricultural self-sufficiency, and pursuing its quest for economic independence.[11]

In sum, the coming to independence of Mozambique really posed no difficult policy choices for the United States. Once a decision had been made to work toward building a new relationship with the country's new rulers, Washington needed only to employ sensitive diplomacy and modest but responsive assistance to put United States-Mozambique relations acceptably on track. There was reason to believe that help in relieving Mozambique's economic dependence on South Africa especially would be appreciated.

For a variety of reasons—the ease with which the modus vivendi was taking shape between Mozambique's new rulers and South Africa, the value attached by American naval analysts to freedom of access for all to Mozambican ports, the routine (instead of privileged) status that FRELIMO-governed Mozambique seemed to be extending to its long-term Chinese and Soviet benefactors, the enthusiasm with which African leaders in neighboring countries had greeted Easum's initiative with FRELIMO—it seemed logical that Washington would respond quickly and decisively to the unexpectedly early willingness of the new Mozambique government to explore avenues of cooperation with the United States. In a way it did.

Upon his return in November 1974 from the wide-ranging tour of southern Africa that had taken him to Maputo, Easum was notified that he was being relieved of his post (after a nine months' incumbency preceded by seven years of service in African countries). A low-key, bilingual intellectual with an open style, Easum inspired confidence because his willingness to listen conveyed genuine concern to African interlocutors. The change became all the more astonishing when Easum was replaced by Nathaniel Davis, a more traditional Foreign Service officer who had never served in Africa and who had been ambassador in Chile at the time of President Salvador Allende's overthrow. Associated in FRELIMO's minds with covert American backing for the political "destabilization" that helped prepare the way for Allende's downfall, the Davis appointment could only be viewed with alarm by a marxist-influenced movement that was committed to building a socialist society. It brought to mind earlier warnings by Harvard Professor Henry Kissinger that a "nationalist communist" regime was to be welcomed in Eastern Europe but deplored in Latin America or Africa where it "would inevitably become a center of anti-Western policy."[1 2]

Did the replacement of Easum by Davis suggest that Mozambique, like Chile, would be considered a potentially "nationalist communist" regime? Or did it merely reveal an insensitivity and indifference reflective of the small importance attached to Africa?[1 3] Wide currency was given to the simpler explanation that Easum had irritated the secretary of state personally by pressing African issues in policy forums where occasional General Idi Amin jokes were much more in style. Whatever the explanation(s), the action provoked public criticism by President Mobutu of Zaire and the Organization of African Unity's Council of Ministers, a sharp retort by the secretary of state in defense, of American "sovereignty" and the "besmirched" reputation of the new appointee,[1 4] and a virtual boycott of the Davis "swearing in" reception by African ambassadors in Washington.

The new FRELIMO government in Maputo marked time in the months that followed, responding coolly to American overtures in the early post-Easum period, including an offer to send an economic survey team "to study developmental problems and assistance potential."[1 5] Washington was pointedly not among those invited to send a delegation to attend the independence ceremonies on June 25, 1975. It was late September before Mozambique's new rulers agreed to "leave the past to history," embark upon a "new phase in relationships with the United States," and establish diplomatic relations on a "basis of mutual respect and mutual benefit." Even then, their response to Washington's restated willingness "to discuss specific projects in which [it] might be of some assistance"[1 6] was cautious.

The Rhodesian Tinder Box

Only one dimension of Mozambique's foreign relations—its policy toward Rhodesia—threatened to deviate from a posture of protective prudence. The African nationalist movement in California-sized Rhodesia had long been divided into two competing parties—the Zimbabwe African People's Union (ZAPU) under the leadership of Joshua Nkomo, and the Zimbabwe African National Union (ZANU) led by Reverend Ndabaningi Sithole. For some time before independence, ZANU guerrilla units had been operating in concert with FRELIMO through the Tete district of Mozambique into northeastern Rhodesia. There was every reason to expect, and ZANU did, that FRELIMO would extend this cooperation after independence, granting ZANU access to the full 800 miles of the common border shared with Rhodesia, and transferring to the Rhodesian rebels the sophisticated mines, SAM-7 ground-to-air missiles, and other weaponry that the Soviet Union had delivered to FRELIMO on the eve of the Portuguese collapse.

Contrary to the expectations of ZANU and many others, President Machel concluded that FRELIMO's highest priority was to consolidate its authority within Mozambique, and thus he took no immediate action to respect United Nations sanctions by closing Rhodesia's rail and sea links to the outside world through the Mozambican ports of Beira and Maputo. Machel's reasoning was that such closure would mean the loss of thousands of jobs for volatile urban workers and of over $40 million in annual revenue, and he was not swayed from this position by prospects of financial compensation from Commonwealth and other countries. ZANU insurgents would be provided with sanctuary and training facilities (notably a base near Vila Gouveia, comparable to bases made available to FRELIMO in Tanzania during the guerrilla war against Portugal) until such time as FRELIMO had secured its own authority. Only then would it consider cutting the railroads and unleashing ZANU in a coordinated effort to end white minority rule in Rhodesia.

South African Prime Minister Vorster understood all this. His decision to deal with FRELIMO, like FRELIMO's decision to deal with South Africa, formed part of a larger design. Recognizing that the exit of Portugal ended the hope of preserving a *cordon sanitaire* of white-ruled states to the north, Vorster displayed a degree of hardheaded pragmatism surprising to his detractors. Using the strength of his position as the unchallenged leader of Afrikaner nationalism, he seized the initiative and threw his energy and guile into a bid for regional détente calculated to concede the margins and save the essentials of Afrikaner power and prosperity. With a flair for theatrical timing, Vorster employed a dramatic diplomatic outreach to cover a careful political retrenchment.

In 1965, Rhodesia's white minority government had proclaimed a defiant Unilateral Declaration of Independence (UDI) from British colonial rule. In 1967, when allied forces of ZAPU and the African National Congress (ANC) of South Africa organized a joint and ill-fated military incursion into Rhodesia from Zambia, Pretoria did not hesitate to send some 2,000 paramilitary police to help guard the Rhodesia-Zambia borders.[17] Prime Minister Vorster's commitment to the defense of Rhodesia's whites had seemed unequivocal in 1967: "We are good friends and good friends do not need an agreement to combat murderers. Good friends know what their duty is when their neighbor's house is on fire ... we shall act in any country where we are asked to act by the government of that country."[18]

The United Nations embargo imposed on trade with Rhodesia in retribution for the white rebellion against Britain was never fully effective. South African and Portuguese nonobservance, coupled with under-the-table connivance by a number of other countries, enabled Rhodesia to find clandestine foreign markets for increased mineral production and to achieve a considerable degree of self-sufficiency by developing local industry. The annual post-1965 real GNP growth rate held at about eight percent. While this was a remarkable achievement under the circumstances, it was a perilous month-to-month existence based on selling cheap and buying dear. Moreover, scarcity of foreign exchange and the costs of counterinsurgency increased Rhodesian dependence on South Africa, where there was growing criticism of Salisbury's failure to move expeditiously toward a settlement in political-demographic circumstances that were bound to get tougher. It was recognized that the dependence would become almost total if Mozambique were to decide to close its railroads and ports to landlocked Rhodesia; in that event, the Salisbury government would have to reroute much of its foreign trade over (1) a single-track railroad via Beitbridge, and (2) the Bulawayo-Mafeking line through Botswana, both leading to already crowded ports in South Africa.

Over time, Pretoria's praetorians grew increasingly impatient with the limited vision of the breakaway Rhodesian Front government of Prime Minister Ian Smith. Although Rhodesia's whites were overwhelmingly outnumbered—an unstable white population of at best 275,000[b] was pitted against an African majority of almost six million—the Smith government staunchly refused to accept any of a succession of British offers to settle and thus legalize independence on terms that would not seriously threaten continued white rule. Unwilling either to move toward genuine multiracialism or to adopt a clear-cut racial policy of separate development ("provincialization" in the Rhodesian lexicon), the Smith government waffled, in a manner reminiscent of their Anglo kinsmen in the opposition United Party of South Africa. The pro-government Afrikaans language press of South Africa, convinced that territorial partition (i.e., creation of African "homelands") had "eliminated" the issue of majority rule in the Republic, decried as "neo-imperialistic" a shortsighted Rhodesian racial policy that failed to take similar steps to accommodate African nation-

[b]In 1974, white emigrants left at about 1,000 a month, about the inflow rate of new immigrants, some 60 percent of whom move on elsewhere within five years. About 100,000 of the country's 275,000 whites are new since UDI in 1965.

alism. By "shirking" its responsibility to face up to the racial issue, the Smith government had created a situation that was a "provocation to aggression" and therefore a danger to South Africa.[19]

In 1974, Vorster concluded that the inept and hapless Smith regime had to go. It had to be replaced by a "moderate" African regime that could (1) maintain order and (2) do business with Pretoria. Bold action was in order. While the United States, Britain, and France saved South Africa from expulsion from the United Nations by resorting to a triple veto, Vorster embarked upon a secret diplomatic offensive that took him as far afield as the Ivory Coast and Liberia. Official South African political statements took on a new tone. In an October 23, 1974 speech before the South African Senate, to which he had especially invited the diplomatic corps, Vorster stated that "Southern Africa is at the crossroads and should choose now between peace or escalating violence." It was time to seek solutions. The framework would be a modernized South African patrimony—a Southern African Economic Community including Botswana, Lesotho, and Swaziland (the "BLS countries"), Rhodesia, Namibia, the "black nations" (bantustans) of South Africa, and, hopefully, Angola, Mozambique, and Zambia.[20] At the UN Security Council the next day, Ambassador R.F. Botha extended an olive branch to black Africa, disarmingly acknowledging that South Africa had "discriminatory" practices and laws but denying that white South Africans had a *herrenvolk* complex." The government was prepared to do "everything in [its] power to move away from discrimination based on race or color."[21]

While assuring his internal constituency that his new initiatives and rhetoric applied to interstate relations and in no way implied a retreat from the principle of separate development or an advocacy of multiracialism within South Africa, Vorster embarked upon an intense diplomatic exchange with Ian Smith on the one hand and President Kenneth Kaunda of Zambia on the other. Kaunda, in turn, consulted with Presidents Julius Nyerere of Tanzania, Sir Seretse Khama of Botswana and Samora Machel of Mozambique. Under South African pressure, Smith in November 1974 released a number of detained nationalist leaders,[22] including ZAPU's Nkomo and ZANU's Sithole.

Flown to Lusaka, the leaders of the two liberation groups were pressed by Kaunda and Nyerere to merge under the banner of the African National Council (ANC), an opposition movement led by Bishop Abel Muzorewa and recognized as quasi-legal by the Smith government. The ZAPU and ZANU leaders were also obliged to accept a December 1974 cease-fire as a step toward a constitutional conference, a new constitution, and a transition to majority rule via an expanded but qualified franchise. Herbert Chitepo, the external organizer of ZANU's guerrilla campaign, balked, fearing that the movement's guerrilla cadres would suspect a sellout and either rebel or disintegrate. In the event of a collapse of efforts to achieve a political settlement, ZANU would be back in square one. ZANU leaders and their Chinese backers also feared that they would come out second best in a compromise settlement that gave Nkomo an opportunity to capitalize on his presumed personal popularity and thus carry Soviet-supported ZAPU into power. These Sino-Soviet and intergroup rivalries were set aside by Kaunda, Nyerere, Khama, and Machel, who imposed at least nominal unity and a cease-fire.

Fear of a "Munich" produced internal convulsions within ZANU. Though its leadership came overwhelmingly from the Shona population (which outnumbered the rival Ndebele, from which ZAPU drew much of its leadership, by a ratio of 11 to 3), ZANU was not immune to ethnic conflict at the level of Shona subgroups. Disagreement over how to respond to an externally imposed strategy of negotiation exacerbated rivalry between Karangas who formed the core of ZANU's guerrilla forces and Manyikas who provided much of its political leadership. ZANU nationalists, turning upon themselves, killed Herbert Chitepo and over 150 colleagues, provoked the arrest of another 75 of their lot by Zambian authorities, and, finally, clashed openly with a Zambian military unit.[23]

President Kaunda was desperate to salvage a sagging, landlocked Zambian economy that was caught between depressed copper prices and an Angolan civil war that closed the (Benguela) railroad outlet for nearly half of his country's copper exports. Accordingly, he bent every effort to promote a negotiated settlement that would reopen the previously (1973) closed Rhodesian route to the sea.

Meanwhile, Smith and his government also faced unrelenting pressure from South Africa to come to terms with the leadership of the catchall ANC. When a mid-1975 ANC-Smith encounter on the railroad bridge at Victoria Falls aborted because Smith refused to grant blanket immunity to prospective ANC participants at follow-up discussions inside Rhodesia, Kaunda and Vorster continued to press for negotiations. When Smith disparaged South Africa's détente policy publicly, Vorster summoned him to Pretoria for a public apology.[24]

In blocking the participation of "militants" (such as Reverend Sithole, who had been allowed to leave Rhodesia but faced rearrest if he returned), Smith encouraged dissension within African ranks. After a spate of complex political maneuvering, the ANC split in two factions, roughly along the lines of the earlier ZAPU-ZANU cleavage. As the head of one wing, Joshua Nkomo, aided by a team of Zambian advisors, pursued the path of negotiations to Salisbury where he entered upon formal constitutional talks with Ian Smith and his Rhodesian Front government in December 1975. The opposing wing of the ANC, headed by Bishop Muzorewa, established an external Zimbabwe Liberation Council (ZLC) to prepare for the test of armed force that it considered the only reliable route to majority rule. As the likelihood dwindled away that Nkomo could obtain concrete assurance from the Smith regime of an expeditious transition to majority rule, therefore, he seemed destined to be shunted aside as anti-Nkomo guerrillas forced the issue with mines, rockets, and rifles.

In March 1976, it was reported from Dar es Salaam that the leadership of a 16,000-man Zimbabwe liberation army training in Tanzania and Mozambique had "fallen into the hands of men unknown to the outside world."[25] The presidents of Tanzania, Zambia, Mozambique, and Botswana, acting under the mandate given them by the Organization of African Unity in June 1975 to "oversee" the liberation of Rhodesia, were said to have encouraged the emergence from guerrilla ranks of a new 18-member high command council based in the camps in Mozambique. According to the Dar es Salaam report, quoting "diplomatic sources," the council consisted of nine former ZANU and nine former ZAPU militants who "want nothing to do with the factional fighting that has paralyzed the movement . . ." In a corollary effort to solidify the movement, the four presidents were said to have arranged for all military aid from communist sources destined for the Zimbabwe liberation forces to be channeled through Tanzania and Mozambique and to have told the Soviet Union and China to avoid direct dealings with the guerrillas. On March 3, 1976, the Mozambique government, after detailing alleged border attacks by Rhodesian troops, announced that it was closing its border with Rhodesia and cutting off all communication with the Smith government.

The prospect of a fierce race war that would ultimately clamp Rhodesia under the stern rule of a radical young military regime posed a new set of difficult choices for Pretoria. If South Africa applied economic sanctions to persuade the Rhodesians to come to terms with the Nkomo "moderates," would the effort succeed? If so, would the maneuver create a precedent for an eventual application of international sanctions against South Africa itself? In the event of a major guerrilla assault on white rule in Rhodesia, how would Vorster deal with domestic pressures to go to the aid of Rhodesian whites, a fourth of whom were born in South Africa?[26] How bitterly would white South Africa be divided by a hardheaded refusal based on military cost-benefit considerations?

On the Rhodesian issue, as on so many African matters, U.S. policy had long been one of treading water. Aware of the ultimately bleak prospects of the go-it-alone 1965 rebellion of Rhodesia's whites, a sequence of Democratic and Republic administrations held to a low-key policy of nonrecognition, support for a negotiated settlement "based on the principles of self-determination and eventual majority rule," and application of UN trade sanctions against the Salisbury regime.[27] Department of State spokesmen openly acknowledged that congressional passage of the so-called Byrd amendment in 1971 (authorizing the purchase of Rhodesian chrome) constituted a significant and deplorable breach of these sanctions. When a modest effort to get the Congress to repeal the Byrd amendment failed in 1975, the position of the executive branch was restated: "In addition to providing the regime in Salisbury with much-needed foreign exchange, the Byrd amendment . . . also provided moral and psychological support to that regime."[28]

These statements notwithstanding, no American president has ever put his prestige on the line to mount a major effort to educate the public and convince the Congress to end American violation of an international commitment to which we were a signatory and regain American political credibility before events in Rhodesia might render repeal irrelevant. If the intransigence of white Rhodesians should result in the emergence of a spartan, marxist-ruled Zimbabwe, the United States government would be left with no real option but to establish a working relationship with the new regime. And no matter how much the United States decried the fact, the Chinese and/or the Soviets would be the godfathers of any African government by virtue of their roles as undemanding benefactors over a long period of time.

From South West Africa to Namibia

The third country to fall within the purview of Vorster's détente policy was South West Africa—now identified on maps and in the United Nations as Namibia. This vast (318,000 square miles) but sparsely populated (850,000) territory, formerly a German colony, was mandated to South Africa under the League of Nations. Pretoria refused to recognize the United Nations' decision to convert all mandates into UN trust territories after World War II, contending that South West Africa's future had become an *intra*state not an *inter*state issue.

The territory is rich. It's approximately 100,000 whites preside over a basically extractive economy that yields diamonds, copper, lead, zinc, vanadium, uranium, fish, and wool from karakul sheep. Whites occupy much of the productive central plateau while the 80 percent of the people that are African are grouped in peripheral, economically marginal "homelands" and in segregated urban townships. Some 396,000 Ovambo, who form over half of the African population and much of the work force for white-run mines, farms, ports, and railroads, exercise a limited degree of self-rule within their northern homeland up against a portion of the 850 mile southern border of Angola. The rest of the country's dispersed humanity is divided into what South African ideology presents as "nations"—Damara, Herero, Nama, Okavango, Eastern Caprivian, Bushmen (or San), Tswana, Kaokovelder, Cape Coloured, and Rehoboth Baster Coloured—numbering variously from 4,000 to 75,000. (Ironically, South African governments have studiously ignored the ethnic differences among the territory's Europeans, two-thirds of whom speak Afrikaans, one-fourth German, and the rest English.) Beginning with the rise of the National Party to power in 1948, Pretoria progressively extended apartheid laws to South West Africa, meanwhile pressing for its outright incorporation as a fifth province of the Republic.

The United Nations General Assembly "terminated" South Africa's mandate in 1966—an action accepted as valid by the United States. In 1971, years of litigation before the International Court of Justice climaxed with an advisory opinion supporting the UN action and declaring South Africa's continued occupation of South West Africa to be illegal. Meanwhile, the General Assembly had established a Council for Namibia to replace South Africa's administration, and named Sean McBride, an Irish statesman and fervent advocate of Namibian independence, as territorial commissioner. In an attempt to force the issue, McBride notified all UN member states on May 20, 1975 that he intended to implement a General Assembly resolution authorizing the seizure of cargoes and vessels departing the territory without specific UN authorization. Since most Namibian exports pass through South African territory, and bear South African markings, it would be difficult to prove their origins. Whether Commissioner McBride could come up with a capacity to interdict remained to be seen, but no one doubted that he would try.

Pilloried in United Nations debate, discomfited by the International Court's decision rendering the argument of *legal* occupancy no longer plausible, shaken by an unexpected and widespread strike by Ovambo workers in 1971-72, and faced with the danger of political and military spillover from Angola to the north, the South African government reconsidered its options in 1974. While maintaining officially that it wished for the *peoples*—not people—of South West Africa to decide their own future,[29] the Vorster government's preferred détente scenario for the territory went like this: (1) The traditionalist Ovamboland Independence Party led by Chief Minister Filemon Elifas in concert with Kwanyama-speaking kinsmen in southern Angola would opt for separate independence and thus out of South West Africa. (2) That would leave the 100,000 whites and smaller black "national" groups south of the Ovambo buffer state to form a loose federation, based on homeland boundaries and close economic ties with the Republic.

The South West Africa People's Organization (SWAPO), recognized by the UN and the Organization of African Unity as *the* principal voice of African interests in the territory, was dead set against such partition. Although its own ethnic genesis and contemporary following was largely Ovambo, SWAPO's multi-ethnic leadership rejected any notion of a separate Ovambo state. And Prime Minister Vorster reportedly learned during a five-hour discussion with a Stellenbosch University professor whom he consulted that most young, socially conscious Ovambos were rejecting the leadership of traditional, chiefly authorities who preached ethnic separatism.[30]

In September 1975 Chief Elifas was assassinated. And when a constitutional conference of presumably pliable politicians convened in Windhoek that same month, it quickly became apparent that South Africa would be pressed to accept a formula not entirely to its liking. In a declaration of intent, local white legislators led by Dirk Mudge joined African delegates such as Chief Clemens Kapuuo (Herero) and Dr. B.J. Africa (Rehoboth Baster) in pledging themselves to draft a constitution that would neither splinter the country into ethnic ministates nor create a state so unitary as to risk "Ovambo hegemony."[31]

The constitutional conference gave itself a leisurely three years in which to design a federal system that would leave each ethnic community with a large measure of autonomy in its own "national" affairs. Although the conference drew prompt fire from SWAPO and other African political organizations for allegedly proposing a bantustan system disguised as federalism,[32] Chief Kapuuo and his associates insisted that they rejected both a bantustan formula and South African "occupation,"[33] and would accept only a unitary, independent state. As for local whites, they apparently calculated that a properly devised federal system could permit them to exercise economic leverage and link up with African traditionalists and Afrikaans-speaking coloureds in such fashion as to preserve white control at the core of an ethno-politically fragmented state.

Timing was as crucial a factor in South Africa's détente policy in relation to Namibia as it was in relation to Rhodesia. To build up "reasonable" nationalists such as Kapuuo and Nkomo would be self-defeating unless there was a timely transfer of political authority to the "moderates." The risk that nationalist leadership would be preempted by more "radical" competitors would increase with each passing month. In South West Africa, the "radical" alternative was SWAPO. Because of the territory's international status, Pretoria had allowed African political organizations a harrassed but quasi-legal existence since their emergence in the 1950s. Constrained by Afrikaner attachment to legalistic (as distinct from liberal) values, the South African administration had failed effectively to repress African/Namibian nationalism. While it banned the African National Congress (ANC) and Pan-Africanist Congress (PAC) in South Africa proper, it permitted a branch of SWAPO to function in South West.

Pretoria clearly perceived SWAPO as an instrument of "international communist conspiracy." That SWAPO enjoyed United Nations support only rendered it more suspect. Though a two- to three-year timetable for a constitutional solution failed to reflect what Western diplomats viewed as an appropriate "sense of urgency,"[39] a revocation of some of South West Africa's segregation laws in 1975 constituted a modest step toward "deracializing" the territory's political system without basically altering the locus of political power. Moreover, it seemed likely that the desire to outmaneuver SWAPO and its external supporters might force the pace of controlled change toward political independence for a single, ethnically federated Namibian state.

Pretoria's willingness to move ahead might also be linked to constitutional clauses guaranteeing white political and economic interests in the territory and the continued presence in Walvis Bay of South African air and naval power. Walvis Bay is a 434 square-mile ex-British enclave that is legally a part of Cape Province but is physically located within South West Africa and forms the principal port and railhead for South West as a whole. The Walvis Bay enclave not only provides South Africa with an ideal base from which to monitor, influence, or intervene in Namibia; it also could be of crucial value to Prime Minister Vorster in gaining acceptance within his own National Party for Namibian independence.

The thrust of South African policy in Namibia thus appeared consistent with the overall idea of the Vorster détente policy: accommodation with African nationalism wherever confrontation would prove costly and threaten the long-range security of Afrikanerdom. In the case of Namibia, unlike that of Rhodesia, Pretoria had the authority to set both the path and the pace of such change. Whether it would act in time and bring all vital parties into a settlement remained to be seen. And it was precisely shortfall on these two counts that could lead to difficult choices for United States policymakers.

U.S. Policy Choices

American policy toward South West Africa has been surprisingly assertive. This may be explained by the fact that it is the one area of southern Africa where law, international law, is on the side of change. As a status quo power with a deep interest in the existing international legal order, the United States has felt obliged to oppose South African occupation of Namibia since the UN terminated South Africa's mandate in 1966. Accordingly, Washington has argued for Namibian self-determination under UN supervision with the participation of "all Namibian political groups."[35] In the face of Pretoria's defiance of what it termed United Nations "interference," the Nixon administration decided in 1970 to: "officially discourage investment by U.S. nationals" in, withhold Export-Import Bank credit guarantees for trade with, and deny government protection for American investors facing claims by "a future lawful government" of Namibia. At the same time, Washington continued "to make clear its opposition to mandatory economic sanctions" and to "any use of force in southern Africa."[36] In May 1975, the United States, Britain, and France vetoed a UN Security Council resolution that found the situation in Namibia to constitute a threat to international peace. South Africa's continued occupation of Namibia, however "deplorable," did not constitute a threat of these dimensions.

In Namibia, modest and timely American action might help further the cause of peaceful black emancipation. If South African détente initiatives sufficiently eased the diplomatic climate, the United States might wisely feel that it could follow the footsteps of Australia and assume a role on the UN Council for Namibia. But if South Africa dallied in instituting constitutional reform or tried to exclude SWAPO from a political solution, domestic pressures from American church groups and other citizen lobbyists could be anticipated, with the objective of forcing American disinvestment in the territory. The withdrawal of U.S. oil companies from all exploration in Namibia in 1975 was a response to just such persuasion.

In any case, quiet diplomacy and economic leverage employed with a minimum of moral posturing seemed to offer the best hope for positive

American influence for constructive progress. South Africa's willingness to make major concessions was in some degree dependent upon the government's ability to preserve the appearance if not the fact that settlements were being generated by direct political discussions between the principal protagonists and not imposed from outside. So long as change resulted or appeared to result from South Africa's own political and diplomatic initiatives, significant concessions might be made and "sold" to the South African electorate, concessions that would be resentfully rejected if proposed by Americans, the United Nations, or other "outsiders."

A key variable, however, was South African political perception. The Vorster government had no intention of making tactical concessions not absolutely necessary to its détente strategy. And if an opportunity arose that seemed to offer a positive possibility of eliminating a "radical alternative" by means of military intervention, there would be no hesitation in undertaking this option.

It was precisely this reasoning—the desire to eliminate SWAPO militants from political contention in Namibia—that enticed South Africa into search-and-destroy military ventures in southern Angola in mid-1975. Beginning in 1966, SWAPO's external organization, under a former Ovambo store clerk, Sam Nujoma, had carried out a series of small-scale military raids from Zambia into the Caprivi Strip, a narrow 300-mile-long finger of South West Africa interjected between the northern border of Botswana and the southern borders of Angola and Zambia (under the terms of an 1890 agreement between Germany and Great Britain) to give Namibia access to the Zambezi River. For years, SWAPO guerrillas had also filtered across southern Angola to raid and politicize in Ovamboland to the west. And following the Portuguese coup in 1974, some two to three thousand young SWAPO supporters crossed from Ovamboland into Angola headed for military training in Tanzania or administrative and technical training at a UN-financed institute in Zambia.[c]

With the outbreak of civil war in Angola in 1975, SWAPO stepped up its organization of Ovambos living on the Angolan side of the border as well as clandestine incursions into Namibia. On October 23, South Africa marched north with the objective of securing the future for "moderate" political alternatives in both Angola and Namibia.

Angola: From Colony to People's Republic

In the unsettling wake of World War II, Britain and France, and to a lesser extent Belgium, begrudgingly allowed Africans under their colonial rule to organize,

[c]The absence of these SWAPO cadres proved politically costly in January 1975 when local authorities managed to turn out over half the Ovamboland voters for a legislative election despite a SWAPO boycott. In Ovamboland proper some 75 percent of the electorate voted whereas less than five percent of the harder to police Ovambos living and working outside the reserve did so. The result was a separatist-oriented government formed by the Ovamboland Independence Party. A SWAPO boycott had limited voter participation in earlier 1973 legislative elections to just 2.5 percent.

politicize, and acquire growing measures of political power. Portugal, too weak
to be assured of economic advantage short of direct political control, remained
implacably hostile to expressions of cultural let alone political dissent in its
African territories. In the 1950s, the government of Premier António Salazar
attempted to root out and destroy individuals and groups suspected of
nationalist sympathies.

The nationalist movements that survived this harsh repression shared common
weaknesses. Their leadership ranks would have been thin in any case, for literacy
ranged from one to five percent in the Portuguese territories and not all who
were literate were politically aware. But the nationalists were additionally
handicapped by travel restrictions, police harrassment, and lack of funds.
Because their range of action (and often their lifespan) was so limited, most were
unable fully to transcend the parochial bounds of primary ethnic (or regional)
loyalties or of class ties. Clandestinity left its mark too. Decimated by
infiltrators and corroded by the insecurities and tensions of underground
politics, Angola's nationalists became obsessively distrustful of everyone, including each other.

In due course, some sought refuge abroad. While the life of a political exile is
insecure, frustrating, and often debilitating, it allowed nationalist movements to
survive, regroup, seek international assistance, and organize among Angolans
living and working within the more permissive political contexts of neighboring
countries, e.g., the Congo (Zaire) and Northern Rhodesia (Zambia). These exiles
helped to spark the outbreak of hostilities. The sprawling territory of Angola (14
times the size of Portugal) shared 1,300 miles of border with Zaire. Drawing
support from an exile-émigré community of several hundred thousand (Bakongo) Angolans resident in Zaire, nationalists operated across that border and
parlayed an ill-organized uprising in 1961 into an ongoing insurgency.

During the 13 years of fighting that ensued, Angolan liberation movements
were never able to overcome their constricted origins and harsh conditioning.
Unlike their counterparts in Guinea-Bissau and Mozambique, they spent much of
their energy fighting one another. Over time, each of Angola's three major
ethno-linguistic communities produced a major liberation movement with a
separate army and separate sources of external support. Behaving as though in a
zero sum game for political and military ascendancy, they checkmated one
another. And when Premier Marcello Caetano's government fell in Lisbon in
April 1974, no one of the three could convincingly claim to be *the* embodiment
of revolutionary legitimacy.[37]

Unable to unite even long enough to accept political authority from the
Portuguese, the three contenders did manage to tack together an uneasy,
short-lived transitional government, but only under considerable pressure from
Portugal and independent African states. Anxious to clear the way for their own
departure and hoping to preclude further Angolan fragmentation, Portugal's
Armed Forces Movement (AFM) decided to oblige all Angolans (including those
in the resident European community of some 335,000) to aggregate within or
about one or another of the three liberation movements. All other political

movements were banned. The AFM further undertook to democratize the form of tripartite competition by scheduling the election of a constituent assembly prior to granting independence to Angola in November 1975.

Molded in clandestinity, exile, and rebellion, Angola's three movements found themselves in unfamiliar territory in the forest of legal electoral politics. Before the common experience and compromise of governmental administration and democratic competition could supersede their blood feuds and allow them to coalesce around a common set of national values and processes, their competition deteriorated into civil war. The distinctive background and qualities of the three movements thus took on a new importance.[38]

National Front for the Liberation of Angola (FNLA). The genesis and basic support for the FNLA came from within the 600,000 to 700,000-strong Bakongo community of northern Angola. Following the outbreak of fighting in 1961, up to 400,000 Bakongo war refugees poured north across the border to join ethnic kin in the Bakongo regions of the Bas-Zaire. Added to an already sizable population of Angolan émigrés (attracted over the years by the comparatively favorable economic and social conditions of the Belgian Congo), these refugees brought to the FNLA a transplanted political constituency. They also helped lodge the FNLA firmly within the confines of the Zaire political system.

Under the leadership of Holden Roberto, a Bakongo émigré politician schooled and socialized in the Belgian Congo, the FNLA became, over time, largely an extension or branch of Zairian politics. Except for the brief period of Moise Tshombe's ascendancy to the prime ministership (1964-65), Roberto enjoyed the support of all successive Zairian central governments. Operating from a secure exile base, he concentrated on military thrusts into Angola, giving minimal attention to political education, organization, and strategic planning. When his movement met with reverses in the face of Portuguese counterinsurgency, he relied on a combination of exile sanctuary and isolated forest redoubts in northern Angola to survive. Political and military reverses (in 1964 and 1970) sparked mutinies and defections, especially among non-Bakongo, within the FNLA. Over time, Roberto eliminated potential rivals, centered authority in his person, and relied on a coterie of mostly Bakongo aides to keep the comparatively unstructured FNLA functioning.

Following Zaire President Mobutu Sésé Séko's dramatic visit to Peking in 1973, Roberto also made a pilgrimage to the Chinese capital that garnered for the FNLA considerable Chinese material assistance as well as the services of a 120-man training mission headed by a Chinese major-general. With Mobutu's support, Roberto had recruited, armed, and (at least partially) trained a military force of perhaps 15,000 by the time the Lisbon coup took place. Enjoying both material (thanks to Zaire) and numerical superiority over its rivals, the FNLA occupied the Uige and Zaire districts of northern Angola and forced some 60,000 suspect Ovimbundu farmworkers to flee southward to their Bailundu home country. In sum, the FNLA embarked upon the 1975 power struggle for control of independent Angola from a position of military but not political strength.

National Union for the Total Independence of Angola (UNITA). The result of a 1964 schism within FNLA leadership ranks, UNITA derived fundamentally from a second ethno-linguistic stream of nationalism. Its leaders came largely from among the well over two million Ovimbundu of the central Benguela plateau, although other central-southern ethnic groups (the Chokwe, Ganguela, Ovambo) were also represented. Under the direction of Roberto's one time chief lieutenant, Jonas Savimbi (*license* in political science, University of Lausanne), UNITA lost its one contiguous exile base in 1967 when it ran afoul of internal Zambian politics. Making a virtue of necessity, Savimbi then shifted all UNITA operations inside the country, maintaining only tenuous outside linkages through an information office in London. Savimbi, who had visited Peking and been received by Mao Tse-tung in 1964, adopted a highly self-reliant, political strategy emulating the Chinese. The Chinese, in turn, extended a modicum of press, training, and financial support. But with only a trickle of material aid coming through Zambia, UNITA forces undertook to seize their weapons locally, quoting Mao Tse-tung to the effect that in any case the enemy should be the "principal source" of guerrilla arms. Reflective of Sino-Soviet competition, UNITA denounced the "modern revisionism" of those (the Soviets) who armed its chief rival, the third insurgent group, the Popular Movement for the Liberation of Angola (MPLA). The MPLA, whose guerrillas outgunned and outnumbered UNITA roughly 4,500 to 800 in the eastern Angolan zones of insurgency, sought, with possibly more dedication than the Portuguese, to wipe out UNITA. Indeed, in order to survive, UNITA may have occasionally collaborated with the Portuguese. Savimbi's advantage in 1974 was that he was on the spot, not in exile, when the colonial regime collapsed, and able to switch swiftly to a legal campaign for political power.

As independence approached, UNITA dropped its maoist rhetoric and adopted a conciliatory posture calculated to effect political alliances within the anxious but disorganized and leaderless white community. Since Lisbon had never delegated substantial political authority to Angola's Europeans, they were in no position to emulate the white Rhodesians and their breakaway independence of 1965. Savimbi's considerable success in cultivating local European support was a counterweight to FNLA and MPLA external backing for a time, but his new allies fled en masse with the collapse of central authority.

Popular Movement for the Liberation of Angola (MPLA). Led by a Portuguese-educated Mbundu physician, Dr. Agostinho Neto, the MPLA was spawned in a third ethno-linguistic bailiwick, the city of Luanda and its hinterland of some 1.3 million Mbundu (Kimbundu-speaking) people. Denied operational bases in

Zaire, the movement had been unable to develop the military potential of its beleaguered partisans in the interior regions north of Luanda. Instead, from bases in the more peripheral contiguous states of Congo-Brazzaville and Zambia, it had organized incursions into the oil-rich enclave of Cabinda and, most tellingly, into the vast savannah lands of eastern Angola.

The MPLA's leadership was more urban, intellectual, socialist, and racially mixed than that of the other two movements, and its uneducated rank and file included the inhabitants of city slums (*musseques*) as well as rural Mbundu. Whereas its principal theater of operations from 1966 to mid-1974, eastern Angola, was inhabited by a variety of peoples—Chokwe, Luena, Luchazi, Bunda—its top leadership remained what it had always been: Mbundu and mixed descent or *mestiço*. Basically, then, the MPLA was as much a captive of its ethnic origins as the other two movements.

Unlike Roberto, who never ventured from exile into Angola during 13 years of insurgency, Neto and other MPLA officials did make occasional sorties into the fighting zones. But they were not able to weave together a cohesive multi-ethnic movement. And in 1973, the principal organizer of the MPLA's eastern campaign, a fiery Ochimbundu, Daniel Chipenda, broke with Neto and led several thousand followers into dissidence and eventual (February 1975) alliance with Holden Roberto. At the time of the Portuguese coup, guerrillas loyal to Neto numbered as few as 3,000.

Also attacked by a group of largely *mestiço* intellectuals (led by the MPLA's former honorary president, Father Joachim Pinto de Andrade) for alleged authoritarian, secretive "presidentialism," Neto, like Roberto, owed his survival to external support. For over a decade the exclusive Angolan recipient of Soviet and East European training and arms, the MPLA, under his leadership, had been closely associated with the Portuguese Left. Thus, after the coup in Lisbon, it enjoyed a preferred position within the councils of the Armed Forces Movement as well as in communist and socialist circles. The acculturated, lusophile nature and Portuguese linkages of the MPLA's leadership were reflected in the prominent roles played in the movement by *mestiços*, and symbolized by Dr. Neto's own marriage to a Portuguese woman. (Roberto, incidentally, helped to solder his ties with Zaire by leaving his first [Bakongo] wife and marrying Mobutu's sister-in-law.) And thus it was that Portugal's new Left-centered government disallowed a Spínola-Mobutu agreement of September 1974 that would have eliminated Dr. Neto and his Luanda/Mbundu based "loyalists" from political competition and recognized Daniel Chipenda's dissidents as the "real" MPLA. It was Dr. Neto's prestige among Portuguese political and military figures that secured his role in the transitional government which was set up in Luanda, his principal political stronghold.

The tripartite transitional government established under Portuguese aegis in late January 1975 constituted a fragile concession to the cause of national unity. Although each of the movements pledged to pool 8,000 men into a common national army alongside an initial Portuguese contingent of 24,000, each of the three strong-willed men who signed the agreement for the FNLA, UNITA, and the MPLA also simultaneously set about recruiting, training, and arming separate autonomous armies with the objective of amassing power unto themselves.

How the MPLA Came to Power

As Lisbon withdrew its forces, its capacity to umpire the zero sum gaming of Angola's contending movements declined. The absence of a forceful move on the part of the Organization of African Unity to take up the role of political arbiter encouraged unilateral intervention by African and extra-African powers at the invitation or urging of the three increasingly reckless protagonists.

The FNLA, whose military superiority was bolstered in mid-1974 by additional Chinese training and arms, began moving from Zaire into Angola in November 1974 and attacked MPLA forces in Luanda and areas to the north beginning in March and April 1975. With the help of Zairian weapons and manpower, FNLA forces took control of the northern Angolan districts of Uige and Zaire, denying their rivals any political or military presence in the region.

Holden Roberto, whose self-confidence was reinforced in early 1975 by a resumption of modest ($300,000) American financial support cut off since 1969, purchased Luanda's largest daily, *A Provincia de Angola*, and a television station and undertook to implant his movement in the capital. In Luanda, however, the FNLA met strong resistance from the pro-MPLA populace of the city's crowded *musseques*, now armed with new Soviet rifles. The Soviet Union had resumed shipping in modest quantities of arms to the MPLA beginning in October 1974 after a hiatus of several months occasioned by dismay at the movement's debilitating internal feuds and schisms. In March-April 1975—with Agostinho Neto confirmed in leadership, and China and Zaire fueling the rival FNLA—Moscow began smuggling large shipments of AK47 rifles, machine guns, bazookas, and rockets via Brazzaville and Pointe Noire to points along the Angolan coast.

By early July the MPLA military had forced the last FNLA units as well as UNITA representatives from Luanda and the transitional government collapsed. MPLA troops operating from bases in the Congo Republic had also taken effective control of Cabinda. That same month, the U.S. government responded to the total collapse of the transitional government, and to importuning from Zaire, by embarking upon a sizable military aid program to the FNLA and UNITA.

As of August 1975, Portuguese estimates of the numerical strength of the three adversary armies were 30,000 for the FNLA, 17,000 for the MPLA, and 22,000 for UNITA. UNITA, whose troops were largely unarmed, received rifles and encouragement from a Zambian government alarmed by mounting Soviet intervention. Meanwhile, Savimbi, who had been most eager for a political as against a military solution given his movement's populous ethnic base, searched desperately for support from any external source that could help ward off imminent defeat at the hands of better armed and organized MPLA troops. He turned to Zambia, France, West Germany, and eventually South Africa.

As an international airlift flew most of Angola's white population to uncertain safety in a Portugal absorbed in its own political crisis, the MPLA extended its control over most Mbundu country from Luanda to Malange and over important urban centers and ports to the south, notably Benguela-Lobito and Moçamedes. By October 1975, Soviet weaponry and the movement's own organizational superiority seemed to hold out the prospect of an early MPLA victory.

Although President Kaunda had privately warned of Soviet designs in Angola during a visit to Washington the previous April, and Secretary of State Kissinger had long held the dour view that liberation movements such as the MPLA were little more than captive instruments of Soviet ambitions, the United States failed to make a formal protest against the Soviet arms buildup in Angola until the end of October. By that time Cuban troops had begun to appear alongside MPLA forces and Soviet prestige had been publicly committed.

All its efforts to promote a cease-fire and create a new coalition government having failed, Portugal held firm to its pledge to grant Angola independence on November 11. As Portugal's High Commissioner and his remnant entourage folded the Portuguese flag and departed Luanda, the MPLA proclaimed a Peoples' Republic of Angola and named Agostinho Neto as its first president. After a week of hard bargaining in Kinshasa, the FNLA and UNITA patched together a loose coalition and proclaimed a Democratic Republic of Angola at Huambo; it was decided that the premiership would rotate monthly between the two movements.

With independence, external intervention in Angola's civil war took on new dimensions. The Soviet Union immediately recognized the MPLA government. Huge Antonov-22 transport planes began disgorging tons of sophisticated arms in Luanda and Henrique de Carvalho, including Soviet T54 and T34 tanks and, most tellingly, 122 mm rockets that would soon tear holes in the FNLA military front that had been pressing in on Luanda from nearby Caxito. To train and assist MPLA troops and several thousand ex-Katangan gendarmes (who had fought against UNITA for the Portuguese before doing so for the MPLA)[39] in the use of this equipment, Cuba flew in an expeditionary force that totalled some 10,000 men by early 1976. Several hundred Soviet technicians accompanied a Soviet input of $300 million in military equipment (U.S. government estimate) during an 11-month buildup ending mid-February.[40]

In support of what media shorthand referred to as the "anti-Communist" side, a "mystery column" emerged from the south out of Namibia in late October 1975. Led by white South Africans, Portuguese, Rhodesians, and assorted "mercenaries" equipped with French-licensed heavy weaponry manufactured in South Africa—including Panhard armored cars—this augmented FNLA-UNITA force quickly pushed the MPLA out of the southern half of the country toward the region of its own Mbundu home base north of Novo Redondo. The origins of this alliance with South Africa could be traced back to a May 1975 visit by freewheeling FNLA convert Daniel Chipenda to Windhoek, South West Africa for "medical treatment.[41] According to press reports, UNITA virtually ceded an 80-kilometer strip of southern Angola, stretching from the Atlantic in the west to Zambia in the east, to South Africa, "Africa's theoretical principal enemy," in exchange for Pretoria's assistance.[42] Indicative of other possible trade-offs involved, Jonas Savimbi announced a few weeks later that the situation in Angola prevented UNITA from extending further assistance to SWAPO, a longtime ally.[43]

Now possessing superiority in arms (Soviet), manpower (Cuban) and organizational discipline, the MPLA swept to a military victory in February 1976. By January 1976, the ill-organized and badly led northern forces of the FNLA had crumbled, abandoning American equipment on the battlefield as they retreated back across the Zaire border. MPLA/Cuban troops then moved southward against poorly equipped and inadequately trained UNITA troops which simultaneously had to face an abortive military challenge from rampaging followers of the FNLA's southern leader, Daniel Chipenda. By late February, Agostinho Neto's government had extended its authority to all of UNITA's Ovimbundu stronghold and pushed the remnants of Jonas Savimbi's army into barren expanses to the southeast. The People's Republic of Angola was then accepted into the OAU, and Zaire's President Mobutu struck a live-and-let-live accord with the regime. With military ascendancy achieved, and the OAU stamp on its legitimacy in hand, the MPLA faced the crucial political test of its will and capacity: the task of creating a truly national, popular, and effective government of Angola.

The Soviet/Cuban Roles: Motivations and Responses

Why did the Soviet Union involve itself in such a major way in the Angolan power struggle? Although the sudden escalation of the USSR to the role of a major actor in the drama appears to be a case of improvisation in response to an unanticipated opportunity, it was not illogical that the USSR would wish to extend and expand aid to a longstanding ally. The MPLA was an ally, moreover, whose tried senior leadership seemed likely to prove ideologically more reliable than had that of some other African protégés.

During a decade and a half of the anti-Portuguese insurgency, Moscow had invested something over $60 million in the MPLA (according to U.S. government sources). In the absence of a sizable educated African elite, the exodus of most

Angolan whites offered the MPLA's leadership cadre of European-educated *mestiços*, supplemented by Soviet and Cuban advisors, a good chance of monopolizing power. This was not a certainty, of course, for African resentment of *mestiço*-intellectual domination, an issue that had long cleaved the MPLA, could backfire against a Soviet policy that seemed to keep *mestiços* in power. There were reports that one of the functions of the Cuban expeditionary force was to protect a "pro-Soviet faction of the MPLA led by Dr. Neto" from resentful opposition elements within the movement.[44]

There were economic and strategic considerations as well. The oil and mineral wealth of Angola preordained that it would become an important regional power; revenue from oil in the Cabindan enclave alone is expected to rise from $450 million to over $700 million annually. Unlike Mozambique, whose economic dependence on South Africa necessitated caution in regional politics, Angola could quickly become a launch pad for political and even military action against white minority rule in Namibia. In the Soviet view, an MPLA victory could catalyze revolutionary forces and speed up the inevitable collision of "progressive" versus "racist/capitalist" forces in southern Africa as a whole.

It did not escape Soviet attention either that Angola shares a 1,300 mile border with Zaire—where a new inflow of American capital into copper mining and smelting was scheduled to raise the total American investment from approximately $800 million to $1.5 billion. With the United States strongly committed to President Mobutu's personal rule, the prospect of a neighboring MPLA regime disposed to harbor and nourish Mobutu's enemies was bound to intrigue Moscow. How tempting it must have been to contemplate getting even with the United States for the expulsion of the Soviet Union from Zaire (Congo) in the 1960s. Zambian President Kaunda's publicly stated apprehensions about Soviet motives[45] were fueled by his acute awareness, almost surely shared by Soviet planners, of the leverage that control of Angola's Benguela railroad provides over the inland mining economies of both Zaire and Zambia.

That Mobutu was confronted with serious political dissidence was scarcely a secret. A sharp fall in copper prices, failure to develop agricultural production above pre-independence levels, and the conspicuous affluence of a governing elite had increasingly undermined support for his regime. In January 1976, Mobutu's prestige was dealt a new blow when work was suspended on the $850 million Tenke—Fungurume copper project in Shaba province after major bank loans fell through because of Zaire's doubtful financial solvency and the unsettling impact of the Angola war.[46] Zaire's position as a regional military power, already put into question by Mobutu's failure to dislodge the MPLA from the Delaware-sized enclave of Cabinda (historically part of Angola, but physically located in Zaire) via support of the separatist Cabindan Liberation Front (FLEC), fell further in early 1976 as the MPLA routed some 1,200 Zairian troops along with all FNLA forces in northern Angola.

Angola held special interest for Moscow for two other reasons as well. The deep water, South Atlantic ports of Luanda and Lobito offer facilities to which the expanding Soviet Navy would welcome access, all the more so because of the importance attached to these facilities by American naval analysts. Angola also presented the Soviets with a promising opportunity to outmaneuver the Chinese, who enjoy a considerable measure of influence in East Africa, especially in Mozambique and Tanzania.[47] Perceiving itself to be a "global power" like the United States, the Soviet Union rejected American contentions that it had no "historic" or "legitimate" interests in southern Africa. Unless Washington could come up with powerful extra-African disincentives, the Soviets had every reason to hold firm to this position. Not to do so, under the circumstances, would risk incurring negative credibility among socialist and Third World powers.

As for the Cubans, the thesis that Moscow was simply collecting on long-term debts by sending Cuban surrogates to an African battlefront does not take sufficient account of the fact that Cuba has had its own history of involvement in Angola. Havana had helped the MPLA in the mid-1960s by employing some of an estimated 1,000 soldiers sent to organize local militia for Congo-Brazzaville to train MPLA guerrillas. Moreover, the legendary Che Guevara offered counsel and moral support to MPLA revolutionaries in Brazzaville in 1965. Clearly ambivalent about the trend toward rapprochement with a giant neighbor whose embrace could be suffocating, Premier Fidel Castro responded to an MPLA request for help by electing to take the risk of reaffirming Cuba's revolutionary mission abroad.

Although the world was astonished by the numbers of troops Castro committed to the Angolan action, Cuba's status as a part of the Third World enabled it to plunge in without provoking the convulsion that would have resulted from an equivalent military intrusion by a great power. The capacity of a nation of Cuba's small size to absorb casualties, sustain or expand such a foreign venture, or exact benefits was obviously limited.

What finally legitimated Soviet/Cuban involvement in the eyes of African opinion leaders such as President Nyerere of Tanzania was the simple fact of South African counterintervention. Nyerere preferred no intervention at all, but he spoke for a spectrum of African opinion when he differentiated between the extension of Soviet aid begun during the period of anticolonial insurgency as against post-coup intervention by South Africa and the United States that, he argued, could only force the MPLA to rely on the Soviet Union "for its very existence."[48]

Not all Africans agreed with Nyerere's rationale. Noting that Moscow had not helped the MPLA "with missiles and Mig-21s" when the Angolans were fighting the white Portuguese, a leading Zairian official commented: "Now that it is a civil war of black against black, yes—they give sophisticated weapons." As for the "80 percent black" Cuban expeditionary force, he alleged, it was in Angola not because of ideology "but because blacks are good for machine guns . . . this we call racism."[49]

South Africa's Miscalculations

South Africa's plunge into Angola (partially motivated by (1) the opportunity it offered to smash SWAPO guerrilla bases and (2) the importance attached to securing a Pretoria-financed hydroelectric project on the Cunene River in southern Angola that was to provide vital power for mining and industrial development in Namibia and water for irrigation in Ovamboland[50]) involved several miscalculations. Prime Minister Vorster's government almost certainly underestimated the extent of Soviet/Cuban commitment to the MPLA. At the same time, Pretoria clearly overestimated the extent to which Vorster's détente initiatives had softened African rejection of the racism which the Republic personifies. Heretofore noncommittal, Nigeria, black Africa's wealthiest state, reacted to South African intervention by promptly recognizing the MPLA government in Luanda. Only an overriding desire not to destroy the Organization of African Unity, and expectations of an MPLA battlefield victory, staved off an early pan-African recognition of the Luanda government at an extraordinary January 1976 meeting of OAU heads of state.

Pretoria also erred if it anticipated that Chinese denunciation of Soviet intervention would help legitimate its own. Having withdrawn its military trainers from FNLA bases in Zaire just prior to Angolan independence, China stood safely aside from the short-lived civil war, limiting its involvement to rhetorical slings and diplomatic nudges. Finally, Pretoria overestimated the likelihood that American and other Western participation could be enrolled in a "free world" crusade against Soviet expansionism in Angola. French, Zairian, Zambian, and (according to some reports[51]) secret American encouragement of South Africa's action could not suffice as casualty lists grew, the scale of battle escalated, and domestic dissension over the involvement mounted.

In mid-January, Minister of Defense Pieter W. Botha announced: "I have on several occasions stated that South Africa's involvement in Angola is part of the involvement of the free world. But I also stated that South Africa is not prepared to fight on behalf of the free world alone."[52] South African troops thereupon withdrew to a defense line some 50 miles north of the Namibian border. A force numbering some 4,000 to 5,000 was assigned to remain in that buffer zone, which included the Cunene hydroelectric project, until, as Botha put it, "we are satisfied that Angola won't be used to overrun the Ovambo with independent elements and refugees."[53] All South African troops were ultimately withdrawn in March 1976.

The Role of the United States

It was in January 1975 that the U.S. government, apparently for the first time since the coup, came seriously to grips with the question of what posture and actions to take in relation to the deteriorating situation in Angola. The three movements were still sharply divided, and the existence of a secessionist movement in Cabinda raised the spectre of a four-way partition (Cabinda, Bakongo, Mbundu, Ovimbundu) after a cruel conflict.

At this point, the United States might have acted expeditiously to forestall competition with the Soviets, modestly improve its diplomatic position in Africa, and also to encourage conciliation in Angola. In particular, the United States might have mustered its diplomatic forces and encouraged the OAU to take up a continuing role of political arbiter, thereby minimizing the hazards of large-scale external intervention. Although nominal Portuguese sovereignty remained, this had been no bar to OAU efforts in the past, and it seems likely that the Portuguese attitude would have been favorable. Whether OAU arbitration would have been successful or not is by now a moot point. The United States could in any case have made clear its commitment to a foundation stone of African unity—resistance to outside intervention—and thereby created real political difficulties for a Soviet intervention as well as gaining needed diplomatic credit in an area of the world where we have little.

Instead, just as the accord establishing a triparte transitional government was being hammered out in Alvor, Portugal, the National Security Council's "40 Committee" authorized a covert grant of $300,000 to the FNLA, the movement with the largest army and the one most disposed to follow a military rather than a political strategy. Curiously, the 40 Committee declined to help UNITA, whose strategy was the most political of the three. Apparently past connections, and an irrepressible habit of seeing things in terms of "our team" and "theirs," enticed the administration into choosing one side.

Almost at once, rumors of "heavy continuing CIA support for the FNLA" became "very prevalent in Luanda," although they were denied by American officials.[54] And others, surely including Soviet intelligence, detected a new rash of conspicuous spending by the FNLA in Zaire.[55] Although apparently intended, in U.S. government thinking, for "political purposes" and to fortify the FNLA in its hitherto neglected political area, this American action was wide open to different interpretation by the Soviet Union and other parties.

In January 1976, Secretary Kissinger explained the reasoning behind the administration's subsequent decision to expand substantially its role in the war. "By mid-July," the secretary said, "the military situation radically favored the MPLA." Zaire and Zambia became "more and more concerned about the implications for their own security," and "turned to the United States for assistance in preventing the Soviet Union and Cuba from imposing a solution in Angola, becoming a dominant influence in south-central Africa, and threatening the stability of the area."[56] The U.S. response was to provide military assistance to the FNLA and UNITA forces through neighboring black African countries. In order to avoid "a public confrontation" with Congress in July, the administration mounted a covert program to beef up the FNLA and UNITA that according to the official reckoning pumped over $30 million in military hardware to the FNLA and UNITA by the end of 1975.[d]

Given the circumstances, American inaction and reaction seemed almost designed to provoke the Russians into seeking maximum advantage. Because the Soviet Union's outreach as a superpower is more military than economic, and because its capacity to intervene is essentially unconstrained by democratic accountability, there was every reason to conclude that the Soviets would enjoy an advantage in the event of an Angola war by proxy. One would have thought that the president and secretary of state would have perceived, as the Soviet leadership must have, that an American public chastened and disillusioned by a lost war in Vietnam would not tolerate even a very modest involvement in another distant, unfathomable, civil conflict.

Did the Ford administration attempt to arrest this escalating arms race with the Soviets between the time when it first became alarmed over Soviet involvement in March 1975 and the point of no return marked by Angolan independence in November? According to the secretary of state himself, it was only at the eleventh hour in October that the United States made any "overtures" to the Soviet Union. Nor is there any reason to believe that, after having made its own January 1975 decision to provide covert assistance to the FNLA, the U.S. government sought either to constrain its client from trying to impose its dominance by force of arms or to allay Moscow's possible misgivings in this regard. Moscow was left to draw its own conclusions about American intentions. In the Angolan circumstances a policy of tit for tat with no communication was doomed to failure.

Why were there no attempts at preventive diplomacy? Why no signal to the Soviets that the United States would be willing to use its influence to safeguard a role for the MPLA in the transitional government on a basis of reciprocity? Why did the administration fail to convey to Moscow—and other interested parties— strong American backing for an inclusive coalition rather than the imposition of any movement by force? And as the Soviet weaponry began appearing in Luanda and elsewhere, why did the secretary of state not sense that the United States would be at a comparative disadvantage playing a "covert game of soldiers" and alert Moscow to his concern for the future of Soviet-American relations?

The answer given by administration sources is that the United States lacked "bargaining chips." Until it had built up a countervailing force to that of the reorganized and rearmed MPLA, it could not usefully converse with the Russians. And since, according to Secretary Kissinger, what mattered was not "America's modest direct strategic and economic interests in Angola," but only the "massive foreign intervention," it had to be met in kind.

---

[d]While the published figure of American arms support to FNLA and UNITA is only $32.3 million, it appears that much of this equipment was undervalued. Senator John Tunney stated in February 1976 that data collected by his aides in Angola and elsewhere showed that "American involvement has been much larger and more pervasive than I previously realized or than the Administration has acknowledged."

To insist upon defining the Angolan issue in global terms to the exclusion of local and regional terms was to exclude the most plausible means of remedying the conditions that had attracted foreign intervention in the first place. And to insist that the only "chips" were military chips was to play from the weakest suit in the American hand. The accompanying notion that one should not communicate intentions and concerns but should allow free rein for others to miscalculate and take reckless risks defies any definition of diplomacy. It betrays an obsessional preoccupation with superpower global antics reminiscent of the grimmest days of the Cold War.

It was, then, in January 1975—or at the latest in July—that it became imperative for the United States to suggest to Moscow the formula actually used in October, a readiness to "use our influence to bring about the cessation of foreign military assistance and to encourage an African solution if they would do the same." (What, one wonders, ever happened to the "hot line"?)

But the offer needed to be made not just to the Soviets—as though they were the only real actors in the play. The president and secretary of state ought at one or both of these earlier dates to have called in the OAU ambassadors and contacted key African leaders—encouraging collective African initiatives and promising U.S. support for them.

By late 1975, as MPLA/Cuban troops got the upper hand in Angola, the apparent tie between the United States and South Africa both destroyed the possibility of collective African support for a compromise solution and undermined the frail and limited acquiescence of those senators and congressmen who had been informed, in accordance with a 1974 law, of the covert actions the United States had been taking since July. When the issue came to a head in December, a phalanx of alarmed senators, sensing a congruence of conscience and a promising election-year issue, derailed the escalation train by voting 54 to 22 to ban further covert aid to Angola. The House of Representatives followed the Senate in January 1976 in voting 323 to 99 not to provide the "trivial sums," the "tens of millions of dollars" with which the administration proposed to bolster FNLA-UNITA forces and induce a military stalemate propitious for a negotiated settlement. The secretary of state compounded his credibility problem by renouncing his remaining leverage with the Soviet Union—ruling out a delay in negotiations on a Strategic Arms Limitation Treaty or a moratorium on massive grain sales to the Soviet Union.

The hapless, would-be beneficiaries of American policy perceived its weakness. In their view, the United States neither persuaded the Soviet Union to moderate its role in the conflict nor provided anti-Soviet forces with enough assistance to be successful. Instead, American rhetoric about a global Soviet threat was counterproductive. As FNLA leader Johnny Eduardo put it: "Whenever [Ford or Kissinger] bang their fists on the table against our enemies, the Russians take them seriously and increase military aid to the MPLA." Indeed, American policymakers seemed intent upon escalating the consequences of not doing something after they knew that nothing would be done.

Aside from sliding into a de facto alliance with South Africa, the United States also fell into another trap as its Angolan policy evolved: it overreacted to the harsh rhetoric of a marxist-influenced liberation movement by identifying it as the "enemy." It responded to the MPLA as a Soviet pawn rather than a discrete, if blemished, African reality. Ironically, the subsequent willingness of the victorious MPLA to respond to American overtures for direct discussions derived from what President Ford has described as the "tragedy" of the Senate action. MPLA officials seized upon the occasion of visits by congressional aides and journalists to Luanda to convey their (1) readiness to welcome the Gulf Oil Corporation back to the Cabindan oil fields that they had left under U.S. government pressure; (2) recognition of the importance of Western markets for their oil, iron, coffee, diamond, and silver exports; and (3) willingness to make a constitutional undertaking not to allow any "foreign power to establish bases" on Angolan territory. Freed from the constraints of global obsession, U.S. policymakers might find that flexibility, time, and flux would erode transient Soviet advantage.

In sum, the most fundamental weakness of U.S. policy in Angola was its total disregard for the realities of African politics. Washington misjudged the character and capabilities of Angolan nationalist movements, jeopardized the future of regimes it sought to support (Zambia and Zaire), and contributed to a further weakening of Africa's aggregate capacity to mount sanctions against external intervention. Above all, American policy failed completely to reckon with the negative importance of South Africa in African politics. The more the United States came to depend on tacit cooperation with South Africa to stem Soviet penetration, the more the United States opened the way to Soviet intervention by removing the risk of united African opposition.

The Nub of the Matter: South Africa

If Prime Minister Vorster reads *The New York Times*, he may well have pondered Hedrick Smith's December 1974 analysis of the state of East-West détente. "It is apparent now," Smith wrote, "that the Soviet leadership—with increasing self-confidence and pragmatism—has found a formula for achieving the foreign policy and economic dividends of accommodation with the West without paying the price of relaxing controls at home." The key lay in keeping "sufficient controls at home to prevent the contamination of free ideas from stirring new creativity among the intelligentsia." These controls include a censored press, limited access to Westerners, and mental wards or exile for especially troublesome dissenters.[57]

For two important reasons, South Africa cannot replicate in Africa the formula for dichotomized détente that has served the Soviet Union so well. First, South Africa is a selectively, not all-inclusively, repressive state. Characterized by Heribert Adam as a "democratic police state,"[58] South Africa pragmatically tolerates "white nonbelievers" in both press and parliament, while ruthlessly suppressing black proponents of majority rule. Second, the longer term external success of Vorster's détente policy depends, as the Soviet Union's does not, on basic internal reform of a racial caste system which the ruling group believes to be vital to the survival of a desirable social order.

But what is internal and what is external? What are the Republic's "real" boundaries? By defining all Africans as members of unassimilable "nations" entitled (obliged?) to preserve their separate "identities," is the Afrikaner-centered government not itself "internationalizing" relations among primary groups within the Republic? Will the Transkei "homeland of the Xhosa people" become an "external" concern when it is granted all the trappings of independence in October 1976, even though it remains crucially dependent economically on South Africa? Is South West Africa, long claimed as an intrinsic part of the Republic, now considered an "external" issue? Are the 2.3 million Afrikaans-speaking coloureds to be add-ins? What about the 700,000 Asians? Are 400,000 English-speaking Natal whites potential add-outs? And how does one apply to all this the Afrikaner dictum against interference in the *internal* affairs of others? Has Pretoria itself not thoroughly befogged the distinction between internal and external?

Over and over, Afrikaner spokesmen invoke the history of their Voortrekker forebears who moved deep into the Transvaal and Orange Free State to escape British rule. When faced with a choice, it is stressed, these pioneers chose identity over property—and persons who cannot accept this fact will "never understand the Afrikaner."[59] Systematic studies of white South African elites substantiate the contention that Afrikaans-speaking descendants of seventeenth century Dutch settlers are more concerned than are English-speaking South Africans with group culture and welfare.

For the Afrikaans-speaking majority (58 percent) of whites, freedom (within a traditional Calvinist ethic) is an important value. Dissent within Afrikanerdom is legitimate, but only so long as it does not threaten the integrity and material interest of the group. High value is attached to disciplined schools, to the political process, to state enterprise, and to collective ethnic (Afrikaner) ascendancy over the more individualistic English-speakers within the white minority. The Afrikaner elite clings to primary group solidarity in maintaining firm control over the country's central political and military structures. At another level, it has stressed *white* solidarity to win support from the more diverse English-speaking community. But it has remained intolerant of any outsiders' (*uitlanders*) demands for a share of power, especially those coming from the African majority.

Although those holding political power have displayed an increasing degree of adaptability and sophistication in recent years, they have shown little disposition to move toward fundamental change in the historic Afrikaner scale of values.

The attitudes of a growing minority of adults within the Afrikaner elite have begun to modify and diversify, however, as a result of professional education, foreign travel, urban secularism, and general exposure to modernization. In recent years, Afrikaner "intellectuals, journalists, writers, and even politicians have publicly criticized petty apartheid, colour discrimination, the lack of meaningful contact between ethnic groups in South Africa, the lack of development in the Bantu homelands and the lack of scope for and low wage levels of Black workers." Even conservative Afrikaners are becoming "more sensitive to the injustices of colour discrimination and petty apartheid in the common area," while liberal English-speakers are becoming "more willing to consider the merits of separate development or grand apartheid, the development of homelands, and the recognition of cultural identity."[60]

Paradoxically, attitude surveys show a preponderance of young Afrikaners to be fearful of social disorder, concerned for the future of their community, and less inclined to compromise than their elders. Among 16 to 24 year olds as a whole, "poverty seems preferable to Black rule and, as among English-speaking youth as well, a majority, albeit slight, would be inclined to think of leaving South Africa if faced with the prospect of Black political dominance as they understand it at present." Afrikaner youth are not shifting politically to liberal opposition parties. Recent polls have shown 57 percent agreeing with the statement, "In spite of many good qualities, Africans will never have the abilities of Whites," and only 16 percent favoring recognition of African trade unions. All of which caused the director of the Institute of Social Research at the University of Natal to conclude: "the profile of attitudes which seems to be characteristic of 16-to-24-year-old Afrikaners offers scant encouragement to those who hope for more enlightened and forward-looking race policies, whether along the lines of Separate Development or that of the common society."[61]

But is it to gradual attitude change that one should be looking for the emergence of a societal consensus for structural change? The answer must be a negative one, since it is impossible to predict future behavior simply on the basis of knowledge about attitudes. Behavior is as much or more determined by environmental pressures as by spontaneous changes of attitude. It was the collapse of Portuguese rule, not a sudden burst of humanitarianism, that brought a radical change in South African diplomatic behavior in 1974. Similarly, most analysts believe that the dismantling of South Africa's internal racial caste system will depend "almost wholly on the bargaining power" of subordinate racial groups. As one of the cited studies of white South African elites concludes: "Internal pressure, sometimes in alliance with pressures from abroad," not attitudes held by those in power, will "largely determine" the course of societal change in South Africa.[62]

What kind of pressures are we talking about? Over the long haul, demographic. Constituting only 17 percent of the Republic's population, South Africa's 4.16 million whites are confronted with an African population of nearly

18 million that is growing at a considerably faster rate. Despite government programs to encourage European immigration, African growth was 30 percent and European 25 percent during the decade 1964-74. Add 2.3 million coloured (mixed descent) and 700,000 Asians, and the white population is outnumbered by a deteriorating ratio of 5 to 1. A leading South African demographer, J.L. Sadie, forecasts that the country's population will more than double by the year 2000 with Asians up 70 percent to 1.2 million; coloureds up 110 percent to 4.9 million; whites (including immigration) up 70 percent to 6.9 million; and blacks up 120 percent to 37.3 million. This would reduce the white population from 17 to 14 percent of the total.[63]

Pressures will also be economic. Out of a total South African work force of 8.5 million, nearly six million are black Africans. And although blacks are underpaid in relation to whites, their skills and purchasing power have become a crucial and integral dimension of the country's complex, industrialized economy. In the process of raising educational and income levels, the system inevitably raises social and, however muted, political awareness as well.

The government has erected a coercive legal and social system aimed at preventing reaction to basic inequities from generating a serious organized challenge to white rule. It has enacted stringent laws such as that which renders a person guilty of "terrorism" if he or she has "committed any act or attempted to commit . . . any act" with "intent to endanger the maintenance of law and order."[64] It has enforced a system of influx and pass controls that has led to the arrest of over 500,000 Africans annually. It has forcibly uprooted and transplanted some two to three million people as a part of an ongoing scheme to "consolidate" white and black areas.[65] It has instituted "banning," a form of social isolation by restriction to limited specified areas or even house arrest; issued one-way exit permits as a means of exporting special troublemakers; and organized (via threats and money) an extensive system of security police informers planted among urban Africans. And to insure that the social system perpetuates "differentiation" among "national" groups, it has established separate school systems that impose parochial "Bantu education," and separate substandard universities organized on ethnic lines.

The social costs of this coercive system are evident in dysfunctional behavior among both whites and non-whites. Among whites it tends to take the form of intensified group isolation, which, in the face of strong external criticism, leads to defensive and messianic behavior and, in turn, to further reliance upon coercive as distinct from rational action.[66] A University of Cape Town psychologist, H.J. van der Spuy, concludes from an analysis of seven recent studies that South Africans as a whole are "more neurotic than most other national groups,"[67] and attributes this to a high level of anxiety related to racial policies. South African whites (especially Afrikaners) manifest "obsessional" behavior, as evidenced in the "petty apartheid" (separate facilities, entrances, and "pass books") by which the life of blacks is regulated and ordered. And studies of Afrikaner students reveal extraordinarily high levels of authoritarian behavior and prejudice.

Of particular relevance to South African politics and foreign policy, these qualities in Afrikaner behavior are reflected in a degree of "national paranoia," a feeling of "national persecution." They produce "the belief that there is some sort of international plot against the Afrikaner; that the English press and other liberals are not really worried about injustice to blacks, but that this is simply an excuse to obtain the cooperation of the blacks and other international forces to fulfil their real aim—the destruction of the Afrikaner nation, or even of White Western civilization."[68] These beliefs, coupled with ideas of grandeur, of being a "chosen people," are manifested most intensely in the fanatic but still small *Herstigte Nasionale* party that emerged on the political scene in 1969. The pathology of white South Africa is revealed as well in the incidence of self-inflicted violence, *viz.* an exceedingly high suicide rate,[69] and in feelings of personal frustration and guilt.[70]

Social dysfunction is even more widely disabling among other racial groups. A four year study by a commission of the Cape Synod of the Dutch Reformed Church concluded that the harshly controlled system of African migratory labor which services the white-run urban economy is breaking up African family life (only one-fourth of married urban African men live with their wives), encouraging sexual promiscuity, fostering high rates of violent crime, and threatening to "affect the whole social and religious life of all the races in our fatherland" like a raging "cancer." The guilt-ridden albeit thoroughly doctrinaire study struck a note of despair. Lifting legal restrictions so as to unite (some 1.3 million) migrant workers' families would either entail the "impossible and excessive burden of providing housing" or multiply untenable squatter towns. "with their terrible evils." Which left only the alternative of inaction, African bitterness, and fated Calvinist punishment: "By virtue of God's laws the Whites will not remain untouched by the sickness which is ravaging the moral life of the African."[71]

Testing for job suitability, a Johannesburg psychologist canvassed several hundred Africans and found that "roughly four out of every ten tested [showed] symptoms of severe neurotic aggression syndromes." Some of their frustration was unleashed in the gang killings and terror that suffused African urban life.[72] Among the 2.3 million, predominantly Afrikaans-speaking, coloureds who are denied Afrikaner "identity" on the sole basis of racial origin, frustration again expressed itself in social anomie, as reflected in rampant alcoholism.[73]

Every effort is made to discourage any African political activity focused on acquiring a share of power within a "common society," and to root out and destroy multi-ethnic nationalist movements, e.g., the African National Congress (ANC) and Pan-Africanist Congress (PAC). While the government may have succeeded in frustrating and deflecting political opposition inward into self-destructive violence, banning of political activity has not expunged political thought. For example, a 1971 analysis of the response of African high school students to tightening social and political restrictions showed a decline of interest in community service and individual economic success and a corresponding increase of interest in politics.[74]

Responding to the separatist/identiy motif in Afrikaner politics, young Africans increasingly eschew multiracialism and articulate a political outlook based on self-reliance and assertive counter-rejection of the "white world" which has rejected them. African bitterness about influx control, low wages, inadequate transport, and personal manifestations of white disrespect projects most strongly against those who most firmly reject the notion of a common South African "nation," the Afrikaners.[75] Fascinated by the evolution of race relations in the United States, young Africans have generated a new "Black Consciousness" movement.[76] It finds organized expression in the South African Students' Organization (SASO) and the adult Black Peoples' Convention (BPC). Setting themselves off against whites, the organizers of these movements define "blacks" as "people who are by law or tradition, politically, economically and socially discriminated against as a group" in South Africa, thus including coloureds and Indians as well as Africans.[77] Though they have not risked articulating specific political programs and have focused instead on educational, social, and cultural issues, they are in the multi-ethnic ("multi-national" in the Afrikaner's lexicon) tradition of the banned and exiled ANC and PAC. As such they are an anathema to the architects of separate development and internal "national" détente. Despite government use of the Terrorism Act to justify arrests of SASO and BCP leadership, the two "black consciousness" organizations survive as embarrassing evidence of black opposition. In December 1975, when white South African soldiers were engaged in combat against the MPLA in Angola, the BCP's fourth annual congress publicly announced its support for Dr. Neto's MPLA government.[78]

The fact remained that black movements such as the BCP and SASO are being unmercifully harassed and have little "bargaining power" with the government. More likely to win concessions—at least in the short term—are those blacks who capitalize on demographic and economic leverage and push for specific advantages within the existing system. Through the first half of the 1970s, the government appeared increasingly intolerant of both black and white forms of extraparliamentary dissent, as witness crackdowns (1973) on such galvanizers of moral conscience as the Christian Institute[79] and threats (1974) to curb the English language press. In the view of a liberal South African sociologist and M.P., F. van Zyl Slabbert: "The general pattern that seems to be emerging is that all forms of dissent or opposition, whether Black or White, will increasingly be forced into government sanctioned organizations or institutions. This will ensure that the Afrikaner Nationalists will play a strategic role in whatever political change may come about."[80]

The Leverage of Separate Development

Apartheid was defined in a National Party pamphlet published for the 1948 election campaign in these terms: "It is a policy which sets itself the task of preserving the racial identity of the white population of the country; of likewise preserving and safeguarding the identity of the indigenous peoples as separate racial groups, with opportunities to develop into self-governing national units . . . The Bantu in the urban areas should be regarded as migratory citizens . . . The process of detribalization should be arrested. . . ." A 17-volume report of a Commission on the Socio-Economic Development of the Bantu Areas (the so-called Tomlinson Report) recommended in 1954 the basic guidelines for a consolidation of the 264 existing Native Reserves into seven (subsequently adjusted to ten) economically viable "bantustans." The Promotion of Bantu Self-Government Act of 1959 and the Homelands Constitution Act of 1971 provided for the four-step constitutional development of each of the black "national groups." As of late 1975, one (the Transkei) was being prepared for full independence (stage 4), five had been proclaimed (stage 3) self-governing territories (Basotho Qwaqwa, Bophuthatswana, Ciskei, Gazankulu, Lebowa, and Venda), one had a legislative assembly indicative of the first stage of development (KwaZulu), and two, Swazi and Ndebele, were but formative.

One stratagem available to Africans in the Republic is to accept this Afrikaner doctrine of ethnic separation and attempt to turn it to the advantage of the majority. Asserting an officially recognized "identity," each ethnic community, or "nation," now has a presumptive right to an independent national future. The extent and character of this independence may be circumscribed by pragmatic (especially economic) considerations, but it is not rigidly foreordained.

Three contrasting working models of this stratagem are the ethno-linguistic states of Botswana, Lesotho, and Swaziland—three former British High Commission Territories long coveted by South Africa and still geographically and economically intertwined with the Republic after a decade of independence. A U.S. government assessment of the BLS states undertaken in 1967 concluded that minerally endowed Botswana was the only one of the three that had demonstrated a commitment to reduce its dependence on South Africa.

Under the able leadership of Sir Seretse Khama, Botswana has undertaken a comprehensive economic development plan grounded in production of diamonds, coal, base metals, and beef cattle. While this effort has not yet led to the degree of economic freedom Seretse Khama would like to achieve, American aid has enabled Botswana to reach out from its near encirclement by white-ruled states to link up by road with Zambia to the north. And it now stands ready to route much of its mineral trade through Rhodesia to Mozambican ports once an African government has been established in intervening Rhodesia. Swaziland (with "some economic resources," notably iron ore and timber) and Lesotho (without "much economic potential") were described as remaining "willingly" in the South African "orbit." Like Malawi under President H. Kamuzu Banda, they have made maximum utilization of substantial support from the Republic in the form of technicians, loans, and grants, and passively suffered the quiet discouragement of any economic enterprise that might be competitive with South African industry (e.g., the proposed establishment of a Japanese auto assembly plant in Lesotho in 1972)[81] as well as spasmodic political intervention by the South African Bureau of State Security (BOSS).[82]

De jure independence does, however, give these states the ability to needle South Africa publicly from time to time as a signal that they are aware of the economic squeeze under which they operate and of the omnipresence of BOSS. For example, Lesotho's foreign minister purposefully prickled Pretoria by journeying to China early in 1975, and later the same year roundly denounced South African "racism" in the UN General Assembly.[83] Swaziland's passivity has been ruffled as a result of the rise of FRELIMO to power in adjoining Mozambique, a development that could, over time, encourage the tiny kingdom to edge away from the constraining customs union that binds its economy so closely to that of South Africa.[84] Swaziland's exports of iron ore, coal, and timber go by rail to the Mozambican port of Maputo.

That the BLS states might invoke South African dicta about the integrity of ethnic "nations" and make irredentist claims to contiguous South African territory inhabited by their ethnic kin emerged as an intriguing possibility in 1975-76. With the aid of a Nigerian expert in international law, the government of Lesotho began preparing a claim to contiguous areas in the Orange Free State and Cape Province on the basis of century-old treaty rights. Should Pretoria refuse to negotiate, Lesotho threatened to carry its case for restitution of Basotho territory lost in 1866 to the United Nations.[85] Some of the land claimed lay within the confines of adjoining bantustans, or, in the words of Lesotho's foreign minister, the "pseudo-states" into which Vorster was fragmenting South Africa. Reinforcing Lesotho's ambitions, 1975 elections in the contiguous Qwaqwa bantustan of the South Sotho resulted in a government that has publicly favored eventual incorporation of that minihomeland into Lesotho.[86]

To complicate matters further, Chief Minister Lukas Mangope of the Tswana Bantustan of Bophuthatswana proposed as early as 1973 that his Tswana-speaking "homeland" be united with contiguous Botswana. His two-step plan would (1) consolidate Bophuthatswana into one territory (not six as planned by Pretoria) and (2) then federate it and its more than 800,000 resident Tswana-speaking people with 600,000 kinsmen of the spacious (222,000 square mile) Republic of Botswana.[87] Although a few Afrikaners have spoken out in support of consolidating Bophuthatswana into one unit as part of a necessary crash program to speed up homeland development,[88] consolidation has been blocked by fierce opposition from Afrikaner farmers. Botswana President Seretse Khama is on record as opposing the South African policy of fragmenting and "herding" blacks "into barren Bantustans,"[89] but he has not picked up on Mangope's suggestions. Meanwhile, there also has been talk of eventually affiliating some of South Africa's 450,000 Swazis with Swaziland.[90]

Within the Republic proper, the Vorster government has scheduled October 26, 1976 as independence day for the only bantustan that in fact consists of essentially one contiguous and thus governable unit of territory, the Belgium-sized Xhosa homeland of Transkei. Chief Minister Kaiser Mantanzima bargained for the incorporation of white enclaves and Xhosa-inhabited border areas[91] prior to accepting an independence that is essential for Pretoria if its policy of separate "national" development is ever to be taken seriously abroad. Pretoria holds to the terms of a 1936 Natives Land and Trust Act under which no more than 13 percent of South Africa's 471,000 square miles is to go to Africans, i.e., for all the ten homelands together. Suggesting that an ever-escalating spiral of territorial demands might well be a logical consequence of Pretoria's disaggre-gating "nations" policy, Mantanzima has appeared intent upon pressing for creation of a Greater Xhosaland extending from the Fish River to the Natal border. He sees independence for 1.8 million Xhosa in present day Transkei as just a first step; over two million more Xhosa live within "common" (meaning white) areas.

Belated efforts are underway to attract foreign investment capital to the undeveloped territory which supplies some 260,000 workers to the Republic and employs less than 50,000 at home.[92] Offering very favorable terms, including a promise of no labor unions, the Xhosa Development Corporation has been able to attract a commitment of modest investment capital for textile and other small industry.[93] Wishful ambitions extend to creation of an international airport at the capital, Umtata, building a harbor at the mouth of the Mtata River (Transkei has no port), and membership in the United Nations, despite a 100 to 0 vote of the General Assembly condemning South Africa's whole policy of separate "national" development for African "homelands."[94] A true test of Transkeian leadership, however, will lie in whether or not it plans and executes a basic reform of the territory's outmoded, feudal land system.

With the nucleus of a national university being set up in Umtata and government advisors at work on the text of a "multiracial" constitution (there would be no apartheid), the Transkei is being thrust forward as a test model of South African intentions. Among those attracted into the nucleus of a diplo-matic corps-in-training has been Tsepo T. Letlaka, a former leader of the Pan-Africanist Congress who reasoned that more could be accomplished by working from within the system than from exile. Slated to be the first Transkeian ambassador to Washington should the new state gain American recognition, Letlaka has predicted that an independent Transkei would act as a vigorous champion of *all* the "oppressed and exploited people" of South Africa. Rather than remain united in oppression, he argues, it is better for "an important section of the victims of apartheid," the four million Xhosa resident in both the

Transkei and the Republic, to deal with the South African government as sovereign equals.[9 5]

Reversing his earlier position, Chief Minister Mangope of Bophuthatswana fell in behind the Transkei in November 1975 and announced that his government would in due course also ask for independence. Frustrated by Pretoria's failure to facilitate the territorial consolidation of Bophuthatswana, he concluded that the way to increase his political leverage with the Republic was to move toward independence, even as a mosaic of discontiguous territory. Would other fragmented homelands follow suit? None seems prepared to accept independence without substantial territorial accretion.

One factor that might influence their leadership, however, is the possible impact of Transkeian independence upon urban blacks. Would Xhosa living in large black townships such as Johannesburg's Soweto gain in social and legal status at the expense of Zulus, Tswanas, Shangaans, and others as citizens of an "independent" state that many had never seen? And if so, might the leadership of other homelands confront pressure to seek the same "independence"?[9 6] Perhaps. But urban black leadership is generally hostile to bantustans, and basutos and Swazis working in the Republic have experienced little benefit from the independence of their countries. Moreover, there is reason to think that South Africa's program of (1) separate development for black (Xhosa and Zulu) but not white (Afrikaner and Anglo) ethnic groups and (2) homelands for less than half of the African population and none of the coloured and Asian, is creating the conditions for its own undoing. Its contradictions are being dramatized by the leadership to which it has given birth.

At the forefront of this officially legitimated leadership is the head of the KwaZulu homeland government, Chief Gatsha Buthelezi. An opponent of ethnic and racial separation even during his days as a student at Fort Hare University, Buthelezi accepted the KwaZulu post in 1970 only after concluding that the government was determined to impose its homeland formula. As a spokesman for four million Zulus, half of whom live in the 29 patches and 200 snippets of Zulu homeland scattered about Natal Province, he has campaigned for a much larger, consolidated territory, for a detribalized and expanded system of education, and for an inflow of foreign investment. But he has refused to limit himself to ethnic (Zulu) politics. As an advocate of racial equality and black solidarity, he has traveled through Africa, Europe, and the United States and won respect for his cause and person. He has joined white liberals in endorsing the concept of a multiracial South African federation. And he has taken a lead in grouping the chief ministers of various bantustans around a common political platform. Thus it was that in March 1974 and again in January 1975, when the homeland leaders met with Prime Minister Vorster, they presented him with common grievances and requests for reform. Instead of limiting themselves to bantustan issues, they moved in to fill the vacuum created by the harsh repression of multi-ethnic nationalist movements since 1960.

At the January 1975 meeting, the homeland leaders delivered a series of memoranda and oral proposals on behalf of urban blacks. They urged that urban Africans: (1) be permitted to own property (Vorster agreed to the kind of 30-year home leases that had been available until 1967, but now only for blacks who become citizens of a homeland); (2) be freed from influx control regulations (Vorster rejected this but suggested discussions on modifications); (3) be given solid budgetary power in their urban councils (no action); (4) be authorized to adopt the same language of instruction in their schools as was used in their ascribed homelands, meaning more English, less Afrikaans (to be discussed further); (5) be placed in administrative control of black universities (acceptance in principle); and (6) be delivered from a host of discriminatory laws concerning business, trade, professional and labor rights, transport, population removal, and the like (few concessions).

Chiefs Buthelezi and Mangope used the occasion to place before the prime minister grievance memoranda from leaders of other sectors of African life who otherwise lacked access to him.[97] Buthelezi's request for amnesty for political prisoners (including Nelson Mandela of the ANC), detainees (including Robert Sobukwe of PAC), and exiles who wished to return to work in the "homelands" was rejected. Assuming a broad accountability function as well, Buthelezi delivered a comprehensive report on the summit meeting discussions to a mass gathering some days later in Soweto's Jabulani Amphitheatre.

As an official homeland spokesman, Buthelezi insinuated himself into a precarious and ill-defined, but fascinating, national role. Included in his well-publicized report at the Jabulani Amphitheatre were accounts of several carefully worded warnings that he had presumed to deliver to the prime minister. Buthelezi cited recent government statements, notably the speech by South African Ambassador to the United Nations R.F. Botha acknowledging, condemning, and promising a "move away from" racial discrimination within the Republic. These statements, Buthelezi stressed, had given rise to new African hopes and expectations of progress toward a more equitable "federal" structure for South Africa based upon a system of "properly consolidated" homelands. Should these hopes for "meaningful change" be dashed, he warned, the "pent-up frustrations" of the people could well lead to "civil disobedience and disruption of services." And he, Buthelezi, could not be "expected to successfully ward off" such a venting of frustration in the absence of a change in government policy.

Linking this suggestive, public warning to prospects for the success of Mr. Vorster's quest for détente with black-governed states of middle Africa, Chief Buthelezi recounted to the Jabulani audience what he had told Vorster in cautionary terms about a recent exchange that he, Buthelezi, had had with President William R. Tolbert of Liberia. "Although the Prime Minister does meet us as equals around the table," he had told Tolbert, ". . . it [is] too early . . . to judge whether we are moving towards real and meaningful equality in South

Africa." Tolbert was reported to have responded that he and his government "would be guided by us, their black brothers" as to what stance they should adopt towards South Africa.[98]

After Prime Minister Vorster made a dramatic pilgrimage to Liberia in February 1975, President Tolbert confirmed that he had brought Chief Buthelezi and Sam Nujoma of Namibia (SWAPO) to Monrovia to provide him with "accurate information" preparatory to his talks with the white South African leader. Underscoring the link between external détente and domestic policy, Chief Buthelezi subsequently revealed that he was in close communication with the Zambian government which was keeping him informed of matters related to détente. Zambia was thereby demonstrating its concern for the interests of blacks in South Africa.[99]

The subtle political theater of Jabulani aside, what bargaining power do bantustan leaders have? The failure of past governments to give more than lip service to the notion of homeland development has left these disparate, undersized territories looking like very improbable solutions to South African racial inequities. Although reduced bureaucratic barriers had encouraged German, Italian, Japanese, and other investors to inject some capital into these impoverished backwaters by 1976, a massive transfer of skills and capital would be required to render them more than impotent client states. This would be true even if they are enlarged, consolidated, and federated.

Arguing that "history itself has divided the land between whites and blacks," South African Minister of Bantu Administration and Development M.C. Botha has described demands for more land as "futile," though "characteristic of the Bantu."[100] Responding to "extravagant" claims by the Lebowa government to over a third of the Transvaal, he warned in 1974 that the (government as) grantor and *not* the grantee will decide what constitutes proper boundaries.[101] In the same year, Botha also dismissed homeland requests for permission to recruit black American science and mathematics teachers, insisting that they can be found in South Africa.[102] "Independence" might be a way around such constraints on skill acquisition. But earlier agreement among homeland leaders to seek strength in unity by federating seemed to be giving way to ethnic nationalism and separate strategies.[103] And although some observers believed that they saw a confirmed tendency in homeland politics for "initial moderate leadership" to be "replaced by more radical and pragmatic leadership,"[104] and for articulate homeland leaders such as Gatsha Buthelezi to mobilize political constituencies and gain powerful outside friends, Pretoria seemed confident in its economic and police power to deal with feisty ministates.

On the one hand, critics of bantustan independence see its acceptance as (1) legitimizing existing land boundaries and (2) conceding that bantustan citizens have "no claim to a share of the capital accumulation of the South African economy."[105] On the other hand, precisely because the homelands are a hopelessly inadequate answer to African economic and political aspirations, they are seen by some as legal instruments, which both their inhabitants and urban Africans ascribed to them may find useful in working for generalized change. To project from one of the system's absurdities, if the government of tiny (200 square miles, 26,000 inhabitants) Qwaqwa is to be treated as the "national" homeland of some 1.5 million South Sotho "citizens" living largely in urban Orange Free State, is it not fated to become an instrument of political protest? The real significance of the homelands may lie with the open-ended process of pressure, conflict, and concession that surrounds their evolution and with the interaction of this process with socioeconomic and political dynamics in the rest of the Republic. Uncertain agents of change, they seem likely to generate cross currents of nationalism, irredentism, and ambition.

The Potential Political Leverage of African Labor

The impact of separate development politics on African labor in the white-controlled economy of South Africa warrants careful attention. For every five economically active men in the rural homelands, six "homelanders" are working in "white areas" as migrant laborers. There they now constitute nearly 60 percent of the black work force in the "modern sector" of the country's economy.

Alongside mounting pressure from separate development politics, black Africans seem to be gaining bargaining power in the economic arena. The highly industrialized, technological economy of South Africa, built upon immense sub- and topsoil riches, achieved a GNP of some $18.4 billion by 1971—before benefiting from a soar (later modified) in world gold prices. Totalling $3.8 billion, gold counted for 36 percent of South Africa's exports in 1974.[106] Abundant and cheap black labor to exploit and process these riches has attracted over $9 billion in foreign investment which commonly earns a 15 to 20 percent annual return, about twice the world average.

Africans provide more than 80 percent of the country's agricultural workers. Over two million are employed in farming, fishing, and forestry. Urban-bound Afrikaners have left Africans in charge of managing and running a large proportion of the country's central *platteland* farms. Despite their indispensability, three-fourths of the some four million Africans living in "white" rural areas have received no schooling—an indication of their standard of living.[107] Meanwhile, black labor rose from 70 percent to 80 percent of the manufacturing labor force in the urban industrial sector between 1960 and 1971. As the economy grows more complex, and requires more and more skilled workers than the white minority can provide, the color bar has floated higher.[108] In late 1974, for example, the government announced that it was establishing eight training centers to upgrade the skills of African workers (electrical, laboratory, machine maintenance, etc.) in white urban areas.[109]

The significance of potential black labor leverage is nowhere more apparent than in South Africa's mines. Although average wages for gold miners tripled between 1972 and 1975 (to roughly $123 a month plus food, accommodation and "amenities"),[110] inflation has eaten up a sizable portion of these gains and labor boycotts, work stoppages, and pit violence have bedeviled the mining industry. For years the gold mines depended upon foreign migrants for three-fourths of their 400,000 black work force. But in 1974-75 Malawi's President Banda banned further recruitment of Malawians (who had accounted for 134,000), several thousand Basotho withdrew in contract disputes, the future availability of 86,000 Mozambican gold miners became doubtful, recruitment rates fell in Botswana, and the gold mines were operating with only 72 percent of full labor complement at the outset of 1975.

Although explanations varied ("A growing political awareness; the presence of agitators; higher wages leading to more spending on alcohol; a greater realization of the power of the strike weapon. . . ."[111]), the implications were sobering. The South African Chamber of Mines began recruiting in Rhodesia, an undependable source for the long term, and, most significantly, had to begin competing on the internal South African job market for an additional 50,000 workers.[112] Intensified recruiting had raised the work force back to 89 percent of requirements by mid-1975, allowing for a ten percent cut attributable to increased productivity.[113] Neighboring states whose political complexions were undergoing drastic change could be expected to drive harder bargains when singly or collectively negotiating terms of employment. Should the governments of Botswana, Lesotho, Mozambique, and Malawi, possibly joined later by homeland governments ("independent" or not), undertake to bargain as a consortium, economic (and thus political?) reality might further alter.[114] In mid-1975, the foreign minister of Lesotho initiated exploratory talks with Botswana and Mozambique with an eye to future "collective bargaining."[115]

In late 1974, Harry Oppenheimer, chairman of the mammoth Anglo-American Corporation, warned that South Africa was heading into a period of serious political unrest. "Unless the representation of Black workers for discussion and negotiation with management is radically and rapidly improved," Oppenheimer said, "that unrest is going to have very serious consequences indeed."[116] Similarly, M.P. Helen Suzman (opposition Progressive Reform Party) pointed out that whites could provide only 1.7 of 3.7 million skilled workers needed by 1980. Job reservation laws and white labor union obstruction, she warned, would have to give way to African pressure for access to technical education and collective bargaining rights, if the economy was not to be thrown out of gear.[117]

Whereas the government has been willing to ease unessential racial restrictions ("petty apartheid") and to abolish such onerous laws as the Masters and Servants Act that had made it a crime for Africans to break employment contracts,[e]

---

[e]This particular reform was undertaken to prevent a ban on the importation of South African coal into Alabama.

demands for collective bargaining rights have been resisted. The hope persists that such bargaining can be limited to "work and liaison" committees and that the effectiveness of pressure for broad-gauged unions would be reduced by mechanization and automation. A new reefboring machine raised hopes that underground labor needs could be reduced by half—that mining could be made capital rather than labor intensive. But even where feasible, costly laborsaving devices will only shift dependency to a smaller but highly trained work force of African operators and technicians.

The white Mine Workers' Union continues to fight black job advancement and the White Confederation of Labor (200,000 members) and the Afrikaner press denounce disruptive foreign "interference" in the labor situation, especially that of the British Trades Union Congress (TUC) in financing training programs designed to promote African trade union organizing.[118] A long history of arrests, bannings, and police intimidation of labor organizers reflects an underlying Afrikaner suspicion that the creation of black trade unions would represent but a "first step in bringing about integrated trade unions."[119]

Under pressure from anti-apartheid activists critical of American investment in and trade with South Africa,[120] the U.S. State Department since 1974 has advised American companies in South Africa to be "prepared to engage in collective bargaining" with black unions "if, as and when they come into existence."[121] In determining their policies in this area, corporations must balance the risks of defying South African government policy (though not law) against the alternative risks of adverse publicity and disrupted stockholder meetings at home.

The dramatic Ovambo strikes of 1971 (Namibia), followed by a rash of unofficial strikes mostly in and around Durban in 1973, alerted the South African government, and Africans, to the potential power of the strike weapon. That they also increased the earnings of some 50,000 Durban area workers by between 15 and 18 percent[122] has fed official fear that the scope of labor's concern would progressively expand from wages and in situ working conditions to related matters of health, housing, family welfare, and education—that is, to matters of public (political) policy. On the other hand, to deny Africans any right to bargain collectively "on the basis of gradually acquired strategic positions in an expanding economy" will risk work boycotts and lowered productivity,[123] and perhaps also a disruptive backlash among increasingly selective African consumers whose spending is expected to be 50 percent greater than that of whites by 1990. Recalling the violent smashing of African labor protest in the 1920s, Francis Wilson, a keen-eyed researcher at the University of Cape Town's School of Economics, is more skeptical than some observers about the significance of the "phenomenal rise" in black participation in worker organizations since 1973. Wilson reluctantly concludes that "the repressive power of the state—including the willingness to use it if White control is threatened—is greater than it has ever been and . . . the possibility of organizing

Black labor effectively, whilst perhaps a little better than it was a decade ago, remains insignificant in comparison."[124]

Labor unions are not the only agencies attempting to aggregate black pressure for change within the "common area." Black urban councils are seeking, with as yet little result, increased local authority as part of the country's system of separate but "parallel" political structures. And at another level of "parallel" development, the Coloured Representative Council (CRC), given increased budgetary and administrative authority over coloured affairs by the Vorster government, has become a focal point of opposition to Nationalist racial policies.[125] After winning 31 of 40 elected seats on the council (the government appoints 20) in 1975, the Labour party led by Sonny Leon pressed demands for direct coloured representation in parliament. The government said "no." Leon then proposed as a compromise interim arrangement a joint body with decisionmaking authority in which white and coloured political parties would be represented proportional to their elective strength respectively in parliament and the CRC.[126] Agreement proved impossible. In November 1975, Sonny Leon refused to pass the CRC budget and the government dismissed him, putting in his place a non-elected government employee.

One public opinion poll has shown a majority of whites willing to accept coloured representation in parliament.[127] Government officials also stress the importance of not making enemies of 2.3 million people, although hard-core Afrikaner opposition to the acceptance of coloureds into a "common" society remains strong. In 1975, Minister of Interior Connie Mulder proclaimed flatly that sharing a language (Afrikaans) is not the same thing as sharing a culture, that coloureds are *not* brown Afrikaners and will not be assimilated with whites.[128] A policy that permits neither assimilation nor separate development, of course, promises only to frustrate and embitter.

As of early 1976, neither the sense of urgency nor the spirit of conciliation was sufficient to unsnarl the internal South African tangle. By denying hope of "shared institutions" but offering outlets for greater economic and educational advancement than before, the government seemed to be motivating "the majority of the politically rightless" to "try the narrow roads open instead of breaking down the barriers to the highways."[129] And yet to assume that government force and guile will succeed in maintaining the status quo indefinitely is unwarranted. Such an assumption ignores, as historian Leonard Thompson puts it, the fact that: "Greater power is now being accumulated by Black rural authorities and urban workers than Africans have possessed in South Africa at any time since they were conquered in the nineteenth century. While it is difficult at this stage to perceive by what precise mechanisms Black power will escalate, it is also difficult to see any way in which the process of escalation can be reversed."[130]

The psychopolitical impact of external events following upon the collapse of Portuguese rule in Mozambique and Angola can only reinforce this assessment.

Photographs of white South African prisoners of war on display in Lagos and Addis Ababa, as well as the retreat of outnumbered South African army units in the face of Cuban/MPLA offensives in Angola, have undermined the myth of white South African invincibility. From the ranks of new black leadership rising within the segmented South African system have come unprecedented warnings. Unlike the Vorster government, the disenfranchised are not mesmerized by the spectre of a communist Soviet/Cuban threat to their existence. Sonny Leon has declared that he will never ask coloured soldiers to fight in support of white baasskap (domination)—"to risk their lives for their country when they are still being treated as second-class citizens." And Chief Minister Hudson Ntsanwise of the Gazankulu homeland has advised: "South Africa should put right its internal situation so that blacks have a stake and are ready to defend the country against the enemy. Now the restless youth are espousing the cause of the Popular Movement [MPLA]."[131]

Insurgency as a Catalyst of Change?

The possibility that the government will be sufficiently flexible, powerful, and ingenious to accommodate and/or deflect black political assertion by means of a complex "conference system" of interlinked structures representing different "nations," races, and territorial entities seems just conceivable; some propose that communities such as Soweto become self-governing black city-states. Any moves toward such accommodation or "internal détente" would doubtless be accompanied by ringing chauvinism, a harsh crackdown on liberals and their press, and denials that any fundamental change is in fact taking place—all designed to provide the government with more room in which to maneuver.[132] Even an optimal sequence of evolutionary change would not, however, preclude spasmodic outbursts of black violence. The government has, as sociologist Heribert Adam has phrased it, reduced political opposition "to ineffectual acts of individual dissent, which require much more courage to carry out than collective action,"[133] but underlying black bitterness is such that a mine disaster or train wreck attributed to white callousness could unexpectedly spark a spontaneous African uprising.

A spontaneous uprising is one thing and organized insurgency is another. Neither the South African ANC nor the PAC possesses a guerrilla force of the size, skill, and means that would be required to penetrate the South African *laager*. South Africa is not a distant colony of those who rule it. It is "home," and it is defended by formidable legions of well-trained, well-equipped, and determined white forces. The government's counterinsurgency specialists are convinced that the intelligence capability as well as the research, training, and equipment possessed by South African security forces makes them more knowledgeable about insurgency than any African guerrilla movement.[134]

For the longer run, however, the best protection against insurgency is for the Vorster regime to capitalize on the gains of its détente policy to effect peaceful racial accommodation within the Republic. The rise to power of FRELIMO in Mozambique and the MPLA in Angola, and the looming possibility of a radical black regime in Rhodesia, are dramatically lessening white South Africa's ability to insulate its black majority from radicalizing outside influences and practical help. In due course, significant numbers of South African blacks may slip out via Botswana, Swaziland, or KwaZulu to coalesce as a serious insurgent force in exile. At minimum, there are likely to be hit and run raids from contiguous states, infiltration of sabotage teams into urban areas or homelands, and radical penetration of black labor organizations, urban councils, and homeland governments. Despite the acknowledged efficiency of the government's security and counterinsurgency forces, it is now conceivable that African insurgents (supported by the OAU, Arab states, the Soviet Union, Cuba, China, or any combination of these) might become an important variable in the unfolding South African drama. The fact that South Africa's scientists are "believed to be hurrying the country's first nuclear weapons into production"[135] is beside the point. If Africans ever gain the organizational capacity and collective audacity to withhold their labor, all the nuclear bombs, tanks, missiles, helicopters and jet fighters that Pretoria could muster would not put the Humpty Dumpty of a fractured race-caste social economy together again.

The Critical Choices for the United States

For the United States, the lesson of Portugal's African wars was that long-term policies should not be grounded on the assumption that white "European" armies do not give up in the face of black insurgents. The subsequent Angolan civil war challenged another dogma that has long played a crucial role in shaping political attitudes and postures throughout southern Africa. While the retreat of South Africa's forces to the southern border of Angola was the result of a political and tactical decision, not a battlefield defeat, the symbolic message of the withdrawal, for Africa's whites and blacks alike, is that the Republic's military might is limited. The precedent set by the large-scale Soviet and Cuban intrusion on behalf of a selected insurgency movement opens up a range of new variables that did not previously have to be taken into account and may have signalled the end of an era when a few hundred white mercenaries could determine the fate of an African nation.

It is too early to say whether South Africa's modified self-perception of its regional invincibility will result in quickened efforts to reach accommodation with "moderate" African nationalists in Namibia and speed the development of small ethnic states (homelands) to provide a kind of vicarious citizenship for some of its disenfranchised African majority. The hope (and in the long run it is

South Africa's best hope) that the government might possibly choose to pursue a rational policy of external and multileveled internal détente was kindled by the remarks of Ambassador to the United Nations R.F. Botha in October 1974: "I would be naive Sir, to pretend that I do not know why it is that members of this Organization, especially the African members, display towards us this antagonism, this lack of goodwill. It is basically because these members think that the Whites of South Africa have some inborn hatred and prejudice against the Blacks, that they consider themselves to be superior to or in some ways better than the Blacks and that on these grounds they discriminate against them in order to deny them fundamental rights and freedoms."[136]

But it may be that Prime Minister Vorster's commitment to détente will not withstand the pressures arising from his own and/or his constituents' ethnocentrism, perception of history, economic values, and rising fear of a "communist" threat from Angola and Mozambique. In that event, the *laager* mentality will prevail and South Africa will become a much more repressive state than it is today.

Whatever policy, or combination of these alternative policies, evolves in Pretoria in the wake of Angola, one overriding fact remains. Unless and until South Africa does achieve some kind of fundamental change in its racial caste system, it will remain a magnet for trouble. And it is the kind of trouble that the United States should avoid.

It would not be easy for the United States—already involved with massive investments (almost $1.5 billion) and trade ($1.1 billion in U.S. exports in 1974); anxious for continued access to platinum, manganese, vanadium, and other metals; implicated, despite a 1964 arms embargo, in agreements to sell enriched uranium suitable for the manufacture of nuclear weapons, as well as "non-lethal dual use" items such as Lear jets and Cessna dual-engine 401s and 402s to the South African defense forces;[137] involved in a secret (1971) relaxation of restrictions on the extension of Export-Import Bank facilities to South Africa;[138] and cooperating in the monitoring of the Cape sea route—to disengage, to dissociate. There would be much argument over the means. But it seems clear that American interests dictate dissociation.

The unprecedented anxiety and confusion with which black Americans responded to the Angolan crisis constituted a portent of what the response might be when the clearcut, black-white issues of South Africa come to the fore. American policymakers would risk a serious threat to domestic peace if they underestimated the extent to which 25 million black Americans share a latent identity with the disenfranchised black millions of white-ruled southern Africa. And the United States could ill afford to allow either racial bias or the Soviet Union to push it into an alliance with an embattled white minority attempting to maintain a privileged status quo from which we continue to enjoy economic profit. Instead, it would do well to encourage South Africa to interpret the loneliness of its intervention in Angola as evidence that, despite perceived anticommunist affinities and vigorous South African lobbying in the United States, acceptance by black Africans is a prerequisite to healthy relations between the two countries.

Restraining a propensity for moral posturing and self-righteousness, and avoiding the traps of commitment for or against any particular solutions—be they "radical" or "moderate"—the United States could achieve the essentials of a constructive policy by adopting some comprehensive guidelines. It should start by concerning itself with such issues as: (1) how visibly, responsibly, and convincingly to convert existing American enterprise in South Africa into a force for social change (through wages, fair employment standards, working with black trade unions); and (2) how sensibly to guide or constrict any future capital, science, or technology inputs (through tax disincentives, licenses, visa policies, public disclosure laws) in conformity with universal principles of social justice.[139] In coming to grips with these issues, special attention might usefully be given to the role of the 20 to 25 companies that hire some 90 percent of the black South African labor that works for American firms, and to the importance of imparting scientific and technological skills to black Africans.

In many areas of difficult choice—whether, for example, to recognize or extend economic or educational assistance to an "independent homeland" such as the Transkei after October 1976—the United States would do best to be guided by the collective judgment of African states as expressed through the Organization of African Unity.

Above all, our objective should be to work within the framework of African realities, promote racial justice, relate to "radicals" and "moderates" alike on a basis of mutuality of interest, and reinforce African regional strength. Building Africa's collective strength and self-reliance offers the best hope for preventing external intervention and avoiding a superpower collision in southern Africa.

American credibility now having become a scarce but vital resource, it should be appreciated that the kind of misleading disclaimers that have surrounded previous dealings with the Portuguese and South African regimes will only further undermine the creative potential of American policy.

Notes

1. See official statements by Assistant Secretary of State for African Affairs, Donald D. Newsom, "United States Options in Southern Africa," *Department of State Bulletin*, Vol. LXIV, No. 1647 (January 18, 1971), p. 83; and President Richard Nixon, "U.S. Foreign Policy for the 1970s, Building for Peace," *Ibid.*, No. 1656 (March 22, 1971), p. 388.

2. The full texts of this review and ten annexes were published in *The Kissinger Study of Southern Africa* (Nottingham, U.K: Spokesman Books, 1975).

3. *Ibid.*

4. António de Spínola, *Portugal e o Futuro* (Lisbon: Arcadia, 1974).

5. See Eduardo Mondlane, *The Struggle for Mozambique* (Baltimore: Penguin Books, 1969).

6. In January 1974, South Africa's Defense Minister P.W. Botha predicted increasing pressure from African insurgents in Mozambique—a "buildup of military power in southeastern Africa" that formed part of a "larger [read communist] strategy" aimed at all southern Africa. *Die Burger* (Cape Town), January 25, 1974.

7. See Bridget Bloom's "Mozambique: Between Revolution and Pragmàtism," in *The Financial Times* (London), November 3, 1975.

8. See statement by Aquino de Bragança in *Expresso* (Lisbon), May 10, 1975.

9. *The Financial Mail* (Johannesburg), Vol. LVI, No. 5 (May 2, 1975), p. 399.

10. *The Washington Post*, December 3, 1975.

11. Julius Nyerere was the first foreign leader to pay a state visit to Mozambique where, in September 1975, he and Samora Machel signed an agreement creating a Joint Commission of Cooperation for the purpose of fostering close economic and diplomatic ties between their two countries. *Daily News* (Dar es Salaam), September 8, 1975.

12. Henry A. Kissinger, *The Troubled Partnership: A Reappraisal of the Atlantic Alliance* (New York: McGraw-Hill, 1965), p. 205.

13. See Frances E. Hill, "Kissinger's Missing Continent," *Worldview*, Vol. 17, No. 10 (October 1974), pp. 29-33.

14. Text of letter from Secretary Kissinger to OAU Secretary General William A. Eteki Mboumoua in Department of State Press Release, No. 98 (February 24, 1975).

15. Department of State, Bureau of Public Affairs, "Mozambique Independence," *Current Policy*, No. 3, (Washington, D.C., June 1975).

16. See "Exchange of Remarks" between Foreign Minister Joaquim Chissano and Secretary of State Henry Kissinger, New York (September 23, 1975).

17. See Anthony R. Wilkinson, "Insurgency in Rhodesia, 1957-1973: An Account and Assessment," *Adelphi Papers*, No. 100 (London: International Institute for Strategic Studies, 1973).

18. "Zambia: Pawn or Primer?" *Background to South Africa and World News* (Pretoria), September 1968, p. 3.

19. *Die Transvaler*, January 18, 1975; January 25, 1975; April 19, 1975.

20. *The Rand Daily Mail* (Johannesburg), October 24, 1974.

21. South African Mission to the United Nations, "Statement by Ambassador R.F. Botha in the Security Council on Thursday, 24 October 1974."

22. For detailed description of the complex negotiations preceding and following the release of the most prominent but not all Rhodesian nationalists, see Colin Legum, *Southern Africa. The Secret Diplomacy of Détente* (New York: Africana Publishing Company, 1975), pp. 2-13.

23. *The Observer* (London), April 27, 1975; *The Star* weekly (Johannesburg), May 24, 1975; *The Times* (London), September 18, 1975.

24. *The Star* weekly (Johannesburg), October 25, 1975.

25. See Tony Avirgan's despatch from Dar es Salaam in *The Washington Star*, March 11, 1976.

26. See Patrick O'Meara, *Rhodesia. Racial Conflict or Coexistence?* (Ithaca, New York: Cornell University Press, 1975), p. 58. In 1975, leaders of the extreme right-wing Herstigte Nationale Party of South Africa met with Ian Smith and formed a South African Solidarity Conference (Sascon) to generate opposition to détente and support for Rhodesian whites. *Die Transvaler*, May 10, 1975; May 12, 1975.

27. See statement by Assistant Secretary for African Affairs Nathaniel Davis (July 10,1975) in *The Department of State Bulletin*, Vol. LXXIII, No. 1885 (August 11, 1975), p. 210.

28. *Ibid.*

29. *Windhoek Advertiser*, November 6, 1974.

30. John Seiler, "The South African Perspective of the World: Can it Serve as the Basis of a Productive Foreign Policy?" Lecture to the Witwatersrand Chapter, South African Institute of International Affairs, July 9, 1974.

31. *The Star* weekly (Johannesburg), September 27, 1975.

32. *Windhoek Advertiser*, September 15, 1975; September 24, 1975.

33. *Ibid.*, March 26, 1975.

34. British Foreign Secretary James Callaghan quoted in *The Star* weekly (Johannesburg), September 27, 1975.

35. See, for example, Department of State, "South Africa: Apartheid and Occupation in Namibia," *Current Policy*, No. 5 (September 1975).

36. National Security Council Decision Memorandum 55, April 17, 1970 (revised May 22, 1970).

37. See Anthony R. Wilkinson, "Angola and Mozambique: The Implications of Local Power," *Survival* (London: International Institute for Strategic Studies, September-October 1974), pp. 217-227.

38. For an analysis of ethnic, racial, class, and cultural variables underlying Angolan nationalist differences, see John Marcum, "The Anguish of Angola: On Becoming Independent in the Last Quarter of the Twentieth Century," *Issue*, Vol. 5, No. 4 (publication of the African Studies Association, Winter 1976), pp. 3-11.

39. These forces, led by General Nataniel Bumba, shared with the MPLA an

antipathy for the government of Zaire. *The Times* (London), September 24, 1975; *The Star* weekly (Johannesburg), September 27, 1975.

40. Secretary of State Kissinger, press conference, February 12, 1976.

41. *Windhoek Advertiser*, May 30, 1975.

42. *The Standard* (Nairobi), January 3, 1976.

43. *Windhoek Advertiser*, June 12, 1975. MPLA-SWAPO relations reportedly remained hostile (*The Financial Times*, September 27, 1975), however, and it seemed possible then that UNITA's ethnic, rural, and racial affinities with SWAPO would prove stronger in the long run than UNITA's alliance of desperation with South Africa.

44. *The Star* weekly (Johannesburg), January 3, 1976.

45. See Kaunda's interview with C.L. Sulzberger in *The New York Times*, December 31, 1975; also *Los Angeles Times*, January 1, 1976.

46. *The New York Times*, January 27, 1976.

47. At least one veteran observer of African affairs views "mutual obsessions between the Russians and the Chinese in seeking to undermine each other's influence in the Third World" as central to understanding the magnitude of Soviet intervention. Colin Legum, "A Letter on Angola to American Liberals," *The New Republic*, Vol. 174, No. 4 (January 31, 1976), p. 18.

48. *The Washington Post*, January 12, 1976.

49. Interview with Nguza Karl-i-Bond, *The Washington Post*, February 4, 1976.

50. As part of the agreement by which it would construct a series of dams by stages (the first stage costing $63 million), the South African government had been permitted by the Portuguese to station a small security force at Cunene construction sites. The overall scheme was slated in due course to generate more electricity than the Cabora Bassa dam in Mozambique. See Ivan Philip's "Why SA Defends Kunene Scheme," *The Star* weekly (Johannesburg), December 20, 1975.

51. *The Star* weekly (Johannesburg), January 10, 1976. *The Washington Post*, February 4, 1976. Secretary Kissinger denied "collusion with South Africa. . . . We had no foreknowledge of South Africa's intervention, and in no way cooperated with it militarily." See "Testimony of the Secretary of State Before the Senate Sub-Committee on Africa," January 29, 1976.

52. *The New York Times*, January 26, 1976.

53. *The Washington Post*, February 4, 1976.

54. Kenneth L. Adelman, "Report from Angola," *Foreign Affairs*, April 1975, pp. 568.

55. Roger Morris, "The Proxy War in Angola: Pathology of a Blunder," *The New Republic*, January 31, 1976, p. 21.

56. "Testimony of the Secretary of State before the Senate Subcommittee on Africa," January 29, 1976.

57. *The New York Times*, December 23, 1974.

58. Heribert Adams, *Modernizing Racial Domination: The Dynamics of South African Politics* (Berkeley: University of California Press, 1971), pp. 53-67..

59. Prime Minister Vorster quoted in *The Star* weekly (Johannesburg), December 21, 1974.

60. H.W. van der Merwe, M.J. Ashley, N.C.J. Charton, and Bettina J. Huber, *White South African Elites. A Study of Incumbents of Top Positions in the Republic of South Africa* (Cape Town: Juta and Company 1974), p. 177.

61. Lawrence Schlemmer, "The Afrikaners: Youth and Change," *Africa Currents* (London), No. 1 (Spring 1975), pp. 24-28.

62. Van der Merwe et al., *White South African Elites*, p. 178.

63. See Martin Spring, "The South African Kaleidoscope," *South Africa International* (Johannesburg), Vol. IV, No. 3 (January 1974), p. 174.

64. Terrorism Act (No. 87 of 1967), described in a UN secretariat document as containing "probably the broadest definition of a crime ever created by any statute." See UN, Unit on Apartheid, Department of Political and Security Council Affairs, *Repressive Legislation of the Republic of South Africa* (New York: 1969), pp. 80-91.

65. See *Uprooting a Nation. The Study of Three Million Evictions in South Africa* (London: African Publications Trust, 1974).

66. See analysis by professor of psychology K. Danziger in "Political Mind-Bending," (lecture at Cape Town, Fall 1963).

67. H.J. van der Spuy "The Psychology of South Africa," *Africa Currents*, No. 1 (Spring 1975), pp. 21-24.

68. *Ibid*., p. 23.

69. The South African suicide rate in 1960 was 14.2 whites as against 4.3 other categories per 100,000. The 1964 figure for the United States was 5.6. Chalmers Johnson, *Revolutionary Change* (Boston: Little, Brown and Company, 1966), pp. 122-124.

70. Responding to a query from liberal white parents who expressed concern that their coerced compliance with South African racial laws would undermine their children's respect for them. Dr. Bruno Bettelheim counselled them to leave the country rather than submit their families to such psychic damage. (Column in *Ladies Home Journal*, June 1968).

71. See Papers Nos. 6a and 7 by Special Commission on Race Relations presented to Cape Synod, Dutch Reformed Church, October 1965.

72. Lawrence Schlemmer, *The Negro Ghetto Riots and South African Cities* (Johannesburg: South African Institute of Race Relations, 1968), pp. 8-9.

73. Journalist Jim Hoagland has described South Africa as a "hard drinking country" in which the rate of coloured alcoholism stands out as "phenomenal": 35 "confirmed" alcoholics per thousand among coloureds, as against four per thousand among Africans and five per thousand among whites. *The Washington Post*, July 2, 1970. See also M.G. Whisson, "The Coloured People," *South Africa's Minorities* (Johannesburg: SPROCAS, 1971), pp. 46-77.

74. K. Danziger, "The Psychological Future of an Oppressed Group," *Social Forces*, Vol. 42, No. 1 (October 1963), pp. 31-40. A 1971 survey of urban African students conducted by government social workers revealed "inadequate political rights" to be their most commonly shared (73 percent) grievance. *The Star* weekly (Johannesburg), September 10, 1971.

75. See *Die Transvaler*, October 21, 1972; October 24, 1972.

76. See Heribert Adam, "The Rise of Black Consciousness in South Africa," *Race* (London), Vol. 15, No. 2 (October 1973), pp. 149-166.

77. *SASO 1972* (Durban, brochure). See Gwendolen M. Carter, *Black Initiatives for Change in Southern Africa* (University of Edinburgh, Centre of African Studies, 1973), pp. 10-13.

78. *The Times* (London), December 23, 1975.

79. F. van Zyl Slabbert, "Afrikaner Nationalism, White Politics and Political Change in South Africa," in Leonard Thompson and Jeffrey Butler (eds.) *Change in Contemporary South Africa* (Berkeley: University of California Press, 1975), pp. 17-18.

80. *Ibid.*, p. 18.

81. See Kenneth Grundy, "Economic Change in Botswana, Lesotho and Swaziland" (paper prepared for Symposium on Change in Contemporary Southern Africa, Seven Springs Center, Yale, Mt. Kisco, New York, May 1975).

82. See John Seiler, "South African Perspectives and Responses to External Pressure," *The Journal of Modern African Studies*, Vol. 13, No. 3 (September 1975), p. 457. *The Sunday Times* (October 6, 1974) of Johannesburg decried these policies toward the BLS countries as a "decade of lost initiatives, tragic blunders, squandered opportunities."

83. Statement by the Honorable J.R.L. Kotsokoane, Minister of Foreign Affairs, at Thirtieth Session of the UN General Assembly, September 29, 1975.

84. P.M. Landall-Mills, "The 1969 Southern African Customs Union Agreement," *The Journal of Modern African Studies*, Vol. 9, No. 2 (1971), pp. 269-271. Lesotho charged that Pretoria's devaluation of the South African rand in September 1975 was carried out without consultation in violation of the terms and spirit of the rand monetary area agreement. *The Star* weekly (Johannesburg), September 27, 1975.

85. *The Star* weekly (Johannesburg), January 4, 1975; January 11, 1975.

86. W.J. Breytenbach, "Change of Government in Qwaqwa," *Africa Institute Bulletin*, Vol. XIII, No. 5 (1975), p. 192.

87. Lukas Mangope, "Will Bophuthatswana Join Botswana?" *Munger Africana Library Notes*, No. 20 (August 1973), pp. 22 and 34.

88. See statement by Professor H. Grobler, Chairman of Western Transvaal Bantu Administration Council, *Die Vaderland* (Johannesburg), June 4, 1973.

89. "Speech by H.E. the President, Sir Seretse Khama, at the Opening of the Second Session of the Third Parliament of Botswana," November 24, 1975, Gaborone.

90. Christian P. Potholm, "The Effects on South Africa of Changes in Contiguous Territories," in Thompson and Butler *Change in Contemporary South Africa*, p. 341.

91. He asked for Elliot, Maclear, Mount Currie, Matatiele, Port St. Johns, Herschel, and Lady Frere as well as Glen Grey (Ciskei), *The Star* weekly (Johannesburg), April 17, 1971; February 8, 1975.

92. *The Financial Mail* (Johannesburg), Vol. LVI, No. 7 (May 16, 1975), p. 574.

93. The Bertrand Group of Milan, Italy, proposed to establish a textile factory at Butterworth, Transkei, that would eventually employ 1,400 Xhosa. *The Star* weekly (Johannesburg), October 11, 1975.

94. *Ibid.*, November 1, 1975.

95. See T.T. Letlaka, "Transkei's Independence: The Historic Breakthrough for a People; The Path to Freedom and Self-Determination in South Africa" (Lecture delivered at California Institute of Technology, Pasadena, December 1, 1975).

96. A former British Ambassador to South Africa, Sir Arthur Snelling, so predicted. *The Financial Times* (London), January 15, 1975.

97. V.M. Motsuenyane of the National African Federated Chamber of Commerce; Mayor Makhaya of Soweto; and Lucy Mvubelo of the National Union of Clothing Workers (SA).

98. The Honorable M.G. Buthelezi, "A Report Back to the Reef Africans on the Conference of Black Leaders with the Honorable B.J. Vorster, Prime Minister of South Africa—On the 22nd January 1975," typescript, February 9, 1975. Also *The Star* weekly (Johannesburg), February 15, 1975.

99. *The Star* weekly (Johannesburg), February 22, 1975.

100. *Die Transvaler*, May 19, 1973.

101. *Ibid.*, May 1, 1974.

102. *Ibid.*, July 28, 1973.

103. A November 1973 "summit" meeting of homeland leaders at Umtata agreed to federation despite some reported fears of Zulu-Xhosa domination. *Die Burger* (Cape Town), November 10, 1973.

104. Breytenbach, "Change of Government in Qwaqwa," p. 192.

105. See Francis Wilson, "The Political Implications for Blacks of Economic

Changes Now Taking Place in South Africa," Thompson and Butler, *Change in Contemporary South Africa*, p. 197.

106. *The Wall Street Journal*, September 8, 1975.

107. See Gwendolen M. Carter, *American Policy and the Search for Justice and Reconciliation in South Africa* (Racine, Wisconsin: The Johnson Foundation, 1975), p. 18.

108. Wilson, "The Political Implications for Blacks of Economic Changes Now Taking Place in South Africa," p. 188. Department of Commerce, "South Africa" in series "Foreign Economic Trends and Their Implications for the United States," FET - 75-078, July 1975.

109. *The Star* weekly (Johannesburg), October 5, 1974.

110. Reporting that "better pay" is "markedly improving the economic lot of blacks," Neil Ulman of *The Wall Street Journal* (September 8, 1975), cited claims by South Africa's Chamber of Mines that with all benefits included "the average amounts to $765 a month, considerably higher than the $140 a month earned in manufacturing."

111. *The Financial Times* (London), October 28, 1974.

112. *The Star* weekly (Johannnesburg), December 12, 1975.

113. *Ibid.*, May 31, 1975.

114. As of April 1974, South Africa (including homelands) provided 114,000 mine laborers; the BLS countries, 103,000; Mozambique, 94,000; Malawi and others, 46,000. See Siegfried Hannig, "The Changing Face of South African Labour," *Africa Institute Bulletin*, Vol. XIII, No. 5 (1975), pp. 184-190.

115. According to then Foreign Minister Joseph Kotsokoane in personal interview, October 7, 1975. For a discussion of this common three-country strategy on migrant labor, see *The Star* weekly (Johannesburg), January 31, 1976.

116. *The Star* weekly (Johannesburg), November 30, 1974.

117. Lecture by Mrs. Suzman, Stanford University, December 6, 1974.

118. *The Rand Daily Mail*, February 2, 1975.

119. *Die Transvaler*, August 15, 1973.

120. These groups include the American Committee on Africa (ACOA), The Washington Office on Africa, the Black Caucus of the U.S. Congress, various church action movements, the Southern Africa Committee (publishers of the monthly *Southern Africa*), and local committees in Chicago, Madison, Denver, Atlanta, and other cities.

121. Department of State, "Statement on Employment Practices of U.S. Firms Operating in South Africa," September 1974.

122. Marcelle Kooy, "Black Worker Unrest in South Africa 1971-1973 in Its Historical Context," *Africa Today*, Vol. 21, No. 4 (Fall 1974), pp. 53-74.

123. See Heribert Adam, *Modernizing Racial Domination*, p. 154.

124. Wilson, "The Political Implications for Blacks of Economic Changes Now Taking Place in South Africa," p. 91. Unlike the 1920s, however, there was no white unemployment in the 1970s. This served to increase black leverage.

125. See Peter Swartz, "The Possibility of Purposeful Political Participation by the Coloured People Through the Medium of the Coloured Persons Representative Council," in Michael G. Whisson and Hendrik van der Merwe (eds.), *Coloured Citizenship in South Africa* (Rondebosch: Abe Bailey Institute of Interracial Studies, 1972), pp. 212-220; and N.J.J. Olivier, "Political Rights in Perspective," *Ibid.*, pp. 247-261.

126. *The Star* weekly (Johannesburg), March 3, 1975.

127. *Ibid.*, February 8, 1975.

128. To accept the coloureds would mean eventually having to accept Indians and urban bantu, Mulder reasons. *Die Transvaler*, March 25, 1975. See also *Die Burger*, August 26, 1974.

129. Heribert Adam, "Internal Constellations and Potentials for Change," Thompson and Butler, *Change in Contemporary South Africa*, p. 314.

130. Leonard Thompson, "White over Black in South Africa: What of the Future?" *Change in Contemporary South Africa*, p. 413.

131. *The Washington Post*, January 24, 1976.

132. See Jeffrey Butler, "The Significance of Recent Changes within the White Ruling Caste," Thompson and Butler, *Change in Contemporary South Africa*, p. 100.

133. Heribert Adam, "Internal Constellations and Potentials for Change," p. 306.

134. Brigadier General Johan Fourie speaking at a Symposium on Political Violence and Revolution at Potchefstroom, *Die Transvaler*, August 25, 1973.

135. *The Christian Science Monitor*, September 20, 1974.

136. South African Mission to the United Nations, "Statement by Ambassador R.F. Botha in the Security Council on Thursday, October 24, 1974."

137. National Security Decision Memorandum 81, August 17, 1970.

138. Memorandum written by White House aide Marshall Wright, March 29, 1971.

139. The full range of issues surrounding Western investment in South Africa is analyzed and argued by 11 observers of diverse persuasions in *Foreign Investment in South Africa: The Policy Debate* (Uppsala, Sweden: Africa Publications Trust, 1975).

IV Lessons to Be Learned from the Sahel Drought

William A. Hance

For six long years, from 1968 to 1974, a large area south of the Sahara suffered a devastating drought that caused the death of tens of thousands of human beings and millions of livestock, severely damaged the physical environment and economies of the countries involved, and disrupted their societies and political institutions. More "normal" rains fell in 1974, but it would be premature to conclude that the drought has ended. Even if it has, its legacy will be felt for many years, presumably for the lifetime of children who were subjected to protein-calorie malnutrition (PCM). In addition, the disaster has focused attention on the long-term need to work toward more effective, less destructive use of the land in the vast arid and semiarid regions of Africa, some parts of which are likely to suffer from drought in any given year. In 1975, for example, parts of North Africa and the Horn, especially Somalia, were experiencing severe lack of rainfall.

The significance of the so-called Sahelian drought extends far beyond the Sahel itself. The issues involved include some of the most difficult problems facing mankind: the growing strain of increasing populations; producing enough food, not just in quantity but also in nutritive quality, to feed the expanding populations; improving the standard of life of the earth's billions; and the potential conflicts arising from inequalities between the more advanced peoples and economies and those that remain among the poor, the underdeveloped, and the nonindustrial.

Other questions are of less global scope but of greater immediacy to the Sahelian nations. Is the Sahara encroaching on its bordering lands? What are the opportunities and limitations of land use in the ecological zones affected by the drought? What sectoral priorities are appropriate for the Sahelian countries? What are the optimum settlement patterns for the areas concerned?

Restrictions of the Physical Environment

Sahel means shore in Arabic, and the term was taken over by the French to delineate a relatively narrow belt of semiarid climate and vegetation stretching across the continent along the northern and southern "shores" of the Sahara. Its rainfall is so low and so variable as to make tillage agriculture precarious and nomadism, either seasonal or year round, the regional occupation. Pastoralism continues into the Sahara at least seasonally and southward into the Sudan belt, a wetter but still semiarid to subhumid zone where the bulk of the population is engaged in tillage agriculture but where livestock are grazed both by sedentarists and by nomads. The drought affected all three of these zones—the Sahara, the Sahel, and the Sudan—although it was called, somewhat erroneously, the Sahelian drought. In fact, lower than average rainfall affected almost all of West Africa, including the humid savanna and rainy tropical zones south of the Sudan, where yields of such crops as coffee, cocoa, and palm oil showed serious declines in some years.

Six countries received most attention in writings on the drought and in relief efforts, and they came to be known as the Sahelian Six (hereafter called The Six). From west to east they are Mauritania and Senegal on the Atlantic, Mali, Upper Volta, Niger, and Chad. Covering an area about 56.5 percent as large as the United States, The Six account for some 19 percent of the area of Africa and contain approximately eight percent of its population. Four of them—Mauritania, Mali, Niger, and Chad—include large sections of the Sahara, and the last three, plus Upper Volta, are landlocked and suffer from geographic isolation. Upper Volta, Mali, and Chad rank among the world's poorest nations as measured by per capita GNP (between $70 and $90 in 1974). For practical purposes, Mauritania and Niger should also be so ranked, since it is only enclave-type mining activities (benefiting a very few people) that raise their per capita GNPs to the still low levels of $230 and $100, respectively. Senegal, with a favorable location, important exports of peanuts, phosphates, fish, and garden produce, and the major port and industrial center of Dakar, is considerably better developed than the others and has a per capita GNP estimated at $325. Except for Mauritania and Senegal, the foreign trade of these countries is heavily imbalanced, their budgetary expenditures are very low, and they remain dependent for development finance on outside aid, mainly from France and the European Economic Community.

It must be stressed again that the drought was not confined to The Six; indeed, tiny Gambia was officially added to the disaster area in 1973. Northern Nigeria was also seriously affected; the reason Nigeria received relatively little attention was that it was able, with large earnings from oil, to handle its own relief efforts. The northern portions of other West African countries were also adversely affected. To the east, the Democratic Republic of the Sudan, which incorporates parts of the Sahara, Sahel, and Sudan belts, experienced considerable losses, particularly in the later years, and a catastrophic drought hit parts of Ethiopia. The human toll in Ethiopia may have been more serious than in The Six, in part because news of the famine was late in reaching the world.

Sharply reduced harvests were reported in Egypt, Kenya, Somalia, Tanzania, and Zaire in 1973 and 1974. Other parts of Africa that are periodically hurt by drought include the Maghreb (Morocco, Algeria, Tunisia) and Libya in the north; Botswana, which experienced a devastating six-year drought in the 1960s; parts of all the other countries of southern Africa; and the western and southern parts of Madagascar.

Africa in fact leads the world in the extent of its dry climate regions. It includes about one-third of the world's arid lands, almost 60 percent of its area being classified as semiarid, arid, or hyperarid—the highest percentage of any continent except Australia. Water must be considered *the* principal physical factor limiting economic advance in more than half of Africa.

The climates of tropical semiarid areas represent a transition from zones of moderate rainfall to true desert. One region grades imperceptibly into another with marked annual differences in the amount of rainfall received. According to a French categorization that became familiar during the 1968-1974 drought, the Sudan zone receives about 25 to 60 inches, the Sahel about 10 to 25, and the Sahara zero to ten inches. The length of the rainy season decreases to the north and lasts only 2.5 to three months in the Sahel.

In the arid areas of Africa, it is normal for the rainfall to be abnormal; "average" is a more or less meaningless term; variability and uncertainty are the keynotes. Rains are uncertain in onset, seasonal duration, frequency, amount per occurrence, and annual total in any one place, and rainfall received in neighboring places may vary considerably. Although good and bad years tend to occur in series, efforts to detect regularity in the patterns have not succeeded.

The vegetation zones of West Africa have a similar transitional character. The Sudan belt is characterized by tall grass and wooded savanna, the Sahel by short, drought-resistant bunch grass with scattered thorn scrub and trees. The grasses and bush become more widely spaced and sparser toward and into the desert, where they finally disappear except in mountain massifs that receive some rainfall.

The appearance of the vegetation varies markedly from season to season. In the Sahel, it is lush green and succulent during the rainy season, but it soon dries out and hardens; some months before the next rainy season, only the dry stream beds have any grasses left, while vast areas resemble a true desert. The desolate appearance is increased by brush fires started by man to stimulate a brief growth of new grass, destroy weeds and scrub unsuitable for animal consumption, and provide some control of harmful insects. Since domestic animals both graze and browse, not only grasses but also shrubs and trees provide forage. Trees and bushes serve other valuable purposes: they bring up nutrients that are later released through decaying leaves and brush to the base-poor soils, anchor the soil to reduce wind and water erosion, and slightly increase the amount of local rainfall. Because trees are also important sources of firewood and hut poles, excessive cutting is likely as the population increases and in periods of severe drought.

Another unfavorable aspect of the physical environment in the arid areas of Africa is the large number of harmful microorganisms, insects, and animal pests found there that adversely affect man, his livestock, and his crops. Malaria remains the single most important disease problem, while smallpox and measles continue to pose deadly hazards in the Sudano-Sahelian areas despite massive vaccination campaigns in the late 1960s. Two diseases are of special importance for the negative constraints they impose: trypanosomiasis (sleeping sickness in humans and *nagana* in cattle), carried by the tsetse fly, which confines cattle-keeping groups to the drier areas and precludes developing an integrated crop-livestock economy in the humid tropics; and onchocerciasis or river blindness, carried by the black fly, which incapacitates several million people in West Africa and prevents use of some relatively rich river valleys of the Sudan belt, particularly in Upper Volta.

Trillions of locusts and billions of weaver or quelea quelea birds consume a large part of the crops grown in semiarid areas. In the Senegal Valley alone, weaver birds consume an estimated 100,000-200,000 tons of grain a year. Campaigns against the locust have had considerable success; those against the quelea quelea bird have not. Poison bait, smoke, noise, biological control, explosive charges in the nesting and roosting sites, flame throwers, and spraying with chemical poisons have all been tried but none has proved adequate.

While most of this vast area depends on rainfall for growing crops and for pasturelands, several large streams—the Senegal, Niger, Volta, and Chari-Logone river systems—and numerous smaller ones provide opportunities for irrigation, floodland farming, and seasonal grazing, and hence support notably denser populations than the surrounding lands. In some cases, underground aquifers are tapped to provide water for people and livestock and for a limited amount of gardening, as, for example, in the close-settled zone around Kano, Nigeria, or in the Dallol-Bosso Valley east of Niamey in Niger. Thousands of deeper wells and bore holes sunk in recent decades sometimes make habitable otherwise unusable areas. Ironically, the inland waters of West Africa constitute an important fishery resource: the four landlocked countries normally export fish to their coastal neighbors.

With some exceptions, then, the Sudan-Sahel-Sahara portions of West Africa are not well endowed from the physical standpoint. Their ecological constraints explain many other deficiencies—the relatively low stage of economic development, the inadequate physical and social infrastructures, and the fragile financial positions of most of the countries.

Human Use of the Area

No one knows the exact population of the drought-affected region. Most of the countries have had only sample censuses, and the three most recent Nigerian censuses—those of 1962, 1963, and 1973—were distorted by false counting. The estimated mid-1975 population of The Six was 26.3 million, to which should be added half a million persons in Gambia and several million in northern Nigeria who were affected by the drought.

These populations are unevenly distributed. The Saharan portion, covering more than half the total area of The Six, has only a few hundred thousand inhabitants, including camel nomads, residents of oases, and persons living in the few coastal towns and mining communities. Numerous pastoralists move into the Sahara on a seasonal basis when pasture is available. The Sahel belt, about 20 percent of the total area, is also sparsely populated except where rivers or underground water make exceptions to the general pattern of water scarcity. A substantial part of its people are seminomadic. Thus the Sudan belt holds the greater part of the populations except in Mauritania and Niger, whose Sudanic portions are small. Although grazing covers more of the belt than does tillage agriculture, sedentary farmers make up the bulk of the population. There are a number of cities, among them Dakar (Senegal), Bamako (Mali), Ouagadougou (Upper Volta), Niamey (Niger), Katsina (Nigeria), Kano (Nigeria), Zaria (Nigeria), and N'Djaména (Chad).

To a significant degree the distribution of population throughout the region reflects the distribution of numerous ethnic groups[1] whose presence or absence may depend on many things—for example, the coexistence of different land use systems in areas having similar physical characteristics; the juxtaposition of several groups in a given area, each depending on a specific set of physical factors; the existence of characteristic ethnic-group densities; reluctance to move away from the base area of the community even when pressure on the land becomes severe; the contrasts in the degree to which economic change and modernization are accepted. While such ethnic differences lead to recognizable contrasts in land use, the ecological conditions of the Sudan, Sahel, and Saharan belts sometimes place rigid limits on just what uses can be made of a given area, and therefore make for broad similarities in land use patterns. This is clearly shown in the correlation between decreasing rainfall and the transition from intensive farming to less intensive cropping, and from sedentary grazing to transhumance and full nomadism. Transhumance involves the seasonal migration of livestock and the people who tend them.

It should not be supposed that relations among the various groups are marked mainly by competition and conflict. Interaction and cooperation result from centuries of contact, the high percentage of the population adhering to Islam, the continuing exchange of goods and services, the shared heritage of French colonialism in six of the countries, and the symbiotic relationship that exists between graziers and farmers in some areas, the former wanting pasturage on the fields in stubble and the latter wanting the enriching manures of the grazing animals.

Crop Production

Only about two percent of Mauritania, 29 percent of Senegal, 41 percent of Upper Volta, perhaps 16 percent of Niger, and 45 percent of Chad are considered to be cultivable. Usually less than half of available lands are cropped and much less than that effectively cultivated. In Niger, for example, only about two percent of the country is cultivated. Nevertheless, tillage agriculturalists considerably outnumber pastoralists in all the countries except Mauritania.

Several types of tillage agriculture are practiced in the Sudano-Sahelian areas, the most common being the cultivation of rain-grown crops in a short-cropping and long-fallow cycle. But in the areas of high population density—for example, some of the crowded mountain areas and the closely settled zones around cities such as Kano, Katsina, and Zaria—much of the farmland is permanently cultivated and the soils replenished by heavy applications of animal and household wastes. Rural populations reach densities as high as 700 to 1,000 per square mile in some of these areas, which is truly remarkable given the rainfall characteristics. Many farmers keep livestock, though there is almost never a true integration of crop and livestock production in a mixed agricultural system such as characterizes Western Europe or the American corn belt.

Varieties of irrigation and floodland agriculture are found in scattered places. Small streams may be used to water kitchen gardens, the balanced-weight lift being a fairly common sight along some watercourses, while elsewhere water is carried laboriously in gourd buckets from ponds to garden patches. More important is the use of floodplains and other areas inundated in the annual rains for the production of grains, sugarcane, and vegetables. Because these plains or *fadama* lands often do not dry out sufficiently to permit planting until after the rain-grown crops have been harvested, their cultivation has the distinct advantage of extending the work year and providing an off-season crop. Though *fadama* land is scarce in most of the region, its cultivation is very important in the Sokoto-Rima Basin of northwest Nigeria, along the middle Niger River in Mali, and on the Senegal River along both the Mauritanian and Senegalese banks.

Examples of more modern types of irrigation agriculture are few. The French invested over $100 million in the years from 1932 to 1959 in the Office du Niger project in Mali, designed to revive the "dead" part of the inner delta of the Niger River and to use more effectively the "live" part, which is inundated annually, for the production of cotton. Today only 124,000 acres are under management, about two-thirds of those being irrigated each year. Explanations for the disappointing results include the poor quality of much of the soil; losses to cotton parasites, locusts, and quelea quelea birds; unattractive work requirements and tenancy arrangements; and the difficulty of training settlers to use a new system of agriculture.

The only other large-scale modern irrigation scheme in the region is the Richard-Toll project in Senegal, the biggest ever undertaken in that country. It uses the Lac de Guiers, filled by the Senegal River during the high water period, as a reservoir from which water is pumped to irrigate land adjoining the river. Beginning in 1947, about 20,000 acres of infertile saline soil were mechanically cultivated to produce rice for domestic sale. Costs have been excessive, some soils have had to be abandoned because of salinity and wind erosion, and rice production has suffered severely from losses to birds. Much of the area is now being converted to sugar, requiring an additional investment of about $50 million.

The staple crops in the Sudan-Sahel belt are sorghum, millet, and peanuts, plus sweet potatoes, cassava, sesame, beans, and cowpeas. In the limited areas where enough water is available, rice is a leading crop; tomatoes, onions, peppers, tobacco, and sugarcane are also grown. In normal times there is a considerable sale of country produce in local markets and some shipment of vegetables to the south, but the two major cash crops are peanuts and cotton. Senegal plans to export about 40,000 tons of irrigated market crops to European markets each year during the off-season, and Upper Volta has been airlifting green beans to France, also in the off-season. Most of the countries have been introducing sugarcane grown on large plantations as a substitute for imported sugar.

Despite such examples, numerous shortcomings in agricultural practices remain. Tools are rudimentary, the short-handled hoe and the all-purpose machete being by all odds the most important. Work animals are used very little. It has been estimated that in Senegal, which is more advanced technologically than the other countries, only four percent of the sown area is cultivated with animal-drawn plows and 23 percent is sown with a drill machine, all the remaining work being done with hand implements. Knowledge and use of seed selection, crop rotation, weeding, and fertilizing leave much to be desired. The result is that each farmer tills only a small area, his labor provides a meager return or only a small surplus beyond subsistence needs, and his crop yields often are incredibly low.

Some groups have developed superior practices. As examples, the Sérér in Senegal have a rudimentary form of integrated farming, the Diolas are skillful cultivators of rice, the Dogon in Mali follow several highly intensive practices that demonstrate real skill in adjusting to a difficult environment, and the Hausa have learned how to farm year after year in areas where adequate fertilizer is available.

Pastoralism

Animals are grazed over much of the Sudan and Sahel belts, which together form one of the main cattle-producing regions of Africa. In the wetter areas farmers often keep some livestock while pastoralists use the intervening areas and, by agreement, graze their animals on the stubble of harvested fields. Northward in successively drier areas, pastoralism becomes predominant and there is a transition from transhumance to full nomadism extending into the desert areas, at least on a seasonal basis.

Transhumance as contrasted with sedentary grazing is necessary in much of the Sahel-Sahara for several reasons: the pasturage varies in a yearly cycle, being available in the inundated areas only in the dry season and in much of the rainlands only after the first rains; water for livestock in the dry season is most readily available along the rivers; requisite trace minerals are obtained by grazing in differing soil regions; trips to salt licks are desirable; and dispersal of the herd in the wet season reduces the loss from animal diseases.

The exact number of pastoralists is unknown but apparently rather small, with two million being a fairly common estimate for The Six. Only in Mauritania does livestock herding surpass tillage agriculture in the total numbers engaged. The main pastoral groups—the Moors, Tuareg, Fulani or Peuhl, and Tebu—range over vast stretches and across national boundaries. Their herds comprise a variety of animals. Cattle predominate except in the driest areas, where the true nomad is dependent on the camel; goats and sheep are also important; donkeys may be used for transporting water and fuel, and horses for riding. Most of the cattle are of poor quality. The zebu are well adapted to the hot, dry climate, but their carcass weights are low—about 600 to 1,200 pounds—and their milk yields are only one to two quarts a day, a tenth or less of what would be expected in the middle latitudes.

The life of the nomad and seminomad is marked by a high degree of self-sufficiency amid physical handicaps and human obstacles that are less evident but no less formidable. Lack of knowledge and certain cultural traditions foster serious malpractices or a lack of interest in improving livestock or in marketing them. Most graziers in sub-Saharan Africa adhere to a "cattle culture" whose common denominator is the recognition of cattle as a measure of wealth—a source of prestige—rather than as animals produced for sale. This leads to an emphasis on quantity over quality. Breeding may reflect a desire for impressive horns, height, or a specific color as well as other traits; too many young males and too many old beasts are likely to be kept; beef is eaten only on ceremonial occasions or when an animal dies. While such practices are not irrational as the cattle culturalists perceive their way of life, and are economically sensible as far as the individual grazier is concerned, they are not scientifically sound. Keeping large numbers of stock in a difficult or impoverished environment may actually decrease the chances of maintaining a healthy nucleus; the emphasis on quantity almost inevitably leads to pressure on the pasturelands and to their impairment; the practice of bringing livestock through the dry season on a semistarvation basis degrades the herd; pasture management based on wet season capacity inevitably is destructive.

So it is not surprising that most of the grazing lands of Africa have been seriously overgrazed. This has contributed greatly to degradation of the vegetation in the Sudan and Sahel and to its destruction along the desert margins. Livestock are selective eaters, choosing the more palatable and nutritious grasses and bushes which, unless proper stocking is practiced, are gradually replaced by less nourishing plants. The accelerating expansion of woody, often thorny growth is a curse in many grazing areas of Africa.

Dynamic Changes

What has been portrayed thus far may appear to be a static situation; indeed, the traditionalism of existing societies contributes to a sense of timelessness. But a number of dynamic factors were affecting The Six long before the recent drought. They must now be examined as the next step toward understanding the area.

Population Pressure

Probably the most important of these dynamic factors is the now rapid rate of population growth, estimated to average 2.2 percent a year for the region. This rate is below the average for the continent, yet the population will double in about 32 years if it is sustained. The major explanation is a drop in the death rate brought about primarily from better control of diseases. There has been no significant change in the birthrate nor is one likely in the near future, for children are wanted and welcome; they sustain the strength of the family, permit a forging of links with other families, supply help when they are young, and provide care in old age.

The impacts of an increasing population are manifold and most of them are harmful. Farmers respond by attempting to intensify the cultivation of their present holdings. Some areas appear to sustain extremely dense populations without deterioration of the environment, as in the closely settled zones around certain cities in northern Nigeria. But for every such example there are others that reveal excessive pressure on the land, evidenced by one or more of the following: deterioration, degradation, or outright destruction of the soil; declining crop yields; changing crop emphases, especially to soil-tolerant but less nutritious crops; reduction of the fallow period and lengthening of the cropping period without measures to retain soil fertility; partial breakdown of the indigenous farming system; food shortages, hunger, and malnutrition; land fragmentation and landlessness; rural indebtedness; and rural unemployment.

The myth that Africa does not suffer from pressure on the land has gained wide credence, which may be explained by common but erroneous references to crude population densities for the continent, failure to consider the low carrying capacity of much of the land, and lack of attention to the problem. Using the indicators listed in the previous paragraph and examining a broad range of documents, I have tentatively estimated that 47.1 percent of the area of Africa and 50.5 percent of the population was experiencing pressure on the land in mid-1967.[2] Nearly all of the region affected by the Sahelian drought was included in the areas subject to this pressure. These estimates, conservative at the time, probably would be somewhat higher today, and are likely to increase with the rapid growth of population now under way.

Mounting population pressure contributes to serious undernourishment whether or not there is a drought. Severe loss of weight is experienced almost yearly by residents of densely populated Sahelo-Sudanic farming areas during the so-called hungry season that precedes the new harvest. That the ratio of food imports to total imports was increasing in four of The Six before the recent drought was in part evidence of increasing pressure of population. When basically agricultural countries such as Upper Volta and Mali must import food valued at about half the value of their total exports, the imbalance reaches serious proportions.

Farmers and graziers sometimes seek new areas to open up in response to population growth, but this strategy is not always feasible. Extension may impinge on other groups, particularly pastoralists, by reducing the available grazing lands. In other cases, lands that should be left in grass are planted to crops; yields may be quite satisfactory in a good rainfall cycle, but plummet in the inevitable dry years; wind erosion may cause a serious loss of topsoil, and the water table is critically affected.

Pastoralists experiencing population growth are likely to see a need for more animals, which only worsens overgrazing. The UN Food and Agriculture Organization estimates that the number of cattle in The Six increased from 18 million in 1960 to 25 million in 1971, while the optimum number was not over 15 million.

Because most of the grazing areas of West Africa and of the continent are incapable of taking either more people or more livestock, there has been a long-term trend toward settlement. Although some settlement takes place by choice, it is often an unwelcome response to necessity. Indeed, there is a vicious circle within transhumant societies caused by the need of an expanding population to grow more crops, thereby reducing the land available for grazing. Seminomads may end up with herds too small to support them and be forced to settle permanently. This may lead to a breakdown of group rights within the community or to conflicts over the rights to occupation and use of the land, especially in the Sahel, where pastoralism and farming are antagonistic forms of rural economy.

Another response to population pressure is migration, either seasonally or permanently. Migration may injure farming if a loss of young, healthy males leaves the heavy work to women and older men; sometimes the migrants go away only for the dead season and return to help plant and harvest crops. Large numbers have migrated from parts of the Sudan and Sahel regions for many years. It is estimated, for example, that about 150,000 people migrate from Upper Volta on a seasonal basis, some 200,000 do so for periods of one to five years, and that an indeterminate number have settled permanently in other countries, mainly Ivory Coast and Ghana.

Population growth has consequences not only in The Six but in virtually all developing countries. It hinders economic development to the extent that a substantial part of new investment must provide the incremental population with the same services available to the extant population, which are already at an undesirably low level. The demographic trend also signifies unusually high rates of dependency. In few African countries—certainly in none examined here—are enough new jobs created to absorb more than a fraction of the new entrants into the job market each year. If population growth interferes with income growth, it may also slow the rate at which industries and services can be developed, since markets are more dependent on income levels than on numbers of people.

Random Intervention

A second kind of dynamic change in the Sudan-Sahel areas is governmental intervention. It is remarkable and tragic that several of the major "benefits" brought by both colonial and independent governments have had adverse effects on the people and the land. More often than not, those effects have occurred because development efforts were focused on one or two specific features, and no attempt was made either to view existing problems holistically or to prepare for the new problems the innovations would create.

In one sense the lowering of death rates through disease control is an example, for with no attempt to lower birthrates or to provide for an increasing population, this was an invitation to tragedy. Of course it was not wrong to improve health standards and lower death rates, but there must be wider recognition that modern medicines can in the long run take more lives than they save if their introduction is not accompanied by other modernizing programs.

Examples of governmental interventions that sometimes have had unfavorable impacts on tillage agriculture include the introduction and expansion of cash crop production, when it has reduced the level and variety of subsistence production, shortened the fallow period without compensating fertilization, or lessened the possibility of developing an integrated mixed agriculture; and the extension of irrigation, which sometimes has deprived graziers of essential pasture and watering areas and invariably has led to increases in the incidence of bilharzia and other diseases. Encouraged by a series of good rain years, governments sometimes have extended agriculture into areas that are not suitable for tillage; the damage inflicted when the inevitable dry period arrives can be catastrophic.

Governmental "assistance" to livestock production offers countless examples of the pernicious impact of one- or two-shot programs. Since water appears to be the main factor limiting grazing in some areas, and since in theory a larger number of water points will disperse grazing more evenly throughout the available land, it has seemed logical to sink a large number of wells and boreholes to provide potable water for man and beast. And since losses of livestock through disease have had catastrophic effects, it has appeared logical to provide, indeed require, vaccination, dipping, and other disease control measures. But if either or both of these programs are applied without other efforts, the result is simply to increase the animal population and overgraze the entire area rather than just a part of it.

Thus in the pastoralist Masai country of Kenya, KAG rinderpest vaccine was introduced in 1942 on a free but compulsory basis and annual inoculations followed thereafter, with perhaps 20 percent of the total cattle population being inoculated in a normal year. Boreholes were sunk in areas where lack of stock water had precluded keeping cattle. By 1960, these measures, plus a generally favorable rainfall cycle and the Masai's continued reluctance to sell their cattle, had resulted in an approximate doubling of the cattle population. Masailand in the process became increasingly overgrazed and the vegetation deteriorated to less nutritious grasses and thorn bush. At this point, nature provided a drastic, painful, but probably necessary solution in the form of a severe drought in 1961-1962. The cattle population was reduced in one year by 30 to 70 percent, and it became clear that the area in fact had been on the verge of catastrophe for a dozen years. It was also shown that the losses would not have been so great if the land had not been so heavily overused, since losses from one section to another were roughly proportionate to the condition of the rangelands.

A variety of forces, including growing numbers of people and livestock and governmental programs to force or encourage offtake, have brought some increase in marketing and a partial breakdown of the cattle culture. The offtake, however, is rarely more than a third of what it should be for proper range management, and many pastoralist groups remain largely outside the money economy.

Other examples of dynamic change include the replacement of camel caravans by modern transport in the Sahel and desert areas; the spread of education, which has been criticized for imparting contempt for traditional rural life and encouraging migration; the drawing of boundaries that have interfered with nomadic circuits or cut off oasis communities from their former lines of communication; and increasing efforts by some independent governments to require nomads to settle down and somehow become more effective contributors to modern economies.

Nomadic life is often considered incompatible with modern civilization. Kenya probably has taken the strongest steps to rationalize grazing, encouraged in part by the striking contrast between ranches developed by the European and the open, often exhausted lands of the African graziers. In the poorer West African countries, governments have been incapable of intervening so drastically, and indeed some have sought to prevent nomads from remaining in farming areas because of the danger of conflicts with farmers.

Short-Term Impacts of the 1968-1974 Drought

Beginning in 1968, the arid and semiarid lands of West Africa, areas that retained many aspects of traditional life yet were undergoing complex dynamic changes, began to be affected by what was to become in the next years the worst drought the region had experienced in at least 60 years. Estimates of the losses sustained vary greatly and accurate data may never be available. Natural catastrophes are likely to stimulate high emotions leading to exaggeration and this drought was no exception. Whatever the exact figures may be, the losses in human and animal life were tragic and the long-term impacts on man and the environment perhaps even more severe.

About 12 million people in West Africa were seriously affected, with some seven million dependent on food aid by 1974. The number of deaths was probably between 100,000 and 200,000, including a disproportionate number of children and old people. Many children, weakened by malnutrition, succumbed to measles; this disease, which can be deadly in Africa, had been almost eradicated a few years earlier in a massive campaign against measles and smallpox, but the youngest children had not been vaccinated. Without being callous, one may perceive the impact of the drought on the long-term health of the area's inhabitants as more serious than the immediate deaths resulting from famine. Because prolonged malnutrition reduces resistance to disease, medical authorities predict markedly higher death rates for at least the next five years. Inadequate nutrition in early childhood also can result in some degree of mental retardation.

Many thousands of nomads and a smaller number of farmers migrated from the drought-stricken areas. Some pastoralists left with their herds early enough to avoid serious loss; most in the northern Sahel were not so fortunate. Others migrated to the cities, where they gathered in refugee camps or in new urban slums, often with miserable housing and deplorable sanitary and health conditions. Dakar alone was estimated to have received 100,000 migrants by mid-1973, while estimates of the total number of refugees from the Sahel run as high as a million people.

Millions of livestock were lost. The FAO has estimated that 3.5 million cattle died in The Six in 1973 alone. Possibly 25 to 35 percent of all livestock were lost, though in some areas the figure is as high as 80 percent. Cattle owners attempted to sell their animals when they realized that there would not be enough fodder for them, but poor quality and glutted markets greatly depressed cattle prices while the costs of fodder soared. Those animals that survived the drought are weakened and prone to disease, as witness recent outbreaks of rinderpest and contagious pneumonia.

Crop production was seriously reduced, though again the estimates vary. Grain harvests were short by 550,000 to 850,000 tons in 1972-73 and by 650,000 to 1,250,000 tons in 1973-74. Total crop yields may have fallen by about 30 percent in The Six, with losses ranging as high as 50 to 90 percent in the worst hit areas. In some places seed reserves were exhausted because several plantings had to be made after the early rains failed or because the famine was so severe that the seed had to be consumed. Yields of irrigated crops declined severely as available water decreased. Agricultural exports fell by one-third or more in most countries.

The hydrology of the area of course was seriously affected. River flows fell off dramatically; the Niger was at its lowest level in living memory and could be forded at Niamey, the Kano River ceased to flow for the first time in history, reservoirs were depleted, and Lake Chad was less than one-third its normal size. Water tables were not adequately recharged, so many wells ran dry. As supplies gave out in one area, herds tended to congregate around the more reliable wells and surface water points, exhausting the surrounding pasture while ample stock water was available.

National economies have been severely hurt by the decline of exports, governmental revenues, and GNPs. Unemployment, already a problem in the cities, has increased. Industries damaged by the drought included not only those that process agricultural raw materials, but others compelled ,by the water shortage to reduce their working time as, for example, the textile mills in Kaduna, Nigeria. The drought has also had political effects. Objections to the way drought relief was handled played a role in the overthrow of governments in Niger, Ethiopia, and Chad.

The rains were sufficiently good in 1974 to produce satisfactory harvests for the first time in seven years, but there is no way of knowing whether this was only a break in a longer series of dry years. What should be clear is that the land and its people will require several good years to recuperate from the injuries they have sustained.

Long-Term Problems and Potentials

The drought shed a penetrating light on a series of regional problems and possibilities, none of which is new: climatic desiccation, food supply, means of improving tillage agriculture in the area, and appropriate strategies for dealing with the nomad population and the areas that are too dry for farming.

Climatic Desiccation or Man's Misuse?

Droughts have occurred many times in this region in the past and will occur just as certainly in the future. It is not surprising that the most recent drought has revived questions that have been debated periodically over the last century: Is the Sahara expanding to encroach on lands to the north and south? Is there progressive desiccation or desertification in the Sahara and adjacent Sahelo-Sudanian areas? If so, is it caused by climatic change or by man's misuse of the area?

Scientists who have studied the evidence suggesting a climatic change do not agree about what is going on, and even the massive studies now under way may not provide adequate answers. More convincing is the evidence that man's actions have degraded the environment, while giving the impression that the climate has become progressively drier. Human errors include overgrazing, tilling the soil in excessively dry areas, overcropping, grass burning, and tree cutting. It is a gross exaggeration to claim, however, as some observers have, that the vast Sahara is largely man-made. The desert is explained by descending and warming air; only in the lands along the margins has man extended the desert, although he has downgraded the vegetation over much of the area. Climate modification is not yet a practical proposition. Nor can the planting of linear forests or shelter belts be expected to result in increased rainfall, as is sometimes claimed.

Assuring Food Supplies in "Normal" Years

The provision of food in the Sahel-Sudan area is not a problem limited to the recent drought; inhabitants of the region are always aware of the danger of running short of food and water. Even in "normal" times the tillage agricultural-ists frequently suffer from inadequate intake of proteins and from shortages of calories as well during the hungry season. Inadequate nutrition during the hungry season weakens the farmer just when his strength is most needed for clearing, plowing, and weeding, which may help to explain his failure to clear and plant adequate areas and grow a greater diversity of crops. Diets of the pastoralists are usually high in protein and somewhat better than those of the farmers, but in periods of severe drought they are likely to be harder hit than the farmers.

The incidence of deficiency diseases in children is high, though in most years it is explained more by cultural practices than by inability of the land to provide a satisfactory diet. It is common, for example, for a child who has just been weaned to be put on a diet that is nearly devoid of proteins, an abrupt change that is a major cause of deficiency diseases. Protein deficiency increases susceptibility to other diseases and, in adults, prevents the proper rebuilding of body tissues. This problem is being attacked on several fronts. Possibly the greatest hope lies in the promotion of high protein foods, but it would be unrealistic to expect large-scale change in the Sahel-Sudan belt in the near future.

Inhabitants of the area, accustomed to periodic droughts, have developed a variety of strategies to reduce their impact. Farmers may plant widely scattered plots and produce a variety of crops, including some whose drought resistance provides a measure of insurance; replant once or twice if the rains fail; and employ dry farming techniques to conserve available moisture. Pastoralists use an even greater variety of strategies, including efforts to gain and hold large and varied grazing lands; keeping a variety of animals; remaining highly mobile and moving as necessary to avoid the worst effects of drought; storing food and water in various ways; sharing animals so that if one herd is lost the family can begin again; maintaining symbiotic relations with cultivators; and having second-ary activities (e.g., trading, transport, production of handicrafts) that can provide at least temporary support or means of reconstructing the herd.

Keeping a diversity of animals is one of the most interesting of these strategies. Since each type of animal has its own ecological niche, the herd may be split to allow use of the most suitable pasture. Cattle and sheep are primarily grazers; goats browse mainly on shrubs and trees; camels both graze and browse. Camels can be taken far afield where water points are widely separated; goats must drink often, but the quantities needed are small enough for water to be carried to them in skins when necessary. The several animals also have different breeding cycles, which means that milk is available throughout the year, while the short gestation period of goats gives them special value in times of severe drought.

What Kind of Aid Helps Most?

Residents of the Sahelo-Sudan areas are enormously self-reliant and usually survive recurrent drought on their own. An extraordinary drought such as that of 1968-74, however, causes enormous loss of human and animal life unless aid is provided from outside the region. The recent drought did bring an impressive enlistment of donors, and, despite some valid criticism of their efforts, the provision of emergency food undoubtedly saved hundreds of thousands of human lives.

More than a score of nations provided one or more forms of aid to The Six. Food was the main need, but transport and medical supplies were essential as well. The United States and France were the principal governmental donors, with aid coming also from many Western European countries, Canada, and on a

smaller scale from several African countries. A remarkable range of nongovern-
mental organizations also provided aid, their contributions having been coordinated by Action for Development of the UN Food and Agriculture Organization.

U.S. famine relief began with emergency shipments of grain in November
1972. Through mid-1974 the American commitment totalled about $130
million, of which $100 million was for food and its delivery. In fiscal years 1973
and 1974, some 506,000 tons of food were provided, or about 46 percent of the
tonnage from all foreign sources. An additional 100,000 tons were allocated for
later distribution while the area was being monitored to determine whether
further allotments would be necessary. In their polemical *Disaster in the Desert:
Failures of International Relief in the West African Drought*, published by the
Carnegie Endowment for International Peace, Roger Morris and Hal Sheets are
highly critical of the U.S. AID effort.[3] While much that they say is true, it is
doubtful if the kind of efficiency they use as a measuring rod, with food
delivered to remote areas when the first hunger pangs are felt, is a practicable
expectation in this imperfect world. In any case, their critique—and the torrent
of other writings on the Sahel disaster—has aroused a great deal of interest in
developing ways of improving performance in future emergencies.

The affected nations made efforts to help themselves by controlling prices
and prohibiting speculation, rationing food and water, raising taxes on employees and companies, allotting funds to relief programs, sending volunteers
including many students to assist in relief efforts, and mounting emergency
inoculation programs. Nigeria, with large and increasing revenues from oil, chose
to handle its own relief program, which it did very effectively, and it also
contributed to other countries.

Several agencies were formed to coordinate the relief effort. The Six, later
joined by Gambia, set up the Permanent Interstate Committee for Drought
Control (CILSS) with headquarters in Ouagadougou, Upper Volta. The FAO's
Office for the Sahelian Relief Operation (OSRO) was charged with coordinating
the emergency efforts of UN agencies and much of the aid coming from other
multilateral and bilateral sources; its offices ultimately were moved to Ouagadougou to be near CILSS and the scene of action. OSRO's major concern in
1973 and 1974 was to provide food, but it also furnished seed, animal feed, and
vaccines, and mounted an emergency effort to deepen wells and water holes. By
1975, the UN Secretariat's Special Sahelian Office had become responsible for
formulating and seeking finance for medium- and long-term assistance programs,
and the World Bank had placed a permanent representative in Ouagadougou to
monitor Bank-sponsored development projects and to facilitate contact with
other agencies.

The delivery of aid was an enormous challenge. With the exception of
Senegal, Gambia, and coastal Mauritania, the region suffers from a remoteness
that increases as one goes eastward toward Chad, one of the most isolated
nations in the world. Transporting food to the stricken areas cost roughly half as

much as the food itself. Only two railways penetrate to the landlocked countries, the lines from Dakar to Bamako in Mali and from Abidjan to Ouagadougou, and neither was equipped to handle the large tonnages of grain supplied. Roads are sparse and many become impassable after the rains, placing tremendous pressure on relief efforts in 1973 and 1974 and requiring the use of aircraft to reach remote localities. The Niger and Senegal Rivers normally can be used for local shipments, but at times the Niger flow fell too low for this purpose, thereby placing still another burden on air transport. The difficulty of moving goods from congested ports to interior points led to the sending of several emergency truck convoys across the Sahara from Algeria.

Several nations provided planes, perhaps with some unneeded effort and expenditure resulting from pressure in donor countries. The U.S. Air Force was the single most important carrier. For all countries it was a costly enterprise: airlifting costs about 14 times as much as land transport and requires sophisticated logistical support that was difficult to provide in West Africa. Varying airport capacities meant that a variety of planes had to be used and that parachute drops were necessary in some areas.

Other problems included failure to provide the right kinds of foods; lack of full coordination among the agencies, whose number was excessive; the inexperience of local governments in managing a large and complex emergency effort, not surprising given the thinness of government establishments in this area; some corruption and discriminatory allocations of food; and totally inadequate medical and health facilities reflected in severe shortages of doctors, nurses, and paramedics, and a near-absence of mobile medical units.

The emergency provision of food and medicine to prevent deaths should be part of a continuing relief effort. Medium- and long-term aid is essential, for the problems of the area certainly will not end with a few good rainfall years. CILSS has suggested that at least $1 billion will be needed for long-term programs. Nine United Nations programs and agencies are reported considering a $150 million, seven-year program, and France has pledged long-term assistance. A study conducted by a multidisciplinary team at the Massachusetts Institute of Technology with financial support from the U.S. Agency for International Development purports to establish a framework for evaluating long-term development strategies for the area.[4] Unfortunately, the proposed program of Integrated Sustained Yield Arid Land Agricultural Production Systems, or ISYALAPS, outlined therein presents such generalized conclusions as to be nearly useless both to the nations involved and to potential donors. AID is examining the possibility of providing perhaps $100 million for a 12- to 15-year coordinated program whose total cost would be from $1 billion to $1.5 billion.

For the present, AID is contributing to a number of medium-term rehabilitation efforts, including the provision of new motors for barges and improved cargo handling equipment on the Niger River, storage facilities in remote areas, seeds, hand tools, supplemental feed for livestock, vaccines, and assistance to medical programs. Attention is also being given to improving food-distribution systems and to more efficient use of floodplains.

In addition, several UN agencies—the World Bank, World Health Organization, the FAO, and the UN Development Program—are joined in a $120 million program to control river blindness, a long-term effort whose pertinence here is the possibility that it may open large, relatively rich areas of West Africa to food production.

Can Food Aid Be Improved in Future Emergencies?

Experience with the Sahelian drought and other catastrophes in Africa and elsewhere suggests a number of steps that might be taken to reduce the terrible losses they cause. These include improved monitoring and early warning systems, preplanning of transport and other systems for relief delivery, more sophisticated reporting and communications during the emergency, measures to assure the provision of foods that are appropriate in protein-calorie content and acceptable in the recipient areas, the training of workers in an international disaster relief center, and the establishment of a permanent organization to carry out several of these functions and to supervise specific relief programs. One of the most important proposals, discussed intensively at the November 1974 Conference on Food in Rome, involves setting up local, national, and international food banks.

It was possible to meet most of the emergency food requirements for the 1968-74 drought in West Africa even though the relief efforts were not perfect. But serious questions surround the provision of food in future catastrophes. The major fear is that the growth in food production will not keep pace with rapidly growing populations, particularly in the developing world. Indeed, this appears to be happening already. As many as 400 million people—some say 800 million to one billion—have diets that are inadequate from the qualitative if not the quantitative standpoint. Several models have been prepared that project catastrophes of unprecedented scale, particularly in the densely populated parts of Asia, if current trends in food production, fertilizers, and population are not significantly changed.

It does not require sophisticated computer exercises to demonstrate that future needs for emergency food are likely greatly to surpass those of The Six in the last few years. It is all too easy for those who become emotionally involved in one crisis to forget that other crises are occurring at the same time. As has been noted, numerous African countries other than The Six were seriously affected, and the arid parts of Africa remain vulnerable to future catastrophic droughts.

But famines may occur not only in arid areas. In densely populated humid regions, pressure on the land may become so great that a relatively small shortfall in food production caused by climatic, disease, or other factors may bring famine to far larger numbers than are likely to be affected in arid zones. Again, contrary to widely held notions, considerable parts of Africa and large numbers of people already are affected by pressure on the land, and many more will feel that pressure, given the present rate of population increase which will double the population in the period 1974 to 2000.

While the outlook for Africa is serious, it does not compare with the prospects for Asia. There, floods are a far greater threat than in Africa and the range of possible catastrophes can affect far more people. The population of the subcontinent and of China are both more than double that of Africa, while Southeast Asia's people number 83 percent of the African total.

Americans face difficult questions in deciding just what responsibility the United States should assume in covering future needs for emergency food. There is also the more technical question as to just how much food this country can produce. The availability of surplus food in the United States up until the past few years made it relatively easy to respond to emergencies. Indeed, the surplus was often an embarrassment; the Department of Agriculture welcomed the chance to dispose of some of it through various free and subsidized programs. Other nations and we ourselves came to take it for granted that this country would respond to crisis needs as they arose. Many believe that we have a continuing heavy responsibility to do so. Those who hold that position often contend that we must furnish relief even if it requires a cut in our own consumption and other sacrifices. We are called upon to avoid waste, recycle materials, drink less alcohol and beer produced from grains, have meatless and breadless days, use lawn and golf course fertilizers sparingly, and reduce the number of household pets. There does, in fact, appear to be rather wide acceptance of a continuing responsibility to assume a major role in emergency relief programs, though there is disagreement as to the appropriate level of aid.

An opposing view is represented by the biologist Garrett Hardin, who writes:

A world food bank coupled with sovereign state irresponsibility in reproduction . . . creates an unacknowledged commons. People have more motivation to draw from than to add to the common store . . . the process finally coming to a halt only when all countries are equally and miserably poor. . . .

We cannot safely divide the wealth equitably among all present peoples, so long as people reproduce at different rates, because to do so would guarantee that our grandchildren—everyone's grandchildren—would have only a ruined world to inhabit.[5]

With respect to this country's ability to produce more food, the potential is very great indeed. Much land that could be productive is not in use; some of it may be marginal by American standards but would not be considered so in many nations. The opportunities for intensifying use are also far from exhausted. But there is an important distinction between a physical or scientific potential and a practical potential. Economic and political considerations impose limits on any programs that are likely to be adopted by the U.S. government or through individual choice. Setting up food banks and supplying emergency food may have costs beyond the value of the food itself. They may worsen the inflation that already has raised domestic food prices dramatically in recent years; they may impair our balance of payments by reducing the quantity of food that could be sold; some programs that have been proposed might lower our own standards by restricting consumption of food and fertilizers.

The will to sacrifice and to share is not boundless. Complaints by farmers in 1973 led to reserving an extra 1.5 million tons of U.S. fertilizers for domestic consumption. Criticism of food sales to the USSR has increased because of their impact on American inflation. Limits have been imposed since 1973 on exports of soybeans and other foodstuffs. It is by no means clear that Americans will convert willingly from feed grain to food grain production. And some farmers still fear that increasing output will again produce surpluses and depress prices.

Differences have also arisen regarding the allocation of available food. Some hold that political favoritism and strategic interests rather than need or moral concerns have directed food aid to Vietnam, Indonesia, Egypt, and Chile. The countries that should be favored vary according to the proposer but usually include India, Bangladesh, The Six, Ethiopia, and Africa in general. Others insist that priority be given to the many Americans who have inadequate diets. Such decisions will seem rather simple in comparison to those that will have to be made when there is not enough food to meet demands from a variety of starvation areas simultaneously.

How Can Tillage Agriculture Be Improved?

More important in the long run to inhabitants of the drought-stricken areas of West Africa than the future of emergency food supplies is the development of their own capacity to produce enough food to provide adequate and well-balanced diets and sufficient surpluses in good years to cover their own emergency needs. How might production and productivity in tillage agriculture be increased?

Proposals to increase production by intensifying output on lands now being farmed include greater use of fertilizers, more rapid adoption of high-yielding seeds, increased use of pesticides to reduce heavy losses to insects and diseases, and proper rotation of crops. Some of these proposals will not be easy to implement because farmers cannot afford their costs. Steps can be taken, however, to collect and use available wastes more effectively, and Acacia albida trees can be planted in regular patterns to enrich soils and reduce evaporation and wind erosion. It has been shown that a combination of relatively simple improvements can raise yields per unit area and per man by two to five times with modest capital inputs. Measures that may not be designed specifically to increase production or productivity, but that are nonetheless important in rationalizing tillage agriculture in the Sudan-Sahel belt, include protection of the land against water and wind erosion, more careful application of dry farming techniques, and the use of drought-resistant and quick-maturing crops. Attention should also be given to improving the quality of food crops. High lysine sorghums can provide most of the protein required in the diet, while sorghums and millets have six times the protein content of manioc per unit weight.

In addition to intensifying output on lands in use, cultivation can be extended by opening up new areas, either by expanding the number of farmers using current practices or by increasing the productivity of existing farmers through the use of better equipment or implements drawn by bullocks or tractors. Circumstances sometimes favor the use of mechanical equipment— when, for example, more fadama land is available than can be planted with traditional tools in the brief period suitable for planting after the soil is no longer inundated but is still storing moisture. Then the use of tractors for plowing permits the local farmers to plant larger acreages. But more often than not, the introduction of mechanical equipment has been a dismal failure, either because the increased value of output was insufficient to amortize the cost, or farmers did not use the equipment effectively, or there were no trained personnel to repair the machines. Moreover, mechanical plowing sometimes damages the local soils.

The use of bullocks usually has proved much more successful. Some 75,000 farmers currently use them for plowing in northern Nigeria. All of the other countries in the area have programs to increase animal traction, but its adoption progresses much more slowly than might be expected. Two-wheeled carts drawn by bullocks may increase productivity by permitting easier and fuller application of fertilizer to the fields. Employing work animals contributes to an integration of crop and livestock production that can increase the yield of both. Feeding the bullocks in the dry season is a problem that needs greater attention, one solution being the use of pit silos to preserve their fodder.

Some of the measures designed to extend farming are not without drawbacks. It has been noted in parts of Senegal, for example, that bullock owners have taken over land that had been communally held, thereby creating a landless class. Animal or mechanical plowing, by allowing the cultivation of larger areas, may shorten the fallow period and lead to gradual deterioration of the soil. It should also be recalled that extending farming may increase pressure on graziers and have damaging consequences, at least in marginal farming areas.

Of course the main obstacle to increasing output in the Sahara-Sahel-Sudan region is lack of water, so it is not surprising that serious attention is being given to various means of improving the use of available rainfall, surface water flow, and underground supplies. Both farmers and graziers may benefit from modest measures such as the digging of wells or drilling of boreholes to provide human and stock water, the construction of earthfilled and subsand (below the stream bed) dams, and the excavation of small reservoirs, called *hafirs*, that usually hold from 10,000 to 80,000 cubic meters of water, much of which may be lost to seepage and evaporation. Building contoured benches and low earthen banks or bunds to slow the runoff of rainwater, increase soak-in, and thus give greater yields of grass or crops, is often not justified in low-capacity grazing areas, but water-spreading measures of these kinds can increase crop yields by two times or more.

National and aid-agency plans call for a massive extension of small-scale water control projects, but there are accompanying dangers. Surface reservoirs, small or large, are subject to rapid silting and must be protected against pollution. Water spreading increases losses to evaporation that may reduce the flow moving downstream, to the detriment of other users. Problems in exploiting underground water arise from lack of knowledge of the amounts available, excessive salinity, the fossil character of some of these resources (these may be large but they are not being replenished and hence can support development for only a finite period), and the unfavorable cost-to-benefit ratio of many water-control schemes.

The 1968-1974 drought renewed interest in large-scale irrigation. Proposed for the Senegal River basin are the $125 million Manantali Dam on the Bafing tributary in Mali, which would permit irrigating 750,000 to 815,000 acres and installing a 100,000 kw hydroelectric station, and a $42 million barrage about 12 miles above Saint-Louis, which would prevent the incursion of seawater, control 74,000 acres for irrigation, and permit year-round navigation of the river to Kayes in Mali. It would be desirable to place dams in the headwaters in Guinea, but the withdrawal of that country from the Organization of Senegal River States (OMVS) has made this politically impractical; recent easing of tensions between Guinea and its neighbors gives hope, however, for greater cooperation in river control projects.

Possible developments in the Niger River basin include headwater dams in Guinea; construction of the Sélingué Dam on the Sankarini tributary, which would permit irrigating about 100,000 acres, provide a more stable water supply to the Office du Niger, and support a 40,000 kw hydroelectric station; and the $167 million Bakolori scheme to control 75,000 acres in the Rima basin in northwestern Nigeria. Other medium- to large-scale irrigation projects include the $17 million Tiga dam in Kano State, Nigeria, which eventually may irrigate 180,000 acres, and proposals for partial control of the Chari and Logone Rivers and the waters of Lake Chad, which would affect four nations sharing the Chad basin.

Large irrigation schemes certainly can make significant contributions to agricultural output, but their importance should not be exaggerated. The total hydrological resources of the Sudan-Sahel belt are not adequate to irrigate more than a small fraction of the total area, though they could support perhaps a fifth of the total population. The limitations in the Sahara are even more severe; excluding the Nile oasis, less than 0.03 percent of the total is thought to be irrigated. Only the Sudan Republic among all African countries has sufficient underdeveloped potential to justify major reliance on irrigation in economic planning.

Factors other than the scarcity of available water militate against developing irrigation as the principal means of increasing food production. Very important is the unfavorable cost-to-benefit ratio of many irrigation projects, well illustrated by the Richard-Toll and Office du Niger schemes already in being and by numerous projects in other parts of Africa. Explanations for the frequently poor ratios include the dearth of good dam sites in a relatively flat area, high rates of silting, heavy losses to evaporation, and very high construction costs in remote areas. Still other factors pertain to the areas to be irrigated: the need for well-drained soils, the danger of wind erosion, increased losses to birds and other pests, interference with seasonal pasturing, and the problems that accompany a shift from traditional agriculture to a new and more intensive system.

The increase in disease rates that accompanies irrigation in the Sudan-Sahel region has led to recommendations against new irrigation projects unless they are absolutely necessary. The incidence of bilharzia already is high in parts of the area and will increase rapidly if irrigation is extended; the available drugs and treatments for this disease are too dangerous and too expensive to permit their application to a large population.

Despite the problems and costs associated with large irrigation projects and the disappointing results of those that exist in the region, prospective donors, including the United States, appear to be planning major commitments to river and lake basin development in West Africa. They are attracted by preliminary studies and by the existence of several commissions (Organization for the Development of the Senegal River, Commission for the Development of the Niger River Basin, and the Lake Chad Basin Commission), by the regional character of the proposed developments (Americans are prone to think that there should be TVAs all over the world), and perhaps by the specific nature of constructing dams and canals (which may, incidentally, bring profitable contracts to the donor states) as compared to the amorphism of dealing with millions of individual farmers and graziers. If this preoccupation with large projects severely reduces the attention and assistance that can be given to the agricultural systems that employ the vast bulk of the populations, there is good reason to question the assigned priority.

How Can Pastoralism Be Improved?

Livestock raising in the region can be improved by a variety of methods. The quality of livestock can be increased primarily through careful breeding of indigenous beasts rather than by crossbreeding with exogenous animals, since adaptability to local conditions and resistance to local diseases are of prime importance. It would be easier to increase the meat yield than the milk yield, given the nature of the grazing land and the high heritability of meat production. To achieve milk yields comparable to those of animals in the middle latitudes may never be possible except under strictly controlled artificial conditions, since such levels require full feeding; in the high temperatures prevalent in the region, full feeding increases the heat burden of the animal and results in a loss of appetite. That most African graziers are less interested in producing beef than milk is one of many examples of conflict between suggested improvements and cultural preferences. Controlling cattle diseases is another obvious way of improving the quality of cattle and the productivity of cattle raising.

Opinions differ as to the desirability of changing the ratio of the several kinds of domestic animals kept. Thus some authorities suggest that the goat be forbidden, since it appears to be the most destructive of vegetation. Others note that the goat has high value because it has the greatest ecological range and toleration of the domesticated animals, and is probably the most efficient in areas where forage is meager. Both of these arguments miss the point. Goats can be destructive to trees, but it is man who is responsible for their bad reputation, for it is man who is unwilling to limit the numbers of goats to the sustaining capacity of the land. Admittedly, it might be easier to forbid goats altogether than to determine and enforce a limit on the numbers kept.

In parts of the Sahara and the Sahel, the camel provides an obvious means of increasing meat production, especially where water points are widely separated and where vegetation is low. Another alternative is the substitution of game for domestic animals and the cropping of game for subsistence use and for sale. This approach has numerous possible advantages and may be feasible in other parts of Africa, but it would be impracticable in West Africa because of the dearth of game and because of cultural obstacles.

The improvement of pasture vegetation is difficult because its low value does not justify a large investment. With foreign aid, superior grasses might be sown from the air as an emergency measure. Or selected grasses might be introduced under a system comparable to the *harig* farming used in Sudan, where old grass is burned after a new growth has sprouted with the first summer rains, killing the new shoots and providing an ash into which seeds are immediately planted. Specialists believe that this time-controlled burning avoids the worst features of grass firing.

A third realm for physical improvement is that of water supply. Many of the small-scale measures mentioned in the previous section are applicable to grazing—wells, bore holes, hafirs, and bunds in particular. Dispersing water points permits more effective use of large grazing areas, and in some cases opens lands that are not otherwise usable for grazing.

But the single most important measure to improve grazing in The Six is to achieve control over the numbers of livestock permitted in any given area. Indeed, without some kind of disciplined use related to the carrying capacity of the land and adjustable to sharp fluctuations in that capacity, one can predict with complete assurance a continuing series of crises, periodic catastrophic losses, and a sporadic but certain extension of desert conditions into the Sahel and Sahelian conditions into Sudan.

Past efforts to control grazing have included the provision of better marketing, transport, and processing facilities; campaigns to encourage a voluntary offtake of animals; and taxation designed to force the selling of cattle. None has worked satisfactorily, mainly because other measures were contributing to an increase in the numbers of livestock, which was exactly what the graziers wanted. It is true that cattle sales have risen as the "cattle culture" has begun to break down, but the annual offtake is often less than a third of what it should be, and overgrazing is ended mainly by recurrent catastrophes.

That proper stocking preserves pasture quality is shown by abundant evidence, including examples of successful ranching in several African countries and the revival of vegetation that occurs after grazing has been eliminated by the advance of the tsetse fly. A dramatic example of the former was the appearance on a satellite photograph of a large hexagonal dark area in a portion of the Sahel. It proved to be a fenced ranch divided into paddocks and scientifically managed. Its good grass-growth was in striking contrast to the surrounding lands made barren not so much by drought as by overuse.

The failure of voluntary or compulsory control of grazing results mainly from lack of acceptance by the pastoralists and the inability of governments to police the vast areas involved. Systems such as closing watering points and rotating forage areas require a degree of supervision and technical knowledge that is rarely available in this part of Africa. Fencing usually is too expensive even if it were acceptable to the graziers, and the rapid rotation of cattle in relatively small paddocks, a system used in southern Africa, would require even greater outlays and supervision.

Kenya is one country that has an ambitious program to modernize the use of its extensive grazing lands. Starting in Masai country, communal lands are being converted into private ranches held by groups that may be given corporate legal powers; it is believed that the group ranches will facilitate a variety of improvements, but the government is prepared to enforce stocking limits if that proves necessary. Two factors were apparently significant in securing acceptance by the Masai of the ranching program—their observation of adjacent European ranches that remained in good condition when Masai lands were deteriorating and their livestock dying, and the provision by government of new bore holes, pumps, and pipelines in return for the Masai's agreement to limit livestock numbers and register their lands.

In addition to controlling numbers, the shortage of pasture in the dry season can be alleviated by other means. These include the planting of fodder crops as well as food crops by pastoralist-farmers and ensilaging a crop for winter consumption; setting up fodder banks that might include high protein concentrates such as peanut cake and cottonseed cake; developing closer relations with sedentary farmers to assure dry-season feed; and setting up commercial feedlots to fatten range-fed cattle before marketing. (Kenya has opened 17 feedlots in the Rift Valley on which it is hoped that cattle will increase their weight 50 percent in 70 days. Botswana, Zambia, and Morocco are also establishing feedlots and fattening ranches.) But most of these measures would require a degree of cooperation and sophisticated management that cannot realistically be expected for some years; others involve governmental intervention on a level that the poorer countries could not afford.

Improvements in marketing and the higher prices that may be expected with increasing world food shortages may increase the offtake of livestock. The marketing of lower quality products (in the form of canned beef and meat extract, for example) has increased the offtake ratio in a number of countries. A potentially valuable program would be to provide for emergency offtake before serious deterioration of the herds had set in, backed by an organized system of restocking when that became possible. As is true of so many technical possibilities, however, the cultural and administrative barriers to such a program, plus the continuing problem of inadequate transport, would work against its successful adoption.

It is frequently suggested that pastoralists should be sedentarized, and some governments appear determined to do so. Explanations for the wish to settle nomads range from the desire to prevent further destruction of pasturelands to the belief that nomadism is a "backward" system that precludes extending modernizing education and other social amenities, and that makes no significant contribution to the national economy.

The effects of the 1968-74 drought and continuing population growth will compel some of the nomads to settle somewhere, either in areas where tillage farming is possible or, more likely, in shantytowns near cities within and outside the area. If they settle in the drier areas, there will be further destruction of the vegetation through overgrazing, overcropping, and overcutting of trees. In any event, it is questionable whether all nomadic peoples should be required to settle. They make use of areas that could not be used by man in any other way, and in normal circumstances they produce a surplus of animal protein that would otherwise be lost. Many nomads prefer their way of life to any other and are well adapted to it. Unless governments are prepared to provide some other reasonably attractive form of employment, it would be wiser to work toward more effective use of the nomadic areas than to prevent their use by compulsory sedentarization.

Conclusions

Of many lessons to be drawn from the Sahelian catastrophe, three seem of paramount importance: that those who would help need to know the area much better; that the United States must strike a delicate balance between limitations and responsibilities in providing future emergency food aid; and that agricultural development and population control in Africa itself are essential if greater catastrophes are to be avoided over the longer term.

Some Research Needs

Intensive research is needed on a variety of subjects of key importance. It might best be conducted by a center for research on crops and agricultural systems of Sudano-Sahelian areas comparable to the International Institute for Tropical Agriculture (IITA), financed by the Rockefeller Foundation, the Ford Foundation, and the official U.S. and Canadian aid agencies and located near Ibadan, Nigeria, in a wet tropical area. Alternatively, existing research centers in the Middle East and in eastern Africa may make advances pertinent to agricultural development in The Six and other semiarid areas of Africa.

Research is needed to improve predictive powers with respect to climate, to achieve more effective pest and disease control, and to extend knowledge of the area's hydrological resources. Pilot schemes would be desirable to test alternative ways of improving farming and grazing. In the human sphere, more should be learned about population movements and a better understanding of human ecology be gained through detailed studies of local groups. (Many of the community studies made by the French under the Office de Recherche Scientifique et Technique Outremer are models in this respect.) But it should not be forgotten that a mass of valuable information already exists—that there is a need for action as well as for research.

The need for an holistic approach in dealing with the problems of the area has been emphasized, and it warrants reiteration. The results of piecemeal approaches have often been destructive, even tragic. Examples include the provision of water points, veterinary services, and predator control without control of livestock levels; extending irrigation without attention to suppressing disease; developing lands for tillage in ways that adversely affect the pattern of transhumant grazing; and focusing attention on cash crops without concern for sustaining the quantity and quality of subsistence crops. It is disturbing to note that some of the national programs adopted for recovery from the 1968-74 drought have among their main components the same one-shot approaches that have had such negative results in the past.

The need for site-specific solutions has also been stressed. The rainlands of the Sudan farming areas, the fadama lands, the irrigation areas, the rangelands of the Sahel, and the usable areas of the Sahara all require solutions related to their particular environmental assets and limitations. At the same time, it should be recalled that certain land-use systems depend on the complementary assets of differing environments. And it should be recognized that there are opportunities for more effective relationships between the peoples of the Sahel and those of the Sudan, and for extending commercial relations between those areas and the wet tropical regions to the south.

The cultural ecology of an area must also be understood if ameliorative steps are to be effective. Here it may be wise to recognize that persuasion and positive inducements are preferable to denial and restriction. But it is also realistic to recognize that man's capacity to engineer society is relatively primitive.

What Should Americans Do Next Time?

The policy choices involved in providing food and other supplies in response to another natural catastrophe such as the Sahelian drought will not necessarily be easy for the United States government or private groups. Moral, economic, political, and strategic considerations may complicate the planning and execution of emergency aid programs.

Past decisions to provide or not provide emergency relief have been relatively simple, with the United States responding frequently and vigorously to natural catastrophes in distant parts of the world. Private donations have often complemented governmental efforts, and Americans have taken pride in the support their country has provided. The existence until recently of chronic food surpluses and our position as the wealthiest nation in the world have made generosity not only appropriate but also possible at small sacrifice.

Because the basic decision may become considerably harder in the future, we should consider in advance some of the issues involved. One is the proper size of emergency stores to be maintained. This must be related, on the one hand, to projected needs and, on the other hand, to production or supply levels in the United States, particularly of foodstuffs.

With rapidly rising populations in the less-developed countries, the number of people affected by future emergencies inevitably will increase, even though it is now predicted that world food production can keep up with population growth for at least several decades. Presumably it will be possible to sell, perhaps at premium prices, an increasing volume of agricultural products, and hence the decision to extend aid may require a degree of sacrifice not necessary in the past.

A decision to increase supplies will also be somewhat more difficult than in the past. One position, held by Secretary of Agriculture Earl Butz among others, maintains that interference with free market forces may result in gross and costly distortions. A contrasting position is that the laissez-faire approach would deplete food stocks and make it impossible to maintain stores required for future emergencies. While there is little question that the United States has the capacity greatly to increase food production, it is politically unrealistic to expect individual farmers to overproduce in order to fill relief stores unless they are given some support or assurance that selling prices for staples will not be adversely affected.

It is my view that preparing for and responding to natural catastrophes in various parts of the world should be seen as an international proposition, not as a United States *national* government responsibility per se. There are few if any operations more appropriate for a multilateral approach than meeting such emergencies, and we should support the proposals to establish a standby international agency. Several reasons can be cited for cooperation of this kind, a crucial one being that it would promote assistance from nations on the basis of their wealth, not their food production capacity, whereas a national operation tends to concentrate on the latter capability.

In this context, projections of population growth and of food production and consumption in the less-developed countries suggest the desirability of United States support for aid programs designed to increase food production and storage and to decrease fertility rates in those countries. The former is not easy, as there is no panacea for improving agriculture in the LDCs, and the latter must be approached with sensitivity and with the realization that no rapid change may be expected. We need to ask ourselves if providing more effective and generous aid now might avoid greater expenditure and friction later. In this area, too, the longer term programs are more appropriate for international action; thus, we should support the Consultative Group on Food Production and Investment set up by the 1974 World Food Conference to coordinate and stimulate national and international efforts aimed at increasing food production in the LDCs.

The provision of food both for emergencies and for improving dietary standards, and the granting of aid to the LDCs to assist in their development, are not unrelated to the United States' desire for free access to raw materials and world markets. Thus political and strategic concerns may become involved in what should ideally be largely a moral response to emergency and longer term needs. Many of the LDCs are calling for a "new world economic order." While the concept is poorly defined and partially inimical to the free enterprise system, we cannot afford rigidly to ignore the aspirations of its proponents. These considerations lead in turn to one of the most pervasive issues facing Americans, namely whether we should reduce the rate of increase in our consumption of raw materials and deliberately plan for a slower rate of growth in our national economy.

The Ultimate Choice Is Africa's

Participating in food banks and perfecting emergency delivery systems are desirable, but their importance should not be exaggerated. Even given ideal circumstances and a high level of self-sacrifice, the United States and other surplus food producers cannot possibly continue indefinitely to meet the needs of the developing world, where populations are growing by 2 to 3.6 percent a year and thus will double within 20 to 35 years. Two conclusions logically follow—that strenuous efforts should be made to promote food production in the developing countries and that those countries be encouraged to work toward lower fertility rates.

The record in recent years in many African countries with respect to agricultural production has not been good, in part because the sector has not been accorded sufficiently high priority in development plans. While there is now wider acceptance that agriculture must be given greater attention and that progress in the service and manufacturing sectors depends heavily on improvements in agriculture, many countries pay only lip service to the need. In Zaire, for example, agriculture was allotted only 2.5 percent of government expenditures in 1973—despite repeated assertions that agriculture was to be the priority of priorities, and despite the facts that about 70 percent of the population is engaged in farming and that distressing declines occurred between 1959 and 1974 in agricultural exports and in agriculture's contribution to the GDP.

Lowering birthrates is, in the long run, the all-important prescription; but it is unrealistic to expect rapid gains in the near future. The danger is that the lesson may not be learned until a massive famine has made starkly clear the relation between food supply and population growth.

Notes

1. W.B. Morgan and J.C. Pugh, *West Africa* (London: Methuen and Company, Ltd., 1969), pp. 15-16.

2. William A. Hance, *Population, Migration, and Urbanization in Africa* (New York: Columbia University Press, 1970), pp. 383-422.

3. Hal Sheets and Roger Morris, *Disaster in the Desert: Failures of International Relief in the West African Drought* (New York: Carnegie Endowment for International Peace, 1974).

4. M.I.T. Center for Policy Alternatives. *A Framework for Evaluating Long-Term Strategies for the Development of the Sahel-Sudan Region*, 2 v. (Cambridge, Mass., December 31, 1974).

5. Garrett Hardin, "Living on a Lifeboat," *BioScience*, 24, No. 10 (October, 1974), pp. 565, 567.

Suggested Additional Reading on the Sahel

Bryson, Reid A. *Climatic Modifications by Air Pollution, II: The Sahelian Effect.* Report No. 9. Madison, Wisconsin: The Institute for Environmental Science, University of Wisconsin, 1973.

Caldwell, John C., ed. *Population Growth and Socio-Economic Change in West Africa.* New York: Columbia University Press, 1975.

_____ . "The Sahelian Drought and its Demographic Implications." American Council on Education, Overseas Liaison Committee. OLC Paper No. 8, December 1975.

Dalby, David and Church, R.J. Harrison, eds. *Drought in Africa: Report of the 1973 Symposium.* London: University of London, School of Oriental and African Studies, Centre for African Studies, 1973.

DuBois, Victor D. "The Drought in West Africa. Part III: The Logistics of Relief Operations." *AUFS Field Staff Reports, West Africa Series 15*, No. 3 (May 1974).

Grove, A.T. "Desertification in the African Environment." *African Affairs*, Vol. 73, No. 291 (April 1974).

Hance, William A. *The Geography of Modern Africa.* 2nd edition. New York: Columbia University Press, 1975.

International Bank for Reconstruction and Development/International Development Association. "World Bank Approach to Economic Development of Sahel." Washington, D.C. (March 18, 1975).

Morgan, W.B. and Pugh, J.C. *West Africa.* London: Methuen, 1969.

Queant-Thierry, de Rouville C. *Agriculteurs et Eleveurs de la Région du Gondo-Sourou.* Ouagadougou: Centre Voltaique de Recherche Scientifique, June 1969.

Savanna, Vol. 2, No. 2 (December 1973).

Stryker, J. Dirck. "The Malian Cattle Industry: Opportunity and Dilemma." *The Journal of Modern African Studies*, Vol. 12, No. 3 (1974).

United Nations. Educational, Social, and Cultural Organization. *Sahel: Economical Approaches to Land Use.* Paris, 1975.

_____ . Food and Agriculture Organization. *Analytical Bibliography on the Sahel.* Rome, 1974.

United States. Department of State. Agency for International Development. *Report to the Congress on Famine in Sub-Sahara Africa.* Washington, D.C.: Government Printing Office, 1974.

V Sub-Saharan Africa in the 1980s: An Economic Profile

Andrew M. Kamarck

If we could first know where we are, and whither we are tending, we could better judge what to do, and how to do it.

—Abraham Lincoln

Because modern economic development in black Africa is still historically quite recent, the amount of structural change likely to occur over the next decade will be limited. Therefore, an understanding of the economic position of Africa in 1975, including the economic trends at work, is indispensable in forecasting what Africa will be like in 1985.

Africa in 1975

The main economic characteristics of Africa in 1975 can be summed up briefly. The continent is one of the two poorest regions in the world and it is still largely homogeneous in its poverty and in its economic structure, which consists of a fairly small modern sector and a large agricultural sector that absorbs most of the labor force. The modern sectors in most countries remain dependent on the export of a few primary products, with economic and financial relations with Western Europe still dominant. As in other developing regions, the rapid pace of urbanization, of growth in urban unemployment, and of overall population increase are becoming major problems. These economic characteristics will be discussed in more detail below.

Some Fundamentals

In 1975, the average gross national product per capita in the less developed countries (LDCs) as a whole was roughly equivalent in money terms to about $300. Africa south of the Sahara (excluding South Africa) had a per capita GNP of around $200. In these terms, Africa was considerably behind Latin America and the Middle East but a little ahead of the noncommunist Asian region, where the average per capita GNP is perhaps $180. The contrast between Africa, Asia, and Latin America can be seen in Table V-1, showing rough estimates of the numbers of people and proportions of total populations that could be classified as being in "absolute poverty" (below $50 income per capita in rural areas and below $75 in urban areas) in the principal LDC regions in 1969.

Although Africa may be slightly ahead of Asia in this economic arithmetic— certainly there are no great masses of people in Africa in such abject poverty and misery as exist in parts of Asia—by other criteria, such as the size of the technological and entrepreneurial elite, Africa is still behind most of the countries of Asia. The UN General Assembly in 1975 was essentially right, therefore, in classifying 18 countries of Africa among the world's 29 least developed, while only eight Asian countries, two Middle Eastern countries, and one Latin American country were so classified.[a]

During the world economic and financial crisis of 1974 and 1975 (associated with the quadrupling of oil prices, the exhaustion of world food reserves, and an acceleration of world inflation), a number of poor countries were particularly

Table V-1
Estimates of Population in Poverty

	Total Population	Total Urban and Rural Population in Poverty* (in millions)	Rural Population in Poverty* (in millions)	Poverty Population as Percentage of Total Population	
				Total Urban and Rural	Rural
Sub-Saharan Africa	270	125	105	46	39
Developing Asia	1080	620	525	57	49
Developing America	250	50	30	19	12

*Defined as below $50 per capita income in rural areas and below $75 per capita income in urban areas, in 1969 prices.

Source: Derived from *Rural Development and Bank Policies* (Washington, D.C.: International Bank for Reconstruction and Development, December 1974).

[a]In Africa: Botswana, Burundi, Chad, Central African Republic, Benin, Ethiopia, Gambia, Guinea, Lesotho, Malawi, Mali, Niger, Rwanda, Somalia, Sudan, Uganda, Tanzania, Upper Volta. In Asia: Afghanistan, Bangladesh, Bhutan, Laos, Maldives, Nepal, Sikkim, West Samoa. In the Middle East: the Yemen Arab Republic and the People's Democratic Republic of Yemen. In Latin America: Haiti.

hurt, and the United Nations tried to organize an "emergency operation" to help them get through the worst of this period. Twenty-six African countries were classified by the United Nations as "most severely affected," among them most of the least developed countries but also several others.[b]

Four-fifths of the African population lives in rural areas. Most Africans still depend on agriculture and most of these, plus some whose families earn a money income (through trading or working in a mine, factory, or office, or in other ways) feed themselves entirely or almost entirely from food they grow themselves. As Table V-2 indicates, most are to a substantial degree still part of a subsistence economy; yet it is also true that few Africans are any longer completely outside the money economy. For more and more people every year, the money economy—represented in the cash crops they produce and sell and in wages, salaries, or even entrepreneurial profits they receive—is becoming an important reality.

Modern economic growth in Africa, as in other tropical areas, began with the production of crops and minerals for export. The money economy continues to be predominantly influenced by the foreign sector, and consequently the pace of a country's economic growth depends largely on the market for its main primary products abroad, on the inflow of external capital invested or made available as economic aid from abroad, and on the import of foreign technical and managerial skills.

African exports consist almost entirely of primary and semi-processed products: foods such as coffee, cocoa, peanuts, and sugar; agricultural raw materials such as cotton, sisal, rubber and logs; or minerals such as copper, industrial diamonds, alumina, and, in very recent years, oil. The list is relatively short for all of Africa, and most countries depend on only a small number of these. The country-by-country chart of basic facts about Africa accompanying this volume lists the principal exports for each African country and shows how the bulk of the exports of any one country are relatively few in number.

Just as modern economic development began in Africa with the production of cash crops or minerals for export, so the physical structure of the economies has been and still is largely shaped by the demands of foreign trade. The infrastructure—the railways, roads, ports, and urban growth—has been primarily shaped by those demands. And since the export-import trade is largely overseas, most lines of communication still lead overseas rather than to other African countries. Some progress has been made in creating new transport and communications links among the African countries in the recent postcolonial years, but economic forces continue to ensure that the most important routes are those that lead to the rest of the world. Even today, it is often easier to travel from one African country to another through London or Paris than it is directly.

---

[b]The May 1, 1975 United Nations Emergency Operation list of Africa's Most Severely Affected Countries: Burundi, Cameroon, Central African Republic, Cape Verde Islands, Chad, Benin, Ethiopia, Ghana, Guinea, Guinea-Bissau, Ivory Coast, Kenya, Lesotho, Madagascar, Mali, Mauritania, Mozambique, Niger, Rwanda, Senegal, Sierra Leone, Somalia, Sudan, Tanzania, Uganda, Upper Volta.

Table V-2
Percentage of Total Labor Force in Agriculture and Manufacturing in Sub-Saharan Africa

| Country | Percent of Labor Force | | Date of Data |
	Agriculture	Manufacturing	
Benin	52	n.a.	1974est.
Botswana	91	1	1964
Burundi	90	–	1975est.
Congo-Brazzaville	65	n.a.	1974est.
Ethiopia	85	3	1973est.
Gabon	84	2	1963
Ghana	58	9	1960
Guinea	85	1	1963
Ivory Coast	39	10	1970
Kenya	28	10	1972
Liberia	80	1	1962
Madagascar	90	n.a.	1970
Mali	80	n.a.	1971
Mauritania	90	n.a.	1965
Niger	95	n.a.	1970
Nigeria	80	11	1965
Rhodesia	73	n.a.	1965
Senegal	74	n.a.	1965
Sierra Leone	75	4	1963
Somali Republic	90	n.a.	1973
Sudan	86	5	1956
Tanzania	91	2	1967
Upper Volta	80	n.a.	1969
Zaire	64	9	1966
Zambia	29	3	1969

Source: U.S. AID. *Economic Data Book* (loose-leaf, various dates, 1973-1975).

The growth rates of African countries have been and continue to be strongly influenced by external economic and financial forces. As is true of very poor developing countries throughout the world, the beginning and early phases of modern economic development are facilitated by a country's possession of rich natural resources to exploit. The most dramatic examples are, of course, the oil-producing countries. But it is also true of countries such as Zambia and Zaire, producers of copper; Mauritania and Liberia, producers of iron ore; and the Central African Republic and Sierra Leone, producers of diamonds. In Zaire, as a result of the disruption accompanying independence, agriculture stagnated and the transportation network deteriorated during the 1960s. Mining, however, continued to develop. In 1973, copper mining alone provided two-thirds of Zaire's foreign exchange earnings and 40 percent of government revenues. By 1975, government revenues and foreign exchange earnings from mining had grown enough to enable the government to begin turning the situation around in the other sectors by using its copper revenues to finance new investment in the other sectors, by training Zairians in Zaire and abroad, and by importing foreign technical skills.

Africa continues to be a region that both needs and uses large numbers of foreign experts. Although the colonial civil servants who held key government jobs at the time of independence have been largely replaced by indigenous personnel, those African countries that have been most successful in promoting economic growth have imported expatriate personnel for technical and managerial positions in numbers equal to or even considerably greater than the departing civil servants. No regular system exists for reporting the inflow of high-level personnel into the private sector; however, the Development Assistance Committee (DAC) of the Organization for Economic Development and Cooperation (OECD) occasionally publishes data on the number of persons made available by the DAC governments and multilateral organizations as technical assistants.

Table V-3, based on the most recent available information, illustrates the scope of this assistance to major African recipients and suggests that Africa is unique in the Third World in its need for, and its willingness to accept, expatriate technical assistance personnel. For black Africa south of the Sahara as a whole, the total number of expatriate personnel working as experts, advisers, operational personnel, and teachers is estimated at around 70,000. The number of Africans supported as students and trainees and on fellowships in the OECD countries is probably about 40,000 a year.

Another essential component of Africa's economic development is the continuing import of capital from abroad. In 1972, for example, the total GNP of the black-governed African countries south of the Sahara was equivalent to some $45 billion. Roughly 15 percent of this, or around $7 billion, was invested. During the same year, the net flow of capital into black-governed Africa from all sources (public and private) in the OECD countries was $2.5 billion, or about 35 percent of total African investment. These figures are, of course, only a rough indicator of the continued importance of external resources. In some extremely poor countries, such as Upper Volta, the external resources largely determine the pace of investment in the country. In other cases, as in Botswana, private foreign direct investment in the development of new mineral deposits may enable the country to break loose from centuries of poverty and for the first time open up to its people the economic vistas modern development provides. In some countries—Nigeria is one example—external capital resources now make only a slight difference in the rate at which the country is able to develop.

Table V-3

Personnel Components of Total DAC and Multilateral Technical Cooperation by the Major Recipients in Africa, 1971

Recipient Country	Disbursements U.S.$ Million	Teachers	"Experts," Operational Personnel, Advisers, Volunteers (other than Teachers)	Students, Trainees, Fellowships
Zaire	51	1,652	1,308	1,483
Kenya	32	1,394	1,972	1,110
Nigeria	28	710	2,042	2,646
Ivory Coast	23	2,395	1,566	628
Tanzania	23	278	1,311	842
Madagascar	21	922	1,074	1,102
Senegal	20	904	1,097	785
Ethiopia	20	499	1,323	1,096
Zambia	19	1,550	2,861	508
Cameroon	18	587	1,273	964
Uganda	16	1,226	1,088	1,322
Ghana	16	789	731	1,684
Total 12 Countries	287	12,906	17,646	14,170

Source: Based on *Development Cooperation, 1973 Review*, Table 30, (Paris: Organization for Economic Cooperation and Development, 1973), p. 224.

Most of the net inflow is on favorable terms. Of the total of $2.5 billion in 1972 and the $3.4 billion in 1973 of recorded net flows of resources from the OECD countries and the multilateral agencies into black Africa, $1.7 billion in 1972 and $1.9 billion in 1973 was bilateral Official Development Assistance (ODA), or grants and credits on concessional terms from multilateral agencies. Most of the difference between these figures and the totals represents private direct investment, the placement of bond issues, and credits on the Eurodollar and other international markets.

A new element in the early 1970s was rapid growth in the flow of private funds to several African countries, particularly Zaire, Kenya, Ivory Coast, Nigeria, and Botswana. Even more important was the rapid growth in loans and credits from the World Bank Group, which by 1975 had become by far the most important source of external capital for African governments (see Table V-4).

Table V-5 sets forth the details for those African countries whose total net inflow of financial resources from OECD countries and multilateral agencies exceeded $50 million in either 1972 or 1973. A glance at the table identifies several countries that depend primarily on Official Development Assistance, including concessional aid from multilateral agencies. For example, Ethiopia in

Table V-4
World Bank Group Loan and Credit Commitments to Black African Countries (Fiscal Year ending June 30)
(millions of dollars)

1964-1968, Annual Average	130
1969-1973, Annual Average	391
FY 1973	519
FY 1974	690
FY 1975	1,105

Note: These figures are not directly comparable to those in Table V-5 for the following reasons: While Table V-5 shows *actual flows* for the calendar year, Table V-4 shows loan and credit *commitments* signed during the fiscal year, which will eventuate in actual flows in future years. Table V-5 figures are net of amortization repayments, whereas Table V-4 figures do not deduce amortization.
Source: Computed from IBRD *1975 Annual Report.*

1972 received $47 million of a total of $48 million in this form, and $64 million of $65 million in 1973. The same relationship characterized Upper Volta's inflow of resources. Zaire, on the other hand, received $139 million in ODA in 1973 of total external capital resources of $515 million—that is, most of its new foreign capital consisted of private investment funds.

Urbanization

As we have seen, Africa south of the Sahara was still mostly rural in the early 1970s, rather less than a fifth of the population being urban. But though

Africa is the least urbanized of continents . . . this demographic fact belies the new importance of African cities. . . . African leaders are no longer traditional chiefs or renegade rousers of unrest, but are the holders of the economic, military and political power of the new nations. The habitat of this new elite is the city. Here is the center of commerce, the seat of government, the source of news and innovation and the point of contact with the outside world.[1]

While Africa has remained the least urbanized of continents, the growth rate of its cities is among the fastest in the world, their population having doubled in a decade or less. Greater Lagos numbered 250,000 people in 1950, 1.5 million in 1967, and around 2 million in the early 1970s. Kinshasa's population was 200,000 in 1950 and 1.2 million in 1970. Abidjan was well under 100,000 in 1950 and surpassed 500,000 in 1970. Nairobi had a population of around 140,000 in 1950 and 500,000 in 1970.

This high urban growth rate has brought with it the problems often faced by

Table V-5
Recorded Total Net Flow of Resources and Official Development Assistance and Resources on Concessional Terms Received by African Countries from OECD Countries and Multilateral Agencies
(millions of dollars)

Country	Total Net Flow of Resources		ODA and Concessional	
	1972	1973	1972	1973
Angola	(110)	62	70	9
Botswana	70	132	31	35
Cameroon	86	90	64	62
Congo	109	179	23	27
Ethiopia	48	65	47	64
Gabon	49	100	27	34
Guinea	63	76	27	21
Ivory Coast	84	155	49	62
Kenya	116	182	72	96
Madagascar	61	56	56	52
Malawi	51	29	36	29
Mali	41	68	39	68
Mozambique	(89)	101	51	4
Niger	42	73	43	70
Nigeria	(217)	131	83	73
Reunion	147	206	147	176
Senegal	58	98	49	77
Sudan	45	95	37	46
Tanzania	99	119	59	95
Upper Volta	35	58	35	57
Zaire	212	515	121	139
Sub-total	1,832	2,590	1,166	1,296
Sub-total, other African countries	712	801	535	642
Total, South of Sahara	2,544	3,391	1,701	1,938

Source: Extracted from OECD, *Development Cooperation, 1974 Review*, Paris, OECD, Nov. 1974, Tables 70, 72, pp. 266-7, 270-1.

Third World cities in these circumstances: neither the volume of housing nor the municipal infrastructure of water supplies, sewerage, streets, and public utilities can keep up. Around every African city, as happened earlier in Latin America, squatter colonies have sprung up. Table V-6 presents estimates of the very high proportions of urban populations in Africa living in slums and squatter settlements in recent years. Indeed, the urban areas are full of marginal laborers,

Table V-6
Slums and Squatter Settlements as Percent of Total Population of Selected Cities

City	Percent	Year of Estimate
Yaoundé, Cameroon	90	1970
Addis Ababa, Ethiopia	90	1968
Douala, Cameroon	80	1970
Mogadiscio, Somalia	77	1967
Lomé, Togo	75	1970
Ibadan, Nigeria	75	1971
Mombasa, Kenya	66	1970
Abidjan, Ivory Coast	60	1964
Dakar, Senegal	60	1971
Kinshasa, Zaire	60	1969
Blantyre, Malawi	56	1966
Accra, Ghana	53	1968
Monrovia, Liberia	50	1970
Nairobi, Kenya	33	1970

Source: Excerpted from UN *World Housing Survey*, January 1974.

the so-called unemployed. An important part of urban growth is caused by these laborers attracted from the countryside to the city by the substantial disparity between urban and rural incomes, and the migration is slowed only when the number of "unemployed" in the city surviving through marginal sources of income (living off relatives, petty theft, small-scale buying and selling, and so on) grows so large that rural subsistence or incomes seem relatively more attractive.

Concurrently, the rapid growth of the cities has tended to outrun their domestic food supply. It is not that the urban population can no longer be fed by the local farmers, but that distribution and marketing have not kept pace. Neither road-building, nor the construction of storage and preservation and processing facilities, nor the organization of new domestic marketing arrangements has matched the increased food needs of the cities. Importers and the world marketing system have taken up the slack, with the result that a growing volume of food imports into African countries is substituting for domestic foods and creating new tastes and demands.

Population Growth

By mid-1975 the population of Africa south of the Sahara (excluding South Africa) totalled roughly 270 million people, and the United Nations demographic yearbook estimated that Africa had the most rapid population growth rate in the world. In 39 of 45 African countries for which data were available, the growth rate was more than two percent. In nine countries the rate was three percent or more. Because of very high birth rates, these growth rates were achieved despite death rates that remain the world's highest. In most African countries a new-born baby can expect to live less than 50 years; in 21 of the countries for which there were figures, life expectancy was less than 40 years. In Sweden, which shows the best statistical record, there were 9.6 deaths per 1,000 live births in 1973; at the other statistical extreme, Liberia had an estimated 159 deaths per 1,000 live births in 1971. It should be noted, as Table V-7 indicates, that the economic progress of the last 20 years has been accompanied by a considerable increase in life expectancy in Africa.

High population growth means that African countries typically have youthful inhabitants: around 44 percent of their populations are under 15 years of age, in contrast to Europe, where this figure is usually around 25 percent. Youthfulness in turn points toward continued high population growth rates. Unlike the other less-developed regions, tropical Africa as a whole shows little indication of a drop in birthrates. In the early 1970s, those rates still tended to be around 47 per thousand in Africa, whereas South Asian birthrates were around 43 per thousand, Latin America, 37, and East Asia, 29. The industrialized countries' birthrates generally were around 19 per thousand.

The economic impact of Africa's demographic trends is suggested by the fact that half to two-thirds of all investment usually is needed to provide for the

Table V-7
Expectation of Life at Birth, 1950-1970
(by five-year intervals)

	1950-1955	1955-1960	1960-1965	1965-1970
Sub-Saharan Africa				
Western	32.3	34.5	36.8	39.2
Eastern	35.0	37.5	40.0	42.3
Middle	34.5	35.7	36.9	39.3
Southern	43.0	45.3	47.3	48.0
Tropical South America	52.0	54.6	57.2	59.7
Middle South Asia	39.5	42.4	45.4	48.3
World Total–Developing Regions	41.7	44.4	47.0	49.0
–Developed Regions	64.6	67.8	69.2	70.4

Source: Excerpted from United Nations May 3, 1973, "Demographic Trends in the World and its Major Regions, 1950-1970," E/Conf. 60/BP/1. Reproduced in World Bank Staff Study, *Population Policies and Economic Development* (Baltimore and London: Johns Hopkins Press, 1974), p. 170.

increase in population rather than to improve the standard of living, while the high dependency ratio inhibits savings. Moreover, the "Asian type" of population problem reflecting a high ratio of population to available resources is not unknown—for example, in parts of eastern Nigeria, Rwanda, and Burundi. The wide-open African spaces are misleading in this context. What counts is resources, such as arable land, that can be used. Large areas in most countries appear to have little or no fertile soil, insufficient rainfall, or rain at the wrong times and in inappropriate amounts. Statistics on the extent of arable land are nonexistent or fuzzy. In fact, whether land can be categorized as arable or not depends in large part on known technology; fertility, for example, may depend on knowing how to add to the soil "trace elements," minute quantities of a mineral such as copper or molybdenum. The available statistics, as shown in Table V-8, indicate that the population-to-cropland (i.e. area actually under crops) ratios in some African countries are comparable to those of India and Pakistan.

International Economic Relations

The modern monetary part of African economies was called into being mainly by demand for African products from overseas, by colonial government action, or by foreign direct investment in mines and trading firms, plantations, or

Table V-8
Cropland in Relation to Population by Countries[a]

Country	Cropland (thousands of hectares)	Total Population (millions)	Agricultural Population (millions)	Hectares of Cropland per Person of	
				Total Population	Agricultural Population
Angola	900	5.5	3.6	.16	.25
Ghana	2,835	8.8	4.8	.29	.59
Nigeria	21,795	76.8[b]	45.4	.32	.48
Rwanda	704	3.6	3.3	.20	.21
Uganda	4,888	8.5	7.3	.57	.67
Zaire	7,200	17.5	13.7	.41	.53
India	164,610	550.4	372.6	.30	.44
Pakistan	24,000	60.0	35.0	.40	.69

[a]Calculations as of about 1970.

[b]The population figures for Nigeria are almost certainly too high. But, even on the basis of a lower figure for Nigeria in 1975, the figure for 1985 will be higher than that in the table.

Source: Excerpted from Annex Table 15, World Bank Staff Study, *Population Policies and Economic Development* (Baltimore & London: Johns Hopkins Press, 1974), p. 182.

factories. As noted, the modern sector remains closely tied to these overseas influences. And the dominant influence has been and continues to be that of Western Europe. Of tropical Africa's total foreign trade, three-fifths is with Western Europe, eight to ten percent is with the United States, six to nine percent is intra-African trade, four to five percent is with the centrally planned communist economies, and the remaining 15 to 25 percent is with the rest of the world (Japan, the Middle East, East Asia, Latin America).

Economic Relations with the United States. Only for a small number of African countries does the United States provide a significant market (ten percent or more of a country's total exports) or an important source of commodities (ten percent or more of its total imports). Black African countries whose trade patterns fit these criteria are indicated in Table V-9.

The leading American imports from black Africa are petroleum, coffee, cocoa, rubber, and iron ore. Total United States imports from black Africa came to about $1.7 billion in 1973 (or about 2.5 percent of total United States imports) and $4.8 billion in 1974 after the oil price rise (or 4.8 percent of total imports). American exports to black Africa totaled about $900 million in 1973

Table V-9
Significant United States Trade Partners in Africa (1972 Trade Data)

	U.S. Purchases 10% or above of Total Country Exports	U.S. Supplies 10% or above of Total Country Imports
	%	%
Angola	16	13
Benin	—ᵃ	10
Burundi	77	—ᵃ
Cameroon	10	11
Central African Republic	19	—ᵃ
Ethiopia	35	1ᵃ
Ghana	13	18
Guinea	—ᵃ	13
Ivory Coast	14	1ᵃ
Liberia	21	30
Madagascar	21	1ᵃ
Mozambique	13	1ᵃ
Nigeria	21	10
Uganda	18	1ᵃ

ᵃLess than ten percent.

Source: Extracted from the Agency for International Development *AID Economic Data Book* (January 29, 1975), pp. 32-37.

and $1.3 billion in 1974, or just over one percent of total U.S. exports in both years. The book value of U.S. direct investment in black Africa totaled around $2 billion in 1973, or about two percent of worldwide United States private direct investments. American direct investments in South Africa, which formerly surpassed American investment in black Africa, were $1.2 billion in 1973. During 1974, American direct investment in South Africa grew by 25 percent while American investment in Nigeria decreased as a result of a transfer of over $200 million in the equity ownership of oil firms in Nigeria from American companies to the Nigerian government. If no allowance is made for the increased value of oil, total book value of American direct investment in South Africa once again surpassed that in black Africa in 1974.

Economic Relations with Western Europe: The Lomé Convention. On February 28, 1975, a convention was signed in Lomé, Togo, between 37 African countries (plus nine small countries in the Caribbean and Pacific) on the one side and the European Economic Community (EEC) on the other, to govern trade, aid, and economic cooperation between the two groups for the period to 1980. Because the convention had to be ratified by parliaments, it did not come into force until April 1, 1976. The sweeping character and importance of this agreement make it a good focal point for our discussion of economic and financial relations between Africa south of the Sahara and the nine countries of Western Europe—Belgium, Denmark, France, the German Federal Republic, Ireland, Italy, Luxembourg, Netherlands, United Kingdom—that compose the EEC.

The convention replaces the so-called association agreements that linked the European Economic Community with the former sub-Saharan territories of France, Belgium, and Italy. It covers, for the first time, countries south of the Sahara, other than the Republic of South Africa and the Portuguese colonies, whether they were former colonies or always independent (Ethiopia and Liberia). And it is open to newly independent countries: thus Guinea-Bissau already is included, and the other former Portuguese colonies and Namibia (South West Africa) are expected to join after independence. In brief, the convention treats the whole area as a single group of countries.

The terms of the agreement give African countries the right to export to EEC countries, without payment of duty or any limitation by quota, all industrial products and any farm products that do not compete directly with EEC products. For those few products (such as edible oils) that do compete, amounting to about 15 percent of present African exports, the barriers to entry will be lower than for any other non-EEC members. In effect, the convention opens up to the African countries a vast free market for their exports, present and potential. In return, the African countries have only to give exports from the EEC no less favorable treatment than they give to exports from third countries. Under previous agreements the EEC nations had required that their exports receive preferences in return for the preferences they gave. The United

States and many other countries had objected to these so-called reverse preferences, which under the new convention no longer exist.

The convention signifies that the EEC has granted the African nations an enormous potential asset for their industrialization, for industries can move freely into Africa and yet remain within the EEC free trade area. It also reinforces and confirms the close ties Africa has had with Western Europe in the past, as contrasted with relations between Europe and the LDCs of Asia and Latin America.

In addition to the trade advantages, the EEC has agreed to make available 3.39 billion "units of account," or around $4 billion, in aid, more than two-thirds of it in grants and the bulk of it for the African countries. (Nigeria has announced it will not take advantage of this aid fund.) This is a substantial increase over the amounts the EEC had made available to the 18 African countries covered in earlier agreements (1957-64, $500 million; 1964-69, $730 million; 1969-75, $920 million).

A most important pioneering arrangement agreed to as part of the convention is a provision that earmarks about $400 million of the aid for use in stabilizing the LDC's earnings from exports of their primary commodities—cotton, tea, cocoa, coffee, bananas, sisal, groundnuts, copra, hides and skins, palm products, and timber—and one mineral product, iron ore. The proposed stabilization scheme, known as STABEX, provides that when export earnings from a product drop below their average level of the previous four years, the countries concerned will be at least partially compensated for the loss in earnings. The poorest 24 countries can claim compensation when earnings drop by as little as 2.5 percent below the average, nor will they be obligated to repay the funds to STABEX when earnings recover. For richer countries the drop in earnings must be at least 7.5 percent, the money to be repaid when and if earnings boom. For sugar producers a special provision guarantees for a minimum of seven years the sale of up to 1.4 million tons of sugar a year at a price indexed to the price of beet sugar fixed under the EEC common agricultural policy. When the world sugar price exceeds the EEC price, the African producers can negotiate for more.

The convention, in short, not only recognizes the special relationship of Africa to Western Europe but also reinforces the economic structure on which that relationship rests.

New Economic Influences: The Soviet Union, China, Japan, the Arabs, and South Africa. During the 1960s and early 1970s, four international economic forces became newly important to black Africa: the communist countries, Japan, the Arab countries, and the Republic of South Africa.

The Soviet Union and Eastern European countries began aid programs in Africa in the early postindependence years of the 1960s; while substantial for a time in a few countries (Guinea, Ghana, Somalia), these programs never provided as much as ten percent of the flow of capital resources from the OECD countries over the same period. By 1975 Soviet and Eastern European economic aid had become negligible, usually averaging less than a total of $100 million equivalent a year. The Soviet Union has tended in recent years to concentrate its aid in the Middle East and South Asia. China appears more interested in black Africa and its total commitments here run around $250-$300 million a year. (See Chapter XI, "The Search for an Aid Policy.") As for trade, while trade agreements with one country or another occasionally have brought a flurry of Soviet imports from Africa, overall African trade with the communist states has remained very small. On the basis of their per capita incomes, Eastern European countries and the Soviet Union should be a major market for African products, but the communist system of state trading monopolies ensures that the potential demand is not realized. This situation is likely to persist as long as the communist countries are unable to produce commodities that the African countries would find attractive to buy and thus provide the offsetting purchases the state trading monopolies require.

It was not until the early 1970s that Japan, the Arab countries, and the Republic of South Africa arose as important international economic influences on black Africa. By 1975, black Africa's trade with Japan was about equivalent to its trade with the communist countries. Although it was not yet an important source of economic aid for Africa, Japan was beginning to include the continent in its aid plans. More important, Japanese firms were making a determined effort to find mineral investments in Africa that would produce exports for Japan—either by entering into partnership with a local government (for example, copper in Zaire) or by providing the assured market needed to sustain local development of a resource (for example, iron ore in Swaziland). As Japan increasingly widens its sources of primary products, semiprocessed goods, and simple manufactures beyond East and South Asia, its importance to Africa will grow perhaps even more rapidly than the Japanese economy itself, already the third largest in the world.

After the jump in oil prices in 1973, the Arab oil-exporting countries began extending aid to African countries, in part to offset the impact of higher oil prices but also for reasons quite apart from the price factor. During 1974, $100 million of a $200 million Special Arab Fund for Africa was to be distributed; during 1975, the second half was supposed to be disbursed.

In June 1974, the Assembly of heads of state and government of the Organization of African Unity requested that the African Development Bank (the regional bank to which most African nations belong) be entrusted with the administration of the Special Fund. In fact, only $25 million was channeled through the African Development Bank and the rest was disbursed by the Arab League directly, using the basic criteria suggested by the ADB. The Kuwait Fund for Arab Economic Development was expanded to $3 billion and its area of activity widened to include developing countries throughout the world, including Africa. It had already become an important source of investment funds for the Sudan. The African Development Bank, starved for funds since its beginning in 1964, now began to receive lendable funds from oil exporters such as Libya and Nigeria ($30 million from each) but still far less than the bank could handle.

Instead of channeling their funds mainly through African institutions, the Arabs apparently intend to keep their money firmly under their own control—if necessary in new Arab institutions. One of these is the Arab Bank for African Development, set up in Khartoum in January 1975, with a capital of $231 million for loans to non-Arab African countries. Also indicative of this trend is the growth in purely bilateral lending. Libya, while disbursing its own funds, also joined with the World Bank in March 1975 in a $200 million mining investment in Zaire. Saudi Arabia, Kuwait, Libya, and Egypt have undertaken to help the government of Guinea (a largely Muslim country) to exploit its bauxite and process it into alumina, which will be exported to the oil-producing countries to be refined into aluminum, using cheap electric power generated from natural gas. Several Arab countries have agreed to help the Islamic Republic of Mauritania to refinance its copper mine, which was severely hurt by the 1975 fall in copper prices, in the process buying out the interests of Charter Consolidated and the World Bank's International Finance Corporation. Saudi Arabian investors, the Kuwait Fund, Abu Dhabi, and other Arab oil interests are investing in Sudan, attracted in large part by the prospects for increasing food output there and, in the longer term, making Sudan an Arab granary.

While the oil price boom lasts, African countries clearly will be able to attract Arab oil money to finance African projects. It is equally clear, however, that the Arabs will give priority to other Arab and Muslim countries and that the funds made available to black African countries will not completely offset the burden of higher oil costs.

Finally, the Republic of South Africa, the continent's most industrialized nation, has entered the aid and investment picture. As a part of Prime Minister Vorster's "opening to the North," South Africa has lent Malawi $12 million toward building its new capital of Lilongwe, $16 million for a rail link to the Mozambique port of Nacala, and $28 million for a new railway between Lilongwe and Mchinji on the Zambian border. By trucking goods to Mchinji, Zambia will have a new rail route to the sea. South Africa has also lent Mozambique and Angola more than $22 million for sugar mills, pipe lines, and dams.

Patterns of Development Since Independence

By historical measures, black Africa has shown a good rate of economic growth since the early 1960s, when most countries of the region became independent. From 1961 through 1973, regional gross domestic product (GDP) grew by about five percent a year in real terms—considerably faster than the industrialized countries grew during the eighteenth and nineteenth centuries and at about the same rate as the industrialized countries have grown in recent years. Because of the much higher rates of population increase in Africa, however, the per capita growth rates were one-half to two-thirds those of the industrialized countries. In absolute terms, the annual rise in per capita GDP in the United States was often as great as the total per capita GDP in the average African country—about $200.

A most important economic trend since 1960 is that growth rates among African countries have differed substantially: some countries have stagnated or even retrogressed, others have grown moderately, and still others have grown rapidly—even very rapidly. By 1975 the difference in arithmetic terms in per capita GNP (even more so in GDP) between the highest per capita black African country, Gabon, and the lowest (for example, Rwanda, Upper Volta, Burundi) was greater—over 20 to 1—than the difference between the United States and Gabon—about 4 to 1.

The causes of this wide spectrum of growth rates are likely to prevail in the future as they have in the immediate past. They fall into sets that sometimes work independently, sometimes reinforce each other, and sometimes offset each other. The first set is the natural environment: location, resources, and climate. The landlocked countries of the Sahel, afflicted by drought and with few known mineral resources, were condemned to very small rates of economic growth or none at all. In other countries, such as Uganda, the government created so much insecurity for its own citizens as well as for foreign technical assistance, foreign aid, and investment, as to halt economic growth or bring retrogression. Insecurity caused by actual or incipient civil war has similar results.

A government's development strategy is another important, even decisive, factor in setting the pace of economic growth. At one extreme is Guinea, seeking to run a centrally planned economy in African conditions and showing a zero rate of growth over the period. At the other extreme is Ivory Coast, basing its economic strategy on decentralized decisionmaking and encouraging foreign private investors, with an average growth rate of about eight percent a year.

The relative priority a country places on economic development is yet another important factor. A rough measure of priority is the ratio of government tax revenues to gross national product—rough because it is relatively easy, for example, for a country with a high ratio of foreign trade to increase its tax revenues, since it is easier to collect taxes on foreign trade than on internal activity. And the fact that tax revenues are higher in one country does not necessarily mean that each unit of revenue will be used as effectively to finance development-serving activities as it might be in another country with lower revenues.

The average tax ratio in the OECD countries in 1969-71 was 26 percent, excluding social security taxes. In his useful book *Development Planning*,[2] W. Arthur Lewis concludes that "most underdeveloped countries need to raise at least 17 percent of gross domestic product in taxes and other government revenues, taking central and local authorities together". Table V-10 shows the tax ratios for a spectrum of African countries, together with a selected group of less-developed countries elsewhere. The African countries do not compare unfavorably at all.

Growth rates are also affected by the amount of economic aid, technical assistance, and foreign investment a country receives. An area like the French Territory of the Afars and Issas, with full access to the flow of French government funds and personnel made available to territories associated with France, has received aid on a per capita basis equivalent to 50 times or more that available to other countries. Tanzania's growth rate has reflected its special attraction for a large variety of aid donors. (These attractions include its socialist and cooperative approach to ownership of the economy, its income redistribution policies preventing enrichment of a small elite, and its moral foreign positions which do not condone tyrannical excesses of power in non-African and African states.) On a per capita basis, however, Tanzania has been far less favorably treated than some of the French-speaking countries.

The country with the highest growth rate in the region, Gabon, combines

Table V-10
Tax Ratios of Selected Developing Countries, 1969-71

Country	Taxes as Percent of GNP	Levels of Government Covered
Zambia	31	All
Zaire	29	Central
Ivory Coast	20	Central
Sudan	18	Central
Senegal	18	Central
Ghana	16	Central
Kenya	14	All
Tanzania	14	Central
India	13	Central
Argentina	13	Central
Mali	13	All
Burundi	11	Central
Togo	11	Central
Upper Volta	10	All
Ethiopia	9	Central
Rwanda	8	All
Nepal	4	Central

Source: Selected from R.J. Chelliah and others, "Tax Ratios and Tax Efforts in Developing Countries" (International Monetary Fund Staff Papers, Vol. XXII, No. 1, March 1975).

several sets of favorable factors: possession of rich natural resources (oil, manganese, uranium, tropical timber), a population of only about half a million with a low growth rate of around one percent a year, stable government, and a large inflow of foreign investment and economic aid.[3]

Africa in 1985

Because Africa's economic and financial weight in the world economy is still relatively small, global economic trends will remain the predominant force in African economies in 1985, and Africa's economic fortunes will have little influence on economic activity in the rest of the world. Consequently, in trying to suggest what African economies will be like in 1985, one must make some basic assumptions about the world economy in that year. My assumptions do not coincide with those of the author of Chapter VIII of this book.

The World of 1985

The OECD countries (the United States, Western Europe, Japan, Australia, and New Zealand) will still compose the most important group of industrialized countries. The relative weight of Japan will be considerably greater within the group, however. The interruption in economic growth of the industrialized market countries that occurred in 1975 will not last long and growth will be resumed as in the 1960s, though possibly at a somewhat slower rate. The USSR and Eastern European countries will have continued to grow industrially and will be somewhat more open to international trade than in 1975. The same is true of China; it will clearly have become an industrialized country with a total industrial output equivalent to that of Japan in 1960. Outside these areas, the number of industrialized countries will have increased considerably. In Asia, South Korea, Taiwan, and Iran should by then be in the industrial category. According to the President of the Inter-American Development Bank, Latin American industry as a whole should be comparable by 1985 to that of the European Economic Community in 1960. Growing industrial areas will exist in Malaysia, Indonesia, India, Pakistan, the Persian Gulf states, Saudi Arabia, Egypt, and Algeria.

In sum, the world in which the African countries must function in 1985 will be a richer, more industrialized world providing considerably greater export opportunities, and therefore development opportunities, for those African countries that are able and willing to grasp them. To a ponderable degree, *ability* and *willingness* will depend on the nature of government in each country. It is impossible, at least for an economist, to predict whether an African country will fall under the control of a tyrant, still less whether a tyrant fearful of his people will govern in such a way as to choke economic development or bring about actual retrogression. In the analysis that follows, it is assumed that the form of government in 1985 will not markedly affect the development of any African country discussed.

Migration of Industry

Between 1975 and 1985 both the Europeans and the Japanese can be expected to export a significant part of their labor-intensive industries to the LDCs. Both areas have largely exhausted their indigenous labor reserves, and low population growth rates ensure that their labor forces will not grow appreciably during this period. Western Europe, with some ten million migrant laborers in 1975, has begun to appreciate the social problems that accompany large-scale immigration and will increasingly focus national policies on exporting labor-intensive, less-technical industries rather than importing foreign labor. Japan, facing a shortage of labor, already has decided against permitting large-scale immigration and has made it a national policy to move such industries overseas. Expansion of industries making large use of natural resources will also be directed to overseas locations.

The United States, in contrast, is likely to continue to have an abundant total industrial labor supply. Although migration from agriculture has practically ceased, children of the post-World War II baby boom are now in the labor market; to the roughly 400,000 legal immigrants allowed to enter the United States each year, around a million political refugees in the last 20 years have been added, along with an unknown but very large illegal immigrant population totalling in the millions. Therefore the export of labor-intensive industry is not likely to be good policy for the United States. On the other hand, the United States, Western Europe, and Japan should find it economical to export energy-intensive industries, such as aluminum refining and other electrometal-lurgical and electrochemical processes, to the oil- and natural gas-producing countries and to African countries with a large hydropower potential, such as Zaire. Even if existing industries are not exported, a substantial part of their growth should take place outside the industrial nations.

The Lomé Convention giving African countries duty-free access to the EEC for their manufactures provides a special attraction for the export of EEC-owned or managed industries to black Africa. Countries such as Senegal, Ivory Coast, Cameroon, Ghana, and Kenya almost certainly will benefit from this movement. Exports of manufactures can be expected to represent an important and growing share of their total exports. Such countries—those that are fairly hospitable to foreign direct investment and have a record of respecting law and judicial processes—have good prospects for attaining GNP growth rates of six to eight percent a year over most of the next decade. By 1985 their per capita GNP should have risen to the $400-$600 range (in 1972 dollars), placing them among the middle-income developing countries. Because of their currently low relative level of development, however, they are not likely to attract as much industry as, say, the Mediterranean or some of the Latin American countries. They will have good rates of growth but not the explosive rates that propelled Taiwan, South Korea, and Singapore into the industrialized class within a decade.

Economic Disparities Will Widen

Aside from the possibility of new industries imported from abroad, other major economic forces in Africa can be expected to continue to operate during the decade as they do at present. This means that African countries will diverge more and more from one another in economic development, the spectrum from the poorest to the richest widening even more than it has in the 1970s.

Barring the unexpected discovery of substantial amounts of oil or natural gas in the Sahel (and there is little exploration for either in this area), the landlocked, resource-poor Sahel countries are not likely to improve their economic condition very much by 1985. As William A. Hance explains elsewhere in this volume, so great are the climatic handicaps, scarcity of resources, and obstacles to increased agricultural production that not much can be accomplished in ten years. Comparable disadvantages have similar consequences in the densely populated, landlocked countries of Rwanda, Burundi, and Lesotho, in the Central African Republic, and in arid Somalia.

At the other end of the spectrum is Gabon, with a high per capita GNP in 1975 but with much of its population still not benefitting from the investment in oil and other mineral developments. By 1985, however, most of Gabon's small population should have moved into the modern sector, making Gabon the first black African country to establish a completely modern economy. Gabon's per capita GNP of $3,000 or more in that year would be comparable with that of Italy or the United Kingdom today.

Most of the other countries will be arrayed between Gabon and the Sahel countries, with more of them nearer the Sahel end than near Gabon. Where a particular country falls in this spectrum will depend partly on its richness of known and exploited resources, partly on the wisdom of its economic and financial policies. A special subset of countries is composed of those that in the short run are giving less priority to economic growth and greater priority to efforts to restructure their economies to increase egalitarianism (as in Tanzania), to eliminate long-entrenched feudal elements (Ethiopia), or to achieve a particular ideological objective (Benin, Guinea, Guinea-Bissau). Whether or not attainment of these objectives would accelerate their economic growth in the longer run, in the 1975-85 decade the attempt almost certainly will cause these countries to have slower growth rates than they could have attained otherwise.

By 1985, their annual per capita GNP figures are unlikely to exceed $150, as against 1973 per capita GNP of $80 in Ethiopia, $110 in Guinea, and $130 in Tanzania (in 1972 dollars).

With per capita GNPs of $200 to $300 in 1975, countries such as Sierra Leone, Liberia, Togo, and Cameroon are not only richer than those just discussed but also likely to make somewhat faster progress. If by 1985 oil in substantial quantities has been discovered off their coasts, where exploration currently is under way, these countries will begin to receive returns that will move them more rapidly across the spectrum in the direction of Gabon.

Congo, Mozambique, Angola, Botswana, Swaziland, and Zambia, with per capita GNPs ranging from $300 to around $400, have good enough resources or locations to double their outputs by 1985. In the case of Mozambique and Angola, doing so clearly will depend on how their postindependence governments are organized and whether they retain, get rid of, or replace experienced Portuguese civil servants, technicians, and entrepreneurs. It would be extraordinary if the political processes of adjustment, regrouping of forces, and learning by trial and error that follow independence went so smoothly that Mozambique and Angola could pursue optimum economic growth policies. This doubt is reinforced by the lack of preparation through degrees of self-government prior to independence. The probability is high, therefore, that Angola and Mozambique will not make rapid economic progress in the next decade.

Zaire

This prognosis is borne out by the experience of Zaire, which became independent in 1960 with a similar absence of preparation. By 1975, Zaire had made progress in the mining, manufacturing, and other modern sectors; but in agriculture, which depends on thousands of small farmers producing for the home market and for export, output had not recovered to the 1960 level. The main obstacle to Zaire's economic growth continues to be a shortage of trained staff and a consequent weakness of governmental functions. In these circumstances, enclave investment often succeeds while broader development suffers, since the latter depends on efficient performance of a multitude of governmental tasks such as routine road maintenance.

Zaire has large mineral resources, including at least a small oil field offshore, that can be further developed, and the enormous energy potential of the Congo River rapids has hardly been tapped. At the Inga site alone (the only one that has been studied in some detail) the hydropower potential is 40,000 megawatts— more than exists in the whole of North America. Since it has become technically and economically feasible to transport electricity as far as a thousand miles, industries based on power generated at Inga could be sited in Nigeria, Cameroon, Gabon, Congo, Angola, and Zambia. The higher costs of thermal energy in industrialized countries dependent on imported oil or coal could make Zaire and the countries within reach of Inga power attractive sites for a whole gamut of electrometallurgical and electrochemical industries. But in view of the time and other factors involved in building hydropower stations and the industries concerned, Zaire probably at best will have doubled its 1973 per capita GNP of $140 by 1985.

Nigeria

The giant among black African countries in size and population,[4] Nigeria is becoming an economic giant as well, with development of its sizable oil and gas reserves. Its GNP rose from $9 billion in 1972 to about $20 billion in 1975, in part through economic growth but in larger measure through the quadrupling of oil prices in 1973-74. At $20 billion, Nigeria's GNP amounted to one-third of the total for the whole of black Africa and approached that of the Republic of South Africa, hitherto far ahead of the rest of the continent. Yet, overall, Nigerians in 1975 were still among the poorest Africans. Leaving oil income aside, GNP per capita was around $130; including oil in the calculations raised per capita GNP to around $300.

The oil revenues give Nigeria an opportunity for development unprecedented in black Africa. Nigerian government revenues from oil rose from just over $1 billion in 1972 to about $2 billion in 1973; in 1975 they were expected to reach $8 billion. Though oil prices in real terms are likely to have receded from their 1974 peak long before 1985, increases in Nigerian oil and natural gas production during this period should offset most, if not all, of the decrease in prices. Even if revenues should drop to between $5 billion and $6 billion a year, Nigeria will have sufficient revenues to finance a massive development effort.

Everywhere in Africa the supply of trained manpower is an important constraint. In Nigeria it will be the main constraint. Close behind is the shallowness of technical knowledge of Africa's agricultural potential and natural resources. Even with money available to invest in improving agriculture, too little is known of better varieties of crops, of better techniques of cultivation, of the kinds and uses of insecticides, pesticides, weed-killers, or fertilizers that are cost-effective in Africa, to make possible dramatic increases in agricultural output and in the living standards of the small farmers who are the mass of the population. By 1985, however, research in progress at the International Institute of Tropical Agriculture (IITA) at Ibadan and at other international research institutes that have been organized in recent years should begin to provide answers to these questions. The IITA was founded in 1967 by the Ford and Rockefeller Foundations and has been sponsored and financed since 1971 by the Consultative Group on International Agricultural Research, composed of the World Bank, the United Nations Food and Agriculture Organization, the UN

Development Program, leading donor nations, the Ford, Rockefeller, and Kellogg foundations, the regional development banks, and other institutions. The Nigerian government joined the Consultative Group in December 1974 and donated the equivalent of $800,000 to help finance four of the international agricultural research centers, three of which are in Africa and one in India.

To meet the need for trained manpower, Nigeria is engaged in a major expansion of its education system. It hopes to introduce universal compulsory primary education throughout the country before the end of the 1970s. It is also expanding its secondary schools, teacher training institutes, and universities. But even with adequate resources and high motivation, education and training take time. By 1985, Nigeria should be well along toward lifting the manpower constraint, but the constraint will still be there.

Industrial development can proceed much faster. Oil and gas will attract industries using them as raw materials and Nigeria's financial resources will make it possible to import other industries as well, together with the technicians and managers needed to run them until Nigerians are trained to take over.

In consequence of these forces, the Nigerian economy should be one of the fastest growing in Africa. By 1985 per capita GNP should reach the neighborhood of $500—still well below that of the poorest of the industrialized countries of today. This projection assumes, of course, that the stresses rapid growth will set up in the society and government will be contained. Growth inevitably will be unequal in different parts of the country and in different industries; non-oil-based industries will have difficulty matching the oil industries' payoffs in wages, salaries, and other benefits. Since it is impossible to distribute the benefits of the new wealth in ways that everyone regards as fair, there will be a tendency to overload potential fault lines in the society, such as ethnic and regional rivalries.

On balance, however, Nigeria should become a major economic power in Africa and command attention elsewhere, even though its per capita income will be relatively low on a global scale. At the end of 1974, the nominal book value of American direct investment in Nigeria was shown at $238 million; in terms of the 1974 balance of payments income to the United States ($346 million) from this investment, a more reasonable estimate of its value would be around $1 billion. (The nominal book value of American direct investment in South Africa was $1,457 million at the end of 1974 and the balance of payments income to the United States was $117 million.) American imports from Nigeria (mostly oil) reached $3 billion in that year, at least five times the value of American imports from South Africa. American exports to South Africa were still greater than to Nigeria, but the latter were catching up fast. In 1975 Nigeria was the second largest source of United States oil imports. Because the largest source, Canada, has announced a national policy of eliminating oil exports to the United States, Nigeria probably will become our most important foreign supplier of oil in the 1975-1985 decade.

Despite its relatively low per capita GNP, Nigeria has begun providing economic aid to its African neighbors. It gave more than $15 million to the Sahel countries to help them overcome drought emergencies in 1974-75 even though Nigeria had a major problem in its own northern states. It is participating in the financing of an iron ore project in Guinea, from which iron ore will be imported for Nigeria's own steel industry in the 1980s, and of cement and sugar industries in Benin. As was noted above, Nigeria will forego receipt of the new EEC aid funds in order to leave more for other African countries. In 1975 Nigeria also lent the World Bank Group $240 million (eight percent, final maturity 15 years), the first long-term lending to an international institution by a sub-Saharan African country ever.

African Trends in 1985 and Their Meaning
for the United States

Africa's leading trends and problems in 1985 should differ little from those of 1975, except that most of them will be more acute. The problems of urbanization—growth of slums, traffic-choked streets, "unemployed"—will be even greater than in 1975. Population growth rates are likely to be even higher, since death rates will have continued to decline while birthrates, at best, will be only beginning to dip.

Economic relations with the EEC will retain their paramount position in most African countries, though the East African states are certain to find their trade and financial relations with Middle Eastern countries—especially Iran, Saudi Arabia, and Egypt—to be more important than in the past. Economic relations between the central and southern African countries and South Africa will presumably retain their importance. Japan will carry more weight in a number of countries, and trade across the South Atlantic with Brazil and Argentina will become significant for the first time in this century. On the other hand, Eastern Europe and China are likely to remain of minor economic importance to Africa. And the United States, except for its imports of oil and gas, is unlikely to be much more important to Africa than it is today.

What does this mean for the United States? Although we import substantial quantities of a few important minerals from Africa—industrial diamonds, cobalt, manganese, chromite, tantalite—and though Africa is an important alternative to the Middle East as a source of oil, the African countries cannot be called essential to the American economy. American investments in the continent are relatively small. On short-term economic grounds, then, the United States could give very low priority to Africa and to African interests.

Over the longer term, the United States posture toward Africa will depend on how much weight is given, *first*, to the general moral and ethical imperative that the affluent United States should help one of the poorest regions of the world improve the condition of its peoples; *second*, to the self-respect of the ten percent of the American people of African descent, who are likely to be increasingly interested in the progress of African countries; *third*, to the importance to be attached to the large number of African votes in the United Nations; *fourth*, to the importance, even in the comparatively brief span of a decade, of increasing the number and diversifying the sources of supply of commodities vital or useful to the United States; *finally*, to the value of establishing close relations with countries, some of which will certainly become significant markets and sources of supply for the United States in the next century.

If the United States decides that the economic development of Africa is worth supporting, it can choose among several options. In trade, the United States can try to match the EEC position by abolishing all or most tariffs and quota restrictions on African exports. This would be more difficult for the United States than it was for the EEC, since we cannot discriminate against our Latin American and Asian suppliers. In this instance, help to the African countries can be extended only in combination with help to other LDCs. Conversely, the United States could parallel the EEC-Africa axis by extending comparable benefits to Latin America, thus discriminating *against* Africa. Refraining from such discrimination in itself is a measure of help to Africa. That the United States was moving toward the alternative of extending tariff concessions to all less-developed countries, African and non-African, was indicated by the elimination, effective January 1, 1976, of tariff duties on about a fifth of United States imports coming from LDCs. Given the favorable current balance of payments that the United States enjoys, there is a potential for greatly increasing this way of helping Africa and other LDCs.

The United States is also beginning to recognize the particular problems experienced by developing countries dependent on exports of primary products whose prices fluctuate much more than the prices of manufactures. For all the major commodities of interest to Africa, the United States government has proposed the establishment of producer-consumer forums and the discussion of problems on a commodity-by-commodity basis. Membership in commodity agreements is decided on a case-by-case basis. During the 1960s, the United States was a member of an International Coffee Agreement that was quite successful in stabilizing coffee prices; in early 1976, Washington was still considering whether or not to join a new agreement worked out by the coffee producers after a lapse of several years. The United States has agreed for the first time to join the long-existing International Tin Agreement. An International Cocoa Agreement, which is of primary interest to the African countries since the bulk of the world's cocoa is produced in Africa, took over a decade to negotiate; the United States has decided not to join until or unless the agreement is renegotiated.

In economic aid, a spectrum of decisions is available. The World Bank Group has stepped up its lending and easy-term credits in capital assistance so much that there is little need for the United States to expand its bilateral capital aid, though there is room for American help in financing the easy-term window of the World Bank Group. In addition, United States capital funds could be made available through the African Development Bank, currently so starved for resources that even relatively small sums would be extremely useful. A contribution of $75 million a year, for example, would make possible a doubling of its activity.

The United States has taken a leading role in securing an expansion of the International Monetary Fund's compensatory finance scheme, which (like the STABEX scheme under the Lomé accord described above) is designed to try to stabilize export earnings of the developing countries by financing shortfalls in revenues. The United States has also supported the setting up of a Trust Fund in the International Monetary Fund to be financed out of the sales of gold held by the IMF. This Trust Fund, which may secure resources of several billion dollars by 1980, will be available to finance on soft terms African countries experiencing particular balance-of-payments difficulties.

But the biggest needs in African development are for thorough surveys of investment possibilities, expert preparation of projects, and technical assistance in carrying them out. Africa's capacity to absorb this type of aid is so great that all the effective technical assistance the United States could provide could be put to good use. Another major need is for United States help in educating and training Africans, particularly in Africa. Again, the need may well exceed American ability to provide suitable personnel.

The United States has taken the lead in proposing that the International Finance Corporation of the World Bank undertake to bring together technical, managerial, and financial expertise to initiate and finance new mineral development. This proposal is of particular importance to Africa because, on the one hand, governments do not have the resources—financial, technical, or managerial—to start new and often necessarily large-scale mining operations, and, on the other hand, the large international mining groups are more reluctant to enter Africa in light of the recent history of nationalizations. Without some solution along the lines of this American proposal, African mineral resources may remain idle, neither contributing to African development nor to the world supply of needed commodities.

In summary, the next ten years will not be easy ones for Africa. Most of the agony of the process of structural change and transformation is still ahead. The African peoples no longer accept sickness and early death as inevitable; they realize they are very poor but that this can be changed for their children if not for them. African governments are keenly aware of the needs, the growing demands, and the impatience of their peoples—and also of their inability to accomplish what must be accomplished without help from the industrialized world.

Notes

1. Horace Miner, "The City and Modernization: An Introduction," in Horace Miner (ed.), *The City in Modern Africa* (London: Pall Mall Press, 1967), p. 1. Quoted in Colin Posser, *Urbanization in Tropical Africa: A Demographic Introduction*, (International Urbanization Survey, The Ford Foundation, 1972), p. 1.

2. W. Arthur Lewis, *Development Planning* (New York: Harper and Row, 1966), p. 129.

3. For a more detailed analysis of the position and background of the African economies at the beginning of the 1970s, see A.M. Kamarck, *The Economics of African Development* (rev. ed., New York and London: Praeger, 1971).

4. The size of Nigeria's population is in dispute. The United Nations has projected a total Nigerian population of 63 million in 1975, or about one-fourth the total number of black Africans (*United Nations, Urban and Rural Population 1950-1985*, ESA/P/W.P 33/RW 1, September 22, 1970). The Nigerian census arrived at a total of 83 million for 1973, implying rates of population growth for some areas that are impossibly high. Because the population of a state may affect its political weight or share of revenue under Nigeria's federal system, there is an incentive to inflate the numbers.

VI The Organization of African Unity

Claude E. Welch, Jr.

The most important single accomplishment of the Organization of African Unity is that it has survived for nearly a decade and a half. Despite bitter political disagreements between its members, no state has resigned since the OAU was founded in May 1963, and none of the 18 countries achieving independence (and eligible for membership) since that time has declined to join. The meetings of the Assembly of heads of state are recognized as critical annual events, with absences sometimes conveying messages as significant as attendance. Despite its many structural and functional weaknesses, of which the most crucial is that the only enforcement power in relation to wayward member states is the ability to exert collective moral pressure, the OAU is more than a token pancontinental ritual. Its failures, but also its success in maintaining a political nucleus around which some level of pan-African unity persists against all odds, can be attributed in part to the absence of any single overriding bloc or dominant leader.

How the OAU Was Shaped

To understand the strengths and constraints that characterize the OAU, we must return to the intellectual and political currents that shaped the organization at its birth in 1963. The founding meeting was preceded by intensive debate among the leaders of the newly independent African states about the degree of practical commitment to be made to the philosophical concept of African unity. It is an oversimplification, but basically accurate, to identify two schools of thought, each characterized by a distinctive set of assumptions. The first school, led by President Kwame Nkrumah of Ghana, believed that the balkanization created by the carving up of Africa at European bargaining tables at the outset of the colonial period could and should be wiped away, and a genuine "United States of Africa" created. Nkrumah had spent a decade (1935-45) as a student in the United States and the motto *E pluribus unum*—"out of many, one"—seemed to him as applicable to the African continent as it had been in creating the American melting pot. Nkrumah described his vision and his fears in an address to the Ghana parliament in 1959:

I look forward to the forging of links that will enable us to achieve what the Americans have achieved: A form of supranational and international organism. For I am firmly persuaded that unless we work towards a close organic identification within some form of constitutional Union of Africa, our Continent will remain what it is today—a balkanized mass of small individual units, used as a political and economic pawn by those external forces which seek to keep us divided and backward.[1]

He drew the parallel again on the eve of the founding of the OAU:

No one today doubts that the welfare and prosperity of the United States would never have been achieved if each state still cherished its petty sovereignty in splendid isolation. Yet in those days there was perhaps less obvious reason for South Carolina to join New Hampshire as members of a continental union than there is today for Ghana and Nigeria, Guinea and Dahomey, Togo and Ivory Coast, Cameroon and Mali, and others, to form themselves into a Union as a first step to the creation of a union of all the states of the African continent.[2]

Flowing against this pressure for amalgamation was what turned out to be a more powerful current—that of protecting newly won sovereignty at the national level. It was better to cement self-government by interstate cooperation, the coalitionists argued, than to enter into a hastily conceived and centralized union of African peoples who did not yet really know each other very well. The acrimonious collapse in 1960 of the Mali Federation, which joined two economically intertwined adjacent states (Senegal and Mali) of the same colonial background (French), strengthened the case of those leaders who saw the Nkrumah vision of unity as either premature or threatening.[3] Even so—especially after the Congo (now Zaire) slipped within a few months of independence from a highly centralized colonial regime into four antagonistic governments with extra-African sponsors, eloquently demonstrating the perils of isolated weakness—the commitment to some form of pan-African organization was widely shared. On one point, all African leaders could now agree with Nkrumah: that any kind of fissure among Africans might be seized and turned to "imperialist" or "Cold War" interests.

A vanguard of coalitionists, accepting the Nkrumah diagnosis if not his prescription, responded to the Congo crisis by creating the foundation for extensive political coordination in December 1960. Twelve newly independent countries formerly ruled by France convened in Brazzaville (the capital of "the other Congo") and hammered out a communique proclaiming their aim to realize "new progress on the road to . . . inter-African cooperation,"[4] and denouncing the "new form of colonization" undertaken by those who were "trying to recolonize the Congo." The mechanism by which the Congo (or any other African states thus afflicted) should be "protected from outside intervention through the intermediary of soldiers or diplomats"[5] was not spelled out.

A more radical (but scarcely Nkrumahist) formula for pan-Africanism was crystallized a month later at a meeting in Casablanca of seven other states— Guinea, Ghana, Mali, Egypt, Morocco, Libya, and the provisional government of Algeria. The call from Casablanca was for "an effective form of cooperation among the African states," including the creation of a consultative assembly representing all African states, a political committee of heads of state, an economic committee, a cultural committee, a military high command (to ensure "the common defense of Africa in the case of aggression against any part of this continent, and with a view to safeguarding the independence of African States"), and a liaison office to coordinate these groups.[6]

What came to be known in the course of time as the Brazzaville/Monrovia-Casablanca split persisted until May 1963, when 30 heads of state and government or their representatives met in Addis Ababa to devise and sign the charter of the Organization of African Unity. Although a small, vocal, and highly committed group, led by Nkrumah, continued to argue for a series of linked economic and political transformations that would permit Africa to deal with industrialized countries on a basis of parity, a clear majority sought a more limited form of pancontinental cooperation that would safeguard the still fragile independence of Africa without radically altering existing national entities. Immanuel Wallerstein has analyzed the contrasts between the two groups, identifying as the "core" those concerned with political unification, and the "periphery" those favoring an alliance among existing units:

For the core, unity was the unity of people, the theme of a revolutionary movement—its intentions were to transform Africa and thereby the world. For the periphery, unity was the ultimate point of an alliance of nation-states whose object was to strengthen the participants in the world power game, to advance them but not transform them. . . . Because they used the same slogan and occupied the same political terrain, the proponents of movement and the proponents of alliance were to work together, found it mutually useful to work together. . . .[7]

Thus the five-letter word "unity" was uttered hundreds of times in the formal presentations preceding the OAU's establishment, even though—or perhaps because—the word held different meanings for each adherent. Emperor Haile Selassie of Ethiopia, host for the founding conference, expressed the tenuous compromise achieved in the OAU charter in these terms: "Unity is the accepted goal. We argue about means, we discuss tactics. But when semantics are stripped away, there is little argument among us."[8] This foundation of a shared sentiment of being African has proved stronger than most observers predicted at the outset. As Zdenek Cervenka observed in 1974, "There is indeed no other international organization which has survived more predictions about its imminent collapse and disintegration. . . . Almost every OAU summit was viewed by the Western press as 'critical'; time has proved them all wrong."[9]

Values and Structure

Member states pledge in the OAU charter to protect seven principles: (1) the sovereign equality of all member states; (2) non-interference in the internal affairs of states; (3) respect for the sovereignty and territorial integrity of each member state and for its inalienable right to independent existence; (4) peaceful settlement of disputes by negotiation, mediation, conciliation, or arbitration; (5) unreserved condemnation, in all its forms, of political assassination as well as of subversive activities on the part of neighboring states or any other states; (6) absolute dedication to the total emancipation of the African territories which are still dependent; (7) affirmation of a policy of nonalignment with regard to all blocs.

The OAU can rightfully claim to represent all states on the African continent recognized as independent, with the exception of the Republic of South Africa, whose policies of apartheid have provided a continuing focus for the organization's activities. Thus, the membership as of mid-1976 totalled 49.

The Assembly

The "supreme organ" of the OAU is the "Assembly of Heads of State or Government." Meeting at least once a year, the Assembly may "discuss matters of common concern to Africa with a view to coordinating and harmonizing the general policy of the organization, and may, in addition, review the structure, functions, and acts of all the organs and any specialized agencies" that might be created under the charter. The sessions are customarily rotated among African states, balancing region (e.g., North, East, Central, or West Africa), language, and other considerations. Provision exists in the charter for emergency meetings of the Assembly, on the basis of a two-thirds majority; although the heads of state have been polled about such matters as the changing of meeting sites, the first extraordinary meeting was convened in January 1976 on Angola.

The Assembly, as well as other OAU organs, has gradually developed structure, continuity, and a pattern of leadership. The most significant change has been the emergence of the chairman as more than a figurehead, to a large extent eclipsing the prime role played by the secretary-general in the early years of the OAU. Although the charter makes no specific provision for executive leadership between the annual sessions of the heads of state, the need for a political spokesman carrying more weight than the secretary-general was a major factor in the gradual increase in the chairman's powers. While the chairman of the Assembly is not, and cannot be under the charter, an executive leader for the continent, he is the closest equivalent to a spokesman for Africa as a whole.

The chairmen of the OAU since 1963, following a predetermined schedule based on states rather than the popularity or length of incumbency of the head of state, have been: President Gamal Abd al-Nasser (Egypt), 1963-64; President Kwame Nkrumah (Ghana), 1964-65; Emperor Haile Selassie (Ethiopia), 1965-66; President Kenneth Kaunda (Zambia), 1966-67; Emperor Haile Selassie (Ethiopia), 1967-68; President Houari Boumedienne (Algeria), 1968-69; President Ahmadou Ahidjo (Cameroon), 1969-70; President Kenneth Kaunda (Zambia), 1970-71; President Moktar Ould Daddah (Mauritania), 1971-72; King Hassan V (Morocco), 1972-73; President Yakubu Gowon (Nigeria), 1973-74; President Siad Barre (Somalia), 1974-75; President Idi Amin Dada (Uganda), 1975-76. In 1976-77, the chairmanship passes to the prime minister of Mauritius.

United States Ambassador to the UN Daniel P. Moynihan's 1975 charge to the contrary notwithstanding, it *was* an accident of history (or ritual) that Uganda's President Idi Amin was elected 1975-76 chairman; the risks of breaking the precedent of choosing the next year's chairman from the state whose turn it is to host the Assembly, of possibly alienating Muslim states, and of questioning the internal sovereignty of Uganda, overrode the grave doubts in many African capitals about Amin's qualifications to speak for Africa in the year of Angola's perilous transition to independence. Those who found Amin's election too unpalatable simply stayed at home.

Precisely how powerful the chairmanship may be depends, in any given year, on the personal competence of the head of state serving his term in the office, the trust vested in him by other African leaders, his energy and effectiveness in dealing with issues that arise, and the complexity of the problems thrust upon him. The degree of agreement among members of the Assembly, and thus the effectiveness of the organization as a whole during a given chairman's tenure, may be based on factors that are largely personal. Scholars of international politics have given these personal factors in OAU decisionmaking only limited attention, in part because scholars are more comfortable with quantifiable factors than with subjective and idiosyncratic explanations of state behavior. But the fact is that the Organization of African Unity, given its present modest level of institutionalization, derives its power from the group norms that affect the behavior of heads of state and, through them, the foreign policies of the countries over which they preside.

Under these conditions, a decision by a head of state to boycott an Assembly meeting represents a calculated, important political act. Perhaps there is no better barometer with which to assess the health of the OAU than attendance records for the summit meetings—although it might be argued that failure to pay dues on time can also reflect disapproval or disenchantment. High attendance indicates general similarity of views among the participants—and a clear correlation exists between the number of presidents in attendance and the willingness of the heads of state to compromise in the interests of (what else?) African unity.

The "old boy" atmosphere of the first years of the Assembly has diminished, of course, with the expansion of the membership and the passing from the scene of many of the founding fathers of African nationalism. In the earlier years, peer pressure could effect extraordinary reconciliations among those who shared a common history in the forging of nations out of European colonies. The statistics alone suggest that personal ties may be weakening as a cement for OAU actions. Of the 30 heads of state who attended or were represented at the inaugural session, 11 attended or were represented a decade later (15 had been deposed, almost all in coups d'etat, and four had died in office). Three of the 11 "survivors" in 1973 were pushed out of office by 1974 through military intervention.

The three most recent chairmen all gained power through coups d'etat, reflecting the military's emergence as the key political actor in contemporary Africa. While the military backgrounds of more than half of Africa's current presidents could provide a set of shared experiences and assumptions facilitating cooperation, the prime concern of most governments dominated by members of the military appears often to be the resolution of the domestic grievances that brought them to power rather than the kinds of foreign policy issues to which their civilian predecessors gave attention. If diminished commitment to pan-African goals shared on a personal level with other heads of state should result from the increasing incidence of military intervention and the growing size of the OAU, the role of the Council of Ministers and the Secretariat in policy formulation could increase in importance.

The Council of Ministers

The Council of Ministers is the second major organ established under the OAU charter. The Council, comprised of the foreign ministers of each member state, has always been more directly involved than the Assembly with the ongoing management of the OAU. Although formal approval of the budget rests with the Assembly, for example, the crucial financial debates occur within the Council. Only once, in 1966, has the Assembly made significant changes in the budget as recommended by the Council.

The influence of the Council of Ministers is enhanced by the greater ease with which its members can convene. At least two sessions are scheduled annually, one preceding the Assembly (in recent years held in May or June), the other (in February) devoted to budgetary and political matters. Since 1966, the February sessions have been held in Addis Ababa, where the permanent headquarters of the Secretariat are located. The pre-summit sessions are scheduled in the city hosting the heads of state. In contrast to the Assembly, which met 12 times in the first 12 years, the Council held 25 regular and ten extraordinary sessions in the first dozen years of the OAU's existence; six of these special meetings were in the first 30 months, as the organization grappled with such diverse issues as the Algeria-Morocco border conflict, the 1964 military mutinies in East Africa, the Ethiopia-Somalia territorial dispute, the use of white mercenaries in the Congo (Zaire) in the 1960s, the locale of the 1965 summit, and the Unilateral Declaration of Independence by the white minority government of Southern Rhodesia in 1965. Resolutions passed by the Council must be approved formally by the Assembly. Since all member states are represented in the Council, and since foreign ministers generally do not stray from the policies set down by heads of state, Council resolutions are normally adopted without amendment, and often without dissension.

The Secretariat

The largest, most expensive, most active, most controversial, and least studied part of the OAU is the Secretariat. The chairman of the Assembly is the strongest political figure within the OAU, but even the most innovative and respected chairman is constrained by the annual rotation of this office. The Secretariat is charged with easing the transition and implementing that which the Assembly and its chairman initiate.

The focal point of the Secretariat is the secretary-general, who leads an inevitably hazardous existence because of the uncertainty of his mandate. Neither in the charter nor in practice has the OAU dealt conclusively with one basic question: is it the responsibility of the secretary-general to carry out the desires and decisions of the Assembly subject to strict supervision (a model necessitating tight controls and frequent reporting), or is he entrusted by the Assembly to implement its general policies in ways he regards as appropriate and feasible (a model allowing for relative autonomy, subject to periodic review)? Given the imprecision of the definition of the secretary-general's power, it is not surprising that filling this position has been among the most divisive issues to confront the Assembly.

According to the charter, the secretary-general is chosen by the Assembly, on the recommendation of the Council, to "direct the affairs of the Secretariat." A two-thirds majority of OAU member states must approve a candidate, who (according to the regulations of the OAU, though not always in fact) then serves for a four-year term. The selection process has become a lightning rod for discontent with the organization as a whole, as well as an arena within which different perceptions of the secretariat's role are aired. Issues of national pride (the "favorite son" phenomenon), of regional and linguistic balance, of personality, and (most fundamentally) of the candidate's expected level of activity all enter into the balloting. Balloting is often protracted, with lobbying and maneuvering behind the scenes.

The three secretaries-general who have served the OAU since its inception have all been from French-speaking Africa, and their backgrounds have been primarily administrative. Diallo Telli of Guinea, who held the position from 1964 to 1972, enjoyed a brilliant academic career before becoming the first Guinean to rise to the highest ranks of the French colonial service. As a government official after Guinea gained independence in 1958 under the presidency of Sekou Touré, he played a key behind-the-scenes role in persuading states to attend the 1963 Addis Ababa conference. Diallo Telli was the only candidate proposed at the 1964 summit, yet he repeatedly failed to receive the required majority of votes. His known penchant for personal and secret diplomacy, and his identification with Touré, aroused disquiet among the more conservative francophone states. Although a conflict of political philosophy clearly was involved, the challenges to the Guinean's candidacy took the form of legal and procedural arguments. In the final analysis, the election of Ambassador Diallo Telli was accomplished through a complex political deal involving distribution of privileges.[10] That these tensions surrounding the secretary-generalship had not abated was demonstrated in 1968, when Telli required six ballots to be reconfirmed in office.[11]

Nzo Ekangaki, elected secretary-general in 1972, grew up in the British Cameroons, but made his political mark in the Federal Republic of Cameroon, created in 1961 following the merger of the former United Nations trust territories of the (British) Southern Cameroons and (French) Cameroun. Ekangaki had studied at the University of Ibadan in Nigeria and at Oxford, and had served as a deputy in the federal Assembly and as Cameroon's Minister of Foreign Affairs, Health and Population, and Labor. His bilingualism helped bridge the language differentiations in the Secretariat, where English is used more than French in deference to the largely Ethiopian clerical staff. Ekangaki emerged from relative obscurity at the 1972 summit, and was elected almost without debate, on the assumption that the role of the secretary-general under his stewardship would revert to one of administration and coordination without illusions of major policymaking powers.[12] As it turned out, Ekangaki's term of office was short and stormy, for he unexpectedly became embroiled in a political controversy touching on the one issue with which the Assembly predictably speaks with an institutional voice. The firm selected by Ekangaki to work with the OAU in examining the impact of increased petroleum prices was one that had extensive investments in Rhodesia and South Africa. Although the secretary-general defended his choice, his position became so untenable that his resignation was accepted prior to the 1974 summit.

The choice of William Eteki Mboumoua of Cameroon as the successor to Ekangaki illustrates the complexity of OAU politics. Two respected foreign ministers, Vernon Mwaanga of Zambia and Omar Arteh of Somalia, were proposed to the 1974 summit. Each represented a distinct bloc within the organization: Mwaanga, English-speaking black Africa; Arteh, the choice of Arab North Africa. Neither could gain more than 25 of the 28 votes required for election. Arteh was at a disadvantage because he came from the same country as the 1974-75 chairman of the Assembly; Mwaanga's position was weakened by a split among French-speaking states. The balloting dragged on for 20 rounds before the heads of state wearily turned to a compromise. President Ahmadou Ahidjo of Cameroon, asked to find a suitable candidate, proposed Eteki, a civil servant with a range of appropriate experience (Special Adviser to Ahidjo, Minister of Education, Youth and Culture in Cameroon, UNESCO Executive Council, and special adviser to the OAU Committee for the Middle East) and a reputation for a low profile, noncontroversial style.

One useful balancing device in the backstage political maneuvering that goes into the choice and monitoring of the secretary-general is the selection of his deputies. The charter provides for "one or more assistant secretaries-general," and general OAU practice has been to name four—a number which allows for geographic and linguistic balance, enlarges the pool of high-level managerial talent, and encourages a search for complementing personal strengths. While the latter two considerations are important to the workings of the Secretariat, the choices made are of states (e.g., Algeria, Kenya, Nigeria, and Zaire in 1973), rather than individuals. Each member country has a de facto veto power over the selection of personnel—despite the charter provision (Article XVII, Section 1) that administrative staff "shall not seek or receive instructions from any government. . . ." In short, the OAU still lacks a cadre of international civil servants owing their allegiance to the organization. Antagonizing a head of state can result in overnight restaffing.

In the area of budget, as in personnel, the OAU is handicapped by the fact that politics are paramount. Although member states are assessed percentages (based on the formula devised for funding the United Nations) of the annual budget, there is no effective means of insuring payment of subscriptions on time. The charter merely notes, "The member states agree to pay their respective contributions regularly." The secretary-general's revelation at the 1965 Assembly that 24 of the (then) 36 member states had neglected to pay *any* part of their dues is illustrative of the financial uncertainty under which the Secretariat must operate. Not until 1968 could the secretary-general announce, "for the first time, we shall have a normal and regular budget. . . ."[13]

Even when member states meet their commitments, the OAU operating budget is extremely modest in relation to the potential scope of OAU interests.

Expenditures during the 1960s, when membership contributions generally fell below the expected levels, ranged between $2.5 and $3 million annually. The total costs of the OAU in its first decade would purchase less than half a B-1 supersonic bomber.

While this financial anemia reflects the economic weaknesses and underdevelopment of Africa as a whole, and the priority that is given to domestic claims (government, education, health, transport, defense), a more basic cause has been the reluctance to contribute substantial sums directly to the OAU or its offshoots because of skepticism about the benefits derived. Individual heads of state extol unity; they participate vigorously at the annual summits; yet they remain unconvinced of the organization's effectiveness below the level of personal palaver among heads of state and foreign ministers, or outside the political realm. The limited achievements of the OAU in such areas as regional planning, scientific cooperation, and in supporting and coordinating movements seeking to achieve majority rule in southern Africa can be related primarily to these unresolved doubts about apolitical pan-Africanism.

The Specialized Commissions

The charter proposed the creation of several specialized commissions under OAU aegis, dealing respectively with educational and cultural matters; economic and social affairs; health, sanitation, and nutrition; scientific and technical research; and defense. The first summit added two additional such commissions, one for transport and communications, and another of jurists. Some started with flourishes of activity; others remained paper entities; all proved costly. Perhaps the most successful has been the Commission on Scientific and Technical Research, based on an existing entity (the Commission for Technical Cooperation and Research South of the Sahara, or CCTA, created in 1950 by France and Britain, with cooperation from other colonial powers). In 1968, the seven special commissions were collapsed into three: Economic and Social; Education, Science and Culture; and Defense.

Generalizations about activities of the special commissions are apt to be misleading, given the extraordinary range of performance. Suffice it to say that (1) the commissions meet irregularly and seem to have little direct impact on the policymaking of individual OAU members; (2) the more technical and less "political" the entity, the lower its status in the organization; (3) the commissions have rarely succeeded in carrying their activities to a (political) level necessitating the approval of the heads of state.

This is not a statement of failure as much as it is an underlining of the reality that the OAU is preeminently a *political* institution. It was not designed to achieve technological objectives, as is the Universal Postal Union, or directed primarily toward defense or economic purposes, as are NATO, the Latin

America Free Trade Area, or the Economic Commission for Africa. These regional and international organizations are not devoid of politics, to be sure, but their success in achieving perceived objectives depends on member states' willingness to subordinate domestic concerns in the hope of greater mutual advance. In the case of the OAU, the political issues with which the member states (and thus the organization itself) are primarily concerned are those related to the protection of national sovereignties.

The fate of the Commission of Mediation, Conciliation, and Arbitration—the only "regular" commission (as opposed to the "specialized commissions" described above) ordained by the OAU charter—is a case in point. The commission was to be composed of 21 individuals chosen by the Assembly for five-year terms, and it was empowered to take jurisdiction over interstate disputes on the request of the Council, the Assembly, or either or both parties to the dispute. Its protocol, which is almost as long as the OAU charter, authorizes the use of mediation, conciliation, or arbitration to resolve issues within its jurisdiction. Despite the importance attached to the commission in initial OAU documentation, it was not established until 1965, did not meet until 1968, and has never functioned effectively.[14] Settling controversies between nations, it soon became apparent, required political compromises only heads of state can bring about. Neither the secretary-general nor the commission has been entrusted with the delicate task of dealing with any major conflict or potential conflict.

Thus, the boundary dispute between Algeria and Morocco, marked by intense fighting near the Tindouf oasis in 1963, was initially mediated by Emperor Haile Selassie of Ethiopia and President Hamani Diori of Niger; their efforts, and continuing pressure from other heads of state, led to a formal announcement of agreement at the 1972 summit. Mediation of relatively minor disputes in 1972 and 1973 between Tanzania and Uganda, Equatorial Guinea and Gabon, Tanzania and Burundi, and Burundi and Rwanda was coordinated by the secretary-general and the Council of Ministers, but the serious crises (especially those involving divisions within nations) required presidential-level pressures. An ad hoc commission, headed by President Jomo Kenyatta of Kenya and including Cameroon, Egypt, Ethiopia, Ghana, Guinea, Nigeria, Somalia, Tunisia, and Upper Volta, was created to monitor the 1964-65 crisis in Zaire, which had led to strained relations with neighboring Congo-Brazzaville. Reconciliation of a dispute between Guinea and Senegal required the presence of nine heads of state in Liberia in May 1972. Mali's refusal to permit a special OAU military subcommission to visit the border zone during 1974-75 clashes (over an unclearly demarcated border with Upper Volta) again required presidential-level activity.

In summary, it has seldom been the OAU as an institution but rather an ad hoc group of heads of state operating under OAU aegis that has registered any success in reconciling African disputes. The record of failures and successes suggests that even presidential-level efforts are more effective in resolving boundary quarrels than territorial ones, and then only if vital national interests are not involved.

OAU mediation efforts have not been confined to intra-African questions. Probably the most significant organizational initiative was directed toward the troubled Middle East. The 1971 summit set up a peace committee—composed, as one would expect, of highly regarded heads of state. The members included Emperor Haile Selassie and Presidents Ahidjo (Cameroon), Gowon (Nigeria), Houphouet-Boigny (Ivory Coast), Kenyatta (Kenya), Mobutu (Zaire), Nyerere (Tanzania), Ould Daddah (Mauritania), Senghor (Senegal), and Tolbert (Liberia). Supplementing the "shuttle diplomacy" of United Nations envoy Gunnar Jarring, a subcommittee of Ahidjo, Gowon, Mobutu, and Senghor made contact with the Egyptians and Israelis, listened carefully to both sides, and suggested ways of reactivating negotiations. Israeli intransigence over the issue of withdrawing to its 1967 boundaries, as urged by both the United Nations and OAU mediators, is said to have accelerated the rupture of diplomatic relations between black Africa and Israel in 1972 and 1973 (see Chapter I), a development consistent with the OAU position on the sanctity of borders.

Limitations on the OAU: Planned and Unplanned

Four civil wars involving casualties in the hundreds of thousands have raged in Africa since the OAU was created. In the Nigerian civil war, the Assembly created a six-state ad hoc consultative commission (under the chairmanship of Emperor Haile Selassie) which succeeded in bringing the two sides together for discussion—but not in moving them toward an agreement. The civil wars in Burundi and Sudan passed essentially unremarked upon, if not necessarily unnoticed. In the case of Angola, it was only after the major powers and South Africa had become directly involved that the OAU moved toward a center-stage role. The Eritrean secessionist movement in Ethiopia has been officially ignored, and the competing claims of Algeria, Mauritania, and Morocco to the Spanish Sahara have been only peripherally considered by the OAU at this writing.

"Sovereign equality of all Member States" and "non-interference in the internal affairs of States" are the first two principles set forth in Article III of the charter. Since changes of government within African states, however achieved, are not in the OAU's province, the organization as such has acquiesced to the changes, most frequently by coups d'etat, that have occurred in half its member states during the past decade. The only two exceptions to the "see no evil" stance have involved the ouster of African leaders with the purported connivance of outside powers.[15] In sum, the OAU is an organization composed of *states*; the process by which heads of member states are selected is not one of direct legal or moral concern to the Assembly. When Nigeria's prestigious

President Yakubu Gowon received news of his overthrow while sitting in the 1975 Assembly in Kampala, Uganda, regrets were privately, not publicly, expressed by fellow chiefs of state; some flew home to make sure the same thing did not happen to them.

The "Liberation" of Southern Africa

Despite the affirmation, in the first clause of the charter's preamble, of "the inalienable right of all people to control their own destiny," and despite the increasingly strident resolutions passed in support of majority rule in Rhodesia and the Republic of South Africa, consensus has never existed within the Assembly on the most effective means of achieving political change in southern Africa. At their first session, the heads of state resolved to (1) break off diplomatic and consular relations with Portugal, Rhodesia, and South Africa, (2) boycott foreign trade with these nations, (3) establish a coordinating committee for liberation movements (thereafter referred to as the "Liberation Committee"), (4) collect voluntary contributions for a liberation fund, (5) train members of these movements, and (6) furnish volunteers to assist the quest for freedom.

Nine states—Algeria, Egypt, Ethiopia, Guinea, Nigeria, Senegal, Tanzania, Uganda, and Zaire—originally constituted the Liberation Committee. Its headquarters were established in Dar es Salaam, Tanzania. Almost immediately, the underfinanced and overcommitted agency became a target of attacks from both left and right—for making exaggerated and impractical military threats beyond its conceivable capabilities, for not being militant enough, for frittering away its limited resources in inefficient support of too many competing groups, for not recognizing the longer term "liberating" potential of dialogue with South Africa.

As a result of this swirl of controversy, the parent organization gradually extended its control over the Liberation Committee's activities. Membership was gradually broadened to include Somalia and Zambia (1965) and six other states (1972) for a total of 17. In 1966, non-voting attendance at committee meetings was opened to all OAU members, and the Council of Ministers officially circumscribed the committee's authority by limiting its competence to action and administration (restricting policymaking to the Assembly), and by placing it under the overall control of the Secretariat.

Yet the criticism persisted. As Cervenka observed in 1968, "Activity has increasingly been paralyzed, on the one hand by the failure of the members to agree on what movements should be recognized, where arms should be bought and the general strategy to be applied, and on the other hand by the reluctance of African states which are not members of the committee to pay their assessments."[16] A special commission consisting of the Central African Republic, Algeria, Ethiopia, Kenya, Morocco, Senegal, and Sierra Leone to study the

Liberation Committee was proposed at the 1968 summit; its report, submitted in 1970, was referred back for "further study." In 1973, a new storm erupted within the Council of Ministers when the secretary-general presented a report proposing that all activities of the Liberation Committee be placed under the immediate supervision of the Secretariat.

The extent to which OAU support has strengthened individual liberation movements is a matter of heated conjecture, in part because rhetoric disguises substance. In some cases, competition for OAU funding may have resulted in the placing of greater stress on lobbying in Dar es Salaam than on undermining minority governments. The most successful African guerrilla group, the PAIGC of former Portuguese Guinea (now independent Guinea-Bissau), mobilized the rural populace and immobilized Portuguese forces without extensive OAU aid. There is evidence thát the squabbles in Angola among the three major rival movements (and between factions in these movements) may have been exacerbated by the attractions of Liberation Committee support. OAU recognition, or indication of preference, can bestow a kind of legitimacy on a particular group and facilitate its access to bilateral aid as well as assistance from United Nations specialized agencies.

Military Cooperation

The unresolved issue of minority rule in Rhodesia and South Africa raises the question of an eventual OAU role in coordinating military strategy if détente and dialogue should give way to open black-white confrontation. Prior to the creation of the OAU, Ghana's Nkrumah lobbied vigorously for an African High Command on the grounds that the weakness of independent African states vis-à-vis South Africa made cooperation imperative; in 1963 South Africa's military budget was one-third of that for all of Africa. The founders of the OAU did not share Nkrumah's sense of urgency sufficiently to tinker with their armed forces by creating a single high command, however. The Defense Commission written into the organization's specialized agencies was largely dormant during the 1960s. By the early 1970s, there was some talk of creating regional defense systems (northeast, northwest, and central/east have been suggested) with individual states deciding which, if any, of their units to assign to the regional command, and the OAU kept informed through a coordinating and intelligence-gathering Council of Military Defense Advisers within the Secretariat. Meanwhile, of course, the military power of some member states had grown considerably.

Relationships with Regional and Functional Subgroups

Proposals for regionalization of military activities raise the more general question of regional and functional groupings of African states. While this is a chapter devoted to the OAU, and not to the panoply of interstate groups, some ephemeral and some flourishing, that have taken shape in Africa, these functional, regional, and linguistic unions warrant brief attention here for three reasons: they fill gaps in the OAU grid; they exemplify the practical and political obstacles to effective coordination in Africa; and they illustrate the distinctive political nature of the OAU itself.

The preamble to the charter (over which the heads of state debated as long as they did over the 33 articles that follow) asserts the desire that "all African states should henceforth unite so that the welfare and well-being of their peoples can be assured." Article II calls upon member states to "coordinate and harmonize their general policies. . . ." But what if the states of (for example) East Africa should decide that they could better progress by intensive regional collaboration than by continent-wide collaboration? Or if countries sharing a monetary system, trade links, and economic structures developed during the colonial period should decide to give these ties priority over all else? The signatories of the charter may have "clearly intended to abandon all former regional and sectional alliances," as Cervenka has observed, but the absence of a specific article declaring this desire, the reluctance with which some of the alliances (especially among francophone states) were dissolved, and the recent reemergence of regional linkages (notably in economic planning, transportation, and military coordination) hint at a renaissance of regional organization.

One of the more promising regional unions that seems to have failed is the proposed East African Federation of Kenya, Tanganyika, and Uganda.[17] In a euphoric communique issued in mid-1963 to announce the intention to federate by the end of the year, the heads of government of the three states made specific reference to the relationship of their endeavor to the OAU: ". . . following the Declaration of African Unity at the recent Addis Ababa conference . . . practical steps should be taken wherever possible to accelerate the achievement of our common goal. We believe that the East African Federation can be a practical step towards the goal of Pan-African unity." When it came to working out the details of federation, however, negotiations broke down on such key issues as distribution of power, location of the federal capital, powers of the legislature, and placement of wealth-generating industries. In May 1964, the deadlocked working party concluded that the heads of state should be informed that a political federation was not feasible and that efforts should henceforth be directed toward strengthening of the East African Common Services Organization (EACSO).[18] Although Tanganyika (subsequently merged with the island of Zanzibar to create the United Republic of Tanzania), Uganda, and Kenya proclaimed an "East African Community" in 1967, the new organization did little more than confirm the maintenance of functional EACSO institutions carried over from the colonial period: a customs union; common services for railways, airlines, and harbors; arrangements for harmonization of industrial development, and advisory councils. Escalating disputes among the three member states, including armed border clashes between Uganda and Tanzania in 1971, subsequently jeopardized the limited consensus on which the East African

Community was founded. As of early 1976, Tanzania's closest ties were with Zambia and Mozambique, and Uganda was East Africa's odd man out.

Shared colonial experiences also formed the basis for what was successively referred to as the UAM (Union Africaine et Malgache, 1961-64), the UAMCE (Union Africaine et Malgache de Coopération Économique, 1964-65), OCAM or OCAMM (Organisation Commune Africaine et Malgache, 1965-present). The original member states were all former French colonies or trust territories. Although the federations of West and Equatorial Africa had been "balkanized" into separate entities in 1956 in a major administrative reform, and each of the dozen states thus created had gained independence separately, several economic links remained, of which one of the most important was a shared currency—the CFA franc. The UAM was defined at its founding conference in Brazzaville as "a union of sovereign independent states whose goal is the cooperation of its members in all domains of foreign policy . . . ," and, as indicated earlier, its membership played a significant role in the final shaping of the character of the OAU.

Under strong pressure from other members of the OAU, the francophone subgroup dissolved itself as a political entity in 1964, to reconvene as the UAMCE, limited primarily to economic coordination. In their next incarnation as OCAM, the "Brazzaville group" moved to a position somewhere between the overtly political UAM and the apolitical UAMCE. Concern at the OAU's continuing impotence in the Congolese crisis, the increasingly radical foreign policy of Ghana (and the latter's alleged subversion of Togo, a UAMCE member state), and a growing conviction, nurtured by the Ivory Coast's economic success story, that Africa needed a new political center of gravity, were all factors in the shift. OCAM gradually expanded its membership, adding countries with other than French colonial backgrounds (Zaire, Rwanda, Mauritius) for a 1970 high of 15. Membership began to drop off in 1971, in part because of squabbles over nonsubstantive issues and in part because two of the major attractions of OCAM affiliation began to lose their significance—the association with the European Economic Community and the assistance thus available from the European Development Fund. British entry into the EEC and the wider reach of the association reduced the economic foundation that (together with the French colonial background of the core members) had held the group together. In addition, domestic policy issues became paramount in many of the OCAM states as more and more governments fell victim to coups d'etat.

The problems involved in moving from logical reasoning to actual interstate unity in Africa are nowhere more clearly demonstrated than in the history of the postindependence relationship between the adjacent states of Senegal and Gambia. The frontier dividing these two countries is surely one of colonialism's greater absurdities. Gambia consists of two narrow bands of territory extending some 300 miles inland along the banks of the Gambia River and, except for its 25-mile ocean frontage, is totally surrounded by Senegal. Trade and travel across the frontier are almost impossible to regulate, since traffic to and from southern Senegal must traverse "alien" territory. Ethnic and (African) linguistic ties run through the two states, which are differentiated only by the fact that Gambia became a British colony and Senegal was part of the French West African Federation.

Prior to Gambian independence, UN-appointed experts proposed various levels of association, and agreements calling for friendship and cooperation in defense and foreign affairs (but not a customs union, or any significant infringement of either country's sovereignty) were signed in 1964. Under the terms of a 1967 treaty of association, an interministerial coordinating committee was created, presidential visits were exchanged, and various cooperative projects discussed but not implemented. "Senegambia" may be a reality in ethnic and geographical terms, but the cultural differences that developed in the elites during the colonial "interlude" have precluded amalgamation. National independence—which means secure employment, the prestige of authority, and a preferential way of life for those who man the bureaucracy—is a tangible and immediate goal not easily exchanged for the unknowns of existence in a larger union.

An even more modest effort, to coordinate the economic development of the Senegal River basin, also ran aground on the shoals of local nationalisms. The Organisation des états riverains sénégalais (OERS) was created in 1968 by Guinea, Mali, Mauritania, and Senegal, but with the stipulation that any one veto could curtail the enterprise. Guinea took this option following a dispute with Senegal over alleged harboring of persons implicated in the November 1970 invasion of Guinea, and the OERS was dissolved. A new organization with similar goals—the Organisation pour la mise en valeur du fleuve sénégal (OMVS)—was formed in 1972 by Mali, Mauritania, and Senegal, but its survival as of early 1976 was threatened by a dispute between Mauritania and Senegal over control of a small island.

OAU involvement with the major and most effective economic coordinating agencies of Africa has been in most cases tangential. The Economic Commission for Africa, housed in Addis Ababa near the OAU Secretariat, continues to report to the United Nations, and ECA-OAU relations have on occasion become strained. The tensions have encouraged, over time, a de facto division of labor between the two organizations—with the better financed ECA concentrating on technical and functional cooperation and the OAU focusing on Africa as a political entity rather than as part of a world system. Only occasionally have these roles intersected, as when the 1974 OAU chairman (Nigeria's Gowon) orchestrated the creation of special machinery to strengthen the African hand in renegotiating the relationship with the European Economic Community. The OAU as such was not involved in the negotiations that led to the Lomé Convention of 1974, but the OAU chairman used his office and prestige to get the talks off to a very different start than would have been possible without his organization and leadership.

While many initiatives toward economic cooperation have come from the ECA, others have originated in extra-African quarters and some in bilateral negotiations between individual African states. The 1975 treaty creating the 16-nation Economic Community of West African States (ECOWAS) resulted primarily from Nigerian and Togolese initiatives, even though the commitments of the signatories to a common tariff and a common internal market involve important political decisions of a type that should be of concern to the OAU.

The African Development Bank, a child of the ECA, has developed modestly in its 11-year history despite limited funds and various tensions over the presidency. The 1975 annual meeting, for example, ended in a stalemate over nominees from Ghana and Libya that is unresolved at this writing. In recent years, moreover, the ADB has fallen into the shadow of the newer OPEC-financed Arab Bank for African Development and the Special Fund for Africa administered through the Arab League. Even with a Nigerian serving as OPEC chairman in 1975, the oil-exporting nations' choice of aid recipients was strongly influenced by Middle East value judgments; some 80 percent of aid given by the OPEC states by 1975 was disbursed to predominantly Muslim countries, and over half to Arab nations.[19]

Four guidelines about regional and continental unity would seem to emerge from these examples and others omitted for lack of space:

1. Although no decision involving a state's resources can be considered to be entirely apolitical or technological, the chosen medium for economic cooperation is likely to continue to be the ECA or regional groups such as EACSO rather than the OAU, which lacks the staff, resources, and interest requisite for an active continental economic role.

2. A continuing personal commitment and conviction on the part of the heads of state involved is a prerequisite to genuine interstate cooperation in Africa, until and unless foreign affairs policymaking becomes more institutionalized.

3. Visible development of the nation is perceived by the leaders of Africa as far more pressing and politically necessary than longer term regional or continental development. In fact, the preoccupation with national solidification has grown rather than lessened in the post-Nkrumah period, and inevitably runs counter to the creation of supranational institutions with autonomous powers.

4. The lack of financial and staffing resources for interstate development creates a vicious cycle: expectations are pitched too high; inadequacies of staff or finance leave hopes unfulfilled; the benefits of joint action are viewed with more cynicism than is warranted.

The Outlook

What politicians have put together, politicians can rip asunder. The constraints on the activities of the Organization of African Unity reflect the preferences—

and fears—of the heads of state who collectively determine what the organization should not do, or try to do. Given the centralization of power in the Assembly, the restrictions placed by the Assembly on the Secretariat, and the limited interest of the heads of state in sustained projects that could lessen member nations' autonomy, the prognosis for the OAU would appear to be what it has been since 1963: weakness. Yet a remarkable feature, noted often in the preceding pages, has been the ability of the heads of state to resuscitate the OAU periodically. Forecasting its future thus requires caution, for Africa has its own way of negating social scientists' predictions.

As part of this caution, consideration must be accorded to the strengths, as opposed to the more obvious weaknesses, of the OAU. Four are of special importance: (1) The survival of the institution for more than a decade has established an accepted pattern of cooperation among heads of state, some norms of conflict resolution, and acceptance by non-Africans of the OAU's focal role. (2) The desire of African leaders to resolve their political problems without extensive external intervention or involvement is undiminished. (3) Basic consensus continues to exist on the desirability of maintaining inherited frontiers as a guard against excessive influence by external or internal powers. (4) The continued denial of majority rights in South Africa remains a unifying challenge and focus.

In the early years, the organization was buoyed by the ebullient optimism that characterized the decolonization process and by the visionary leaders of the 1960s, but was impeded in practice by the weakness of the Secretariat resulting from the centralization of power in the Assembly. With unity resting on the lowest common denominator of agreement—the ability of a rising number of heads of state to reconcile their differences and to plan effective action on the basis of three to four days of intensive discussion and socializing once a year—the OAU was and is a far cry from a suprastate. Nonetheless, the commitment to air differences on a regular basis at the highest level of decisionmaking is a significant accomplishment unparallelled by any pancontinental body outside Africa. Even the deadlocked special 1976 summit on Angola did not diminish the importance of the OAU as the chief forum within which African issues are confronted.

The OAU's commitment to the maintenance of inherited (colonial) frontiers will be severely tested in the late 1970s. How will this principle be applied in the Cabinda enclave, historically administered by Portugal as part of Angola but coveted by Zaire and possessing its own homegrown independence movement; in France's one remaining dependency, the Territory of Afars and Issas, a possible bone of contention between Ethiopia and Somalia; in the vast formerly Spanish (now Western) Sahara coveted by Morocco, Mauritania, and Algeria; in the Transkei, the first of the South African "homelands" to be broken off and accorded official independence? A partial answer is that, even if one or more of these difficult cases become exceptions to the general pattern, the wholesale redrawing of frontiers some analysts expected in the early 1960s is increasingly unlikely. While Africa's economic development might be enhanced by the effective amalgamation of ministates under modernizing regimes, as Nkrumah argued in 1963, the protection of frontiers has probably stabilized politics in Africa in the short run, and thereby facilitated peaceful development.

The positive accomplishments registered to date by the OAU have resulted primarily from the collective determination by the heads of state to resolve African issues in African ways. A constant leitmotiv in both debates and activities is minimization of extra-African impact on the continent. The Congo crisis of the mid-1960s and the Angola civil war of the mid-1970s have caused the greatest concern, even though the OAU was less effective in the face of these major power confrontations on African soil than in pressuring neighboring African states to resolve border disputes with minimal use of imported arms. It is a basic principle of the OAU that non-African disengagement from the continent as a whole is a sine qua non for political progress—and nowhere more so than in southern Africa.

Indeed, the issues of southern Africa are second only to protection of national sovereignties in the scale of values that have held the OAU together. When the foreign ministers of the African states met in 1963 to prepare the way for the OAU's creation, they became so ensnarled in complex organizational disputes that they could not come up with a clear course of action. The heads of state cut the Gordian knot by focusing on the unifying issue of colonialism and minority rule in southern Africa. As Cervenka recounts:

The turning point [at the Addis Ababa conference] came with the speech of the President of Algeria, Ahmed Ben Bella, who made the Conference turn from the discussion of African Unity to a real devotion to the problem of decolonization. . . . Ahmed Ben Bella brought the whole Conference to its feet with an impassioned speech lasting little more than three minutes in which he pledged 10,000 Algerian volunteers to free African nations still under white minority rule or under colonial oppression. . . . Subsequent speeches took the same line. The Conference had become seized by a genuine urge for immediate action. . . . Such was the impact of Ben Bella's speech on his colleagues that the proposed Charter was being interpreted as a common weapon for the liberation of Africa. The growing enthusiasm of the assembled leaders over the issues of the decolonization of Africa and the war against apartheid gave birth to what has been called the *spirit of Addis Ababa*.[20]

That the "spirit of Addis Ababa" has been sorely tested needs no further substantiation at this point. On balance, the OAU has been strengthened by its involvement in efforts to press decolonization and majority rule. Although serious divisions opened over the activities (or inactivity, depending on the point of view) of the Liberation Committee, these disagreements were more over means than ends. The only serious challenge to the OAU's position came in 1970-71, when the president of the Ivory Coast proposed that the organization officially endorse "dialogue" with the government of South Africa, an initiative rejected by a 28-6 vote of the Assembly.

Paradoxically, the greatest strength of the OAU—the high degree of agreement reached at most summits—may be its greatest weakness. Unity has been achieved to a great extent by muting the areas of disagreement. Pressure for consensus is intense and highly personalized. A leader who raises delicate issues, or impugns the motives of another, risks weakening the equilibrium on which the OAU rests. Houphouet's "dialogue" proposal was such an issue in that it threatened to undercut a consensual prop of the organization. Use of the annual summit meeting to attack a fellow OAU member constitutes a breach of more than good manners; domestic sovereignty is the cornerstone of the OAU charter.

Thus, the Organization of African Unity cannot escape an inherent dilemma. It is a creation of states jealous of their domestic sovereignty. Any significant expansion of the organization's (especially the Secretariat's) autonomous power will come at the expense of this domestic sovereignty and will require, in effect, the unanimous concurrence of all members. The foundation of agreement built to date is insufficiently strong for such moves, although steps can be, and have been, taken in regional cooperation and in attempting to reduce external pressures on Africa.

The issues the OAU confronts in the rest of the twentieth century may be far more knotty than those confronted thus far. Passing resolutions of escalating rhetoric on apartheid and giving modest financial support to an array of guerrilla movements are not comparable to an all-out offensive in southern Africa, or to the negotiation of a peaceful settlement with the white redoubt. Resolutions condemning the unequal division of world income cannot bring about redistribution—nor can an inadequately funded African Development Bank effect a breakthrough into sustained economic development. Increasing agricultural productivity, moving 18 African countries from the World Bank's list of the world's 29 poorest, preparing for the next drought before it comes—these are economic challenges that call for effective international cooperation, but the OAU has not equipped itself to lead the African search for solutions to these challenges.

As each African country further develops its own foreign policy mechanisms and conception of its "national interest," centrifugal pressures within the OAU are likely to be strengthened. The complexity and intractability of the economic and political issues confronting Africa may encourage OAU members to become more reliant on special or ad hoc groupings of countries (such as ECOWAS) or on purely domestic props (growing Nigerian, Zairian, and Gabonese self-sufficiency). Thus, regional and functional emphases will emerge to complement the continent-wide political approach which is the OAU's raison d'étre.

In sum, the OAU is, and is likely to remain, a concert of heads of state primarily concerned with coordinating the foreign policies of African states to limit external involvement, while avoiding entanglement in the domestic policies of any member state. The organization was not designed to prepare the way for an African union. The several rebuffs given Nkrumah made it abundantly clear that coalition rather than amalgamation was the desired end, not a beginning.

Nor was the OAU designed to be a technological coordinating body. The reservation of powers to the Assembly, the limitations placed on Secretariat initiatives, and the general lack of emphasis on bread and butter economic issues underline the political nature of the OAU. It is an institution reflecting the desire of the African governing elite, after the colonial "interlude," to enhance Africa's own identity: by insistence on the sovereign powers of each government; by insistence on the importance of continental solidarity to resolve African issues which might undermine the sovereignty of individual nations or invite extra-African intervention in support of one faction or another; by ensuring a cohesive African presence in international bodies, as a trade-off for support of the cause of majority rule in southern Africa.

One should thus view the OAU as no more, and also as no less, than a shared desire to make concrete the individuality which Africa was denied during the century its many segments were second-class appendages of Europe.

Notes

1. Government of Ghana, *Debates*, First Series, Vol. XVI, Col. 369 (July 10, 1959).

2. Kwame Nkrumah, *Africa Must Unite* (London: Heinemann, 1963), p. 190.

3. William J. Foltz, *From French West Africa to the Mali Federation* (New Haven: Yale University Press, 1965), pp. 166-196.

4. Reprinted in Colin Legum, *Pan-Africanism: A Short Political Guide* (London: Pall Mall, 1962), p. 179.

5. *Ibid.*, p. 180.

6. The Casablanca resolutions are reprinted in Legum, pp. 187-192.

7. Immanuel Wallerstein, *Africa: The Politics of Unity* (New York: Random House, 1965), pp. 20-21.

8. Haile Selassie, "Towards African Unity," *The Journal of Modern African Studies*, I, 3 (September 1963), p. 284.

9. Zdenek Cervenka, "The Tenth Anniversary of the OAU," in Colin Legum (ed.), *African Contemporary Record: Annual Survey and Documents, 1973-1974* (New York: Africana Publishing Company, 1974), p. A29.

10. Zdenek Cervenka, *The Organization of African Unity and Its Charter* (New York: Praeger, 1969), pp. 62-63.

11. *Africa Research Bulletin*, Political, Social and Cultural Series, V, 9 (September 1968), col. 1175A.

12. *Ibid.*, IX, 6 (June 1972), col. 2498B.

13. *Ibid.*, V, 2 (February 1968), col. 972A.

14. Cervenka, *The Organization of African Unity*, pp. 98-99.

15. The ouster of President Milton Obote by General Idi Amin stirred a lengthy controversy within the OAU, as pressure was brought to bear by some states to avoid seating the Amin delegation at the Council and to change the meeting site for the 1971 summit from Kampala to Addis Ababa. For details, see Claude E. Welch, Jr., "The OAU and International Recognition Questions: Lessons from Uganda," in Yassin El-Ayouty (ed.), *The Organization of African Unity in Comparative Perspective* (New York: Praeger, 1975), pp. 103-117. The lingering distrust of President Nicholas Grunitzky, who assumed power in Togo in 1963 following the assassination of President Sylvanus Olympio, led to pressure on him to stay away from the Addis Ababa meeting, and unsuccessful efforts were made in 1966 to preclude the Ghanaian delegation sent by the newly established National Liberation Council from attending the Council of Ministers' session. The representatives of Guinea, Kenya, Mali, Tanzania, and the United Arab Republic left that session in protest; delegates from Algeria and Somalia also departed, protesting the weakness of resolutions dealing with Rhodesia.

16. Cervenka, *The Organization of African Unity*, p. 18.

17. For details, see Joseph S. Nye, Jr., *Pan-Africanism and East African Integration* (Cambridge: Harvard University Press, 1965), pp. 175-210.

18. *The Nationalist* (Dar es Salaam, June 2, 1964).

19. Ali A. Mazrui, "Black Africa and the Arabs," *Foreign Affairs*, LIII, 4 (July 1975), p. 741.

20. Cervenka, *The Organization of African Unity*, pp. 12-13.

VII Through a Glass Darkly: The Media and Africa

W.A.J. Payne

In 1869, James Gordon Bennett of *The New York Herald* sent Henry Morton Stanley off to Africa with these cosmic instructions: "I want you to attend the opening of the Suez Canal and then proceed up the Nile. Send us detailed descriptions of everything likely to interest the American tourists. Then go to Jerusalem, Constantinople, the Crimea, the Caspian Sea, through Persia as far as India. After that you can start looking around for Livingstone. If he is dead, bring back every possible proof of his death."

More than a hundred years later, the American press is still engaged in a voyage of discovery in relation to Africa. In contrast to Britain and France, where journalists have made a prestigious lifetime career of becoming authorities on Africa, an American journalist is expected to approach Africa as a short-term assignment in the safari tradition. The reward for those who explore their domain conscientiously is promotion to an area of greater journalistic (and diplomatic) priority. For a range of reasons set forth in the following pages, the practice of sending talented and innovative generalists to Africa produces the kind of "zingers" that please editors but results in an incomplete mosaic and a lack of institutional memory.

Africans also receive a distorted view of the world from their media, but for quite different reasons. With the passing of political control from colonial governments to fragile and yet restrictive African regimes, newspapers in Africa have become increasingly the interoffice memoranda of the new elite. Radio, the medium of the masses, remains mired in catch-as-catch-can programming only occasionally addressed to the real problems and needs of the urban and rural poor. In both the press and radio, any given African country's news of the world beyond its immediate borders still comes largely from non-African sources; even

219

the details of the Angolan and Nigerian civil wars were reported to the rest of Africa via Agence France Presse, UPI, BBC, ORTF, VOA, Deutsche Welle, Reuters, AP, Tass, and the New China News Agency.

American Journalism and Africa

The Transitional Years

The small corps of Western journalists covering Africa in the transitional years of the late 1950s and early 1960s had a power within Africa out of all proportion to their place in the pecking order of the journalistic and political world beyond Africa's shores. John Hughes, now the editor of *The Christian Science Monitor*, described the working conditions of this period in his autobiographical book, *The New Face of Africa*: "When I arrived [as the *Monitor's* correspondent in Africa in 1955] there were only two other American foreign correspondents stationed in my territory. For some while thereafter, the three of us, from *The New York Times*, *Time-Life*, and *The Christian Science Monitor*, were the sole full-time resident correspondents of the American press covering Africa South of the Sahara."[1]

These rajahs had Africa to themselves, saw every European official on demand, and built very close ties to many of the rising African nationalist politicians who were to head governments sooner than most then dared to dream. When Ghana's independence in 1957 signalled the beginning of the end of colonial rule in West Africa, the correspondents were on the ground floor. African politicians who were (and are still) making local African reporters wait for stories while giving the news first to the foreign correspondents justified this practice by saying, in effect, "We must reach the Western audience in order to legitimize our struggle." Among the correspondents, it became a form of upmanship to recount to each other what "Tom," "Ken," "Julius," "Milton," "Francis," or "Zik" had told them.

The picture of the African leaders that both Western journalists and the rising nationalist politicians found it self-serving to have depicted in the foreign media was of men who were angry, but not too angry; responsible but not Uncle Toms; energetic but not wild; and open to dialogue with the former colonial masters. In short, the perfect brokers who would be trustworthy and could thus be rewarded. The title of Kenyatta's autobiography, *Suffering Without Bitterness*, could have been the public motto of most of the African nationalist politicians in the transition period. Europeans would not have to fear that African revenge would be visited upon them. Catharsis was not suggested. By not embarrassing the symbolically retreating colonialists, African politicians were bargaining to ensure access to the aid cookie jar.

The foreign correspondents' presence became a status symbol, a sign of power either waxing or waning. African leaders came to believe that they controlled these foreigners, that they were somehow upgraded by having the correspondents at their beck and call. To eat and drink socially with the eager European and American newsgatherers was a sign of the transition from dependence to independence. Clearly the local nationalist cadres were impressed that their leaders had powerful contacts. Bound by a common need, foreign journalists and upwardly mobile African politicians walked into the sunlight of independence. The ritual of complaint that the Western media were racist was a set piece in the togetherness that was forged in these days and nights of camaraderie.

But even as the journalists and the nationalist leaders exploited each other to fulfill their respective needs, African politicians consciously or unconsciously looked forward to the time when they could control the flow of news, expel the unaccommodating. The foreign correspondents, on their part, realized that their very success in cultivating news sources in Africa would be the ticket to another better-paying assignment elsewhere, and that the African interlude would provide a lifetime store of stirring anecdotes for the cocktail and dinner party circuits at home. The "been to" correspondent who could retail these intimacies at editorial conferences and at social encounters with the home office brass knew that he would be measured as a newsman by his ability to tell his anecdotes with just enough cynicism to demonstrate that he had not gone native and that Africa was still exotica. No one on either side would remember the promises, explicit or implicit, that the correspondents and the nationalist politicians had made to each other in the heady last days of empire.

This symbiotic relationship between the foreign press corps and the rising African leaders could be dismissed as a rather unimportant footnote if it had not led to some otherwise inexplicable cleavages in the nationalist movements. The politicians who elected to become involved in this trade-off (i.e., to be "open" with Western correspondents) were perceived as the "good guys" of African nationalism; those who were "uncooperative," for one reason or another, were labeled the "bad guys." The Western intelligence services—whose assessments of African nationalists were based in considerable part on the coverage of the activities and attitudes of the various leaders in the media—followed the journalists' trail through the open door to extend helpful material and psychological attention to the receptive "good guys." Perhaps it is not an exaggeration to say that the interaction between the foreign correspondent and African nationalism profoundly affected the course of post-independence history, at least in some African countries.

Independence for Whom?

Independence significantly changed the attitudes of the leaders of the nationalist movements (or at least those who inherited the power of government) toward both the African and foreign press. The nationalist struggle now being over, so the new rulers declared, the need was for the press to set aside its role as gadfly and become fully committed to nationbuilding. Accordingly, the indigenous press was urged, prodded, and "channelled" into becoming a claque for flag independence—no matter that in most countries flag independence meant that a black urban elite replaced a European elite and that the problems of Africa's rural majority often worsened. Having seen the European-owned press used to reinforce colonial rule, having used the nationalist-controlled press as a counter-weapon against colonial governments, the political leaders carried with them into independence the preconception that a press not under government control is a potential fifth column against that government.

Over the longer term, the methods used by the new governments to neutralize the potentially troublesome press included nationalizing or buying out existing European- and African-owned papers and creating new government-controlled or government-owned newspapers. Local journalists were expected to become praise-singers of the new Jerusalem, or at least to accommodate themselves to the government's usually velvet-gloved guidance. Foreign correspondents enjoyed more latitude, but the old days of camaraderie were gone, and visas were implicitly conditional.

The image to be set forth in the local media was of the nation as a citadel of peace. The masses would be spared the destructive effect of exposure to controversy. Fathers of the nation—or, in most cases, one Father of the Nation—would watch over the masses, cuffing the recalcitrant and patting the cooperative. News was expected to be uplifting, and "responsible" journalists were those who aided in this inspirational team-building process. The media were to spread the new myths and to add to the legend of the charisma of the new leaders. There was nothing radically new about this concept, of course, since traditional African society had often sought unanimity or at least overt agreement.

To read a newspaper in present-day Africa is to learn to read between the lines, to calculate by its omissions as much as by its content what the government is thinking and doing. Only by working and living in a country does one collect over a period of time the storehouse of past events, rumors, and innuendos that flesh out the bare bones of the seemingly dull local coverage. Those who know this technique for decoding the African press amplify and elaborate the published "facts" in the various bars and in the drinking groups that meet daily in the capital cities to hammer out the real news of the political world. The skilled reader knows which ethnic group is in favor by reading the name of a key appointee. The placement of a particular project or institution suggests which region is being rewarded by the government, and it is a fair assumption that the leaders of this region are playing ball with the government in some game of reciprocity. In short, the African media mirror the elite's detachment from the masses.

Parodoxically, African politicians still "sunflower," turning toward the bright light of foreign coverage and reading foreign papers in preference to their own. In 1975 even more than in 1955, the super status newspapers and magazines in Africa are those published in the Western industrialized countries. The international editions of *Time* and *Newsweek, L'Express*, the British weeklies, the major French newspapers, and the *International Herald Tribune* (Paris) are a window on the modern world of which the African elite likes to think it is a part, and also a more interesting source of news about Africa as a whole (or at least of how Africa is perceived abroad) than anything published on the continent.

African intellectuals outside the inner power circle are also mesmerized by Western journalism. They often deride these papers and newsmagazines, yet there is a kind of pained envy of the freedom to comment so critically on governments and leaders. And there is always the titillating hope that one day some of the truth about the African reader's own country may be written in one of these imported publications—a hope fed by the knowledge that the bootlegging of locally unacceptable stories to foreign correspondents is one way that African newsmen eke out a living. When African governments ban copies of these foreign publications from time to time, the desire for a peek into the forbidden world of the free press only increases. There is almost certainly a correlation between the availability of these external sources of enlightenment and the passivity about the lack of unfiltered information and of genuine critical debate permitted in the local press.

Some Practical Problems

One reason given for the sending of enterprising younger correspondents to Africa for seasoning is that only the sturdy and physically resilient can endure the exasperations of hopping from one newsbreak to another in a vast and fragmented continent where travel, communications, visas, accommodations, and access to news sources are substantially improved but still difficult. As Henry Kamm reported in a Paris-datelined roundup in *The New York Times* early in 1976, the foreign correspondent is increasingly becoming a casualty of the self-assertion of the Third World toward the West; the number of countries that grant entry visas more or less routinely sharply diminished in 1975, and the practice of allowing journalists to visit a country while carefully restricting his contacts and his travel opportunities is on the rise in both Africa and Asia. In much of Africa, particularly in countries formerly colonized by France, visiting correspondents are treated as if they were (like the journalists of the country) part of the official apparatus of their own governments, and interviews with officials must be arranged through diplomatic notes from the journalist's embassy to the information ministry.[2]

A related frustration, described by David Ottaway of *The Washington Post* in a February 1975 despatch from Ethiopia, is that of bridging the gap between the realities of newsgathering in Africa and the preconceptions of home base editors:

Reporting on the war in Ethiopia's distant northern Eritrea province has become a veritable nightmare for the journalists and the Ethiopian officials alike. No issue is more sensitive to a sovereign government than a civil war, and probably no single event attracts more foreign correspondents.

Recently, there were more than 50 foreign newspaper, radio and television correspondents here in Addis Ababa to cover the Eritrea war story. But the Ethiopian military government stubbornly refused to meet with any of them, barred all from the war zone, provided no reports on the military fighting and acted as if everything in this mountain kingdom were normal and the "imperialist" Western press out to "sabotage the Ethiopian revolution" with exaggerated and fabricated war stories.

The result has been a cacophony of all too often false or misleading war reports and screeching Ethiopian denunciations of the Western media that has served no one's interest, not that of Ethiopia, of the correspondents or the reader. The true story of what is happening in Eritrea is not being told because it cannot be told. What the reader is getting is only a vague approximation of the ebb and flow of fighting in the war.

The sad fact is that not a single correspondent here has witnessed a battle, seen a dead guerrilla or soldier, taken a picture of any fighting or been able to assess the situation in the province first hand outside the provincial capital of Asmara itself. (One Ethiopian journalist and three Americans did manage to spend one night huddled in an Asmara hotel listening to rocket, artillery and heavy arms fire outside, and a day touring hospitals and refugee centers, however). The Eritrean war is probably the first one in history covered almost entirely by long distance telephone calls to the battle front.

Little wonder then that more and more frustrated correspondents "stuck" at the Addis Ababa Hilton Hotel, with its hot thermal water swimming pool, nine-hole minature golf course and high-priced drinks served by Ethiopian women, have begun muttering the word "scoop" under their breath with increasing frequency as they ponder the improbable situation in which they find themselves.

Scoop is the classic work of the late Evelyn Waugh, who wrote in 1938 a hilarious and still all too relevant satirical account of foreign correspondents covering a largely imaginary war in a make-believe African republic called Ishmaelia, with a disturbing similarity to Ethiopia.

As in *Scoop*, we have here in Ethiopia today correspondents not beyond resorting to their imaginations as to what may be taking place in the Eritrean war in the absence of hard facts and under the pressure of deadlines and fierce competition. We also have the main hotel (the Liberty in 1938 and the Hilton today) where "war reports," improving in the sound of gunfire and the heat of battle, circulate furiously among correspondents as the reports pass from pillar to post and find their amplified way into one dispatch after another.

We have too the news agency reporters (British correspondents in *Scoop*) in bitter, 24-hour competition to beat each other onto the world's front pages and often feeling themselves obliged to turn believable rumors into hard war reports in order to keep editors back home happy and hopefully to win the morning or night cycle of news on Ethiopia. Under the best of conditions, news agency reporting is a tough, extremely competitive sport in which the writer with a sharp dramatic war lead is certain to win hands down over his more cautious colleagues.

Finally, we have the intriguing foreign powers interfering in the internal affairs of Ethiopia and perhaps even hatching some infernal plot to get their respective men into power. While it was Soviet agents in *Scoop*, today you can have your choice. It can either be the Arabs (the official government version) or it can be the Americans with their Central Intelligence Agency hard at work to keep the military government afloat or plotting its overthrow, depending on your ideological propensity. But one European news agency has settled instead on the Chinese, picturing Peking's little men in Mao tunics as habitual visitors to the government palace where they are virtually dictating the course of events and getting "their boys" into the saddle.

A few examples of the strange art of news alchemy as it is being practiced here in Ethiopia seems in order. One of the most imaginative and image provoking news reports yet put out by the agencies (reprinted by *The Washington Post* on February 6) was a story of a large Ethiopian army convoy, including 52 tanks and 20 armored vehicles, toiling for days through the "heavy fighting" in the province and making its way around a blown up bridge to reach the "beleaguered" capital of Asmara. We now know that no such convoy of tanks and armored vehicles ever existed and that there was at that time no bridge destroyed on the road involved to hold up the imaginary convoy. Indeed, it is the judgment of the Western military experts here that it is practically impossible to get a tank by road from Addis Ababa to Asmara because of the incredibly tortuous mountain terrain and passes between the two cities.

The same dispatches, quoting "reliable sources," told of an Ethiopian air force plane being shot down by Soviet surface to air missiles, presumably the shoulder fired SA-7. However, both Western military experts and Ethiopians, including one whose plane had reportedly been shot down, say the Eritrean guerrillas do not yet have such missiles, or at least have yet to use them.

On another occasion, an American news agency, on a quiet weekend, reported soldiers and civilians engaged for an hour in "street fighting" on the very outskirts of Addis Ababa. But all other journalists could verify was a handful of shots fired when police attempted to arrest a single Eritrean. The agency, however, had added authority to its report by quoting "diplomatic sources," and what editor, or indeed reader, could then doubt its authenticity?

. . . It is easy to criticize this kind of journalism but all too easy to become swept up in the game under the pressure to give editors and readers some version at least of developments in the war. With no newsmen on the spot and the military deliberately refusing to confirm, deny or provide reports ("we are too busy to do that," said one military spokesman), correspondents are reduced to two main sources of information, Western diplomats and a few brave Ethiopians still willing to risk prison and perhaps their lives.

There are some unsung and unnameable heroes among these Western diplomats and Ethiopians to whom correspondents and readers owe an enormous debt of thanks. But there are also some diplomats playing their own games and some Ethiopians who have proven unable to tell the difference between gun firing and heavy fighting, and tanks and armored vehicles. Then, too, most of the Ethiopians in Asmara still willing to answer the telephone calls of journalists in Addis Ababa live in an atmosphere hardly conducive to unbiased reporting.

Reporting on the war in Eritrea is thus a very imperfect art which will not improve until the government lifts its blackout and correspondents give up their uncontrollable lust for scoops and revive their concern for accuracy in the news.[3]

The Afro-American Factor

Reflecting the special interest in Africa that exists among the 25+ million Afro-Americans whose forefathers came to this country in slave ships, the major Afro-American newspapers have long devoted a higher proportion of their newsspace to coverage of Africa and to cultural exchanges between the two continents than do the general interest mass media. While the African content of *Bilalian News* (successor to *Muhammed Speaks*), Harlem's *Amsterdam News*, the Baltimore-based *Afro-American* chain, the *Pittsburgh Courier* chain, and the *Chicago Defender* chain is qualitatively uneven, no other area of the world outside the United States receives such extensive coverage in these papers.

The interest of the black press in Africa long predates the "Afro" renaissance of the 1960s. Although the focus has shifted in various directions over the years, the tradition is rooted in the heated editorial debates of the nineteenth century anti-slavery press on the options facing the free Afro-American in the United States. The American Colonization Society, an organization created by white elitists with some black support, was the most coordinated effort advocating creation of an African homeland for both freed slaves and freeborn Afro-Americans. Strong sentiment also developed among some Afro-Americans for emigration to the West Indies, especially in light of Haiti's achievement of independence in 1804. John B. Russwurm, who joined with Samuel E. Cornish in 1827 to found *Freedom's Journal*, the first Afro-American newspaper, finally rejected his own paper's anti-emigrationist position and left for Liberia, the geographical focal point of the emigrationist movement.

The North Star, the anti-slavery newspaper published by Frederick Douglass, was the leading spokesman for the anti-emigrationists. Together with likeminded publications, *The North Star* argued that the struggle for identity must be carried on by a united front within the United States. The flight of the better educated to the safety of Africa or the West Indies would amount to abandonment of less-advantaged brothers, leaving the masses leaderless and in permanent bondage.

Although the concentration of the Afro-American press on the emigration issue lessened during times when economic and political stresses diminished, the question of identity remained a continuing concern of Afro-American editors and writers. Thus it was no accident that much of the early writing on pan-Africanism was by Afro-Americans; they were born pan-Africanists in that their black ethos was rooted in Africa but divorced from the divisive pull of tribal loyalties and European colonial acculturation. The best known of the Afro-American pioneers of modern pan-Africanism was W.E.B. DuBois, who, among his many other activities, opened the pages of the NAACP organ *Crisis* to African issues. Carter G. Woodson founded the monthly *Negro History Bulletin* and the quarterly *Journal of Negro History*, both actively linking Africa and the struggle for equality in the United States. The Associated Negro Press, the first news agency specifically keyed to the interests of Afro-American editors, was founded in 1919; these interests were assumed to include a heavy volume of news of Africa and of cultural exchanges between Africans and Afro-Americans. In the 1930s, the Afro-American press became deeply concerned with the Italian-Ethiopian war, and a number of Afro-Americans subsequently went to Ethiopia to aid in the development of an English-language press there.

After 1945, the leadership of pan-Africanism shifted from Afro-Americans to Africans, and became more directly connected to the rise of African nationalist movements. As a consequence of this shift, and the quickening pace of politics in Africa, the relationships between blacks from the two continents became more structured and more complex. Some Afro-American myths were jostled in the encounters with postindependence Africans in the Third World conferences, and especially in pan-Africanist congresses, for the new loyalties of the African elite to several dozen individual nation-states sometimes were overriding. Efforts to supply new nations of Africa with news of Afro-Americans through Afro-American channels were less successful than hoped, though economic rather than other factors are said to be responsible for the short life of the popular African edition of *Ebony* in the 1960s and for the failure of the Associated Negro Press (ANP) service to find a rewarding African market. Even so, the special feeling for Africa in the Afro-American press has remained a powerful one, and the most authoritative English-language voice of cultural pan-African-ism was (until its demise in April 1976) Johnson Publications' monthly *Black World* (formerly the *Negro Digest*). The quarterly *Freedomways* (New York) and the monthly *Black Scholar* (Sausalito, California) represent the socialist view of the African and Afro-American world. Sociologist Nathan Hare, who founded *Black Scholar* in the late 1960s, resigned in 1975 in protest against the magazine's leftward movement, but the magazine continues to grow among black intellectuals.

As the push for integration gained momentum in the United States in the 1960s, attention to both Afro-American and African news increased in the general interest "white" mass media. As a consequence, the Afro-American press lost ground in two crucial areas. Black professionals found it in their interest to become more serious readers of *The New York Times, The Washington Post, The Los Angeles Times*, and other mainstream media. At the same time, these papers (and radio and television as well) were raiding the Afro-American press for talented writers with specialized skills to cover areas previously ignored. The folding of many marginal Afro-American newspapers was part of this phenome-non.

   To say that Afro-American newspapers no longer have a monopoly on the coverage of African news for Afro-American readers is not to suggest that they do not still wield important influence, particularly in monitoring (and usually protesting) the character of U.S. policy toward African issues. The weekly *Bilalian News*, the voice of the Nation of Islam, deserves special attention for two reasons. Not only does it carry more news of the African world on a regular basis than any other newspaper in the United States, but its circulation (almost three quarters of a million and growing) is largely lower and middle class. This inculcation of a sense of identity with Africa in social strata heretofore largely untouched by print media may have implications for the future development of an "African constituency" in the United States warranting further study.

The Media of Africa

The relating of news was a major African preoccupation and tradition long before the arrival of Western technology and terminology. The griots, the praise singers, and ordinary social encounters have for centuries been charged with the passing of information. Witness this exchange among a group of the nomadic Masai in East Africa, reported by Henry R. Ole Kulet in his novel, *Is It Possible*?:

Saaya told him their names. He then went on to tell him how he found us. In turn, the stranger told us how he came from beyond Arusha. He told us every village he slept at, what he ate, what time he started the previous morning, and all the minor details. This is one very good custom the Masai people have. Even when two people meet who do not know each other, it is customary for each of them to tell all that he knows about where he has come from. In turn, the other person does the same, giving news of the places he has come from. This is important because one always knows what is happening in the place one is going to visit. This way of exchanging news serves instead of newspapers and radio.[4]

   The traditional system of communication among the Kikuyu has been described in more formal terms in Donald Barnett's and Karari Njama's *Mau Mau from Within*:

Given the relatively high degree of mobility found among the million or so Kikuyu of the Central Province, Rift Valley, and Nairobi, news and information normally spread with unbelieveable rapidity. Largely by word of mouth, news could often be transmitted great distances in the space of a few hours through the informal networks of dispersed kin and neighborhood relations.[5]

Or again:

... events considered of some importance to an individual will usually be reiterated by him time and time again in his dealings with other people. Upon meeting friends, relations or neighbors Kikuyu customarily bring one another up to date on all significant happenings in their lives since they last met.[6]

Illiteracy is too often equated with ignorance and a lack of respect for knowledge. We see an example of this in the first Western study of the Swahili language by the German missionary Reverend J.L. Krapf, who wrote in 1850:

We do not expect that the African mankind will ever perform considerable achievement in philosophy, or in the theoretical branches of science, but we believe that it will cultivate the body or practical point of civilization and Christianity.[7]

Even Krapf had to express astonishment, however, at some aspects of the language he was studying: "We must be surprised at the vigor, moveableness, tendency to clearness, and other grammatical phenomena, which this language manifests throughout."

If it is axiomatic that language reflects culture and enables men to deal with abstractions, it also becomes axiomatic that we must retrace our steps, discard some cultural baggage, and recognize that all African societies have been concerned with knowledge and its transmission to succeeding generations since long before the first missionary arrived under colonial auspices to teach "the word." The significance of the head in traditional African culture is not incidental. The entering of the gods into the head in spirit possession, the rendering of head (facial) masks in West Africa, the devotion African artists give to the head in their work all reflect a preoccupation with the receptacle of knowledge. The emphasis placed on information transmission as a means of socializing the young is indicated in another passage from *Mau Mau from Within*:

In the absence of a writing system the Kikuyu, as with other African peoples, were traditionally dependent upon oral history, often reinforced in song, proverb and verse, in their efforts to preserve and transmit to future generations important happenings and events. The transference of this knowledge was an extremely important aspect of the upbringing and socialization of children. Historic events of significance, along with a wide variety of other information which could not be stored in books for future reference, simply had to be remembered or stored in the human mind if it were not to be lost for all time.[8]

An understanding of this oral tradition in Africa prepares one for the importance of gossip and the importance of radio in modern African communications. The radio resembles the oral tradition and gossip dovetails with it. Gossip and rumor are not ends in themselves but also serve as forms of social control—in effect, an informal "government" in an era of weak national states. Anyone who has frequented Africa's capital cities, witnessed the function of bars as centers for rumormongering, and the "what-will-happen-next" theme of all dinner parties, recognizes that oral communication has a power and importance undiminished by the parallel existence of other forms of mass communication.

To say that Africans are more inclined to accept the validity of information received verbally is not to suggest that print journalism does not have a fascinating history in every country on the continent. The number of books that have been published on the development of the African press leaves no doubt that newspapers have been around for a very long time.[9] But what these historical accounts also tell us is that the pattern of development was distinctly different in (1) areas which attracted heavy European settlement (East, Central, and southern Africa) and (2) populated areas, notably West Africa, where there was extensive European contact but where Europeans did not bring their kith and kin and had no main aim other than groundholding to keep other colonial powers out, trading and related economic activity, and conversion of the local population to Christianity.

In technical terms, the press of East Africa reached a higher level of development earlier than anywhere else in black Africa. In contrast to the "protest-oriented" press of West Africa, the major newspapers of East Africa were "news-oriented." The reasons, of course, were that the media of East Africa were created by and for European settlers and mirrored their interests and concerns. The Standard chain of newspapers (founded in Mombasa, Kenya, in 1910 by an Asian and later bought out by Europeans) predominated in all three British territories. Africans and African aspirations were not regarded as "news" in their pages until the Mau Mau Emergency of the early 1950s, and then the coverage became fearful and hostile for the remainder of the preindependence years. Meanwhile, largely ignored by the colonial government, an indigenous press gradually took form. The first African-owned publication, the Kikuyu-language *Mwigwithania*, appeared in 1928 under the editorship of Jomo Kenyatta. The organ of the Kikuyu Central Association, *Mwigwithania* ceased publication in 1934 when Kenyatta went to England to lobby for Kikuyu land grievances. A number of other African-language newspapers—or, more often, news sheets—began to appear in the 1940s, but most of those not controlled directly or indirectly by colonial governments were suppressed in 1952 during the Emergency. The founding of the *Nation* series of newspapers by the Aga Khan in 1959 was a watershed in the development of a truly African-oriented press in East Africa.

In Central Africa, press and radio also catered to settler rather than African interests, but the orientation was toward South Africa rather than Britain. Argus South African Newspapers Ltd., installed in Southern Rhodesia along with Cecil Rhodes in 1891, finally arrived in Northern Rhodesia, now Zambia, in 1951. Even as late as 1956, all four newspapers published more than twice a week in the Federation of Rhodesia and Nyasaland were Argus-owned. An African-oriented weekly, *The Central African Post*, financed in part by Astor interests in England, was begun in 1960. In 1964, the multinational Lonrho corporation purchased the *Zambia Times* and *Zambia News* from South African interests, as well as the Argus-owned *Northern News*, and gained effective control of the print media of the independent country. (In 1975, the Zambian government nationalized all papers.)

In the media field, Johannesburg is to anglophone sub-Saharan Africa what New York and London are to the United States and the United Kingdom. The Republic has the longest journalistic tradition in Africa, with an English-language newspaper dating from 1800, and now supports 21 dailies among some 500 newspapers, periodicals, and journals, most of them published in English or Afrikaans. For obvious reasons, South African newspapers have historically concentrated on white interests and viewpoints, with the African press lagging far behind; by 1967, however, there were 30 publications oriented toward African readers, and the number has continued to grow. One major Johannesburg daily, *The World* (circulation 100,000+) is African-edited and caters exclusively to African readers. Although the white press has always been relatively unfettered, the freedom of the African press to speak for its constituency is decidedly limited by financial factors and more direct controls of content.

West Africa had intensive contact with Europe for several centuries before colonial rule was introduced, and Sierra Leone—the mecca for freed slaves from within the British orbit and the intellectual center for the English-speaking coastal countries—had a *Royal Gazette* by the beginning of the nineteenth century. It was only after the first printing press arrived in Liberia in 1826, however, that an African- (as opposed to a European-) oriented press began to emerge. In contrast to East and Central Africa, where the major newspapers were European-owned and the news focus was heavily tilted toward settler interests right up to the time of independence, the press in British West Africa became an agent of the nationalist movement and a spokesman for the African elite. Nnamdi Azikiwe, the first president of Nigeria, was editor of the Gold Coast's *African Morning Post* and the founder/owner/editor of the *West African Pilot* and newspapers in Ibadan, Onitsha, Port Harcourt, and Kano. Ghana's first president, Kwame Nkrumah, founded the *Evening News* in 1948 to forge unity around the independence movement and the Convention People's Party. Altogether, there were 227 newspapers during the colonial period in British West Africa: 52 in Sierra Leone, 70 on the Gold Coast, 100 in Nigeria, and five in Gambia.

In French West Africa (now Senegal, Ivory Coast, Guinea, Benin, Mali, Upper Volta, Mauritania), the development of the pre-independence press followed a somewhat different course. The French "civilizing mission" aimed at the assimilation of Africans into a cultural sphere centered in Paris, and thus French was the language of schools, government commerce, and the favored local media. French publications entered francophone Africa duty free, and taxes on imports of newsprint and printing presses (as well as government policy emphasis on the use of French as the lingua franca) served to discourage the growth of a vernacular press. In Dakar, Abidjan, and other capitals of former French West and Equatorial Africa, the elite papers of the colonial era have survived to the present day, although often under new ownership and new names. There has also been an explosion of new publications of various types. As in anglophone Africa, the sales area of the print media was and is limited within each country by geographical, economic, literacy, and demographic factors. On the other hand, interstate circulation of major newspapers is more institutionalized in francophone Africa than it is among the anglophone states outside East Africa, with the result that a publication originating in Dakar may be available as far away as Kinshasa.

Most of the serious magazines and journals covering Africa at large continue to have their publishing bases in Europe (e.g., *Africa, Jeune Afrique, Afrique-Asie, Africa Confidential, West Africa*). Of the few magazines published in Africa for Africa-wide audiences, the glossy monthly *Drum* (which originated in South Africa in 1951 under the editorship of British journalist Anthony Sampson but now has editions in Lagos and Nairobi as well as Johannesburg) is the best known. Dakar's *Bingo* was established in 1954 as an equivalent in French-speaking Africa. These publications were designed to appeal to African city people, with the emphasis on politically safe uplift and success stories, bizarre photos, advice-to-the-lovelorn columns, and other light reading. What is interesting about such publications is their symbolic importance: the very possession of a copy of the relatively costly *Drum* is a sign to other Africans that the possessor is "with it," is potentially one of those on the way up. That the content is pure froth and the ultimate ownership of the publishing chain expatriate rather than African is beside the point.

The African Journalist

Although various U.S. organizations concerned with Africa set out with characteristic missionary zeal in the 1960s to participate in crash programs to train African reporters, American journalists (whose status is unparalleled even in Europe) have never been comfortable with the milieu in which the African journalist-in-training must be prepared to function. By the mid-1970s, most American foundations had turned to funding training programs managed by Europeans and (in some French-speaking areas) Canadians. The rationale is that basic training for journalists should be conducted in Africa and that the training programs should be shaped to meet the peculiar needs of African journalism—how to live with suspicious African governments, how to live on low wages, how to survive low social esteem, how to live with a shortage of trained personnel, and how to better one's craft. It is understating the point to observe that expatriate instructors have some difficulty in combining this approach with their commitment to the ideology that the kind of journalism that has met the needs of the Western industrial countries should be the goal of Africa as well. A further complication is the differing philosophical styles of North American, British, and French journalism.

By 1976, there were established training schools and/or university-based schools of journalism in Algeria, Cameroon, Egypt, Ghana, Kenya, Madagascar, Nigeria, Senegal, South Africa, Tanzania, Tunisia, Uganda, Upper Volta, Zaire, and Zambia. In addition, many churches offer short journalism and Christian literature workshops and correspondence courses, and governments conduct various types of courses for their information officers.[10] There is always a risk in overgeneralizing about Africa, but it is basically accurate to note that the university programs are patterned on North American (including Canadian) models while the non-university training institutes tend to be patterned on British or French models. While Africanization of staff is accelerating in the university programs in some countries (notably Nigeria, Ghana, and Kenya), many others remain African only juridically.

The most active single agency concerned with raising the professional quality and status of African journalism has been the International Press Institute, a print-oriented institution based in Zurich. Financed by the Ford Foundation, among others, IPI conducts training programs and annual meetings in Asia, Africa, and Latin America, and has Africans on its board of directors. It has operated training facilities in Lagos and Nairobi since the 1960s, and publishes a useful quarterly newspaper treating problems of the African press, *The African Journalist*, under the editorship of Frank Barton.

The African journalist who accepts too literally the ideology of Western mentors about the responsibility of the press to assert its freedom is being programmed for disillusionment. This is a particular peril for the journalist who trains in a prestigious school of journalism in the United States or Europe. When he experiences preventive detention (or "cooperates with the police," an Aesopian way of dealing with the indignity of being picked up by police for questioning), when he is warned off covering certain news stories, when he sees his colleagues being fired for persisting in peering too closely at the behavior of certain politicians—then he will begin to understand that many of the objective conditions for the practice of journalism in Africa are not to be found in American or European textbooks or experience. An African who received his Master's degree at the Columbia University Graduate School of Journalism told me of his disillusionment at awakening to the fact that his impressive credentials had no validity when he returned home: "One of the biggest mistakes I ever made in my life was to become involved in journalism. What can I do in Africa? I feel I am a laughing stock."

The experience of Peter Mwaura, a Kenyan graduate of Ohio State, illustrates the point. Mwaura, one of the most competent journalists on Nairobi's *Nation*, was detained by police in mid-1973 after publishing a splendid story detailing government/business corruption that would have won him a Pulitzer award for investigative reporting in Ohio. Most disheartening of all was that it took a

question in the Kenya National Assembly to bring out the fact that the reporter
had been in detention for three days. Mwaura's editor at the *Nation* did not tell
his readers what had happened and why. Neither the Kenya Union of Journalists, the journalist's trade union, nor the more ceremonial Kenya Press Club went
on the public record with a protest. There were private efforts and private
handwringings, but it was deemed impossible to go further. When Hilary
Ng'weno, a colleague of Mwaura's, followed up (in his then regular weekly
Nation column, "With a Light Touch") with a satirical commentary on the
affair, the rumor in Nairobi was that Ng'weno too would be picked up. That
Ng'weno's gentle column was seen as an act of courage is indicative of the
atmosphere in which African journalism must function.

A window on the world of the African journalist can be found in several
works of popular African fiction. In Cyprian Ekwensi's *People of the City*, the
major character, Sango, is perceived by his fellow Nigerians as a hedonist, a
leader of a dance band, and a womanizer; the fact that his profession is
journalism is beside the point. Ekwensi, who has himself worked in the steamy
pit of Nigerian journalism, can depict with compassion the double world of West
African newspapermen: "Yet Sango's one desire in this city was peace and the
desire to forge ahead. No one would believe this, knowing the kind of life he led:
that beneath his gay exterior lay a nature serious and determined to carve for
itself a place of renown in this city of opportunities."[11] When Sango is evicted
from his dwellings, he has no power, no automobile, and is forced to carry his
belongings in a hand cart through the streets. Despite his success, measured in
terms of bylines in the local newspapers, he is of low status, no one that the
landlord has to fear. He is buoyed when he is complimented by his (European)
editor for the story he writes on the funeral of an African leader liked by his
editor. But when he gets too close to the truth in another story, the expatriate
British editor fires him with a perfunctory apology: "You understand how it
is—a matter of policy. *The Sensation* does not stand for playing one section of
the community against the other. Personally I have nothing against you or your
writing in this tragic affair. . . . But I do not own *The Sensation*."[12] Aubrey
Kachinewe, Wole Soyinka, Can Themba, and Onuora Nzekwu also deal compas-
sionately with their journalist characters in their novels. But the image of the
journalist that emerges is not a positive one. What all these novels tell us is that
the individualism that marks Western journalism is not a luxury that this
generation of African leaders is prepared to allow to take root.

In this environment, it is not surprising that so many of the promising young
journalists one encounters in Africa or in training abroad decide to leave the
profession before they become fully proficient or adapt their skills to the more
secure and often prestigious niches available within government, or in the
blurred area of quasi-government journalism. Other havens for these bright
young people capable of expressing themselves passably in written European
languages are the multinational corporations operating in contemporary Africa.

The second class status and limited access to major news sources accorded by governments to African journalists of uncertain political reliability is one reason so few Africans are employed as correspondents or stringers by European and American agencies or newspapers. In addition, the Europeans complain that African reporters do not take care to be precise and meticulous in their reporting; clearly this is partly a culture conflict. Language can be another problem. In a continent where literacy is so limited and where the number of local languages used in the homes of various ethnic groups can number in the dozens in a single country, print journalism starts off with a major strike against it. More so in anglophone than in francophone Africa, beginning African journalists may have difficulty writing in the syntax required by the world press. However fluent their verbal English, they are likely to write and think in an African-tinged European language unless they have had intensive specialized training.

That other factors may also be involved is suggested by the experience of Thomas Johnson of *The New York Times*, the first Afro-American assigned as a regional correspondent in Africa by a major U.S. newspaper or news agency. Johnson takes particular pride in the extent to which he Africanized the stringer network of the *Times* during his assignment in West Africa. Only one of 20 stringers were Africans when he arrived in 1972, and 12 of 16 were Africans when he left in 1975. In undertaking this restructuring of the *Times* staff in West Africa, Johnson presumably took into account the irony that the African reporter with international "strings" enjoys a status, i.e., an access to news sources, several notches above that of the reporter writing only for local media.

If there are no African and few Afro-American journalists working as full-fledged correspondents in Africa for the American media, the even greater anomaly is that there are so few African correspondents reporting to their own compatriots on the world beyond Africa. Almost everything that Africans read or hear or see on film about the United States through what we have come to call "the media" is written or spoken or photographed by non-Africans. There are only three full-time journalists representing African papers in Washington, all from South Africa. Other papers have part-time correspondents or stringers in the United States, but seldom are they Africans. As noted in the introduction to this chapter, most African papers get their news of the world beyond Africa's shores (and often of other parts of Africa) from European or American press agencies, or from handouts of USIS and its sister information agencies of the industrialized world.

Scarcely a Smile

Although there is much humor and warm laughter in African societies, as evidenced in the designs of masks, the antics of the village funnymen, and the satirical songs sung about leaders and peasants, the current crop of African leaders are very, very serious men decidedly on the defensive. There are smiles, light jokes, and hearty laughs in public, but anyone who pokes fun (especially in print or on stage) at some of the foibles of the nation-builders or of nation-building takes a decided risk. In this context, the appearance in Kenya in 1973 of a monthly (now ,a fortnightly) called simply *Joe* is a phenomenon of considerable significance.

Joe is the creation of the aforementioned Hilary Ng'weno, the first African editor of the Ismaili-owned *Nation* chain of newspapers in East Africa, and Terry Hirst, an English artist who had been teaching and working in Kenya for a number of years. Although *Joe* includes essays, cartoons, book reviews, and even serious political reportage, the engine of the magazine is a fictional everyman named "Joe Kihara"—a stubble-chinned, fortyish, portly, balding urban African dressed in an outsize cast-off British army overcoat—who spends a lot of time in bars arguing about life in Kenya. Usually he is arguing with Ng'weno, who plays the straight man to the volatile Joe. "Joe" has become so familiar and real to Kenyans that the government persuaded his creators to use him as the vehicle to inform citizens how to avoid damage to their eyes during a total eclipse of the sun in June 1973. The circulation by 1975 was more than 20,000 and climbing.

In early 1975, Ng'weno sold his interest in the enterprise to Hirst, but Ng'weno still writes his column for the magazine. The two founders' view of Joe Kihara as a "survivor," a portrait of resilience, explains perhaps why he is so important in Kenya:

Joe is nobody in particular. He is everybody. If you are an average fellow, born with no silver spoon in your mouth, condemned by all manner of circumstances to always miss the boat wherever it may be going, but always hopeful that you'll make it one of these days . . . you are Joe.

If you can get taken by con-men of all kinds—salesmen, landlords, church-men, politicians, relatives or whatever—and at the end of it all have faith in the nobility of mankind . . . you are Joe.

If when things are going fine for you, as fine as they ever go, you can retain a suspicion that it will not last, that somehow, somewhere, something is bound to happen to spoil everything for you . . . you are Joe.

If you can look over your neighbor's fence and see that the grass is greener but never entertain any ideas about it . . . you are Joe.

If you can hold to some semblance of sanity while all about is falling to pieces . . . you are Joe.

And even if in the process, you should lose your sanity, provided that you can accept the fact that you have lost it . . . you are Joe.

Joe, in other words, is everyman as he or she copes with the hypocrisy, the chaos, the stupidity and the pain that abounds in the world today.

The important fact about Joe is that he is capable of laughing. He laughs at the world. He laughs at himself too. And the world laughs with him. It may not laugh with him always. But it laughs sometimes. And that is what counts.[13]

Radio and Television: The New Oral Tradition

Sometimes a five minute experience in Africa can convey reality more forcefully than a carefully researched academic study. In 1972, I struck up a conversation with a Kenyan about a recent event I had witnessed and that had been reported in the press. "I know, I know, I have read it too," the African responded, "but now tell me with your voice; then I will believe it." The palaver tradition, the long nights of recounting legends and myths, folktales, proverbs and riddles, and the marketplace chatter—in short, the greater acceptance of the spoken word— help to explain why radio is now and is likely to remain the most acceptable and effective modern information medium in Africa. There are practical consider- ations as well. As Sydney Head has observed, "Radio is the only medium in Africa able to scale the triple barrier of illiteracy, distance, and a lack of transportation; broadcasting uses scores of local languages, most of which never appear in print."[14]

It is an accurate measurement of their relative importance that, while some newspapers have been allowed to remain outside of government control in some African countries, direct access to the major radio facilities (and television where it exists) is regarded as an essential part of the governing process. For the same reasons, Africa's broadcasting stations generally have larger, better-paid staffs and more modern equipment than newspapers. One of the elementary steps in any attempted coup d'etat in Africa—and certainly any successful one—is to take over the radio station in the capital city. Many analysts of Zairian politics still argue that Patrice Lumumba's downfall in the Congo (Zaire) in 1961 can be directly related to his inability to regain control of the broadcasting station in Leopoldville (now Kinshasa) and use it as a means of rallying his forces. That control of the radio station is *thought* to be important is as real and vital as whether it *is* important.

According to the UNESCO's 1971 *Statistical Handbook*, every 1,000 Africans shared 45 radio receivers while 1,000 shared 11 newspapers. According to a 1972 survey in Zambia, 77 percent of those responding did not read even a non-daily newspaper, and 67 percent learned of news events only through radio broadcasting. In *Muffled Drums*, William Hachten provides these statistics for Africa as a whole, excluding Egypt, as of 1971:

only about 175 newspapers circulated about 2.7 million copies daily; some 98 radio stations broadcast to 12.5 million radio receivers; 32 television stations transmitted to roughly 428,000 receiving sets; about 525 weeklies and fortnight- lies had a combined circulation of more than 3.8 million; about 5,000 indoor motion picture theatres had about 1.3 million seats and some 3,800 local libraries contained almost 14.8 million books.[15]

Nigeria and South Africa have the lion's share of the media south of the Sahara;

indeed, the 21 daily newspapers in South Africa account for more than 30 percent of all daily newspaper circulation in sub-Saharan Africa; Nigeria had 18 dailies in 1969, though only 11 by 1975. According to the minimum standards for "adequate communications" established by UNESCO in 1961, a country should be able to assure for each 100 of its people at least ten copies of daily newspapers, five radio receivers, two movie seats, and two television receivers. In Africa, only radio is approaching that minimum.

While the government-controlled broadcasting station in the capital city is the crucial keystone of African radio in immediate political terms, the overall mosaic of radio is far more complex than this declaration would suggest. Various facets of the European intrusion can be seen in the overlapping and intersecting layers of local governments, supranational agencies, and religious and other private interests involved in radio. Sydney Head speaks, as of 1972, of 115 separate administrations under as many auspices in the broadcasting systems of 58 countries studied:

. . . . although typically each country has one single monolithic government system, actually the range of administrative variations in Africa is still consider- able. Nigeria has its federal Nigerian Broadcasting Corporation but it also has regional services owned by the States and independent of the N.B.C. The Portuguese territory of Mozambique is alone in having no government station, with all official programming carried by one of several private stations. There were in 1972 more than 40 private, non-government radio stations in Africa, most of them owned by radio clubs in the Portuguese territories, but several in independent countries. This is not counting missionary-operated radio stations, of which there were at least seven. A dozen radio installations on African soil are owned by foreign governments—France, Germany, Great Britain, the Nether- lands and the United States. There is even a student-operated station, run by a high school in Mozambique; and a foreign television station run by the American Forces Radio and Television Service in Ethiopia.[16]

Not only do African listeners have a variety of radio sources from within Africa. The outside world is also omnipresent via short wave. According to Head,

in 1972 some 40 nations outside of Africa and 19 within Africa were pumping propaganda by radio into and around the continent. In addition, several religious stations operating within the continent, as well as the United Nations in New York, added their perhaps less self-serving share of the traffic to the over- crowded short-wave spectrum. As African colonies won independence and as colonial hegemonies faded, rival European and Asian powers began to compete for markets, ideological converts, and third-world leadership. At the same time, the operation of an external service became a status symbol among the new nations themselves—alongside such luxuries as television, jet airlines, and embas- sies abroad. The result is a stunning babel of voices issuing from the short-wave receivers of Africa. Many of these would-be international voices are drowned out in the general hubbub, overwhelmed by the signals of major international broadcasters who, using immensely powerful transmitters equipped with sophisticated directional-antenna arrays, occupy six or eight different frequencies simultaneously. Some, like the Voice of America's relay complex at Monrovia, Liberia, are even located on African soil, where their massive wattage can be even more effectively deployed.[1,7]

This flow of international communications into Africa is only an intensified and diversified continuation of the largely one way cultural contact that began between Europe and Africa even before colonial rule. Radio stations were first established to help European settlers keep in touch with what was taking place in the metropole. From the outset, radio had been an organ tying Africa to Europe, with Africans gradually joining the audience. In the English-speaking colonies, the vernacular was used for broadcasts catering to African listeners, but the emphasis in French-speaking Africa was on teaching and appealing to Africans through the French language. In neither case were the broadcasting systems inherited by African governments at independence equipped to educate, mobilize, and politicize the masses for African nationhood as the new leaders had promised and envisaged. What was left behind instead was an apparatus consciously and unconsciously designed and heretofore employed, with varying degrees of enthusiasm and success, to make Africa a kind of cultural appendage of Western Europe.

Thus the African leaders who had dreamed of taking over and reorienting their communications systems toward more authentically African goals found that they did not have the personnel, the funds, the expertise, the equipment, or the concrete concepts needed to make radio a central part of the nation-building process. Many African leaders, contrary to pre-independence hyperbole, are now more wary of their own artists and intellectuals and information ministry civil servants than they are of supposedly depoliticized European advisors. Radio is not an area in which to take risks—not yet anyway. Except for a few countries, of which Tanzania is a notable example, the packaging of the culture of independence has fallen to European experts who have returned—or never left. Not unsurprisingly, both the capitalist and socialist worlds have found it in their interest to offer technical aid of various kinds in the restyling of independent Africa's radio facilities.

Given the ambivalence of African governments toward radio's potential, there is no immediate prospect that the experience of China in using it as the prime medium in overcoming geographical, cultural, and linguistic barriers to nationhood in an area of vast dimensions will be recognized as strikingly applicable to the needs of Africa. Even so, it is worth noting that Ithiel de Sola Pool's introduction to Alan P.L. Liu's *Communications and National Integration in Communist China* offers a sound prescription for mending Africa's dual society dichotomy:

The real problem was the national integration of a backward country almost totally lacking the prerequisite conditions for the creation of a nation: a common language, adequate roads and railroads to tie the land surface together, literate people capable of communicating over distance, an effectively organized bureaucracy to govern the nation, and radios, newspapers, telephones, and telegraph to provide normal modern communication.

To an extraordinary extent, Chinese efforts surmounted these obstacles by creating a novel and innovative mass communications system at fantastically low capital costs, though very high labor costs. During mass campaigns, discussion meetings attended weekly or more often by hundreds of millions of people substituted for scarce newspapers, magazines, and books. A highly economical wired loudspeaker system that reached almost all Chinese villages substituted for radios that even in battery-transistor form would have been too expensive. The wired radio network also provided secure communication for military mobilization for much of the country, and did double duty as a telephone system for official business. Movies are shown in fantastic number by mobile projection teams who may move the equipment by bicycle. Newspapers are rented by the hour at the post office to people too poor to buy them. Confidential information bulletins brought by delivery boy and picked up again after being read tell the cadres what is going on in the world. During campaigns the walls are covered by *tatzpao*—posters with short, handwritten, large character slogans which everyone is asked to write."[18]

At the same time, it would be unfair to ignore altogether, simply because they barely touch the surface of the problem, the experimental efforts of a few African countries to use radio to reach out from the capital city to extend a helping hand to the rural peasantry. In several African countries, the United Nations Development Program and FAO have lent their support to projects designed to reduce the isolation of the rural peoples and help them to cope with the difficulties of subsistence in situations of distress. The Rural Radio project undertaken since 1968 in the West African nation of Benin—where the Sahel drought of 1968-74 worsened the already marginal rural economy—is an example of the use to which radio is being put in a number of states that were formerly French territories. The citizenry in each of some 700 villages in Benin gather together under straw-roofed canopies, called *apatams*, to listen to the broadcasts on transistor radios:

.... the farmers listen to advice on such matters as caring for palm trees and treating cotton with insecticides or learn how animal traction can influence rural economy. Subjects for the broadcasts are initially chosen by a National Committee comprising representatives of the Ministries of Information, Rural Development, Economy, Public Health and Education. They are then prepared in French and subsequently translated into the country's ten principal spoken languages: Fon, Adja, Yoruba, Mina, Wama, Dendi, Ditamari, Bariba, Pilapila and Peulh. Every evening, Monday through Friday, the National Radio's sole channel devotes an hour to the broadcasts, and as half hour segments in each of two languages are aired each evening, every language group receives one half hour of programming a week. . . .

As overall development of the farming regions is the Rural Radio's primary objective, agricultural broadcasts are supplemented by those designed to promote general health and community development. Topics treated have included: drinking water; care of wells; need for giving blood; fighting malaria; precautions to take to avoid getting sick during the "harmatan"; child feeding and protein; the importance of reforestation; creating cooperatives. There has even been a broadcast entitled "Health lies in the stewpot, not the glass" which counselled against excessive use of palm wine.

Where social customs permit, women listen to the broadcasts along with their husbands. All programmes are followed by discussions, conducted jointly by "animateurs", villagers elected to their posts by their peers, and counsellors from the Ministry of Agriculture's Extension Service. At this time, farmers are given the opportunity to comment on what they have heard and question any points not fully understood. In order to prevent the discussion from becoming unwieldy, membership in each club is limited to 31. Once a month, reports from participating villagers are filled out and returned to Rural Radio headquarters in Cotonou and these are used in the preparation of occasional "feedback" programmes which respond to questions of common concern. . . .[19]

The pre-independence illusion that television would be the great nation-builder has also faded as the hard realities—the cost of the receiving sets and their maintenance, the costs of program production, the limited geographical range of the telecasts, and the resulting small audience—were brought home to the new governments. Another deterrent, as in the case of radio, is that today's leaders are uneasy with African artists and reluctant to give a free hand to innovative producers and writers outside the orbit of the government studios. Even in those countries where television is most developed, free programs provided by the foreign information services fill much of the schedule; the hours in which telecasts are available are limited, and the cost of a set is prohibitive for most Africans. Only Zanzibar has opted to use its resources from the sale of cloves to build a color television system. Yet, given the vast and unevenly populated nature of Africa, television's potential as an educational medium for both children and adults is very great indeed.

What's on at the Movies?

Urban Africans are enthusiastic movie-goers. Despite its somewhat patronizing tone, an article by an anonymous contributor to the bimonthly magazine *Africa Report* captures some of the flavor of going to the Cinema Rex in Lomé, the capital city of Togo:

Programs change daily, and are announced on billboards in front of the theatre and in Lomé's only newspaper, *Togo Presse*. The Rex is a popular theatre, and it shows mostly Italian or Spanish Westerns, German war films, grade C French espionage thrillers, gladiator films, and occasionally an American Western. Sometimes you can catch a 10-year-old Great, such as a James Bond film, and once we saw a silent Laurel and Hardy. Togolese or European newsreels are often part of the program. On Sunday, you might see "King of Kings," or "The Bible."

You can watch the whole show for free standing on the northwest corner of the rue d'Atakpamé and the avenue des Allies. You get a fairly clear view (no sound), and the kids who collect there are good company. Otherwise, seats for evening programs (8:30, 2 films) are 50fr., 100fr., or 150fr. Matinees (6:30, 1 film) are 30 fr., 50fr., or 100fr. Foreigners beware! You will always be sold the most expensive seats unless you insist on your choice.

If you're looking for comfort rather than participation, the 100fr./150fr. section, at the back of the theatre, has individual metal armchairs and fans that sometimes work. The audience is an interesting but rather subdued combination of older professionals, wealthy market mammies (the Togolese economy is in the hands of these enormous, savvy women), girls from nearby nightspots, and French embassy and AID staff.

The soundtrack is inaudible from here if the other sections are noisy, as they invariably are during a cowboy or 007 film. The chief peril in this section, however, is rain. It is the only part of the theatre with a roof, and if it rains during a showing, the seats are taken by storm from the other sections. Since the citizens in the cheap seats have to hurdle two metal barriers before they reach shelter, they are likely to have built up considerable momentum by the time they get to you. Hold fast; and remember that few people will understand why "your" seat can't hold two.

The 100 fr./50fr. seats are the author's choice. The seating is reasonably comfortable: straight-backed benches made of wooden slats, with an armrest here and there to lean on. The benches are easily moved back and forth to put your feet up on and suit your slouch. You sit in the center of the house, the right distance from the screen. And the audience in this section is good people, made up of yourself, young professionals, parents whose children are sitting in cheaper seats, and occasional Peace Corps volunteers.

Nothing, however, can equal the cheap (30fr./50fr.) seats for participation. This section is always the first to be sold out, so if you want to try it, you should get there early (or buy a black-market ticket outside the theatre before the showing). The seating consists of a few backless benches and lots of low stone blocks. The audience is largely teen-agers and impecunious persons of every description, friendly and rowdy. (But watch for pickpockets.)

Remember that the audience at the Rex will more often than not entertain you as much as the film. Some people will be asleep, some will be empathizing out loud with the film, some will be passing back and forth visiting friends in various parts of the house. And then, if you don't want to look at the film or the audience, the part of the night sky you can see through the roof will usually be putting on a pretty good show of its own—floating clouds, bright constellations, a shooting star every once in a while.

If there is a scene of prolonged violence, the best thing to do is to sit very still as the whole section erupts with empathy. Once we were at the Rex for a German war movie called "Ten Against Death" when audience participation got very intense, and the management called in the police to clear the 50fr. section. It was during a 20-minute scene of climatic violence when everyone on-screen was being machine-gunned, falling from heights, and so on. In one sequence a whole platoon of the *Wehrmacht* was electrocuted with blue flames and lots of twitching bodies.

That's what did it. The theatre was in an uproar, especially the 50-francers up front. Half the audience was standing on the seats, cheering the victors and helping them machine-gun the Germans; the other half was mock-machine-gunning the people standing up.

The involvement between the audience and the screen that you sense at the Rex is a distant but exhilarating reflection of how Africans usually approach entertainment. The atmosphere in a western theatre is so repressive: don't smoke, don't move around, don't make comments or someone's going to get the usher, don't fall asleep, what do you think we came here for?

In traditional African entertainment, such as a village dance, the focus is in the *middle* of the crowd, where the dancers are; and the performance usually isn't specialized, anyone can do it. More important still, the performers *need* the audience to do their thing: people step up to wipe the dancer's face, or thank him with small change. Often everyone makes the music.

There's the same lack of specialization at the Rex, as if people didn't realize that movies can be shown to an empty house. You will sense the focus of the attention shift, depending on where the action is. You will feel freer as you shake your conventional passivity; and dimly but deeply you may feel somehow *better*, because humanity is still in charge here.[20]

The cultural cleavage left over from the colonial period is nowhere more evident than in Africa's nascent film industry. In English-speaking Africa, the emphasis is almost exclusively on documentary films, travelogues, and newsreels. Film-making in formerly French Africa is of higher professional quality, though the content varies from froth to the world-renowned cinema-*engagé* of Senegal's Ousmane Sembene. Following the OAU Cultural Festival in Algiers in 1967, it was the francophone group which most energetically undertook to challenge Western control of the film industry in Africa; one of the results of this effort was the creation of a rebel African federation of filmmakers which holds its own cinema festival every other year in Ouagadougou, Upper Volta. Even now, however, most of the theaters in which films are shown in Africa are owned by Europeans or Lebanese or Americans rather than Africans. Although government participation in the distribution machinery has improved the situation in recent years in francophone Africa, extraordinary problems still arise in arranging for the showing in English-speaking Africa of films made in French-speaking Africa. One reason is that the real power in anglophone African distribution is in New York. Of the new film processing laboratories in Africa, only a minority are owned by Africans.

Even African filmmakers who make films for their own governments have trouble getting together the equipment to do the job, and the amount of time and energy required to get an "approved" project through the bureaucratic maze that African governments maintain is staggering. Governments are slow to pay bills on schedule, and costs increase because the funds to finish films-in-process tend to get wrapped up in red tape in some civil servant's "in-basket."

The London monthly *Africa* observed in February 1975:

If African cinema is to survive, it needs more cinema halls because they are the central point of contact with the African public, and the very audience that this cinema is created to serve. When filmmakers can show their films in their own and other African countries, in cinemas of their choice, and know how much money the film makes, so that the profits can be used to finance other films; in short, when the proper economic base is secured, then African cinema can begin to develop normally. This reality is clear to filmmakers, but, unfortunately, not to many of the policymakers in various governments.

Most puzzling of all is the insensitivity of most governments to films and their symbols. I remember being astonished to find that Ousmane Sembene's *Mandabi* was to be shown in 1973 as a part of the *French* Information Service's film festival in Nairobi. There was no protest in the press, no discussion, no overt concern that the showing of this distinguished African's work was not being sponsored by the government of Kenya instead of that of France. (Of course, Sembene's social message is regarded as too strong for the masses in Senegal too; it is in the elite theaters of Dakar, not the *medina*, that his films are usually shown.)

Conclusion: What Are the Choices?

If we measure American media coverage of Africa in terms of relative space allotment and accuracy of basic geographical, economic, and governmental desiderata, then there can be no argument over the judgment that significant improvements have occurred in recent years. Even the ever-changing names of countries, capitals, leaders, and ethnic "ins" and "outs" are now more often than not correctly spelled and identified. What has not changed perceptibly, however, is the prism through which American journalists since Livingstone have looked at Africa. We have not yet come to terms with Africa as it is, but continue to package it in boxes that fit our expectations of the ways in which governments ought to make decisions, armies ought to fight wars, and people ought to choose leaders.

As David Ottaway's chronicle of war reporting in Ethiopia illustrates, there is no way that even the best-intentioned correspondent can bridge the gap between the cultural and technical constructs of his profession and the way things are in Africa. The Africa he reports is inevitably a partly mythical Africa, in which selected facts and observations are patched together to create stories responsive to his readers' (and his editor's) needs, expectations, and concerns. Even if he knows that these needs, expectations, and concerns are not those of the Africans about whom he is writing—and some Western journalists do know or sense this reality—the demands of his profession are overriding. The assignment is to produce instant history in the language of familiar models, and to identify the "good guys" and the "bad guys." More often than not, these identifying labels are based on the subject's perfunctorily overstated rhetoric on extra-African matters and have little to do with his probable competence or compassion in responding to the needs of his own people. The longer term choice for the American press, then, is in the area of consciousness-raising.

In the interim, there are choices that could be made to bring greater expertise, authenticity, and continuity to the reporting of African news in American media. Almost two decades have elapsed since the end of colonial rule began in Africa, and the time has surely come to allow some American journalists—not all who are sent to Africa, but some—to make a career of understanding Africa's complexities in historical context without being labeled special pleaders.

It is not enough, however, to send area specialists to Africa and park them there for long periods of time. One of the traditional strengths of European coverage, for example, has been that senior correspondents commute regularly between their home offices and Africa. When this occurs, editors aren't allowed to file Africa away in some obscure corner of their minds between crises, and the dialogue between home office and field encourages more systematic treatment at both ends. Perhaps the most important by-product of this cross-fertilization is that the correspondent is available from time to time to pose hard questions at Foreign Office press briefings in Paris or London. Contrast this with Washington, where the knowledge of Africa among American diplomatic correspondents covering the State Department appears to this observer to be nil. Sharp, well-timed, knowledgeable, and persistent questions that should have been asked of senior officials as our relations with Africa deteriorated over the past decade were never posed.

The major difference between the mythmaking that characterizes so much of American news coverage of Africa and the purveying of myths in the African press is that the first is unconscious and the second is quite deliberate. That African governments overtly restrict the role of the media is not surprising if one remembers that the several hundred years of African history before 1960 did not create paradigms for popular democracy, representative government, private capital enterprises, or a free press. Neither colonial codes nor practice established the model we inexplicably expected Africans to follow after independence. Even as African journalists become technically more proficient, the media in which they work will continue to be instruments of an authoritarian elite until or unless there is a fundamental reorganization of African society.

Notes

1. John Hughes, *The New Face of Africa* (London: Longmans, Green & Company Press, 1961), p. 275.

2. Henry Kamm, "The Third World Rapidly Turning Into a Closed World for the Foreign Correspondent," *The New York Times*, January 14, 1976.

3. David Ottaway, "Covering a War—By Long Distance Telephone Calls," *The Washington Post*, February 26, 1975. Reprinted with permission.

4. Henry R. Ole Kulet, *Is It Possible?* (Nairobi: Longman Kenya Ltd., 1971), p. 68.

5. Donald Barnett and Karari Njama, *Mau Mau from Within* (New York: Monthly Review Press, 1966), p. 18.

6. *Ibid.*, p. 19.

7. Rev. Johann Ludwig Krapf, *Outline of the Elements of the Kisuaheli Language, 1850* (Tubingen, West Germany: Tubingen Press).

8. Barnett and Njama, *Mau Mau from Within*, p. 18.

9. See, for example, the following: Rosalynde Ainslie, *The Press in Africa* (London: Victor Gollancz, Ltd., 1966); Frank Barton, *African Assignment* (Zurich: International Press Institute, 1969); Frank Barton, *The Press in Africa* (Nairobi: East African Publishing House, 1966); William A. Hachten, *Muffled Drums* (Ames: Iowa University Press, 1971); Tom Hopkinson, *In the Fiery Continent* (New York: Doubleday & Company, 1962); Tom Hopkinson, *Two Years in Africa* (Zurich: International Press Institute, 1965); Helen A. Kitchen (ed.), *The Press in Africa* (Washington, D.C.: Ruth Sloan Associates, Inc., 1956); and Anthony Sampson, *Drum: A Venture Into The New Africa* (London: Collins, 1956).

10. Information supplied by Professor William A. Hachten of the School of Journalism and Mass Communication, University of Wisconsin, and Professor Robert L. Nwanko of the Department of Journalism, University of Rhode Island. See also *Training of Journalists: Africa*, a pamphlet of limited distribution published in March 1973 by UNESCO's Division of Development and Application of Communication.

11. Cyprian Ekwensi, *People of the City* (London: Heinemann Educational Books, Ltd., 1963), p. 127.

12. *Ibid.*

13. "My Friend Joe . . . as he really is" by Hilary Ng'weno and Terry Hirst, *Daily Nation*, April 20, 1973, p. 15. Reprinted with permission.

14. Sydney Head (ed.), *Broadcasting in Africa* (Philadelphia: Temple University Press, 1974), p. 3. Reprinted with permission.

15. William A. Hachten, *Muffled Drums*, p. 15.

16. Sydney Head (ed.), *Broadcasting in Africa*, p. 6.

17. *Ibid.*, p. 175.

18. Alan P.L. Liu, *Communications and National Integration in Communist China* (Berkeley: University of California Press, 1971), (Foreword by Ithiel de Sola Pool), p. xiii. Copyright © 1971 by The Center for Chinese Studies, University of Michigan; reprinted by permission of the University of California Press.

19. *Africa* magazine, #42 (February 1975). London, England. Reprinted with permission.

20. Anonymous, "Now Starring, at the Rex Cinema Lomé! . . . ," *Africa Report* (New York), July-August 1973, pp. 43-44. Reprinted with permission.

VIII

Who Will Rule Africa by the Year 2000?

Philippe Lemaitre

Following World War II, the entire world entered into three decades of steady economic expansion, and the demand for Africa's primary products grew accordingly. Partly because of this enhanced interest in Africa's primary products, expansive changes occurred at many other levels: more extensive and intensive use of land for cash-crops, development of infrastructure, population growth, accelerated urbanization, an increase in the numbers of Africans receiving cash wages for their work, rapid growth in the numbers of Africans receiving training both in formal educational institutions and within private and governmental enterprises, a greater flow of outside private investment into the continent, multiplication of government and business bureaucracies. In short, the period from 1945 to 1976 was one of remarkable overall growth. This growth was quite uneven, however, and left some Africans untouched, many worse off than before.

These three decades following World War II were also marked by major political transformations, perhaps nowhere more so than in Africa. When the United Nations was founded in 1945, four states on the continent were eligible for membership as sovereign entities: Egypt, Ethiopia, Liberia, and South Africa. The rest of Africa was composed of colonial territories subject to one or another European power (except South West Africa, ruled by South Africa since the departure of the Germans in World War I). In the next 30 years, virtually all of Africa came to consist of sovereign states—48 in all by 1976, with more in prospect. Indeed, Africa accounted, by 1976, for almost a third of the membership of the United Nations. With minor exceptions, the boundaries of these sovereign states were identical with those of the colonial territories of 1945.

Economic growth and decolonization were closely linked, for the visible quickening of the economic pace in Africa after 1945 created unprecedented strains on the colonial system. On the one hand, it produced large strata of persons in the urban areas whose economic and political aspirations, whetted by wartime rhetoric about self-fulfillment of free peoples, could not be satisfied within the limitations necessarily imposed by a colonial framework. On the other hand, it inevitably accentuated exploitation and the differences between the new "haves" and the old "have nots" in the rural areas, creating resentment and resistance to the pressures for greater productivity associated with economic growth.

In the towns, there were not only more people each year, but also a larger number of persons at each educational level. The pressure for more and better jobs in the two urban sectors that employed most people—the colonial government and the· export-import firms—came up against one of the basic givens of the colonial situation. This was that the decisionmaking and more prestigious positions were allocated (exclusively or predominantly) to whites from the colonial metropole, and secondarily to selected "third" groups such as the Asians in East Africa. In those areas where favorable climate and economic factors encouraged the growth of large white settler populations—for example, Kenya, Algeria, Southern Rhodesia, South Africa—this formal and informal discrimination against African promotion penetrated further and further down the occupational hierarchy. Thus the barrier to individual African advancement that had existed from the beginning of colonial rule was now felt more acutely and by larger numbers of persons, precisely because of the visibility of overall development.

This frustration of individual mobility in the urban areas was compounded by a slow but steady price inflation which affected the real wages of an initially largely nonunionized wage force.[1] Whites, on the other hand, found life in Africa more palatable than before, not only because the colonial wage differentials worked to their benefit but also because the expanded infrastructure enhanced the quality of their *lifestyle*. Indeed, the relative privilege of the colonial administrators and settlers became more blatant in the postwar years.

In the rural areas, expansion of cash-crop areas and expansion of production involved various kinds of disruptions and reorganizations affecting traditional social structures and practices. These changes had many consequences, including de jure or de facto reallocation of collective land to private owners and the relative enrichment of one segment of the African rural population in relation to the others. The segment which prospered from these changes in rural Africa consisted for the most part of high-ranking persons (traditional chiefs) of certain, though not all, tribal groups. This process of creation of African rural landowning classes, and the concomitant creation of African rural classes that earned their living by working on the land of others, inevitably created dissatisfaction among those who were being proletarianized.

But even the new African rural bourgeoisies were not necessarily content. Particularly in East and Central Africa, they had to contend with government-assisted, legally privileged white farmers. In all areas, they had no alternative but to sell their produce to buyers—either export-import firms or marketing boards of the colonial governments—whose bargaining position was very strong. Colonial governments were, by the nature of things, less concerned with promoting the interests of African owners of cash-crop farmland than they were with the realities of a world commodity market subject to manipulation by the large purchasers in the Western world.

The discontent in the rural areas—among those workers of the land being proletarianized and those becoming rural landowning classes under less than ideal groundrules—led to various forms of resistance and slowdown. Despite absolute economic growth and persistent world real demand, the situation at the grass roots level was not conducive to optimal productive effort.

It is here that the nationalist movements enter into the story. Long before 1945, there had been sporadic "primary resistance" to colonial rule in African rural areas, just as there had been quasi-political organizing by educated elements in the larger cities for better treatment, less discrimination, and a voice in their fate. But it was rare before 1945 to find territory-wide organizations that brought together rural and urban elements, the more- and the less-educated, around specifically political objectives. Only in the post-1945 period did such political organizations begin to arise, in a kind of chain-like effect. These groups came to be known as "nationalist" movements, since their demands evolved over time, from however, apolitical beginnings, into a demand for the end of colonial rule and the creation of a sovereign state more or less within the colonial territorial boundaries. The ideology of these movements—whether in the British Gold Coast, the several territories of French West Africa, or Belgium's Congo— was "nationalist" in two senses. They asserted a collective right of their "nation" to peer relationship with the former colonial power and all other nation-states. And they asserted the primacy of national rights and loyalties over those of any other corporate ethnic, religious, or racial group.

Although the details varied from country to country, the process of decolonization followed the same basic pattern in most African states: (1) The nationalist movement started as a small number of political activists, usually drawn primarily from the urban educated. (2) Frequently more than one pretender group claimed to represent the true interests of the future nation. (3) The initial response of the colonial power to the claims of these pressure groups was rejection, on the grounds that they were unrepresentative of the population as a whole and lacking in effective organizational strength.

The organizations that eventually succeeded in moving colonial governments to take them seriously were those that were able to weld together various dissenting groups in diverse areas of the country, in both urban and rural areas, among both more and less educated. This process was carried forward by political propaganda and militant action against the colonial power, which led to repression of varying degrees of severity, which in turn broadened the recognition and appeal of the nationalist leaders. In a few territories ruled by an economically weak colonial power (Angola, Mozambique, Guinea-Bissau), or where the presence of white settler farmers complicated the confrontation (Algeria, Kenya, Southern Rhodesia), this phase involved guerrilla warfare. Organizing within the context of official negativism or repression is always a politicizing phenomenon. In Africa, it led to the political education and eventually the effective "radicalization" of peoples previously less-concerned with the larger national and international scene.

When the nationalist movement in a particular African country was able to demonstrate genuine organizational strength, the colonizing power was usually faced with two alternatives: to invest in the political and financial cost of further repression, risking further mass politicization and radicalization of the population; or to attempt to effect a compromise with the leadership of the nationalist movement, by trading political concessions (ultimately independence) for minimal changes in the economic structure of the country and particularly in its international economic relations.

The choices confronting the European colonial powers at mid-century in relation to their African territories were not a matter of indifference to other world powers. This was the period of the so-called Cold War, and the USSR, theretofore excluded from contact with the colonized world, had much to gain and little to lose by unequivocally supporting nationalist demands for African control of Africa's destiny. Although the United States was in a more ambiguous position because of its NATO association with the colonial powers, Washington had a lively interest in the prospect of freer and more direct access to Africa as seller and buyer, and was also pulled into Africa by a concern that a radicalized and hostile nationalist movement would develop interests in common with the USSR.

Britain was the first European power to accept the Disraelian logic of concessions in the hope of cooptation. Beginning with the granting of independence to Sudan in 1956 and Ghana in 1957, London had by the mid-1960s applied this logic to 16 of its African holdings, all except Southern Rhodesia.

Once de Gaulle came to power and was able to ensure that decolonization could be brought about without rending the internal fabric of French society, the French followed suit. Indeed, de Gaulle demonstrated in Algeria that compromise with nationalist leadership was possible even after a long and bitter guerrilla war had taken place. De Gaulle's conversion to decolonization, combined with pressure from Washington growing out of a late 1950s policy decision that United States interests would be better served by advocacy of "Africa for the Africans," led Belgium to shift course abruptly and try to cut its economic losses by granting independence to the mineral-rich Congo in 1960—before the Congolese nationalist movement was yet a coherent force.

Portugal was the most reluctant European power to decolonize, perhaps primarily because it was the poorest. The Portuguese economy was relatively more dependent on colonial monopolies than that of the other colonizing powers, and Lisbon had less grounds for optimism about the possibility of retaining economic advantage in a postindependence era, in the face of the kind of competition for the significant resources of Angola and Mozambique likely to come from the United States and other industrial countries. In the end, it required a liquidation of the heart of the Portuguese regime in Lisbon in 1974 to bring about a willingness to decolonize, the liquidation itself having been precipitated by the costs (both economic and political) of the colonial wars.

There has been an observable correlation, though not a perfect one, between the degree of European resistance to decolonization and the degree of African mass politicization and radicalization. Algeria, Mozambique, and Guinea-Bissau are cases in point. Overall, however, the requirement for armed resistance in the decolonization of Africa has been small, and consequently the level of mass radicalization has been relatively low. In the short run, then, the gamble that timely political concessions on the part of the colonial powers could abort the development of strong revolutionary currents in Africa proved successful. Britain and France (and probably also Belgium) minimized their losses; while they could not be said to be stronger in Africa in 1976 than in 1946, either politically or economically, they were not drastically weaker. It is doubtful that alternative modes of handling the political discontent would have served them better. The effect of the decolonization of Angola, Mozambique, and Guinea-Bissau on Portugal is yet to be measured.

Both the USSR and the United States gained from the decolonization of Africa, albeit probably less than either anticipated in the early 1960s. For the USSR, decolonization has permitted direct contact and some slight diplomatic advantage. From the point of view of the United States, the modesty of the Soviet gain is seen as a positive American gain, as is the extent of United States influence and economic penetration achieved at modest political cost. There has been an overall net gain for multinational corporations and banking institutions, not so much in terms of immediate profit figures as in the preparation of the ground for profitable investment in Africa in the coming decades.

As for the Africans themselves, the middle classes have everywhere been the major beneficiaries of the decolonization process. In North, West, Central, East, and the self-governing parts of southern Africa, it is the middle classes which have gained control of the state structures, eliminated internal barriers to their individual advancement, and augmented their annual income by a considerable margin. They have gained international status and local authority, and, for the most part, they welcome profitable collaboration with outside economic investors.

By contrast, the mass of the African populations, both in rural and urban areas, seem to me to have lost ground overall. To be sure, there have been some visible improvements in their lot: the humiliations of legal discriminations have ended; primary schooling has expanded enormously; health conditions have improved, though spottily; and a small segment of the mass has moved upward into the middle class. But there is another side to the ledger. The twin phenomena of ecological exhaustion and population increase have resulted in mass starvation in parts of rural Africa. And malnutrition is endemic among the ever-expanding ranks of effectively landless and jobless urban residents or squatters. The form of political expression, and hence of democratic involvement, open to rural and urban workers in the nationalist movements in the last years of colonial rule has in most cases been eliminated by the widespread installation of authoritarian military regimes, or, in the nonmilitary states, by the fossilization of most of the nationalist parties. To appreciate the extent of this disenfranchisement, we should take a careful look at the politics of the postcolonial regimes.

The Governments Since Independence

On the day that independence came, almost all of the African states were governed by a major nationalist movement that had emerged during the post-1945 period and had demonstrated substantial support in large parts of the country. In a few cases, such as Nigeria, Benin, Zaire, and Sudan, the strongest movement was too weak to govern alone and entered into a coalition with one or more other smaller groups, usually regionally based. In virtually all cases, there were groups of varying vitality in "opposition."

Within months in some cases, or a few years in others, most states moved from government by a dominant party to a formalized single-party regime. Often, the single party became a structure of the state itself. The transition to a single-party regime was usually brought about by a combination of methods: entry of opposition leaders or whole parties into the dominant party; gerrymandering; imprisonment of opposition leaders; expulsion of opposition members from the legislature; dissolution of opposition parties; constitutional amendment.

In those cases where a single-party regime was not achieved for various reasons (Nigeria, Benin, Zaire), a military coup created the functional substitute. And where one-party regimes were created, many were eventually replaced by military regimes (Ghana, Uganda, Togo, Niger, the Somali Republic, etc.). In no independent African state has there been a steadily functioning multiparty system with alternation in office by electoral means.

Why has Africa fallen victim to this pattern of rotation of governments by palace coups? The answer lies, on the one hand, in the very high expectations created by pre-independence rhetoric. Pressures for immediate government assistance in improving the level of income and the quality of life came from the educated and relatively well-off elements in both agricultural and urban areas, as well as from the rural poor and the swollen ranks of "unemployed school-leavers" looking for jobs in the towns and cities, and preferably jobs that offered a level of income and prestige above the bottom stratum. The ability of the African governments to meet these demands was sharply limited by the decline of revenue (in relation to world prices) of the 1960s and the thin bureaucratic superstructure inherited from colonial rule.

It has been argued that, in the end, the dilemmas were more or less the same whether a government took a "radical" or a "conservative" policy stance,[2] if by "radical" one means resistance to bedding down with Western-based multi-national corporations and a foreign policy line at odds with that of the United States. In any case, it is clear that all regimes, whatever their ideological stance, were subject to threats of tribally based regionalism and even secession.

In summary, the political trend of the period 1960-1976 was, in many ways, to reverse the dominant political trend of 1945-1960. Whereas pressures from World War II to 1960 forced governments to contend ever more openly with mass political interests, the period from 1960 to 1976 has been marked by a steady trend back to a form of administrative politics in which decisions are made behind a screen by a small inner circle, and opposition is coopted or repressed instead of confronted with a view to negotiating compromises.

While the form of the political process in the mid-1970s is reverting to an earlier style, the content of the politics is, of course, quite different. New groups now have access to the government, and the kinds of political decisions that governments face are indicative of changing economic structures.

The New Social Forces

If it is accepted that the principal difference between African polities of 1976 and those of 1945 lies in the degree and form of influence of internal social forces on the government, it is crucial to examine these newly important forces. They can be divided into four groups: the indigenous middle classes (or bourgeois elements), the intelligentsia (to the extent that they can be said to constitute a group separate from the middle classes), wage-earning workers, and so-called subsistence farmers.

In the history of the Western world, bourgeoisie is a term that connotes primarily entrepreneurs—whether merchants or industrialists—who have no legally or customarily established privileged status. That is, they are *not* nobility. It is the bourgeoisie who were the progenitors of capitalist enterprise and presumably the economic makers of the modern world. Yet, if one were to think exclusively in these terms with reference to African economic history, the picture would be very distorted.

There were, obviously, groups of African merchants who were involved in the early trade with the Western world. Indeed, as this trade expanded in the period from the sixteenth to the nineteenth century, the merchant strata prospered, particularly in the coastal regions. But one of the most significant consequences of the imposition of colonial rule throughout Africa in the late nineteenth century was the elimination of these indigenous merchant classes from a major role in the export-import trade of the colonial era. The elimination of the African merchant class was largely deliberate[3] and partly inevitable, given the structural discriminations of a colonial society.

Thus, the African middle classes were at their economic ebb during the core years of European colonization in most of Africa, the years after conquest but before decolonization, roughly 1900-1945. They controlled few enterprises, and the ones they did control were small in size and largely at the retail level. Africans occupied virtually no managerial positions in private enterprises and very few responsible positions in government, church, or educational bureaucracies; there was a sprinkling of doctors, lawyers, and clergymen in the French, British, and Portuguese territories, but only the latter in Belgian Africa. The generally minimal role of Africans receded to infinitesimal in those areas where white settlers were a power factor.

As political activity became more legitimate in the period after World War II, the nationalist leadership arose from among the middle class elements most familiar with the vulnerabilities of the colonial regimes. Those who had managed to hold on to a position of minor privilege in the prewar years were, on the whole, significantly less "militant" than Africans whose aspirations for middle-class privilege were as yet unfulfilled; but the differences were not fundamental.

In their private lives, many middle-class Africans alternated between entrepreneurial activity and nationalist agitation in the late colonial period. Some managed to make of their entrepreneurial activity itself a form of nationalist agitation (as for example, in the establishment of a Nigerian-owned bank in the 1950s by Nnamdi Azikiwe, who was later to become his country's first president). Throughout Africa, the net result of nationalist political activity was to place nearly all top managerial positions, both in and out of government, in the hands of members of the African middle class, who received for their work high remuneration, especially high in relation to the standard of living of the vast majority of the indigenous population in each country. In addition, most of these "bureaucrats" supplemented their incomes by establishing, either in their own name or that of their spouses, a series of small enterprises (house rental, truck farming, transport, etc.) which increased their real income enormously— and frequently created conflicts of interest in relation to their responsibilities as ministers or civil servants. There is, of course, no way of calculating the extent of illicit income, but circumstantial evidence of conspicuous consumption almost everywhere suggests that corruption was, and is, substantial. Only in a few countries, notably Tanzania and Guinea, did the government after independence make a serious attempt to deny to ministers and civil servants these forms of supplementary income, and, even in these more militantly egalitarian states, the core income (government salary) was relatively high.

The role of the African urban middle class takes on additional interest because of the significant ties that professionals, politicians, civil servants, private businessmen, and managers in the private sector maintained with the rural areas from which they or their families originally came. This took the form not merely of land claims, but the actual establishment of enterprises (agricultural, commercial, and/or artisanal) located in these areas. In effect, the political leader (or aspirant) from the new urban middle classes sought the status of a sometime-resident patron with a rural clientele. What the patron offered his clientele was individual political protection and service as a spokesman for economic claims to the largesse in the government pork barrel (schools, dispensaries, roads, and also access to jobs). The clientele, on its part, gave the patron a political base for his own personal claims vis-à-vis the state, and also, more often than not, underpaid service in his various enterprises.

The "chiefs" of the intricate maze of tribes that comprise rural Africa evolved through the late nationalist period and the era after independence as the rural-based managerial link of this urban-patron/rural-peasant client nexus. In exchange for a share in the various entrepreneurial activities, the resident chief acted as the de facto enforcer of the numerous unwritten contracts that came into being over time between the patron and his clientele.

The most efficient and politically most important of these urban middle-class elements also sought to establish links with the multinational corporations when and where these corporations sought entry into the more promising economies. Of course, there were many countries which had too little to offer in immediately exploitable products to make it worthwhile for outside corporations to invest in any significant way. And there were others where such activity was largely channeled through the state; in the early years, this was one of the marks, although not a very reliable one, of a "radical" state. But the number of states where such mixed operations were feasible and profitable for all concerned was impressive. In, for example, Ivory Coast, Kenya, Zaire, Nigeria, and Morocco, there was a direct correlation between the economic and political strength of that sector of the bourgeoisie serving as local agents of the multinational corporations.

The principal internal conflict within these middle-class strata has thus far had less to do with economic specialization than with the simple squeeze on the availability of profit-making positions—in the state apparatus, with the multinationals, or in quasi-monopolistic national enterprises. Since few Africans were in a position to accumulate capital in the colonial period, the new middle classes largely relied on control of (or at least access to) the state for their access to credit, subsidy, and speculative capital. Factional quarrels at the center were endemic because of the crucial role of the state apparatus as broker or guarantor for most economic transactions. Since the major political resource that could be mobilized by individual members of the middle classes was their rural clientele and its urban offshoots, the quarrels between these new middle-class factions took the form of "ethnic rivalries." Periods of acute conflict tapered off into temporary quiescence, when one group or combination of groups won effective control of the state apparatus; but the basic condition was one of inherent instability.

The intelligentsia was really a segment of the middle classes, but it has sufficiently specific characteristics to warrant further identification. In the Belgian and Portuguese territories, educational opportunities above the primary level were so limited prior to 1960 that this group could barely be said to exist. In some of the other territories—notably British West Africa, French North Africa, Senegal, Benin, Togo, Uganda, Madagascar, and South Africa—small but significant numbers of students were sent or went on their own to universities in Britain and France (or, in the case of the British colonies, sometimes to the United States). Many spent long years in student exile, often living at a low-income level.

During the period of pre-independence nationalist agitation, strains often developed between these students attending universities in the metropoles and the less-educated nationalist leadership engaged at home in negotiating the route to decolonization. Many of the older leaders had no more than secondary or even primary schooling, and the student "radicals" were inclined to look down upon them and chastise them for their timidity and "incompetence." The leaders actually in toe-to-toe encounter with the colonial regimes, on the other hand, accused the students of dilettantism, verbal radicalism, and political irrelevance. But most of the students who eventually returned to Africa, and most of them did as independence became a reality, tended to be incorporated into middle-class economic, political, or professional positions in their home country (or in some other country with the same linguistic and colonial heritage).

This is not to suggest that the problem of the absorption of the intelligentsia was resolved for all time. In a sense, it was just beginning, for one of the major effects of the rise of nationalism and the achievement of independence was the very rapid expansion of educational opportunity at all levels. The fact that the expansion of education far outpaced the expansion of appropriate occupational opportunity has created acute social problems, ranging from the crisis of the unemployed primary school-leaver with illusions of a better life to the tensions arising from the inability of a growing reservoir of university graduates to find appropriate employment in their own countries.

While the term "appropriate" is a function of social expectation, there unquestionably was and is a shortage of positions, insofar as these graduates use a reference group of parallel graduates in Western industrialized countries. This shortage has been complicated in those countries (particularly in such former French colonies as Ivory Coast, Senegal, and Gabon) where the governments still use expatriate personnel to fill a significant number of the relatively few professional positions available. Independent governments continue to employ expatriate personnel for various reasons: uncertainty concerning the political reliability of returning graduates, politico-economic appeasement of the ex-metropole, and financial savings insofar as expatriate personnel were paid for by aid funds from the ex-metropole.

What happens to the surplus graduates? Some have become part of the international "brain drain" and have been lost to Africa. Some have found gilded exile in international agencies. Some went home, entered into political opposition, and ended in prison, or worse. Some accepted positions below their "station" (as schoolteachers, etc.). Thirty-nine African countries now have from one to four universities and/or other institutions of higher learning; Egypt and Nigeria each has seven and South Africa has 22. Since, in addition, many Africans were still studying in universities outside of Africa by 1976, this problem is not easing. Africa may yet see the emergence of a self-conscious and discontented intelligentsia, in the original nineteenth century Russian usage of the term—an economically frustrated but uncohesive stratum growing more distinct from fellow graduates with direct access to the state machinery.

It is my view, however, that the intelligentsia as a social force in gestation is, in Africa at least, far less important for the longer term than the wage-earning workers. Although the wage-earning workers emerged as a socially visible category during the colonial era, analysis of their role is complicated by the fact that their numbers, both in absolute and relative terms, are unevenly distributed between countries, and between regions within countries. Almost all of those employed in urban areas are employed for wages; and, even if one deducts those who might be considered to be performing "managerial tasks," the numbers are significant and growing. Most of these urban wage-earners are in administrative, commercial, or service sectors; but in a few countries (Algeria, Morocco, Nigeria, Zaire, South Africa, among others) there is now a sizable and growing industrial work-force. In the rural areas, increasing numbers of wage-workers are involved in cash-cropping and mineral extraction, although statistics show that the bulk of the rural population still ekes out its living from so-called subsistence farming.

This picture is not as simple as it seems, however, because many Africans play multiple roles. In the first place, a large number of Africans are "migrant workers" in the sense that they spend part of their lives (or part of each year) as wage-earners in mines, on cash-crop farms, or in towns, and the rest of their lives as rural cultivators, often in "subsistence" farming. Many of the workers in the mines of South Africa, for example, are migrants from outside the Republic. Some Africans—especially in francophone West and North Africa—even migrate back and forth as "foreign workers" to France. The situation is further complicated because many of those living in rural areas combine cash crops with "subsistence" crops, and also obtain wages for working on the cash-crop farms of others from time to time. Moreover, wage-workers may be employed sporadically, or seasonally, or remain unemployed for long periods of time. The flow to the towns of "school-leavers"[4] increased markedly with the increase of educational facilities and the removal of the remaining political and psychological barriers at independence. Nairobi, Lagos, and Kinshasa offer only the most graphic examples of the large and growing unemployed stratum of newly urban Africans living marginally on relatives and showing many signs of evolving into a permanent lumpenproletariat.

While some of these unemployed urban elements became active in the nationalist movement during the years just before independence, the actual achievement of independence has removed this social framework for their existence. Under President Kwame Nkrumah, Ghana established a "Builders Brigade" within a few months of independence to engage the landless young, and many other governments have subsequently improvised various busy-work schemes for this potentially destabilizing element. But most of these paramilitary agencies have been able to provide slots for no more than a token number of school-leavers, and many have degenerated into a form of political patronage.

The fourth and least visible, but sometimes largest, social stratum in African countries is comprised of so-called subsistence farmers. The "so-called" is important, because the rural African thus labeled does more than sustain himself by his agricultural activities. He also provides sustenance for those of his extended family who emigrate somewhere after childhood and return to the village as old age approaches. As the percentage of aged has grown in the colonial and postcolonial periods, and as people have begun to live longer because of general improvement in sanitation, subsistence farmers have in fact been called upon to support larger and larger numbers of persons by their labors.

This has not only placed an additional productive burden on them and their land, usually without any infusion of technology to compensate; it has also served as a constraint on the wage levels of wage-workers by reducing the effective minimum lifetime sum required for sustenance and reproduction of the wage work-force. In addition, this system of rotation of labor (rather than rotation of crops) has served to involve the "subsistence" farmer in the wider political concerns which his brothers who return from the cities bring to his attention.

Pastoralists (including nomads) are a specific kind of subsistence farmer. Some of Africa's livestock raisers are full-fledged cash-crop "farmers," of course, but the majority serve the larger economy in ways similar to subsistence food-crop growers, with two differences. Some of the nomadic groups provide a smaller proportion of the urban migrants than do sedentary agriculturalists, and thus to this extent are less fully integrated into the system. On the other hand, nomads tend to be located in land that is marginal and very susceptible to climatic fluctuations. Because these groups are hit hardest in the famines, they may be largely liquidated in the coming ten to 25 years.

One of the factors relatively special to Africa, distinguishing it from Asia and

Latin America, is the degree to which these four strata—bourgeoisie, intelligent-sia, wage-earners, and "subsistence" farmers—can be found linked together in kinship groups. No doubt this is becoming less true as the years go by, but the familial links between middle-class elements and lower strata remain surprisingly difficult to cut. The aged mother of an African nation's president may indeed continue to live in a small village. Certainly his second cousin may. And this limited degree of correlation of family ties and class ties has its effects on political developments.

Who Governs Africa Today?

It is not an exaggeration to say that the governments of independent Africa have been governments operated by and for the middle classes, even in the so-called radical states. That is, the initial concern of all African states after independence was to build a government coalition that included the middle-class representa-tives of every important geographical area and ethnic group; or, failing that, to build a coalition of sufficient strength so that those sectors not included (for any reason) were too weak to threaten the state by rebellion, secession, or sabotage.

Such a coalition of middle-class elements was the essential point of the single-party system that attained such vogue in the 1960s. In those cases where the political leadership lacked sufficient skill in the political arts of manipula-tion, cooptation, and legerdemain, and was pressed (either actually or poten-tially) in the direction of acute repression, the army often took over. The replacement military regimes were constrained to build coalitions identical to those of the predecessor civilian ones, and it is no surprise that they met with about the same degree of political success. It has made virtually no difference to the daily functioning of an African state whether the cabinet is composed of politicians or army officers. In this sense, military regimes can be regarded as a functional alternative to a single-party system. (Ethiopia is likely to be a special case, since the military regime that succeeded the deposed Emperor Haile Selassie will almost certainly diminish, if not abolish, the powerful social and political role of the stratum of large noble-landowners, a group which had no historical equivalent in most other African states.)

What the middle-class clientele demanded of these various middle-class dominated regimes in newly independent Africa was the use of government apparatus to enhance the way of life of the middle classes in various ways: by direct expenditure on national infrastructure (major transportation facilities, the university, large hospitals in the urban centers, recreational facilities, even large merchandising outlets); by redistribution of revenue among middle-class ele-ments through subsidy of enterprises as well as growing perquisites of state employment; by a search for external grants, loans, or investment which would have local payoff. Some governments acceded to these pressures wholeheartedly and were rewarded, in the short term at least, with a high degree of prosperity. The Ivory Coast under President Houphouet-Boigny and Zaire under Mobutu are two of the most obvious middle-class "success" stories. Benin, Sierra Leone, and Chad were among the countries which tried the Ivoirian route but were unable to attain the economic momentum to stay rising political unrest.

But the middle classes were not the only strata to give political expression to economic and social demands. In a number of countries, the urban wage-workers and the unemployed sectors contingent to them erupted in protest against the growing disparities of income resulting from declining real wages, increases in relative tax burdens (through across-the-board impositions on salaries), and concentration of government expenditures in areas from which primarily the middle classes profited. The 1964 general strike in Nigeria, the "three glorious days" in Congo-Brazzaville in 1963, the trade union demonstrations leading to the army coup in Benin in 1963, and the Sekondi-Takoradi strike in Ghana in 1961 occurred precisely because these disparities had become too patent, and were triggered by particular government actions (or non-actions) of a provocative nature.

In some of these urban worker eruptions, the leaders of the trade unions (albeit themselves a sector of the middle classes) were swept along by events and sought to channel the furor by joining it. In others, the unions were bypassed. In some cases, notably Benin and Upper Volta, worker rebellions led directly to changes in government, which did not always accomplish the improvements the workers demanded but indicated the longer term worker potential. Generally speaking, the major consequence of workers' rebellions in independent Africa has been to weaken the position of the civilian leadership, either immediately (Benin, Upper Volta), or in a delayed fashion (Ghana, Nigeria). Discontent among small rural cash-crop farmers has led to explosions less frequently, but in at least one instance farmer discontent provided the base for a sustained uprising. This was the Mulelist rebellion in the Kwilu in Zaire (1963-64).[5]

The lot of the "subsistence" farmer has been to suffer in obscurity and to resist on an individual basis. It has been only since the acute famines of the 1970s began to strike in the Sahel, Ethiopia, and East Africa that these farmers became politically perceptible. Thus far, however, they have not organized, albeit their plight has served as one excuse for at least two military coups (the overthrow in 1974 of the governments of President Hamani Diori in Niger, and of Emperor Haile Selassie in Ethiopia).

But Africa is not an island unto itself, and one cannot analyze the politics of African regimes without taking note of the fifth significant "internal" social force—the Western world, as expressed through the governments of the ex-colonial powers and the United States and through the multinational corporations and banks. The role that these extra-African participants have played has been largely supportive. They have sustained friendly governments with economic and humanitarian assistance, and, at critical junctures, with direct military aid (France in Gabon in 1963, Belgium and the United States in Zaire in 1964, the United States in Zaire in 1967, Britain in the case of the East African military mutinies in 1964, France in Cameroon and Chad over many years). They have withheld crucial economic aid for disciplinary purposes at critical junctures (France in Guinea in 1958-59, the United States and Britain in Ghana in 1965, and for the Tan-Zam railroad project circa 1965). They have served as a useful prop of white regimes in southern Africa (the ten-bank consortium loans to South Africa in the period 1961-64, direct and indirect military support of fellow NATO member Portugal during the period of the colonial wars in Mozambique, Angola, and Guinea-Bissau). In general, however, the Western world has not had to face the issue of intervening "massively" anywhere in Africa to sustain its interests (except possibly in Zaire in 1960-64), in part because internal elements whose interests were not believed to be fundamentally or permanently inimical to the interests of the West were largely in effective control of Africa.

In addition to each African nation taken separately, there has been, since 1958 at least, a pan-African political arena in which these social forces have also played. Pan-African politics have been in part determined by, in part determinative of, what has gone on in the national political arenas.

The establishment of the Organization of African Unity (OAU) in 1963 was the culmination of a five-year struggle between those who wished an interstate agency that would primarily serve as a reflection and a mechanism for coordination of the national governments, and those who envisaged a unifying organization that would act as a "radicalizing" force not only in the world arena but in Africa itself. It can be said in summary that the more cautious "Monrovia" forces prevailed over the so-called Casablanca forces just as and just because they prevailed within most of the African states. The most significant way in which the pragmatists prevailed was in writing into the OAU charter both a "noninterference" doctrine, and in establishing a practice of "automatic recognition." Automatic recognition meant that changes in regimes by coups would result in no interruption in the rights and role within the OAU of the state involved. As the years passed, the OAU was occasionally pained to accept automatic recognition in all its implications—as reflected in its hesitation when President Sylvanus Olympio of Togo was assassinated in 1963, when Moise Tshombe became prime minister of Zaire (then Congo/Kinshasa) in 1964, when Kwame Nkrumah of Ghana was ousted in 1966, and when Idi Amin came to power by coup d'etat in Uganda in 1971. In each case, however, the basic tenet was eventually honored by the OAU.

According to the doctrine of noninterference, it is illegitimate for any African government to provide or offer concrete forms of political support to opposition elements in another African state, particularly if the opposition is defined as illegal by the incumbent government. This doctrine was regularly defied only by Nkrumah, and opposition to it became sporadic and underground after his overthrow in 1966.

The effect of both these doctrines, along with the decision to regard pre-independence colonial boundaries as sacred, was to lessen the possibilities of social upheaval anywhere in Africa. To be sure, the OAU did commit itself to active support of independence and liberation movements in colonial and white settler territories. To this end, the OAU established the African Liberation Committee (ALC), which has given money and other forms of support to African movements in such areas. While the ALC support was important in furthering the decolonization of Portuguese Africa, as well as in keeping alive the fires of resistance to white rule in Rhodesia and South Africa, the ALC has been, on balance, a moderating force in that it has furthered the integration of the liberation movements into the standard African middle-class nationalist pattern.

In summary, despite all the newspaper headlines to the contrary, the years 1960-1975 were ones of surprisingly homogeneous political arrangements in Africa. Most governments have been, relatively speaking, status quo oriented. Although particular regimes sometimes changed faces frequently, the basic politics of the state did so far less often. Genuine civil wars have occurred in only a few states, and, except for Sudan, Nigeria, and perhaps Ethiopia and Chad, have been relatively short lived. No guerrilla movement arose in the independent states that showed much depth as a revolutionary movement, except perhaps in Zaire in the early 1960s. The forms and modes of class conflict have been muted and repressed. Behind surface instability lay political continuity, that of a series of governments effectively controlled by middle classes using this control to advance themselves economically. If many of these national middle classes were doing only fairly well at best by international measurements, they were doing very well indeed by internal national measurements. That is, the inequality of income distribution seems to have increased noticeably in the postindependence period.

The Next Quarter Century

Thus far, we have talked of how Africa has evolved in the period since the nineteenth century partition of the continent. Now we turn to what we may expect to occur in the coming decade or decades on the basis of extrapolation from past trends and some assumptions about how the rest of the world will respond to the new social and economic problems of the 1970s. These "predictions" must necessarily be speculations, if informed ones, and it will only be possible to suggest general trends, from which particular states may deviate to one degree or another because of special circumstances.

One basic and controversial assumption will be made by this writer, which is that the entire world is now in the beginning of an economic "contraction" or "crisis" of longer duration than the two to three year recessions that regularly occur, a contraction more like the 15 to 25 year downturns that the world has also experienced in the nineteenth and twentieth centuries. Within such an assumption, and to the degree that it is correct, what will happen in Africa? What kinds of pressures, external and internal, will confront its governments and its political forces? Will there be "opportunities" that did not exist in earlier periods? And will these pressures and opportunities be the same for all regions or states of Africa? Finally, how will the governments react to these pressures and opportunities? And will the changing economic circumstances of Africa generate important social and political change?

One of the manifestations of a worldwide economic downturn is that producers of manufactured goods experience difficulty in finding enough buyers for their goods. In the normal course of events, unsold inventories, reduced production, and increased unemployment lead to relative price reduction. Insofar as the world momentarily becomes in this sense a buyer's market (especially for capital goods, and to some extent for manufactured goods in general), there is likely to be sharper competition than previously between the principal sellers, presently located in North America, Europe, and Japan.

In these circumstances, the primary concern of a producer in the developed countries and in the special world of the multinational corporation will be to maintain a profit level—by production restriction, government subsidy, price wars, inflationary cost-push price rises, or a combination or alternation of these devices.[6] The governments of the developed countries must, however, be concerned not only with overall "profit" (that is, balance-of-payments considerations) but also with maintenance of employment at levels that preclude major internal social crises. Thus one form of international profit-making may be preferable to another, if one form involves lower unemployment rates for the industrialized nation housing a choice of profit-making operations. In a protracted period of economic slowdown, industrialized countries may want to move in increasingly protectionist directions, even if this may not be the optimal solution for some multinational corporations.

How does this complex interplay affect Africa? Insofar as the industrialized nations must search for new market outlets to rebuild "demand" to appropriate levels, the bargaining position of the African purchaser of manufactured goods would seem to be improved. Insofar as the early stage of the downturn is characterized by a discrepancy between the rate of worldwide industrial production and the rate of worldwide commodity production, the terms of trade for those African states with key commodities to sell (oil, obviously, but probably also copper, phosphate, bauxite, etc.) would probably be enhanced, primarily because of the competition between various industrial users to retain or expand their percentage of the world market. Insofar as rising unemployment figures and inflation lead to decreased consumer demand in the industrialized countries, the market for African commodities geared to food-processing or light industry (cocoa, coffee, cotton, tobacco, etc.) will suffer. Insofar as this competition between such highly industrial countries as the United States,

Germany, and Japan grows more acute, the ability of any one of them to impose and enforce unequal political and economic relationships on African countries would diminish. On the other hand, insofar as climatic eccentricities or long-term soil exhaustion of subsistence-cropping areas in Africa lead to acute famine conditions, the ability of a country with food surpluses for export (such as the United States in the case of grain) to offer a crucial rare resource obviously enhances its overall political strength.

Quite clearly, then, not all countries in Africa would be affected in precisely the same way by a world economic downturn. In relation to such a downturn, it may be suggested that the African states would fall roughly into two categories: those whose conditions are such that a downturn for the industrial nations represents an "opportunity" for significant improvement of their national economic situation, and those for whom it represents no change or even further stagnation.

A combination of factors characterizes the states for which the present situation involves an "opportunity": a relatively large internal industrial base, a relatively large potential domestic market, an effectively functioning state structure, location within its boundaries of one or more key or scarce resources required by the industrialized world, a growing stratum of skilled personnel and facilities to generate more, and some degree of food self-sufficiency. While no African state ranks uniformly high on all points of this scale, those at the top of the list would seem to be Algeria, Nigeria, Zaire, the politically special case of South Africa, possibly Egypt, perhaps Zambia and Morocco, one day (but only later in time?) Angola. Those states whose scores are weakest on the "opportunity" criteria scale include all or most of those in the "famine belt" of the Sahel, the Horn, and East Africa, and most of the continent's ministates.

Let us for ease of discussion refer to the first group as the "semi-industrializing countries" and the latter group as the "largely agricultural" countries. Such nomenclature is by no means exact, since it singles out a single feature of the complex, which is not necessarily the key one in causal terms. In any case, our argument is that the next 15 to 25 years present relatively positive opportunities for Africa's semi-industrializing countries, but a bleak picture for the largely agricultural ones.

If one leaves out for the moment South Africa, the probable pattern for Nigeria and other semi-industrializing states would seem to be as follows. The altered terms of trade for their major raw material exports should put them in a position to acquire a considerable stock of capital. They should be able—by a partial redistribution of this collective profit to their own population, or at least to segments of it—to create sufficient domestic demand to sustain the creation of import-substitution industries. Another portion of this collective profit may go to state-building, by which we mean an expanded civilian bureaucracy and better armed, better equipped, better trained armed forces. To set these processes in motion requires a certain prior level of availability of skilled personnel, industrial equipment and experience, and a reasonable level of food production. But once set in motion, this process would itself enable the state to develop all of these resources.

Such a process would involve strengthening the state apparatus not only internally but also internationally. If the ability of the industrialized powers to intervene is weakened because of their own acute competitive rivalries, played out precisely in terms of courting the rising semi-industrializing powers, these two factors would not merely serve to "protect" economic growth in the Nigerias and Algerias and the Zaires but would also enable such countries to begin to serve as significant exporters of manufactured goods to their neighbors. They would have the advantage of increasingly competitive costs of production and low transportation costs to their markets.

One clear problem arises here. Too many semi-industrializing cooks could spoil the broth. Algeria and Morocco might compete for the trade of their neighbors, as might Nigeria and Cameroon, Zaire and Zambia, or Zaire and Angola. There might not be effective room for both, and one of the two might be forced out of the semi-industrializing category by the success of the other, or perhaps become its secondary associate.

Discussion of the economic potential of South Africa obviously entails taking into account the degree to which the racial character of the internal class hierarchy is likely to compromise that nation's ability to take full advantage of its economic opportunities. There are some clearly limiting factors. The reluctance to develop an adequate reservoir of skilled black labor and resulting strains within the labor sector are among the most obvious. Internal apartheid may set political and cultural limits to the creation of as wide an internal market as purely economic wisdom would dictate. Prime Minister Vorster's bridge-building successes aside, the racist symbolism of the South African regime may set limits on the degree to which neighboring countries will be comfortable entering into a South African export sphere. And ultimately, of course, the political oppression of the country's system may generate political turmoil, up to and including full-fledged civil war, that would seriously interfere with economic production.

One says "may," but the fact is that it almost surely will unless the South African regime is able to achieve a major political compromise with both internal and neighboring external black political forces that would involve some combination of de facto or de jure political partition and some sharing of the collective profit with these forces, or at least some of them. The degree to which such a solution is feasible is discussed elsewhere in this book.

The alternative, of course, is a political revolution that would result in a black government. Once again, the likelihood of this occurring is discussed elsewhere. But if it occurred within five to ten years, a black South African government could benefit very substantially indeed from the processes favorable to "semi-industrializing" countries, as described above. I believe that this might even be more true if the change in regime followed a protracted civil war. For what the post-transformation regime would have lost in actual physical resources (both machines and men), it might more than have compensated for in the form of political solidity and the ideological commitment of the working classes to expanded production.

The structural economic changes that might occur in Africa's half dozen countries-of-opportunity comprise only part of the picture. These structural changes would also entail class formation. A substantial increase in an industrial-urban proletariat seems certain, along with a reduction in the ranks of subsistence farmers (who could be eliminated by more efficient, market-oriented, and semimechanized farming). Some of the ex-subsistence farmers might be recruited into wage-earning positions; but it is doubtful there would be a place for all of them. Thus, the numbers of the urban lumpenproletariat would probably grow, creating a major sociopolitical problem for the governments.

As economic opportunities expand at the managerial level, the stratum of the intelligentsia-in-limbo described earlier may well disappear and simply be absorbed into the strengthened and enlarged middle classes. I would certainly anticipate a very great expansion of the state bureaucracy (including the military). Whether there would be a corresponding expansion of non-state bureaucracies and of entrepreneurs would in part depend on which of the alternative policy routes is chosen by specific governments. These alternative routes to the future will be discussed below.

The prospects for Africa's "largely agricultural" states with no major bargaining power would seem to be very different indeed. The short-run prognosis for these countries is pessimistic: a relatively high rate of malnutrition, if not starvation, due to stagnation in subsistence agricultural production, and rising population rates; soil exhaustion; reduction of worldwide food surpluses available for relief purposes; increased balance-of-payments difficulties because of rising relative energy and fertilizer costs; and a weak international market for their low-priority exports because of the inability of the industrialized countries to return to full employment. In the short run, chances of creation of import-substitution industries would be reduced both because of capital shortage and because of the growth of competitive industries in relatively strong neighbors.

Acute revenue crises would inevitably weaken popular support for existing state structures in these poorer states, with a succession of marginally stable military regimes a typical pattern. Such regimes would, more likely than not, be as addicted to corrupt misuse of collective resources as their civilian predecessors. While the fear of neocolonialist controls from the great powers might recede in this period of great power balancing, a new specter would rise in the ability of semi-industrializing neighbors to interfere in the internal affairs of the economically peripheral states.

To the extent that significant economic structural change occurred, it might take the form of creating large units of agricultural or pastoral land under single ownership (of individuals, corporations, or the state) to produce food and raw material exports to sell to semi-industrializing neighbors and perhaps to the developed world as well. Since this would involve external investors working with politically influential internal elements, the result could be a steady drain of both products and profits at a scale reminiscent of the more rampant years of colonial economic exploitation of Africa. In these circumstances, total economic stagnation might actually become a favorable alternative.

The class formations likely to take place in the poorer states would be different from those of the semi-industrializing states. The numerical growth of the internal middle classes might be stunted, and an urban proletariat scarcely exist. On the other hand, a socially separate intelligentsia might solidify itself, while the refugees (or the expellees) from deserted rural areas might swell urban squatter settlements of intensifying squalor. Substantial pockets of subsistence farming would remain, partly because there would not be an external demand great enough to justify utilizing *all* the land for cash-cropping, and partly to serve as a political and economic safety valve, areas to which overconcentrations of urban squatters could be returned or relocated by desperate governments— thus creating new long-term strains on the land. One compensating feature might be the sustenance or revival in some of these rural areas of low-level handicrafts, which could satisfy some immediate needs with minimal cash expenditure.

What will be the political consequences if economic and social developments in Africa follow the script outlined above over the next 15 to 25 years, with the continent divided into a few semi-industrializing states in a position to benefit from world economic trends, and a lesser endowed majority of states that would almost surely suffer from it?

In the year 1960, it was unquestionable and unquestioned that the two grand political-military coalitions in the world were that of the West, led by the United States, and including Britain, France, Germany, and Japan, and that of the Soviet bloc, led by the USSR and including China. In the year 1976, it would be an audacious analyst who would forecast the alignment of 1990. There are clearly a host of alternative possibilities. The alignment of 1960 seems the least likely of them.

No matter what the alignment, it is doubtful that African states will fall entirely outside the major coalitions, nor unanimously cooperate with one or another. Nor can it be predicted that all the states identified as "semi-industrializing" (even excluding South Africa) would necessarily fall on the same side. The new factor, given the previous analysis, is that the "semi-industrializing" states now have some choice and will seek to coordinate their political alignment with direct economic advantage.

By contrast, the "largely agricultural" states would have a narrower range of options. While the likelihood of intervention by the major powers of the world might diminish, the prospect that a nearby "semi-industrializing" regional power might take a direct interest in maintaining smaller, weaker neighbors in its small orbit would become very real and immediate.

The crystallization of Africa's class structures is also hard to predict, because economic developments will be both a consequence and cause of whatever degree of crystallization takes place. The clearest picture is likely to emerge in the economically most successful "semi-industrializing" power centers, where a fairly self-confident middle class seeks self-consciously to mark out its boundaries and decide its course. In some of these countries, mixed private-public companies might enter into quasi-monopolistic arrangements with particular multinational corporations, assuring a flow of technology, military equipment, and advanced machinery into the state in exchange for certain key products. The corporations and the major extra-African countries in which they were based would gain assured markets, profits from the sale of invisibles (patents, etc.), and the flow of needed raw materials. In return, the middle classes of semi-industrializing countries would be in a position to obtain advanced equipment, enhance the military security of the state, and carve out a local sector of the world market for intermediate industry.

Several problems arise with this formulation. It would require relatively high salary scales to create a sufficiently buoyant internal market for intermediate industry, which might in turn outprice such goods on the external market and require severe protectionist measures (unpopular with the cooperating industrialized countries). The examples of South Korea, Singapore and Malaysia in Asia, and Brazil in Latin America, suggest that suppression or taming of trade unions, restriction of political opposition, and the according of only marginal attention to the unemployed sectors and remaining subsistence farmers might be the route followed to keep the lid on the wages of this growing industrial work force. Assuming that labor costs could be controlled, the manufactured products of a semi-industrializing African state might find outlets both in the home market and in neighboring agricultural countries, within a world "sphere of influence" framework, guaranteed in part by the world coalition to which the semi-industrializing state had attached itself.

Two groups would be intensely unhappy with such a development. First, there would be those major powers, as well as those worldwide corporate structures, excluded from the benefits of the arrangements. This could be reflected locally in an internal split in the middle classes of a semi-industrializing state. Acute struggles for "influence" and palace coups would, or could, become endemic.

A second group hurt by this kind of success story would be the majority of the urban work force (especially the semiskilled and so-called unskilled workers), the landless rural laborers, the unemployed, and the subsistence farmers. If the dominant middle classes were able to build a relatively competent bureaucratic infrastructure and maintain the image of nationalism in their international juggling, these less-favored elements would not be in a position to organize politically. But if—either because of excessive outflow of profits to allied but extranational forces, excessive consumption of surplus by rentier-type elements, or the draining of energies by regional warfare—the governments showed administrative weakness and seemed on the road toward increased direct subordination of the new industrial network to external forces, revolutionary movements might grow. One can envisage such movements bringing together "nationalist" elements from the middle classes, some segments of urban wage-workers, marginally successful market-oriented peasants, and politicized urban unemployed and subsistence farmers.

If such a group were to come to power in a given state, it could be expected to seek first of all to strengthen the country's economic, political, and military defenses against outside intervention; expand the internal market by substantial internal redistribution; sacrifice, at least temporarily, the export trade with weak neighbors; and attempt even tighter exchange bargaining with external forces in the industrialized world. This would be accompanied by considerable internal ideological training.

In summary, the essential choice of patterns for the relatively strong candidates for the semi-industrializing role in Africa in the next 15 to 25 years is likely to be between the Brazil 1976 model and the China 1976 model. Since perceptions of both Brazil and China vary widely, it is essential that I share with the reader the meaning I attach to the terms "Brazil 1976" and "China 1976" as models against which to measure African development.

Writing from Rio de Janeiro for the July 28, 1974 issue of *The Washington Post*, correspondent Leonard Greenwood described the economic landscape of Brazil in terms immediately meaningful to one concerned with alternative futures for Africa's most "promising" semi-industrializing states:

... The scale of "benefits" has gone wild, as Brazilian and foreign firms compete for administrators and technocrats to fill jobs in an economy that has doubled in eight years to become the fastest-growing in the world.... (An) American executive, Wayne Gibson, president of J. Wayne Gibson Associates, industrial psychologists, said his firm has studied salaries in the banking, manufacturing, computer, petroleum, petrochemical, and pharmaceutical industries this year. What he and other researchers have found is a severe jolt.

"At the upper technical level, a firm pays a Brazilian 20 percent more than a man doing the same job in the United States," Gibson said. "A chief of a factory, marketing, industrial relations or a finance department gets 30 percent more. At the top level, there's no limit. The director of a Brazilian bank may earn $300,000 a year and he enjoys 'perks' undreamed of by a U.S. executive...."

If Brazil pays its executives the highest salaries in the world, how is it able to compete on world markets? How, in fact, is it able to increase its exports year after year as it has done recently? Economic specialists say the trick is in the very low salaries paid to the mass of workers lower down the scale, and in low research and development costs.

Most Brazilian workers receive only a fraction of what a worker in the United

States gets. The minimum wage—all millions of Brazilian workers get, and more than many receive—is about $50 a month. Most factory workers earn less than $100 a month, and since strikes are illegal companies have no breaks in production.

Brazil spends very little on research and development, buying the technology developed elsewhere for a fraction of development costs. . . . A multinational corporation that is expanding rapidly here was so desperate for technicians that it sent recruiting teams to England. Not only did England have the men it wanted, but the company found it cheaper to hire Englishmen and bring them, their families and their belongings to Brazil than to pay the salaries and benefits demanded by Brazilians. . . .

Can the high salaries for Brazilian executives continue? Probably, say experienced observers. The trend will last as long as security forces are able to continue repressing the work force—an iron control that so far shows no sign of breaking.[7]

The China 1976 model also involves a considerable amount of industrialization and no doubt an ability to profit in the coming 15 to 25 years from improved terms of trade resulting from the prospective downturn in world production. But there the similarities between the China and Brazil models abruptly end.

In China, the internal allocation of reward is at the other extreme from the Brazil model. Salaries of managers, bureaucrats, and other cadres are relatively very modest by the world scale. Real income of the lowest paid workers in both urban and rural areas is markedly above the mean level for countries in the Third World, especially if one remembers that no one starves in China. The result of this more egalitarian allocation of reward is a larger per capita internal market than in the case of Brazil and a reduced need, at this stage of economic growth, to market products in neighboring countries or seek regional political hegemony.

The China model also differs significantly from the Brazil model in the degree to which agricultural production is a function of world demand. While both countries are under economic pressure to produce in terms of the needs of the world market (the pressure taking the standard form of economic reward or profit), the Chinese regime finds the pressure unsettling, whereas the Brazilian regime accepts it as natural. To maintain the "China model" requires utilization of the mass political process as a major weapon, and thus the political process takes a highly ideological form.

The rise of Brazil model states in Africa, albeit not as headily prosperous as the model itself, would require only the reinforcement of some trends already strongly established in each of the semi-industrializing countries. To follow the China model would require a kind of large-scale political mobilization which does not seem immediately likely in any semi-industrializing African state. An exception to this generalization might conceivably be South Africa if an extended civil war, ending in an overthrow of white minority rule, were to create the kind of social upheaval in which a revolutionary movement might flourish.

A subcategory of semi-industrializing Africa will be comprised of those states marginally capable of a semi-industrializing role, but which fail, or at least only partially succeed, in grabbing the rung. For these states which do not quite make it into the ."boom" stratum, but cannot be grouped with the "primarily agricultural" poorer states, a different sort of development can be envisaged. By definition, the middle-class elements would not be strong enough to bargain effectively in the international marketplace, either Brazilian or Chinese style. Depending upon their location in relation to more powerful semi-industrializing centers, the states in this in-between position might even lack the strength to impose their industrial exports on their neighbors. To ward off internal turmoil, a state in this position might decide that the optimal course of action would be to buy off urban elements by state redistribution, suppress incipient peasant rebellion, and bolster its funds through some international client relationship. The outward form of such a regime might well be a pseudo-"revolutionary" military regime, tied closely to one power bloc, with acute repression and/or expulsion of the intelligentsia. Populist slogans without popular involvement could be used to disguise slow economic stagnation, consumption austerity for the majority of the population, and corrupt profiteering by the governing groups.

In the case of the largely agricultural states, where the economic picture is particularly bleak in the near future, the political choices narrow. Two varieties of "largely agricultural" states seem to be taking shape in Africa. One possibility is that a state in this category will support the growth of a relatively strong commercial farmer class, even a landlord class, enabling it to dominate the internal economy and, directly or indirectly, the state apparatus. Relatively conservative governments with relatively little internal turmoil can be expected in a largely agricultural state managed in this way, provided the state can remain solvent.

Of course, this proviso of solvency is important, since the relatively long-term contraction of the world economy assumed earlier in this chapter is not reassuring to marginal economies. Solvency would depend in large part on a given country's export crops and the degree to which the country, however small, was self-sufficient in food supplies. In any case, even if insolvency precipitated changes in regime, few changes in reality could be anticipated.

There are, however, other agricultural states in which, for various historic reasons, commercial farming and other forms of small enterprise have not yet bred a dominant stratum of private indigenous owners. In such countries, we may see the emergence and/or strengthening of "socialist" regimes, sometimes calling themselves by original names (Tanzania's doctrine of *ujamaa*) and sometimes marxist (Congo-Brazzaville and Somalia).

The "socialism" of such countries means primarily the effective hostility of the regimes in power to the rise of private indigenous groups owning significant segments of the economy, and the achievement by the state of an effective monopoly of export and import operations. This can have important consequences for foreign affairs, giving more latitude to the government in both economic and political relationships. It may mean less internal disparity of wealth, as in Tanzania, but also perhaps less total national income. The ability to resist the predatory thrusts of semi-industrializing neighbors may be stronger in a state professing "socialism," but its ability to move along the semi-industrializing path itself to any great degree in the next 15 to 25 years will be limited by the state of the international economy. Exceptions may occur if a "socialist" country controls some important resource, such as hydroelectric power in the case of Mozambique; but, by and large, these African "socialisms" are primarily techniques of resisting the path of increasing dependence on which the other largely agricultural states seem to be headed.

Thus, the degree to which African states will express their political options in ideological terms will vary. If any of the successful semi-industrializing states follow a "China model," they may become very ideological; in all probability they will be "marxist-leninist." Those which follow a "Brazil model" may eschew ideological language entirely; or they may invent various original ideologies, largely nationalist and a bit xenophobic in content. The doctrine of "authenticity" now preached in Zaire may be a foretaste of such ideologies. Those semi-industrializing nations which don't quite make it may also try a variation of the Zairian theme, perhaps with an added dash of populism to appease the frustrated.

As for the agrarian states, there will be some ideological militants among them and a tendency toward formulations that are simultaneously "original" and in tune with world socialist terminology. Tanzania's *ujamaa* might be the model, or Somalia's "scientific socialism," but one that is "not incompatible with Islam." Essentially, the verbal juggling game will continue. Some agrarian states that are not socialist may nonetheless call themselves so, if and when it serves some short-run purpose, but no one will take such claims seriously.

In all these developments, it is likely that there will be few boundary changes. Some of the physically larger states may be prey to secessionism if for any reason the central state apparatus is acutely jostled (as seemed possible in Ethiopia in 1975 and in the future in Angola and Kenya). But even in these cases, the prospect is for a militarily imposed reassembling of the pieces (as has already occurred, for example, in Zaire, Cameroon, and Nigeria). It is possible that one or more of the semi-industrializing states might be tempted to acquire valuable pieces of a neighbor's territory, or at least encourage its secession. In the end, however, the rivalry among competing potential beneficiaries would almost surely result in a falling back to the status quo. Maneuvers over the future status of the oil-rich enclave of Cabinda in Angola could turn out to be a case in point.

The future of those largely agricultural states which stay firmly on a "socialist" path over the next 15 to 25 years may be different from that of states which keep their heads above water by ad hoc improvisations. There will surely be a difference, 25 years from now, between those semi-industrializing states which go down a "Brazil path" and any that find themselves on a "China path." But analyzing the differences would require too high a degree of speculation, not merely on internal developments but on the state of the world as a whole.

In the nearer future, the essential option of African states seems to be between governments controlled by internal middle-class groups openly allied to governments and corporations in the industrialized world, and the more "socialist," more autonomous, and more self-consciously indigenous regimes. The differences between these two will not necessarily be in amounts of total economic growth or degrees of political liberalism. And depending on how the world political coalitions develop, there may not even be major differences in terms of international option. The differences will be in the way the internal economic structure develops, the paths of class-formation, and the focus of political education. The ultimate impact of these differences on Africa and the world may only be properly and seriously weighed in the period after next, the one beginning about the year 2000.

Notes

1. See Elliot Berg, "Real Income Trends in West Africa, 1939-1960," in Melville J. Herskovits and Mitchell Harwitz (eds.), *Economic Transition in Africa* (Evanston: Northwestern University Press, 1964), pp. 199-238.

2. See Immanuel Wallerstein, "The Range of Choice: Constraints on the Policies of Governments of Contemporary African Independent States," in Michael F. Lofchie (ed.), *The State of the Nations* (Berkeley: University of California Press, 1971), pp. 19-33.

3. See John E. Flint, *Sir George Goldie and The Making of Nigeria* (London: Oxford University Press, 1960).

4. The original description of the problem of the unemployed school-leavers is to be found in Archibald Callaway, "Unemployment Among African School Leavers," *Journal of Modern African Studies*, Vol. I, No. 3 (1963), pp. 351-371. See also Peter C.W. Gutkind, "The Energy of Despair: Social Organization of the Unemployed in Two African Cities: Lagos and Nairobi," *Civilisations*, Vol. XVII, No. 4 (1967), pp. 380-402.

5. See Bénoit Verhaegen, *Rébellions au Congo* (Bruxelles: Les Etudes du C.R.I.S.P. 1966), Vol. I, Part I, pp. 35-186.

6. For the consequences of one such sequence, see Lars Bordestam, "People and Capitalism in the North-Eastern Lowlands of Ethiopia," *Journal of Modern African Studies*, Vol. XII, No. 3 (September 1974), pp. 423-440.

7. Stanley Greenwood, "Report from Brazil," *The Washington Post*, July 28, 1974. Copyright, 1974, *Los Angeles Times*. Reprinted by permission.

IX How a Defense Planner Looks at Africa

William H. Lewis

In the three decades since World War II, one constant in American policy toward Africa has been the tendency of defense planners to think of Africa as an appendage of United States security interests in Western Europe, the Middle East, and Asia. The long periods of benign neglect, punctuated by the interventions in the Congo in the 1960s and in Angola in 1975, can only be understood in this contextual framework.

Historical Evolution

Throughout the period of the Cold War, five major factors shaped American political-military thinking about Africa: (1) The general sense of economic insecurity and fear of Soviet intentions that pervaded Western Europe for the first decade following the fall of the German Reich; (2) the emergence of the state of Israel, and the decolonization of the Arab world, which combined to strengthen Arab nationalism and thus challenge traditional Western influence in the southern Mediterranean area; (3) the strong residual ties that the United Kingdom, France, and Belgium retained with their former colonial possessions in sub-Saharan Africa, ties which were viewed favorably by American military strategists of the Cold War period as in the United States national interest; (4) the emergence of several Middle Eastern states as major oil producers; and (5) technology requirements. The latter are of particular interest. Just as the intercontinental ballistic missile downgraded the importance assigned to forward basing of bomber forces, so satellite tracking systems have replaced fixed installations as the favored means of intelligence collection. Similarly, the acquisition of long-range military transport aircraft has reduced the military establishment's need for a large number of logistical support bases; indeed, the remarkable strides made in aerial refueling, as well as resupply and replenishment at sea, have diminished drastically, though not eliminated, the need for backup facilities abroad.

In the sections that follow, the interplay of all these factors is traced as United States security relationships with Africa waxed and waned during the 1945-1975 time frame.

The Late Colonial Period (1945-1955)

During the bulk of the years when deterrence in the form of nuclear superiority was the touchstone of American security policy, the United States also was the preeminent political, military, and economic power in the "free world." In this position, the United States gave generously of its resources to selected other countries and regions; in exchange, under the strategy of containment and forward defense, it acquired base rights and other military privileges from those countries with which it was formally or informally allied. Africa, particularly the northern periphery, was regarded during this 1945-1955 period as a strategic hinterland providing urgently needed defensive depth to the narrow waist of a beleaguered Western Europe.

Shortly after World War I, the English military adviser Halford MacKinder wrote: "Who rules East Asia commands the Heartland [essentially the Soviet Union, mainland China, and Iran]: who rules the Heartland commands the World-Island [Eurasia and Africa]: who rules the World-Island commands the world."[1] The rejoinder of the American geostrategic thinker Nicholas Spykman was a variation on the same theme: "Who controls the Rimland [the peripheral areas of the Eurasian land mass] rules Eurasia; who rules Eurasia controls the destinies of the world."[2] The American political-military perception of Africa during the period just after World War II mirrored the Spykman axiom.

For United States strategic planners, the "Rimland" was of special importance. From this Rimland, nuclear-armed B-36 bombers could strike at Soviet military concentrations if required; war supplies could be prestocked with assurance they would not fall into adversary hands; Soviet maritime and naval activities could be kept under surveillance; facilities in North Africa and Middle Africa could be used to transport weapons and related support equipment into the Middle East; communications and other intelligence activities could be carried out in comparative security; antisubmarine patrols in the Atlantic, the Red Sea, and the Indian Ocean could be facilitated. For all of these reasons, the African possessions of Britain and France were viewed as immensely important, replete with ports, airfields, and other valued facilities. Conceptually, if not diplomatically, security considerations relegated the principle of self-determination to secondary status in such councils as the United Nations. While not embraced formally as a part of NATO, the African protectorates and colonies obviously were regarded in American policy circles as associated appendages.

In schematic terms the relationship of Africa to United States security interests approximated the pyramid shown in Figure IX-1.

North Africa was girdled with American and allied military installations. From Gibraltar in the west—an important naval chokepoint—to Libya in the east, a wide range of facilities came into being. The United States constructed three Strategic Air Command bases in Morocco shortly after the outbreak of the Korean conflict, and bolstered the United States naval air facility at Port Lyautey. In Libya, a major air base, Wheelus Field, was implanted to fulfill a wide variety of military missions in the middle Mediterranean region. Wheelus was "legitimated" in 1954 through the instrumentality of a bilateral agreement with the government of King Idris, Libya's first and only ruling monarch, more than two years after the country became independent. Below the Sahara, the United States enjoyed special landing and overflight rights in Liberia, where $5.5 million had been disbursed during World War II for the construction of Roberts Field. The special U.S. communications installation in Ethiopia, Kagnew Station near Asmara, also dates from World War II. Its status was "regularized" under a base agreement concluded with the government of Emperor Haile Selassie on

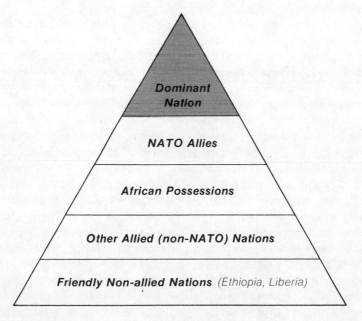

Figure IX-1. Pyramid of Relationship of Africa to United States Security Interests

May 22, 1953. On the same date, a military assistance agreement was signed with Ethiopia. The nature of United States military aid programs in Africa is addressed in following sections; what is significant at this juncture is the absence of mutual defense agreements in United States relations with Ethiopia, Liberia, and Libya; in all three instances, American economic and military assistance was the official quid pro quo.

During this period, Africa was relatively unimportant to the United States as a source of industrial raw materials and unprocessed foodstuffs. Annual American imports from Africa immediately prior to World War II were approximately $50 million, or about two percent of the U.S. worldwide total. As a market for American goods and services, Africa accounted for only $100 million on annual average. Capital investments tell a similar story: of $6 billion in external capital investment below the Sahara, the American share was less than three percent ($160 million). Even this compared favorably with North Africa, where the American investment portfolio was but $40 million, concentrated primarily in Egypt. By 1956, total imports from Africa had grown to $590 million, or more than ten times the prewar value; however, imports from Africa still constituted less than five percent of the worldwide U.S. total. American exports had grown commensurately—to some $563 million or more than five times the prewar total—but remained under four percent of American global exports. With respect to capital account, American investments had ballooned to approximately $1 billion by 1956—largely in the northern and southern geographic extremities of Africa—but this fivefold increase represented only two percent of total American investments abroad.

The NATO allies, on the other hand, commanded vast capital investments in Africa. By conservative estimate, they were on the order of $10 billion by 1954-1955. Consequently, the string of military installations which had been implanted over the years in the southern part of the continent now had a dual purpose—to provide strategic depth as already noted, and to insure the measure of internal order needed to perpetuate the colonial system. For the United Kingdom, African military facilities also were of importance as way stations for its forces assigned to East Asia.

In North Africa, despite legal precedents to the contrary, the French bases at Casablanca, Mers-el-Kebir, and Bizerte were regarded as informal assets for the NATO command system. British facilities in Libya, notably at Tobruk and el-Adem, had comparable utility. Below the Sahara, from a contingency point of view, the giant Belgian base at Kamina in the Congo, British facilities at Takoradi in Ghana, Kaduna in Nigeria, and Mombasa in Kenya, and French facilities in Somaliland, on Madagascar, and in Dakar were all regarded as being of potential value to Western security interests.

In the early and mid-1950s, major efforts were launched to integrate Western defense planning in Africa:

... Conferences were held at Nairobi in 1951 and Dakar in 1954 to discuss the improvement of transport and communications facilities. Today, the Union of South Africa is campaigning for a leading role in Africa's defense. Conferences between the Union and Britain in 1955 and 1957 resulted in an agreement to sponsor a future Southern Africa Defense Conference to be held in the Union. Belgian, French, Portuguese, and Rhodesian officers have also visited South Africa recently to confer on military coordination. When Britain transferred the Simonstown naval base to South Africa in 1955, the latter agreed to make its facilities available to Britain and to all of Britain's allies in time of war whether or not South Africa was at war. The United States has sent observers to some of these defense conferences. ... Moreover, important defense developments are discussed in NATO.[3]

On the political plane, as might be anticipated in these circumstances, our African policies were ambiguous at best. In the interest of "stability," "order," and "security," the United States government maintained a posture of benign noninvolvement in the issues of colonialism and self-determination that were beginning to arise. Wartime rhetoric about "free peoples" notwithstanding, the simple fact was that Africa was not populated by "free peoples" and that United States policy largely followed a path of expediency toward Africa during the immediate postwar years. In 1951, the United States blinked the passage into exile of Tunisia's future president, Habib Bourguiba; it ignored the outcry of Algerian nationalists against blatant election rigging by French officials; it spent little time trying to fathom the attitudes and concerns of Jomo Kenyatta, the putative leader of Kenya's Mau Mau movement.

Legal niceties were also ignored on occasion by the United States in the name of "free world" security. For example, as a result of the perceived threat of Soviet military aggrandizement in Western Europe while American forces were engaged in Korea, a special agreement was concluded by U.S. Ambassador to France Jefferson Caffrey and Foreign Minister Georges Bidault in December 1950 to construct Strategic Air Command bases in the French Zone of Morocco—without consulting King Mohammed V, as required under the Protectorate Treaty of 1912. Three years later, the United States government was otherwise occupied when the French Resident General at Rabat determined that Mohammed V had become too closely identified with the Moroccan nationalist movement, ousted him on August 20, 1953, and dispatched the king into exile for two years. By contrast, the United States was unstinting in its support of Libya's King Idris I who, from the date of his country's independence in December 1951, served as its principal stabilizing influence.

Why did security interests so overshadow and overrule moral precepts in U.S. government councils during the decade immediately following World War II? This was a time of testing vis-à-vis the USSR, a time when Washington was far from convinced that Soviet forces would remain east of the Elbe River, that Greece and Turkey could survive as free nations, or that the African "Rimland" would remain uncontested territory. The outbreak of hostilities on the Korean peninsula reinforced American sentiment in support of a policy of tough-minded forward defense. Collective security was seen as the only valid course available to Washington, given the crisis atmosphere of the period; the principle of "self-determination" was allocated a lower priority. Thus, during the period from 1945 to 1955, the United States played only a marginal role in the resolution of the colonial issue.

Decolonization and Debasement (1956-1975)

The weighting of the military balance in favor of the West during much of the decade of the 1950s, in addition to keeping the Soviet Union firmly in check, had the following important consequences: (1) It permitted the British and the French to keep vital lines of communication to Indochina and East Asia intact; (2) Western Europe was assured continued access to Middle Eastern oil; (3) the West, for a transitory period, served as the principal arbiter of political forces in the Middle East and Africa; and (4) the United States served as the primary security shield and arms supplier for selected independent nations.

The availability of base facilities in the Mediterranean region for British and American forces proved a decisive strategic advantage. Virtually all the militarily significant targets in European Russia and Eastern Europe were within reasonable flying distance from the eastern Mediterranian. Moscow, the industrial complex in the Urals, and even Omsk in central Siberia were within 2,400 miles of Cyprus. From bases in England, the distance was 2,800 miles. From bases in North Africa, all of Central Europe and the Balkans could be targeted. In addition, carrier aircraft could range over the Balkans and the Crimean region of the Soviet Union.

The decade that followed (1955-1965) witnessed major political and military changes. British forces were withdrawn from the Suez Canal; Morocco and Tunisia, after several years of internal tension, terminated the French protectorate in March 1956; in Iraq, a bloody coup toppled the regime of Nuri-as-Said in 1958 and ended prospects of that country's participation in the "northern tier" security system then being fashioned by the United States and the United Kingdom. This was a time of political awakening in much of what is now known as the Third World, and sub-Saharan Africa was to become one of the principal beneficiaries of the forces unleashed.

Four sets of events shaped the American and European reactions to the rise of Third World nationalism: (1) the French withdrawal from Indochina in 1954 following the ignominious defeat at Dienbienphu, and the rise of Algerian nationalism, set in motion some reevaluation of the United States posture on the question of colonial rule; (2) the abortive 1956 Anglo-French invasion of Egypt produced a definitive rupture within the Western camp on the issues of security and colonialism, as the United States foreclosed on European assumptions that NATO was linked to the preservation of empire; (3) the Soviet achievement in launching "Sputnik" in 1957 stimulated new advances in military research and technology that ultimately redounded to the benefit of American security interests, in time reducing the need for Strategic Air Command bases in North Africa; and (4) the accession to power of Charles de Gaulle in 1958, under conditions of severe political stress in France, led to a reappraisal of French policies in Africa and to a decision by the new president to follow the British lead and cut French losses on the colonial issue. With the passage of time, it became apparent to most of Europe that the preservation of empire in the face of rising nationalist opposition was a foolishly wasteful venture. Obduracy gave way to flexibility—except in Portugal and to a lesser extent Spain—and the pellmell rush to independence was underway.

In the mutated world that evolved from these events, Western security objectives inevitably came into question. Most of the colonial territories now emerging as nations shared neither the Cold War security concerns of the United States and Western Europe nor their basic political values. As a result, a slow erosion of the old security symbols occurred, a wasting away of the sense of community they once evoked. The terms "free world," "communist camp," "bipolarity," and "commitment" underwent redefinition and began to lose their former validity. In Africa, there was now measurable incongruence in the policies of the United States and its NATO allies. While United States policy increasingly focused on such concepts as "political development," "stability," "pro-Americanism," and "regional cooperation," the former colonial powers concentrated on "trade preferences," the development of a "Eurafrican community," and "special military-economic relationships." The first generation of African political leadership, on its part, was directing its energies toward the consolidation of power, the muting of the residual economic and political "influence" of the former metropoles, and the creation of conditions that would assure the preservation of the political systems that were being forged by the new elite.

In this transitional period, the United States belatedly undertook various well-meaning efforts to establish a foundation for common understanding with Africa's new leadership. Within a time span of 18 months, beginning in 1961, American embassies were established in virtually all of the newly independent nations. Several years previously, the United States had agreed to withdraw from its three Strategic Air Command bases in Morocco as an earnest of the desire to "normalize" relations with the king. In 1961, Washington also embarked upon a program of concentrated economic development assistance in Africa, selecting four "bellwether states"—Tunisia, Nigeria, Ethiopia, and Tanzania—as the primary beneficiaries of American assistance.

In dealing with the new states, however, American policymakers found that communication was hampered by the very different ways in which American and African leaders perceived the world. The United States, both in its rhetoric and in fact, had no desire to substitute itself for Western Europe in a proconsular relationship. Washington offered its assistance, albeit at modest and sometimes token levels, to the leaders of many of the states as they grappled with the twin problems of political and economic development, and encouraged the efforts of the Organization of African Unity to resolve local boundary disputes (Ethiopia-Somalia, Morocco-Algeria). Aside from the Congo, where the United States actively took sides in a civil war,[4] Washington sought to come to terms with the new Africa in low-key terms, to deter the polarization of political forces in the continent ("radical" versus "conservative," "white redoubtist" versus African "liberationist"), and to encourage Africans to take the lead in resolving regional problems. It was assumed that more investment by American-based multi-national corporations would be good for the United States, for the corporations, and for African development.

United States defense policies throughout most of the 1960s reflected a new reading of the altered political-military situation in Africa. It was expected, however, that European economic recovery would permit the former colonial powers, particularly France and Britain, to remain the principal protectors, armorers, and trainers of the former colonies. This de facto assignment, it was recognized, would not serve as a fully reliable substitute for the "hinterland" concept that had guided Western strategic thinking during much of the previous decade, but it was anticipated that advances in military research and technology, together with the nuclear "shield" still provided to Europe by the United States, would more than offset the erosion of the West's military position in Africa. Technological advances in the missile field, for example, had already diminished the overall utility of Strategic Air Command bases in North Africa. This factor, together with the rising tide of nationalism, led to the liquidation of virtually all the West's military facilities in North Africa in the course of the 1960s: the SAC air bases in Morocco were closed down in 1963, the French military evacuation from Morocco having taken place the previous year; the removal of the French military presence in Tunisia (at Bizerte) occurred in 1963. While the French-Algerian agreement of 1962 accorded French forces special facilities for a period of up to 15 years, all had been closed before the decade was out. In the case of Libya, the British and American withdrawal from Tobruk, el-Adem, and Wheelus Air Base followed shortly after the deposition of King Idris by military officers in September 1969.

In sub-Saharan Africa, however, France and Britain undertook to maintain modest networks of residual facilities—for reasons of prestige and influence in the case of France, and to ensure air and naval transit elsewhere in the case of the United Kingdom.

As its dozen colonies in *Afrique noire* moved toward independence, France negotiated agreements allowing French military forces to retain access to important air and naval installations in Senegal in the west, Chad in the center of the continent, and Madagascar in the east; these bases, together with Djibouti in the one remaining dependency, French Somaliland, enhanced the French capacity to assist client governments anywhere in Africa in dealing with local crisis situations by deploying strategic reserve forces based in Africa and/or southern France, as well as to play a modest security role in the western reaches of the Indian Ocean. As late as 1968, some 77,000 French forces were still actually based in sub-Saharan Africa, and in 1969 France maintained 18 military assistance missions with a total of some 2,500 French staff.

During this period, the French military presence was quietly emphasized by the occasional despatch of French forces on joint exercises and maneuvers in African states, ostensibly to enable French and African units to gain common experience and French troops to become "acclimated" to tropical conditions. Some 10,000 French and Ivoirian troops and French air and naval forces, for example, participated in a 1967 exercise ("Alligator III"), and there were French-Niger maneuvers ("Damergou 1968") in 1968. The theme of such exercises was usually related to hypothetical local conditions involving externally aided subversion plus an enemy *coup de force* to be jointly repelled by Franco-African units.

To say what manner of conflicts may have been averted by the French presence during these early postcolonial years would be pure speculation. However, a close examination of the political stresses of the 1960s suggests a correlation between this presence—even when it was not employed—and the absence of military coups in Senegal, Niger, Ivory Coast, Mauritania, Chad, Gabon, and Madagascar.[5]

By the end of 1975, the overt French military role in Africa had sharply diminished. With the evacuation of the major French installation at N'Djaména following a prolonged 1975 dispute with Chad's new military regime over the handling of the kidnapping by antigovernment rebels of a distinguished French archaeologist (the "Claustere affair"), only Dakar and Djibouti remained of the network of bases formerly available to French forces. Other incidents had already led to the de facto termination of French operating rights in Congo-Brazzaville, Niger, and Madagascar. The number of defense accords with states in *Afrique noire* had been reduced from 12 to four—Gabon, Cameroon, Senegal, and Togo. Mutual facilities agreements with Benin, Gabon, Ivory Coast, Mauritania, and Niger were still on the books. And technical assistance agreements remained in force with Congo-Brazzaville, Benin, Gabon, Cameroon, the Central African Republic, Mauritania, Senegal, Togo, and Upper Volta. The nature of each of these three classes of agreements remains quite distinctive: (1) a defense agreement generally covers "external acts of aggression" against the African signatory state and binds France to provide assistance in a form to be determined at the time of the crisis; (2) mutual facilities agreements allow French access to local African airfields and support bases, usually on a joint use basis involving sharing of costs and overhead charges; and (3) technical assistance agreements involve military training and instruction and, in some cases, transfers of military equipment to African recipient countries.

Not only have French military capabilities within Africa withered perceptibly in recent years; the lessened political motivation for rescues of friendly incumbent regimes suggests that it is unlikely that there will be repeat enactments of scenarios such as that in which President Leon M'Ba of Gabon was restored to power through the intervention of French paratroops during an attempted coup in February 1964. Even so, most states formerly under French rule still perceive considerable advantage in retaining some linkage to Paris. This linkage assures continuity of training and doctrine, availability of military equipment, and the presence of advisors in such technical fields as fiscal management and logistical support.

The future French military relationship with non-francophonic states—most notably South Africa—is likely to be more enigmatic. Although President Giscard d'Estaing affirmed on a visit to Zaire in mid-1975 that "we shall sell no more arms to South Africa," subsequent performance suggested little basic change in France's pragmatic policy of selling aircraft and arms wherever there is a market. That the discrepancy may lie in the area of semantics was suggested by the fact that South Africa, by the end of 1975, was meeting most of its major requirements through local production under license of such equipment as Mirage interceptor aircraft, AMX tanks, and the Crotale missile.

Britain's residual defense ties with its former African colonies were far, more limited—both in concept and in fact—than those of France. Only in Nigeria, Mauritius, and Kenya were modest facilities maintained after independence, and a 1968 White Paper made clear that even these capabilities were to be eliminated as a result of austere financial policies that were to be adopted with respect to missions, roles, and basing of British forces east of Suez.

The United Kingdom passed the high water mark of its postcolonial military influence in responding to the request of the East African governments of Kenya, Tanganyika (now Tanzania), and Uganda to assist in quelling military mutinies that threatened elected civilian authority in these countries in 1964. As of 1975, Uganda had turned primarily to the Soviet Union for military supplies; Tanzania's modest military equipment needs were being met by China and selected Eastern European nations; and even Kenya had begun to diversify its arms, with an increased U.S. role indicated by two small-scale 1975 agreements covering sales and training assistance.

Elsewhere, the decline of British military ties and influence was even more dramatically demonstrated. The unilateral declaration of independence by a white minority government in Rhodesia in November 1965 brought no British military response. Arms sales and military associations with South Africa were the subjects of heated domestic debate until 1975, when a defense White Paper confirmed that the special relationship with the Republic (including a provision for access to the naval facilities at Simonstown) was being terminated, and that other British facilities in the western Indian Ocean islands of Gan, Mauritius, and Masirah were being phased out.[6] The one exception to the general pattern of disengagement was the joint effort initiated by the United States and Britain in the mid-1960s to buttress the UK defense capability from a base in the Indian Ocean—a remarkable venture that is described more fully later in this chapter.

With the granting of independence to Angola in November 1975, several centuries of Portuguese military presence in Africa came to an end. The decade of increasingly costly and painful conflict with African liberation forces in Guinea, Angola, and Mozambique is analyzed elsewhere in this volume. Suffice it to say here that no Portuguese combat forces were to be found in any of these territories by the end of 1975, and that the new military rulers in Lisbon had no inclination to assume a significant peacekeeping or peacemaking role in Angola.

The "BIOT" Venture

In the early and mid-1960s, a confluence of forces and events led American and British defense planners to examine with increasing seriousness the feasibility of establishing a "Commonwealth" route from Britain to the Persian Gulf/Indian Ocean area, and thence eastward to East Asia. The forces and events included difficulties with the militantly nationalist Nasser regime in Egypt that raised serious doubts about unfettered passage through the Suez Canal "in time of need"; the reduced political feasibility of relying on South Africa's naval and air facilities should an emergency arise in East Asia or the Persian Gulf, as Pretoria became increasingly isolated due to international censure of its racial policies; and the weakened prospects for long-range dependence on the intervening black-governed area, a result of the increasing incidence of military coups and other manifestations of instability.

As a result, the British government, with the active encouragement and financial support of the United States, created the British Indian Ocean Territory (BIOT) in 1966. BIOT comprised four widely separated island groups that had been carved away from Mauritius and the Seychelles, after agreed compensation to these governments. The compensation covered, inter alia, the anticipated costs of evacuating small nonindigenous populations—totalling some 700 persons—to Mauritius and resettling them there. (An exposé initiated by the London *Sunday Times* in 1975 revealed that the £650,000 paid by the United Kingdom to the Mauritius government to cover the costs of appropriate resettlement of the island residents, mostly copra-workers, was not so used, and that the living conditions and employment opportunities of the evacuees fell far short of the standards specified by the British negotiators in the settlement agreement.)

Two of the islands, Aldabra and Farquhar, were off the coast of East Africa, and Diego Garcia in the Chagos Archipelago was approximately 1,000 miles south of India (2,000 miles due east of Dar es Salaam, Tanzania, and 2,400 miles southwest of Bangkok). The stated objective was to construct a chain of airbases and naval support facilities that would permit Britain and the United States to airlift forces and dispatch naval units to the Persian Gulf, Hong Kong, and Singapore without total reliance on African overflight, landing, or bunkering privileges. British security and economic interests were still substantial at this time, including: (1) protectorate and special responsibilities for maintaining the internal security of the Persian Gulf emirates; (2) a leading role in CENTO; (3) concern with unfettered access to Persian Gulf energy sources; and (4) participation in the Five Power defense arrangements for Singapore and Malaysia.

The idea of having clear military throughput capacities in the Indian Ocean for British forces was generally regarded as a well-conceived stroke of defense planning, but the BIOT concept suffered from three major defects: (1) some of the islands selected for the BIOT grouping were unsuited for military construction; (2) Britain shortly thereafter found itself beset by far-reaching financial and economic woes that led the Wilson government to contract out of most of its lesser security obligations east of Suez—a course that reduced British needs for a major chain of bases within BIOT; (3) the governments of most of the nations in or bordering the Indian Ocean received the news poorly, some publicly denouncing the decision and calling for the creation of a "Zone of Peace" in the area, others expressing quiet misgivings about the projection of Cold War rivalries into the region.

The technical feasibility issue is particularly instructive. It involves several key elements—notably aircraft lift capacity, overflight, and BIOT basing itself. The first two elements interact closely; given the long distances to be covered and the heavy payloads involved, a broad range of requirements arose that could not readily be met. For example, the payload of the C-130 Hercules, the principal transport aircraft of this period, was such (20,000 pounds over 3,700 miles) that an aircraft starting from the United States would have to be refueled in mid-air or on the ground in Africa before arriving at Aldabra or Farquhar. Moreover, to move 5,000 men on light scales of equipment would involve 1,000 tons of freight and necessitate 200 sorties to transport the full unit. Mid-air refueling at this level would be exceedingly difficult without landbase support on the African continent.

The problem was further compounded by the growing awareness, upon closer study, that neither Aldabra nor Farquhar was suitable for an airbase. Aldabra was one of the few sanctuaries left in the world for certain rare species of wild-life; the presence of birds in large numbers not only constituted a hazard to aircraft, but also aroused the unwanted attention of environmentalist groups as prestigious as the Royal Audubon Society and the Smithsonian Institution. It has been said that the decision not to proceed with the construction of an installation on Aldabra represented the first peacetime or wartime defeat of the United States Air Force by an effective joint force of pink-footed boobies, huge land turtles, and flightless rails; in fact, the issue was never fully joined. Meanwhile, the secretary of the air force determined that Farquhar could not be used as a suitable substitute because of the small size of the island; the proposed runway would have had to be constructed hundreds of feet into the Indian Ocean at quite prohibitive costs. While the larger C-5A aircraft coming onstream later would be able to cover the distances under light loading, even it could not make the Atlantic/Indian Ocean transport legs without aerial refuelings, a costly and technically difficult operation.

Diego Garcia was more promising. In 1968, the United States Navy secured the approval of the Department of Defense to construct an austere naval communications and support facility on the island. The justification for the facility came in three parts—as a fallback base for MIDEASTFOR, should it be compelled to relinquish its basing privileges at Bahrein; to provide point-to-point communications for U.S. naval ships in the Indian Ocean; and to monitor Soviet naval activity in the same region. Events between 1973 and 1975 in the East Africa, Persian Gulf, and Indian Ocean areas lent additional military importance to the Diego Garcia facility.

Evolving U.S. Strategic Interests: The Petroleum Factor

Shortly after World War II, as noted earlier, the concept of "continental defense" was interred and replaced by the principle of "containment"; in due course, as the Soviet Union gained access to the Middle East and as Moscow became the principal source of arms for Egypt, Syria, Iraq, the Peoples' Democratic Republic of South Yemen, and the Somali Republic, the reactive policy of the United States also moved in the direction of "special relationships" with responsive leaders in the area. Deterrence and the policy determination to seek to achieve a regional balance of force were seen to require the linking of our interests and resources to the fate of nations threatened by what in the 1950s and 1960s was perceived as a Soviet quest for hegemonic power. As a result, American military power was projected into the Mediterranean Sea, the Persian Gulf, and, more recently, into the Indian Ocean.

By the mid-1970s, however, global military priorities had been drastically altered. Détente with the Soviet Union, initial progress on the SALT front, improvement of trade relations with Moscow, and the establishment of diplomatic ties with the People's Republic of China seemed to suggest that the cork was finally being placed in the Cold War bottle. "Containment," "forward deployment of forces," and "alliance maintenance" were no longer universally accepted by defense analysts as priorities on the agenda of American concerns.

This new sanguinity was not shared, however, by all senior U.S. government officials. The fact could not be ignored that there had been a steady and continuous acceleration in recent years in the quality of Soviet armed forces, the quantity of weapons and equipment held in active inventory, the emphasis on offensive capabilities, and the Soviet ability to project power at greater distances. The advances of most concern to American defense planners were those in the evolution of Soviet naval and air forces. By 1975, the striking power of these forces extended into the Persian Gulf/Indian Ocean area (facilitated by new bases at Aden and the Somali port of Berbera) as well as the mid-Atlantic region. The Atlantic capability was enhanced by port and replenishment rights in Guinea and Cuba, and the availability of Guinean airfields to Soviet naval surveillance aircraft. These developments led some defense planners to counsel a more prudent approach to the dismantling of alliances and special security relationships, and maintenance of a high level of defense preparedness, while the exploration of avenues for the reduction of tension and the normalization of relations with the Soviet Union continued.

Those officials who hold the more guarded view of national security interests note with concern the erosion of the West's position of predominance in Africa since 1960, and the reduced ability of the United States to shape the course of events in adjoining geographic areas. The "southern flank" of NATO has been weakened by the 1974 Cyprus crisis, political instability in Portugal, Spain, Italy, and Turkey, and by the monetary and economic squeeze resulting from inflation and spiralling energy costs. In their view, the traditional military-economic importance of the eastern Mediterranean basis, northeast Africa, and the Red Sea/Persian Gulf areas, which seemed to be declining in the mid-1960s, has been reaffirmed in the 1970s. For various reasons, including lack of foresight and overly optimistic misjudgments on the pace of progress toward technological breakthroughs in the area of alternative energy sources, dependence of the industrial nations on Middle Eastern energy resources has mounted rather than declined since 1965. The OPEC decision in 1973 to increase the posted oil price by a factor of four set in motion forces that could lead to an international monetary crisis of the first magnitude. At minimum, events in the Middle East/African area since the Arab-Israeli hostilities of October 1973 suggest the following:

- A new power constellation has emerged which has the capacity to disturb the economic equilibrium and political stability of virtually all Western nations, including the United States.
- The oil-producing nations in the Middle East have the capacity to strengthen or erode the economic foundations of a large number of less-developed nations, particularly those in Africa.
- The growing political and economic linkages between the Middle East and Africa suggest the possibility of a longer term community of interest between the OPEC nations and many African states, with significant implications for the future of the United Nations.
- The Soviet Union, which has developed the ability to project its own

conventional military forces at long distance, is now a major external influence in key areas of the Middle East and in at least two strategically placed countries of Africa.

- The West in general and the United States in particular confront major political difficulties in acquiring and sustaining long-term military over-flight, port, and other throughput capabilities in Africa.
- Clearcut disparities in economic and military power are emerging within the less-developed Third World. For a variety of reasons discussed elsewhere in this book, the American role in mitigating these disparities and their political ramifications is likely to be marginal.

In this new period in which security can no longer be defined primarily in terms of geography and no particular piece of foreign territory is, in itself, critical to American security, it can be argued that United States security interests "in the affairs of minor powers, in the peripheral regions . . . and in local balances of power, will be limited to those matters which in turn have an effect on the overall global balance of power."[7] The most immediate challenge to this global balance is the effective organization of OPEC as an energy cartel. The world's energy consumption, by all reasonable estimates, will continue to expand over the coming decade at an annual rate of growth exceeding that of the 1960s. Petroleum almost certainly will remain the principal source of the world energy supply, accounting for approximately one-half of global needs. In developed countries, the linear expansion of consumption will increase dependence on Middle East sources of supply through the next decade.

The Persian Gulf/Africa Nexus

The commodity factor in United States defense planning has become a vexing subject, particularly for members of the Joint Staff and for National Security Council Staff advisers. In attempting to anticipate crisis situations that could affect vital national interests, and in devising strategies to cope with them, it was simpler to wargame United States moves in the Pacific before 1941 or to devise a conceptual approach for the defense of Western Europe after World War II than it is to define the role of military power in assuring the United States and Western Europe access to raw materials deemed essential for the maintenance of economic stability.

In 1974, the U.S. Naval War College at Newport, Rhode Island, organized a symposium on "Resource Scarcity as a Possible Source of Future Conflict" to address the following questions:

- Can the military contribute anything to the resolution of an essentially economic issue?

- Can the availability and display of military force prevent other nations from taking actions inimical to our interests?
- Is military action an acceptable means of forcing the removal of nonbelligerent embargoes or sanctions?
- Would stockpiling necessary raw materials be preferable to an equivalent investment in military forces?

While most of the senior-level officers and civilians attending the meeting rejected the view that military power is of only marginal value in dealing with resource leverage situations, no clear view emerged as to (1) the circumstances under which resource scarcities are likely to develop; or (2) those conditions and contingencies in which military force would have any efficacy in reducing resource scarcities. Vice-Admiral John M. Lee (USN, Ret.), among others, argued that "military operations are of declining utility" in achieving national goals in a period when military forces of the United States and the Soviet Union are coming into balance, and that "the truly vital problems of the human race . . . aren't susceptible to military solutions."

The United States government, while subscribing to the general thrust of Admiral Lee's remarks, concluded that the situation in the Middle East nonetheless warranted a new look at Diego Garcia. In February 1974, the Congress was notified that the Department of Defense intended to expand the existing communications facility on the island into a permanent support base which would provide logistical backstopping for "the more regular deployment of a carrier task force in the Indian Ocean." In June 1975, Secretary of Defense Schlesinger outlined to the Congress plans to extend the 8,000-foot runway on Diego to 12,000 feet (to accommodate C-5As and B-52s, if necessary), to dredge an anchorage capable of sheltering carrier task force groups; and to provide additional storage facilities for naval units operating in the area (see Appendix IXA to this chapter). To defray the costs of expansion of the Diego Garcia facility, the administration requested congressional approval for $29 million in a fiscal year 1974 Defense Department supplemental bill, and $3.3 million more in the regular fiscal year 1975 Defense Department appropriations bill. In addition, more than $5 billion in military equipment had been sold to Iran and Saudi Arabia by 1975, for the express purpose of "enhancing their capacity to protect their national interest in the Red Sea-Persian Gulf area."

Seymour Weiss, then director of the Department of State's Bureau of Political-Military Affairs, summarized United States objectives in the Indian Ocean area in the following terms in March 1974 hearings before the Near East Subcommittee of the House Foreign Affairs Committee:

. . . . let me emphasize that our deployments and support facilities in the Indian Ocean are not a threat to any nation or group of nations. It is a simple fact, however, that powerful maritime nations are active in the Indian Ocean, including the Soviet Union, which had virtually no forces there . . . prior to 1968 and which of late has maintained a presence approximately four times that of our own. We do not believe that either our interests, or those of the littoral states, are served by our inability to operate effectively in the area.

We are not in any arms race with the Soviet Union in the Indian Ocean area, and our requirements for a facility at Diego Garcia are related to an entire spectrum of U.S. interests and considerations, only one of which bears on the level of Soviet deployments there. . . .

We seek nothing more than an ability to stage forces in the area similar to the ability the Soviet Union presently has using port facilities at Berbera in Somalia and Aden, plus the anchorages they routinely use off the Island of Socotra. Our capacity to deploy in no way prejudices future agreements on levels of forces to be deployed. Thus, while we remain open to constructive possibilities for an arms control arrangement bearing on specific deployment levels in the area, we see no reason to believe that such an agreement would preclude the need for the capability which Diego Garcia would provide.

And finally, while we sympathize with the principles which motivate some of the nations in the area to promote concepts such as the "Indian Ocean Peace Zone," major maritime powers, including the United States and the Soviet Union, have been doubtful about this initiative because of its implication that littoral states somehow have a special right to limit or control the use of the high seas by others. The United States has long held the view that there must be unimpaired freedom of navigation on the high seas; this is a basic tenet of our position with respect to the forthcoming International Law of the Sea Conference. . . .[8]

With the opening of the Suez Canal, the likelihood of a year round Soviet naval presence in the Red Sea/Persian Gulf/Indian Ocean area seems virtually assured. This development, together with rising political instability in "choke-point" regions, is a matter of some concern to Western defense planners. Successful insurgent movements in Eritrea, the Yemen Arab Republic, and Oman could, under some circumstances, lead to the interdiction of the narrow arteries of the adjacent waters—thus "choking" Israel's commercial lifeline, and/or that of the Sudan, Ethiopia, Saudi Arabia, and Iran. In addition, the possibility of political instability in the post-Kenyatta period in Kenya, in the post-Nyerere period in Tanzania, as well as in Mozambique and Angola, encourages defense planners to give new attention to such matters as port facilities, access, and overflight privileges. In the light of these future uncertainties and the importance attached to the Cape of Good Hope sea routes to and from the Middle East, facilities available at Simonstown, South Africa, must be discussed.

Simonstown, avoided by American ships since 1967, offers a complex overhaul, repair, dry docking, and storage capability unequalled elsewhere in the area, indeed comparable in sophistication to that of Singapore. Diego Garcia, even with the maximum development now proposed, will be primarily a fueling station with only a modest replenishment capability. Thus, the reaffirmation of American defense-related policy toward southern Africa in July 1975 before the

Subcommittee on Africa of the Senate Committee on Foreign Relations is of particular interest. In his testimony on July 29, Deputy Assistant Secretary of Defense for Near Eastern, African and South Asian Affairs James H. Noyes said:

. . . . I would like to emphasize that the role of the Department of Defense is essentially supportive of the Department of State in the implementation of U.S. policy toward southern Africa. In contrast to the broad range of problems associated with United States support of the various United Nations Resolutions seeking to encourage equal rights for the native peoples in the Republic of South Africa, Namibia, Rhodesia and the Portuguese Territories of Angola and Mozambique, the DOD's specific responsibilities are relatively limited.

Our strategic security interests in the area derive from the fact that the continental land mass of the southern African littoral interdicts the vital sea lanes to the Indian Ocean and the underbelly of the Middle East. The ultimate and potential importance of these sea lanes was brought sharply into focus when the Suez Canal route was closed in 1967 and remained closed until last month. While Suez is now open we must remember that another closure always remains possible.

I would like to refer briefly to our support of current policies on the UN arms embargo on South Africa and that country's disputed presence in Namibia, the UN resolutions condemning Rhodesia's illegal secession from the United Kingdom without provision for the rights of its native population, and finally movement toward independence by the Portuguese African Territories, including Angola and Mozambique.

In the Republic of South Africa, defense activities are confined to an exchange of military, naval and air attachés in Washington and Pretoria, and the now reduced operation of the USAF missile and satellite tracking station at Pretoria which is run by civilian contractors for recurring use when specific satellite programs are in process. This station is serviced by periodic deliveries of supplies by MAC aircraft and visits by technical personnel from the U.S. The facility is the terminal station on the Air Force Eastern Test Range and played a key role in our missile and space program during the 1960s. The DOD has adhered strictly to the U.S. arms embargo policy which was established even before the UN Resolutions of 1963. Since that time, we have excluded South Africa from DOD sales of U.S. military equipment, training, and even correspondence courses that might help South Africa to enforce its apartheid policy of racial discrimination. In addition, we have suspended normal U.S. Navy ship visits to South African ports since 1967, making use of facilities elsewhere. I should emphasize that while South African ports and other facilities have highly significant capabilities when viewed in the sense of potential need in case of world conflict, we have found it possible to meet current requirements elsewhere.

In the cases of Namibia and Rhodesia, the DOD has no current or anticipated security requirements. We maintain a complete hands-off policy with them and have no basis for any military exchange or reciprocal arrangements. Until both countries become legally independent nations there would be no basis for seeking such cooperation. As you may be aware, the issue of the U.S. purchase of high quality Rhodesian chrome has been viewed by some as a breach of U.S. policy to support the UN resolutions against Rhodesia. In that connection, the Byrd Amendment that made such U.S. purchases possible is still being considered for repeal by Congress. The DOD believes that Rhodesian chrome is not

required to meet anticipated defense requirements as these needs are a comparatively minor part of overall U.S. consumption of chrome. . . .[9]

From the perspective of the defense planner, "the Simonstown option" is
seen as chancey on grounds other than those cited by Noyes. Like South
Africans themselves (see Chapter III, "Southern Africa After the Collapse of
Portuguese Rule"), the U.S. defense establishment has become aware that the
Republic no longer sits comfortably behind a security buffer along its northern
frontiers. Pretoria has responded to the emergence of what is perceived as a
marxist state in Mozambique, the prospect of black rule (one way or another) in
Rhodesia, the 1975-76 civil war in Angola, and an uncertain future for Namibia
(South West Africa) by simultaneously (1) pursuing a strategy of détente with
black-governed Africa, (2) involving itself in the Angolan outcome, and (3) de-
voting an increasing portion of its resources to buttressing its military defenses
to hold the line. The South African military budget for 1976-77 is estimated at
[940-950 million rand] approximately 19 percent of the national budget, as
against [700 million rand] 16 percent in 1974-75. As Marcum indicates,
peripheral tactical initiatives in relation to Rhodesia and Namibia, early independence for the Transkei "homeland," and technical assistance to selected African
governments are measures that may gain time over the next decade—if the
unexpectedly activist South African role in the Angolan war does not drastically
change the scenario.

In sum, the United States government now must view South Africa through
an additional set of lenses. Quite aside from the political and moral issues
involved, the prudent planner would not choose to have the United States
locked into a dependency relationship with the South African military establishment if—or when—the Republic becomes a garrison state. Following precisely
the same reasoning in reverse, South Africa continues to take imaginative
initiatives to woo Western nations into such a relationship.

Angola and Ethiopia

Perhaps no defense-related American policy decision since that of the mid-1960s
(to provide limited logistical air support to the Kinshasa government during the
disorders in the Congo)[10] generated such deep divisions in Washington as the
1975 decision to intervene militarily via Zaire in the Angolan civil war. In both
instances, the triggering factor was growing Soviet logistical support of a
marxist-oriented faction which stood a good chance of coming to power. In the
case of Angola, the basic argument was that the establishment in power in
Luanda of a regime beholden to Moscow could and probably would result in the
basing there of Soviet naval and air forces. Combined with the Soviet aircraft
already based in Guinea, such a development would—the argument ran—virtually
assure the Soviet Union's domination of the South Atlantic.

Critics of the 1975 executive branch decision to take sides in Angola contended that it was based on outdated Cold War clichés and several dubious assumptions about African psychology. The historical record of the French in Chad and the Soviets in Sudan and Egypt were cited as only the most clearcut examples of the countervailing principle that there are few moods as transient as gratitude for aid, even when such aid has played a major role in permitting a country to survive as a unit. A second doubt, dealt with at length in this book by contributors Marcum, Halpern, Jones, and Lemaitre, is whether a purportedly "marxist" African government of the 1970s is likely to seek or endure any binding client relationship with one of the two communist power blocs.

The decision to continue military assistance to Ethiopia following the overthrow in 1974 of Emperor Haile Selassie was less divisive, but only because there was no strong conviction in the Washington bureaucracy that there was a "right" way of resolving the post-Selassie policy dilemma. Three elements compounded the problem confronting American strategists in dealing with the avowedly radical military junta which supplanted the Emperor: (1) the close and symbol-laden association that had existed between a succession of American presidents and the Lion of Judah during his half century reign; (2) the near total dependence of the Ethiopian military on U.S. arms and training since World War II; and (3) the strategic geographical location of Ethiopia on the eastern Horn of Africa. The major U.S. communications installation at Kagnew, for which earlier military aid had been the quid pro quo, was virtually phased out by now and no longer a factor.

On Ethiopia's borders, the neighboring Somali Republic, itself also under stewardship of a "revolutionary" military command, was laying claim to stretches of Ethiopian territory inhabited by pastoral Somali tribesmen, and had permitted the Soviet Union to construct a sizable and sophisticated naval support facility at the port of Berbera. While the base was a source of some embarrassment to the Somalis, indications were that the facility would remain at the disposal of the Soviet Navy—at least as long as Somali resentment of American military support of the Ethiopian regime continued, and/or until the United States offered counter-aid to Somalia.

A further complicating factor was the significant Arab support—financial, military, and moral—for the secessionist movement in Ethiopia's largely Muslim province of Eritrea. By the end of 1975, the two contending factions of Eritrean dissidents—the Eritrean Liberation Front (ELF) and the Popular Liberation Forces (PFL)—appeared to have buried their differences, and the excesses of Ethiopian troops in suppressing the rebellion had drawn Eritrean Muslims and Christians closer together. From the perspective of Addis Ababa, Eritrean secession was regarded as a life-or-death struggle, for the loss of the coastal province would end otherwise landlocked Ethiopia's access to vital seaports on the Red Sea and could open a Pandora's Box of balkanization in a country composed of many ethnic communities.

Projections on United States relations with Ethiopia were also constrained by uncertainty about the nation's new power structure. While the military was clearly the only nationally organized force in the country, and broad consensus seemed to exist within the ruling Provisional Military Administrative Council (PMAC) on basic negative goals (e.g., elimination of feudal institutions, the vast landholdings of the Coptic Church, and any leftover aspects of traditional rule that would block "modernization"), consensus did not exist on positive goals. In part because the PMAC was a motley grouping of officers, NCOs, and enlisted men of differing educational levels, experience, sophistication, and worldviews, perceptions of the desired egalitarian society were uneven. Two years after the revolution first began to take shape, deep disagreements were still evident on the scope of reform needed, the type of new political system that should be fashioned, and the degree of participation to be permitted labor organizations, student groups, and various ethnic communities.

The PMAC had disposed of military challenges from its own "far left" in October 1974 (technical services officers who supported a return to civilian rule); the so-called "right" in November 1974 (general officers who wanted to make concessions to the Eritrean dissidents); the intelligence services in April 1975; and a group of enlisted men who tried an unsuccessful countercoup sparked by pay grievances in June 1975. Yet PMAC Chairman Teferi Banti remained a figurehead, and no effective military chain of command yet existed. Even the ability of the PMAC to control its major units—for example, the Second Division in Eritrea—was tenuous. Meanwhile, food shortages had developed as a result of declining local productivity, the balance of trade was adverse and worsening, and inflationary pressures were creating new problems for an already deteriorating economy. It seemed unlikely that the United States, through the provision of military assistance or its denial, would be in a position to influence appreciably the future course of events.

In these circumstances, it could be argued—indeed was argued within the Washington bureaucracy—that it was not in the American national interest, and perhaps not in Ethiopia's, to underwrite the weak post-Selassie regime. But, as *Washington Post* correspondent David Ottaway reported from Addis Ababa in February 1975:

The arms issue has now taken on a life of its own in U.S.-Ethiopian relations and has become nearly an obsession with the country's new military leaders. They feel seriously threatened by neighboring Somalia, which has recently obtained large quantities of sophisticated arms and is as persistent as ever in its claim to about one third of Ethiopia's land. . . . The Ethiopians for two years have been seeking several hundred million dollars worth of new American arms, including heavy M-60 tanks, missiles and Phantom jets to deal with the array of sophisticated arms piling up in Somalia. . . .[11]

In the end, the "careful" 1974-75 review of American policy toward post-Selassie Ethiopia concluded with a decision to continue to assist the beleaguered regime. To terminate all assistance after so many years of virtually total dependency would alienate the new leadership, it was determined, and could result in a lurch toward sources of aid perceived as inimical to American interests. Moreover, a failure of central authority in Addis Ababa could set a precedent that would open other areas of East Africa to the fissiparous forces of ethnic and tribal particularism. Sudan, Chad, Kenya, and Uganda were all seen as vulnerable.

As a result of this decision not to abandon Ethiopia, the level of American military aid—grant and sales—rose appreciably in the year following the assumption of power by the military, as did the sophistication of the weaponry provided. From a base of $11 million to $13 million (entirely in grant assistance) in much of the decade of the 1960s, U.S. assistance totaled $22.3 million in weapons and equipment during fiscal year 1975, equally divided between grants and sales. In addition, the United States had approved the sale to Ethiopia of $53 million worth of arms over a two-year period.

Yet the fact remained that the United States government had little familiarity with most of the members of the Military Council, and lacked the leverage and skills to influence the outcome of the policy deliberations of this unstable coalition, or to temper the summary dispensations of justice against dissidents. Ethiopia, in short, seemed at the brink of major if not revolutionary change, and the hope that a new omelet could be cooked without breaking eggs was generally agreed to have little foundation.

Military Regimes and Military Assistance

Elsewhere in Africa, the growing role of armies in politics posed military-related foreign policy issues of lesser dimension. The principal imperative of all Western policy toward Africa in the 1970s and 1980s appears to be to encourage some measure of domestic stability and self-reliance, with less and less attention to whether the ruling elite wears a khaki uniform or is in civilian attire, or how "representative" a government may be. As the weekly *West Africa* (London) observed in November 1975, the military is now viewed as "part and parcel of politics" and no longer "some political *deus ex machina* imposing artificial, alien standards of behavior." In short, military intervention may not be "constitutional," but it is now accepted as "institutional."

As of 1976, military-dominant regimes in Africa fell generally into two categories, guardian or reformist. Guardian regimes, by far the more numerous, were represented by officer-politicians who seized power to preserve and enhance the social and economic status quo. Reformist regimes, on the other hand, were characterized by a commitment on the part of the leadership to promote some degree of social and economic change, but in an orderly and generally gradualist manner. Both types are clearly middle class, and the distinctions between them are likely to blur as economic pressures mount in Africa—that is, both types of military-dominant regimes will continue to be most deeply and immediately concerned with order preservation and the maintenance of the state as a viable entity within the international community. Under these circumstances, the United States is likely to continue to deal with military regimes on a case-by-case basis in shaping political relationships and arms supply policies.

Heretofore American military aid to Africa has been relatively limited, less than one percent of the global program of the United States, and the criteria straightforward. The grant military assistance Africa program for fiscal year 1973 was approximately $13 million out of a worldwide figure of $582 million (excluding emergency aid to Israel and Vietnam assistance, funded out of the Department of Defense budget). Assistance to Africa has been distributed as set forth in Table IX-1. Virtually all of the lesser dollar programs were for military education and training—i.e., they did not involve grant equipment transfers. Of the remaining country programs, all were phased out by the end of fiscal year 1975 with the exception of Ethiopia.

Africa does not loom large on the foreign military sales (credit) horizon either, representing less than three percent of the U.S. government's proposed fiscal year 1975 account. The Ford administration, in its presentation to

Table IX-1
U.S. Military Assistance Program (MAP)
(thousands of dollars)

Country	FY 1973	FY 1974	FY 1975[a] (est.)
Ethiopia	8,495	11,300	11,300
Ghana	51	40	70
Liberia	200	100	100
Mali	4	40	50
Morocco	108	850	860
Senegal	19	20	25
Sudan	–	–	50
Tunisia	1,787	1,200	2,000
Zaire	227	350	300
Regional (for training programs)	61	80	30
Total	10,952	13,980	14,785

[a]The overwhelming majority of FY 1975 African country programs were to provide military training exclusively.

Source: Compiled by author from unclassified U.S. government data.

Congress, proposed to allocate only $24 million in sales credits to Africa out of a total program of $550 million. The African distribution was to be as shown in Table IX-2. Several aspects of the proposed levels of arms transfers to Africa are noteworthy.

The first is the existing congressional regional ceiling of $40 million on grants and government-to-government cash or credit sales to the continent in any one fiscal year. This constraint, incorporated in the Foreign Assistance Act of 1961 (amended), can be waived by presidential determination. Commercial arrangements between American companies and African governments do not fall under this ceiling; they are, however, subject to review and licensing by munitions control authorities in the Department of State. Second is the trend away from MAP and toward credit sales. It has been a basic tenet of recent security assistance policy to encourage MAP recipient nations to become self-reliant—i.e., to use their own resources to plan and program for their national military establishments.

Having encouraged the termination of MAP for Morocco, Liberia Tunisia, Libya, and Zaire, the United States would seem to be contradicting itself if it were to invoke a regional arms transfer ceiling, particularly one that ignores inflationary factors in weapons production, as well as the capacity of several African countries to pay their own way in the defense procurement field.

Theoretically at least, if constraints are to be established for the U.S. arms transfer program in Africa, these constraints might more realistically be placed on the types and quantities of weapons to be made available. Even here, however, we are confronted with major policy choices. For example, what weapons are we prepared to sell to Middle Eastern countries, yet to deny to Africa? How do we weigh such considerations—i.e., in favor of regional arms balances or in favor of arms control desiderata? What importance do we assign to follow-on costs to the purchasing country? To that country's overall absorptive capacity? Should we refuse to sell arms to African governments when other

Table IX-2
U.S. Foreign Military Credit Sales
(thousands of dollars)

	FY 1973	FY 1974	FY 1975
Ethiopia	–	5,000	5,000
Liberia	–	–	500
Morocco	9,800	12,000	14,000
Tunisia	–	2,500	1,500
Zaire	6,227	3,500	3,500
Total	16,027	23,000	24,500

Source: Compiled by author from unclassified U.S. government data.

industrial nations stand willing and able to provide viable equipment alternatives? How much weight should be given to U.S. export promotion, balance of trade, and related economic factors?

Traditionally, arms sales or grant military assistance have been viewed by major powers as a means of extending political influence or winning "strategic advantages." Put more bluntly, arms have been provided to selected nations to acquire or to maintain base rights or access to port facilities, and the like; or to retain the friendship of cooperative regimes and/or secure their support on international issues deemed to be of significance to the supplying nation. In recent years, however, these simplistic criteria for determining where to give or sell arms have been rendered obsolete by the perceived requirement to take account of the appearance of alternative suppliers, particularly if they are hostile.

In general, the military in Africa is not a heavy institution—i.e., its demands for an increasing share of national resources are relatively limited. In most instances, national armies are numerically small (less than 10,000 men), are weighted in favor of infantry and light artillery, have a highly circumscribed technical absorptive capacity, and, therefore, are not likely to be consumers of sophisticated weaponry, at least in the immediate future. (In terms of size, Nigeria's 1975 standing army of more than 200,000 men is one notable exception to the general rule. See "armed forces" panel of country-by-country chart, "Some Basic Facts about Africa," accompanying this book.) This situation is reinforced by the low incidence to date and for the foreseeable future of interstate conflict in Africa; the principal preoccupation is with internal security.

Finally, because of the modest scale of African military requirements, and the continuing ties of cooperation with the former colonial powers, Africa is the only region of the world where neither the United States nor the Soviet Union is the primary supplier of weapons. A conscious decision by the United States to restrict its export of arms to much of Africa would not necessarily have a decisive impact with respect to the balance of forces in the continent. On the other hand, a decision to play a major role as arms supplier would diminish whatever prospects exist—admittedly unspectacular—for controlling the arms trade in Africa. In recent years, African states have resisted efforts in international fora to establish arms transfer restraints for their continent. They regard such efforts as a form of neocolonialism and paternalism and hence deeply offensive to their drive for status.

Future Choices

Within recent years, there has been a growing breadth and depth to our relations with the African continent. Private American investment has been mounting at the rate of 14 percent each year, and now exceeds $4 billion for the continent as a whole. Our economic assistance (see Chapter XI) is substantial. Despite this larger presence, the United States has no overall strategy or conceptual approach to Africa and African problems. Each agency and bureaucracy of the government, and sometimes various layers within a single agency, seeks to attain objectives which, while individually unexceptional, are not always compatible. As a result, most African leaders have an impression of American policy as inherently unstructured and lacking in focus.

Part of the difficulty involves perception. In a world of fast-moving events where political change is constant, limited means and contingent ends are likely to become the essence of policy. In the area of defense planning, for example, we seem to be leading toward, in Thomas Schelling's words, a "balance of prudence" rather than a balance of power. Moreover, having learned to distinguish between power and force, we are now actively aware that it is progressively more difficult and expensive to apply both at long distance. The question of their relevance also arises since the fundamental threat to international stability today derives less from purely military considerations than from inflation, widespread famine, and the cartelization of control over the production, cost, and sale of basic commodities.

Yet, perception is important. Détente is not a synonym for alliance or for friendship, but a limited tacit agreement to avoid escalation of differences to a state of war, while continuing to compete for ideological, political, economic, and strategic gains. Within the context of détente, the Soviet Union has become the principal external influence in South Asia and in parts of the Middle East, and is pursuing a more active role in Africa and Latin America. The Soviet presence does not represent a decline in American power so much as an increase in Moscow's capabilities. But this unfolding pattern confronts us with a choice. How do we choose to perceive Soviet ambitions? Do we perceive the spreading Soviet presence as a challenge to vital U.S. interests or as part of a natural process in which we both have a role to play and in which our fundamental interests are not threatened? Do we return to the dogma of the past in which power was regarded as a zero sum game (and in which the preeminent feature of international politics was the conflict between communism and the "free world"), or do we search for a basis for accommodation? The answers to these questions will influence most profoundly how the United States evaluates its security interests in Africa in the years immediately ahead. The answers will also shape decisions on the distribution of resources to friends and allies, and even how we define friends and allies. The sale of military hardware to African armies must be considered.in the broader context.

Our policy choices also expand or contract depending on our perception of our economic interests. Is the commanding imperative for the United States in relation to Africa access to raw materials, or a more broadly based consideration of the interrelationship of this access with African needs for training, price stability, and assured markets? If our approach is confined to the raw materials end of the policy spectrum, we will continue to be obsessed with such desiderata as stability, lines of communication, and military access. If our approach is broader and more encompassing of African needs, then purely political-military considerations are likely to be downgraded.

There are few signs at present that the United States is prepared or is preparing to make clearcut choices. The prospects are that we will pursue our present approach, which simultaneously emphasizes détente and security. In this context, we are likely to seek to maintain or to establish special bilateral relations with African nations that fall into one or more of the following categories: (1) is a major producer of commodities considered essential to the defense readiness and economic well-being of the United States and Western Europe—e.g., petroleum, chromium, cobalt, tantalum, uranium, etc.; (2) is capable of playing a significant political-military or economic role in a particular subregion—e.g., Nigeria and the Ivory Coast, Zaire and Zambia, South Africa; (3) occupies a strategic geographic location—Morocco, South Africa, Zaire, Ethiopia, perhaps Kenya; or (4) has been a traditional friend or dependency of the United States—Liberia. Since these categories are not congruent, bureaucracies and bureaucrats can be expected to continue to engage in lively debate over the merits of each, or the lack thereof.

In short, until—or unless—there is an early sorting out of overall American priorities, the ambiguities in United States policy toward Africa will persist for the foreseeable future.

Notes

1. Halford MacKinder, *Britain and the British Seas* (New York: Appleton and Company, 1922).

2. Nicholas Spykman, *America's Strategy in World Politics* (New York: Harcourt, Brace and Company, 1942).

3. Vernon McKay, "External Pressures on Africa Today," *The United States and Africa* (New York: Columbia University Press, 1958), p. 83.

4. George W. Ball, "American Policy in the Congo," Chapter 8, in Helen Kitchen (ed.), *Footnotes to the Congo Story* (New York and Toronto: Walker and Company and the Ryerson Press, 1967).

5. Chester A. Crocker, "France's Changing Military Interests," *Africa Report*, Vol. 13, No. 6 (June 1968), pp. 22-23.

6. *Survival* (London: International Institute of Strategic Studies), XVII, No. 3 (May-June 1975), p. 145.

7. Samuel P. Huntington, "After Containment: The Functions of the Military Establishment," *The Annals* (March 1973), p. 13.

8. Seymour Weiss, Statement before the House Foreign Affairs Subcommittee on the Middle East and South Asia, U.S. Congress (April 10, 1974).

9. James H. Noyes, Statement before the Senate Committee on Foreign Relations Subcommittee on Africa, U.S. Congress (July 29, 1975).

10. George W. Ball, "American Policy in the Congo."

11. *The Washington Post*, February 18, 1975, p. 11. Copyright 1975 *The Washington Post.* Reprinted with permission.

Appendix IXA

Statement of
James R. Schlesinger
Secretary of Defense
Before the
Senate Armed Services Committee

June 10, 1975

Mr. Chairman and Members of the Committee, I appreciate this opportunity to clarify for you our reasons for proposing an augmentation of facilities on the island of Diego Garcia in the Indian Ocean. As I have indicated in previous appearances before this Committee and elsewhere, we believe this project is necessary to provide logistical support for our forces which operate periodically in the Indian Ocean.

Since my last appearance here, the President has signed the Military Construction Act of 1975 (Public Law 93-552), which authorized $18.1 million to begin construction of these facilities, subject to certain qualifications. In response to Congressional request, as specified in Section 613(a)(1) of that Bill, the President certified to the Congress on May 12 that he had evaluated all the military and foreign policy implications regarding the need for United States facilities at Diego Garcia and concluded that the construction of such a project is essential to the national interest of the United States. In the absence of any negative action by Congress, it will be possible to commence construction of the support facilities this fall. An additional $13.8 million in military construction funds has been requested in the FY 76 Budget.

At the present time we have a limited communications station on Diego Garcia. The purpose of the new construction would be to expand this station to include certain support functions beyond its present communications role. The proposed expansion would include the following:

— The runway would be lengthened to 12,000 feet from its present 8,000 feet to permit the operation of larger cargo aircraft as well as high performance tactical aircraft under a variety of circumstances in the tropical climate;
— The fuel storage capacity would be increased from the present 60,000 barrels of aviation fuel to a total of 380,000 barrels of aviation fuel and 320,000 barrels of fuel oil for ships;
— An anchorage would be dredged in the shallow coral lagoon which could accommodate the ships of a carrier task group, and a pier would be constructed to provide about 550 feet of berthing primarily for the rapid loading or unloading of fuel;
— Various airfield improvements would include additional parking aprons, an arresting gear for emergency use, and limited aircraft maintenance facilities;
— Additional quarters for approximately 300 officers and men would be constructed; and
— Storage, power, and other ancillary facilities would be expanded proportionate to the intended support functions.

The military construction funds required for this project would be approximately $37.8 million, to be carried out by SEABEE units through FY 79. At the present time, there are approximately 600 SEABEES on the island completing previously authorized work on the communications station and harbor, which is expected to be finished during this calendar year. There are about 430 U.S. military personnel currently assigned to operate the communications station and the airstrip. With the expansion program, this number would rise to approximately 600.

The total cost of the improvements we have requested on Diego Garcia, including the salaries of the construction personnel, their food and fuel, the replacement costs of equipment used in the construction process, the procurement of hardware for the communications station, and all other operating and maintenance costs would be about $108 million, or roughly the cost of a single navy oiler. In view of the flexibility which the proposed installation on Diego Garcia will offer to our forces, and the operational economies it will make possible, we feel that this is a prudent investment.

Our principal objective in requesting this facility is to provide secure access to logistical support for our forces operating in the Indian Ocean. For example, our naval forces operating there today must rely either on local sources of fuel or else must be replenished by a chain of tankers stretching over 4,000 miles from U.S. facilities in the Philippines. The additional fuel storage we have proposed would permit a normal carrier task group to operate for about 30 days independent of other sources of supply. That margin of time could spell the difference between the orderly resupply of our forces and a hasty improvisation which could place unwieldy demands on our support assets in other areas. The same is true of the repair and maintenance which could be performed on ships and aircraft.

In short, the proposed facility would provide the assurance of U.S. capability to deploy and maintain forces in an area which has become increasingly important over the past decade.

Mr. Chairman, for nearly two centuries the Indian Ocean was the military preserve of Great Britain, which exercised control over the vital sea lanes to India and the many outposts of the British Empire. From the early nineteenth century Britain opposed Czarist attempts to extend Russian rule into South Asia, just as it later cooperated in countering postwar Stalinist efforts in Azerbaijan to extend Soviet influence in the direction of the Persian Gulf.

In the economic environment of the 1960s the British were forced to reorient their priorities toward Europe and away from Asia and the Indian Ocean. It is an interesting coincidence that 1968—the year the British announced their intention to withdraw—was also the year when the USSR first established what has now become a permanent naval presence in the northwest Indian Ocean.

While this transition from British dominance to a more diffuse power structure has been in progress, the interests of the United States in the Indian Ocean region have been growing. We have become increasingly dependent on the oil which is constantly moving in tankers along the sea lanes in the Indian Ocean, and our allies are even more dependent. We have an immediate stake in the stability and security of this very large body of water where half of the world's seaborne oil is in transit at any given time.

Consequently, we have been concerned at the steady growth of Soviet military activity in the region. I would like to review briefly the sequence of events by which this increase of Soviet military presence has developed.

The first Soviet deployments to the Indian Ocean in 1968 were small and tentative in nature. Lacking any shore facilities, the original contingents of Soviet ships were satisfied to remain mostly quiescent, spending most of their time at anchorages in international waters, with only occasional brief port visits to break what must have been a monotonous existence. This cautious probing of unfamiliar waters is very reminiscent of Soviet initial deployments into the Mediterranean some five years earlier.

When the Soviet Navy began to deploy to the Mediterranean in 1963, following an abortive earlier attempt to introduce submarines into Albania, there were very few ports open to them and they spent most of their time sitting idly at anchor. But the Soviets grew more confident with time, and when Egypt made port and airfield facilities available to them after 1967, they were quick to increase the scope and intensity of their operations. By the time of the Arab-Israel War of October 1973, they were able to introduce and sustain an armada of more than 90 ships, including the most modern in their inventory.

As early as 1962, the Soviets agreed to assist the government of Somalia in constructing port facilities in Berbera, a small port overlooking the entrance to the Red Sea. The harbor was completed in 1969, and 16 Soviet ships paid visits to the port by 1971. In 1972, Marshal Grechko visited Somalia for the signing of a Soviet-Somali Agreement, and this was soon followed by an increase in Soviet use of facilities at Berbera, including the establishment of a naval communications site and the arrival of a barracks and repair ship which has remained as a permanent feature ever since. In late 1973, the USSR began initial construction of what has subsequently been identified as a missile storage and handling facility at Berbera, suggesting that the Soviets had plans for such a facility even before the events of the October 1973 war and the introduction of a more frequent US presence.

In July of last year, the USSR signed a Treaty of Friendship and Cooperation with Somalia, similar to those signed with Egypt, Iraq, and India. Several months later, approximately coincident with a visit by the Commander of the Soviet Navy, Admiral Gorshkov, we noted the beginning of a significant expansion of Soviet facilities at Berbera, including expansion of the POL storage, construction of additional housing ashore, and the beginning of a very long airstrip. The emerging configuration of a missile storage and handling facility became apparent. It is evident that the USSR is in the process of establishing a significant new facility capable of supporting their naval and air activities in the northwest Indian Ocean.

The USSR has also provided assistance to the Government in South Yemen in managing the former British port of Aden, which was the fourth largest bunkering port in the world when the Suez Canal was in operation. This port lies directly across the Gulf of Aden from Berbera and commands the northern side of the entrance to the Red Sea. In addition, the USSR is assisting Iraq in the construction of a port, Umm Qasr, at the northern tip of the Persian Gulf. However, Soviet development and use of these two facilities has been much more modest than at Berbera.

The Soviet Union has become a major sea power only in the last decade. The first display of Soviet global naval power—the so-called OKEAN Exercise in 1970—was intended to demonstrate Soviet capability to conduct coordinated naval operations in every ocean of the world. A similar worldwide exercise was held in April of this year. For this event, the number of Soviet ships in the Indian Ocean was approximately doubled. Activity was centered in the northern Arabian Sea, at the crossroads of the tanker lanes from the Persian Gulf. The exercise was supported by long range aircraft operating from the Soviet Union, and, for the first time, by maritime patrol aircraft operating from airfields in Somalia.

It is worth remembering that the entire Soviet buildup in the Indian Ocean which now averages approximately 19 ships on a regular basis, has occurred during the period since the Suez Canal closed in 1967. We anticipate that, with the canal once again open as of last week, we will see an increase in the level of Soviet merchant ship traffic and commercial activity with South Asia. We will be watching very carefully for any change in the pattern of their naval deployments. As you know, the opening of the canal reduces the distance from the Black Sea to the Arabian Sea from 11,500 miles to only 2,500 miles—a difference in sailing time of 24 days. It also reopens to the USSR a warm water transit route from European Russia to the Soviet Far East, which will undoubtedly be important for the transfer of naval units between eastern and western fleets. Whether this will mean an increase in Soviet naval presence on a regular basis is not certain, but it will certainly increase Soviet flexibility in supporting or reinforcing its units in the Indian Ocean.

The level of U.S. presence in the Indian Ocean has been prudent. We have had a small permanent presence in the Persian Gulf and Red Sea since 1949, consisting of the command ship and two destroyers of the Middle East Force centered in Bahrain. In addition, since October 1973, we have conducted more frequent and more regular deployments to the area from our Pacific Fleet. Over the past 18 months, there have been seven such deployments, including five visits by carrier task groups and two visits by major surface combatants. Over the past year, we have had an augmented presence in the area approximately one-third of the time.

Although we would strongly prefer to see no Soviet buildup of military presence in this region, it appears that the USSR intends to undertake such a buildup. Since an effective military balance is essential to the preservation of regional security and stability in this area of great importance to the economic well-being of the industrialized world, we feel we should have logistical facilities which will permit us to maintain a credible presence. In a period of historical transition toward a new set of power relationships, only the United States among the Western nations has the stature to insure that the balance is maintained.

X   An American Banker Looks at Africa

David L. Buckman

[Editor's Note] *This chapter reflects Mr. Buckman's personal and institutional viewpoint on American trade and investment in sub-Saharan Africa. Although observations derive from his own nine years of practical experience in Africa-related banking (seven of them resident in West Africa and two as Vice President and Division Executive for Africa of the Chase Manhattan Bank in New York), his assessment of the circumstances, opportunities, and choices in Africa is directed toward the questions and concerns of the American business community as a whole.*

The oil crisis of 1974 made us realize that the United States is dependent on developing countries for many essential products and that the earth's resources may not be infinite, or at least not infinitely affordable at the prices exporting countries may be able to charge. Only in the past generation has our interest in the mineral wealth of Africa come to be matched by an appreciation of its magnitude and its importance to world developments.[1]

The extent to which the American business community can participate in the development of Africa's resources will depend on the role it plays in initiating trade and investment opportunities. Not only will Americans benefit from increased trade and investment, but the nations and peoples of Africa also have much to gain. There is an increasing awareness among African leaders that measures can be taken to assure mutual advantages to the host country and the investor, and that private investment can assist a country in meeting its development goals, including those financed on a long-term basis through aid programs.

Problems for the Coming Decade

A major problem for the coming decade is that both investors and host countries believe that their bargaining power in determining the objectives of a project has been increased vis-à-vis the other party. Investors sense that capital will be the scarce resource in the next decade and that their access to world money markets gives them a bargaining advantage over the host country. On the other hand, host countries feel that the scarcity of raw materials puts them in the superior bargaining position. This tension over the relative importance of the host country's contribution of raw materials and the investor's access to capital is likely to intensify rather than diminish. It must be resolved at the negotiating table in each case, in a manner satisfactory to both parties, or investors will continue to be tempted to walk away from unfinished projects and host countries will continue to contemplate forced nationalization.

In addition, the United States faces two new developments in the economic side of its relations with Africa.

Although African-American trade reached slightly more than $10 billion in 1974 (see Table X-1), or about five percent of our total foreign trade, we incurred close to a $3 billion deficit in that year because of the sharp rise in oil prices. As Table X-2 indicates, most of this deficit was with Nigeria, as a result of massive U.S. petroleum imports from that country. There were also substantial deficits with Angola and Gabon because of petroleum imports. While there is no serious reason for the United States to attach high priority to maintaining a positive balance of trade with Africa, some concern is inevitable when the value of imports outpaces exports by almost two to one. Attention needs to be given to the export side of the ledger.

Second, the White House study on raw materials—declassified in December 1974—confirms the importance of Africa's raw materials to the United States in the last quarter of this century and after. If it is agreed that Africa's petroleum and minerals are important to us, then we must accept that we will have to compete for them with Britain, Europe, Japan, and others—not to mention Africa itself. The question is *how* do we compete? Until now, the rules of the game have required American companies essentially to "go it alone" while their competitors have enjoyed considerably more encouragement and direct support from their governments—in the form of insurance-tied aid, subsidies, and "economic statesmanship."

Clearly, a new chapter in economic history is opening in Africa, and the U.S. private sector can be a part of it. The ability of American businessmen to function in the unfamiliar and sometimes difficult conditions of the African marketplace of the late 1970s and 1980s can have a direct influence on the American balance of payments, on African economies, and on African political attitudes toward the United States.

Table X-1

U.S. Trade with African Countries, 1973-74

(millions of U.S. dollars)

	1974	1973	Percent Change
1. World Total			
Exports	98,506.3	71,338.8	38
Imports	100,972.3	69,475.7	45
Balance	−2,466.0	1,863.1	
2. Africa			
Exports	3,659.4	2,305.8	58
Imports	6,617.3	2,582.9	156
Balance	−2,957.9	−277.1	`
3. Africa (excl. North Africa)			
Exports	2,478.8	1,643.1	50
Imports	5,414.4	2,079.8	160
Balance	−2,935.6	−436.7	
4. Africa (excl. North Africa & South Africa)			
Exports	1,318.9	896.8	47
Imports	4,863.7	1,702.9	185
Balance	−3,544.8	−806.1	
5. Principal Commodity Trade Exports			
Exports			
Capital goods (excluding automotive)	1,291.6	1,011.3	27
(Non-electric machinery excluding consumer type)	(865.6)	(586.3)	47
(Civilian aircraft and parts)	(237.5)	(276.4)	−14
Food and feed grains	754.8	408.0	85
Imports			
Petroleum	4,750.9[a]	892.8	432
Coffee	445.6[b]	422.9	5
Gem diamonds	155.6	177.6	−12
Cocoa beans	117.3[b]	124.1	−4
Copper	86.1	35.9	139
Fish and shellfish	82.7	70.3	17

[a]Africa supplied 29 percent of U.S. crude petroleum imports in 1974.

[b]African countries supplied 37 percent of U.S. imports of cocoa and 30 percent of coffee imports in 1974.

Source: Bureau of African Affairs, U.S. Department of State.

Table X-2
U.S. Trade with Principal Trading Partners in Africa, 1974
(millions of U.S. dollars)

	Exports	Imports	Balance
South Africa[a]	1,159.9	609.2	550.7
Egypt	455.2	69.8	385.4
Algeria	315.5	1,090.6	−775.1
Nigeria[b]	286.4	3,286.3	−2,999.9
Morocco	184.0	19.7	164.3
Zaire	145.2	68.0	77.2
Libya	139.4	1.4	138.0
Tunisia	86.9	21.4	65.5
Ghana	76.8	125.6	−48.8
Liberia	70.1	96.3	−26.2
Zambia	68.0	5.7	62.3
Sudan	64.3	26.8	37.5
Angola	61.8	378.2	−316.4
Tanzania	51.4	26.4	25.0
Ivory Coast	49.0	95.4	−46.4
Kenya	48.7	39.4	9.3
Senegal	34.1	2.5	31.6
Ethiopia	33.3	63.6	−30.3
Gabon	32.5	162.3	−129.8

[a]South Africa was the eighteenth most important market (worldwide) for U.S. exports in 1974.
[b]Nigeria was the seventh most important source of U.S. imports (worldwide) in 1974.
Source: U.S. Department of Commerce.

Where Do We Stand Today?

Substantial American economic relations with Africa began to develop just before World War II, but only with the advent of postwar "internationalism" did the United States government play an active part in increasing these relations. The growing official interest in stimulating African trade and investment was motivated in part by idealism and the desire to "foster economic development," in part by a number of foreign policy considerations aimed at increasing American influence, offsetting communist trade and investment initiatives, and encouraging the creation or continuation of stable governments.

Implicit in those goals was the assumption that they could be achieved by increased private investment and trade as well as by aid. When the 1957 Special Congressional Committee to study the Foreign Aid Program issued a report on

"American Private Enterprises, Foreign Economic Development, and the AID Programs," it emphasized the importance of private investment:

What we need to do is to place reliance on expanded private investment and the building of foreign private economies. Private investment . . . is the most effective way of helping other people to improve their levels of living. . . . [The] presence of American enterprise abroad also does much to widen the local enterprise base, an indispensable requirement if the less-developed countries are to achieve their maximum rate of growth and economic improvement is to proceed on a self-sustaining base.

An American response was handicapped, however, by unequal competition from the large British and European-based companies that had been established in Africa during the colonial era and subsequently had expanded throughout most of the continent. With some notable exceptions, American goods were essentially excluded from Africa until the beginning of World War II. Then the American need for African raw materials—especially rubber, copper, iron ore, and palm oil—and the inability of Great Britain and France, absorbed in the war, to meet African commodity needs led to increased trade and, to a lesser extent, investment. Aggregate average annual trade between the United States and Africa amounted to under $200 million before World War II, according to the 1957 United States *Statistical Abstract*, but by 1960 it had risen to $1.3 billion annually. Africa then was supplying four percent of our imports and taking three percent of our exports. In 1960, total American direct investment in Africa mounted to $925 million, or 2.8 percent of our total worldwide investment, as is shown in Table X-3.

As they became independent, the African countries opened up as a "new" area of investment and trade for many American companies. In general, however, American business knew little about Africa or Africans and was unprepared to appraise systematically the opportunities and problems. American

Table X-3
U.S. Direct Investment in Africa by Industry, 1960

Category	Dollar Value (millions)	Industry Share (percent)	Share of U.S. Worldwide Investment (percent)
All industries	$925	100.0	2.8
Petroleum	407	44.0	3.7
Mining	247	26.7	8.2
Manufacturing	118	12.7	1.0
Other	153	16.6	

Source: U.S. Department of Commerce. *Market Indicators for Africa.* World Trade Information Service, Statistical Reports, Part 3, 62-20, 1962.

visitors to Africa abounded in the euphoric transitional years, but it was difficult for African governments to identify "the serious investor"—in part because the visitors themselves didn't know if they were serious. By the end of the 1960s, general interest had dwindled, though several multinational companies had recognized the long-term prospects for African markets and had established manufacturing or assembly plants to serve them.

By 1973, American-African trade (total of imports and exports) had increased in absolute terms to $4.9 billion a year or more than triple 1960. U.S. imports from Africa were around four percent of total American imports, and exports to Africa were around three percent of total American exports. This meant that, compared to 1960, Africa had maintained its position as buyer of our goods and as supplier of raw materials, whereas most other developing areas declined in importance to the United States during this period.

During the period 1960-74, American investments in Africa grew faster than trade. Direct investment more than quadrupled, maintaining an annual compound growth rate of 12.1 percent. In contrast, our worldwide investment grew at a much slower pace, 9.5 percent. In absolute terms, American investments in Africa of $925 million in 1960 had grown to $4.23 billion by 1974. Even so, investment in Africa represented a rather small portion (3.8 percent) of total American investment abroad. As is shown in Table X-4, investment in manufacturing represented only 1.5 percent of our worldwide commitments in 1973, though the percentages for petroleum (7.7) and mining (7.4) are more substantial.

The importance of petroleum is hardly surprising, especially since these calculations were made before much of the U.S. investment in Libya was nationalized. What is surprising, however, is that our investments in manufacturing ($701 million) were by 1973 larger than those in mining ($555 million). In contrast, we had invested $129 million more in mining than in manufacturing in 1960. This important shift probably reflects a number of trends, in particular

Table X-4
U.S. Direct Investment in Africa by Industry, 1973

Category	Dollar Value (millions)	Industry Share (percent)	Share of U.S. Worldwide Investment (percent)	Growth Rate 1960-73 (percent)
All Industries	4,070	100.0	3.8	12.1
Petroleum	2,276	55.9	7.7	14.2
Mining	555	13.6	7.4	6.5
Manufacturing	701	17.2	1.5	14.7
Other	539	13.2	—	10.1

Source: U.S. Department of Commerce. *Survey of Current Business*, January 1974.

increased American investment in local Nigerian and South African manufacturing as well as increased local African participation in mining projects. In short, manufacturing in Africa became an increasingly important focus of interest for American firms in the decade ending in 1973, even to the point of having a faster growth rate (17.2 percent) than the petroleum sector (14.7 percent).

Although Africa's primary economic importance to the United States and to the rest of the world still lies in its commodities and raw materials, we are beginning to realize that the continent is also a significant potential market for increasingly sophisticated manufactured goods, whether exported from the United States or manufactured locally in selected African countries. Today, American business can neither ignore these wider world markets nor dominate them. What the trade and investment statistics will record a decade from now will depend on the interest, ingenuity, and initiative shown by American businessmen in developing new trade and investment opportunities, and on the support they receive from the United States government.

An Appraisal of American Business Practices

A major problem confronting American business in Africa is the lack of aggressiveness among American investors and exporters. Many African businessmen, especially in non-English speaking areas, have had no active contact with an American company, yet many of them express interest in the quality and marketability of U.S. products. They say they would welcome anything we offer so long as it is competitive in the marketplace. Any reasonable offer from United States investors or exporters would be seriously considered. But taking advantage of this African market calls for an aggressive posture, since few African businessmen are motivated to find out which American companies supply what products.

Prerequisites for Trade Expansion

Clearly, the first requirement for expanding trade with Africa is to know and respond to African markets. Some American businesses fail to answer letters requesting catalogues and information. Their low level of interest in African inquiries results from a lack of knowledge of the potential market; a lack of initiative in finding out; and/or from an assumption that there are easier, more profitable, alternatives. Many firms neglect their African contacts after they have been established. The African businessman is not actively urged to push American products. He receives virtually no assistance in the form of advertising and promotion. This failure to follow through is a real and important obstacle to development of the American business presence in Africa, despite ample room for investment and export growth in the former French- and English-dominated areas. While many American companies might consider that most individual African countries present too small a market, their outlook may change when they take a broader look at the size and potential of the markets in which they could be competitive.

If efforts to expand trade are to succeed, changes will be needed in the relationship between American business and the United States government. As a general principle, the relationship should be strengthened to be more competitive with other governments' support for their corporate entities. For example, the Departments of State and Commerce are sometimes overly cautious in their attempts to be impartial, contacting not just the most-qualified American companies for a particular project but including some which may have no relevant African experience. There is also a reluctance—or, at least, a failure—to make full use of the banking community's expertise. Banks have extensive contacts with potential project participants. Some of the larger banks have technical advisers in agriculture, mining, and transportation. Increasing coordination between the information systems of the Departments of State and Commerce with those of the commercial banks would increase ability to act positively on a project rather than merely react to specific inquiries.

American embassies abroad could play a central role as a conduit of information to the private sector. They are in the best position to identify priorities of host governments and act on investment and trade opportunities. But information received by the private sector is valuable only if it is timely. What is needed is computer quickness, to provide sufficient lead time for the American investor or exporter to prepare his case and compete effectively.

Credit and foreign exchange are of critical importance to the African businessman and, of course, to the American firm in its preliminary negotiations. Most American companies require cash deposits before delivery. This poses difficult problems for African businesses, which often must resort to local loans. An intrinsic part of every transaction should be a satisfactory arrangement for payment that protects the domestic consumer as well as the overseas supplier. Too often this essential payment mechanism is not considered until after the negotiations concerning price, quantity, and other details. American banks involved in Africa should be encouraged to improve their contacts and knowledge in order to provide better service within the constraints and trading practices of African countries.

In countries where the lingua franca is not English, language can be a serious deterrent to interaction between American business and African firms or governments. The effort and expense required to obtain a translation into French, Arabic, or a local language can terminate a transaction in the early stages of negotiation. Appropriate advertising, promotion, and consumer communication at the retail level all are dependent on a planned capacity to use the lingua franca.

Defining an "Acceptable" Profit

Two questions probably cause more disagreement during contract negotiations than any other: (1) What is an "acceptable" rate of return on invested capital in the eyes of the investor? (2) What do the governmental authorities of the host country consider "acceptable"?

The answers are not easy. Many governments do not recognize that the return on invested capital is not a standard formula but depends in many ways on the overall position of the parent company in its international and domestic operations. The purpose of the project, the type of industry, the sales market, and alternative opportunities all contribute to determining what is an "acceptable" return. No rules prescribe whether five percent is too low or 25 percent is too high. Some companies may be satisfied with a low rate of return on a project to gain access to raw materials or to enter a new market. On the other hand, some countries may find the higher rate acceptable if the investment yields substantial benefits in employment or hard currency savings.

The company's viewpoint usually reflects its responsibility to its shareholders and directors to earn a return commensurate with the risks of operating in a developing country. Higher returns are demanded where the risks involve political stability, transportation, labor, technology, or other special factors. The host government, on the other hand, may take a simplistic view of the return on invested capital it will allow the company to repatriate. A misunderstanding can deter investment in a project or persuade the company management to move on to other investment possibilities in countries allowing a more acceptable rate of return.

In such cases, one approach to the problem is for the government and the companies to agree at the outset not only on the return on invested capital but also on the accounting methods employed in arriving at that figure. Whatever approach is used, both the government and investors should look behind simplistic formulas for determining what is an "acceptable" return. For return cannot be separated from a detailed analysis of risk.

Are We Sending the Right People?

The selection of personnel is critical to the success of American business in Africa. As previously mentioned, language facility and ability to adapt to the ways of business in Africa are decided advantages. In another area, one of unique interest to American business, interviews conducted with Nigerian businessmen in Lagos in 1974 brought out some forthright views on the relative acceptability of black and white representatives.[2]

In response to the question, "Do you feel that black Americans would be more acceptable than white?" the consensus was that "acceptance in Nigeria is based on the attitudes and conduct of the individual, not race." Further, "When it comes to business, we still want assurance that our money is in safe hands and that the people with whom we are conducting business really know what they are doing. This doesn't mean that we wouldn't deal with an Afro-American, or even that we might not give him first consideration. We just want to know that he is competent, that he is well supported by the organizations he claims to represent, and that he will be respectful both toward us and our institutions."

One Nigerian executive commented, "My general feeling is that, if two Americans come here, one black and one white, the black American probably will receive quicker acceptance simply because Nigerians will relate to him easily. However, as an American, he must prove himself no less than the white American and, once the white American has shown himself to be trustworthy, competent, and sympathetic, he will receive no less acceptance than anyone else regardless of race."

Some Favorable Trends

Africa is no longer a "mysterious" continent. In many ways it is becoming a better place for American business to seize opportunities and an easier place for businessmen to measure, analyze, and understand. For example:

1. Africa is more accessible now than before, from both a transportation and a communications viewpoint. With most countries possessing their own airlines, and with frequent and regular flights to African capitals from London, Paris, Brussels, and Rome, getting to Africa is not the problem that it was even a decade ago. In addition, the amount of printed information about the countries has never been greater, although quality has not improved as much as quantity. Airmail editions of London's *Financial Times, The Economist, West Africa,* and *The Financial Mail*, among others, are readily available in the United States. Detailed information on specific development plans, with financial statistics, are obtainable in most major American city libraries and from American international banks.

2. Increasing numbers of African-American Chambers of Commerce, trade associations, conferences, and seminars are specifically keyed to promoting economic ties between the United States and sub-Saharan Africa.

3. Every year, more Africans study abroad in American or European universities, at financial institutions, and at banks in training programs. The number of businessmen and government officials with a working knowledge of international finance and commercial practices is growing fast.

4. Although many economies around the world (and some desperately so in Africa) are depressed by higher oil prices, the wealth flowing into countries possessing scarce commodities (oil in Nigeria and Gabon, sugar in Mauritius, copper in Zambia, and so on) enables many to accept and actively seek out American trade and investment.

5. If the newly rich Arab nations in fact carry out their announced investment plans in African countries such as Sudan (see Chapters V and XI), the resulting need for expertise in design and management, and for equipment for road building and agriculture, will open up new opportunities to which the United States could respond effectively. American business should begin now to establish the necessary contacts on the continent to ensure a future role for itself as investment by the Arabs materializes.

6. Some countries, though independent since the early 1960s, have only recently stepped up their efforts to diversify their economic relations away from their former colonial rulers. This means that American, German, and Japanese interests can share with those of France and Britain in French-speaking and English-speaking Africa.

7. American bankers have become increasingly active in Africa within the last few years in correspondent banking, term lending, trade financing, and project financing. They often have far easier access to senior government officials, including ministers of finance and trade, and to key persons in the private sector, than do their counterparts in Asia or Europe. Their knowledge of government attitudes, the marketplace, political trends, and trade activity is large and growing. It can be tapped by American investors to learn the best ways to mesh their interests with the needs of host countries.

Learning from a Failure

Ideally, foreign investment should serve the purposes of both the investor and the host country. Their objectives usually are substantially different but need not be mutually exclusive. Harmonizing their objectives should be the primary concern of both investor and host.

From the viewpoint of the host country, the importance of foreign investment lies primarily in the transfer of technology, additional capital, and increased employment, all of which can help the country to develop its natural resources or agricultural potential. Second, investment can expand the infrastructure, create other industries, bring more people into the money economy, and raise living standards through provision of medical services, education, more consumer goods, and so on. From the investor's point of view, any investment must provide, first of all, an adequate profit. Second, it may open new markets, assure access to essential raw materials, make use of lower cost labor, and foster the host country's development.

The challenge of any investment project is to harmonize these goals so that each participant is satisfied with his perceived benefits. Many failures of foreign investment in Africa can be traced to disregard or ignorance of the partner's expectations. Unless investment objectives are debated, clarified, and agreed upon *at the negotiating stage*, the risk of conflict and misunderstanding is enormously increased.

The following case of the "Afra Sugar Corporation" in the imaginary
Republic of Afra shows how an American investor failed to understand the
realities of doing business in Africa:

The Afra Sugar Corporation: A Hypothetical Case

Great Expectations

In 1967, the Republic of Afra at last adopted its First Development Plan
(1965-1970), which included a pledge to get an integrated sugarcane plantation
and refinery under way by December 1970. The project was given highest
priority because, when completed, it would be the country's largest industry as
measured by output and employment. It was also essential to the country's first
attempt at national planning for its predominantly agricultural economy. A
publicity drive was launched throughout Afra to draw attention to the new plan
and specifically to the sugar project. Because the plan got off to a very slow
start, it soon became a political issue. At a special meeting of the cabinet, the
minister of economic planning and national development outlined specific goals
the sugarcane project would accomplish. It would

● Exploit the ongoing irrigation program being financed by the International
Bank for Reconstruction and Development (World Bank).

● Increase employment, adding 13,000 jobs in growing, harvesting, manufacturing, and transport. Those jobs would be of critical importance when Afran
laborers working abroad returned home in a few years.

● Increase agricultural production by six percent a year (as against an annual
net population growth rate of 2.9 percent).

● Reduce imports, by producing and refining locally the total domestic sugar
requirement.

● Increase exports, making one-third of the total sugar output available to
foreign markets.

● Enlarge the industrial base, adding plant and capital equipment.

● Add to the country's infrastructure, even though the sugar project was
basically an "enclave project."

● Extend education to new segments of the population by establishing a sugar
research school (initially staffed by expatriate agronomists).

● Help to establish a credit rating for the Republic in international capital
markets. (In 1967, Afra had little experience in external borrowing on commercial terms.)

● Diversify the country's economic ties abroad, thus decreasing Afra's
neocolonial dependence on the European country—the metropole—whose
colony it had been until 1957.

The cabinet decided that no more than 50 percent of the export sugar would
be sold to the metropole and that the technical partner in the project should not
be from the metropole. At the same meeting, the prime minister asked the
minister of economic planning to use his contacts made at the University of
Chicago Business School to interest a United States sugar company in the
project. The first person to come to the minister's mind was Ed Oakes, president
of the Agricultural Bio-Chemical Company of St. Louis, who had been a
classmate at Chicago. The minister decided to refrain from advertising for
technical partners in order to prevent one selected by the metropole from
bidding. He didn't want to risk rejecting the metropole without a commercially

valid reason, for at this stage of Afra's development correct relations with the former colonizing power required sensitive handling.

Soon the minister made a private approach to the American Embassy. In a meeting with the ambassador and his commercial attaché, the minister mentioned his friend at the Agricultural Bio-Chemical Company and stressed the prime minister's urgent wish for immediate action. The minister underlined several points: "We feel that this project must have a technical partner that is willing to form a *real* partnership. We don't want a boss; we want a partner who respects *our* priorities and wishes. We've had our fill of companies that tell us what's best for us. And certainly we don't want this partner to ignore the lowest cost sources of equipment just to give business to companies in his own country. Help us find the right people."

Using normal communication channels, the attaché asked the Department of Commerce to help identify a qualified U.S. investor. At the same time, he approached two private organizations directly: the First Chartered Bank of St. Louis and the Agricultural Bio-Chemical Company. The attaché already knew of Bio-Chemical's prominence as a multinational sugar company, but he took this step primarily because of the minister's personal relationship with the company's president and his own knowledge of the company's strength in the U.S. domestic market.

Because the minister wished to appear impartial (he came from the region where the project would be located), he called on three other embassies. At the Japanese Embassy, he and his permanent secretary were enthusiastically received by the ambassador and his economic, commercial, and labor attachés. They were joined by a Japanese sugar expert who had been summoned to Afra soon after the Japanese government had obtained a copy of the Development Plan. The ambassador personally contacted the president of Japan's largest multinational bank and a related multinational trading company, and asked another friend, the president of the Japanese Export-Import Bank, to discuss the project with the minister of foreign affairs, the bank, and the trading company. The ambassador promised to follow the situation personally and report promptly to the Afran officials. On leaving the Japanese Embassy, the minister of planning remarked that he was impressed by their reception and believed Afra should consider Japan as a technical partner.

Later calls at the German, British, and Soviet embassies were, in varying degrees, repetitions of the Japanese encounter. The permanent secretary in particular came away with high expectations.

Making the Decision

On learning of these talks, the ambassador of the former colonizing power used the occasion of a small dinner with metropole businessmen resident in Afra to discuss how the Afra government could be dissuaded from using a third-country corporation. Long-range metropole planning assumed a steady supply of sugar from Afra, which could be assured only if the state-controlled metropole sugar company invested in and managed the Afra Sugar Corporation.

A coordinated effort was made to sow doubts about the capabilities of other foreign firms. It was pointed out to senior government officials and Afran businessmen that it would be better to deal with "people who know Afra in depth, identify with the government's objectives, have extensive experience in doing business in Afra, and speak the language." The inverse was true of the Americans, who "have little patience and limited language ability, and demand extensive legal agreements—all of which override their acknowledged expertise in agriculture." The Japanese were basically an unknown quantity in Afra whose efforts to secure and protect export markets amounted to "economic neocolonialism." The Germans were unacquainted with the idiosyncrasies of doing business in Africa. The Russians were characterized as politically motivated and likely to create political unrest. As for the British, they had done well in their former colonies but did not understand Afra. As the metropole ambassador continued to press against the selection of any non-metropole technical partner, he thought of an ace in the hole to use with the minister of planning: A few years ago he had helped the minister's wife buy a fleet of metropole trucks at very favorable prices and terms. Perhaps this would pay off now.

With the pressures building, the prime minister and minister of economic planning decided to approach the Agricultural Bio-Chemical Company. They weighed many factors, including what they considered "excessive pressure" from the metropole, but the decision turned on two simple points: the prime minister wanted to involve a third country, and the minister of planning knew the president of Agricultural Bio-Chemical. Little attention was given to the relative technical expertise of potential partners. Politics overruled economics. The minister of planning called on the president of Agricultural Bio-Chemical in his office in St. Louis, where the two old friends discussed the background and details of the project frankly and openly. That weekend, the minister gave a member of the board of the First Chartered Bank a full briefing on the project.

The president of Agricultural Bio-Chemical had some reservations about joining the project, one of which was his company's lack of experience in Africa. He pointed out that the company's overseas experience was limited to the Far East and Central America, where it had successfully operated refining and plantation companies since just after World War II. The minister discounted this reservation and emphasized Afra's need for sugar industry experience, which he felt was easily transferable to Afra.

For convenience, the final negotiating meetings were held in London. As in other recent negotiations abroad, the Agricultural Bio-Chemical team was headed by a young attorney from the company's legal department, together with a technical staff. No one from the executive office of Bio-Chemical was present at the signing, though regrets were given. Afra was represented by the minister of economic planning, since this was the most important project in Afra's First Development Plan.

In June 1968, a partnership called the Afra Sugar Corporation was formed with the following ownership:

Agminco, an Afran government corporation	25 percent
Agricultural Bio-Chemical Company of St. Louis	50 percent
Overseas Corporation for Development, an investment corporation of the former colonial power	25 percent

Although it had raised the largest share of the capital, Agricultural Bio-Chemical failed to obtain a controlling interest of 51 percent, primarily because Afran government policy precluded the formation of companies with controlling expatriate participation. ABC received no help in financing the project from the U.S. Agency for International Development or from the Export-Import Bank because First Chartered failed to present the project in a manner acceptable to those organizations. The Overseas Corporation for Development was brought in to satisfy the former colonial government, which may have anticipated that even minor participation would place it in position to pick up the pieces if Agricultural Bio-Chemical should fail.

Collapse of the Project

While the negotiations were still in progress, the American ambassador learned of significant changes in Afra's sugar marketing plans. In essence, the new regulations would prohibit the Afra Sugar Corporation from selling to the metropole and would curtail the quantity of sugar available for export. Not wishing to interfere in the negotiations because of his commitment to neutrality relative to American firms, the ambassador did not convey this knowledge to Bio-Chemical. The news was a serious blow, for Bio-Chemical had entered the project with the intent of increasing its market penetration in the metropole with sugar from Afra.

The introduction of the restriction on marketing also caused severe strains within the board of Afra Sugar Corporation. The managing director from Bio-Chemical assumed that the local director of the metropole-affiliated Overseas Corporation for Development had known in advance of the changes through his membership on various corporate and governmental boards—a charge that was emphatically denied. To ease the tension, the director eventually was recalled to Europe and subsequently replaced by an Afran director.

By December 1971, Agricultural Bio-Chemical had spent $24.5 million on the Afra sugar project with no return on its investment. Meanwhile, on the advice of the ministry of finance but without consultation with the ministry of economic development, the Afran government unilaterally increased the tax rate on all companies in which there was foreign participation, including Afra Sugar Corporation, to gain revenue for its Second Development Plan (1970-1975)—and specifically for a second satellite sugar scheme hundreds of miles north of the original project. The tax was imposed by a complicated formula that levied a certain percentage against gross income, thus reducing cash flow for dividends and debt service. A withholding tax that severely hurt foreign lenders was introduced. The government of Afra also imposed strict "indigenization" requirements on managerial employees, along with a progressive income tax that hit very hard at anyone earning more than $6,000. Together, these measures reduced the number of expatriate employees below the level necessary to operate the project efficiently. The tax reduced the net pay of expatriate employees to the point that employment in Afra was unattractive compared to other opportunities in the international sugar industry.

Obviously, Bio-Chemical's negotiators had taken too much for granted, having failed to consider the "worst case." No guarantees of tax concessions or maintenance of the existing tax structure were agreed to before the fact. This inexcusable omission was a major factor in the collapse of the project, and the error was compounded by the fact that other companies doing business in Afra did have "untouchable" tax concessions.

At the end of 1973, Agricultural Bio-Chemical showed a substantial loss on its Afra investment, not including its opportunity costs and negative rate of return on capital. Bio-Chemical sold its shareholdings to Proprietary Holdings Ltd., a conglomerate from the metropole introduced by the Overseas Corporation for Development.

In 1974, the government of Afra announced a new policy of "popular socialism" that called for nationalizing foreign investment. Soon the metropole sent a delegation of high government officials to Afra to promise substantial aid on concessional terms if Afra would protect Proprietary's investment with a grandfather clause. Subsequently the United States recognized a "security" interest in Afra and called attention to assistance that might be available if the government of Afra would limit its socialist revolution to rhetoric. But it didn't suggest to Afra that it should compensate American companies for their losses resulting from Afra's restrictions on marketing and higher taxes.

The collapse of Bio-Chemical's venture in Afra had several consequences. Not only did the American firm lose money, but the investment community as a whole received an unfavorable impression of Afra. The Afran government changed its attitude towards foreign investment, especially American investment. The investment climate in Afra might be far more hospitable today if the sugar project had been handled better. In addition, trade between the United States and Afra was inhibited, and the Afran market remained a preserve of the colonial power which had previously ruled the country.

Evaluation of the Afra Sugar Corporation

With hindsight, we can see what went wrong in Afra. Certain problems should have been identified during negotiations, analyzed, and solved. Through ignorance, indifference, and the tyranny of a misplaced sense of urgency, Agricultural Bio-Chemical went about things all wrong. At the same time, the Afran government was not above blame.

The following diagnosis of the Afra Sugar Corporation case is organized topically, for simplicity and focus. In reality the topics are neither clear nor distinct but overlap and blend together in a way entirely familiar to the investor experienced in project management in developing countries.

Ownership. The three shareholders of Afra Sugar were delighted to reach a compromise that divided the equity 25 percent to Agminco, 50 percent to Agricultural Bio-Chemical, and 25 percent to the Overseas Corporation for Development. The government of Afra thought this arrangement would bring in the essential equity contributions while minimizing the risk of "economic neocolonialism." In fact, the shareholder agreement allowed for tie votes in meetings of the board of directors, which substantially delayed decisionmaking, in particular with respect to the marketing of sugar products. The error here seems to rest with the Afran government, which should have been willing either to invest in more equity or cede majority control to the technical partner. Agricultural Bio-Chemical, for its part, should have known better than to yield on this critical point, and should have warned Afra of the possible consequences of an even equity split.

Equity Valuation. Some of Agricultural Bio-Chemical's equity was in the form of equipment, both new and used, and a dispute arose over its valuation. Having failed to identify this problem in advance, neither Bio-Chemical nor the government saw the need to agree on an independent expert's valuation. Since some of the new equipment was custom-made for local conditions—climate, energy, labor—it was expensive to Afra Sugar Corporation; but because it was customized it was worth much less when valued for resale on the international market. The Afran government felt that the cost-price differential constituted an excessive markup by Agricultural Bio-Chemical.

Some of the equipment purchased for the project had been used in the United States, but was rebuilt and certified by an engineering consultant before shipment. It was selected as ideal for Afra because it was labor-intensive and would assist the government in alleviating unemployment. Agricultural Bio-Chemical failed to explain the logic of this action to the minister of economic planning in advance, however, and the result was that unnecessary mistrust, suspicion, and hard feelings developed. The government believed it was being sold obsolete equipment that would impair the project as well as the country's stature in the world sugar community.

Conflicting Investment Goals. The government of Afra fully expected that the integrated sugar project would suffice to meet its goal of a six percent annual increase in agricultural production. Unconsciously and implicitly, the government made Afra Sugar Corporation, and ultimately the Agricultural Bio-Chemical Company, responsible for attaining this level of performance. When the target was not met, members of the National Assembly made speeches criticizing Agricultural Bio-Chemical and accusing it of not fulfilling its contract with the government. Neither the government nor Agricultural Bio-Chemical recognized the need to define the limits of the project and free Bio-Chemical from responsibility for achieving Development Plan goals. This is one reason that the government went ahead with the Satellite Sugar Cane Refining and Plantation Scheme at the expense of Afra Sugar Corporation profits.

Agricultural Bio-Chemical, as a worldwide sugar marketing firm, was primarily interested in producing and selling sugar according to its competitive worldwide market needs. It expected to make an adequate return on its investment in Afra Sugar Corporation but, more important, it expected that its head office in St. Louis would profit substantially from sales activities. This goal implied some price cutting for competitive purposes, though Bio-Chemical never spelled this out to the Afran government. Since the government wanted to maximize export earnings on the one-third of total sugar available for foreign sales, this difference in corporate and government goals created constant tension.

Investment Incentives. Recognizing at the outset that it would have to offer incentives to prospective investors, the government of Afra looked to its Investment Code for possibilities. Incentives were unusually important in the case of Afra Sugar Corporation because the nation's allowable rate of return on investment was not competitive with sugar schemes elsewhere in the world. The major incentives offered to Afra Sugar were a tax holiday for five years and a concessional tax rate for years six through 20, conveyed by discretionary authority of the head of state on the recommendation of the ministry of finance.

In subsequent years a new minister of finance became restive as he watched hard currency leave the country. The ministry of finance began to visualize ways in which Afra could profit from additional tax revenues. Agricultural Bio-Chemical's local managers were unaware of this change of attitude until fairly late and were unable to deter the 1971 tax increase. In retrospect, they realized they should have continued to press for more incentives than they expected to get even after negotiations were concluded, to keep the pressure on the government not to rescind the concessions already granted.

For the Republic of Afra, the sugar project was so important that finding a suitable partner with technical ability, management skill, and adequate capital was sufficient incentive for the government to accept Bio-Chemical's offer.

Lack of Concessional Finance. As the principal domestic bank for Agricultural Bio-Chemical, the First Chartered Bank of St. Louis was asked to prepare a "financing package" for the new company. First Chartered lacked experience in dealing with U.S. AID, the U.S. Export-Import Bank, the World Bank, and related institutions, but, rather than admit its weakness and ask for outside help, it took all the debt for itself and its syndicate partners, which were equally unfamiliar with soft loan alternatives. Nor did Agricultural Bio-Chemical bring much assistance to Afra on concessional terms. Despite its knowledge of international finance, Bio-Chemical accepted the Afran government's assurances that multilateral aid was not needed, again mistaking pride for determination. The bank and Bio-Chemical wrongly assumed that the senior Afrans with whom they were dealing understood U.S. banking practices.

Interest on senior debt of the Afra Sugar Corporation was based on the prime lending rate of American banks lending to the project. But because Afra Sugar was unable to maintain the compensating balances normally required of loan customers, the banks charged a premium over the prime rate. They assessed additional markups reflecting the fact that this was a foreign loan (country risk premium) and that the customer lacked a proven credit record (credit risk premium). The resulting interest was high enough to provoke severe criticism from the Afran directors of Agminco; they were accustomed to the local rate on bank bills, which at times was a full six percent less than the rate charged to Afra Sugar Corporation. Never mind that the local rate was funded differently, making the comparison irrelevant.

In addition, the Afran directors were unfamiliar with the floating rate concept that American banks applied to long-term loans. They sensed, quite rightly, that they had no control over the interest costs charged to Afra Sugar, and some spoke of a conspiracy among the American bankers and Agricultural Bio-Chemical to bleed the country.

The interest rate issue exemplified Bio-Chemical's failure to recognize the special requirements in dealing with an African country whose officials might not know the terms and conditions accepted as routine by American business. Agricultural Bio-Chemical should have explained these terms and conditions carefully in advance, informing the Afran government of the basis for interest costs and warning it of possible fluctuations caused by changes in the money market. Unless interest rates are seen and understood from the outset as a reality by the host government, they can breed serious misunderstanding.

To arrange financing on terms more acceptable to Afra, First Chartered Bank could have asked the project finance division of Bio-Chemical's international bank to arrange the financing package. That division, as financial adviser to Afra Sugar, would have analyzed the project in each significant aspect and assisted in devising a financial structure combining equity, Eximbank finance for equipment, and long-term debt from the Eurodollar market, Afran insurance companies, or commercial banks. In addition, the bank would have aided both partners by acting as a sounding board and a communication channel. Bio-Chemical would have learned that the project's blended cost of capital might have been lowered by the use of some Eximbank financing, and that insurance was available from the Overseas Private Investment Corporation against expropriation, war, or inconvertibility of currency.

Personal and Cultural Differences. In its ventures in Central America and the Far East, begun soon after World War II at the request of the United States and host governments, Bio-Chemical settled down to relatively smooth and profitable operations after several years of start-up problems. Now managed completely by local citizens, these projects yielded a generous return on invested capital and required little supervision other than periodic reporting and occasional technical assistance. Thus Bio-Chemical in St. Louis had high expectations but little real knowledge of the idiosyncrasies of project management in a developing country. Afra's minister of planning and the president of Bio-Chemical both overestimated the company's ability.

Afra's decisionmakers were accustomed to doing business with the locally based general managers of companies whose head offices were in the European country whose colony Afra had been for many years. Most of those managers were long-time residents who knew local political and economic conditions in Afra and were thoroughly familiar with all aspects of their companies' business. Most were over 45 years old; though they were effective, they never seemed in a hurry.

In contrast, the businessmen from Bio-Chemical were younger Americans in very much of a hurry. They swooped into the capital for short meetings, then left in a rush. From Bio-Chemical's point of view, they were expensive assets to be used as efficiently as possible. They had little knowledge of Africa's political past or present, and most had been only superficially briefed on the Afra Sugar Corporation and its goals. As specialists who knew a great deal about their particular fields of interest, they assumed that their expertise was applicable everywhere. Reassignments, promotions, and executive training programs led to their frequent replacement by other experts similarly conditioned.

From the Afran government's point of view, the "in-and-out" American businessmen provided no continuity. The predominance of lawyers at the negotiating stage and the Americans' insistence on contracts, letters of agreement, letters of intent, and a proliferation of other documentation were intended to compensate for this lack of continuity, but the government officials inferred that the Americans didn't trust their hosts. While American business presupposes that individuals are eminently replaceable, Afrans think more of the irreplaceability of key people. After several months of negotiations, the government wondered just who was ABC. Did these people who swooped in and out know what they were doing? Did they care about Afra at all? Could such an impersonal entity as Agricultural Bio-Chemical be trusted?

From the time the first shovel of dirt was hoisted until the last ribbon was cut, no member of Bio-Chemical's top management appeared in Afra. Meetings were held in Europe, a convenient midpoint for Afran officials flying north and Bio-Chemical officials flying east. Although this arrangement saved executive time, Bio-Chemical's failure to send more senior people to Afra increased Afran government doubt that the Americans could be trusted. When the refinery was opened, the head of state sent a personal invitation to the chairman of the board of Agricultural Bio-Chemical to join in a celebration, but the chairman couldn't work it into his schedule. Bio-Chemical continued to rotate its staff, to fly in auditors quarterly, and every six months to send an assistant vice president from a Bio-Chemical subsidiary in Europe—for a one-day inspection tour.

American businessmen are comfortable with the idea of delegated power. Usually they speak for their bosses and have negotiating flexibility. In contrast, African officials are sometimes uncomfortable with delegated power and are less able or free to speak and negotiate with complete assurance. Thus, in dealing with the government of Afra, Agricultural Bio-Chemical often thought it had agreement on an issue, or permission to make certain changes, only to find that the contact person in the government was overruled by higher authority. When

Bio-Chemical moved ahead on the basis of what it thought was valid agreement or permission, its actions were received with hostility and criticism. In time it was Bio-Chemical's turn to wonder with whom it was dealing, to question whether the designated official knew what he was doing or would be backed up by his superiors.

Quite unintentionally, Bio-Chemical's resident American manager gave the impression that there just wasn't time for him to explain to Afran directors, managers, and trainees what he was doing and why. Having been opposed on marketing issues, the government of Afra first felt resentful, then vengeful. Bio-Chemical lacked understanding of the political dynamics of the Afran situation. All would have benefited if the company had talked to more expatriate businessmen in Afra and to diplomats in addition to the Americans, to get a feel for the political goals the government had in mind when it put together the sugar scheme.

But Agricultural Bio-Chemical was dealing not only with the government but also with the people of Afra. The citizenry were encouraged to see the project as a natural resource, as a promise for the future, and in many ways as a gift of the government. Laborers at the project expected Bio-Chemical to fulfill its obligations as they saw them. Soon the workers began complaining about the absence of three important incentives the company had not considered. First, they missed a medical clinic that would treat local residents, whether or not they were employed by Afra Sugar Corporation. Such clinics are important in most countries in Africa. Because medical services are generally inadequate in relation to population, employers are expected to provide medical care free or for a nominal payment, and Bio-Chemical should have been prepared for this "cost of doing business" in Africa. The other two incentives—employee housing and educational facilities for employees' children—were not discussed during the negotiations because the government assumed that the company would know they were customary. Some of the resentment toward Agricultural Bio-Chemical was directly traceable to worker unrest about these missing services conveyed through local political party representatives at the project site.

If Afran employees expected more from the company in the form of non-salary benefits, they also expected less from themselves in the form of commitment to their employer's goals. Afrans are accustomed to exchanging labor for pay, but unlike Americans they are unwilling to exchange their lives around the clock for still more pay. Misunderstandings about nonprescribed duties were compounded by Bio-Chemical's acceptance of the Afran government's wishful estimate of how rapidly the workers could be trained, how productive they would be, how flexible they would be in their jobs, and how willing they would be to work extra hours when production scheduling demanded it. Frictions arose over workers' absences for seemingly inexplicable reasons and over management's violation of taboos against putting African workers in supervisory positions over persons older than themselves, or, in some cases, of different tribal (ethnic) origin.

Eventually Bio-Chemical went outside the company and recruited a manager with previous experience in Nigeria, Malawi, and Cameroon. His strong points were forceful but tactful diplomacy, an empathetic understanding of the Afran government's position, facility in French, and, perhaps more important, an awareness of the real world of African business. In his previous assignments, he had shown the ability to motivate his expatriate staff in difficult circumstances. He understood that "African time is different time," and his temperament matched his understanding. At his urging, the company began providing preventive as well as curative medical care, a high protein midday meal, and other benefits that seemed to increase the Afran workers' productivity. But for Agricultural Bio-Chemical, time already had run out.

In summary, "good" reasons existed for the Afran government's attack on Agricultural Bio-Chemical's participation in Afra Sugar Corporation. They are "good" in the sense that they remove suspicion that Afra acted arbitrarily and without cause, but they are not "good" in the sense that they were so easily avoidable.

Toward a Framework of Common Interests

The discussion in this chapter has assumed throughout that the United States should be actively concerned about expanding its economic relations with Africa—not only to assure supplies of oil, copper, and other commodities essential to the American economy, but also to contribute to development of the continent through the export of American technology, skills, and capital. The case of the Afra Sugar Corporation was a hypothetical example of some of the pitfalls that can halt constructive pursuit of those mutual interests. In the light of its lessons, the remainder of this chapter examines a range of possibilities for mutually beneficial trade and investment.

Making Sense of Diversity

Africa is not, and is not likely soon to become, a homogeneous group of developing nations. From a businessman's point of view, at least four important characteristics distinguish the 50-odd countries that make up "Africa":

1. the legal structure and business language imposed during the colonial period,
2. the relative wealth of each country in human and natural resources,
3. the ethnic origin of the dominant group in each country or group of countries, and
4. membership in economic communities or monetary unions.

A glance at a map of Africa during the colonial era suggests the extent of European influence on the linguistic, legal, governmental, and business environment, as well as on philosophies of development. In most countries, the legal system, financial structure, and mode of administration introduced during the colonial period have persisted. In addition, the same European companies prominent in the pre-independence period often still constitute the largest foreign business element.

Andrew Kamarck's economic profile of Africa, elsewhere in this volume, differentiates between those countries that are poor simply because they lack resources that can be developed; others that are potentially prosperous or even rich but lack an adequate trained labor force, modern technology, transport facilities, and capital equipment; the few (notably Nigeria and Zaire) already well on the way toward semi-industrialization; and the special case of South Africa.

Rich or poor, most of the countries have passed through at least a decade of what they consider to have been "economic neocolonialism" and are experimenting with ways of managing their factors of production without foreign interference. The Africanization phenomenon varies widely from country to country, in accordance with ethnic histories and colonial experience. The governments of Guinea and Tanzania have practiced their respective forms of "African socialism" for well over a decade, and the prospective investor should recognize and respect this groping for authenticity in other countries as well. But whatever path they choose, most governments and most Africans seem to recognize the continuing value of foreign expertise.

Host governments often express part of their goal as a desire for the latest technology, leading the prospective investor to stress innovation in preparing proposals for investment in Africa. Often, however, the real challenge is to transfer existing knowledge to the African setting. The best methods and equipment may be old ones that are labor-intensive, energy-saving, simple to operate, and easy to repair, since these characteristics suit Africa's current level of economic infrastructure and its ample but as yet largely untrained labor force.

It would be equally wrong to assume that the transfer of technology and investment of capital are all that the African governments are seeking. To do so understates their needs. Increasingly they look for training in management and organizational skills, employee upgrading, and health care and even housing for workers. The time is past when the pure willingness to invest is a sufficient condition for entry.

Historically, many African economies have depended on non-African businesses and investors for all but a few small-scale activities. This too is changing, as African governments require foreign investors to accept (as in "Nigerianization") substantial African participation, either private or government. This trend has aroused suspicion and considerable fear of nationalization among American investors. In fact, there are few recorded instances of nationalization without compensation in postcolonial Africa, though in some cases negotiations toward settlement have lasted up to five years.

In contrast to this good record for investments, American businessmen have experienced some losses in the export market, usually because they failed to check the reputation of their customers. Foreign exchange restrictions have sometimes presented American exporters with problems, though the larger markets have remained relatively open. Obviously the key to trading with Africa is consultation with international banks familiar with the often intricate trade regulations and credit risks of Africa.

Given a United States interest in expanding economic relations with Africa, could American businessmen adapt to the peculiarities, frustrations, and new realities of the African market with sufficient flexibility to avoid forfeiting opportunities to Europe, Japan, and the communist countries? The first step would be simply to understand the continent's diversity. Some countries thrive on the rhetoric of economic nationalism, others have economies more open than our own. Some countries immerse potential investors in red tape and endless negotiations; others can approve foreign investments quite rapidly. The growing success of investors from other nations in Africa suggests that it would be both possible and profitable to adjust American ways of doing business to the African marketplace.

Though it is all very well to speak of "the African marketplace," a businessman needs to choose among "significant" markets, which in turn may be defined from several points of view. Despite widespread use, estimates of the size and real growth of gross national product per capita often provide an inadequate indicator. As Kamarck demonstrates, some countries with a low GNP per capita have a small but thriving economy. A large part of the population may be nomadic or living at a subsistence level, yet from an investor's standpoint the country may offer compensations such as a favorable business environment, governmental stability, or abundant natural resources.

The Special Case of South Africa

According to statistics used by the U.S. Departments of State and Commerce, the book value of direct private American investment in South Africa as of 1974 has been estimated at $1.48 billion and involved some 360 American firms, including 12 of the top 15 on *Fortune*'s first 500 list. This represented an increase, in dollar terms, of over 100 percent in the previous decade. Although American direct private investment amounted to less than four percent of total domestic and foreign investment in South Africa (i.e., 17 percent of total foreign investment of 20 percent), it is noteworthy that more than 50 percent of the American share was in manufacturing, and the remainder well diversified throughout various other sectors of the economy.

It has been suggested that these figures may understate the extent of the role of the American private sector in the South African economy. Not included in the official roster are many companies (such as Polaroid, Holiday Inns, Hertz, Avis) which have agency or distributorship relationships with South African firms, or some major American banks with interests in non-American firms active in South Africa. According to a study by Donald McHenry of the Carnegie Endowment for International Peace, published in 1975,[3] a South African government agency has estimated that at least 6,000 American firms maintained (as of 1970) agency relationships in South Africa. While this may be factually correct, it is also misleading. American companies have dealer/agency relationships in virtually every country in the world, and even in some of the economically more destitute countries one could probably find 500 to a thousand American dealer/agency relationship arrangements with local firms. Therefore, such figures, in my opinion, are poor indicators of the extent of American private involvement in any given country's economy. Another variable that renders lists misleading is the wide disparity in the size of the American firms operating in the Republic; of the 360 companies in the official accounting, no more than 25 or 30 employ 90 percent of the work force involved. Some are one-man operations.

However one interprets the statistics to support one point of view or another, there can be no doubt that investment in South Africa is highly profitable. Between 1958 and 1961, the U.S. Department of Commerce compiled statistics indicating that average American earnings on direct investments in the Republic were 17.1 percent overall—higher than in Australia (15.6 percent), the United Kingdom (12.3 percent), Sweden (10 percent), Japan (9.8 percent), Canada (8.4 percent), Latin America (8 percent), or France (7.6 percent). As of 1973, South African officials placed the return at some 19 percent a year after tax for all sectors (as compared with 16 percent worldwide for American investors).[4]

Confirming that American investment in South Africa was continuing to increase by 12.8 percent a year, former Assistant Secretary of State for African Affairs David D. Newsom referred in 1973 congressional testimony to the "growing market, sophisticated infrastructure and generally favorable climate for investment" of South Africa as "particularly attractive to much of the United States private sector."[5] In diplomatic language, Newsom's statement broaches the paramount fact that it is easier for an American firm to do business in businesslike South Africa than it is in young black nations such as the imaginary Republic of Afra, which often warily resist the operating procedures that are routine in the mainstream of world commerce. South African government statements encouraging further American investment point to the fact that all political parties in the Republic are committed "to the principles of free enterprise" and that "no private sector organization has ever been nationalized."[6]

Investors must continually weigh their impressive returns from their South African operations, however, against the actual or potential costs to their corporate image—both in black Africa and among concerned stockholders and humanitarian organizations in the United States. Somewhat surprisingly, the pressures for disengagement have been much stronger from outside Africa than from within. Although corporations operating in black-governed Africa as well as in South Africa anticipated that they might be forced to choose between the two markets, the fact is that black African governments have not exerted more than token pressure against American firms with dual operations. More important to the affected host governments has been the immediate question, "how much is this American company contributing to *our* people's standard of living and to *our* economy?"

By 1975, a subtle shift could also be seen in the vocally adversary stance that many civic and church organizations and scholars in the United States and Europe had taken for many years against *any* U.S. corporate (or, indeed, governmental) ties with the Republic; the call for total disengagement was still a tactical ploy, but no longer the basic issue. At the Johnson Foundation's April 1975 Wingspread Conference on "South Africa: Policy Alternatives for the United States," for example, it was implicitly accepted by those attending that American businesses already operating in South Africa will probably stay there as long as it is economically feasible to do so. The emphasis by 1975 was on discouraging any further corporate involvement, and, especially, on the need to press the American businesses operating in the Republic to use every means available to them to aid the position of black workers through upgrading wages, providing technical and management training facilities, job advancement opportunities, and pension and health benefits. Above all, American firms were being encouraged to facilitate the organization of African trade unions and to respect their use as bargaining agents.[7]

Professor Gwendolen M. Carter, in her background paper for the Wingspread Conference, stated the case in these terms:

My own preference is not to have American firms involved in South Africa. But while new investments should be discouraged, I believe it is impossible to persuade those already established to withdraw from such profitable opportunities. The best we can do, therefore, is to put maximum effort into publicizing their inadequacies as well as their advances in labor relations, and to press for further improvements.

American companies are frustratingly reluctant to provide exact figures for the wage structures, preferring, not surprisingly, to put any advances into percentages that sound more promising than in fact they are. Moreover, they use poverty datum levels as criteria for estimates of an acceptable level for African wages, instead of productivity as they should. They are not much involved, if at all, in training programs for Africans whereas they could be in the forefront. I can find no evidence that their managements are taking the lead to encourage the formation of African trade unions and to bargain with them in a responsible fashion. These steps are the minimum I feel American companies should undertake to justify their South African investments and profits.

In February 1973, the United States Department of State issued a paper entitled *Employment Practices of U.S. Firms in South Africa* that picked out American companies that had been raising African wages and improving African working conditions. It also suggested gently where improvement was still needed. In September 1974, a shorter but more precise paper was issued entitled "Statement on Employment Practices of U.S. Firms Operating in South Africa." It outlined six "goals" for such firms:

> To pay the "rate for the job" or "equal pay for equal work";
> To provide supplementary educational facilities for employees and their children;
> To assist employees and their families to obtain adequate housing;
> To provide skills training on a regular basis aimed at high productivity;
> To provide opportunities for advancement based solely on merit.

The statement also declared that "considerable attention" should be given to "improve communications between employers and employees using all available channels of communications." This would encompass, it declared, "being prepared to engage in collective bargaining with legitimate representatives of unregistered workers if, as and when they come into existence."

While strongly endorsing these proposals, and American government concern in this matter, I feel that American firms should go further and deliberately encourage the formation of African labor organizations. . . . American firms, which have a wide experience in labor relations, should in my view deliberately encourage the formation of proper bargaining units on as wide a basis as possible, and if necessary try to shield their representatives from South African government restraints.[8]

Some American firms have already taken initiatives along these lines, but there are many whose managers subscribe to the view that a company must follow the lead of the host government on labor practices. Clearly this is an area in which choices should and demonstrably can be made by American firms, including the careful selection of courageous and progressive local managers and senior personnel. It was observed at the Wingspread Conference that "United States firms are doing considerably better than earlier, but were not—with a few exceptions—in the lead of economic advancement for Black workers."

The opening of the door to outside investment in the ten black "homelands" adds a new dimension to the South African picture as viewed by foreign investors, in part because it suggests a way of demonstrably helping blacks toward greater self-sufficiency and less reliance on migratory labor without unduly disrupting the existing investment climate. Although ideological battlelines remain sharply drawn on the homelands issue (see Chapter III), American investors are likely to be increasingly responsive to the beckoning voices of those black leaders who are urging help in furthering the economic development of those areas set aside for particular ethnic communities.

During a 1975 visit to the United States, Chief Gatsha Buthelezi, chief executive councillor of the KwaZulu homeland, urged American firms to invest in the homelands and to contribute more generously to the education and training of blacks. His theme was that American firms, which have profited handsomely from the labor of blacks in South Africa, have an obligation to reinvest some of their profits in black communities to help them break through the ignorance and ·poverty that block their advancement. While sympathizing with church groups and others advocating withdrawal of American investment from South Africa, Chief Buthelezi said the firms would do more for Africans by remaining. Chief Wessels Motta of Basotho Quaqua put the case more bluntly in an interview with the (London) *Economist* in 1974: "Many American and European owned companies are growing fat in South Africa. Many more would like to invest here, but for fear of the wrath of their shareholders. My message to all of you is simply to stop pussyfooting around. If you want a nice, fat, highly profitable overseas operation, invest in South Africa. But at the same time, make sure you build your factory in a Black area. That way the Blacks will benefit too, because you'll be creating jobs where jobs are most needed."[9] While the homelands do not offer the investor anything like the opportunities for profit available in the mainstream of the South African economy, they do offer opportunities to salve corporate consciences.

In this fluid period in southern African history, it is worthwhile to recall that South Africa is part of a much larger region that embraces one of the earth's rich mineral belts. If the recent improvement in South Africa's relations with Zaire, Zambia, and other nations to the north should continue, détente could lead to changes as profound as those of the 1960s—and to new opportunities for American trade and investment in the region as a whole. To make the assumption that this South African goal of normalcy will be achieved is, of course, beyond the guidelines of this chapter.

Whatever happens in South Africa, however, American investors can scarcely err if they take up the option of setting an example in upgrading the wages, skills, and working conditions of African, coloured, and Asian employees. The laws of South Africa in these areas are subject to a wide spectrum of interpretation by individual managers. To assume a leading role in opening up new training and job opportunities would be not only a humanitarian gesture, but also one of enlightened self-interest. If present economic projections materialize, there will be a need for at least four million skilled laborers in the economy by 1980, compared with only 2.3 million in 1970. Since the pool of white labor is not infinite, it is estimated that most of the newly skilled will have to come from other racial groups.

Priorities for the Decade Ahead

How might Americans, as a nation and a government, change their business practices and official posture in Africa if they decide that greater attention to the continent is warranted? One way is to avoid the kinds of errors discussed in our hypothetical case study. Another is to play a less cautious social role in South Africa. But other more positive ways suggest themselves in the preceding pages.

The first is a change of attitude in both the private and public sectors. American businessmen tend to underestimate their assets in Africa, in particular the high regard in which their technology, products, and abilities are held. Despite the apparent price disadvantage of American goods resulting from their relatively costly labor inputs, certain kinds of American products and services are known to be superior and thus are preferred. Americans could be much more outgoing in their efforts to secure markets for such goods.

Perhaps equally important is the need for a change of attitude in the United States government and in its diplomatic and consular posts abroad. Preoccupied with reporting or with administrative and representational chores, U.S. missions in Africa have tended to give little more than lip service to promoting American trade and investment where it counts—on the ground in Africa. Recognition of the growing importance of international economic relations might well justify a reordering of priorities in American Foreign Service posts. At the minimum, they might be motivated and equipped to provide assistance roughly equivalent to that traditionally accorded Western European businessmen by their official representatives, even though differences in the basic government-business relationship at home will necessarily be reflected abroad.

African opportunities seldom can be developed from a home base in the United States, nor are country studies conducted 8,000 miles from the market very reliable. The American businessman should visit Africa himself, and often, to gain a feeling for the unwritten subtleties of doing business and, even more important, to understand governmental priorities that often are unstated or misstated in development plans and invitations to invest.

Alert businessmen should recognize, too, that the traditional areas of American superiority are changing. High-technology capital goods remain important, especially in transportation, communications, mining, and information processing. But the new areas of American advantage are related to agriculture, including farm implements, fertilizers, and food processing and storage facilities. With changes in the pattern of world food production, American agribusiness should reexamine the African market periodically to identify new zones of opportunity.

Financial services are another area of growing demand. American banks can assist in recycling petrodollars to developing countries in Africa, serving as advisers and catalysts both to countries with surplus funds and those with deficits.

Lastly, American business should take care to minimize appearances of power and monopoly control if it is to be accepted in Africa in coming years. The multinational corporation, with its strengths resulting from diverse locations for manufacturing, sales, and administration, may be welcome in a number of African markets. Some countries may be wary of such an association because of the prolonged adverse publicity surrounding the power of multinational corporations. On balance, however, the argument for association with an American firm, whether large or small, should rest on the firm's ability to serve the customer's needs as understood by both parties.

Notes

1. For descriptions of these resources, see Chapter V, "Sub-Saharan Africa in the 1980s: An Economic Profile"; Chapter XI, "The Search for an Aid Policy" (subsection "The Africa We Aid"); and "Some Basic Facts About Africa," the country-by-country chart accompanying this book.

2. Based on interviews conducted for the Africa Area Study in December 1974 by Robert I. Fleming of Life Flour Mill Ltd., Lagos, Nigeria, with O.N. Rewane, O. Efueye, and other West African business executives.

3. Donald McHenry, *United States Firms in South Africa. A Study Project on External Investment in South Africa and Namibia* (Bloomington, Indiana: The African Studies Program, Indiana University, on behalf of the Africa Publications Trust, 1975).

4. Dr. Nicholas Diederichs, South African Minister of Finance (a speech, October 1973).

5. David Newsom, Assistant Secretary of State for African Affairs (testimony before the House Sub-Committee on Africa, Washington, D.C., March 27, 1973).

6. "360 U.S. Companies Have $1.2 Billion Direct Investment in South Africa," *South African Scope*, October 1975.

7. *South Africa: Policy Alternatives for the United States*, Report of a Wingspread Conference convened by the Johnson Foundation, April 1975 (Racine, Wisconsin: The Johnson Foundation, 1975). The Johnson Foundation encourages the examination of a variety of problems facing mankind and reprints various papers and reports. Publication by the foundation does not imply approval.

8. Gwendolen M. Carter, *American Policy and the Search for Justice and Reconciliation in South Africa*, a discussion paper for the 1975 Wingspread Conference on South Africa. Reprinted with permission.

9. *The Economist*, April 27, 1974. Quoted with permission.

XI

The Search for an Aid Policy

William I. Jones

Should America aid Africa? If not, why not? If so, why? And how much? What kind of aid should be given, and who should be in charge of giving it? What should the "terms" be? Should America expect to get paid back, and if so, when and in what way?

These questions are constantly answered in practice in congressional debates and votes, in administration pronouncements and budget proposals, and in the appeals of private charities for funds. Precisely because the questions about American aid to Africa are answered so steadily and in detail, inertia inevitably characterizes each decision. Faced with many small choices, policymakers tend to ask what was done last year and to repeat it with small variations.

This chapter provides a broad look at American options in African aid, in an effort to transcend the immediate and put the whole phenomenon into perspective.[a] In this sense it takes its place as one of several "new looks" at the American aid program that have been inspired by a decade of declining support and by a shrinking program.[1]

To achieve a useful perspective on the alternatives America might weigh in deciding on its African aid, I first owe the reader a brief explanation of what I mean by aid. Then we can take a hard look at what aid the United States has been giving to Africa and can compare it with the aid of others. We can analyze why America aids Africa and review Africa's basic situation and its potential as they affect America. These steps may suggest reasonable possibilities for the United States and what might be expected of these possibilities.

[a]While responsibility for errors is mine, I acknowledge my debt to a host of Americans, Africans, and others who have assisted me, but especially to Bruce Oudes, who persuaded me to undertake the task, traded ideas with me, and contributed to the section on the U.S. bilateral aid record; and to Kanella Vasiliades, Fernando Manibog, and Karen Nurick, who performed the tedious task of aggregating aid data.

341

Some Definitions

Aid is one of several kinds of transfers of real resources from one country to another. It is not like trade, where the transferred resources are paid for. Aid, as I define it, is not paid for. Some paid-for resource transfers are also sometimes called aid, but if they are fully paid for, they will not be considered aid here. Many transfers are a mixture of trade (export sales) and aid. The two cannot be separated to everyone's satisfaction.

The Development Assistance Committee (DAC) of the Organization for Economic Cooperation and Development (OECD), comprising the major non-communist industrial countries, has attempted to distinguish the two. Thus, in calculating what it calls net "official development assistance" (ODA), the DAC ignores purely commercial and nearly commercial transactions, and deducts debt service. Net ODA does not, however, distinguish between outright gifts and credit that is less expensive (more attractive to the recipient) than commercial credit. The DAC's "grant equivalent" measurement attempts to make that distinction by subtracting from a "concessional" loan the present value of all debt service payments, discounted to the present at ten percent yearly.[2] Thus a $10 million gift has a grant equivalent of $10 million, a $10 million loan with no grace period amortized at ten percent interest over any number of years has a grant equivalent of zero, and a loan of $10 million for 50 years at 0.75 percent interest with only interest paid during a ten-year grace period and the principal amortized thereafter has a grant equivalent of $8.4 million.

The two DAC measures have many shortcomings. They do not account for the fact that aid "tying"—forcing the recipient to buy goods or services in the donor country—may distort the value of aid to the recipient because he may be forced to procure high-priced or low-quality products. They do not account for the fact that giving (or receiving) a million dollars worth of sorghum may cost (benefit) the donor (receiver) less (or more) than giving (receiving) a million dollars worth of tractors. Moreover, with the acceleration of world inflation and higher interest rates since 1974, the loans of several organizations that are usually considered aid (those of the African Development Bank, World Bank, and International Finance Corporation, for example) no longer meet the definition of ODA. Those objections aside, the DAC's net ODA and grant-equivalent figures give the best available picture of what aid costs the giver, hence the best way of separating it from trade.

Besides being unpaid for, aid is a voluntary transfer, which distinguishes it from tribute, another form of transfer more common than governments like to admit.

Foreign investment is another kind of voluntary international resource transfer. Some consider it aid on grounds that it stimulates economic growth. Be that as it may, I mean by aid a transfer whereby ownership passes with the resource. Foreign investors keep, or at least intend to keep, title to the resources they transfer. (See Chapter X, David L. Buckman, "An American Banker Looks at Africa," for a discussion of the options for American private investment in Africa.)

So, aid is a voluntary international resource transfer that is unpaid for and involves a change in ownership.

Should only government-to-government transactions be called aid? I think not. Private American aid to Africa has been small—perhaps one-tenth the volume of transfers by the Agency for International Development (AID) alone in recent years. However, it is hard to separate private from official aid, and it has some of the same objectives as government transfers. Moreover, it has important impacts both on Africa and on the way Americans view Africa.

Many use development assistance as a synonym for aid, but I will not. To do so presumes that aid is intended to bring about development—a presumption fraught with difficulties. First, development is a much fuzzier concept than economic growth. Does taking over the commanding heights of the economy by the state constitute development? Is saving the souls of heathens development? Each construction has its partisans. Second, intentions are difficult to know. Certainly one cannot accept at face value the reasons for which people and governments *say* they give and receive aid. To get behind their declared intentions is hard, as will become evident in seeking to fathom why the United States has been giving aid to Africa. Third, despite the difficulty of discovering real intentions, it is clear that aid serves many purposes other than development. In some cases the intent to develop may be minimal or absent altogether, and of course no development may actually take place.

Having been as clear as possible about definitions, let me be clear that all is still not clear. Unpaid for does not mean entirely unrequited. In return for aid, governments may receive United Nations votes or military bases, contributors to Oxfam or CARE may receive lighter consciences, and so on. The OECD grant-equivalent formula is quite unable to take such factors into account. Other difficulties could be cited, but they should become sufficiently evident in the record of American aid and Africa.

The U.S. Bilateral Aid Record

Aid for Africa has roots in our society going back long before the period just after World War II, when the formal structure of international assistance as we know it today was established. Perhaps Americans have had a clearer conscience about aid to Africa than to Latin America or to Asia, feeling its motives to be less suspect because neither the American flag nor trade has been much in evidence there. And perhaps the American conscience suffers a special kind of guilt for that particular type of trade under which the ancestors of one American in ten were brought to these shores as our first major raw material import from Africa.

Americans who have been bombarded by dramatic television reports and fund-raising appeals may share the impression that Africa is hopelessly dependent and that American aid is keeping the continent alive. In fact, U.S. bilateral aid to Africa has been modest, far less than that of the European Economic Community. U.S. food assistance to Africa has been less than one-twentieth of our total worldwide food aid. The American effort in the sparsely populated Sahel region adjacent to the Sahara has been by far the largest American food relief effort ever undertaken in Africa, yet it has been a mere trickle compared to the mammoth U.S. food aid programs in India or Southeast Asia.

Multilateral aid to Africa has been expanding rapidly, principally through the leading multilateral conduit, the World Bank (IBRD) and its concessional-lending sibling, the International Development Association (IDA). American contributions to these organizations have made up a decreasing share of their resources but they are still important.

Africa has been getting an increasingly large slice of the growing World Bank pie. World Bank and IDA lending to Africa in the 1974-78 period is expected to be almost ten times larger than it was in the comparable period a decade earlier. Whereas a decade ago Latin America was receiving more than twice as much as Africa from the Bank, Latin America and Africa will be receiving about the same amount in the years just ahead. Given the fledgling nature of Africa's industrial base and its lagging agriculture, Africa would be the continent most seriously affected by any weakening of the fabric of multilateral assistance.

But U.S. aid to Africa, bilateral *and* multilateral, is a quite modest share of the total aid Africa receives. European aid to Africa dwarfs American aid. And African governments have established other friendships that have led to aid, particularly from China and the Arab world. Combining all these sources, Africa gets more aid per person than any other continent. All that aid—a small portion of it American—may help Africa develop, but is not necessary for Africa's survival.

Africa's low population density is its great strength in survival power but a great problem in development. Even though Africa has a large number of seats in the UN General Assembly, Africans make up only about ten percent of the world's population and 17 percent of the less-developed countries' population. The same high usable-land/man ratio that helps assure survival (when it rains) also means high costs for transportation and communication. Africa's very poverty in producing what the world wants (the mineral enclaves aside) makes even that low population density a development problem: how to find the money to educate the next generation, to attend to its health and nutrition.

As Ghana became independent in 1957, Guinea in 1958, and a host of African countries in 1960, Americans became fascinated with these new and little-known states. For a time they excited great interest among U.S. policymakers, but the policymakers' fascination with Africa, and consequently with aiding Africa, has faded with the passing years. Policy interest in the Third World has gravitated toward Asia, where the majority of the developing world's people live and where U.S. foreign policy involvement is greater. Africa's share of U.S. bilateral aid peaked at 15 percent in the early 1960s, having since declined to less than ten percent.

Missionary Beginnings and Private Aid

American missionary endeavor in Africa—the first American aid to Africa and the precursor of all modern private-sector aid—preceded government aid by a century. After an early start in Liberia, American churches have sent an important but indeterminate number of missionaries to other parts of Africa throughout this century. This form of aid, which does not appear in official aid figures, has paid and is paying for some of the same goods and services for which official aid pays. Many present-day leaders of Africa studied in schools partly staffed and financed by American missions.

In recent years, church aid has become increasingly secular and secular private aid has begun doing many of the same jobs of helping people. The Agency for International Development (AID) has an advisory Committee on Voluntary Foreign Aid to register American voluntary agencies engaged in aid,[3] some religious in affiliation, some not.

Since 1970 the Development Assistance Committee of the OECD has been collecting data on private, as well as public, aid flows from all rich Western countries to all less-developed countries. Since there is negligible private aid from centrally planned or poor states, the DAC figure should cover most of the world flow. They are far from perfect, undoubtedly missing many transfers that are technically aid. Still, they give a rough indication of the size of the private effort.

According to the DAC, the worldwide volume of private (or voluntary) aid has been as much as one-eighth to one-seventh that of net ODA in recent years. Seven-eighths of the world flow comes from the United States, West Germany, Canada, and Great Britain. The United States alone gives two-thirds of the voluntary aid.[4] The French are particularly stingy, contributing less than one percent of the DAC total of private aid.

Africa's share of the total, though small, has been rising. American figures for registered private aid show Africa receiving less than one percent of the flow in 1946, six percent in 1960, and seven percent in 1973. That seven percent represents $38 million—a total exceeding the net flow from the entire Soviet official aid program for Africa in the same period. However, $20 million of the $38 million was transferred in the form of food, much of which was actually paid for by American taxpayers and given to CARE and Catholic Relief Services under Title II of Public Law 480.

To put the voluntary flows to Africa into perspective, note that 48 percent of the U.S. worldwide flow went to Israel—roughly $82.53 per Israeli compared to about $0.11 per African. Also, though the record of American voluntary aid organizations is generally good, some private collectors are much more efficient in transferring resources overseas than others. For every dollar given in 1973 to the largest registered giver, United Israel Appeal, $0.003 went for administration and promotion and $0.997 reached Israel. Oxfam-America did have a hand in alleviating famine in the Sahel, but in 1973 it spent 65¢ of every dollar it collected in the United States on administration and promotion, 35¢ on its overseas programs. Only 28¢ per dollar spent by the Unitarian Universalist Service Committee was devoted to overseas programs; 57¢ went for administration and promotion, and 15¢ for domestic programs.

The Growth of Official Aid

The concern for human well-being, spiritual and physical, that has long motivated American private aid to Africa has always played a part in justifying the government program too. However, it played a minimal role in the government program's beginnings. Strategic and commercial considerations were more important.

Harvey Firestone wanted a cheaper source of rubber than Malaya and Indonesia when his firm negotiated a million-acre concession with the Liberian government in 1925. Official ties between the United States and Liberia were largely sentimental until World War II, when Vichy French control of North Africa and Senegal created an urgent need for alternative Allied communication routes across Africa to Asia. The United States built a modern airfield in Liberia near Firestone headquarters that accommodated Allied traffic during much of the war, and after the war built a seaport at Monrovia. Except for Liberia and distant, landlocked Ethiopia, Africa in those days had no independent governments to receive U.S. official aid.

Formal American government-to-government aid was born after the war. Originally designed to rebuild a Western Europe considered threatened by Soviet expansionism, it consisted almost entirely of grants. Americans had learned from World War I that Europeans (except Finns) do not repay loans. By aiding Europe, America probably gave Britain, France, and Belgium, among other things, the economic strength they needed to prolong their colonial rule another 15 years; in a sense, the U.S. Marshall Plan also made possible British aid transfers (the Commonwealth Development and Welfare schemes) and French aid to African colonies. America's direct official aid to Africa between 1945 and 1952 was about a million dollars. There were few ways to give directly.

In the 1950s, with the doctrine of containment at its peak, Africa's northern and eastern coasts gained a place in U.S. strategic thinking. In March 1950, defending President Truman's Point Four proposal before the Senate Foreign

Relations Committee, Secretary of State Dean Acheson said, "The free way of life is under attack in every part of the world, including those areas of the world which we call 'underdeveloped'. These areas include parts of Latin America, Africa, the Middle East, and the Far East where two-thirds of the world's people live, many of them in the shadow of hunger, poverty, and disease."

Aid in those early years was distributed by the Mutual Security Agency and its immediate successor, the Economic Cooperation Administration. Between 1953 and 1961, 73 percent of American aid to Africa went to northern and northeastern countries flanking NATO and the Suez Canal route to Asia, notably Morocco, Tunisia, Libya, and Ethiopia. In three of those countries the United States had military installations carried over from wartime or the immediate postwar period: in Morocco, airfields and a naval communications facility; in Libya, Wheelus Field, at one time the largest American airbase outside the United States; and in Ethiopia, an important communications, intelligence and relay station near Asmara in the province of Eritrea. Economic aid and military assistance became the quid pro quo for continued use of these installations. (See Chapter IX, William H. Lewis, "How a Defense Planner Looks at Africa.")

In the late 1950s other parts of Africa, still European colonies, received small amounts of U.S. food, economic assistance, and other benefits indirectly through Europe. Leading members of both of the major American political parties were agreed that the granting of independence to black Africa was the best way to forestall communist penetration of the region. Aid followed independence. Thus Vice President Nixon attended Ghana's independence ceremonies in 1957, and $25 million in U.S. aid followed in the next four years. In 1958 the State Department established a separate Bureau of African Affairs, and in subsequent years several dozen American embassies were established across the continent.

The Kennedy administration is remembered for having expanded U.S. relations with and aid to Africa. In fact, the United States and Africa knew so little about each other that the need to set priorities soon became evident. The United States had succeeded in its objective of preserving Zairian (then Congolese) territorial integrity, but at a cost of $231 million in aid during Zaire's first three years of independence. The experience led to soul-searching about the containment doctrine and its applicability to Africa. The Kennedy administration, wanting to distinguish its position from Secretary Dulles's policy toward "left-leaning" governments exemplified by Dulles's refusal to finance Egypt's Aswan High Dam, approved strong U.S. participation in Ghana's Volta River Dam project and maintenance of a substantial aid program in Guinea. This initiative encountered a great deal of criticism on the grounds that African states that were friendlier toward the United States were being penalized.

The former French territories posed still other problems. The Kennedy administration established 14 AID missions in the erstwhile French colonies, but the personnel assigned to them often found little program to carry out and strong French hostility. Many asked themselves why, since the French *wanted* to pay those countries' bills, the U.S. AID mission had come. Simultaneously, in the then-classified Operation Vanguard, the United States was picking up most of the cost of the Republic of China's aid program in Africa. Clearly, some goals had to be set and guidelines established.

Finding a Rationale

In late 1962, Kennedy named General Lucius Clay to head a special Committee to Strengthen the Security of the Free World, with 90 days in which to prepare a report on the foreign aid program. Unlike similar commissions appointed in the 1950s, the Clay committee criticized the executive branch for trying to do too much in its aid program abroad. The Clay Report singled out Africa, recommending that, since the continent was not geopolitically "adjacent" to the communist "bloc," the United States should gradually eliminate its bilateral aid. "As these commitments are completed, further U.S. aid should be confined to participation in multilaterally supported programs," the committee concluded. It made a limited exception for some bilateral programs in North and northeast Africa because those regions were closer to the Soviet "perimeter."

Africa is "an area where the Western European countries should logically bear most of the necessary aid burden," the Clay committee concluded. "In the light of its other responsibilities, the United States cannot undertake to support all of the African countries, especially when their ties with other Free World nations are largely elsewhere."

Minor bilateral programs persisted in French-speaking Africa, but the Clay Report's recommendations were already being implemented even as it was being written. The State Department rescued the AID mission in Senegal by moving the entire embassy—with room to spare—into the downtown Dakar office space that AID, in its initial enthusiasm, had leased solely for itself. In Niamey (Niger), to the embarrassment of the American Embassy, a bridge across the Niger River that was to have been an independence gift became a loan and somehow took a decade to complete. (The Soviets, too, were learning some of the frustrations of aid relationships in francophone Africa. During the Cuban missile crisis, Guinean President Sékou Touré refused the Russians landing rights at the Soviet-built Conakry airport, thus limiting Moscow's options during those tense days. It wasn't long before Soviet and American diplomats in French-speaking Africa began to meet occasionally for a purely social evening. Some of the earliest signs of détente appeared in a part of the world where each power, for its own reasons, was concluding that the game wasn't worth the candle.)

The United States found itself more at home in the former British colonies in Africa. In Nigeria, AID rented an entire ten-story Lagos office building and built up its program so rapidly that for a time in 1965, until it was eclipsed by operations in South Vietnam, the U.S. AID technical assistance program in Nigeria was the largest anywhere.

The Clay Report's recommendations were never fully implemented but, the Nigerian experience notwithstanding, the trend in U.S. bilateral assistance to Africa was downward. During fiscal years 1962-65, U.S. bilateral economic assistance to Africa totaled $2,101 million in gross ODA terms and current dollars. In the budgets prepared for 1966 through 1969—President Johnson's elected term—the figure dropped to $1,402 million. For 1970 through 1973—President Nixon's first term—the total dropped to $1,157 million. Of course U.S. AID levels were falling worldwide, not just in Africa, and not just in constant dollars, but in ever-shrinking current dollars as well. But U.S. bilateral aid to Africa was declining somewhat faster than the rest. On a gross ODA basis, it represented 13 percent of total U.S. economic aid in the 1962-65 period. This figure dropped to just under ten percent in the 1966-69 period and then to nine percent for 1969-73.

In 1966, on the heels of the escalation of U.S. involvement in Vietnam, President Johnson asked American Ambassador to Ethiopia Edward M. Korry to prepare a report on the future of U.S. aid to Africa. Constrained by a set of global political assumptions that hardly favored Africa, the Korry Report ("Policy for Development in Africa") nevertheless recommended some modest increases in aid.

The Korry Report was built upon Clay, accepting the idea that Africa was principally Europe's aid burden, but it diverged from the Clay Report in recommending that there be a U.S. bilateral program in Africa. Korry noted that multilateral lending to Africa through the World Bank was still in its infancy and would need several more years before its potential as a conduit could be realized.

On the subject of rural development, the Korry Report said, almost prophetically, "[Now is] . . . the time to concentrate on economic development if Africa is to realize its potential as a major producer of foodstuffs in a hungry world. . . . There should be no further delay in getting solutions to the complex and obdurate socioeconomic problems of rural development. Better an orderly development effort today than a wasteful crash program in the 1970s." Korry urged that the United States make a major effort in agriculture: "If there is any field in which Americans can claim a measure of expertise in developing both theory and sound practice, it is in agriculture."

The report's authors recognized France's aid preferences and the fact that, with limited funds, "we cannot pretend to conduct economic development programs in 33 countries." They tried to make a virtue of necessity in recommending that U.S. bilateral aid in Africa should be concentrated on a selected list of ten countries with a secondary emphasis on programs supporting regional integration goals.

When the report was written, three-fourths of U.S. bilateral aid to Africa already was concentrated in eight countries. Seven of these—Zaire, Ethiopia,

Liberia, Morocco, Nigeria, Sudan, and Tunisia—continued to be so-called concentration countries, in fact if not always officially. Ghana and the East African Community states of Kenya, Tanzania, and Uganda were included; Sudan dropped out by severing diplomatic relations with the United States after the 1967 Middle East war.

The authors of the Korry study found "surprisingly little difficulty" in determining that infrastructure should be the sector for concentrated U.S. efforts. Otherwise, they suggested, U.S. aid should be concentrated in rural development; secondary education, teacher training, and certain areas of advanced education; disease control and population programs; and, lastly, the promotion of private enterprise. But infrastructure remained the report's focal point. "We can make the greatest impact in the next few years on our long-range development goals by focusing investment in basic infrastructure (communications, transport, and power) which will tie countries together," the report concluded. "Infrastructure is the base on which development must take place, a base that in many parts of Africa is lacking or inadequate. Then, too, in a very real sense, infrastructure creates the regional groupings within which rational economic development must take place." Nevertheless, it cautioned, "Infrastructure by itself is not sufficient to transform traditional societies. We can look to the time when basic African infrastructure needs will be satisfied by the IBRD and African institutions, freeing more of U.S. resources for complementary uses. But we are far from that time."

Commentators on the Sahel drought point to the irony of stressing food production in Africa while recommending against aid to the ecologically fragile Sahel states. Yet the Korry Report as a whole was pro-African in outlook and one of the most important policy benchmarks of its era. Its tempered tone indicated that the United States had been disabused of some of the naive notions with which it had begun aid to Africa only a few years earlier. The report was classified "confidential" for several years because its authors concluded that some in Africa would regard it as being too harsh with respect to certain of the continent's problems and propensities. This classification, in retrospect, is probably more indicative of the authors' and classifiers' sensitivity toward Africa and interest in Africa than of the sensitivity—in the national security sense—of the report's observations and conclusions.

Indeed, in 1966 the national security rationale for U.S. aid to Africa was so remote a concern of the authors of the Korry Report that their sole recommendation in the arms field was left to the very last. The Clay Report had concluded that "limited" military aid programs might be justified in the "few [African] countries where we maintain bases," but it warned, "We believe the problems created by military assistance programs in the African countries generally would be greater than those they would forestall or resolve." The Korry Report added a new wrinkle by recommending that the United States declare itself "ready to support OAU initiatives for a program of arms limitation and control." "We believe that a calculation which takes fully into account the wastage of our own resources, the diversion of the recipient's resources and the probable tendency of some of the recipient's neighbors to enlarge their military establishments should in most cases lead to a decision against an arms program," the Korry study concluded, echoing the findings of the Clay committee. In the context of this study, I do not consider military assistance to be aid. (For discussion of military assistance policies, see Chapter IX.)

The Bilateral Result

As Table XI-1 shows, U.S. bilateral aid to Africa measured as gross official development assistance grew with Africa's independence to a half billion dollars a year in the early 1960s. It has subsequently declined, even in inflated current dollars, to just over half that amount. U.S. bilateral aid worldwide, again in current dollars, has declined by about one-third since the mid-1960s. But the point here is not the declining commitment of the United States to aid anywhere; it is the decline in Africa's *share* that tells what administrations and Congress have thought about Africa's importance.

The figures in Table XI-1 reflect Africa's independence and the growing number of small independent states that attracted attention to the continent in 1960 and for a few years thereafter. It was a period when the Cold War was still quite open and when dramatic articles on such questions as "Which Way Africa?" were very much in vogue. Soon, however, the undramatic but significant downward trend set in. Africa's share of bilateral aid has always been lower than its share of the less-developed world's population, and it has been falling. Has Africa then been "short-changed," as a president of the African-American Institute has argued?[5] The question and its answer may be more emotional than empirical, but Africa's declining share of U.S. bilateral aid surely stems from the perception of American policymakers that Africa was being given more than its share in the aid programs of our allies. This perception and a low evaluation of Africa's strategic importance for the United States have led to a reduction of Africa's aid share and in the number of U.S. AID missions in Africa. By 1975 there were only 11 bilateral programs.

The withdrawal of Portugal from Africa in 1975 and the Soviet and Cuban involvement in Angola brought Africa once more to the attention of U.S. global strategists. Among other developments in 1976, previously unallocated AID funds were promised to Mozambique. Still, it is questionable whether the crisis atmosphere will last, whether policymakers are now committed to American involvement in the area and, if so, whether they will wish to use aid as a policy tool.

Referring again to Table XI-1, the importance of P.L.480 food aid—more valuable than the entire AID package in some years—is striking. Food was one of

Table XI-1
U.S. Bilateral Aid and Export-Import Bank Economic Loans to Africa, 1949-74
(Gross ODA and Eximbank loans in millions of dollars)

	1949-1952[a]	1953-1957[a]	1958	1959	1960	1961	1962	1963	1964	1965	1966	1967	1968	1969	1970	1971	1972	1973	1974
AID[b]	1	36	82	150	191	266	368	311	203	167	180	206	160	154	155	176	175	163	144
Percent of U.S. total	75	67	85	70	67	54	58	50	45	42	50	53	50	46	56	54	59	63	45
P.L. 480 food	..	18	14	67	93	230	255	297	221	203	150	156	134	157	99	127	104	72	154
Percent of U.S. total	25	33	15	30	33	46	40	48	49	51	41	40	42	47	36	39	35	28	48
Peace Corps	..	..	..	..	..	..	6	14	24	26	32	25	23	21	20	21	19	23	24
Total gross ODA	1	54	96	216	284	496	631	623	450	397	363	388	318	333	275	324	300	258	322
Africa as percent of world total	..	2	4	8	10	15	14	15	12	11	8	11	9	11	9	10	9	8	8
Eximbank loans Amount	11	30	..	11	13	62	41	17	12	34	31	5	41	37	27	57	101	281	262
Percent of world total	5	10	..	2	5	7	21	11	4	11	11	1	8	8	4	9	7	17	7

[a]Annual average.
[b]Includes assistance from AID's predecessors: the International Cooperation Administration, the Foreign Operations Administration, the Mutual Security Agency, and the Economic Cooperation Administration.
Source: Agency for International Development, *U.S. Overseas Loans and Grants and Assistance from International Organizations: Obligations and Loan Authorizations, July 1, 1945-June 30, 19--* (1967, 1972, 1974, 1975).

the easiest forms of aid to give to new countries for which there were essentially no aid programs. Before the Indian crop failures of 1965-66, American food was plentiful. Afterward, supplies were shorter and increasingly were allocated to Southeast Asia, where the U.S. government thought it had strategic interests. Moreover, civil servants in AID and the Department of Agriculture began to ask themselves whether fostering Indian-style dependence on American food in Africa was a good idea. Like other kinds of American aid, then, food aid to Africa has been declining; although the 1969-72 Sahel drought resulted in an upward bound in 1974.

The second-largest element of bilateral American aid to Africa has been technical assistance from AID. It averaged $80 million a year for the 1969-72 period, when it was past its heyday; Peace Corps technical assistance for the same years, also past its prime, averaged $20 million. Between them, they accounted for 32 percent of gross American ODA to Africa for those years, and for 37 percent of the net amount. The concentration of Peace Corps volunteers in Africa has been unusual; in contrast to other parts of the U.S. aid package, the Peace Corps has sent Africa one-third of its volunteers, double Africa's population share, despite expulsions from individual countries.

The Export-Import Bank does not fit my OECD-inspired definition of aid, since it is essentially an export-promotion agency. Nevertheless, it provides an indication of U.S. interest in the African economy and, as such, is of interest in relation to aid. Table XI-1 shows that Eximbank economic loans to Africa, while subject to yearly fluctuations dictated by promotional priorities, have moved within a range reflecting a view of Africa similar to that of the aid policy-makers—that the continent is less important than its population share, yet significant.

The shrinking of United States bilateral aid programs, in Africa and world-wide, has coincided with diminishing "burden-sharing" pressures on allied industrial nations, and increasing multilateralization of aid, particularly through those agencies in which decisionmaking rests principally with the donors. The share of American aid to Africa distributed by multinational organizations rose from one-quarter in 1969 to over half in 1973. Over the years, the United States has been more generous than most industrial nations to agencies controlled by the UN General Assembly, such as the UN Development Program and the World Food Program; but the African Development Bank, completely African con-trolled, has yet to receive its first American contribution. A resolution ex-pressing U.S. willingness to provide capital assistance to the ADB was part of the 1965 AID bill, but has never been acted on.

The increasing multilateralization of American aid has moderated the decline in our overall aid to Africa despite the significant bilateral decline. The rise in multilateral aid is ironic, however. For example, our share of contributions to the International Development Association, the UNDP, and other organizations has been declining, but our multilateral contributions to Africa are nevertheless larger because several of those organizations, particularly IDA, have been expanding their African programs. Thus, the decisions of UN aid organizations, including their World Bank sub-family, to increase Africa's share of their aid, affect U.S. figures.

U.S. Aid in Global Context

I have characterized U.S. bilateral aid to Africa as "modest," specifically as about 66¢ per African per year or $1.20 per American per year on the average for 1969 to 1973 on a net official development assistance basis. But how "modest" is that amount? Comparison with other countries' African aid, and with the growing volume of cooperative aid-giving to which America contributes heavily, helps put the American bilateral figures into context.

Unfortunately, the accounting problems that arise when we attempt to measure aid flows worsen when we try to compare them internationally. Donors are most likely to announce *commitments* to aid. Frequently they don't announce the *disbursement* of those commitments or the *terms* under which they are given. Knowing the disbursement rate and terms, we could calculate the present worth of the aid to the recipient (or cost to donor), provided we were prepared to forget about such problems as "tying" and non-fungibility.

The DAC countries have the least deficient system of aid reporting. Since 1969, it has been made uniform. To calculate official development assistance, the DAC excludes private transfers (investments and donations), transfers where economic development is not the "principal objective" (for example, military transfers), and transfers on commercial or near-commercial terms (defined as containing a 25 percent grant element or less). The DAC countries report commitments of ODA, terms of the commitments, disbursements, and service payments on the loan portion. Starting in 1974, similar information is available on OPEC bilateral aid.

We would like to be able to compare aid in two ways. First, we could find the present value of the stream of benefits (and repayment costs for loans) that will arise from aid commitments made this year. We could do that with a list of commitments, their terms, and a disbursement schedule, which would permit us to discount the stream of disbursements and repayments (for loans) to the present at some arbitrary discount rate. The ten percent used by the DAC would do.

This *commitment* method emphasizes the future since it is based on the present value of commitments to aid over a period of time. Aid programs that are recent and growing, such as the Chinese program in Africa, look big under this method; programs that are living off a pipeline of earlier commitments, such as the Soviet program in Africa, look smaller.

Published DAC figures give us only a global look at aid terms by donor in the average grant element of new loan commitments by year. We could assume that terms are nearly uniform worldwide for the same donor and calculate the present value of new African commitments, but commitments are not uniformly reported and disbursement schedules are unpredictable.

A second method of comparison is preferable for the DAC countries and OPEC countries since 1974. Since donors report disbursements and returning debt service annually, we can find *net official development assistance* by donor and recipient continent by year. This flow counts annual disbursements, which may be quite different from commitments, and reduces them by the same year's service payments on earlier debt, instead of by the discounted present value of service payments on that year's disbursements. The *net ODA* method will reflect rapidly expanded commitments—such as China has made to Africa since the Cultural Revolution and the OPEC countries since the energy crisis—much more slowly than the *commitment* method; it doesn't count flows until they happen. Net ODA, on the other hand, reflects flows from slowly implemented projects even if the donor has stopped making new commitments; it also highlights debt service from the commitments of the past.

The DAC countries still provide, either bilaterally or through multilateral organizations, 70 percent of Africa's aid and recently provided as much as 95 percent. The remainder, provided mostly by "centrally planned" countries and now also by OPEC countries, is more difficult to account for. DAC reporting has its difficulties. What DAC donors report they gave never matches what the less-developed countries tell the World Bank and IMF they received! The centrally planned countries' reporting is largely limited to press releases. These, plus trade statistics for the Soviet Union and the receivers' trade and payments statistics, are scrutinized by scholars, the DAC, and the U.S. State Department's Bureau of Intelligence and Research.[6]

We have fairly good information on aid commitments by all non-DAC donors, and a general idea of their terms. Chinese aid is almost all in the form of loans bearing no interest and repayable in 30 to 40 annual installments after ten years' grace; Russian aid consists almost entirely of loans, characteristically at 2.5 percent interest with payments amortized over 12 years after completion of construction; East European terms are usually harder than Russian terms, and so on. This is general information, but better than none. The best bet for the centrally planned economies is to multiply annual commitments by an estimate of the grant element, even though this method counts as aid such items as the Russian commitments to Ghana and Ethiopia that have been undisbursed for years and are likely to remain so.

Of the significant centrally planned donors, Russia alone provides trade statistics that allow identification of aid disbursements. Thus, for the USSR we can compare the net ODA method and the commitment grant equivalent method. Not surprisingly, they give widely different results.

Another problem arises for countries, notably the centrally planned ones, that conduct their trade and aid on a barter system. Many analysts believe that the Russians (and others practicing the barter system) cheat by charging higher than world prices for goods and services provided in their aid programs, while assigning lower than world prices for goods the poor countries use to repay the loans. One scholar analyzed the relevant statistics up to 1969 and found overcharging averaging 15 percent and underpayment averaging 15 percent.[7] Another scholar checked the average unit price paid by the Soviet Union for goods taken in payment of African aid loans from 1961 to 1966 where those goods could be standardized (cotton, cocoa beans, peanuts, olive oil) and compared them with world prices. On the average, the Russians paid slightly higher than world prices.[8] No consensus exists.

The barter prices issue is analogous to the aid-tying issue for DAC countries. Just as most observers believe that countries that receive aid on barter terms generally lose by being constrained in what they can buy and how they can pay back, so most observers believe that, on the delivery side at least, DAC aid-tying permits donors to unload what they could not sell otherwise or to charge prices they could not charge otherwise. Eminent economists have estimated the costs of DAC aid-tying to be as low as 12 percent and as high as 35 percent.[9] Since both of these alleged price distortions are controversial, since both distort the value of aid to the recipient but less so the cost to the donor (since they probably reflect the allocation inefficiencies of his own economy), and since both are allegedly of the same order of magnitude, we need not pursue the matter.

Flows from multilateral agencies present no special accounting problems; the main ones all report their activities according to the DAC system. As indicated earlier, new OPEC multilateral aid agencies—the Special Arab Fund for Africa, the Arab Fund for Economic and Social Development, the Islamic Development Bank, and the Arab Investment Bank for Africa—have been since 1974 among those making data available on a basis comparable to the DAC system.

A multilateral accounting problem does arise when we try to assign to specific donors their net ODA or aid given on some other basis. It is not hard to find out how much the UN Development Program gave away in Africa each year and, since we know who contributed how much, we can assign its aid to the original donors. The same is true of the International Development Association, which passes the hat among its members every three years. But how can we assign the aid of the banks (International Bank for Reconstruction and Development and the small but growing African Development Bank) or, harder still, the International Finance Corporation, which is partly a foreign investor as well as a bank? These banking institutions exist because their founders—preponderantly the DAC countries for the IBRD and IFC, African countries for the ADB—paid in capital, but the aid they lend "comes from" that capital only in the most limited sense. The savers behind IBRD aid are principally the persons and institutions who buy the bank's bonds, and they make little sacrifice because they are paid the going bond-market interest rate. In the following discussion, therefore, the aid given by most multilateral organizations is allocated to the donors, while for the IBRD, IFC, and ADB it is not.

Tables XI-2 and XI-3 present estimates of aid flows to Africa for five recent

Table XI-2
Net Official Development Assistance to Africa by Donor,[a] 1969-74
(millions of dollars)

Donor	1969	1970	1971	1972	1973	1974
European DAC countries	1,208	1,221	1,391	1,569	1,924	2,276
United States	370	370	443	355	317	471
Canada	43	67	101	132	138	212
Asian DAC bilateral	5	10	14	6	21	51
IBRD, IFC	58	51	107	179	148	[178][f]
First World	1,684	1,719	2,056	2,241	2,548	3,188
Percent of total	*94*	*91*	*88*	*85*	*80*	*69*
People's Republic of China[b]	...	50	150	200	200	300
USSR[b]	45	30	15	35	25	25
Six Eastern European countries[b,c]	15	20	30	40	35	35
Second World[b]	60	100	195	275	260	360
Percent of total	*3*	*5*	*8*	*10*	*8*	*8*
OPEC[b]	20	40	75	105	340	1,015
African Development Bank	1	2	7	12	20	[23][f]
Third World[b]	21	42	82	117	360	1,038
Percent of total	*1*	*2*	*3*	*4*	*11*	*22*
Other[d]	20	20	25	30	35	50
Percent of total	*1*	*1*	*1*	*1*	*1*	*1*
Total[e]	1,800	1,900	2,350	2,650	3,200	4,650

[a]Aid through UNDP, IDA, WFP, UNRWA, UNICEF, UNFPA, UNHCR, EDF, SAFA, OAPEC, and AFESD is allocated to donors; IBRD, IFC, and ADB aid is not so allocated.

[b]Author's estimates.

[c]East Germany, Poland, Czechoslovakia, Hungary, Rumania, and Bulgaria.

[d]Non-DAC bilateral (Spain, Finland, etc.), non-DAC European and Asian DAC multilateral, other Third World bilateral (India, Israel, etc.), and other Second and Third World multilateral, most of which is reported to DAC.

[e]Details do not add to totals because of rounding.

[f]No longer meet ODA criteria in 1974 due to higher interest rates.

Sources: OECD Development Assistance Committee, "Geographical Distribution of Financial Flows from DAC Member Countries and Multilateral Organizations to Developing Countries, 1969-73" (Paris: OECD; processed); U.S. Department of State, Bureau of Intelligence and Research, *Communist States and Developing Countries: Aid and Trade in 19--*, various years; annual reports of multilateral organizations.

years. For reasons already explained, the figures for non-DAC countries involve heroic assumptions about disbursements and terms; they are orders of magnitude at best.

Patterns and Trends

The Preponderance of Western Europe

The most striking feature of the global aid-to-Africa figures is the preponderance, even in 1974, of Western Europe. Whereas Europe contributed about 45 percent of aid to poor countries worldwide during the 1969-74 period, it contributed nearly 60 percent of the total aid to Africa. Of DAC bilateral and multilateral aid, the European DAC countries accounted for roughly one-half worldwide and for 70 percent in Africa.

Within Western Europe the predominant feature is French bilateral aid, and within French bilateral aid, technical assistance to former French colonies. France's bilateral program for the six years averaged $656 million a year, some 30 percent of all flows, bilateral and multilateral, from DAC countries, and more than double the U.S. bilateral program for Africa.

Two features of the French program stand out. The first is the size of technical assistance grants, averaging $459 million a year, or 70 percent of France's Africa program and over half of all DAC technical assistance to Africa during the period. African ministries still have Frenchmen as key advisers, and in many schools French instructors are teaching the French language or other subjects in French.

The second striking aspect is the concentration of French bilateral aid in French dependencies, both formal dependencies called "overseas departments" and "overseas territories," and informal dependencies—former French colonies now sovereign. In 1974, some 95 percent of French bilateral aid to Africa went to the one-fourth of the population now or recently under French rule. Less than one percent went to non-francophone African states. France's massive support to Reunion ($370 per person per year in 1973) counts as bilateral aid—one-fourth of the French total to Africa.[10]

Similarly, Belgium's aid was highly concentrated in its former African colonies. Belgium, unlike France, has maintained aid programs in a large number of countries, but these are very small compared to those in states formerly Belgian-ruled—Zaire, Rwanda, and Burundi. These three accounted for from 84 to 92 percent of Belgian bilateral aid to Africa between 1969 and 1974.

A large proportion of French and Belgian multilateral aid also went to former colonies because it was channeled through the European Development Fund, the funnel for the EEC's aid program, which until 1975 permitted the French and Belgians to share the burden of aiding their former colonies with their Common

Table XI-3
Major Programs of Bilateral Aid to Africa, 1969-74
(millions of dollars)

Donor and Basis	1969	1970	1971	1972	1973	1974
Net ODA						
France	548	523	562	679	774	849
United States	276	254	312	236	170	284
Germany	112	120	132	126	201	297
United Kingdom	132	125	128	118	123	136
Belgium	70	78	87	110	134	155
Canada	30	52	84	115	114	172
Saudi Arabia	n.a.	n.a.	n.a.	n.a.	n.a.	518
Portugal	57	27	88	139	46	0
Kuwait	n.a.	n.a.	n.a.	n.a.	n.a.	96
USSR[a]	34	16	30	43	23	n.a.
10 other DAC countries	102	125	133	131	280	346
7 other OPEC countries	n.a.	n.a.	n.a.	n.a.	n.a.	242
Estimated grant equivalent of commitments[b]						
People's Republic of China	9	411	294	196	329	196
USSR	62	23	236	0	5	2
6 Eastern European countries[c]	3	25	72	63	59	24

[a]Estimated repayments based on assumption of five percent grants and 95 percent loans at 2.5 percent interest for 12 years with no grace period.

[b]Assumes disbursement in the same year as commitment and grant equivalents as follows:

	Percent grants	Percent loans	Grant equivalent of loans (percent)
China	5	95	90
USSR	5	95	43
6 Eastern European countries	0	100	30

[c]East Germany, Czechoslovakia, Poland, Hungary, Rumania, and Bulgaria.

Sources: OECD Development Assistance Committee, "Geographical Distribution of Financial Flows from DAC Member Countries and Multilateral Organizations to Developing Countries, 1969-73" (Paris: OECD; processed); U.S. Department of State, Bureau of Intelligence and Research, *Communist States and Developing Countries: Aid and Trade in 19--*, various years; John D. Esseks, "Soviet Economic Aid to Africa: 1959-73," in Warren Weinstein (ed.), *Chinese and Soviet Aid to Africa* (Praeger, 1975).

Market partners, principally Germany. France and Germany each contributed 34 percent of the Fund's resources while the other four EEC members made up the other third, but 88 percent of those resources aided countries with special links to France, and almost all of the rest went to former Belgian colonies.

Until 1974, Portugal's entire aid program was devoted to its African "overseas provinces." The DAC considered Portuguese net ODA, excluding purely military transfers, to have amounted to an average of $71 million a year between 1969 and 1973; this was three percent of all net ODA flows to Africa and more than twice the Russian flow. These flows were an integral part of Portugal's effort to hold on to its African dependencies in the face of growing opposition; now that Portugal has abandoned that struggle, the aid flow has ceased. Remember that aid is never given solely to help poor countries develop!

British aid was only a little less concentrated in colonies and former colonies than was French, Belgian, or Portuguese aid. Eighty-eight percent of bilateral British aid to Africa went to former colonies and to the Seychelles in 1974. Britain (unlike France, Belgium, and Portugal) did not have virtually all of its colonies in Africa. Consequently, though Africa receives a disproportionate share of British aid, the disproportion is not so great as for the other three major former colonial powers. Africa's share of net British aid fell from 37 percent in 1966-69 to 27 percent in 1970 and to 22 percent in 1971 as Britain broadened its aid perspectives.[11]

The African aid programs of the European countries without great-power pretensions and without recent African colonial ties are growing most rapidly. They are not concentrated in colonies and in ex-colonies, but are more widely distributed. Countries such as Germany, the Netherlands, Sweden, and Norway have been increasing the share of the aid burden they bear, while Britain, France, and Portugal have been reducing theirs.

Canada

Outside Europe, Canada's rapidly growing African program devoted 35 percent of bilateral aid in 1973-74 to the 17 percent of the less-developed world's population that is African, and 18 percent to the five percent of the less-developed world's population that lives in French-speaking Africa.[12] This distribution is heavily influenced by Canada's dual culture, which attracts francophone Canada to francophone Africa and requires that aid to the latter be balanced by aid to English-speaking Africa. But Canada also devotes an increasing share of its expanding program to multilateral agencies, and its citizens give increasing amounts of private aid through voluntary agencies. Both phenomena also characterize the aid programs of the northern European countries without an African colonial past.

Eastern Europe and China

A striking feature of the global aid-to-Africa figures is the diminishing and barely significant place of Soviet and Eastern European aid, set against a resurgent Chinese interest following the Cultural Revolution. Table XI-4 shows the trend

Table XI-4

Aid Commitments to Africa by the USSR, China, and Eastern Europe,[a] 1957-74

(millions of dollars)

Year	USSR				China				Six Eastern European Countries			
	Egypt	Other North African	Sub-Saharan Africa	All Africa	Egypt	Other North African	Sub-Saharan Africa	All Africa	Egypt	Other North African	Sub-Saharan Africa	All Africa
1957	200	...	...	200								
1958	75	...	...	75								
1959	...	...	181	181								
1960	225	...	62	287								
1961	5	34	116	155	←85→	←52→	←248→	←385→	←507→	←79→	←200→	←786→
1962	54	...	34	88								
1963	...	100	...	100								
1964	452	130	78	660								
1965	...	...	36	36								
1966	...	46	32	78	...	...	41	41	...	...	...	...
1967	...	...	9	9	21	...	22	43	22	...	47	69
1968	...	...	...	...	...	...	...	...	...	66	...	66
1969	...	...	135	135	...	...	10	10	...	...	11	11
1970	...	44	7	51	...	...	454	454	...	74	10	84
1971	299	189	27	515	...	40	285	325	142	...	99	241
1972	...	...	...	...	...	40	177	217	...	150	59	209
1973	...	...	10	10	28	...	335	363	100	98	...	198
1974	...	...	5	5	...	...	217	217	...	...	80	80

[a]East Germany, Poland, Czechoslovakia, Hungary, Rumania, and Bulgaria.

Sources: U.S. Department of State, Bureau of Intelligence and Research, *Communist States and Developing Countries: Aid and Trade in 19–*, various years; John D. Esseks, "Soviet Economic Aid to Africa: 1959-73," in Warren Weinstein (ed.), *Chinese and Soviet Aid to Africa* (Praeger, 1975); James Carter, *The Net Cost of Soviet Foreign Aid* (Praeger, 1969).

of new aid commitments by countries with centrally planned economies. The Russian commitments have been so small of late that debt service obligations in the continent soon will catch up with Russian disbursements if the trend continues; the same is true of commitments by the six Eastern European states belonging to the Council of Mutual Economic Assistance (CMEA). Russia's only major recent commitments have been associated with Guinean bauxite and Moroccan phosphate—two raw materials that the Soviet economy soon will have to import in appreciable quantities—and with an Algerian steel complex and Soviet agreements with Egypt. Egypt also has received a large share of recent commitments by other Eastern European countries.

The Chinese trend has been quite different. China scattered numerous small aid programs around sub-Saharan Africa in the early 1960s, when it was waging the battle of admission to the United Nations with Taiwan and the United States. Aid stopped during the Cultural Revolution but was resumed in 1970 with a Chinese commitment of $402 million to Zambia and Tanzania for their railroad. China's aid commitments to Africa since then have been large by Chinese as well as by African standards—some $1,576 million or 68 percent of worldwide commitments totalling $2,301 million during 1970-74. The only other countries that have so concentrated their aid in Africa are France, Belgium, and Portugal, whose historical and commercial reasons for doing so are a good deal clearer than China's motives.

Scholars have speculated about Chinese purposes without producing what seem to me to be convincing explanations. Yet the commitments appear to be serious, since disbursements are rapid. China now has more bilateral aid programs in Africa than does the United States, and its aid is less concentrated. Tanzania, Zambia, and Zaire receive a substantial share, leading to theories about a Chinese "copper policy." Those three countries plus Somalia and Ethiopia in the strategic Horn of Africa account for about half. However, a number of singularly unstrategic West African countries—Upper Volta, Chad, Benin, and Togo—have been promised from $40 to $50 million by the Chinese, perhaps only because of China's tradition of supplanting Taiwan-Chinese influence in that region.

The World Bank Group

Parallel to resurgent Chinese aid has been a boom in aid by the World Bank group and the European Development Fund to African countries. The UNDP is also an important donor, as Table XI-5 shows, but 1976 brought grave budget problems that have forced UNDP to retrench. Among the truly multinational organizations, aid from the World Bank group has been growing most rapidly and is now the most important. World Bank projections of its future operations, which have been accurate in the recent past, call not only for rapidly expanding

Table XI-5
Major Programs of Multilateral Aid to Africa, 1969-74
(Net ODA in millions of dollars)

Donor	1969	1970	1971	1972	1973	1974
United Nations Group						
UN Development Program	89	102	118	123	109	147
FAO World Food Program	32	48	61	43	68	102
Other UN	31	32	29	26	51	91
World Bank Group						
IBRD	45	40	106	178	139	[172] a
IDA	63	69	74	91	143	155
IFC	13	10	1	1	9	[6] a
European Community						
European Development Fund	108	140	170	158	238	342
Africa						
African Development Bank	1	2	7	12	20	[23] a
Arab Group						
Special Arab Fund for Africa						96
Special Account of OAPEC						58
Arab Fund for Economic and Social Development						2

aNo longer meet ODA criteria due to higher interest rates.
Source: OECD Development Assistance Committee, "Geographical Distribution of Financial Flows from DAC Member Countries and Multilateral Organizations to Developing Countries, 1969-73" (Paris: OECD; processed).

lending worldwide, but also for a continuing increase in Africa's share. Its new "third window"—designed to make development loans on "medium-soft" terms—expects to give 41 percent of its loans to Africa. Since the World Bank group now accounts for over seven percent of world aid to Africa, these projections are important. The IBRD can realize its projections if it can increase its capitalizatioñ, continue to sell its bonds, and maintain their high investment rating by warding off the embarrassment of defaults. The IDA and the "third window" will continue to depend on the generosity of donors.

UN Agencies

The UNDP and, recently, other UN aid agencies have expanded in Africa thanks to increased generosity from such countries as Sweden, Germany, the Netherlands, Canada, and Japan, which are not seeking great-power status and hence are content to let the United Nations distribute their aid. A complicated series of events has led to crisis and retrenchment at UNDP, with consequences for Africa and other recipients. The world food crisis, marked by soaring demand and prices, stymied the World Food Program. Since the November 1974 Rome World Food Conference, however, initiatives have been made to expand food aid and multilateral investment in food production. Africa may benefit.

The African Development Bank

The African Development Bank, negligible as a source of aid for several years after its founding in 1966, has now begun to generate a significant flow of resources. Unlike other regional development banks, the ADB has not until recently gone outside Africa in search of share capital, which has been slow to come in. Firmly in African control, the bank now feels strong enough to seek non-voting capital from outside Africa—for example, $200 million promised by OPEC, of which only $25 million had been paid in 1975. In addition, the U.S. Congress has authorized a token contribution of $5 million to the bank's African Development Fund. If the bank can convince observers that it is prudent, responsible, honestly run, and able to collect its debts, there is no doubt that non-African donors will allow the Abidjan bankers to administer more of their aid programs for them.

OPEC: The New Factor

OPEC aid is the newest and most difficult piece of the puzzle. The OECD's Development Assistance Committee makes a major effort to keep track of OPEC aid. For years prior to 1974, its figures are tentative.[13] DAC estimates that net disbursements of OPEC economic aid worldwide, both bilateral and multilateral, rose from $380 million to $530 million annually from 1970 to 1973, and to $2.6 billion in 1974. OPEC *commitments* in 1974 were an astounding $9.6 billion, a little more than the DAC countries actually gave in 1973. If commitments are a guide to future net disbursements, OPEC will soon rival Europe as Africa's chief aid supplier.

A large part of OPEC aid goes to countries on the front lines of the Arab-Israeli struggle: Egypt, Jordan, and Syria, of which Egypt is by far the biggest recipient. Egypt received $619 million from OPEC donors, net of repayments, in 1974. Of that amount, $471+ million was given by Saudi Arabia, with most of the rest from Kuwait and Iran. OPEC aid to the rest of Africa totalled $393 million in 1974. Of this amount, $156 million was disbursed by OAPEC multilateral agencies, of which the Special Arab Fund for Africa gave $7

million or less to 33 African countries, while the OAPEC Special Account gave
to four, two-thirds to the Sudan. African OPEC members contributed $90
million in bilateral aid, mostly from Algeria to the Sudan and from Libya to
Uganda and Guinea.

Some observers dismiss OPEC aid because such a high percentage is related to
the struggle over Palestine, but it is no less "aid" than was American aid to
Southeast Asia. "Front line" Egypt did get 61 percent, but the Sudan—which
the Arabs would like to develop into a major food source—received $128
million. Arabic-speaking Africa (Egypt, Sudan, Mauritania, Morocco, and Tunisia) accounts for 83 percent of OPEC aid; adding predominantly Muslim
Somalia, Guinea, and Mali accounts for 90 percent.

Where the United States Fits In

Despite its recent declines, the U.S. aid program still accounts for about
one-tenth of total aid to Africa. Not many years ago it provided one-fifth. Thus,
what the United States does about aid to Africa does matter.

Of all the aid given worldwide by all donors, the American share is lower for
Africa than it is for other less-developed regions. Of all DAC and multilateral aid
to Africa for 1969-72, the United States provided 20 percent; of DAC and
multilateral aid worldwide for that period, the United States provided 43
percent. Estimates of all aid, DAC and non-DAC, indicate that the U.S. share for
Africa in 1969-72 was about 18 percent, and for the world, 37 percent.

Why is this so? First, America has attached relatively low priority to African
aid and has given the continent less aid than its share of the less-developed
world's population. Second, other donors give Africa a good deal *more* aid than
its population share would indicate. We have seen the extent to which European,
Chinese, and Canadian aid is concentrated in Africa.

A strikingly large part of U.S. aid to Africa has consisted of food, which at
first blush seems anomalous for a continent with so much underused farmable
land. If Africa cannot produce enough food for itself and for export, what *can* it
produce? Another large part of U.S. aid has been technical assistance, however,
more obviously in line with African needs.

Finally, American aid to Africa is increasingly multilateral. The United States
has less than a decisive say over the allocation of this aid—in some cases, very
little say. We can give to the UNDP or not, but we cannot dictate where the
UNDP will spend its money.

Summing Up

Europe has been the dominant factor in aid to Africa, just as it has been in trade
and in colonial dominance. But the British, French, and Portuguese share has

been declining while that of other European countries has been increasing. This diversification of aid away from the former colonial metropoles has led to some decline in Europe's total share, but Europe is still the single major source of aid and the former colonial powers, especially France, are still the major European donors.

The recent upsurge of assistance from OPEC is manifestly related to the oil situation. Whether it be regarded as reflecting OPEC's growing sense of international responsibility, or as conscience money paid for having gouged the poor on oil prices, or as a bid for support in international forums, we should remember that several OPEC countries are now giving a higher share of their GNPs in aid than anybody else. Nor are all of them rich. The question for the African recipients is: how stable is this welcome new source of funds?

Current trends point toward a pessimistic answer. The oil-rich nations are learning how to spend their new money more quickly than seemed possible when they quadrupled the price of oil in 1973. Current World Bank projections suggest that only four OPEC countries will be running significant balance-of-trade surpluses by 1978; Iran has used its surplus and has sought loans in the international money markets again. Far from being flush with funds and having to worry about their effect on international monetary equilibrium, most OPEC aid givers will soon be choosing between foreign aid and domestic investment. In the circumstances, African states would seem well advised to press for the early commitment and disbursement of OPEC aid.

Specialists on China seem hard put to explain the growing importance of aid from China which now accounts for about one-fifteenth of all aid to Africa, roughly equal to that of the World Bank family. This trend is in contrast to the declining volume of aid given by the United States, the USSR, and other Eastern European countries.

The surge in Soviet and Eastern European aid to Africa in the early 1960s seems to have been linked with hopes of pushing the more progressive "national democratic states" or "revolutionary democracies" along a noncapitalist path of development leading to scientific socialism.[14] Most Soviet aid went to states that were so designated—Ghana, Mali, Algeria, and Guinea. Optimism about the ease of transition from African socialism to scientific socialism declined with the overthrow of President Kwame Nkrumah in Ghana in 1966 and of President Modibo Keita in Mali in 1968—and aid declined, too. Since then, Soviet commitments seem to have been closely tied to strategic considerations, including access to raw materials needed by the Soviet Union. Eastern European aid has had such a low grant element that it resembles export promotion.

Decreases in Soviet bloc and, to a lesser extent, U.S. aid have been compensated for by increased aid from Western countries without great power ambitions. Such aid, like China's, may be particularly valuable because it is tied to no obvious strategic ambitions of the donor. To the extent that it is less self-interested, it may also be more valuable to the recipient; it may, indeed, be development assistance.

Since they seek no strategic advantage, some of these countries have been sharply increasing their donations to multilateral aid-givers. Thus the Netherlands and Sweden have been particularly generous in contributing to the UN Development Program and to replenishments of the International Development Association. Their influence in the United Nations and in the World Bank group has favored aid distribution on the basis of need, which in turn favors Africa.

Between 1969 and 1973 the IBRD and IDA gave 20 percent of their aid to Africa—somewhat more than its share of the poor world's population—and roughly one-fifteenth of the aid Africa received from all sources. During the 1974-78 period the absolute level of aid from the World Bank and IDA is expected to triple. Africa then would receive 23 percent of all aid provided by those agencies and on easier terms than are given other recipients, because of Africa's larger share of "soft" credits from IDA. Such aid, too, is likely to be development assistance.

Who Cares About American Aid to Africa?

We have looked at the record of American aid to Africa first by itself, then in the context of other countries' aid. The record speaks for itself, but it does not speak very clearly without some explanation and interpretation.

"It would be naive," as Griffin and Enos have written, "to assume that the major objective of foreign assistance is economic development."[15] Similarly, it would be cynical to assume that economic development is not an objective at all. When Dr. Samuel Adams, AID's former deputy director for Africa, testified before Congress that the purpose of AID activity was to develop Africa, he certainly spoke from the heart and was speaking truth, though undoubtedly not the whole truth.

Except for that small part of private voluntary aid not paid for by the federal government, the aid Africa gets is what is proposed by the administration *and* authorized and appropriated by Congress. For more than a decade now, the administration generally has been proposing much larger aid programs than Congress has been willing to approve. In addition, Congress has been attaching more and more conditions governing the kinds of aid given and the ways of giving it. The faltering of support for aid, not just for Africa but for every poor country, has become a commonplace reflected in smaller administration proposals, in dwindling congressional majorities for the passage of AID bills with heavy cuts and restrictions, and in continuing appropriations to keep some aid flowing when Congress fails to agree on appropriations bills. The results are apparent in the fall of U.S. global aid levels as a percentage of GNP and in the fall of the United States from its position as one of the more generous aid donors in the DAC to one of the least generous. The trend is shown in figures from annual reports of the chairman of the Development Assistance Committee:

Net Official Development Assistance
as a Percentage of GNP

	United States	DAC Average
1962	0.56	0.52
1963	0.59	0.51
1964	0.56	0.48
1965	0.49	0.44
1966	0.44	0.41
1967	0.43	0.42
1968	0.37	0.37
1969	0.33	0.36
1970	0.31	0.34
1971	0.32	0.35
1972	0.29	0.34
1973	0.23	0.30
1974	0.25	0.33

Scholars and concerned observers offer several explanations. Thus, Francis Colaço has correlated yearly foreign aid appropriations for six DAC countries with various factors that might explain variations in the level of aid—notably the size of the donor's budget deficit, rate of inflation, and balance-of-payments deficit. For the United States between 1962 and 1970, these factors, properly adjusted, accounted for 69 percent of the variation.[16] Colaço cautions against generalizing too much from these figures, but they suggest, at a minimum, that donors are less generous when they feel poor and buffeted by forces of economic change. When American inflation was on the rise, and the balance of payments falling more into deficit, the administration and Congress produced less official aid.

What administrations and the Congress do cannot be entirely explained by such a small number of variables. A worsening balance of payments, increasing inflation, and declining aid coincided historically with a perception that the Cold War was abating. In view of innumerable statements made by AID supporters to Congress on the strategic significance of aid, the Cold War as a motive for aid-giving should not be discounted altogether.

Unpublished statistical analyses of global U.S. aid from 1946 to 1968 indicate that the distribution of U.S. bilateral aid during that period was somewhat correlated with the recipients' public position on the Cold War. Worldwide, countries that have supported U.S. positions received, on the average, somewhat more American aid than those that did not.[17] The correlations were stronger for military than for economic aid and, surprisingly, stronger for the Kennedy-Johnson years (1962-68) than for the longer 1946-68 period. For Africa, however, the Cold War variables gave a reverse indication, though again a statistically weak one. A former American ambassador to Senegal, Mercer Cook, maintained in the 1960s that America gave aid preference to African countries that threatened to "go communist" and slighted its friends. The data seem to bear him out.

But statistical analyses, while instructive, cannot explain the complicated cleavages between support for and opposition to aid in Congress and in the administration. Since, except for voluntary aid, American aid to Africa is what the administration proposes and the Congress approves, the attitudes of both are important—especially in Congress, where positions are a matter of public record.

Alfred Hero of the World Peace Foundation has been studying congressional and constituent attitudes toward aid for more than a decade. According to Hero, liberal congressional positions on social legislation, fiscal matters, and civil rights were highly correlated with support for foreign aid; up to the mid 1960s conservative positions were correlated with opposition to aid.[18] (Ironically, constituent attitudes ran in the opposite direction. Support for aid was weakest among the ill-informed, who were often poor and consequently had liberal views on social and fiscal issues, and vice versa.)

To "sell" aid to conservative congressmen, administrations combined it with military assistance, often appealing to Cold War arguments as well as to the corollary advantages to American private business. This strategy is now of dubious value, given the reaction to the Southeast Asian debacle symbolized by former Senator Fulbright's belief that aid was partly responsible for getting the United States involved in Vietnam. Many liberals on domestic social and fiscal issues can scarcely be called internationalist today. Conservative skepticism has been joined by liberal disillusionment about the capacity of aid to help people, to win votes in the UN General Assembly, or to promote more open and democratic societies, let alone to induce take-off into self-sustained economic growth.

Does congressional disillusionment reflect a broader public disenchantment? Probably not. Public attitudes toward aid never have had much effect on congressional actions, because aid is not an important issue for most Americans. The number who are deeply affected by it—AID employees, the ancillary bureaucracy, and technicians who depend indirectly on AID appropriations—constitute a small lobby. Hero's exhaustive analyses of surveys by the American Institute of Public Opinion, the National Opinion Research Center, the Survey Research Center, and others, show that the vast majority of Americans have had little knowledge of the aid program and that few have held strong or well-articulated views on the subject. Hero concluded in 1965 that there was "... almost no correlation between constituent attitudes and either roll-call votes or the attitudes of Congressmen pertinent to foreign aid."[19] In contrast, there was a strong correlation on questions of civil rights and welfare economics. As a result, "Success of Congressmen at the polls has in most instances depended little, if at all, on their behavior toward foreign assistance or on local general opinion on the matter."[20] The link between constituent opinion on aid and congressional votes has been weak or nil.

There is little or no evidence of declining public support for aid. Hero's analyses of public opinion surveys up to 1965 show support for the general idea of aid (50 to 60 percent for, about 30 percent against, the rest undecided), with

large majorities supporting technical assistance to the Third World, emergency
aid through food and other relief to the unfortunate, and economic aid to
"allies."[21] Military assistance to the same allies was less favored; capital aid for
"neutralist" or communist countries was opposed by the majority. Most people
knew very little about aid and most radically overestimated the amounts being
given; the more people overestimated, the more they favored reducing the
program. Proposals to expand assistance through multilateral organizations in
which the Second and Third Worlds predominated (for example, the UN General
Assembly) were opposed by most, though channeling more economic aid
through the World Bank was not.

In 1972 the Overseas Development Council sponsored a careful, broad-based
survey of American attitudes toward aid. The results supported Hero's earlier
findings, except that general acceptance of aid proved not to have been
weakened by developments in Southeast Asia; it was 68 percent—higher than in
any previous survey.[22] The Cold War rationale had lost most of its public
acceptance and "moral and humanitarian reasons" had become the strongest
justification for aid.

It should be emphasized that American public opinion on aid, diffuse and
inchoate as it is, supports aid not for development, but to meet minimum human
needs, as a philanthropy, to alleviate suffering. Hero reminds us,

... only a relatively small minority, concentrated among the college educated,
have thought of non-military aid to underdeveloped societies in terms of helping
to make possible basic, long-term economic growth. Most below the college level
(and many college educated as well) have tended to view aid ... as humanitarian
charity, a sort of international community chest and relief for the unfortunate
around the world ... emergency relief has been more popular than capital
assistance.[23]

How does Africa fit into this picture? Surveys in the 1950s and 1960s show
that Americans, particularly white Americans, were less enthusiastic about aiding
Third World countries than they were about the Marshall Plan for Europe. Even
in the Marshall Plan period, aiding Germany got more support than aiding Japan,
aiding Greece more than aiding Nationalist China. When asked to choose the part
of the Third World in which the United States should spend the most foreign
aid, 66 percent of the 1,620 people interviewed in Public Opinion Survey 655 in
1965 who expressed a preference chose Latin America; only 20 percent chose
Africa and 14 percent chose Asia. Africa would have fallen to last place but for
the votes of the 182 black Americans in the sample.[24]

Black Americans do differ significantly from white Americans in attitudes
toward aid to Africa and toward aid in general. Black Americans have shifted
"from relative isolationism prior to the 1950s to relative liberalism in respect to
foreign policy in the 1960s," and "have been more favorably inclined than their
white compatriots in recent years to foreign aid."[25] This is all the more

significant in that it occurs despite the fact that, on the average, black Americans are less informed about foreign affairs and less schooled than whites, conditions that usually are coupled with conservatism toward foreign affairs and opposition to aid. In the survey mentioned above, 60 percent of blacks stating a preference for the less-developed continent where America should spend most for aid chose Africa; only 16 percent of white Americans did.

These differences in racial attitudes have led to efforts to mobilize black support for aid to Africa. AID's Africa Bureau has convoked black scholars, tried to involve predominantly black American institutions in technical assistance to Africa under the AID program, and has increased the percentage of black Americans on its staff. In the field of private voluntary aid, C. Payne Lucas, former Peace Corps director for Africa, has worked energetically at mobilizing black support through Africare, a private voluntary agency founded primarily to aid countries affeeted by the Sahel drought but now expanding its scope. Contributions from more than 50,000 Americans were recorded by Africare in 1974 alone, and the organization had chapters in 50 American cities by 1976.

The Black Caucus in the U.S. Congress consistently monitors aid appropriations for Africa, but the most effective advocate of more aid for Africa on the Hill probably has been Senator Hubert Humphrey. Through his efforts, a paragraph was added to the 1974 AID act stating the intention of the Congress that Africa's share of American aid should be increased to a "more equitable share of United States economic assistance."[26]

What are the chances that the "constituency for Africa" will succeed in mobilizing enough public support to influence significantly aid appropriations for Africa? In Alfred Hero's view:

Undoubtedly a gradual shift in general public opinion . . . toward more widespread support for expanded economic aid for Africa . . . could facilitate changes in federal policy in several directions by the Executive, with the approval of Congress. However, such shifts in opinion would not necessarily result in significant changes in policy. Moreover, given the prevailing mass attitudes, most of low intensity, federal policy could probably be changed considerably without much change in opinion—especially if such changes were supported by most of the small minority who exert some influence on foreign policymaking relevant to Africa.[27]

The record of America's declining share of aid for Africa says clearly that the "small minority" to which Hero refers believes that Africa has little strategic value, that aid is not needed to protect access to whatever African raw materials the United States may need, that aid has not bought and could not buy African support in world forums, and that any foreseeable level of U.S. aid to Africa probably would make little difference in Africa's economic evolution.

Has recent American policy been well-founded? Is Africa relatively unstrategic and, if so, might that be an argument for sending *more* aid, given the bitter harvest of the strategic Cold War aid we furnished in Southeast Asia? Does our increasing dependence on oil imported from Nigeria call for a change of position toward that country and others whose goodwill would be indispensable in the event of another embargo by the Organization of Arab Petroleum-Exporting Countries (OAPEC)? A closer look is required at the Africa we aid.

The Africa We Aid

Africa's character influences American attitudes toward giving aid and conditions what American aid can do. Striving to avoid sentimentalism and cynicism, and without glossing over Africa's diversity, let us consider Africa in this context.

Economically, Africa's most striking feature is its low density of human population and overwhelmingly rural character. The Nile Delta is the exception. Elsewhere, rural population densities that are high by African standards (Rwanda, Burundi, northern Nigeria, the Mossi Plateau) are low by European or South Asian standards. Most African cities are of very recent origin and are predominantly administrative and commercial, not manufacturing centers. Consequently, farmers and pastoralists make up a higher proportion of Africa's population than they do in any other continent.

Africa's farmers and livestock-keepers do not, for the most part, use the land very intensively. They do not need to. The usable-land-to-population ratio is high, making land virtually a free good in much of Africa. Therefore, bush-fallow farming systems predominate. Unused land is cleared, planted with minimal preparatory tillage, harvested after minimal weeding and pest control, and abandoned for other unused land when soil fertility declines. Similarly, most African livestock raising is done on communally owned (and hence unimproved) range. Both systems are appropriate for high land-to-man ratios that are only a little lower than ratios that would permit a hunting/gathering lifestyle. Indeed, hunting/gathering lifestyles still predominate in many of Africa's remote corners and were replaced by low-input agriculture only within the past three centuries in many other parts.

Bush-fallow agriculture and open-range pastoralism imply little or no investment in permanent improvements to land because families, clans, and villages move from time to time. In such societies, people are most interested in producing to consume, less so in capitalizing their labor in heavy things that will be left behind or be difficult to move. Except for the Mediterranean coast and isolated examples in the East African highlands, Africa's rich past has left very few monuments. The legacy of today's Africans from their ancient ancestors includes much accumulated knowledge (human capital) about how to produce crops and meat under often difficult conditions while economizing on inputs, but very little physical capital—land improvements, irrigation systems, permanent buildings, transportation investments, and the like.

Africa's predominantly low population density means that distance is important. Distance is a benefit in avoiding imperialist invaders (Europeans dominated Asia and the Americas before they conquered Africa) but a cost when it comes to moving goods. Because low accumulation characterized most of African traditional society, investments to reduce transport costs were not made. In precolonial Africa, a great deal of traffic in goods moved by the most expensive mode: head portage. When European conquest brought railways and rudimentary roads early in this century, transport costs were drastically lowered and interzonal African trade blossomed.[28] Nevertheless, high transport costs still constitute a major factor perpetuating local self-sufficiency in Africa and impeding the integration of African economies and of Africa with the world economy.

Despite recent investments in ports, roads, and railroads, transporting cotton from a farm in the West African savannah to the coast costs about one-third of what the farmer is paid; for peanuts, a crop with a lower value per unit weight, the transport cost equals what the farmer gets; for sorghum, the farmer's situation is even worse.[29] These transport costs are no problem when production is intended for home use, but countries wishing their farmers to compete on the world market must face the world price. Transport costs are real and represent a part of the world price African farmers don't get, thereby greatly decreasing their incentive to become integrated into the world market and to toil for the rewards that such integration would bring.

Although not all Africans are in so difficult a situation as the farmers of the savannah and the Sahel, Africa's geography isolates much of its population by imposing high transport costs. Isolation has never affected the peoples of coastal North Africa, numbering 70 million or about one-fifth of the continent's population. Elsewhere, however, tropical Africa's coast has few harbors and such an inhospitable climate that most Africans preferred to live away from it until this century. West Africa's great medieval empires were in the interior Sahel and savannah; the coasts were left to pygmy hunter-gatherers and the losers of wars, who were ravaged by disease in the fetid malarial forests. The slave trade, European navigational innovations, and the development of tree crops for the humid tropics—oil palm, cocoa, coffee, rubber—and of food staples—manioc, Asian yams and rice—changed that balance. Still, Africa's rivers have not become low-cost routes to the interior. Virtually all of them are blocked by rapids near the coast as they fall from the central plateau to the narrow coastal plain. The Congo and the Niger are navigable *in* the interior but not *into* it (though the Niger might be made so at reasonable cost).

Africa's poverty is not limited to transport infrastructure but extends to all physical infrastructure or "capital." No other continent derives so little of its GNP from processing as Africa does, or has so little capital investment in manufacturing plant and equipment. The result is a continental economy that lacks articulation. An input-output matrix of the Gambian economy, for example, would consist mostly of zeroes. The Gambian economy is integrated into the European economy, which consumes its peanut products and furnishes tourists and virtually all of the sophisticated manufactured goods Gambia uses for consumption and investment. The African economy as a whole is more integrated with Europe, which is Africa's preponderant trading partner, than with itself. Intra-African trade is dwarfed by European and other "foreign" trade.

Because the physical infrastructure is limited and economies are little articulated, the institutional infrastructure is also sparse. The type of economy that characterized traditional Africa lacked uniform business and administrative norms and customs, nor was there much development of the other institutions that transfer ideas, services, and ownership of resources, as well as goods. The large business organizations and banks that have characterized post-agricultural economic development elsewhere are few in Africa, and most of those few are barely assimilated imports.

Africa's geographically extensive food production, high transport costs, low processing capacity, and lack of economic articulation show up in measures of wealth such as GNP, gross domestic product, or national income. Excluding South Africa, the continent's GNP at market prices of roughly $90 billion is about equal to that of Czechoslovakia and East Germany combined, or less than one-fourth of Japan's. Sub-Saharan Africa's GNP of $55 billion (also excluding South Africa) is comparable to that of Australia alone.

Even at Africa's low population densities, GNP per capita is small. Excluding South Africa, the continental GNP per capita is about $200—a low figure, though not so low as in South Asia, China, and Indochina. Of 34 countries listed by the World Bank as having had a GNP per capita of $200 or less in 1974, 22 are in Africa.

These figures do not translate into the conclusion that Africa accounts for over half the world's misery. First, Africa gives a misleading impression because it is divided into many small states. Though 65 percent of the poorest countries as identified above are in Africa, the 22 countries in Africa thus categorized contain a mere 15 percent of the total number of people in the group. Asia, particularly South Asia, is the dominant center of world deprivation; Africa is not.

Second, most of Africa's poverty is not misery—at least in years of normal rainfall. Normally, the lot of the average sorghum and peanut farmer in Niger is incomparably better than that of a landless or near-landless laborer in India or Bangladesh, though their poverty may be equal in terms of GNP per capita. The African has access to land and, with normal rains, hard work will bring rewards; the South Asian has only his labor to sell in a society in which there is too much labor and not enough land.

Third, sociologists tell us that what hurts most is relative deprivation. Most rural Africans are isolated, and not confronted daily with the relatively opulent life-style in their own capitals. Most may suffer protein malnutrition, but they are not hungry. Their shelter and clothing are simple, but adequate to the environment. It is in health and education that they see themselves as deprived, and in the shortage of cash to buy what the outside world produces and they do not. Cash is painfully scarce for most Africans because their rural society produces so little of what the world will buy.

As in any general statement about Africa, there are many exceptions to the generalities sketched here. The factory cities of Egypt are far removed from the Africa we have described. The main exceptions, though, are the mineral enclaves. Most of the countries that are rich in terms of income per capita (Libya, Gabon, Algeria) or in balance-of-payment terms (Nigeria) are mineral exporters. Of 40 African countries eligible for World Bank loans in fiscal year 1974, two did not receive any because they were too rich and six were judged well enough off to take credit on straight IBRD terms.[b] Of the eight, four were oil exporters, one a copper exporter, one a phosphate exporter, one an iron ore exporter, and only one had wealth based on other than mineral sources. Take away the oil enclaves from Nigeria, Libya, Algeria, and Gabon; the copper enclaves from Zambia, Zaire, and Botswana; the phosphate from Morocco; the iron ore from Liberia and Mauritania, and the rest of the economy in those countries is as poor as the poorest. A country such as Guinea is kept in business by its bauxite. Only a very few countries rise above the lowest levels of poverty by virtue of value added in agriculture—usually tree crops (Ghana's cocoa, Ivory Coast's coffee and cocoa and others, Kenya's coffee and tea)—or by value added in industry (Egypt).

Mineral enclaves are good for earning foreign exchange and financing governments. With present prices for energy and recent prices for industrial raw materials, it would be absurd to advise against mineral exploitation. But it would be equally absurd to suppose that Gabon and Libya have strong, developed economies merely because they are rich. Links between mineral enclaves and other productive activities in the economy are usually weak. Mineral development, after all, inspired the conception of enclaves of the rich economies existing within the poor ones popularized by development economist Hans Singer.

Now having the money they need to develop, Africa's mineral-rich countries have a chance to show whether development really is their priority, or whether they are more interested in foreign policy adventures, higher living standards for bureaucrats, and consumption for townfolk in the form of subsidized imported food, free health services, and education. A look at the older mineral-rich countries outside Africa suggests that few have had the commitment to development and the discipline needed to invest their mineral wealth in building articulated, broad-based, productive economies.

Although several African countries have enjoyed a boom based on high prices for their mineral exports, the interests of suppliers of industrial raw materials do

[b]Not including six other countries that received some mix of IBRD loans and IDA credits to soften the terms.

not run parallel to those of energy producers. High energy prices have hurt the economies of industrial countries, which have invested less and built fewer houses and bought less copper, with dire consequences for Zambia and Zaire. Still, relative to other continents, Africa's mineral resources have not been fully surveyed (except in South Africa) and most of those now being exploited lie near the surface. For the longer term, one must suppose that vast undiscovered reserves will be detected by ERTS satellites and exploited in response to rising world demand and prices. Those resources probably will be discovered by foreign technology and brought into production by foreign engineers working for foreign companies or hired from foreign consulting firms by African companies. The African shortage of human capital, with its profound implications for social and political development, is precisely what inspires pessimism about the way Africa's mineral-rich governments will spend and manage their wealth.

As a continent, Africa ranks at the bottom in availability of medical service and life expectancy, in literacy, in schooling (whether measured by the percentage of various age cohorts in school or the output of engineers per capita), and in availability of contraceptives and maternal and child health care. It is at the top in infant and general mortality, and its population growth rate is exceeded only by Latin America. Such rapid population growth is not yet the problem it is in densely peopled parts of Asia, thanks to Africa's relatively abundant land. In the context of Africa's poverty, however, it makes the task of improving the human capital—of schooling more people and keeping them healthy—exceedingly difficult.

In their political rhetoric, all of Africa's governments proclaim development as their goal and almost all declare themselves socialist. Given these commitments, it is striking that—mineral-producing countries apart—the governments save very little. One consequence is that a high proportion of investment in the public sector depends on foreign funds obtained as gifts or loans. According to World Bank estimates, Africa's public and private *savings* as a proportion of GNP have been lower than the Third World average in most years since 1960. Yet Africa's proportion of GNP *invested* has caught up with and recently surpassed the Third World average because a somewhat higher than average share—one-fifth to one-eighth, depending on the year—is financed by foreign savings.[30] In other words, Africa has been receiving more aid per capita than other continents. Socialist governments pledged to develop their countries rapidly and to take over (and hold) the commanding heights of their economies will need to save more from their own resources and manage their commanding heights extremely well if they are to avoid becoming ever more dependent on foreign donors.

Just as disquieting as the paucity of public savings (except in the mineral-producing states) is a related phenomenon that is pervasive but impossible to measure—the low "development quality" of African public investment. There is no way of proving that "development quality" is lower in Africa than it is in other regions at similar stages of development, but a wide spectrum of observers, African and other, share my judgment that it is. A great deal of investment seems to be going to sectors with dubious and distant links to production. Some of the most spectacular blunders are associated with foreign donors: the United States' John F. Kennedy Hospital in Liberia, Britain's East African Goundnut Scheme, France's Office du Niger, Russia's snowplows in Guinea, Yugoslavia's slaughterhouses in the Sahel, the European Development Fund's reservoirs in Upper Volta—is there a Chinese disaster yet? Misallocations by Africans include "investments" in training and in vehicles for extension workers who never visit farmers, in larger bureaucracies and the buildings to house them, in schools for which there are no books or trained teachers. How can these examples of low "development quality" be explained?

Colonial regimes seldom tolerated criticism, and the trend of African politics since independence has certainly been to curtail criticism too. Arguments against the "luxury of an opposition" in a country mobilizing for development were voiced even before independence. The movement toward one-party democracy was justified by making the party a mass organization that would allow expression to all shades of opinion, which would then be harmonized in the interest of development. The political structure that evolved—the "party state" that Aristide Zolberg analyzed in 1966[31]—has been much less tolerant of criticism than its proponents anticipated and much more an instrument of control. As party and government coalesce, the party loses much of its utility as a feedback mechanism. Few are the African states today in which a fundamental change in the government could be brought about by the party or in any other nonviolent way.[32]

The fragility of African states may have preordained this evolution. Aside from Somalia, Lesotho, and Egypt, few states can realistically claim to be nations in cultural or ethnic terms. They are small and their average population a mere eight million. Yet even the smallest states represent a process of *aggregation* in African society, whose fragmentation is reflected in the most powerful expression of culture: language. Africa, with about ten percent of the world's people, has about 25 percent of its languages. Governing Africa's ministates requires juggling and balancing the competing interests of several or many cultural or ethnic groups within state boundaries.

Cultural fragility and the lack of a tradition of legitimacy may explain why political feedback is cut off, but they do not justify the consequences. A lack of such feedback tempts rulers to arbitrariness. A policymaker whose aid program is not justified primarily by the amoral standards of realpolitik must ask what he is accomplishing by strengthening governments such as those now existing in Equatorial Guinea, Burundi, Uganda, or the Central African Republic. The list could be lengthened or shortened according to the reader's ideological preferences, yet it is clear that the governments mentioned operate with a high degree of arbitrariness.

Arbitrariness makes a poor climate for investment; it does not encourage craftsmen to invest in bicycle assembly, or farmers to invest in planting rubber trees that will yield no income for seven years. The *possibility* of arbitrariness signals still other disincentives to development. Without political feedback, a ruling group that is not particularly inclined toward despotism is nevertheless under no direct pressure to respond to mass needs. The outlines of Myrdal's "soft state" emerge. Subtle and not so subtle forms of corruption are easy. Civil servants and workers in the capital city (who can riot and obstruct) are favored at the expense of the rural majority. Marketing boards tax farmers to keep prices down in the cities or to endow the capital with the housing, schools, health facilities, water supply, and national stadium that only accentuate the urban-rural imbalance. Is it any wonder that rural people crowd into slums around the capitals? For the rural majority, the indicators of Africa's limited social infrastructure and social development—high infant mortality, high birth rate, low newspaper circulation, little technical education—remain virtually unchanged.

If political performance belies a single-minded devotion to development goals in the public sector, the African record in encouraging domestic private investment is mixed at best. Most of the resources for economic growth will have to come from African savings and investment, especially from the private sector if savings in the public sector are inadequate. Without attempting to generalize for the continent, one may assume that arbitrary rule does not encourage future-orientation. The marketing-board syndrome impedes the making of many small investments by many small farmers that would bring broad-based development (though Ghanaian and Nigerian cocoa farmers provide an example of such development *despite* heavy taxes). The "soft state" is more apt to stimulate entrepreneurship in obtaining import licenses and government contracts than the entrepreneurship that builds new productive capacity.

Finally, despite the fact that the average African state of eight million people represents a step toward social integration, the average gross national product of $1.5 billion must be regarded as economically divisive. Excluding South Africa, the average GNP and hence market in the sub-Saharan countries is about $1 billion. If pan-African aspirations had been realized or the many paper customs unions really worked, these small markets would present little problem. As it is, in its economically negative political divisions as in its general lack of political feedback and the "softness" of its states, Africa has been following the road René Dumont called "Latinamericanization," and is following it to an extreme.

Strategically, the economic position of the mineral-rich enclaves is quite different from that of the rest of Africa. The "rest of Africa" produces little of what the world wants, giving it little capacity to buy. Access to the products and to the small markets of the majority of countries is of little strategic interest to outsiders. Their sluggish export growth promises ominous foreign debt burdens, where they do not already exist. Most countries are poor candidates for commercial credit; their balance of payments prospects do not encourage foreign investors to assume that they will be able to repatriate any profits they might make. (For the present, however, it should be noted that continent-wide debt service in Africa is a lower percentage of export earnings than in Asia or Latin America.)

In marked contrast to these generalities are the five countries—Nigeria, Libya, South Africa, Algeria, and Zambia—that produce more than 80 percent of Africa's mineral wealth. (The remaining less-than-20 percent may loom large in the economies of smaller countries such as Gabon, Guinea, or Mauritania.) The oil exporters in particular—Nigeria, Algeria, Libya, Gabon, and Angola—enjoy some strategic importance based on the demonstrated effectiveness of oligopolistic pricing. Having quadrupled the price of a commodity vital to other states, the oil exporters have shown their power. Production costs and oil company profits now account for less than ten percent of the f.o.b. price of crude; more than 90 percent consists of royalties paid to governments under whose land the oil happens to lie.

Oligopoly profits inevitably inspire trust busting—in this case more oil exploration, diversification of energy sources, and exploiting the divergent national interests of members of the cartel. Such efforts eventually will bring OPEC down. But the lead time for finding a commercial oil field and bringing it into production is four years at the very least; so is the construction time for nuclear power plants. *If* OPEC can limit production and resolve the divergent interests of its members, the oligopoly should hold at least through 1978 and quite probably until 1980, to judge from the confused and ineffective response of oil-consuming countries to the Arab oil embargo of 1973-74. This suggests that African oil producers can command respect for several years. It also means, for them, that the foreign currency scarcities and debt problems so often associated with development are reduced or removed, at least for a time. Purchasing power in their markets is expanding rapidly.

Nigeria, Canada, and Venezuela are our major foreign suppliers of oil. Had Nigeria joined the Arab oil embargo in 1973-74, the economic consequences for the United States would have been serious indeed. American policymakers, most of whom are not accustomed to thinking of African states as serious forces to be reckoned with, are going to have to stop confusing Nigeria with Niger, at least for a few years. In 1974, America's current account balance-of-payments deficit with Nigeria alone was $3 billion—the same amount as our worldwide balance of trade deficit! Strategic considerations strongly suggest that we find ways of selling more consumer goods to Nigeria and of providing goods and services for its investments. Nigerian actions make a difference to the United States, and so, in lesser measure, do the actions of other African oil producers.

In addition to contributing one-seventh of the world's current oil production, African countries produce a variety of other industrial raw materials. The litany is familiar to every Africanist: The United States now imports 98 percent of its manganese, 40 percent of which comes from Africa. We depend on Ghana for six percent of our imported aluminum, on South Africa for 29 percent of our chrome. Zaire alone provides 49 percent of our cobalt. Six percent of the iron ore and seven percent of the natural rubber we import comes from Liberia. It has been roughly estimated that Africa has 96 percent of the noncommunist world's diamonds, 42 percent of its cobalt, 60 percent of its gold, 34 percent of its bauxite, 17 percent of its copper, and 28 percent of its uranium. South Africa and Rhodesia together have an awesome share of the world's known reserves of chromite. Africa's iron reserves are twice those of the United States and two-thirds those of the USSR.[33]

It would be easy to overstate the strategic importance of Africa's mineral resources. In every instance it depends on the availability of alternative sources, the availability of substitutes, the importance of the mineral, and, of course, price. Rhodesian petalite is important to Corning Glass, but it is difficult to imagine a military operation—or an aid program—designed to preserve our access to petalite. The same could be said of long-fibered amosite and crocidolite asbestos. No one questions the strategic significance of uranium, but numerous non-African sources could come into production as prices rise. Copper is a similar case.

Ironically, as already noted, the success of the oil cartel has been bad news for other producers of industrial raw materials. The West's recession, induced by high energy prices, has travelled along the backward linkages to the raw material suppliers. Demand for copper has faltered and the price of the metal has fallen despite all that Zambia, Zaire, and other members of CIPEC, the would-be copper cartel, could do. From now until about 1980 an effective energy cartel probably will thrive at the expense not only of the industrialized processors, but also of the raw-material suppliers. Under these conditions the copper market is a buyers' market. The strategic importance of Africa's industrial raw materials is reduced.

Reduced, but not eliminated. The Russians have been sufficiently concerned about their future supply of bauxite to try to secure it through aid to Guinea, and about their future supply of phosphates for fertilizer to use their aid in an effort to tie up some of the Moroccan production. Most of the minerals the United States needs and cannot easily get elsewhere, however, come from white-ruled southern Africa: diamonds and manganese from South Africa and chrome from Rhodesia.

A discussion of aid in Africa's strategic context returns us to the question of political instability. Aid is sometimes used in an effort to gain strategic advantage—but should the United States aid Ian Smith's Rhodesia for the sake of America's chrome supply? Leaving moral compunctions aside, few would bet on the longevity of the white Rhodesian regime or be willing to invest aid in cultivating it. What applies to Rhodesia applies, perhaps less dramatically, to other parts of Africa. Just as political instability impairs the climate for domestic investment, so does it lessen the attractiveness of cultivating a regime for strategic purposes. Instability gives rise not only to the possibility of a regime's replacement by force, but also to the possibility of arbitrary action. After Russia's careful cultivation of Guinea, that country's refusal to allow Soviet planes to land at the Russian-built airport during the Cuban missile crisis must have seemed arbitrary indeed in Moscow. The Russians may wonder whether such behavior (or an equally unpredictable coup) will destroy the returns on their investment in Guinean bauxite as well.

Four Alternative Reasons for Aiding Africa

Certain of the characteristics and potentials of Africa described in the preceding sections stand out when one weighs the alternative reasons for aiding Africa. In one way or another, as Griffin and Enos have said, an aid giver "wishes . . . by means of granting assistance, to influence the behavior of those countries to which she gives it."[34] The wish to influence becomes trivial unless one specifies the donor's purposes. Consequently, we need to focus now on Africa's characteristics and potentials from the standpoint of U.S. *strategic* concerns, *commercial* concerns, *philanthropic* concerns, and *development* concerns.

American behavior seems to reflect the belief that Africa has little *strategic* importance to the United States. This is not to say that Africa is perceived as having none. As William H. Lewis notes in an earlier chapter of this book, American aid to Ethiopia during the Haile Selassie period was partly a payment for the use of the Kagnew telecommunications station, evidently of some importance to the National Security Agency; aid to Liberia has been partly payment for being allowed to retransmit Voice of America broadcasts from there and for Liberian willingness to communicate American positions to other African states.

Aid can also be used to win influence or, more crudely, to buy votes in international forums. Africa has many such votes, particularly in the UN General Assembly, where states have equal representation regardless of population or economic or military strength. Certainly the two Chinas and the two Germanies used aid in Africa to influence Assembly votes on seating and national recognition policies.

If the modest American aid program to Africa was meant to serve such goals, it could hardly have been less successful. In most international organizations, America's positions and those of most African states, including those the United States aids, are currently poles apart on most issues. But, more to the point, recent years have brought an evolution of American understanding that international resolutions passed on a one-country-one-vote basis have little strategic importance. The dominance of many international meetings by small Third World countries has led to resolutions less and less in tune with power realities, causing the United States and other countries to take such resolutions less and less seriously. Africa's strategic advantage in being divided into many small countries is thus devalued.

It is argued that American perceptions of Africa's low strategic priority are mistaken, particularly in view of Africa's important stock of nonreplenishable raw materials. Might not aid be used to influence the disposal of those resources?

It might. But a failure to learn from history could lead to overemphasis on the strategic importance of Africa's raw materials. The world economic boom of the late 1960s and youthful anomie in the industrialized West, resulting in part from the war in Vietnam that helped cause the boom, led to the current preoccupation with the world ecosystem and to Meadows' and Forrester's "Limits to Growth" projections for the Club of Rome.[35] The boom also led to high prices for raw materials. The notion that we are running out of everything was lent credence by the oil producers' oligopolistic coup of 1973. The boom recalled the Korean War boom in raw materials prices and the Paley Commission[36] and stockpiling.

Growth pessimists emphasize the importance of Africa's raw materials, forgetting that the essence of economic development is the ability to make more sophisticated goods from *less* raw material, with the result that raw materials prices usually fall relative to other prices. Meadows and Forrester ignore these trends and instead based their projections on what was happening in 1972.[37] When such anomalies are corrected, Africa's mineral resources look less like a strategic trump, as African copper producers have already learned. If a synthetic substitute for industrial diamonds is not found, South Africa may hold a strategic position based on its dominance of supply; South African and Rhodesian chrome and manganese are strategically important despite alternative sources in the Soviet Union, the Philippines, Morocco, and Turkey. Nevertheless, it is a safe bet that much of the next century will see buyers holding the upper hand in negotiating for Africa's nonreplenishable resources.

Africa's *commercial* significance to the United States is reflected in the continent's small share of U.S. trade and investment. Again, small does not mean negligible. Afro-American trade may expand somewhat as Africa gradually lessens its economic dependence on the former colonial powers. How much other countries will be able to expand their trade depends in part on how effectively the new Lomé Convention serves Europe's interest in tying sub-Saharan Africa to the expanded EEC. What we know of the African economy suggests, to me, that the prospects for expansion are not immense, nor is their strategic importance great.

Oil and natural gas will hold a special position over the next five years. As noted, U.S. oil purchases from Nigeria created a $3 billion bilateral deficit in 1974 and were more than 11 times U.S. sales there. If the United States starts importing liquified natural gas from North Africa as proposed, similar deficits could appear with respect to Algeria and Libya. Deficits of such magnitude would create problems that could be better handled by an export-promotion agency such as Eximbank than by aid.

If our dominant aid-giving motive is *philanthropic*—to help meet basic human needs—then Africa can be very important to the United States. While no rival of South Asia in sheer misery, Africa holds abundant potential for human disaster.

The low-intensity agriculture and livestock systems will become increasingly inadequate at higher population densities, which seem assured by present population trends and official attitudes toward population policy in much of Africa. At higher human densities, farmers move into lands with marginal rainfall formerly left to pastoralists. As William A. Hance explains in his chapter on the Sahel drought, this process increases both the potential for and the consequences of severe drought.

The most basic human need is food, and Africa seems destined to experience famine or malnutrition that will elicit American food aid. The question is whether the humanitarian concern that sanctions sending food to *alleviate* the famine will also sanction aid that increases food production to *avert* famines.

Even without catastrophic disaster, Africa's endemic poverty and deprivation should suffice to elicit American aid. It would be unfortunate, however, if aid interest groups were to overemphasize Africa's undeniable poverty to build a case for aid and for their own jobs; American perceptions of Africa, already warped by Tarzan movies, would be warped in a new way.

To the extent that *development* is the American aid motive—and evidence suggests that it is of small moment outside policymaking circles—Africa presents formidable obstacles. By now it should be clear that the main obstacle is not just a lack of money. Africa could absorb unlimited quantities of money, but that would not necessarily lead to economic development. The underlying problems of know-how, institution building, policy improvement, and fostering human and institutional change call as much for technical as for capital assistance.

It is important to recognize the development difficulties that Africa's social, political, and economic conditions create. But even though development is not a major American policy goal, it is a goal of African leaders, regardless of the aid donors' motives. Bearing the difficulties fully in mind, we consider next how the United States might aid Africa in the coming decades.

The "Critical Choices"

In the abstract, America's options in aiding Africa are limited only by the fertility of our imagination. The possibilities can be narrowed to a smaller number of more realistic choices by taking account of the preceding discussions of what Africa is like, why America gives aid, and of the weight of tradition in our aid program. Even then, the possibilities must be further limited by describing what we expect the future world economy to look like. Predictions, Ambrose Bierce said, are "What will happen if nothing happens."[38]

At least since World War II, except for a brief interval during the Korean War, the world economy favored processors of raw materials over the producers of primary products. Energy and industrial raw materials were cheap by historic standards. By the end of the 1960s, the processors' boom was over. Earlier low prices for primary products had lessened the incentives to find and produce them, while the boom itself had stimulated demand; shortages led to price rises, and many primary producers stopped complaining about how their terms of trade had deteriorated since the Korean War. The oil producers' economic coup of 1973 turned the terms of trade significantly against the processors, cutting the processors' real standard of living and inducing a recession that has hurt the traditional aid-givers in the OECD. It has also hurt non-oil primary producers in that the recession in processing countries has backward linkages that have lowered demand for their products.

We have noted Colaço's work showing that aid-giving is closely linked to how prosperous the donor feels. Hero's work suggests that Americans support aid to those they perceive to be in want. Consequently, a reasonable aid policy should take into account not only the economic prospects for the United States and the other OECD countries, but also for Africa.

From 1976 to 1980 the terms of trade should favor the energy producers, who probably can maintain their oligopoly until then. The processors will work to destroy the OPEC cartel and to find substitutes for and ways of economizing oil. They will succeed, but success will take several years. In the meantime, producers of industrial raw materials will find their prices depressed—and they may well find the processors too preoccupied with their own problems to give much thought to foreign aid.

After 1980, energy will be relatively cheap. Oil producers that have not transformed themselves into processors in the interim will be out of luck. The economies of the processors will pick up, as will their feelings of generosity and their aid. Backward linkages will eventually help the industrial raw-material producers too.

The United States, for all its agricultural exports and its production of industrial raw materials and energy, is primarily a processor. Since it is less dependent on processing than Europe or Japan, it will pull through the 1973-80 "processors' eclipse" better than they will. But after 1980 the American recovery should be less dramatic than the European or the Japanese. All this is "if nothing happens."

Africa contains a few oil and uranium exporters and a mixture of industrial raw material exporters and countries that are poor and scarcely a factor in the world economy. The world economic conjuncture will have diverse effects on them. Libya, Algeria, Nigeria, Gabon, and Angola will benefit until 1980 and may even feel rich enough to consider giving aid to influence other countries. Thereafter they will have to adjust to falling energy prices. Zambia, Zaire, Mauritania, Liberia, Guinea, and a few others will be struggling to maintain export earnings and growth with lower real import levels until 1980 and a little beyond before their struggle eases. Ivory Coast, Ghana, Kenya, Ethiopia, and other exporters of agricultural specialities for the processors probably will be little affected by these events; the recession in the processing countries has not been so severe as to collapse the demand for coffee, cocoa, and tea. Chad, Upper Volta, Mali, the Central African Republic, Lesotho, and some others will continue to be poor. Perhaps additional aid from energy exporters and countries relatively isolated from the gyrations of the world market (China, for example) will compensate them for reduced aid from OECD processors.

The likely fall in aid flows from the OECD will be accentuated if the rich countries continue to lose interest in their ideological pursuits. A certain cycle of sanguinity, discovery, and retrenchment has affected Russian and Eastern European economic aid substantially (and American aid to a lesser extent); it could also set in for Chinese aid. Only a major ideological confrontation in southern Africa would be apt to reverse these trends. OPEC aid will be much reduced after 1980.

Assuming that these predictions are close to the mark—that is, if nothing happens—what are the reasonable options for American aid to Africa? Let us look in turn at the possible range of American aid *levels*; at alternative *distribution* policies to determine which countries receive aid; at the possible *vehicles* by which aid can be delivered; at the *terms* on which it is provided; and, most important, at the *content* of our aid program, both as it might affect Africa and as it is viewed in the United States.

Levels: How Much Aid? In the context of the probable future I have described— one of continuing decline in the level of U.S. aid in real terms—to discuss a significant increase in the level of aid to Africa between now and 1980 might seem academic. Even so, Africa may not come off badly. In the light of obvious and deep disenchantment with American involvement in Southeast Asia and with "strategic" aid in general, Africa's perceived lack of strategic importance may prove to be an asset. Aid to Africa holds obvious attractions for administrations and any Congress that would like to make aid more philan- thropic or even more developmental. And public opinion surveys show that the American people want to have *some* aid program, and want it to be philan- thropic.

Realistic levels of American aid range from roughly double to roughly one-half the present level, or annual programs ranging from 50¢ to $2.00 per African or between $200 million and $800 million a year. After all that has been said about the low strategic priority the United States attaches to Africa and about the difficult problems Africa poses for development, as well as about the relatively generous aid that is extended by others to Africa relative to other poor continents, it may seem surprising even to consider such an upper limit. At second glance, the prospect is not impossibly remote.

The lower limit could be consistent with no U.S. bilateral aid program for Africa at all. Congress has authorized (but not appropriated at this writing) the

U.S. contribution to the fourth IDA replenishment, having accepted the negotiated reduction in the U.S. share from about 40 percent to 33 percent. With IDA lending to Africa increasing rapidly, even the reduced share implies American aid to Africa through IDA that will average $160 million a year during the 1974-78 period.[c] Adding another $90 million for U.S. contributions to the UNDP, the World Food Program, and the lesser UN programs produces $250 million in U.S. aid to Africa even before one considers a bilateral program or possible American contributions to the African Development Bank.

In these circumstances, even a bilateral program maintained at present levels in shrinking current dollars would produce an aid-to-Africa package larger than the present one. Moreover Congress might shift some bilateral aid priority from Southeast Asia and the Middle East to Africa precisely because Africa is not regarded as strategic, and because it is so obviously needy. A concerted push by a well-organized interest group, such as a black constituency, might expand the package to the higher limit considered realistic. However, given the stresses on the U.S. economy resulting from the energy crisis, with their implications for the balance of trade and inflation, a total aid program larger than $800 million a year is probably out of the question between now and 1980. Subsequently, the United States may feel richer and more inclined to give aid, though by then other forces may be affecting aid levels.

Whether those levels are near the top, the middle, or the bottom of the realistic range will depend largely on the design of the aid program. The chance that an administration will propose and Congress approve larger expenditures would be increased if the program responded to Americans' vague feeling that a certain amount of aid is good if it responds to human need rather than serving military or strategic purposes or promoting private profit. Although the general constituency cares little for promoting economic development, neither does it oppose development. By the same token, aid could be strategic and philanthropic at the same time.

Distribution: Who Receives Aid? This question would pose little difficulty at the low end of the range of aid levels, since all of our aid to Africa would flow through multilateral channels and we would not have a decisive voice in distributing it. In the much more likely event that the United States will continue to operate bilateral aid programs, the question remains.

Flexibility of distribution would be essential because, with a high percentage of the total African package funnelled through multilateral channels, the

---

[c]IDA's Africa program for 1974-78 projects credits averaging $480 million per year, of which the United States has pledged to pay for 33 percent or $160 million per year. The comparable 1969-73 program *committed* credits averaging $200 million per year, of which the United States paid for 40 percent or $80 million per year. Due to the rapid buildup of IDA credits to Africa, disbursements lag considerably behind commitments. IDA *disbursements* to Africa for 1969-72 averaged $75 million per year, of which the U.S. 40 percent share was $30 million annually.

bilateral program would be the only part the United States could control. To respond to the philanthropic motive, distribution would have to be flexible enough to meet emergencies and disasters that cannot be predicted. At the same time, the United States would continue to have *some* strategic interests in Africa; inevitably, discretionary control over an occasional timely grant would be wanted in case an African government had to be influenced in a hurry, say, to grant American access or to deny someone else access to an airfield or port.

To suggest a large discretionary element in distributing aid runs counter to the tradition of AID that economic assistance should be planned and that it should fit into the recipients' development plans in an orderly way. This tradition underlies the Korry Report's recommendation that American aid to Africa be concentrated in a few countries where it could attain a "critical mass." It assumes that aid can make a big difference in development, especially in countries having favorable social, political, and economic conditions and that are ripe for a takeoff into self-sustained growth. It assumes the existence of serious development plans and of substantial AID missions that will tailor aid to the country's needs and plans.

The discretionary alternative is less planned and more ad hoc. It would distribute relatively more aid on the basis of obvious need; it would deemphasize missions and emphasize reliance on letting the recipients formulate and present their requests for assistance. Aid distributed under the discretionary alternative would probably go to more countries than is now the case, but with smaller amounts to each; it could be used to promote development, but it would not be linked to attempts to induce takeoff, which most Americans are not interested in giving aid for, and the consequences of which would frighten them if they understood them.

To these two options might be added another: distributing aid to maximize African support for U.S. positions on international issues. I give this option short shrift because I doubt that the amounts of American bilateral aid likely to be distributed to Africa would buy much support among so many countries with so many aid alternatives. Such support would be shortlived; Africa's political characteristics have seldom fostered a long-term "climate of cooperation" or "partnership" between donors and recipients, and those characteristics seem unlikely to change. Moreover, the United States seems to be realizing how little consequence attaches to support in the one-country-one-vote bodies where Africa looms large.

Vehicles: Who Should Distribute? If official American aid were to fall to the lower limit discussed above, this question would answer itself; between now and 1980 all aid would travel multilateral routes. Unlikely as that eventuality is, its perpetuation after 1980 would be even less likely. By then America probably will feel rich enough to increase its aid and will have recognized the foibles of international aid organizations as it has recognized the weaknesses of bilateral agencies. Therefore, now and even more for the period after 1980, decisions will be required about the vehicles used in distributing American aid.

Under the present system, for example, private voluntary organizations such as CARE and Catholic Relief Services distribute part of U.S. food aid. This arrangement, worked out many years ago, represents a subsidy to private organizations that may have interests of their own to pursue in Africa. In most cases the governmental subsidy conveyed through the Food for Peace program represents more money than the voluntary organizations raise on their own.

Whether to continue this subsidy of long standing is a critical issue facing the aid system. It is seldom discussed aloud because the voluntary organizations often represent interest groups whose support the AID bureaucracy is loath to risk alienating. On the one hand, many of the voluntary organizations are efficient food distributors whose networks a government agency could duplicate only with difficulty and at great cost. On the other hand, private donors may express in their distributions special interests that are not shared by Americans at large. In their appeals for funds, they may project an image of Africa that is not only demeaning to Africans, but also misleading to the American people. These complex issues need to be faced squarely, as they have not been for some time.

The choices between multilateral and bilateral vehicles are equally complex. No doubt the United States will continue to support a variety of aid organizations controlled by the UN General Assembly, of which the UNDP is the biggest, provided that these agencies avoid highly political and controversial acts such as UNESCO's expulsion of Israel. It is difficult, however, to believe that a larger share of American aid will take these channels. Virtually the only influence the United States has over these organizations comes at pledging time, when the choice is to give or not to give. As Hero's analysis shows, public opinion dislikes having American aid controlled by bodies in which the Third World and the "centrally planned economies" can call the shots. The history of various UN capital funds shows that Congress and several administrations have felt the same way. Givers like to get public credit for their giving.

The World Bank family of institutions gives donors a say in management that is only a little less than their contribution to the institutions' resources. The U.S. voting share, now 25 percent, gives Washington an important voice in World Bank management, though the consensus whereby the United States joined other rich nations in controlling Bank policy in earlier years has evaporated on many issues. Still, Hero's analysis indicates that U.S. public opinion would support increased use of World Bank or kindred institutions to distribute our aid. The question is whether that is a wise course to follow.

The World Bank institutions are expanding their aid rapidly and plan to continue to do so; they are also increasing Africa's share of that aid, as we have seen. Since the United States no longer exerts a decisive influence in those organizations, U.S. policy decisions tend to be made at pledging time: every three years for IDA (1974, 1977, 1980, and so on); whenever the call goes out for more paid-in capital for the Bank; and for the Bank group's "third window," which now makes loans on terms midway between the Bank's and IDA's. Despite its influence, the United States has had to accept Bank policies, a situation that Congress and the administration occasionally find frustrating. In 1974, Congress first defeated the bill to authorize the IDA replenishment before passing it, and has yet to appropriate the money. Nevertheless, the World Bank group, unlike the UN General Assembly, is generally regarded as "responsible."

In 1966 the authors of the Korry Report considered a division of labor in which the Bank group would provide an alternative to U.S. bilateral aid for infrastructure. It concluded that the Bank was too new to Africa to handle this job, but since then the Bank has gained much experience. In addition, the costs of American contractors have risen so high that AID can seldom build infrastructure projects at prices competitive in the world market. For both reasons, the argument for a division of labor between bilateral American aid to Africa and World Bank aid—with the latter concentrated in infrastructure and other large capital projects—becomes increasingly persuasive.

Americans might be willing to increase aid through other international organizations as well. Although its first five years were unimpressive, the African Development Bank now seems to be on a firmer footing and might warrant support if Americans wish to encourage Africans themselves to make some of the difficult aid-allocation decisions. Much depends on the kinds of policies the ADB pursues, for Congress and the administration will be watching closely. If they like what they see, and if the results of any American contributions to the ADB's African Development Fund could be made visible, this vehicle could prove an attractive one.

There are probably strict limits to multilateralizing American aid, however, even in the short run. Multilateral organizations have lives of their own and cannot be expected to specialize in the kinds of aid America will want to give. Banks in particular are massive but often blunt instruments, well-suited for large capital projects but less so for technical assistance or, perhaps, institution-heavy projects in agriculture, education, and health. As in its distribution policies, the United States probably will wish to maintain the flexibility inherent in a substantial bilateral aid program. But what kind of bilateral program?

The smaller the bilateral program in a country, the less sense it makes to have a mission there, primarily because administrative costs consume a disproportionate share of program funds. Worldwide, AID proposed in fiscal year 1976 to support a bilateral "functional development assistance" program of net loans and grants worth $1,177 million with operating and administrative expenses of $208 million,[39] or an administrative: substantive ratio of 1:6. The ratio must be higher in Africa, where programs are smaller than the average. At the lower levels of U.S. aid discussed previously, in-country missions would become luxuries. Indeed, AID already has sharply reduced the number of its missions in Africa.

In such circumstances, ambassadors could provide aid from discretionary funds as they already do in countries without AID missions. But that need not be the limit of U.S. bilateral aid. There is no reason potential recipients should not be expected to prepare and submit project proposals for bilateral aid financing. Unlike the present system, which sometimes "sells" recipients projects they do not really want, such a policy would at least assure that recipients were interested in the projects they sought. Many short inspection trips by American officials could be financed for the cost of a small resident mission; but AID might lose the assurance that its projects were closely integrated into country development plans. At certain aid levels, a no-mission option resembling current arrangements in most francophone African countries might be worth considering.

The whole complicated system of bilateral AID missions raises other questions of cost and efficiency. AID's FY 1967 budget of $208 million for operating and administrative expenses creates jobs and expenditures in the United States that might go abroad if a larger share of our aid were multilateralized. Putting more money through IDA or the ADB would bring competitive international bidding in which foreigners would win many of the contracts. Africa would gain, but to the real resource costs of our aid would be added balance-of-payments costs of a kind that has been practically eliminated from U.S. bilateral aid through tying. Under certain kinds of balance-of-payments constraints, foreign exchange costs of aid might become a major consideration. What might those costs be under a multilateral option?

From 1969 to 1973, the United States' 40 percent share of IDA's average annual commitment to Africa of $200 million was $80 million; about 15 percent of procurement under IDA credits in these years was won by the United States. This implies annual exports of $30 million and an annual balance-of-payments cost of $50 million. Projections for the 1974-78 period call for annual IDA commitments to Africa of $480 million, of which the United States probably will contribute 33 percent, or $160 million annually. The 1969-73 procurement figures reflect a period of dollar overvaluation and a loss of competitive position in many U.S. industries, which they have subsequently regained. If procurement in the United States rose modestly to 20 percent for the 1974-78 period, the additional U.S. balance-of-payments cost for the more than doubling of IDA aid to Africa would be $38 million. If procurement in the United States rose to 25 percent, the balance-of-payments cost would fall. Thus the attractiveness of options that would multilateralize American aid depends not only on our balance-of-payments position but also on our competitive position—on our ability to win in international competitive bidding.

Terms: Grants, Loans, or Both? The choice of terms on which to provide aid revolves around the hoary question of loans versus grants and, if loans are chosen, the rate of interest and terms governing the repayment of principal. This is not the place to rehash the venerable arguments on these options. Suffice it to point out three factors in the debate.

First, loans, unless they are converted into grants, require repayment. Repaying, even for aid projects that have worked, is always unpleasant, and relationships with creditors are always strained. States that try to put the muscle on their aid debtors may find it hard to foster a "climate of cooperation" with them. If threats must be made to secure repayment of aid debts, donors might well prefer to have an international collection agency, such as a bank, do the dirty work.

Second, as a result of the repayment problem, the contention of communist states that their loan aid is more dignified for the receiver than capitalist grant aid has worn thin. The Soviet Union has had to threaten several debtors and to reschedule repayment of its loans to Ghana and several other countries. If Russian and Eastern European aid continues on present trends, the net flow will soon be to the donors, a situation sure to provoke mounting unpleasantness.

Third, loans are clearly preferable for some purposes, such as large, revenue-generating capital projects, and grants for others, such as technical assistance for research. Deciding on the grant-loan mix depends on the donor's willingness to assume a landlord-tenant type of relation with aid recipients and on the content of the donor's aid program.

Content: The Basic Question. Content options are many and essential, both in determining whether the program will "play in Peoria" from the American point of view and, from the African viewpoint, in determining the extent to which American aid will actually be useful.

1. *Food Aid and Technical Assistance for Agriculture.* Probably the kind of aid Americans most strongly support is food aid for the needy. Even *The Washington Post*'s discovery that Food for Peace is sometimes used to develop markets probably will not change this attitude. Africa will need food aid, but on an episodic basis. A widely recognized danger inherent in this form of aid is that it may reduce incentives to improve local agriculture. The joint tendency of receiving governments to count on future food aid and of donor governments to regularize the flow through long-term programming may lead to dependence. Since Africa ought to be able to produce its own food and even exportable surpluses, *regular* food aid could be bad for African economies and for African-American relations.

To paraphrase Lao-tse and Chairman Mao, can the American people understand that it is better to teach a man to fish than to give him a fish? Hero's finding that the American public strongly supports technical assistance to transfer American know-how suggests that they can. Helping to increase food and other agricultural production would also be justified by the Korry Report's finding that the United States is exceptionally qualified in this field.

But building up African agriculture to avoid the need for future food aid is a

difficult business. Though America's worldwide leadership in agricultural research is recognized, applying it to African problems is another matter. The
Consultative Group for International Agricultural Research already supports
large-scale studies in international centers such as the International Institute for
Tropical Agriculture (IITA) at Ibadan. The principal need is for applied research
on adapting agricultural knowledge to local conditions. Much of such agricultural research in Africa is isolated, with researchers not knowing what their
colleagues elsewhere are doing—especially across the English-French linguistic
divide. There is ample scope for more adaptive research and for the coordination
and pooling of knowledge (or ignorance)'of the kind now being supported for
rice by the West African Rice Development Authority in Monrovia and also by
IITA.

Could highly paid Americans do these kinds of jobs better than trained
Africans? Conducting farm management studies to learn whether innovations
pay, and diffusing good innovations through extension services are essential tasks
best done by Africans. Through judicious technical assistance, however, foreign
knowledge and organizational ability may fit into the system at critical
junctures. For instance, many of Africa's pressing food problems are found in
semi-arid regions extending from the West African savannah to Tanzania and
Botswana. Agricultural scientists currently have little practical advice for African
farmers in those areas. However, the United States has a wealth of research
experience in its own arid Southwest that might be adaptable. Several dry-zone
crops that are promising in the American Southwest—the jojoba bean, whose oil
has the high quality of sperm-whale oil, or the intriguing buffalo gourd—also
show promise for the drier parts of Africa.

Any rural development aid would have to clear the difficult hurdle of
adapting to African conditions and leaving American capital-intensive methods
back in America. Commercial production of jojoba beans should not be blocked
in Africa, as it is in America, for want of a mechanical harvester. American
attempts to go directly into food production in Africa—for example, through
mechanized irrigated rice-growing at Gbedin and mechanized rainfed rice
growing near Buchanan, both in Liberia—have ended in disaster. Though the
United States is the world leader in farm machinery, it remains to be seer
whether we can adapt that leadership to African conditions and compete with
small power-tillers from China, Japan, and India.

Similarly, we will have to see whether the tradition of the open range and the
Chisholm Trail is such a distant memory for American livestock experts tha
they will be unable to comprehend and cope with the open-range ranching and
cattle treks of the Sahel and other parts of Africa. Our fertilizer technology i
impressive, yet it is not so much an option as an open question whethe
American fertilizer experience can be adjusted to African farming intensities an
price expectations. The task is not to transfer American modes of foo
production to Africa, but to invent improved ways for Africa to produce foo
with the help of American experience.

2. *Infrastructure*. Making industry part of the aid package is an option that would depart from American aid traditions. Given the strong American predilection for leaving industry to the private sector, it seems unlikely that government aid will be used in Africa to build industries, though training and technical assistance might be given to local entrepreneurs.

American tradition is more accepting of having infrastructure in the public sector, especially in other countries. The Korry Report emphasized Africa's need for infrastructure, arguing that U.S. bilateral aid should help provide it pending greater maturity of World Bank and IDA programs in Africa. The preceding assessment of "the Africa we aid" pointed to the economic need for better transport and communications as well as for those more elusive kinds of administrative and institutional infrastructure that are vital to development. What part should they have in America's aid to Africa?

Infrastructure options ought not to be simply for or against, but should distinguish among the many forms of infrastructure. In my judgment, the most crucial distinction is between infrastructure embodied in heavy construction and that which is principally high technology. Ports, roads, dams, conventional power plants, even telephone lines require engineering, the application of well-known techniques, and usually earth moving and cement pouring. Though the United States is the world leader in earthmoving equipment, American contractors usually are not able to be competitive in international bidding for such projects. Multilateral aid based on an international division of labor would leave AID out of this business.

Satellites that gather information on mineral resources and crop conditions; computerized inventories, tax systems, and payrolls; microwave data transmission and switching systems; nuclear power plants; television employed in literacy and agricultural extension campaigns—these are infrastructure too, but the inputs are more apt to be American know-how than tons of cement. They are highly capital- and technology-intensive, yet not all would throw poor people out of work. Some high-technology infrastructure does jobs that no number of laborers could do. Finding such jobs that need to be done in Africa and doing them cheaply may prove a formidable task. Nevertheless, whatever kind of content is chosen for American aid, the high-technology infrastructure in which the United States has a unique and absolute advantage certainly should be well represented.

3. *Health and Shelter*. A program addressed to basic human needs would consider not only food, but health and shelter as well. AID has encouraged urban Africans to invest in homes, often through aided self-help. The prevailing view among urbanologists is to let people build for themselves while the government, often with foreign aid, prepares sites and provides services. Such programs save money and seem to fulfill personal wants better and to foster more orderly communities than do housing projects where government builds houses.

Decisions on housing programs should take into account some of their consequences. Making people owners of solid houses may render them more satisfied and conservative. Such programs may also attract rural people into capitals to take advantage of these and other subsidies to town-dwellers. Housing programs, even of the sites-and-services variety, touch only the urban minority of Africans, and necessarily only a small minority of them. The urban poor are likely to be more noticeable than the rural poor, but they are likely to be less poor and less numerous.

In my opinion, some of AID's clearest successes in Africa have been in the health sector. They range from preventing smallpox and measles and supplying potable water for humans to controlling rinderpest and trypanosomiasis in animals. Moreover, health aid to Africa obviously conforms to the popular impression of what aid ought to be. But alleviating Africa's health problems could easily swallow far more aid than America could provide. Africa's general economic situation suggests ways of setting priorities within the sector. Saving a life in Monrovia's J.F. Kennedy Hospital is far less cost-effective than saving a life by preventing smallpox. Preventive medicine generally wins the cost comparison with curative medicine. But that choice is not the only one.

Africa's parents and governments are investing their energy, resources, and love in bringing millions of children to maturity, only to have them robbed of their social productivity by blindness or debilitating diseases like bilharzia (schistosomiasis), iron-deficiency anemia, malaria, and intestinal parasites. Some of these productivity-destroyers can be attacked at low cost with existing methods. Where salt manufacture is fairly centralized, the addition of iron to the salt supply can control iron-deficiency anemia, which robs farmers of their energy when peak exertion is required. A trial international program to control river blindness (onchocerciasis) is now underway in West Africa, promising to open vast fertile lands to cultivation. Inexpensive techniques may be available soon to permit wider control of bilharzia, malaria, trypanosomiasis, and even protein deficiency, the last through the breeding of grains with more usable protein. American doctors and nurses are less essential to the success of such programs than American biological and medical research, which has had a major part in finding solutions in the past, and local paramedical workers, who might be American-trained.

4. *Population Planning.* Programs to improve African health can concentrate on the living or on the yet-to-be-born. For balance, they should include both.

A population program makes sense as part of almost any African development plan for two reasons. First, succeeding generations will need health and education services, both of which consume government resources. Africa's leaders are far from satisfied with the health care and schooling they can give the present generation, even with massive aid. Population growth will compound this problem. Second, though people in most parts of Africa are far from running out of land, rapid population growth will compel farmers in some areas to shift to more intensive agriculture more rapidly than their present skills permit, with serious consequences for soil fertility and health.

Most African governments do not now recognize the advantages of restraining population growth. The United States government is convinced of those advantages. American aid to Africa should help those governments that wish to slow population growth and stand ready to help the others. Where African governments are ready, American population technology has some things to offer—not so much new techniques for preventing births as new methods of diffusing techniques that are well known. Applying American marketing skills to condom distribution seems to work in Indonesia and Sri Lanka; combining maternal and child health care with incentives to limit births works on South Indian tea estates. Similar programs would work in Africa, if African governments wanted them. Any population aid program will cost only a small fraction of the total amount devoted to aid.

5. *Training.* Training would have a place in any American aid package for Africa, being a vital part of programs in agriculture, health, population, infrastructure, and industry. If Africans were expected to prepare and present their own development projects for AID to sift, they would also need training in how to go about it.

Training is not always directed to such specific development tasks. Much of Africa's education system, still highly reminiscent of the colonial education systems that preceded it, aims at training people to enter the bureaucracy. Such education consumes a large share of African governments' budgets. Its contribution to development is debatable, and its cost is so great that American aid perforce would seek a specialized niche in training and education rather than support the whole system. (Nonetheless, many African governments would welcome suggestions on how to save money and to improve the cost-effectiveness of general education.) Concentrating on "specialized niches" would call for limiting American aid to training that is specifically related to development goals, and for applying educational methods developed in America but suitable in Africa—the teaching of business administration, for instance, in which America's world preeminence is recognized.

The Balance Sheet. This review of content options for American bilateral aid suggests that *technical assistance may be more important than capital assistance.* The latter is not excluded; especially when there is international cooperation and a division of labor, U.S. participation in capital projects may be entirely appropriate. The development of the Senegal River basin may be the first instance in which American aid will have been mingled in a single project with Chinese, French, UN, Russian, and World Bank aid. But when such international specialization is not possible, Africa would seem to have better sources of support for its major capital projects than the U.S. bilateral program.

We have noted that large capital projects usually are suited to loan financing, while projects that consist mainly of technical assistance are more appropriately financed by grants. The catalog of content options is filled with activities that require a high input of technical assistance and, probably, grants to support it.

But U.S. technical assistance is expensive, perhaps even more expensive relative to the competition than are American construction contracts. AID estimates that it now costs $50,000 to $60,000 in salary, perquisites, and overhead to keep a U.S. technician in Africa for a year. At such costs, American technicians had best not be doing things that Africans could do.

We have all heard about American technicians in Africa who did less than an African could have done in the same position. But a technician who provides a unique and needed skill is definitely worth the current price and much more. If he is worth having there, he is worth supporting adequately, and it is worth taking the time to define what he is supposed to do.

The Peace Corps provides a less costly source of limited technical assistance, but even a Peace Corps volunteer costs about $12,500 a year. That cost might be lowered another 20 percent or so by contracting with nongovernmental volunteer organizations such as International Voluntary Services, but even $10,000 a year far exceeds typical African salaries. Whether it is provided by professional technicians or by volunteers, technical assistance should furnish skills that are absent locally and in crucial demand. Otherwise, the technician is wasteful aid and the volunteer aids only himself.

In the United States, popular perceptions of aid and competing demands on our national resources impose bounds on aid policy. Within those limits lie a host of possibilities that are more or less congruent with what Africans want, more or less conducive to African development, and more or less efficient in their use of American resources.

I have suggested a number of alternatives regarding the content of aid, who gets it, and how. The art of the possible—politics—is to choose those options that build on America's strengths, do jobs as cost-effectively as possible, and concentrate on things Africans want done. Most Americans favor aid, if vaguely and lukewarmly. How the popular mandate is translated into technical assistance or telephone systems—in short, which options are chosen—could make a surprisingly significant difference to Americans and to Africans.

Notes

1. These "new looks" are reviewed in Andrew F. Westwood, *Foreign Aid in a Foreign Policy Framework* (Washington, D.C.: Brookings Institution, 1966); and Goran Ohlin, *Foreign Aid Policies Reconsidered* (Paris: OECD Development Centre, 1966), pp. 15-26. For a more recent "new look," see Report to the President from the Task Force on International Development, *U.S. Foreign Assistance in the 1970s: A New Approach* (March 1970). The 1966 Korry Report ("Policy Report for Development in Africa") remains the most recent "new look" at specifically African aid within the U.S. government.

2. For a more thorough explanation of the DAC measures, see *The Flow of Financial Resources to Less-Developed Countries, 1961-1965* (Paris: OECD, 1967), particularly pp. 141-46 and pp. 192-96 on the "discounted present value method."

3. For more detail, see *Voluntary Foreign Aid Programs*, an annual publication of AID's Office of Private and Voluntary Cooperation, from which these and subsequent figures are drawn unless otherwise noted.

4. See "Development Cooperation: Statistics for 1973 and Earlier Years," an unpublished statistical annex to *Development Cooperation: Efforts and Policies of the Members of the Development Assistance Committee* (Paris: OECD, 1974), pp. 212-35.

5. William R. Cotter, "How Africa Is Short-Changed," *Africa Report* magazine (November-December 1974).

6. The State Department's Bureau of Intelligence and Research produces the annual *Communist States and Developing Countries: Aid and Trade in 19--*, an unclassified document that is published in the spring of the following year by the Office of Media Services of the Bureau of Public Affairs. Two excellent studies of Russian aid are John D. Esseks, "Soviet Economic Aid to Africa: 1959-73," in Warren Weinstein (ed.), *Chinese and Soviet Aid to Africa* (New York: Praeger, 1975), pp. 83-119; and James Carter, *The Net Cost of Soviet Foreign Aid* (New York: Praeger, 1969). No comparable work exists for aid from the People's Republic of China, East Germany, Czechoslovakia, Hungary, Poland, Rumania, or Bulgaria, for which we have no disbursement figures. Until 1974, OPEC aid was the preserve of journalists. The best tentative analysis is "Flow of Resources from OPEC Members to Developing Countries," Working Document DD-403, 1st Revision (Paris: OECD, DAC Secretariat, December 6, 1974).

7. Carter, *Net Cost*, pp. 35-43.

8. Esseks, "Soviet Economic Aid," Table 3.

9. For an excellent summary of this research, see Francis X. Colaço, *Economic and Political Considerations and the Flow of Official Resources to Developing Countries* (Paris: OECD/DAC, 1973), pp. 65-76.

10. For more on this subject, see Falih Alsaaty, "The Distribution of Grants by DAC Members among Recipients, 1969-72" (draft study prepared at the International Bank for Reconstruction and Development, 1974), pp. 17-21.

11. Figures from Table A-1 in Bruce Dinwiddy (ed.), *European Development Policies: The United Kingdom, Sweden, France, EEC, and Multilateral Organizations* (New York: Praeger, 1973).

12. Canadian International Development Agency, *Annual Review, 1973-1974* (Ottawa).

13. OECD, "Flow of Resources from OPEC Members."

14. For the most convincing discussion of Russian motives in aiding Africa, see Esseks, "Soviet Economic Aid," pp. 15ff.

15. Keith B. Griffin and J.L. Enos, "Foreign Assistance: Objectives and Consequences," *Economic Development and Cultural Change*, Vol. 18 (April 1970), p. 314.

16. For detail, see Colaço, *Economic and Political Considerations*, pp. 22-29 and 99-102.

17. Based on research by William Rich and Michael Sculnick done under my direction at Oberlin College in 1969-71. Rich ran simple regressions between aid received per capita by each country in years between 1946 and 1968 and a large number of economic, social, and political variables. Correlation between U.S. aid received (dependent variable) and support for the United States position on China's UN representation (high), and rejection of Soviet aid (high) is given below for different measures of aid. Figures are tau factors.

	China UN Vote	Soviet Aid
Global, net US economic aid, 1946-68	.182	.303
Global, net US economic aid, 1962-68	.271	.319
Global, net US military aid, 1946-68	.230	.090
Africa, 3 variables of US aid combined	−.029	−.180

18. See especially Alfred Hero, "Foreign Aid and the American Public," *Public Policy*, Vol. 14 (1965), pp. 72-116.

19. *Ibid.*, p. 108.

20. *Ibid.*, p. 114.

21. *Ibid.* Also see Appendix B of his later unpublished paper, "American Public Reactions to Development Assistance" (Washington, D.C.: The Brookings Institution, October 1967).

22. See Paul A. Laudicina, *World Poverty and Development: A Survey of American Opinion* (Washington, D.C.: Overseas Development Council, October 1973). Pages 4-5 summarize conclusions; questionnaires, careful documentation, and useful figures are provided.

23. Hero, "Foreign Aid and the American Public," p. 94.

24. Results reported in detail in Hero, "American Negroes and U.S. Foreign Policy: 1937-1967," *Journal of Conflict Resolution*, Vol. 13 (June 1969), p. 244.

25. *Ibid.*, pp. 231-32.

26. Public Law 93-559, Sec. 49, December 30, 1974.

27. Alfred Hero, "Africa and the U.S. Public" (unpublished paper prepared for a meeting sponsored by the African-American Institute in Los Angeles, 1969), p. 9.

28. A classic description of this process can be found in Jean Tricart, "Les échanges entre la zone forestière de la Côte d'Ivoire et les savannes soudanniennes," *Cahiers d'Outre-Mer*, Vol. 35 (July-September 1956), pp. 209-38.

29. For example, see John C. de Wilde and others, *Economic Development in Mali*, Vol. 2, (Washington, D.C.: IBRD, 1970; restricted), pp. 11 and 18.

30. World Bank/IDA, *Annual Report 1973*, and World Bank, *Annual Report 1974*. See, for example, Table 1A in the statistical annex to the 1974 report.

31. Aristide Zolberg, *Creating Political Order: The Party-States of West Africa* (Chicago: Rand-McNally and Company, 1966).

32. See the eloquent general remarks on military rule in Africa in Ruth First, *Power in Africa* (New York: Pantheon Books, 1970).

33. Based on remarks by Donald B. Easum, Assistant Secretary of State for African Affairs, "The African Potential: Markets and Materials—A Fair Exchange for Capital and Know-How," (address delivered to the African American Chamber of Commerce, New York, May 17, 1974). Updated with information from the Bureau of Mines *Commodity Data Summaries—1975* and various individual commodity reports by the Bureau of Mines.

34. Griffin and Enos, "Foreign Assistance," p. 314.

35. An excellent summary of Dennis H. Meadows and others, *The Limits to Growth* (New York: Universe, 1972) appears in *Development Digest*, Vol. 12 (October 1974), pp. 3-31, with a graphic model on pp. 1-2.

36. The President's Materials Policy Commission, known as the Paley Commission, inquired into high prices and apparent shortages of raw materials during the Korean War boom of 1951-52. Its report, *Resources for Freedom* (1952), emphasized that such "shortages" were economic, not physical, and that higher prices would call forth supplies adequate for long-range needs.

37. One of many telling critiques is *Report on the Limits to Growth*, a World Bank report by Mahbubul Haq, N.G. Carter, E.K. Hawkins, D.H. Keare, B. Varon, C. Weiss, and K.C. Zachariah. It is summarized in *Development Digest*, Vol. 12 (October 1974), pp. 32-43.

38. Ambrose Bierce, *Devil's Dictionary* (New York: Dover, 1911).

39. See *Fiscal Year 1976 Submission to the Congress; Summary* (AID, 1975), p. 22.

Index

Index

About the Authors

HELEN KITCHEN, Director of the Africa Area Study of the Commission on Critical Choices since 1974, is a distinguished editor and writer who specializes in African affairs. Her books include: *The Press in Africa* (1956), *The Educated African: A Country by Country Survey of Educational Development in Africa* (1962), *A Handbook of African Affairs* (1964) and *Footnotes to the Congo Story* (1967). She was editor-in-chief of *Africa Report* Magazine from 1961 to 1968.

MANFRED HALPERN, Professor of Politics at Princeton University, is the author of *The Politics of Social Change in the Middle East and North Africa* (Princeton, 1963) and of chapters in twelve other books dealing with problems of personal and political change and violence. His recent research has concentrated on the comparative study of modernization as mankind's first common, worldwide revolution. A resulting volume, *The Dialectics of Transformation in Politics, Personality, and History* is forthcoming.

ALI A. MAZRUI was born in Kenya and educated at the University of Manchester, Columbia University, and Oxford. Formerly Dean of the Faculty of Social Sciences at Makerere University in Uganda, he has been Visiting Professor at the Universities of London, Manchester, Harvard, Singapore, Australia, Stanford, and Cairo. He is now Professor of Political Science at the University of Michigan, but travels widely in connection with his current research on Africa in world affairs. Among his many publications are ten books, including one novel.

JOHN A. MARCUM is Provost of Merrill College and Professor of Politics at the University of California, Santa Cruz. Among other works, Dr. Marcum is author of *The Angolan Revolution:* Vol. 1, *The Anatomy of an Explosion* (M.I.T. Press, 1969), and Vol. 2, *Exile Politics and Guerilla Warfare*, forthcoming. He is a past president of the African Studies Association.

WILLIAM A. HANCE, Professor of Economic Geography at Columbia University, New York, is the author of *The Geography of Modern Africa* (2nd ed. rev., 1975), *Population Migration and Urbanization in Africa* (1970), *African Economic Development* (1967), and numerous articles on African development problems. He is past president of the American Geographical Society and of the African Studies Association.

ANDREW M. KAMARCK, a professorial lecturer on African economic problems at Johns Hopkins University's School of Advanced International Studies, is the author of *The Economics of African Development* (rev. ed., 1971). He has been a Regents Professor at UCLA, a Research Associate at the Center for International Affairs at Harvard, and Economic Adviser on Africa, Director of the Economics Department, and Director of the Economic Development Institute of the World Bank.

CLAUDE E. WELCH, JR. is Professor of Political Science at the State University of New York at Buffalo, and was Chairman of the University's Committee on African Studies from 1966 to 1975. His specialities include civil-military relations, pan-African thought, and political change in sub-Saharan Africa. Among his books are *Soldier and State in Africa: A Comparative Analysis of Military Intervention and Political Change* (1970); *Military Role and Rule* (1974); and *Dream of Unity: Pan-Africanism and Political Unification in West Africa* (1966).

W.A.J. PAYNE has been a practicing newspaperman in both the United States and Africa, and now is pursuing his interest in communication as an Associate Professor of Anthropology at California State College, Sonoma. He has been a reporter for the *Washington Post*, United Nations correspondent for the Associated Negro Press, a *New York Times* correspondent in Zambia, assistant editor of *The Northern Star* (Lusaka, Zambia), a Ford Foundation fellow in Kenya, and Moderator of Black Experience Lectures at the Graduate School of Journalism, Columbia University.

PHILIPPE LEMAITRE is a pseudonym for a Europe-based scholar and international civil servant with long experience in African affairs.

ABOUT THE AUTHORS

WILLIAM H. LEWIS wrote the chapter for this book as a Senior Fellow at the Brookings Institution, Washington, D.C. He has held a broad range of African- and defense-related positions in the Departments of State and Defense. Dr. Lewis is a frequent contributor to scholarly journals, and is co-author of six books on Africa.

DAVID L. BUCKMAN, now principal representative of the Chase Manhattan Bank in the Soviet Union, wrote his contribution to this book while serving as Chase Manhattan's Vice President and Division Executive for Africa. He lived in West Africa from 1961 to 1968.

WILLIAM I. JONES received his doctorate from the Universite de Geneve; has taught at Oberlin College and at Johns Hopkins University's School of Advanced International Studies; and has served with the U.S. Department of Agriculture, the U.S. Agency for International Development, the National Planning Association, and the World Bank's Economic Development Institute. He is former editor of the quarterly *Development Digest*, and author of *Planning and Economic Policy: Socialist Mali and Her Neighbors* (1976).